THE JEWISH TRAVEL GUIDE 1997

Published in association with
The Jewish Chronicle, London

Editor
STEPHEN W. MASSIL

VALLENTINE MITCHELL

First published in 1997 in Great Britain by
VALLENTINE MITCHELL & CO. LTD.
Newbury House, 900 Eastern Avenue,
London IG2 7HH

and in the United States of America by
FRANK CASS
c/o ISBS, Inc.
5804 N.E. Hassalo Street, Portland, Oregon 97213-3644

ISBN 0 85303 327 7
ISSN 0075 3750

Printed in Great Britain by
Redwood Books Ltd., Trowbridge, Wilts.

CONTENTS

IMPORTANT NOTICE

Extensive research is undertaken for every annual revision of the Jewish Travel Guide and every effort is made to ensure accuracy. Nethertheless, no responsibility can be accepted for any errors or omissions, or for kashrut and other claims by establishments listed in the guide.

Particular attention must be drawn to the fact that many kosher establishments change hands often and suddenly, in some instances ceasing to be kosher. It is in travellers' best interests to obtain confirmation of kashrut claims before completing their arrangements.

Readers are asked kindly to draw attention to any errors or omissions. Forms are provided for this purpose at the end of the book.

EXPLANATION OF SYMBOLS

(K) An hotel, restaurant, caterer or other establishment under the supervision of a recognised Jewish religious authority (e.g. the London Kashrus Commission, Kedassia, the local Beth Din or rabbi). In most countries, there is no central Jewish kashrut authority as in Britain.

★ An establishment which, while claiming to be strictly kosher, is not under official supervision. Such an establishment is stated to possess three essential characteristics:

(i) That the meat, and all other foods, utensils, etc., are strictly kosher;

(ii) that the separation of meat and milk in the kitchens and at table is assured;

(iii) that Shabbat and the Holy-days are observed by strict adherence to all rules including – "No Smoking" – and, where possible, that religious services are held.

Establishments without a star are not kosher. They have been included because they may be of interest to readers of the *Jewish Travel Guide* for other than dietary reasons.

A figure in brackets after an establishment's name shows the number of rooms.

(V) Vegetarian establishment. A list of vegetarian organisations is given on p. 363.

ABBREVIATIONS

Accom.	*Accommodation*	M.	*Minister*
Admin.	*Administrator*	Mon.	*Monday*
Assoc.	*Association*	Opp.	*Opposite*
Av.	*Avenue*	Pde.	*Parade*
Bdway.	*Broadway*	Pk.	*Park*
Bldg(s).	*Building(s)*	Pl.	*Place*
Cl.	*Close*	Princ.	*Principal*
Cnr.	*Corner*	Sat.	*Saturday*
Cong.	*Congregation*	Sec.	*Secretary*
Cres.	*Crescent*	Sq.	*Square*
Dr.	*Doctor, Drive*	St.	*Saint, Street*
Evg(s).	*Evening(s)*	Str.	*Straat, Strasse*
Fri.	*Friday*	Sun.	*Sunday*
Gdns.	*Gardens*	Syn.	*Synagogue*
Gr.	*Grove*	Ter.	*Terrace*
Grn.	*Green*	Thurs.	*Thursday*
Hd.	*Headmaster/Headmistress*	Tues.	*Tuesday*
Inf.	*Information*	Wed.	*Wednesday*
Inq.	*Inquiries*		

Festivals and Fasts in 1997 (5757–5758)

Fast of Esther	Thursday	March 20th
Purim	Sunday	March 23rd
First Day Pesach	Tuesday	April 22nd
Second Day Pesach	Wednesday	April 23rd
Seventh Day Pesach	Monday	April 28th
Eighth Day Pesach	Tuesday	April 29th
Holocaust Memorial	Sunday	May 4th
Israel Independence Day	Monday	May 12th
Jerusalem Day	Wednesday	June 4th
First Day Shavuot	Wednesday	June 11th
Second Day Shavuot	Thursday	June 12th
Fast of Tammuz	Tuesday	July 22nd
Fast of Av	Tuesday	August 12th
First Day Rosh Hashanah	Thursday	October 2nd
Second Day Rosh Hashanah	Friday	October 3rd
Fast of Gedaliah	Sunday	October 5th
Yom Kippur	Saturday	October 11th
First Day Succot	Thursday	October 16th
Second Day Succot	Friday	October 17th
Shemini Atseret	Thursday	October 23rd
Simchat Torah	Friday	October 24th
First Day Chanucah	Wednesday	December 24th

Yizkor in 1997

Yizkor is recited in synagogues on the following days: Eighth day Pesach, Tuesday, April 29th; Second day Shavuot, Thursday, June 12th; Yom Kippur, Saturday, October 11th; Shemini Atseret, Thursday, October 23rd

Some Notable Days in 1998 (5758–5759)

First Day Pesach	Saturday	April 11th
Eighth Day Pesach (Yizkor)	Saturday	April 18th
First Day Shavuot	Sunday	May 31st
Second Day Shavuot (Yizkor)	Monday	June 1st
First Day Rosh Hashanah (5758)	Monday	September 21st
Second Day Rosh Hashanah	Tuesday	September 22nd
Yom Kippur (Yizkor)	Wednesday	September 30th
First Day Succot	Monday	October 5th
Shemini Atseret (Yizkor)	Monday	October 12th

GREAT BRITAIN

GREATER LONDON

Well over half the 300,000 (1991) Jews of Britain live in London. Numbering about 210,000, they are spread throughout the Metropolis, with the largest concentration in North-Western districts like Golders Green, Edgware and Hampstead Garden Suburb. There are also large communities in North London (Stamford Hill) and in the East (Barkingside, Clayhall and Newbury Park). Once it was in Stepney that the biggest part of London Jewry lived and, in spite of many changes there, Aldgate and Whitechapel should be visited, not only for the many reminders of their Jewish heyday, but also for the bustling life which is still to be seen there.

THE CITY

There are many historically interesting sites in the City, that square mile of Central London which adjoins the East End. The Bank of England, with its Underground station of the same name, is a useful starting point.

One of the numerous streets which converge on this busy hub is Poultry, leading quickly to Cheapside. The first street on the right is **Old Jewry**. Here, and in the neighbourhood, the earliest community lived before England expelled all its Jews in 1290. There were synagogues in this street and in Gresham and Coleman Sts., not far from historic **Guildhall**, which is itself a "must" for tourists.

Inside the **Royal Exchange**, situated opposite the Bank of England in Threadneedle Street, there is a series of murals including one by Solomon J. Solomon, R.A., of "Charles I Demanding the Five Members", and a portrait of Nathan Mayer Rothschild, who founded the London house of the famous banking firm. There was a time when the south-east corner of the Royal Exchange was known as "Jews' Walk".

The **Rothschild headquarters** is not far away, in St. Swithin's Lane. To reach this handsome building (which has in its entrance-hall more Rothschild portraits, as well as a large tapestry of Moses striking the rock), cross carefully from the Royal Exchange to the Lord Mayor's Mansion House and then turn left into King William St.

Cornhill, which stretches eastwards from the Bank, leads to Leadenhall Street and its shipping offices and, after a short walk, to Creechurch Lane and the **Cunard building**, on the back of which is an interesting plaque. "Site of the First Synagogue after the Resettlement 1657–1701. Spanish and Portuguese Jews' Congregation" is the inscription. Here the post-Expulsion Jews whom Oliver Cromwell welcomed to England set up their house of prayer. In 1701 they built a synagogue in **Bevis Marks** (close by), modelling it on the famous Portuguese Synagogue in Amsterdam. It has been scheduled by the Royal Commission on Ancient Historical Monuments as "a building of outstanding value", and is considered one of the most beautiful pieces of synagogue architecture extant. In it are some benches from the Creechurch Lane Synagogue. Visitors wishing to see the Bevis Marks synagogue the oldest in the British Commonwealth should ☎ 0171-626 1274.

London's chief Ashkenazi place of worship, the **Great Synagogue**, stood, until it was bombed during the Second World War, in Duke's Place, which adjoins Bevis Marks. The "Duke's Place Shool" (as it was called) was the country's best-known synagogue, the scene of many great occasions and a popular choice for weddings. On the wall of International House, which has replaced it, there is a plaque informing the visitor that the synagogue stood there "from 1690 and served the community continuously until it was destroyed in September, 1941".

After the Second World War and until the 1970s, the Great Synagogue was in Adler St., named after the two Chief Rabbis of that name, Rabbi Nathan Marcus Adler and his son, Rabbi Dr. Hermann Adler. Duke's Place leads to Aldgate High St. where, on the opposite side, Jewry Street marks another centre of the pre-Expulsion community. At the time of Richard I's coronation many Jews, escaping from rioting mobs, moved here from Old Jewry.

THE EAST END

Further eastwards, along Aldgate High St., is Middlesex St., which becomes the crowded **Petticoat Lane** every Sunday morning. The cheerful and cheeky language of the stall-holders has made "The Lane" famous throughout the world. On week-days an offshoot, Wentworth Street, continues the market. Eastwards again, to Whitechapel, which has changed almost out of all recognition since the days before the Second World War, when it had a teeming Jewish population. Just beyond Aldgate East Underground station, two familiar spots remain Whitechapel Art Gallery and Whitechapel Library.

The library's extensive Yiddish collection has been transferred to the Taylorian Library, Oxford University's modern-language library. The next turning on the left is Osborne St., which leads to Brick Lane. A large and sombre building in Brick Lane (at the corner of Fournier St.) represents more than anything else the changes that have taken place in the East End over the years. The Huguenots built it as a church, the Jews turned it into a synagogue (the Machzike Hadass), and now the Bengalis, who have replaced the Jews, have converted it into a mosque.

The former synagogue in **Princelet St.** (No. 19) is being converted into a museum by the Spitalfields Trust, which is collaborating with the Jewish Museum to develop the building to show the history of the different immigrant groups which have inhabited the Spitalfields area during the past 300 years. For further information about activities at the Princelet St. Building, contact the Museum ☎ 0171-284 1997.

In **Brune Street**, it is possible to see the building of the former Soup Kitchen for the Jewish Poor, that was established in 1902. Its work of distributing food to the small elderly Jewish community still resident in the area is now undertaken by Jewish Care, the largest Jewish social service organisation in Britain. Before Pesach, it distributes matzot and other kosher le-Pesach items.

Further along Whitechapel Road, outside **Whitechapel Underground station**, stands a drinking fountain. It was erected in 1911 "in Loyal and Grateful Memory of Edward VII Rex et Imperator from subscriptions raised by Jewish inhabitants of East London".

Next to the former offices of the Federation of Synagogues in the former Synagogue Community Centre is the Kosher Luncheon Club. This establishment maintains a strong Jewish tradition and still caters for local as well as business people who require a wholesome dairy meal at lunchtime. This is provided in an informal atmosphere and visitors can learn from the clientele something of the former glories of the East End.

Brady St. is the site of an old cemetery, opened for the New Synagogue in 1761 and subsequently used also by the Great Synagogue. The cemetery became full in the 1790s, and it was decided to put a four-foot thick layer of earth over part of the site, using this for further burials. This created a flat-topped mound in the centre of the cemetery. The cemetery is perhaps the only one where, because of the two layers, the headstones are placed back to back. Among those buried here are: Solomon Hirschel, who was Chief Rabbi from 1802–1842, and Nathan Meyer Rothschild (1777–1836), the banker. To view the cemetery, contact the United Synagogue Burial Society. ☎ 0171-387 7891.

In Mile End there are three more old cemeteries: two Sephardi and one Ashkenazi. Behind 253 Mile End Rd., where the Sephardi Home for the Aged (Beth Holim) was located before moving to Wembley, is the first Resettlement cemetery, the oldest existing Anglo-Jewish cemetery, opened in 1657.

Abraham Fernandez Carvajal, regarded as the founder of the modern Anglo-Jewish community, is buried here, and also Haham David Nieto, one of the greatest of Sephardi spiritual leaders. At 329 Mile End Rd., the Nuevo Beth Chaim, opened in 1725, contains the grave of Haham Benjamin Artom. This is among the 2,000 graves remaining on the site. Some 7,500 were transferred to a site in Brentwood, Essex, during the 1970s. The earliest Ashkenazi cemetery, acquired in 1696, is in Alderney Rd., and here the founders of the Duke's Place Synagogue, Moses and Aaron Hart and others, and also the "Baal Shem of London" (the Cabbalist, Haim Samuel Falk), lie buried. In **Beaumont Grove**, on the south side of Mile End Rd., is the Stepney B'nai B'rith Clubs and Settlement, managed in co-operation with Jewish Care, which caters primarily for the needs of the 7,500 Jews still living in the East End.

In Commercial Rd., **Hessel Street**, another Jewish market centre, is now occupied by Bengali traders. **Henriques Street** is named after Sir Basil Henriques, a leading welfare worker and magistrate, and founder of the Bernhard Baron St. George's Jewish Settlement, who died in 1961. On the same side, three turnings along, is **Alie Street**. At the Jewish Working Men's Club here in July, 1896, Theodor Herzl addressed a meeting which was effectively the launching of the Zionist movement in Britain.

WEST CENTRAL

Chief Rabbi Hermann Adler (1891–1911) is honoured at the Central Court, the **Old Bailey** (Underground station: St. Paul's), where a mural over the entrance to Court No. 1, entitled "Homage to Justice," includes the figure of Dr. Hermann Adler. By the City Boundary High Holborn is the Royal Fusiliers City of London Regiment Memorial. The names of the 38th, 39th and 40th (Jewish Batallions) are inscribed on the monument together with all other batallions which served in the First World War. At the western edge of the City, Chancery Lane Station, Holborn, is a useful centre for several points of interest. To the east, Furnival St. has the "Jewish Chronicle" office. Northward, Gray's Inn Rd. leads to Theobald's Rd. There, at No. 22, a plaque on the wall recalls that it is the birthplace of **Benjamin Disraeli**. Further to the north is Great Russell Street, which runs along part of the south side of the **British Museum**. When visiting the Museum, one should certainly see its collection of illuminated Haggadot, in particular its copy of the 15th Century Ashkenazi Haggadah. No. 77 Great Russell Street was the headquarters of the Zionist organisations from 1919 to 1964. Westward, in Chancery Lane, the **Public Record Office** has in its vast collection many documents of Jewish historical value, including the petitions to Cromwell.

Commonwealth House, 1–19 New Oxford Street, is the new centre of British Jewry's communal activities, housing the Board of Deputies and a range of other offices.

B'nai B'rith-Hillel House, the student centre, is at 1–2 Endsleigh St., in Bloomsbury at the heart of the University neighbourhood and the Council of Christians and Jews in Gordon Street is close by. In the building of University College in Gower St., the **Jewish Studies Library** houses the *Altmann, Mishcon* and *Mocatta Libraries* and the *Margulies* Yiddish Collection. And the School of Oriental and African Studies in the University precinct includes Judaica and Israelitica in its library.

WEST END

A permanent art collection has been accumulated by the **Ben Uri Art Society** – at 21 Dean St., Soho.

In the **Marble Arch** district, in the part of Hyde Park known as "The Dell", a Holocaust Memorial Garden was dedicated in June, 1983. The garden plot was given over by the British Government to the Board of Deputies, which commissioned Mr. Richard Seifert to design the memorial centre-piece rocks bearing a quotation from the Book of Lamentations. Also in the Marble Arch area, you will find an important associate of the United Synagogue (the recently amalgamated Western and Marble Arch Synagogues in Great Cumberland Place), the West End Great, as well as the West London (Reform) Synagogue (Upper Berkeley St.) and the magnificent Victorian New West End Synagogue in St. Petersburg Place, just off Bayswater Road. The Jewish Memorial Council and Bookshop is in **Enford St.**

The British Zionist Federation was inaugurated at the Trocadero Restaurant in **Piccadilly Circus** in January, 1899. At 175 Piccadilly was the London bureau of the Zionist Organisation, set up in August, 1917. Here, Dr. Chaim Weizmann and other Zionist leaders worked, and here, in November, 1917, the Balfour Declaration was delivered by Lord Rothschild. The **Westminster Synagogue** in Rutland Gdns., Knightsbridge, houses the Czech Memorial Scrolls Centre, where there is a permanent exhibition telling the story of the salvaging from Prague in 1964 of 1,564 Torah Scrolls confiscated by the Nazis during the Second World War, and of their restoration and the donation of many to communities throughout the world. The exhibition is open from 10a.m. to 4p.m. on Tuesdays and Thursdays, and at other times by appointment.

In **St. John's Wood** are three more interesting synagogues: the New London (Abbey Rd.) and the St. John's Wood (Grove End Rd.), where the Chief Rabbi, who lives in near-by Hamilton Terrace, generally worships. The third synagogue of great interest in St. John's Wood is the Liberal Jewish, opposite Lord's Cricket Ground recently rebuilt and renovated.

STAMFORD HILL

Of London's many synagogues, one remarkable group is the series of Chasidic "shtiblech" in Stamford Hill (and the yeshivot which are attached to some of them). **Cazenove Rd.** contains several of these, and it is here and in the vicinity that the long coats and wide hats of Chasidim and the curled sidelocks of their children are to be seen. The Lubavitch Foundation headquarters and the Yesodey Hatorah Schools are in Stamford Hill.

AJEX House at East Bank, Stamford Hill houses an interesting military museum. In this district, also, are North African, Adeni, Indian and some Persian Jews and their synagogues.

NORTH EAST

The migration of the Jews from the East End took many of them eventually to the London borough of Redbridge where today the greatest density of London's Jews reside. To obtain a flavour of this large Jewish community one should visit the Redbridge Youth and Community Centre, Sinclair House, Woodford Bridge Road, Ilford, Essex. ☎ 0181-551 0017. Sinclair House is a large modern, purpose-built Jewish community centre and it is the base for a number of organisations and the focal point of many Israeli & Zionist communal events. It also houses the Clayhall Synagogue, the Redbridge Jewish Programmes Material Project and community representative councils.

NORTH WEST

The **Jewish Museum** has moved from Woburn House and recently opened at new premises in Albert Street, Camden Town. It houses Britain's major collection of ritual articles and Anglo-Judaica (see p. 19).

The starting point for visiting North-West London is **Golders Green**. Jews first settled here during the First World War, and the **Golders Green Synagogue** (United) in Dunstan Rd., was opened in 1922. Walk down Golders Green Rd., from the Underground station for half a mile or so, and you will come to Broadwalk Lane on the right-hand side, where the **Lincoln Institute** is. This is the home of Ohel David, a congregation of Indian Jews, many of whom came to England when India was partitioned in 1947. Their forebears went to India from Baghdad.

On the opposite side of the road, at the end of a short turning called The Riding, is the **Golders Green Beth Hamedrash** – formerly known as "Munk's" after its founder in the 1930s, Rabbi Dr. Eli Munk. This very Orthodox congregation, mainly of German origin, adheres to the religious principles of Rabbi Samson Raphael Hirsch. There are many other strictly Orthodox congregations in Golders Green, including Chasidic groups.

Any of the buses travelling along Golders Green Rd. away from the Underground station will take you to Bell Lane, in Hendon. A few hundred yards down on the left-hand side is Albert Rd., where you will find **Jews' College** – established in 1855 as an Institute of Higher Education and associated with London University for many years. A group of Persian Jews holds Shabbat morning services there. Its 70,000-volume library is open to the public.

Also in **Hendon** in Egerton Gardens, a turning opposite Barnet Town Hall in The Burroughs 10–15 minutes walk from Bell Lane, is **Yakar**, which provides a wide variety of adult educational and cultural programmes and has a lending library. Several minyanim are held here on Shabbat and festivals. Further information is available on ☎ 0181-202 5552.

Return to Golders Green Underground station from Hendon Central, either by Underground or by bus. Once there, take a bus northwards along Finchley Rd. for two miles or so, getting off at **East End Rd.**, which is more or less opposite the bus stop. On the right-hand side is the **Sternberg Centre**, the largest Jewish community centre in Europe. The Georgian former manor house contains **Leo Baeck College**, with its library of 18,000 books, which trains Reform & Liberal rabbis; the offices of the **Reform Synagogues of Great Britain**, and the **London Museum of Jewish Life**, now the second centre of the Jewish Museum. In addition to permanent displays, the museum, one of

London's newest, also mounts special exhibitions and runs walking tours and educational programmes. In the Centre's grounds, you will find a Holocaust memorial, as well as a biblical garden and such more mundane places as a bookshop and a dairy snack bar.

You can return to Central London by bus or Underground. (The nearest station is Finchley Central.) Jewish travellers wanting up-to-date information on current religious and cultural programmes should purchase the "Jewish Chronicle" available on Fridays and the monthly "New Moon" magazine.

Synagogues & Religious Organisations

United Synagogue
The offices of the **United Synagogue**, the **Chief Rabbinate** and the **Beth Din** transferred from Adler House at the end of 1995 to:
735 High Road, Finchley, N12 0US.

Chief Rabbi: Rabbi Dr Jonathan Sacks;
Executive Office: Dir. Jonathan Kestenbaum. ☎ 0181-343 6301. Fax 0181-343 6310.

Beth Din (Court of the Chief Rabbi)
Registrar: Jeremy Phillips
☎ 0181-343 6270. Fax 0181-343 6257.

United Synagogue
Chief Exec.: J. M. Lew
☎ 0181-343 8989. Fax 0181-343 5262.

Synagogues
Barking & Becontree, 200 Becontree Av. Becontree, Essex, RM8 2TR.
Barnet & District, Eversleigh Rd., New Barnet, Herts., EN5 1NE.
Belmont, 101 Vernon Dr., Stanmore, Middx., HA7 2BW.
Borehamwood & Elstree, Croxdale Rd., Borehamwood, Herts., WD6 4QF.
Bushey, 177–189 Sparrows Herne, Bushey, Herts., WD2 1AJ.
Catford & Bromley, 6 Crantock Rd., SE6 2QS.
Central,. 36–40 Hallam Street, London, W1N 5LH
Chelsea, Smith Ter., Smith St., SW3 4DL.
Chigwell and Hainault, Limes Av., Limes Farm Estate, Chigwell, Essex IG7 5NT.
Clayhall, Sinclair House, Woodford Bridge Rd., Ilford, Essex, IG4 5LN.
Cockfosters & N. Southgate, Old Farm Av., Southgate, N14 5QR.
Cricklewood, 131 Walm Lane, NW2 3AU.
Dollis Hill, Parkside, Dollis Hill Lane, NW2 6RJ.
Ealing, 15 Grange Rd., Ealing, W5 5QN.
Edgware, Parnell Close, Edgware Way, Edgware, Middx. HA8 8YE.
Elm Park, 75 Woburn Av., Elm Park, Hornchurch, Essex, RM12 4NQ.
Enfield & Winchmore Hill, 53 Wellington Rd., Bush Hill Pk., Enfield EN1 2PG.
Finchley, Kinloss Gdns., N3 3DU.
Finsbury Park, Green Lanes, N4 2NT.
Golders Green, 41 Dunstan Rd., NW11 8AE.
Hackney & East London, Brenthouse Rd., E9 6QG.
Hammersmith & West Kensington, 71 Brook Green, W6 7BE.
Hampstead, 1 Dennington Park Rd., NW6 1AX.
Hampstead Garden Suburb, Norrice Lea, N2 0RE.

Harold Hill, Trowbridge Rd., Harold Hill, Essex, RM3 8YW
Hemel Hempstead, Inq. to 1 Devereux Drive, Watford, Herts WD1 3DD.
Hendon, Raleigh Close, NW4 2TA.
Highams Park & Chingford, 74 Marlborough Rd., E4 9AZ.
Highgate, Grimshaw Cl., North Rd., N6 4BJ.
Hounslow, 100 Staines Rd., Hounslow, Middx.
Ilford, 22 Beehive Lane, Ilford, Essex, IG1 3RT.
Kenton, Shaftesbury Av., Kenton, Middx., HA3 0RD.
Kingsbury, Woodland Cl., Kingsbury Green, NW9 8XR.
Kingston & Surbiton, 33–35 Uxbridge Rd., Kingston-upon-Thames, Surrey KT1 2LL.
Mill Hill, Brockenhurst Gdns. NW7 2JY.
Muswell Hill, 31 Tetherdown, N10 1ND.
New Victoria Community Centre, Egerton Rd., N16 6UD
Newbury Park, 23 Wessex Close, Suffolk Rd., Newbury Park, Essex, IG3 8JU.
New West End, St. Petersburgh Pl., W2 4JT.
Northwood, P.O. Box 112, Northwood, Middx, HA6 2EZ.
Palmers Green & Southgate, Brownlow Rd., N11 2BN.
Pinner, 1 Cecil Park, Pinner, Middx, HA5 5HJ.
Potters Bar & District, Inq. to R. Drexler, P.O.B. 119, Potters Bar, Herts, AL9 6DB.
Radlett, P.O. Box 28, Radlett, Herts WD7 7PN.
Richmond, Lichfield Gdns. Richmond-upon-Thames, Surrey, TW9 1AP.
Romford, 25 Eastern Rd., Romford, Essex.
Ruislip, Shenley Av., Ruislip Manor, Middx., HA4 6BP. ☎ 01895-622059.
St. Albans, Oswald Rd., St. Albans, Herts, AL1 3AQ
St. John's Wood, 37–41 Grove End Rd., NW8 9NG.
South Hampstead, 20 Eton Villas, Eton Rd., NW3 4SP.
South London, 45 Leigham Court Rd., SW16 2NF.
South Tottenham, 111–113 Crowland Rd., N15 6UL.
South-West London, 104 Bolingbroke Gr., SW11 1DA.
Staines, Westbrook Rd., South St., Staines, Middx, TW18 4PR.
Stanmore & Canons Park, London Rd., Stanmore, Middx, HA7 4NS.
Sutton, 14 Cedar Rd., Sutton, Surrey, SM2 5DA.
Wanstead and Woodford, 20 Churchfields, E18 2QZ.
Watford, 16 Nascot Rd., Watford, Herts., WD1 3RE.
Wembley, Forty Av., Wembley, Middx., HA9 8JW.
West Ham & Upton Park, 93-95 Earlham Gr., E7 9AN.
Willesden & Brondesbury, 143-145 Brondesbury Pk., NW2 5JL.
Woodside Park, Woodside Hall, Woodside Park Rd., N12 8RZ.
Associate Synagogue
Western Marble Arch, 32 Great Cumberland Place, W1H 7DJ.

Federation of Synagogues
Headquarters: 65 Watford Way, London, NW4 3AQ. Admin: 0181-202 2263.
Burial: 0181-202 3903. Fax 0181-203 0610.

Beth Din
Dayan Yisroel Yaacov Lichtenstein is Rosh Beth Din.

Synagogues
Ahavath Shalom (Neasden), Clifford Way, NW10.
Croydon & District, The Almonds, Shirley Oaks, Croydon, Surrey.
East London Central, 38–40 Nelson St., E1 2DE.
Fieldgate St. Great, 41 Fieldgate St., E1.
Finchley Central, Redbourne Av., N3 2BS.
Finchley Road (Sassover), 4 Helenslea Av., London, NW11.

Great Garden St., 7 Greatorex St., E1 5NF.
Greenford Oldfield Lane, Greenford, Middx.
Ilford Federation, 16 Coventry Rd., Ilford, Essex, IG1 4QR.
Leytonstone & Wanstead, 2 Fillebrook Rd., E11.
Loughton, Chigwell & District Borders Lane, Loughton, Essex, IG10 3HT.
Machzike Hadath (Spitalfields), Highfields Rd., NW11.
Notting Hill, 206-208 Kensington Park Rd., W11.
Sha'are Shomayim (Clapton), 47 Lea Bridge Rd., E5.
Shomrei Hadath, 527a Finchley Rd., NW3.
Sinai, 54 Woodstock Av., NW11 9RJ.
Springfield, 202 Upper Clapton Rd., E5.
Stamford Hill Beth Hamedrash, 50 Clapton Common, E5 9AL.
Tottenham, 366 High Rd., N17 9HT.
Waltham Forest 140 Boundary Rd., E17
West End Great 21 Dean St., W1.
West Hackney, 233 Amhurst Rd., E8 2BS.
Woolwich & District, Anglesea Rd., SE8.
Yavneh, 25 Ainsworth Rd., E9 9JE.
Yeshurun, Fernhurst Gdns., Edgware, Middx., HA8 7PH.

Union of Orthodox Hebrew Congregations
Headquarters: 140 Stamford Hill, N16 6QT. ☎ 0181-802 6226-7.
Adath Yisroel (Parent) Synagogue, 40 Queen Elizabeth's Walk, N16 0HH.
Adath Yisroel Tottenham Beth Hamedrash, 55/57 Ravensdale Rd., N16.
Ahavat Israel Synagogue D'Chasidey Viznitz, 89 Stamford Hill, N16.
Beit Knesset Chida, Egerton Rd., N16.
Beth Abraham Synagogue, 46 The Ridgeway, NW11.
Beth Chodosh Synagogue, 51 Queen Elizabeth's Walk, N16.
Beth Hamedrash Beis Nadvorna, 45 Darenth Rd., N16 6ES.
Beth Hamedrash D'Chasidey Belz, 99 Bethune Rd., N16.
Beth Hamedrash D'Chasidey Belz, 96 Clapton Common, E5, and 49 St Kilda's Rd., N16.
Beth Hamedrash D'Chasidey Gur, 2 Lampard Grove, N16, and 98 Bridge Lane, NW11.
Beth Hamedrash D'Chasidey Ryzin, 33 Paget Rd., N16.
Beth Hamedrash D'Chasidey Sanz Klausenburg, 42 Craven Walk, N16.
Beth Hamedrash D'Chassidey Square, 22 Dunsmure Rd., N16.
Beth Hamedrash Divrei Chaim, 71 Bridge La., NW11.
Beth Hamedrash Hendon, 3 The Approach, NW4 2HU.
Beth Hamedrash Imrey Chaim D'Chasidey Vishnitz-Monsey, 121 Clapton Common, E5.
Beth Hamedrash Kehillas Yacov, 35 Highfield Av., NW1 9EV.
Beth Hamedrash Ohel Moshe, 202B Upper Clapton Rd., E5.
Beth Hamedrash Ohel Naphtoli (Bobov), 87 Egerton Rd., N16.
Beth Hamedrash of the Agudah Youth Movement, 69 Lordship Rd., N16. Also 95 Stamford Hill, N16.
Beth Hamedrash Spinke, 36 Bergholt Cres., N16 5SE.
Beth Hamedrash Torah Etz Chayim, 69 Lordship Rd., N16.
Beth Hamedrash Torah Chaim Liege, 145 Up. Clapton Rd., E5.
Beth Hamedrash Toras Chaim, 37 Craven Walk, N16 6BS.
Beth Hamedrash Vayoel Moshe, 14 Heathland Rd., N16.
Beth Hamedrash Yetiv Lev, D'Satmar, 86 Cazenove Rd., N16. Also 26 Clapton Common, E5.
Beth Shmuel Synagogue, 171 Golders Green Rd., NW11.
Beth Sholom Synagogue, 27 St. Kilda's Rd., N16.

Beth Talmud Centre, 78 Cazenove Rd., N16.
Beth Yisochor Dov Beth Hamedrash, 2-4 Highfield Av., NW11.
Birkath Yehuda (Halaser) Beth Hamedrash, 47 Moundfield Rd., N16 6DT.
Bridge Lane Beth Hamedrash, 44 Bridge Lane, NW11 0EG.
Etz Chaim Yeshiva, 83/85 Bridge Lane, NW11.
Finchley Road Synagogue, 4 Helenslea Av., NW11.
Garden Suburb Beth Hamedrash, Jacob & Alexander Gordon Hse., 5 The Bishop's Av., N2.
Heichal Hatorah, 27 St. Kildas Rd., N16.
Hendon Adath Yisroel Synagogue, 11 Brent St., NW4 2EU.
Kehal Chasidim D'Munkatch Synagogue, 85 Cazenove Rd., N16.
Kingsley Way Beth Hamedrash, 3-5 Kingsley Way, N2.
Knightland Road Synagogue of the Law of Truth Talmudical College, 50 Knightland Rd., E5. Corr: 27 Warwick Grove, E5 9HX.
Lubavitch Synagogue, 107-115 Stamford Hill, N16.
Mesifta Synagogue, 82-84 Cazenove Rd., N16.
North Hendon Adath Yisroel Synagogue, Holders Hill Rd., NW4 1NA. corr.: 31 Holders Hill Crescent, NW4 1NE.
Ohel Israel (Skoler) Synagogue, 11 Brent St., NW4.
Shaare Zion, 10 Woodberry Down, N4.
Stanislowa Beth Hamedrash, 93 Lordship Park, N16
Yeshiva Horomoh Beth Hamedrash, 100 Fairholt Rd., N16 5HH.
Yeshuath Chaim Synagogue, 45 Heathland Rd., N16.
Yesodey Hatorah Synagogue, 2/4 Amhurst Pk., N16.
Zichron Shlomo Beth Hamedrash, 9 Elm Park Av., N15.

Spanish and Portuguese Jews Congregation
Vestry Office, 2 Ashworth Rd., W9 1JY. ☎ 0171-289 2573. Fax 0171-289 2709. Admin.
Bevis Marks, EC3. ☎ 0171-626 1274.
Lauderdale Rd., Maida Vale, W9. ☎ 0171-289 2573.
Wembley, 46 Forty Av., Wembley, Middx.

Other Sephardi congregations in London include:
Aden Jews' Cong., 117 Clapton Common, E5.
Gan Eden, 140 Stamford Hill, N16.
Holland Park, St. James's Gdns., W11.
Lincoln Institute, Broadwalk Lane, NW11.
Neveh Shalom, 352-354 Preston Rd., Harrow, Middx.
Ohel David (Ilford) Cong., Newbury Pk Stn., Newbury Pk., Essex.

Assembly of Masorti Synagogues
Admin. Office of Assembly of Masorti Syns., 1097 Finchley Rd., NW11 0PU. ☎ 0181-201 8772. Fax 0181-201 8917. E-mail: Masorti.uk@ort.org
Edgware Masorti Syn., Chaim Pearl Community Centre, Traditional Way, Station Rd., Edgware. ☎ 0181-952 4987.
New Essex Masorti Cong., Services held at Prince Regent Hotel, Woodford Bridge, Essex. Inq.: ☎ 0181-554 0158.
New London Syn., 33 Abbey Rd., St. John's Wood, NW8 0AT. ☎ 0171-328 1026. Fax 0171-372 3142
New North London Syn., The Manor House, 80 East End Rd., N3 2SY. ☎ 0181-346 8560. Fax 0181-346 1710
New Whetstone Masorti Syn. Services, Oxford and St. George's 120, Oakleigh Rd. North, N20. Inq.: ☎ 0181-368 3936.
St. Albans Masorti Synagogue. P.O.B. 23, St. Albans, AL1 4PH. Inq. A. Hoffman: ☎ 01727-860642.

Independent Synagogues

Belsize Square Synagogue, 51 Belsize Square, NW3 4HX. ☎ 0171-794 3949.
Golders Green Beth Hamedrash Cong., The Riding, Golders Green Rd., NW11 8HL. ☎ 0181-455 2974. Rav: Rabbi H.I. Feldman.
Lubavitch, 107/115 Stamford Hill, N16 5RP. ☎ 0181-800 0022. Fax 0181-809 7324
Machzike Hadath, 3 Highfield Rd., NW11 9LU. Hon. Sec.: R. Shaw. ☎ 0181-204 1887, M. Bitami. ☎ 0181-455 0449.
Ner Yisrael Community, The Crest, off Brent St., NW4 2HY. ☎ 0181-202 6687. Fax 0181-203 5158. Rabbi A. Kimche, B.A. ☎ 0181-455-7347. Sec.: Mrs L. Brayam
Persian Hebrew Congregation, East Bank, Stamford Hill, N16 5AL.
Sephardi Minyan, 62 Brent St., NW4.
Walford Road Syn., 99 Walford Rd., Stoke Newington, N16 8EF. Sec.: Mrs. S. Raymond, ☎ 0171-249 5604.
West End Great, 32 Gt. Cumberland Place, W1H 7DJ. ☎ 0171-724 8121. Fax 0171-723 4413.
Western Marble Arch Synagogue, 32 Gt Cumberland Pl., W1H 7DJ. ☎ 0171 723 9333. Fax 0171-224 8065. Admin. Malcolm E. Howard.
Westminster, Rutland Gdns., Knightsbridge, SW7 1BX. ☎ 0171-584 3953.

Reform Synagogues

Headquarters: The Sternberg Centre for Judaism, 80 East End Rd., N3 2SY. Chief Exec.: Rabbi Tony Bayfield. ☎ 0181-349 4731. Fax 0181-343 0901. Mikvah on premises.
Bromley & District, 28 Highland Rd., Bromley, Kent, BR1 4AD. ☎ 0181-460 5460.
Edgware & District, 118 Stonegrove, Edgware, Middx., HA8 8AB. ☎ 0181-958 9782. Fax 0181-905 4710.
Finchley, Fallowcourt Av., N12 0BE. ☎ 0181-446 3244. Fax 0181-446 5980.
Hampstead. Chairman: Helene Bromnick, 22 Welbeck Mansions, Inglewood Rd., NW6. Services are held at Hashomer House, 37A Broadhurst Gdns, NW6.
Hendon, Danescroft Av., NW4 2NA. ☎ 0181-203 4168. Fax 0181-203 9385
Kol Chai - Hatch End Jewish Community, 434 Uxbridge Rd., Hatch End, Middx. HA5 4RG. ☎ 01923-771856.
Middlesex New, 39 Bessborough Rd., Harrow, Middx., HA1 3BS. ☎ 0181-864 0133.
Milton Keynes & District. Chairman: Stan Cohen, Mailing address: 11 Fairways, Two Mile Ash, Milton Keynes MK8 8AL. ☎ 01908-569661.
North Kensington, Beit Klal Yisrael. Services in Notting Hill Gate. Chairman: Shulamit Ambalu, 63 Habingdon House, Elmington Estate, Notley St., SE5 7NW. ☎ 0171-703 1611.
North-West Surrey, Horvath Cl., Rosslyn Pk., Oatlands Dr., Weybridge, Surrey, KT13 9QZ. ☎ 01932 855400.
North-Western, Alyth Gdns., Finchley Rd., NW11 7EN. ☎ 0181-455 6763. Fax 0181-458 2469.
Radlett & Bushey, 118 Watling St., Radlett, Herts., WD7 7AA. ☎ 01923 856110.
Southgate & District, 45 High St., N14 6LD. ☎ 0181-882 6828. Fax 0181-882 7539.
South-West Essex & District, Oaks Lane, Newbury Park, Essex, IG2 7PL. ☎ 0181-559 0936.
Sukkat Shalom, Hermon Hill, London, E11 1PA. ☎ 0181-508 9327 (Answerphone).

West London Synagogue, 33 Seymour Pl., W1H 6AT. ☎ 0171-723 4404. Fax 0171-224 8258.
Wimbledon & District, 44-46 Worple Rd., SW19 4EJ. ☎ 0181-946 4836. Fax 0181-944 7790.

Liberal & Progressive Synagogues

Headquarters of Union of Liberal and Progressive Syns.: The Montagu Centre, 21 Maple St., W1P 6DS. ☎ 0171-580 1663. Fax 0171-436 4184. Admin. Dir. Michael Burman.
Barkingside Progressive Syn., 129 Perrymans Farm Rd., Barkingside, Ilford, Essex. ☎ 0181-554 9682.
Chiltern Progressive Syn., 39 Broadacres, Bushmead, Luton LU2 7YF. ☎ 012334-21837.
Ealing, Lynton Av., Drayton Gr., W13 0EB. ☎ 0181-997 0528
Finchley, 54a Hutton Gr., N12 8DR. ☎ 0181-446 4063.
Harrow & Wembley Progressive Syn., 326 Preston Rd., Harrow, Middx. ☎ 0181-904 8581.
Hertsmere Progressive Syn., High St., Elstree, Herts. ☎ 0181-953 8889.
Kingston Liberal Syn., Rushett Rd., Long Ditton, Surbiton, Surrey. ☎ 0181-398 7400.
The Liberal Jewish Synagogue, 28 St John's Wood Rd., London, NW8 7HA. ☎ 0171-286 5181.
North London Progressive Syn., 100 Amhurst Pk. N16 5AR. ☎ 0181-800 8931.
Northwood & Pinner, Oaklands Gate, Northwood, Middx. HA6 3AA. ☎ 01923-822592.
Settlement Synagogue, c/o Stepney Jewish Settlement, 2-8 Beaumont Gr., E1 4NQ. ☎ 0171-790 6262.
Southgate Progressive Syn., 75 Chase Rd., N14 4QY. ☎ 0181-886 0977.
South London, Prentis Rd., Streatham, SW16 1QB. ☎ 0181-769 4787.
West Central, The Montagu Centre, 21 Maple St, W1P 6DS. ☎ 0171-636 7627.
Woodford Progressive Synagogue, Marlborough Rd., South Woodford, E18. ☎ 0181-989-7619.

Kashrut Authorities, etc.

Federation Kashrus Board (Federation of Synagogues), 65 Watford Way, London NW4 3AQ. *Admin:* 0181-202 2263 Fax 0181-203 0610. Dir. of Kashrus: Dayan M. D. Elzas.
Kashrut Division, The London Beth Din, 735 High Rd., N12 0US. ☎ 0181-343 6255. Fax 0181-343 6254. *Dir.,* Rabbi Jeremy Conway. Kashrut Hotline 0181-343 6259. Website http://www.kosher.org.uk.
Joint Kashrus Committee-Kedassia (Union of Orthodox Hebrew Congs.), 140 Stamford Hill, N16 6QT. Admin.: Y. Feldman. ☎ 0181-800 6833. Fax 0181-809 7092
London Board for Shechita, P.O.B. 579, Adastra Suite, NAD House, 401-405 Nether St., N3 1YR. ☎ 0181-349 9160. Fax 0181-346 2206.
Sephardi Kashrut Authority, 2 Ashworth Rd., W9 1JY. Ch.: E. H. Silas. ☎ 0171-289 2573. Fax 0171-289 2709. Dir: Rabbi I. S. Abraham.
Shatnez Centre, 22 Bell Lane, Hendon, NW4 2AD. ☎ 0181-202 4005

Mikvaoth

Adath Yisroel Synagogue Mikvah, 40a Queen Elizabeth's Walk, London, N16 0HH (corner 28 Grazebrook Rd.). ☎ 0181-802 2554.
Craven Walk Mikvah, 72 Lingwood Rd., N16. ☎ 0181-800 8555 (day: Mrs. Dunner) 0181-809 6279 (eve).

Edgware & District Communal Mikvah, Edgware United Synagogue grounds, Approach from path alongside 22 Warwick Ave Drive., or from Synagogue car park. ☎ Mrs. M. Estrin 0181 958 3233.

Ilford Mikvah (Fed. of Synagogues), 463 Cranbrook Road, Ilford, Essex. ☎ 0181-554 8532 (eves.) or Mrs. Matlin 0181-554 2551 (day). All correspondence to 367 Cranbrook Rd., Ilford, Essex.

Kingsbury Mikveh See below: United Synagogue Mikveh.

Mikvaot (Union of Orthodox Hebrew Congs.). Central Mikvaot Board, 40 Queen Elizabeth's Walk, N16 0HH. ☎ 0181-802 6226/7.

North West London Communal Mikvah, 10a Shirehall Lane, Hendon, NW4. ☎ Day 0181-202 1427. Eves 0181-202 8517/5706.

Reform Mikvah, The Sternberg Centre, 80 East End Rd., N3 2SY. ☎ 0181-349-2568 (for appointments).

Satmar Mikvah, 62 Filey Av., N16. ☎ 0181-806 3961.

South London Mikvah, 42 St George's Rd., Wimbledon, SW19 4ED. ☎ 0181-944 7149.

Stamford Hill and District Mikvah, Margaret Rd., N16. ☎ 0181-806 3880; 800 5119/809 4064.

United Synagogue Mikveh, Kingsbury United Synagogue, Kingsbury Road, NW9 8XR. ☎ 0181-204 6390.

There are also Mikvaoth in many provincial towns.

News and Media

Visiters to London and tourists in Britain should be aware of the following newspapers, magazines and other listings of events and services:

Communal Enquiry Desk and Communal Diary (Board of Deputies). ☎ 0171-543 5421/0171-543 5422 (see JCi below).

Jewish Chronicle (Est. 1841), 25 Furnival Street, London EC4A 9 1JT. ☎ 0171-405 9052. Fax 0171-405 9040. (Weekly newspaper).

Jewish Year Book (Est. 1896), Vallentine Mitchell, Newbury House, 900 Eastern Avenue, Newbury Park, Ilford, Essex IG2 7HH. ☎ 0181-599 8866. Fax 0181-599 0984. (Annual directory).

London Diary of Jewish Events, 12 Holne Chase, London N2 0QN. ☎ 0181-458 2466. Fax 0181-458 5457. (Monthly listing).

New Moon, 28 St Alban's Lane, London NW11 7QE. ☎ 0181-731 8031. Fax 0181-381 4033. (Monthly Jewish arts listings, etc.).

An increasing number of institutions and organisations are now establishing internet addresses and web pages through universities and other servers, in particular @ort.org. Details are included where forthcoming.

JCi (Jewish Community Information).

A comprehensive service of communal information is under development between the Board of Deputies and B'nai B'rith, B'nai B'rith Hillel House, 1-2 Endsleigh St., London WC1H 0DS. ☎ 0171-383 3272. Fax 0171-387 8014. Contact: Peter Reichwald.

Brijnet (Internet services to the UK Jewish community), 11 The Lindens, Prospect Hill, Waltham Forest, London E17 3EJ. 0181-520 8331. Email: rafi@brijnet.org. Web site: http://shamash.org/ejin/brijnet. Dir: R. Salasnik.

Representative Organisations

Anglo-Jewish Assoc., 5th Floor, Commonwealth House, 1-19 New Oxford St., W1A 1NF. ☎ 0171-404 2111.

Assoc. of Jewish Ex-Servicemen & Women (Ajex), Ajex Hse., East Bank, N16 5RT. ☎ 0181-800 2844. Fax 0181-880 1117.

Assoc. of Jewish Refugees in Gt. Britain, 1 Hampstead Gate, 1a Frognal, NW3 6AL. ☎ 0171-431 6161. Fax 0171-431-8454.

Assoc. of Jewish Women's Orgs. in the U.K., 24-32 Stephenson Way, NW1 2JW. ☎ ☎ 0171-3877688. Fax 0171-387 2110.

B'nai B'rith, B'nai B'rith Hillel Hse., 1-2 Endsleigh St., WC1H 0DS. ☎ 0171-387 5278. Fax: 0171-387 8014. Exec. Dir.: Mark Marcus. There are more than 30 B'nai B'rith lodges in Britain & Ireland, & 12 B'nai B'rith Youth Organisation (BBYO) chapters. Further details from ☎ above.

B'nai B'rith Hillel Foundation, B'nai B'rith Hillel Hse., 1-2 Endsleigh St., WC1H 0DS. ☎ 0171-388 0801. Fax 0171-916 3973. **(K)** Yoffi's Kosher restaurant open in term-time 12.30 p.m. to 2.00 p.m. Mon.-Thurs.; Friday night Shabbat dinners available if booked and paid in advance by Thursday 11 a.m. Students, graduates & adults from home & abroad welcomed. Closed Shabbat & festivals.

Board of Deputies of British Jews, Commonwealth House, 1-19 New Oxford St., London WC1A 1NF. ☎ 0171-543 5400. Fax 0171-543 0010. Email: bopd@ort.org. The officially recognised representative body of British Jewry, founded in 1760. Central Enquiry Desk, 0171-543 5421/22.

Commonwealth Jewish Council, BCM Box 6871, WC1N 3XX. ☎ (0171) 222-2120. Fax (0171) 222-1781.

Council of Christians & Jews, Dir: Paul Mendel, Drayton House, 30 Gordon St., WC1H 0AN. ☎ 0171-388 3322. Fax 0171-388 3305.

Federation of Jewish Relief Organisations, Polish Jewish Refugee Fund, 143 Brondesbury Pk., NW2 5JL. ☎ 0181-451 3425. Sec.: Mrs. R. Gluckstein.

Cultural and Educational Organisations, etc.

Ben Uri Art Society & Gallery, 4th floor, 21 Dean Street., W1V 6NE. ☎ 0171-437 2582. The aim of the Society, which is a registered charity founded in 1915, is to promote Jewish art as part of the Jewish cultural heritage. The Gallery provides a showcase for exhibitions of contemporary art as well as for the Society's own collection of over 700 works by Jewish artists, including David Bomberg, Mark Gertler, Jacob Epstein, Reuven Rubin and Leon Kossoff. Open Mon-Thur 10-5, Sunday afternoons during exhibitions 2-5. Closed Jewish Holy-days, Bank holidays. Curator: Julia Weiner.

British Library, Oriental & India Office Collections, 197 Blackfriars Rd., SE1 8NG. Inq. ☎ 0171-928 9531, ext. 262. The Hebrew section contains about 70,000 printed books and 13,000 manuscripts and fragments. Daily 9.30 a.m. to 4.45 p.m.: Sat, 9.30 a.m. to 12.45 p.m.

British ORT, 126 Albert St., NW1 7NE. ☎ 0171-446 8520. Fax 0171-446 8654.

College for Higher Rabbinical Studies, Tifereth Shalom, 37 Craven Walk, London N16 6BS, ☎ 0181-800-3868. Mr A. Y. Landau, Main Office, 101, Osbaldston Rd, N16 6NP.

Institute of Contemporary History and Wiener Library, 4 Devonshire St., W1N 2BH. ☎ 0171-636 7247. Fax 0171-436 6248. Email: lib@wl.u-net.com. With 50,000 books and periodicals, and over 1,000,000 press cuttings, etc., the library serves as a research institute and reference centre for 20th-century history (especially Germany), modern Jewish history and anti-semitism, minorities, refugees, fascism, etc. Mon. to Fri., 10 a.m. to 5.30 p.m.

Institute for Jewish Policy Research (JPR), 79 Wimpole St., W1M 7DD. ☎ 0171-935 8266. Publications, lectures, seminars on contemporary issues affecting world Jewry. Reference library available (by appointment).

Jewish Historical Society of England, Office: 33 Seymour Pl., W1H 5AP. Hon. Sec.: C. M. Drukker; Admin: Mrs. J. Cannon. ☎/Fax 0171-723 5852. See also Jewish Studies Library entry.

Jewish Memorial Council and Bookshop, 25 Enford St., W1H 2DD. ☎ 0171-724 7778. Fax 0171-706 1710.

Jewish Museum, Raymond Burton House, 129/131 Albert Street, London

NW1 7NB. ☎ 0171-284 1997. The Jewish Museum holds a Ceremonial Art collection of world importance and a major collection on the history of the Jews in Britain. Open Sun-Thursday 10.00a.m.-4.00p.m. Closed Fri, Sat. Jewish Festivals and Bank Holidays. Groups by previous arrangement with Secretary. Entrance £3.00, students and children £1.50. Incorporating **The London Museum of Jewish Life**, The Sternberg Centre for Judaism, 80 East End Rd., London N3 2SY, (nearest tube Finchley Central). Permanent exhibition traces history of London Jewry with reconstructions of a tailoring workshop, an immigrant home and East London bakery. Also organises temporary exhibitions, educational programmes and guided tours of Jewish London. Curator: Rickie Burman, MA., M.Phil, Education Officer: Ruth-Anne Lenga. ☎ 0181-349 1143. Open Mon.-Thurs., 10.30 a.m. to 5 p.m.; Sun. (except during August & Bank Holiday weekends), 10.30 a.m. to 4.30 p.m. Closed Fri., Sat, Jewish Festivals, public holidays and 25 Dec. to 4 Jan. ☎ 0181-349-1143. **The Jewish Studies Library** within University College London Library, Gower Street, London WC1E 6BT. ☎ 0171-387 7050, Fax 0171-380 7373. In addition to materials purchased for the College's Department of Hebrew Studies it incorporates the Mocatta Library, Altmann Library, William Margulies Yiddish Library and the Library of the Jewish Historical Society of England. Applications to use or view the collections should be made in advance in writing to the Librarian.

Jews' College, Albert Rd., NW4 2SJ. ☎ 0181-203 6427. Fax 0181-203 6420. The library, which contains 80,000 volumes, 20,000 pamphlets, 700 manuscripts, and over 1000 audio and video cassettes is open as follows: Mon.-Thurs., 9 a.m. to 6 p.m. (5 p.m. during vacations); Fri., 9 a.m. to 1 p.m.; Sun. during term-time, 9.30 a.m. to 12.30 p.m. Closed on all Jewish Holy-days, festivals & public holidays. Erev Yom Tov, closed 1 p.m.

Leo Baeck College, The Sternberg Centre for Judaism, 80 East End Rd., N3 2SY. ☎ 0181-349 4525. Fax 0181-343-2558. Email: Leo.Baeck.College@mailbox.ulcc.ac.uk. Vegetarian Cafeteria.

London Academy of Jewish Studies (Kollel Harabbanim), 2-4 Highfield Av., NW11 9ET. Hon. Princ.: Rabbi G. Hager. ☎ 0181-455 5938 (office), 0181-458 1264 (students).

Lubavitch Foundation, Lubavitch Hse., 107-115 Stamford Hill, N16 5RP. ☎ 0181-800 0022. Fax 0181-809 7324. University Council – Rabbi Z. Telsner. Small communities – Rabbi I. Sufrin. Adult Educ. – Dr T. Loewenthal. Women's Centre ☎ 0181-809 6508 – Rachel Bernstein. Hospitality – Rabbi Z. Telsner. Librarian – Z. Rabin ☎ 0181-800 5823. Publ. Lubavitch Direct.

ORT (World Ort Union), Dir.-Gen.: Dr. E. Isler. ORT Administration Ltd., ORT Hse., 3 Sumpter Cl., NW3 5HR. ☎ 0171-431 1333. Fax 0171-435 4784.

Yeshivat Dvar Yerushalayim of London, Princ.: Rabbi J. Freilich, Ph.C. Adult education courses, 24 Templars Av., NW11 0NS. ☎/Fax 0181-455 8631.

Welfare Organisations, Hospitals, etc.

Jewish Blind Society (incorporating Jewish Assoc. for the Physically Handicapped), see: 'Jewish Care'.

Jewish Care, Stuart Young House, 221 Golders Green Rd., London NW11 9DQ. ☎ 0181-458 3282. Exec.Dir.: Melvyn Carlowe, (created by the merger of the Jewish Welfare Board and the Jewish Blind Society in January 1990).

Jewish Deaf Assoc. (Centre and Club), 90-92 Cazenove Rd., N16 6AB. ☎ 0181-806 6147. Dir.: Mrs. Pat Goldring. Fax 0181-806 2251. Advisory and Resource Centre for hearing impaired people; Contact 0181-806 2028. A second centre at 21a Accommodation Rd., NW11 8EP. ☎ 0181-455 1557. Fax 0181-455 1943. Hours are 10-4, Mon.-Thurs.

Jewish Home & Hospital at Tottenham (formerly the Home & Hospital for

Jewish Incurables), 295 High Rd., S. Tottenham, N15 4RT. ☎ 0181-800 5138. General Man; Tony Shepherd, R.M.N., M.R.S.H., Cert.Ed., RNT. M.H.S.M.
Jewish Marriage Council, 23 Ravenshurst Av., NW4 4EE. ☎ 0181-203 6311. Connect The Jewish Marriage Bureau. ☎ 0181-203 5207.
Jewish Welfare Board, see: 'Jewish Care'.
League of Jewish Women, Voluntary Service Org., 24-32 Stephenson Way, NW1 2JW. ☎ 0171-387 7688. Fax 0171-387 2110.
Miyad, National Jewish Crisis Helpline, ☎ 0181-203 6211.
Nightingale House (The Home for Aged Jews), largest nursing/residential home for the aged in Britain and largest Jewish home in Europe, 105 Nightingale Lane, SW12 8NB. ☎ 0181-673 3495. Fax 0181-675 2258. Exec. Dir.: Asher Corren. Dep.: Dir. Leon Smith.
Norwood Child Care, Norwood House, Harmony Way, NW4 2BZ. ☎/Fax. 0181-203 3030. *Contact:* Sara Kyte.
Ravenswood Foundation, field work services, residential care and special education of mentally handicapped children and adults. Head Office: 2nd Floor, Broadway House, 80-82 The Broadway, Stanmore, Middx. ☎ 0181-954 4555. Fax. 0181-420 6800.
World Jewish Relief, Drayton Hse., 30 Gordon St., WC1H 0AN. ☎ 0171-387 3925. Fax 0171-383 4810. E-mail. WJR@ort.org.

Student and Youth Organisations
Assoc. for Jewish Youth, AJY Hse., 128 East Lane, Wembley, Middx. HA0 3NL. ☎ 0181-908 4747, Fax 0181-904 4323. E:mail: ajy@ort.org. Minicom for hard of hearing 0181-904 4393. The AJY is able to give information on a wide range of Jewish youth clubs, centres, projects and movements throughout the country.
Bachad Fellowship, Friends of Bnei Akiva. Chairman: Arieh L. Handler, 2 Halleswelle Rd., NW11 0DJ. ☎ 0181-458 9370. Fax 0181-209 0107. Bnei Akiva Youth Centres: London, Alexander Margulies Youth Centre, 2 Halleswelle Rd., NW11 0DJ; Manchester, Bnei Akiva Youth Centre, 72 Singleton Rd., Salford 7, Manchester; Leeds, Bnei Akiva Youth Centre, Street Lane Gardens, Leeds 17.
Bnei Akiva, 2 Halleswelle Rd., NW11 0DJ. ☎ 0181-209 1319, Fax 0181-209 0107. Email: bnei.akiva@ort.org
Habonim-Dror, 523 Finchley Rd., NW3 7BD. ☎ 0171-435 9033, Fax 0171-431 4503.
Hanoar Hatzioni, 31 Tetherdown, Muswell Hill, N10 1ND. ☎ 0181-883 1022-3.
Harold Godfrey Hillel House, 25 Louisa St., E1 4NF. ☎ 0171-790 9557 (office), 0171-790 5426 (students).
Jewish Lads' and Girls' Brigade Inc. Headquarters: 'Camperdown', 3 Beechcroft Rd., S. Woodford, E18 1LA.
Jewish Scouts and Guides.
Inf. about **Scouts** from Peter Russell, 9 Graham Lodge, Graham Rd., NW4 3DG. ☎ 0181-202 8613, and about **Guides & Brownies** from Mrs D. Simonson, 61 Bute Rd., Ilford, Essex IG6 1AG. ☎ 0181-554 9195.
Jewish Student Centre, B'nai B'rith Hillel Foundation, Hillel Hse., 1-2 Endsleigh St., WC1H 0DS. ☎ 0171-388 0801. Fax 0171-383 0390. Facilities include meeting rooms, common-room. (K) Kosher restaurant open Mon.-Thurs., 12.30 p.m. to 2.00 p.m. termtime only. Fri. night meal available if booked and paid for in advance by Thursday 11 a.m.. Students, graduates and adults from home and abroad welcome. Closed Shabbat & festivals.
Kisharon Senior Centre, 37 Moss Hall Grove, London N12. Principal: Mrs. Ch. Lehman. Centre for Education and job training including Bet Aviezer Workshop. for ages 16-24.

ב"ה

CROFT COURT HOTEL
CROFT GARDEN RESTAURANT

44 Ravenscroft Avenue
London NW11 8AY

STRICTLY
KOSHER

כשר למהדרין

חלב ישראל

TELEPHONE: 0181 458 3331
FAX: 0181 455 9175

The hotel is situated in Golders Green, and is well positioned for easy access into the West End and City, only 20 minutes away. A number of Shuls and Mikvaot are located at close proximity to the hotel.

We pride ourselves on setting a high standard, and are small enough to care for the individual needs of guests. All rooms have en suite facilities and are equipped with: **Direct dial telephone; Tea/Coffee facilities; Remote Control Colour Television; Hairdryer.**

— oOo —

Enjoy a new experience in dining in the elegant and relaxing surroundings of the
CROFT GARDEN RESTAURANT
serving French cuisine
Open 11am to 11pm (Last orders 10.15pm)
The restaurant can also be booked for a Simcha (eg. Sheva Brachot, Engagement, etc.)

— oOo —

Fax and safe facilities are available at Reception
The hotel has a beautiful garden where guests can relax

The Hotel is strictly orthodox and is under the supervision of the London Beth Din. A fully cooked breakfast is included. Shabbat meals are available (Glatt Kosher), and should be ordered by Thursday morning.

Under supervision of the Kashrut Division of the London Beth Din.

Maccabi Union, Gildesgame Hse., 73a Compayne Gdns., NW6 3RS. ☎ 0171-328 0382. Fax 0171-328 9118. Sec. will give inf. about youth clubs in London & the provinces.

Noam (Masorti youth movement), 97 Leeside Crescent, NW11 0JL. ☎ 0181-201 8773. Fax 0181-201 8917.

Union of Jewish Students of UK & Eire, Hillel Hse., 1-2 Endsleigh St., WC1H 0DS. ☎ 0171-387 4644, 0171-380 0111. Fax 0171-383 0390.

Zionist Organisations

Most of the principal London Zionist offices are now centred at Balfour Hse., 741 High Rd., N12 0BQ. ☎ 0181-446 2277. Fax 0181-343-9037. They include the following: World Zionist Organisation, Zionist Federation, Jewish Agency for Israel, Joint Israel Appeal & British Aliyah Movement.

British Emunah, Norwood House, Harmony Way, off Victoria Rd., NW4 2DR. ☎ 0181-203 6066. Fax 0181-203 6668 (Reg. Charity no. 215398). Chairman: Mrs. R. Sachs.

British WIZO, 107 Gloucester Pl., W1H 4BY. ☎ 0171-486 2691. Fax 0171-486 7521. H. Sec: Mrs. B Harding. Chairman: Mrs. R Sotnick.

Children & Youth Aliyah Committee for Great Britain & Eire, 960 High Rd., North Finchley N12 9YA. Exec. Dir.: Sion Mehdi. ☎ 0181-446 4321. Fax 0181-343 7383.

Hadassah Medical Relief Assoc., Trafalgar House, Grenville Place, NW7 3SA.

Jewish National Fund for Israel in Great Britain & Ireland, Harold Poster Hse., Kingsbury Circle, NW9 9SP. ☎ 0181-204 9911.

Mizrachi-Hapoel Hamizrachi Federation and **National Zionist Council**, 2b Golders Green Rd., NW11 8LH. ☎ 0181-455 2243. Fax 0181-455 2244. Admin. Mrs M. Davila.

National Zionist Council, 2b Golders Green Rd., NW11 8LH. ☎ 0181-455 2243-4. Fax 0181-458 7472. Gen. Sec.: Mrs. N. J. Herman.
Poale Zion Labour Zionist Movement, c/o Hon. Sec.: Henry Smith, 82 De Beauvoir Rd., N1 5AT.

Israel Embassy

2 Palace Green, London W8 4QB. ☎ 0171-957 9500. Fax 0171-957 9555. Israeli Consulate-General, 15a Old Court Place, London W8. Nearest Underground Station: High Street, Kensington. Consular Office hours: Mon.-Thurs., 10 a.m. to 1 p.m.; Fri., 10 a.m. to 12 noon.
Internet site: Travel Information http://www.israel-embassy.org.uk/london

Booksellers

London Jewish booksellers are listed on page 367.

Hotels, Restaurants, etc.

In the lists of hotels and restaurants the following note applies:

(K)   An establishment (hotel, restaurant or caterer) under the supervision of a recognised orthodox Jewish religious authority.

LBD   London Beth Din.

KED   Kedassia

FKB   Federation of Synagogues Kashrut Board.

LBS   London Board of Shechita.

SKA   Sephardi Kashrut Authority.

★   An establishment which, while claiming to be strictly kosher, is not under official supervision.

The **Kashrut Division** of the London Beth Din is approved by the Chief Rabbi. The Division's offices are at 735 High Rd., N12 0US. ☎ 0181-343 6255.
Kedassia is under the authority of the Joint Kashrus Committee of the Union of Orthodox Hebrew Congregations, Adath Yisroel Synagogues and Golders Green Beth Hamedrash. *Admin.:* Y. Feldman. *Sec.:* R. M. Hirsch, F.B.S.C., 67 Amhurst Park, N16. ☎ 0181-802 6226-7 & 0181-800 6833. Fax 0181-809 7092.
The **Federation of Synagogues Kashrus Board** (FKB) *Ch.:* W. Ungar; *Dir.:*

Dayan M. D. Elzas, under the authority of the Beth Din of the Federation of Synagogues, 65 Watford Way, NW4 3AQ. ☎ 0181-202 2263. Fax 0181-203 0610.
The **Sephardi Kashrut Authority** is under the supervision of the Ecclesiastical Authorities of the Spanish & Portuguese Jews' Congregation. 2 Ashworth Rd., W9 1JY. ☎ 0171-289 2573. Fax 0171-289-2709. *Dir.:* Rabbi I. S. Abraham.

The following is a select list of establishments in the London area. For fuller details, please request lists of kosher affiliates from the respective authorities listed above.

Hotels

★ **Mrs. Abramsky**, 26 Highfield Av., NW11 9ET. ☎ 0181-455 7136. Bed & Breakfast. Other meals by arrangement.
★ **Andrews Hotel**, 12 Westbourne St., Hyde Park, W2 2TZ. ☎ 0171-723 4514, Fax 0171-706 4143; (office), 0171-723 5365 (guests) (Hebrew spoken).
(K) Croft Court Hotel (LBD) (20), 44 Ravenscroft Av., Golders Green, NW11 8AY. ☎ 0181-458 3331. Fax 0181-455 9175. Meals need to be pre-booked.
(K) Eshel Hotel, Stamford Hill, N16. ☎ 0181-800 1445.
(K) Golders Green Hotel, 147-149 Golders Green Rd., NW11 9BN. ☎ 0181-458 7127-9.
★ **Hampstead House Residential Hotel**, 12 Lyndhurst Gdns., NW3 5NR. ☎ 0171-794 6036. B. Newton.
★ **Mrs. Herskine**, 13 Brook Ave., Edgware, Middx., HA8 9XF. ☎ 0181-958 4409.
★ **Kacenberg's** (Guest House), 1 Alba Gdns., NW11 9NS. ☎ 0181-455 9238 or 3780. Bed & breakfast. Shabbat meals.
(K) Kadimah Hotel (LBD) (21), 146 Clapton Common, E5 9AG. ☎ 0181-800 5960/1716. Fax 0181 800 6237.
(K) (Ked.). Menorah Hotel & Caterers, 54-54a Clapton Common, E5. ☎ 0181-806 4925 (reception) & 6340 (guests).
★ **Pension Strom** (8), 22 Rookwood Rd. N16 6SS. ☎ 0181-800 1151. Bed & breakfast. Other meals to order.
★ **Mrs. H. Shaer** (Guest House), 3 Elm Cl., NW4 2PH. ☎ 0181-202 0642. Bed & breakfast. Other meals by arrangement.
★ **Woodstock Guest House**, 68 Woodstock Av., NW11 9RJ. ☎ 0181-209 0637 (bookings) & 0181-455 4120 (guests).
Brookland Guest House, 220 Golders Green Rd., NW11 9AT. ☎ 0181-455 6678/455 6135.
Buckland Hotel, 6 Buckland Cres., NW3 5DX. ☎ 0171-722 5574. Fax. 0171-722 5594. Bed & breakfast (16).
Carmel Guest House, 137 North End Rd., NW11. ☎ 0181-455 0891.
Central Hotel (40), 35 Hoop Lane, NW11 8BS. ☎ 0181-458 5636. Fax 0181-455 4792.
The Churchill Inter-Continental (450), Portman Sq., W1A 4ZX. ☎ 0171-486 5800. Fax 0171-486 1255.
Clive Hotel at Hampstead, Primrose Hill Rd., NW3 3NA. ☎ 0171-586 2233 (96).
Cumberland Hotel (907), Marble Arch, W1A 4RF. ☎ 0171-262 1234.
Hendon Hall Hotel, Ashley La., off Parson St., NW4 1HF. ☎ 0181-203 3341. Fax 0181-203-9709.
London Regents Park Hilton, 18 Lodge Rd., NW8 7JT. ☎ 0171-722 7722.
London Hilton on Park Lane (446), 22 Park Lane, W1Y 4BE. ☎ 0171-493 8000.
Radisson SAS Portman Hotel, 22 Portman Sq., W1H 9FL. ☎ 0171-208 6000. Fax 0171-208 6001.

Restaurants

(K) **Amor** (Ked), 8 Russell Pde., Golders Green Rd., NW11. ☎ 0181-458 4221.
(K) **Bloom's World-Famous Kosher Restaurant** (LBD), 130 Golders Green Rd., NW11 8HB. ☎ 0181-455 1338. Free delivery service. Fax 0171-247 3767. Fully air-conditioned.
(K) **DD's Kosher Dairy Sandwich Bar** (LBD), 41 Greville St., EC1. ☎ 0171-242 5487.
(K) **Deli at West London Synagogue**, 33 Seymour Place, W1. ☎ 0171-723 4404.
(K)**Dizengoff** (SKA), 118 Golders Green Rd., NW11 2HB. ☎ 0181-458 7003. Fax 0181-381 4902
(K) **Elite**, 225 Golders Green Rd., NW11 9PN. ☎ 0181-455 8195
Harry Morgan, 31 St Johns Wood High St., NW8. ☎ 0171-722 1869.
(K) **Hillel Restaurant** (LBD), Yoffi's, B'nai B'rith-Hillel Foundation, Hillel Hse., 1-2 Endsleigh St., WC1H 0DS. ☎ 0171-388 0801. Mon.-Thurs., 12.30 to 2 p.m. Fri. night Sabbath meal available if booked in advance by Thursday 11 a.m. Closed June/July/August; re-opens mid-September.
(K) **Kaifeng** (LBD), Kosher Oriental Restaurant, 51 Church Road, Hendon, NW4 4DU. ☎ 0181-203 7888. Fax 0181-203 8263. Delivery and Take-Away service.
(K) **Marcus's** (LBD), 5 Hallswelle Pde., Finchley Rd., NW11 0DL. ☎ 0181-458 4670.
Milk n'Honey, 124 Golders Green Road, NW11. ☎ 0181-455 0644.
★ **Morry's Milk Bar Restaurant**, 4 Windus Rd., N16.
(K) **New Connaught Rooms** (SKA), Great Queen St., WC2B 5DA. ☎ 0171-405 7811.
The Nosherie, 12-13 Greville St., EC1. ☎ 0171-242 1591.
(K) **Old Jaffa** (SKA), 27 Finchley Lane, NW4. ☎ 0181-203 0750.
Rabin's Salt Beef Bar, 28 Gt. Windmill St., W1. ☎ 0171-434 9913.
Reubens (SKA), 20a Baker St., W1. ☎ 0171-935 5945.
Richoux, 3 Circus Rd., NW8. ☎ 0171-483 4001.
(K) **Solly's Restaurant** (LBD), 148a Golders Green Rd., London NW11. ☎ 0181-455 0004.
Sally's Exclusive, 146-150 Golders Green Road, NW11. ☎ 0181-455 2121.
Stars Restaurant, 11 Soho Sq., W1V 5DB. ☎ 0171-437 6525 & 9535.
(K)**Tasti Pizza** (LBD, Ked), 23 Amhurst Parade, Amhurst Park, N16 5AA. ☎ 0181-802 0018/455 0004. 252 Golders Green Road, NW11. ☎ 0181-209 0023.
(K) **Uncle Shloime's** (Ked), 204 Stamford Hill, N16. ☎ 0181-802 9355.
(K) **The White House Kosher Restaurant** (LBD), 10 Bell Lane, London NW4. ☎ 0181-203 2427.

Fish Restaurants

★ **Grahame's Sea Fare Restaurant**, 38 Poland St., W1V 3DA. ☎ 0171-437 3788 & 0975. Fax 0171-294 1808.
Café Fish & Café Fish Wine Bar, 39 Panton St., SW1. ☎ 0171-930 3999.
Redford's Fish Restaurant, 313 Hale La., Edgware, Middx. ☎ 0181-958 2229.
Rudland & Stubbs, Green Hill Rents, Cowcross St., EC1. ☎ 0171-253 0148.
Sea Shell, 49 Lisson Gr., NW1 6UH. ☎ 0171-723 8703 & 0171-724 1063; 424-426 Kingsland Rd., E8. ☎ 0171-254 6152.
Upper Street Fish Shop, 324 Upper St., N1. ☎ 0171-359 1401.

Vegetarian Restaurants

Barrow House, 45 Barrow Rd, SW16 5PE. ☎ 0181-677 1925. B&B.
Bibacq Vegetarian Restaurant, 2 Gillespie Rd, Highbury N5 1LN. ☎ 0171-704 0088.
Blah Blah Blah, 78 Goldhawk Rd, Shepherds Bush, W12. ☎ 0181-746 1337.
Cherry Orchard, 241 Globe Rd, Bethnal Green E2 0JD. ☎ 0181-980 6678.

Cordon Vert, 136 Merton Rd, Wimbledon SW19 1EH. ☎ 0181-543 9174.
Cranks Restaurants, 37 Marshall St., W1V 1LL. ☎ 0171-437 9431; 9 Tottenham St., W1P 9PB. ☎ 0171-631 3912.
(K) Dahlia, 11 Bell Lane, Hendon, NW4. ☎ 0181-202 1188.
Diwana Bhel Poori House, 121 Drummond St, NW1 2HL; 50 Westbourne Grove, W2 5SH. ☎ 0171-387 5556.
Food for Thought, 31 Neal St., Covent Garden, WC2H 9PK. ☎ 0171-836 0239.
Futures!, 8 Botolph Alley, EC3R 8DR. ☎ 0171-623 4529, and Futures!! Cafè Bar, 2 Exchange Square, EC2A 2EH. ☎ 0171-638 6341
The Greenway, (Jewish Vegetarian Society), 853 Finchley Rd., NW11 8LX. ☎ 0181-455 0692.
Greenhouse, 16 Chenies St, WC1E 7EX. ☎ 0171-637-8083
Indian Veg Bhal Poori House, 92 Chapel Market, Islington, N1 9EX. ☎ 0171-837 4607.
Mandeer, 21 Hanway Place, off Tottenham Court Rd, W1P 9DG. ☎ 0171-323 0660.
Millward's Restaurant, 97 Stoke Newington Church St, N16. ☎ 0171-254 1025.
Mrs. Poynter's, 102 Arthur Rd, Wimbledon Park, SW19 7DT. ☎ 0181-946 - 0902, B&B.
Rani, 3 Long Lane, N3 2PR. ☎ 0181-349 2636.
Raw Deal, 65 York St., W1H 1PQ. ☎ 0171-262 4841.
Sabras, 263 High Rd, Willesden Green, NW10 2RX. ☎ 0181-459 0340.
Seasons Vegetarian Restaurant, Harcourt St, W1. ☎ 0171-402 5925.
Shan Vegetarian Restaurant, 200 Shaftesbury Av., WC2H 8JL. ☎ 0171-240 3348.
Surya Indian Vegetarian Restaurant, 59 Fortune Green Rd, NW6 1DR. ☎ 0171-435 7486.
Veganomics, 314 Lewisham Rd, SE13 7PA. ☎ 0181-852 7978.
Wilkins Natural Foods, 61 Marsham St, SW1P 3DP. ☎ 0171-222 4038.
Windmill Wholefood Restaurant, 486 Fulham Rd, SW6 5NH. ☎ 0171-385 1570.
Yours Naturally, 45 Shelton St, Covent Garden, WC2E 9MJ. ☎ 0171-497 0079.

Bakeries

The Cake Company (LBD), Basement, 3-4 Sentinal Square, NW4 2EL. ☎ 0181-202 2327.
Carmelli Bakery Ltd (LBD, Ked), 128 Golders Green Road, NW11. Tel: 0181-455 2074.
Cousins Bagel Bakers (SKA), 109 Golders Green, NW11. ☎ 0181-201 9694.
Creme de la Creme (LBD), 5 Temple Fortune Parade, Bridge Lane, NW11 1QN. ☎ 0181-458 9090.
Daniel's Bagel Bakery (LBD), 13 Hallswelle Parade, Finchley Road, NW11. ☎ 0181-455 5826.
Dino'z Bakery (LBD), 11 Edgwarebury Lane, Edgware, Middx. ☎ 0181-958 1554.
Galillee Bakery (LBD), 388 Cranbrook Rd., Ilford, Essex. ☎ 0181-518 3567.
J. Goide (caterers) Ltd (LBD), 4 Stepney Green, E1. ☎ 0171-790 3449.
M&D Grodzinski (LBD), Hot Bread Shop, 223 Golders Green Rd, NW11. ☎ 0181-458 3654. 9 Northways Parade, NW3. ☎ 0181-722 4944. 53 Goodge Street, W1. ☎ 0171-636 0561. 6 Edgwarebury Lane, Edgware, Middx. ☎ 0181-958 1205.
Keene's Patisserie (LBD), Unit 6, Mill Hill Ind Est., Flower Lane, NW7 2HU. ☎ 0181-906 3729. 192 Preston Road, Wembley, Middx. ☎ 0181-904 5952.

Mr Bagels Factory (SKA), 1 Kings Yard, Carpenters Road, E15 2HD. ☎ 0181-533 7553.

Parkway Patisserie Ltd. (LBD), 326 Regents Park Road, N3. ☎ 0181-346 0344. 30a North End Road, NW11. ☎ 0181-455 5026. 204 Preston Road, Wembley, Middx. ☎ 0181-904 7736.

Rensow Patisserie Ltd (LBD), Unit a, 8-10 Timber Wharf Rd, N16. ☎ 0181-800 2525.

Taboon Continental Bakery (SKA), 17 Russell Parade, NW11. ☎ 0181-455 7451.

Delicatessen, etc.

Kosher World, 46 Vivian Av., NW4. ☎ 0181-203 8108.

Pelter Stores, 82 Edgware Way, Edgware, Middx. ☎ 0181-958 6910.

Sunshine Deli, 122 George Lane, South Woodford, E18. ☎ 0181-989 8109.

Butchers

(K) L. Botchin (LBD), 423 Kingsbury Road, NW9. ☎ 0181-204 2236.

(K) Stanley Cohen (LBD), 93b Upper Clapton Road, E5. ☎ 0181-806 5035.

(K) D. Gilbert (LBD), 880 High Road, N12 9RH. ☎ 0181-445 2224.

(K) J.M. Glass (LBD), 100 High Road, Bushey Heath, Herts. ☎ 0181-420 4443.

(K) N. Goldberg (LBD/Ked), 12 Claybury Broadway, Redbridge, Ilford, Essex. ☎ 0181-551 2828.

(K) Gold Bros. (LBD), 222 Jubilee Street, E1. ☎ 0171-790 1572.

(K) L.D. Greenspan (LBD), 9/11 Kyttelton Road, N2. ☎ 0181-455 9921.

(K) H. Gross & Son, 6 Russell Parade, Golders Green Road, NW11. ☎ 0181-455 6662.

(K) Ilford Kosher Meats (LBD), 7 Beehive Lane, Ilford, Essex. ☎ 0181-554 3238.

(K) Miss G. Ismach (LBD), 230 Regents Park Road, N3. 181-346 6554S.

(K) L. Kelman (LBD), 49 Streatham Hill, SW2. ☎ 0181-674 3626.

(K) La Boucherie (LBD), 145 High Street, Barkingside, Essex IG6 2AJ. ☎ 0181-551 9215.

(K) M. Lipowicz (LBD), 9 Royal Parade, W5. ☎ 0181-997 1722.

(K) Louis Mann (LBS), 23 Edgwarebury Lane, Edgware, Middx. ☎ 0181-958 3789.

(K) Mehadrin Meats (LBS), 25a Belfast Rd., N16. ☎ 0181 806 7686/3002.

(K) Menachem's (LBS), 15 Russell Pde., Golders Green Rd., NW11. ☎ 0181-201 8629.

(K) A. Perlmutter (LBD), 1-2 Onslow Parade, Hampden Square, Soughgate, N14 5JN. ☎ 0181-361 5441/2.

(K) Jack Schlagman (LBD), 112 Regents Park Road, N3. ☎ 0181-346 3598.

(K) Ivor Silverman (LBS), 4 Canons Corner, Stanmore, Middx. ☎ 0181-958 8682/2692. Fax 0181-958 1725.

(K) I. Silverman (Grant) (LBD), 360 Uxbridge Road, Hatch End, Middx, HA4 4HP. ☎ 0181-428 6564.

(K) C. Solomons (LBD), 646 Cranbrook Road, Barkingside, Essex. ☎ 0181-554 6562.

(K) S. Samuels (LBD), 30 Red Lion Street, Richmond, Surrey. ☎ 0181-940 3060/6282.

(K) R. Wolff (LBD), 84 Edgware Way, Edgware, Middx. ☎ 0181-958 8454.

Fishmongers

(K) Leveyuson (LBD), 47a Brent St., NW4. ☎ 0181-202 7834.

(K) Sam Stoller (SKA), 28 Temple Fortune Parade, NW11. ☎ 0181-455 1957.

REGIONS

ALDERSHOT (HANTS.)
Inq. to Senior Jewish Chaplain H.M. Forces, Rev. M. Weisman, 25 Enford St., London, W1H 2DD. ☎ 0171-724 7778. Fax 0171-706 1710.

AMERSHAM
South Bucks Jewish Community (ULPS). Enquiries to David Sacker. ☎ 01494 431885.

BASILDON (ESSEX)
Syn: (Affiliated to Southend Hebrew Cong.). Inq.: M. Kochmann, 3 Furlongs, SS16 4BW. ☎ 01268 524947.

BIRMINGHAM (W. MIDLANDS)
This Jewish com. is one of the oldest in the Provinces, dating from 1730, if not earlier. Birmingham was a centre from which Jewish pedlars covered the surrounding country week by week, returning to their homes for the Sabbath.
The first synagogue of which there is any record was in The Froggery in 1780. But there was a Jewish cemetery in the same neighbourhood in 1730, and Moses Aaron is said to have been born in Birmingham in 1718. The synagogue of 1780 was extended in 1791, 1809 and 1827. A new and larger synagogue, popularly known as 'Singers Hill', was opened in 1856.

Representative Organisations
B'nai B'rith Joint Lodge. Jt. Sec.: Frank & Herta Linden, 7 Westbourne Gdns., Edgbaston B15 3TJ. ☎ 0121-454 5042.
Representative Council of Birmingham & Midland Jewry. Sec.: L. Jacobs, 37 Wellington Rd., B15 2ES. ☎ 0121-236 1801 (day), 0121-440 4142 (eve). Fax 0121-236 9906.

Synagogues & Religious Organisations
Birmingham Hebrew Congregation, Singers Hill, Ellis St., B1 1HL. ☎ 0121-643 0884. M.: Rabbi L. L. Tann, B.A.
Central, 133 Pershore Rd., B5 7PA. M. Rabbi C. Rapoport; Sec.: S. Cohen. ☎ 0121-440 4044. **Mikveh** on premises. Inq. Mrs Arkush, ☎ 0121-440-5853. Malcolm Locker Banqueting Hall. ☎ 0121-440 4439.
New, 11 Park Rd., B13 8AB. M.: Rabbi R. Goodman. ☎ 0121-449 3544.
Park Rd. Assembly Hall, B13 8AB. ☎ 0121-449 3435.
Progressive, 4 Sheepcote St., B16 8AA. ☎ 0121-643 5640. M. Rabbi Dr M. Jacobi.
Shechita Board, Singers Hill, Ellis St., B1 1HL. Sec.: B. Gingold. ☎ 0121-643 0884

Cultural & Educational Organisations
Cultural Society. Hon. Sec.: G. Lesser, 15, Crookham Close, B17 8RR. ☎ 0121-429 6773. Publishes 'Birmingham Jewish Recorder' (monthly).
International Jewish Genealogical Resources. Co-Directors: Dr. A. P. Joseph & Mrs. Judith Joseph. Same address & ☎ as Jewish Historical Society.
Jewish Historical Society, Birmingham Branch. Ch.: Dr. A. P. Joseph, 25 Westbourne Rd., B15 3TX. ☎ 0121-454 0408.
Lubavitch Centre, 95 Willows Rd., B12 9QF. ☎ 0121-440 6673. Dir.: Rabbi S. Arkush.
Reference Library. Syn. Offices, Singers Hill, Ellis St., B1 1HL. ☎ 0121-643 0884.
Birmingham Jewish Education Board, Chairman: J.Berg. ☎ 0121-449 2111.

Welfare Organisations, Hospitals, etc.
Birmingham Jewish Housing Assoc. Ltd. Same address & ☎ as Birmingham Jewish Welfare Board.
Birmingham Jewish Welfare Board, 1 Rake Way, B15 1EG. ☎ 0121-643 2835.

Home for Aged. Andrew Cohen House, River Brook Drive, Stirchley, Birmingham B30 2SH. ☎ 0121-458 5000. Inq. to Birmingham Jewish Welfare Board, 1 Rake Way, B15 1EG. ☎ 0121-643 2835. The Joseph & Doris Cohen Day Centre is also at this address.
Jewish Blind Society. Sec.: David Winroope, 3, The Hollies, Plymouth Road, Barnt Green, B45. ☎ 0121-447 7477 (home), 0121-552 1645 (office).
World Jewish Relief. Tr. D.Winroope

Student & Youth Organisations
Birmingham Jewish Youth Trust, Youth Office, c/o Youth Centre, King David School, Alcester Rd., B13 8EY. ☎ 0121-442 4459.
Birmingham Union of Jewish Students, c/o Hillel House. Address as below. ☎ 0121-454 5684 & 0121-455 8116.
Hillel House Students' Hostel, 26 Somerset Rd., Edgbaston, B15 2QD. ☎ 0121-454 5684. Further inf.: Frank Linden. ☎ 0121-454 5042. Mrs. Ruth Jacobs. ☎ 0121-440 4142. Chaplain: Rabbi Fishel Cohen. ☎ 0121-440 1359.
Youth Centre, 19 Sandhurst Rd., Moseley, B13 8EU. ☎ 0121-442 4459.

Zionist Organisations
Israel Information Centre & Bookshop, Singers Hill, Blucher St., B1 1QL. Dir.: Mrs R. Jacobs. ☎ 0121-643 2688.
J.N.F., address as Israel Information Centre above.

Miscellaneous Organisations
Council of Christians & Jews. Hon. Sec.: Mrs. L. F. Gompertz, 325 Pershore Rd., B5 7RY. ☎ 0121-472 0117.
Jewish Graduates' Assoc. Sec.: S. Rose, 40 Lordswood Sq., B17 9BS. ☎ 0121-427 9259.

Bookseller
Lubavitch Bookshop, 95 Willows Rd., B12 9QF. ☎ 0121-440 6673.

Butchers & Delicatessen
(K) A. Gee, 75 Pershore Rd., B5 7NX. ☎ 0121-440 2160.

Caterers
(K) B'tayavon, 20 Hampton Ct., George Rd., Edgbaston, B15 1PU. ☎ 0121-456 2172.
(K) Golda, 125 Salisbury Rd., B13 8LA. ☎ 0121-449 2261 & 440 1925.

BLACKPOOL (LANCS.)
Synagogues & Religious Organisations
United Hebrew Cong. (Orthodox), Synagogue Chambers, Leamington Rd., FY1 4HD. ☎ 01253 28164. Daily services 7.45 a.m. and 7 p.m. (7.30 p.m. in summer). M.: Rev. David Braunold. Hon. Sec.: Mr. D. Lewis or Mr. F.H. Freeman.
Ladies' Guild: Chairman Mrs. Cynthia Lefton, 98 W. Park Dr., FY3 9HU. ☎ 01253 63584.
Reform Jewish Cong., 40 Raikes Pde., FY1 4EX. ☎ 01253 23687. Chairman: Leon Tax, 110 Worcester Rd., FY3 9SZ. ☎ 01253 761763.

Miscellaneous Organisations
Blackpool, St. Annes & District Ajex. Inq. to N. Futter, 7 Kingscote Dr., FY3 8HB. ☎ 01253 32510.
Blackpool & Fylde Jewish Welfare Soc. Hon. Treas.: N. L. Marcuson, 184 High Cross Rd., Poulton-le-Fylde, FY6 8DA. ☎ 01253 883026. President: Gene Kay, 15 Crestway, Blackpool. ☎ 01253 392513.

Council of Christians and Jews. Rev. D. Braunold at United Hebrew Congregation (as above).
League of Jewish Women. Mrs D. Jacobs, St Anne's Synagogue, Orchard Road, St. Annes.
St. Annes and Fylde Jewish Literary Society. Hon. Sec.: Mrs. Gene Kay, 15 Crestway, Newton Dr., Blackpool FY3 8PA. ☎ 01253 392513.

Delicatessen
Lytham Delicatessen, 53 Warton St., Lytham St. Annes. ☎ 01253 735861.

BOGNOR REGIS (W. SUSSEX)
Ch. & Hon. Sec. of Cong.: J. S. Jacobs, 'Elm Lodge', Sylvan Way, West Sussex, PO21 2RS. ☎ 01243 823006.

BOURNEMOUTH (DORSET)
The Bournemouth Hebrew Congregation was established in 1905, when the Jewish population numbered fewer than 20 families. Today the town's permanent Jewish residents number 3,500 out of a total population of some 151,000. During the season and at the Holy-days and festivals, however, there are many more Jews than this in Bournemouth, for it is an extremely popular resort, with its Jewish hotels, guest houses and other holiday accom.

Synagogues
Bournemouth Hebrew Cong. (Orthodox), Synagogue Chambers, Wootton Gdns., BH1 1PW. ☎ 01202 557433. M.: Rabbi. G. Shisler. Mikva on premises.
Bournemouth Reform Syn., 53 Christchurch Rd., BH1 3PN. ☎ 01202 557736. M.: Rabbi D. M. B. Soetendorp. ☎ 01202 514788.

Representative Organisations
Bournemouth Jewish Representative Council. Ch.: Mrs. H. Green, P.O. Box 2287, BH3 7ZD. ☎ 01202 762101.. Hon. Sec. Mrs. M. Perry.
Council of Christian & Jews, 108 Avon Rd., BH8 8SF. Sec.: Mrs. R. Falkenberg, 8 Wimbledon Hall, Derby Rd, Bournemouth. ☎ 01202 552286.

Welfare Organisations
(K) Braemar Royal, Grand Av., Southbourne, BH6 3SY. ☎ 01202 423246. Adminstered by Jewish Care.
(K) Home for Aged. Hannah Levy Hse., 15 Poole Rd., BH2 5QR. ☎ 01202 765361.
Holiday Home for Physically Handicapped,
(K) 'Carlton Dene', 21 Stourwood Av., Southbourne, BH6 3PW. Administered by Jewish Care. Inq. ☎ 0181-458 3282.

Miscellaneous Organisations
Friendship Club. Inf. from Sec.: S. Mazin. ☎ 01202 551255.

Hotels, etc.
★ Grove House Hotel, 61 Grove Rd., BH1 3AT. ☎ 01202 554161.
(K) New Ambassador Hotel (LBD) (112, all with bathroom en suite), E. Cliff, BH1 3DP. ☎ 01202 555453. Fax 01202 311077.
(K) Normandie Hotel (71) (Ked), Manor Rd., E. Overcliff Dr., BH1 3HL. ☎ 01202 552246. Fax: 01202 291178.
Anglo Swiss Hotel, Gervis Rd., BH1 3EQ. ☎ 01202 554794.
Cliffeside Hotel (64), E. Overcliff Dr., BH1 3AQ. ☎ 01202 555724.
Cumberland Hotel, E. Overcliff Dr., BH1 3AF. ☎ 01202 290722.
Durley Dean Hotel, Westcliff Rd., BH2 5HE. ☎ 01202 557711
Durlston Court Hotel, Gervis Rd., BH1 3DD. ☎ 01202 291488.

THE NORMANDIE HOTEL

Manor Road, East Cliff, Bournemouth, Dorset, BH1 3HL
Telephone: (01202) 552246 Facsimile: (01202) 291178

ON ENGLAND'S SOUTH COAST • IDEAL FOR SUMMER HOLIDAYS • SPRING AND AUTUMN BREAKS

We cater for business conferences, weddings, Bar Mitzvahs & Sheva Brochos

Under Kedassia Supervision (s)

East Cliff Court Hotel (70), E. Overcliff Dr., BH1 3AN. Mr. & Mrs. P. Proctor. ☎ 01202 554545.
Norfolk Royale Hotel, Richmond Hill, BH2 6EN. ☎ 01202 551521.
Queens Hotel, Meyrick Rd. ☎ 01202 554415. (115 rooms).
Royal Bath Hotel, Bath Rd., BH1 2EW. ☎ 01202 555555.
Taurus Park Hotel, 16 Knyreton Rd., BH1 3QN. ☎ 01202 557369.

Kosher Meat, etc.
(K) Louise's Deli (Ked), 164 Old Christchurch Rd., BH1 1NU. ☎ 01202 295979.

BRADFORD (W. YORKS.)
The Jewish com. although only about 130 to 140 years old, has exercised much influence on the city's staple industry: wool. Jews of German birth developed the export trade of wool yarns and fabrics. The Syn. of British and Foreign Jews, 'Reform' in character (later called the Reform Syn. and still later the Bradford Syn.), was built in 1880 in Bowland St. An Orthodox syn. came into being in 1886, in Snowden St. Today's syn. in Springhurst Rd., Shipley, was built in 1970.

Synagogues
Bradford Hebrew Cong. (Orthodox), Springhurst Rd., Shipley, BD18 3DN. ☎ 01274 728925. Services: 10 a.m. monthly on Shabbat Mevarchim, High Holy-days & certain festivals. Hon. Sec.: Mrs M.D. Freund, 513 Harrogate Rd., Leeds LS17 7DU. Pres.: A. A. Waxman. Chairman: K. Fabian. ☎ 01274-390783
Bradford Syn. (Reform) Bowland St., Manningham Lane, BD1 3BW. ☎ 01274 544420. Services: Fri., 6 p.m.; Sat., 11 a.m.; Festivals, 6 p.m. & 11 a.m.

Representative Organisations
B'nai B'rith West Riding, Shalom Lodge, Bradford. Hon. Sec.: Mrs. A. Fabian, 26 Thorndale Rise, Poplars Farm, Kings Rd., BD2 1NU.
W.I.Z.O. Bradford. C/o Bfd Hebrew Congregation, Springhurst Rd., Shipley, BD18 3DN.

BRIGHTON AND HOVE (E. SUSSEX)
The first known Jewish resident of Brighton lived there in 1767. The earliest synagogue was founded in Jew St. in 1789. Henry Solomon, vice-president of the congregation, was the first Chief Constable of the town. He was murdered in 1844 by an insane youth. His brother-in-law, Levi Emanuel Cohen, founded the 'Brighton Guardian' and was twice elected president of the Newspaper Society of Gt. Britain. Other 19th-century notables living in Brighton and

Hove included Sir Isaac Lyon Goldsmid and numerous members of the Sassoon family. The town's Jewish population is now about 8,000.

Synagogues
Brighton & Hove Hebrew Cong.: Middle St. Syn., 66 Middle St., Brighton, BN1 1AL. ☎ 01273-327785. M.: Rabbi Pesach Efune.
W. Hove Syn., 31 New Church Rd., Hove, BN3 4AD. Hon. Sec.: M. Shaw. ☎ 01273-776170.
Hove Hebrew Cong., 79 Holland Rd., Hove, BN3 1JN (Orthodox). ☎ 01273 732085. M.: Rabbi Vivian Silverman; Sec.: S. Farrell.
New (Reform), Palmeira Av., Hove, BN3 3GE. ☎ 01273 735343. M.: Rabbi Dr. J. Collick. Sec.: Jan Green. ☎ 01273 735343.
Progressive Syn., 6 Lansdowne Rd., Hove, BN3 1FF. Ch.: Peter Vos. ☎ 01273 737223 9.30 a.m. to 1 p.m. M.: Rabbi W. Wolff.
There is a mikva in the Prince Regent swimming pool complex, Church St., BN1 1YA. For further inf., ☎ 01273 21919.

Representative Organisation
Jewish Representative Council. Ch.: Mr. A. Milstein. Sec.: Mrs. D. Levinson. Fax 01273-504455.

Welfare Organisations
Brighton & Hove Jewish Welfare Board. Inq.: Mrs. J. Markham, ☎ 01273 722523.
Brighton & Hove Jewish Home, 20 Burlington St., Brighton, BN2 1AU. ☎ 01273 688226.

Miscellaneous Organisations
Brighton & Hove Jewish Centre & Friendship Clubs, Ralli Hall, 81 Denmark Villas, Hove, BN3 3TH. Administrator:- Norina Duke. ☎ (01273) 202254.
Brighton & Hove Joint Kashrus Committee. Hon. Sec.: H. Breger, 5 The Paddock, The Droveway, Hove. ☎ 01273 506574.
(K) Hillel House, 18 Harrington Rd., Brighton, BN1 6RE. ☎ 01273 503450. Closed during summer vacation. Further inf. from Mrs. A. Lee. ☎ 01273 880596. Fri. evg. meals available.
Lubavitch Chabad Hse., 15 The Upper Dr., Hove BN3 6GR. ☎ 01273 21919. Dir.: Rabbi P. Efune. (Torah Academy)

Newspaper
Sussex Jewish News. Ed. D. Levinson, P.O. Box 1623. ☎ 01273-504455.

Delicatessen
★ Cantor's of Hove, 20 Richardson Rd., Hove, BN3 5BB. ☎ 01273 723669.

Caterer
(K) Glassman's Catering. Under supervision of Brighton & Hove Kashrus Com.

Restaurant
Angela Samuels, 5 St Keyne Ave., Hove.

BRISTOL
Bristol was one of the principal Jewish centres of medieval England. Even after the Expulsion from England in 1290 there were occasional Jewish residents or visitors. A community of Marranos lived here during the Tudor period. There was next a Jewish community in Bristol some time before 1754 and its original Synagogue opened in 1786. The present building dates from 1871 and incorporates fittings from the earlier building. The Jewish house at Clifton

College (known as Polacks House) was founded in 1878 and is the only remaining Jewish house in a public school. The Progressive Synagogue was founded in 1961 and their present building was consecrated in 1971.

Synagogues
British Hebrew Congregation, 9 Park Row, BS1 5LP. M.: Rabbi Hillel Simon. ☎ 0117 9255160. Enq. to: L. Tankavitch. ☎ 0117 970 6938. Fri. night services, Winter 7.30 p.m./Summer 8.30 p.m.; Sat., 9.45 a.m.
Kosher delicatessen, alternate Sundays 10 a.m.
Bristol Progressive Syn. (Bristol & West Progressive Jewish Cong.), 43 Bannerman Rd., Easton, BS5 0RR. ☎ 0117 9541937. M.: Rabbi Hadassah Davis. ☎ 01734 543768. Inq. Mrs I. Wagen. ☎ 0117 9738633. Services Friday 8p.m., Saturday at 11a.m. Judaica shop.

Miscellaneous Organisations
Bristol Jewish Liaison Com. Chairman: B. Barnett 0117 9424837. Sec.: Michael Romain, ☎ 0117-973 9312.
Bristol University Jewish & Israel Society. Inq. to Jewish Soc. Ch., c/o Hillel Hse.
Hillel Hse.: 45 Oakfield Rd., Clifton, BS8 2BA. ☎ 0117 9466589. Contact A. Holt. Accommodation ☎ 01454 261208.
Davar, The Jewish Institute in Bristol, a cultural–educational organisation, aims to encourage and enhance the widest possible spectrum of Jewish identity in Bristol and the south-west. ☎ 0117 970 6594.
Polack's House, Clifton College. H.M. Mr. J. Greenbury. ☎ 0117 973 7634.

Restaurants
(V) Cherries, 122 St Michael's Hill, BS2 8BU. ☎ 0117 9293675.
(V) Millwards Vegetarian Restaurant, 40 Alfred Place, Kingsdown, BS2 8HD, ☎ 0117 9245026.

BROMLEY (GREATER LONDON)
Bromley & District Reform Syn., 28 Highland Rd., BR1 4AD Kent. Tel/Fax 0181-460 5460. M.: Rabbi Sylvia Rothschild.

BUCKHURST HILL (ESSEX)
Sukkat Shalom Reform Synagogue, Hermon Hill, London E11. ☎ 0181-551 5351.

CAMBRIDGE
Syn/Student Centre, 3 Thompson's Lane, CB5 8AQ. Daily, morn & eve services during term time. Sat. morning during vacations, other services by arrangement). Inq.: R.R. Domb, Cambridge Traditional Cong. ☎ 01223 68346; or 01223 354783. Kosher food is available. ☎ 01223 352145.
There is a (K) kosher canteen during term time serving lunch most weekdays and on Sat., and supper on Fri.
Beth Shalom Reform Syn.: Inf. from Jonathan Harris, 30 Malcolm Place, CB1 1LS. ☎ 01223 365614.
Cambridge Jewish Residents' Assoc. welcomes visitors to all activities. Inq. to Ch.: Mrs. E. Shepherd. ☎ 01223-246751.

CANTERBURY (KENT)
Canterbury Jewish Com. Contact: Irving Morris. ☎ 01227 71145.
The Old Synagogue, an 'Egyptian-style' building of 1847 stands in King Street and is now used by the Kings School for recitals.

Restaurant
(V) Teapot Mother Earth, 34 St Peter's St., CT16 1BK. ☎ 01227 463175.

CHELMSFORD (ESSEX)
The cong. holds regular services, Hebrew classes and a lively social and cultural programme, c/o Merlin House, 23 Parker Rd., CM2 0ES. ☎ 01245 248976.

CHELTENHAM
The congregation was established in 1824 and the present synagogue opened in 1839. However after two generations, the congregation declined, until the synagogue was closed in 1903. At the outbreak of the Second World War, the Synagogue was re-opened following the influx of Jewish newcomers to the town. The congregation has its own cemetery on Elm Street, purchased in 1824.
Syn.: St. James's Sq. Inq.: H. Bazar, Kynance, 22 Sydenham Rd., GL52 6EA. ☎ 01242 525032.

Restaurant
(V) The Barleycorn, 317 High St., GL50 3HN, ☎ 01242 241070.

CHESTER
Inq. to Mrs. A. Mayorcas, 5 Lache Lane, CH4 7LP. ☎ 01244 675240.

Restaurant
(V) Abbey Green Restaurant, 2a Abbey Green, Off Northgate St., CH1 2JH. ☎ 01244 313251. 12-2.30, Mon-Sat; 6.30-10, Tues-Sat.

CHIGWELL (ESSEX)
Syn: Limes Av., Limes Farm Estate, Chigwell, IG7 5NT.
Abridge Golf & Country Club: Epping La., Abridge, Stapleford Tawney (near Chigwell), RM4 1ST. ☎ 0140 28 396.

COLCHESTER (ESSEX)
Colchester and District Jewish Community, the Synagogue, Fennings Chase, Priory St. CO1 2QB. Services held Friday evening and on all Festivals. The Community has many families with young children and there is a Cheder every Sunday morning. The community has close links with the University of Essex at Colchester which is a popular choice for Israeli students wishing to study for a law degree. For information about services, Cheder and social events please contact: the Hon. Sec. Mrs. N. B. Stevenson. ☎ 01206 45992.

COVENTRY (W. MIDLANDS)
There were Jews in Coventry in 1775, if not earlier. Today's Jewish population is about 50 families. The present synagogue was consecrated in 1870.
Syn.: Coventry Hebrew Congregation, Barras Lane, CV1 3BW. ☎ 01203 220168. President: R. Starr. Sec.: L. R. Benjamin. ☎/Fax 01926-49902.
Coventry Jewish Reform Community; Chairman Dr. M. Been. ☎ 01203-672027.
Coventry Jewish Social Committee; Chairman: Mrs M. Berger. ☎ 01926-55246.

CRAWLEY (W. SUSSEX)
Progressive Cong.: Inf. from Hon. Sec.: Lynda Bloom, 44 Brighton Rd., Southgate. ☎ 01293-534294.

CROYDON (GREATER LONDON)
Syn.: The Almonds, Shirley Oaks, Croydon. Inq. to the Sec. ☎ 0181-684 4726.
Restaurant: (V) Hockney's, 98 High St., CR0 1ND. ☎ 0181-688 2899.

DARLINGTON (DURHAM)
Darlington Hebrew Congregation, 13 Bloomfield Rd., Darlington, Co. Durham. Chairman: Martin Finn, 17 Thornbury Rise, Darlington, Co. Durham DL3 9NF. ☎ 01325 467902.

EASTBOURNE (E. SUSSEX)
Syn.: 22 Susans Rd., BN21 3HA. Hon. Sec.: Mrs. M. Mindell, 'Woodthorpe', Forest Pl., Waldron, Heathfield, TN21 0TG. ☎ 01435 866928. Fax 01435 865783.

EPPING (ESSEX)
★ Gaynes Park, Coopersale, nr. Epping CM16 7RJ. ☎ 01378 76021/72566. Weekend seminar & conference centre.

EXETER (DEVON)
In pre-Expulsion times Exeter was an important Jewish centre. The synagogue was built in 1763, while the cemetery in Magdalen Road dates from 1757. Syn.: Synagogue Pl., Mary Arches St., EX4 3BA. ☎ 01392 51529. Services, fortnightly Fri./Sat. and High Holydays.

Restaurants
(V) Brambles, 31 New Bridge St., EX4 3AH. ☎ 01392 74168.
(V) Herbies, 15 North St., EX4 3QS. ☎ 01392 58473.

GATESHEAD (TYNE & WEAR)
Syn.: 180 Bewick Rd., NE8 1UF. ☎ 0191-4770111. M.: Rabbi B. Rakow, 138 Whitehall Rd., NE8 1TP. ☎ 0191-4773012. Hon. Sec.: M. Guttentag, 205 Dryden Rd. ☎ 0191-4773871.
Mikva, 180 Bewick Rd., NE8 1UF. Appointments: ☎ 0191-4773552.

Educational Organisations, Schools, etc.
Beis Hatalmud, 1 Ashgrove Ter., NE8. ☎ 0191-4784352. Princ.: Rabbi S. Steinhouse.
Beth Midrash Lemoroth (women teachers' training college), 50 Bewick Rd., NE8. ☎ 0191-4772620. Princ.: Rabbi M. Miller.
Gateshead Jewish Boarding School, 37 Gladstone Ter., NE8 4HE. ☎ 0191-4771431. Princ.: Rabbi N. Lieberman.
Institute for Higher Rabbinical Studies-Kolel, 22 Claremont Pl., NE8 1TL. Sec.: S. Ehrentreu. ☎ 0191-4772189.
Jewish High School for Girls, 6 Gladstone Ter., NE8 4DY. Principal: Rabbi D. Bowden. ☎ 0191-4773471.
Jewish Primary School, 18-20 Gladstone Ter., NE8 4EA. Principal: Rabbi S. Wagschal. ☎ 0191-4772154.
Kindergarten, Alexander Rd. ☎ 0191-4783723.
Sunderland Talmudical College, Prince Consort Rd., NE8. Princ.: Rabbi S. Zahn. ☎ 0191-4900195.
Yeshiva, 88 Windermere St., NE8 1UB. ☎ 0191-4772616 & 0191-4785210.
Yeshiva L'Zeirim Tiferes Yaacov, 36-38 Gladstone Ter., NE8 4EF. Principal: Rabbi E. Jaffe. ☎ 0191-477 1317.

Bookseller
J. Lehmann, 20 Cambridge Ter., NE8 1RP. ☎ 0191-490 1692.

Baker, Confectioner & Grocer
(K) Stenhouse, 215 Coatsworth Rd., NE8 1SR. ☎ 0191-4772001.

Butcher
(K) K. L. Kosher Butcher, 83 Rodsley Av., NE8. ☎ 0191-4773109.

Caterer
Mrs. J. Rose, 14 Limetree Gdns., and J. Poznanski, 9 Ashgrove Ter. ☎ 0191-477 2880.

GREENFORD (GREATER LONDON)
Syn.: 39-45 Oldfield Lane South, UB6 9LB. Inq. to Hon. Sec.: R. A. Hyams.

GRIMSBY (S. HUMBERSIDE)
Syn.: Sir Moses Montefiore Synagogue, Heneage Rd., DN32 9DZ. Services: Fri., 7 p.m. Sabbath, Services: First Saturday in month. 9.30 a.m. Hon. Sec.: M. M. Lewis, 18 Crescent St., DN31 2HB. ☎ 01472 342579.

GUILDFORD (SURREY)
Guildford & District Syn., York Rd., GU1 4DR. Inq. to Hon. Sec., Mrs. H. Gould, Lynwood, Hillier Rd., GU1 2JG. ☎ 01483 576470.
Enquiries about the recent discovery of a medieval synagogue in the town may be addressed to the Guildford Museum.

HARLOW (ESSEX)
Syn.: Harbert's Rd., CM19 4DT. Constituent of Reform Synagogues of Great Britain. Services: Fri., 8.15 p.m. Ch: Ian. Jackson 34 Greenhills, Harlow, Essex CM20 3SX. ☎ 01279 416138.

HAROLD HILL (GREATER LONDON)
Syn.: Trowbridge Rd. Inq. to Miss D. Meid, 4 Portmadoc Hse., Broseley Rd., RM3 9BT. ☎ Ingrebourne 48904.

HARROGATE (N. YORKS)
Syn.: St. Mary's Walk, HG2 0LW. Services: Fri., 6 p.m. in winter, 7 p.m. in summer; Sabbath, 9.30 a.m. Hon. Sec.: P. E. Morris, Crimple Lodge, Fulwith Mill La., HG2 8HJ. ☎ 01423 871713.
Harrogate Zionist Group (WIZO). Inq. to Mrs. E. Rosenhead, Flat 7, Majestic Court, Spring Grove, HG1 2H7. ☎ 01423 569226.

Hotel/Restaurant
(V) Amadeus, 115 Franklin Rd., HG1 5EN, ☎ 01423-5-5151.

HASTINGS (E. SUSSEX)
Includes Bexhill, Battle, Rye & St. Leonards. Inq. about Hastings District Jewish Soc. to Mrs. Ilse Eton, 6 Gilbert Rd., St. Leonards-on-Sea, East Sussex, TN38 0RH. ☎ 01424 436551. Meetings, 7 p.m. on first Fri. of every month at Hugh Smith Hall, 45 Eversley Rd., Bexhill.

Hotel
(V) Tower House Hotel, 26-28 Tower Road West, St. Leonards-on-Sea, TN38 0RG. ☎ 01424 42717. Propr. Roy & Jean Richards.

HEMEL HEMPSTEAD (HERTS.)
Syn.: Morton Hse., Midland Rd., HD1 1RP. Hon. Sec.: Harry Nathan. ☎ 01923 232007.
Lady Sarah Cohen Com. Centre, Midland Rd., HD1 1OR.

HIGH WYCOMBE (BUCKS.)
Hebrew Cong (U.S.). Inq. to Mrs. R. Weiss, 33 Hampden Rd., HP13 6SZ. ☎ 01494 529821.

HIGHAMS PARK (GREATER LONDON)
Highams Park and Chingford Syn., 74 Marlborough Rd., E4 9AZ. M.: Rev. M.K. Lester, M.A. Sec.: Mrs. S. R. Benjamin, 77 Royston Av., Chingford, E4 9DE. ☎ 0181-527 4750.

HORNCHURCH (GREATER LONDON)
Syn.: Elm Park (Affiliated) Syn., Woburn Av., Elm Pk., Hornchurch, Essex, RM12 4NG. Hon. Sec.: Mrs S. Gaynor. ☎ 01708 449305.

HULL (HUMBERSIDE)
In Hull, as in other English port towns, a Jewish community was formed earlier than in inland areas. The exact date is unknown, but is thought by some to be the early 1700s. Certainly, there were enough Jews in Hull to buy a former Roman Catholic chapel, damaged in the Gordon Riots of 1780, and turn it into a syn. Previously, services had been held in a substantial private house in the High St. A cemetery is believed to have been acquired in the late 1700s.

Hull was then the principal port of entry from northern Europe, and most of the Jewish immigrants came through it. In 1851 the Jewish community numbered about 200. Today it numbers some 350 families. Both the Old Hebrew Synagogue in Osborne St., and the Central Synagogue in Cogan St., were destroyed in air raids during the Second World War. On the Osborne Street site a new synagogue was consecrated in September, 1955, and a new synagogue hall was opened in 1956. The two Orthodox congs. merged in 1994 and moved to the new Pryme St. building in the Western suburbs, where most of the com. now live.

Synagogues & Religious Organisations
Hull Hebrew Congregation, 30 Pryme St., Anlaby, HU10 6SH. Hon. Sec.: E. Pearlman, 277 Beverley Rd., Kirkella, HU10 7AQ. ☎ 01482 653398.
Board of Shechita. Hon. Ch.: Dr. C. Rosen. Contact Mr E. Pearlman.
Reform Synagogue. Great Gutter Lane, Willerby, HU10 7JT. Chairman: Mrs. C. Sugarman. Hon. Sec. Mr. L. Sugarman, 36 Kerry Pit Way, Anlaby, HU10 7NB. ☎ 01482-656469.

Representative & Welfare Organisations
Board of Guardians, 1 Tranby Ride, Anlaby, HU10 7ED. Hon. Sec.: Mr. V. Appleson. ☎ 01482-653018.
Jewish Representative Council. Pres.: Mrs. A. Rowland. Hon. Sec. Mrs. A. Segelman, 251 Beverley Rd., Kirkella, HU10 7AG. ☎ 01482-650288.

Museum
Hull Synagogue Museum, Linnaeus St., HU3 2PD. Correspondence: 771 Anlaby Rd., HU4 6DJ. ☎ 01482-26848. Fax 01482-568756.

Student & Youth Organisations
Hillel Hse., 18 Auckland Av., HU6 7SG. ☎ 01482 48196. Inq. to I. Dysch, 1000 Anlaby High Rd., HU4 6AT. ☎ 01482 54947.
Provincial Hillel Foundation. Co-ordinator: Jack Lennard, 771 Anlaby High Rd., Hull, HU4 6DJ. ☎ 01482 53981 or 26848. Fax 01482-568756.
University and Colleges Jewish Students' Society. Inf. from Hon. Sec., c/o Hillel Hse. Address above.

LANCASTER (LANCS.)

Lancaster University Jewish Society, Interfaith Chaplaincy Centre, University of Lancaster, Bailrigg Lane, LA1 4YW. ☎ 01524 65201, Ext. 4075 (answerphone). Jewish rooms and kosher kitchen. Visitors welcome.

Restaurant
(V) **Fairview**, 32 Hornby Rd, Caton, LA2 9QS. ☎ 01524-770118. B&B.

LEEDS (W. YORKS.)

The Leeds Jewish community is the second largest in the Provinces, and numbers about 12,000. The community dates only from 1804, although a few Jews are known to have lived there in the previous half-century. Until 1846 the community worshipped in a small room. The first synagogue building was erected in 1860, when there were about 60 Jewish families.

Synagogues & Religious Organisations

Beth Hamedrash Hagadol Syn., 399 Street Lane, LS17 6HQ. M.: Rabbi Y. Shemaria. R. Chazan D. Apfel. Exec. Officer: Mrs. M. Wilson. ☎ 0113 2692181. Chairman: D. Apfel.
Chassidishe, c/o Donisthorpe Hall, Shadwell Lane, LS17 6AW. All inq. to M. Kent, Flat 8, Sandhill Lawns, Sandhill La., LS17 6TT.
Etz Chaim, 411 Harrogate Rd., LS17 7BY. M.: Rabbi Y. Angyalfi; M. Rev. G. Harris. Ch. Rev. A. Gilbert. Office 584 Harrogate Rd., LS17 7DP. Sec.: ☎ 0113 2662214.
Shomrei Hadass, 368 Harrogate Rd., LS17 6QB. Independent Orthodox cong. M.: Dayan Y. Refson. ☎ 0113 2681461. Mikva at rear of premises.
Sinai (Reform), Roman Av., off Street Lane, LS8 2AN. ☎ 0113 2665256. Office hours 9.30 a.m.-2 p.m. (Mon-Fri). Services, Fri., 8 p.m., Sat., 10.30 a.m.
United Hebrew Cong., Shadwell La. Syn., 151 Shadwell La., LS17 8DW. M.: Rabbi I. Goodhart. Ch. Rev H. Miller. Admin.: Mrs A. Silver. ☎ 0113-2696141; Fax 0113-237-0851.
Beth Din, Etz Chaim Synagogue, LS17 6BY. ☎ 0113 2696902. Fax 0113-237 0893. Inf. about kosher food & accom. from the Registrar, Rev. A. Gilbert, B.A.
Mikva, 411 Harrogate Rd., LS17 7BY. ☎ 0113-2371096 (answerphone).

Representative Organisations

Leeds Jewish Representative Council, Shadwell La. Syn., 151 Shadwell La., LS17 8DW. President: Mr T. Friedman. Inf. from Exec. Officer: Barry Abis, JP. ☎ 0113 2697520. Fax 0113-2370851. Pub. Year Book.
B'nai B'rith Lodge of Leeds. Pres.: Hon Jt. Presidents Sandra & Tony Felston. ☎ 0113 3944519.

Cultural and Educational Organisations

Jewish Education Board (Talmud Torah), 2 Sandhill Lane, LS17 6AQ. ☎ 0113 2683390/2680836. Contact Mrs. E. Fligg.
Jewish Library, Porton Collection, Central Library, Municipal Bldgs., LS1 3AB. ☎ 0113 2462016.
Jewish Resources Centre, (Makor), 411 Harrogate Rd., LS17 7TT. ☎ 0113 2680899.

Welfare Organisations, Hospitals, etc.

Residential/Nursing House for the Jewish Elderly, Donisthorpe Hall, Shadwell Lane, LS17 6AW. Admin.: S. Stone. ☎ 0113 2684248.
Hospital meals & Visitation. Non-residents of Leeds who may be admitted to one of the city's hospitals should contact the Exec. Officer, Leeds Jewish Representative Council. ☎ 0113 2697520.
Leeds Jewish Blind Society, 311 Stonegate Rd., LS17 6AZ. ☎ 0113 2684211.
Leeds Jewish Welfare Board, 311 Stonegate Rd., LS17 6AZ. ☎ 0113 2684211. Chief Exec.: Sheila Saunders.

Student and Youth Organisations
Bnei Akiva, 'Bayit', Street Lane Gdns., Street Lane, LS17 6PZ. ☎ 0113 2692324.
Jewish Lads' & Girls' Brigade. Commanding Officer: Garrey Haase, ☎ 0113 2661020.
Jewish Scouts: 15/16th Northvale (Hillel) Cubs & Scouts, Fir Tree Lane Headquarters, Leeds 17. Leader: Anthony Taylor. ☎ 0113 2671180.
61st Jewish Guides, Fir Tree Lane Headquarters, Leeds 17. Guide Leaders: Tracey Sapier. ☎ 0113 2682660; Linda Lee. ☎ 0113 2370224.
61st Leeds Brownies, Contact: Wendy Benedict. ☎ 0113 2685557.
Jewish Students' Assoc. Inq. to Warden, Hillel Hse., 2 Springfield Mount, LS2 9NE. ☎ 0113 2433211. Male & female students may apply for residence at Hillel Hse., where (K) meals are provided, by writing to Dr. R. D. Pollard, Dept. of Electronic Engineering, University of Leeds LS2 9JT.
Chaplaincy: 17 Queens Rd., LS6 1NY. ☎ 0113 2789597/2671805.
Youth Activities Contact: Louise Williams. ☎ 0113 2370751.

Zionist Organisations
All information about Zionist orgs. and activities in Leeds can be obtained from the Area Director, Leeds Zionist Council, 411 Harrogate Rd., LS17 7BY. ☎ 0113 2693134. Fax 0113 2668419.

Club: Moor Allerton Golf Club Ltd., Coal Rd., Wike, LS17 9NH. ☎ 0113 2661154-5 (members), 0113 2665209 (professional).

Newspaper
Jewish Telegraph, 1 Shaftesbury Ave., LS8 1DR. ☎ 0113 2666000.

Kosher Bakery
(K) Chalutz Bakery, 378 Harrogate Rd., LS17. ☎ 0113 2691350.

Kosher Butchers and Delicatessen
(K) Fisher's Deli, 391 Harrogate Rd., LS17 6DJ. ☎ 0113 2686944.
(K) Gourmet Foods, Sandhill Pde., 584 Harrogate Rd., LS17 8DP. ☎ 0113-2682726.
(K) Myers Famous Kosherie, 410 Harrogate Rd., LS17 6PY. ☎ 0113 2682943.

Hotels, Restaurants, etc.
Beegee's Guest House, 18 Moor Allerton Dr., Moortown, LS17 6RZ. ☎ (0113) 2935469. Fax (0113) 2753300. Props.: Mr. & Mrs. B. Gibbs.
(K) The Club, Lubavitch Centre, 168 Shadwell Lane, LS17 8AD. ☎ 0113-2663311.
(V) Hansa's, 72 North St., LS2 7PN. ☎ 0113-2444408.

LEICESTER (LEICS.)
There have been Jewish coms. in Leicester since the Middle Ages, but the first record of a 'Jews' synagogue' dates from 1861 in the Leicester Directory. The present synagogue was built in 1897 and consecrated by Chief Rabbi Dr. Hermann Adler.
Syn. & Com. Centre: Highfield St., LE2 0NQ. M.: Rabbi A. S. Hill, ☎ 0116-2706622. Hon. Sec.: G. J. Louis, 4 Lyndhurst Ct., London Rd., LE2 2AP. ☎ 0116-2 700997.
Mikva: Synagogue bldg., Highfield St.
Progressive Jewish Cong. ☎ 0116-2 832927. Services, Fri. and festivals. Hon. Sec.. J. Kaufman, ☎ 0116-2715584. Religion school.
Ajex. Ch.: B. Besbrode, 50 Arden Way, Market Harborough. ☎ 01858 466480.

Bookshop: Com. Centre, Highfield St., LE2 0NQ. Inq.: J. Markham, 74 Wakerley Rd., LE5 6AQ. ☎ 0116-2737620.
Hillette. Inq.: Monty Simmons, 125 Carisbrooke Rd., LE2 3PG. ☎ 0116-2 706600.
Jewish Library: Com. Hall, Highfield St., LE2 0NQ.
Maccabi Assoc., Leicester Communal Hall, Highfield St., LE2 0NQ. ☎ 0116-2540477.
WIZO. Ch.: Mrs. Helen Naftalin, 15 Knighton Grange Rd. ☎ 0116-2 703358.
A limited range of kosher delicatessen is now stocked by Tesco at their Beaumont Leys store.

Vegetarian Restaurants
The Ark, St. Martin's Sq. ☎ 0116-262 0909.
The Chaat Hse., 108 Belgrave Rd., LE4 5AT. ☎ 0116-2 660513;
The Good Earth, 19 Free Lane, LE1 1JX. ☎ 0116-2 626260;
Blossoms, 17b Cank St., LE1 5GX. ☎ 0116-2 539535.
Bread and Roses, 70 High St., LE1 5YP, ☎ 0116-2532448. 10-4, Tues-Sat.
Sharmilee, 71 Belgrave Rd., LE4 6AS, ☎ 0116-2610503. 12-2.30, 6-9, Tues-Thurs; 12-9, Fri-Sun.

LINCOLN
Lincoln was one of the centres of medieval Jewry. One of England's oldest stone houses in the city is known as Aaron the Jew's House. The site of the old Jewry is remembered now at Jews' Court. In the cathedral is a recent token of ecclesiastical apology for the 13th-century incidence of the Blood Libel retold in Chaucer. Jews came again to the area in the 19th century. The current community is of very recent date.
Lincolnshire Jewish Community (Associate ULPS). Enquiries to Edna Creed, Plot 62, Hales Lane, Chapel Heath, Navenby, LN5 0TP.

LIVERPOOL (MERSEYSIDE)
There is evidence of an organised community before 1750. It is believed to have been composed of Sephardi Jews and to have had some connection with the West Indies or with Dublin, but some authorities believe that they were in the main German Jews.

This small community, which was known to John Wesley, the religious reformer, declined at first, but was reinforced, probably in about 1770, by a new wave of settlers, mostly from Europe. The largely Ashkenazi Jews were to some degree intending emigrants for America and the West Indies, who changed their minds and stayed in Liverpool.

By 1807 the community had a building of some size in Seel St., the parent of the present synagogue in Princes Road, one of the handsomest in the country. It celebrated its centenary in 1974.

Synagogues & Religious Organisations
Allerton, cnr. Mather & Booker Avs., L18 9TB. ☎ 0151-427 6848. M.: Rabbi M. Barron M.A.; Sec: R. Hyman.
Childwall Hebrew Cong., Dunbabin Rd., L15 6XL. Mikva in syn. precinct. ☎ 0151-722 2079. M.: Rabbi M. L. Cofnas. Admin.: Mrs A. Reuben.
Greenbank Drive Hebrew Cong., Greenbank Dr., L17 1AN. ☎ 0151-733 1417. M., Sec. & Registrar: Rev. H. M. Chait.
Old Hebrew Cong., Princes Rd., L8 1TG. ☎ 0151-709 3431. M.: Rev. S. Cohen.
Ullet Road Hebrew Cong., 101 Ullet Rd., L17.
Liverpool Progressive Syn., 28 Church Rd. N., L15 6TF. ☎ 0151-733 5871. M.: Rabbi N. Zalud.

Liverpool Kashrut Commission (incorporating Liverpool Shechita Board) c/o Shifrin House, 433 Smithdown Rd., Liverpool L15 3JL. Hon Sec.: Rodney Berman. ☎ 0151-733 2292. Rav to the Bd: Rabbi L. Cofnas. Hon. Sec.: Rodney Berman. ☎ 0151 421 0055.

Representative Organisation
Merseyside Jewish Representative Council, 433 Smithdown Rd., Liverpool L15 3JL. ☎ 0151-733 2292. Hon. Sec.: Mrs. D. B. Salamon.

Welfare Organisations, Hospitals, etc.
Home for Aged Jews, Stapely North, Mossley Hill Rd., L18 8BR. ☎ 0151-724 3260. Hospital wing, ☎ 0151-724 4548.
Merseyside Jewish Welfare Council, Shifrin House, 433 Smithdown Rd., Liverpool, L15 3JL. ☎ 0151-733 2292. Chief Exec. Marilyn Fetcher.

Student & Youth Organisations
Hillel House, 12 Greenbank Drive, L17 1AW ☎ 0151-735 0793. Annexe, 16 Borrowdale Rd., L15 3LE. For Hillel House self-catering accom. for students, contact Mrs. C. Lewis. ☎ 0151-722 5021.
Jewish Students' Society, Inq. to Sec., c/o Guild of Undergraduates, 2 Bedford St. N., L7 7BD or Hillel Hse. As above.
Jewish Youth and Community Centre, Harold Hse., Dunbabin Rd., L15 6XL. ☎ 0151-475 5671. Fax 0151-475 2212. (K) Restaurant on the premises. ☎ 0151-475 5825.
Bnei Akiva; Harold Hse. Youth Club; Haroldeans Football Club; H.Q. of J.L.B.; Shifrin Drama & Music Centre; Tennis Club; Kindergarten; Resource Centre. ☎ 0151-722 3514; JIA office: 0151 475 8707; J.N.F. office: 0151 475 8025. Liverpool Jewish Telegraph office: 0151 475 3999. There is a (K) restaurant at the Centre, open Sun., Tues. & Thurs., 6.30 to 11 p.m. Licenced Bar. Out-of-town visitors welcome. Also take-away service. ☎ 0151-475 5825/5671. Many other facilities available.
Student accom. Liverpool University's halls of residence contain more than 2,000 single bedrooms. These are available during vacations for conferences, student groups, tourists, etc. No kosher catering facilities available, however. Also available, self-catering flats. Inq. to: Conference Office, Liverpool University, P.O. Box 147, L69 3BX. ☎ 0151-794 6440.

Zionist Organisations
These are concentrated at the Zionist Offices, Harold Hse., Dunbabin Rd., L15 6XL. ☎ 0151-475 8707.

Sports
Lee Park Golf Club, Liverpool, L27 3YA. Sec.: Mrs. D. Barr. ☎ 0151-487 3882.
Sir George Bean Memorial Sports & Tennis Centre, c/o Harold Hse., Dunbabin Rd., L15 6XL. ☎ 0151-722-8736.

Books, etc.
A Jewish book and gift centre operates at the Jewish Youth and Community Centre, Dunbabin Rd., L15 6XL on Sun. from 11 a.m. to 1 p.m. ☎ 0151-475 5671.
Liverpool Jewish Resource Centre, Harold Hse., Dunbabin Rd., L15 6XL. Large range of audio-visual and printed materials for sale or hire. ☎ 0151-722-3514. Mon.-Thurs., 2.30 p.m. to 5.30 p.m.; Sun., 11 a.m. to 1 p.m. Answerphone.

Newspapers
Jewish Telegraph, Harold Hse., address above. ☎ 0151-475-6666. Fax 0151-475-2222.

Caterers
(K) M & E Stoops Catering, 23 Montclair Dr., 18. ☎ 0151-722 7459.
(K) Elaine Marco, 20 Beauclair Dr., L15 6XG. ☎ 0151-722 1536.
(K) Celia Clyne, 54 Chapeltown St., Manchester M1. ☎ 061-273 8888.

Restaurants
(K) Harold House, Dunbabin Rd., L15 6XL. ☎ 0151-475 5825.
(V) Munchies Eating House, Myrtle Parade. ☎ 0151-709-7896.

LONDON AIRPORT (HEATHROW) (GREATER LONDON)
A Jewish chaplain is on call at the airport. Chaplaincy Office, TW6 1JH. ☎ 01784 50498.
Heathrow Penta Hotel (636), Bath Rd., Hounslow, TW6 2AQ. ☎ 0181-897 6363.
The Edwardian International Hotel (459). ☎ 0181-759 6311.
Kosher (LBD) sandwiches available at Terminal 1 adjacent to El Al departure lounge.

LOUGHTON (ESSEX)
Syn.: Loughton, Chigwell & District Syn., Borders Lane, IG10 1TE. ☎ 0181-508 0303. Services: Fri. evg., 8 p.m.; Sat. morn., 9.30 a.m. M.: Rev. J. D. Lorraine, 93 The Lindens, Loughton, Essex. ☎ 0181-508 0270.

LUTON (BEDS.)
Syn.: P.O. Box 215, Bury Park, LU1 1HE. ☎ 01582 25032. Hon. Sec.: H. Podgorney, P.O. Box 215, LU1 1HW. Services: Fri. night & Sabbath morn. Office open Sun., 9.30 a.m. to 12.30 p.m.
Friendship Club: Adj. the syn. Open Sun. afternoons, 2-4.30 p.m. Ch.: S. Gonshor. ☎ 01582 26761.
Hebrew Parent-Teachers' Assoc. Inq. to Syn.
Chiltern Progressive Syn., 39 Broadacres, LU2 7YF. ☎ 012334-21837.
Judean Youth Club, PO Box 215, LU1 1HE. Chairman: M.N. Brooker.

MAIDENHEAD (BERKS.)
Maidenhead is a growing Jewish area. The syn. (membership, 550 families) covers Berks. and Bucks. area.
Syn. (Constituent of Reform Synagogues of Gt. Britain): 9 Boyn Hill Av., SL6 4ET. Services, Fri., 8.30 p.m., Sat., 10.30 a.m. Inq.: Rabbi Dr. Jonathan Romain. ☎ 01628 73012.

MAIDSTONE
Kent Liberal Jewish Community (ULPS). Enquiries to John Lloyd. ☎ 01622 728180 or Judi Taylor. ☎ 01233 50738.

MANCHESTER (GREATER MANCHESTER)
The Manchester Jewish community is the second largest in the United Kingdom, numbering about 35,000.
There was no organised community until 1780. A cemetery was acquired in 1794. The present Great Synagogue claims with justice to be the direct descendant of this earliest community.
The leaders of Manchester Jewry in those early days had without exception come from the neighbouring relatively important Jewish community of Liverpool. After the Continental revolutions of 1848, the arrival of 'liberal'

Jews began. One of them, a Hungarian rabbi and soldier of the Revolution, Solomon Schiller-Szinessy, became minister of a Reform synagogue established in 1856.

In 1871 a small Sephardi group from North Africa and the Levant drew together and formed a congregation, which extended to fill two handsome synagogues, one in Cheetham Hill Rd., and the other in W. Didsbury. However, the Cheetham Hill Rd. congregation has now moved to Salford, and its former house of worship has been turned into a Jewish museum.

Synagogues & Religious Organisations

Adass Yeshurun, Cheltenham Cres., Salford, M7 0FE. M.: Dayan G. Krausz. Sec.: S. Gluckstadt. ☎ 0161-792 1233.

Adath Yisroel Nusach Ari, Upper Park Rd., Salford, M7 0HL. Sec.: Rev. S. Simon. ☎ 0161-740 3905.

Bury Hebrew Cong., Sunnybank Rd., Bury, BL9 8EP. M.: Rabbi B. Singer. Admin.: Mrs. M. Wilson. ☎ 0161-796 5062.

Central & North Manchester (incorporating Hightown Central and Beth Jacob), Leicester Rd., Salford, M7 4GP. M.: Rabbi J. Rubinstein. Sec.: M. Green. ☎ 0161-740 4830.

Cheetham Hebrew Cong., 453-5 Cheetham Hill Rd., M8 9PA. ☎ 0161-740 7788. Min. Rabbi Yakov Abenson. Sec.: J. E. Freeman.

Cheshire Reform Cong., Menorah Synagogue, Altrincham Rd., M22 4RZ. M.: Rabbi Dr. M. Hilton. ☎ 0161-428 7746.

Congregation of Spanish and Portuguese Jews, 18 Moor La., Kersal, Salford, M7 0WX. Hon. Sec.: Mrs. B. Kesler. ☎ 0161-773-2954.

Hale & District Hebrew Cong., Shay La., Hale Barns, Ches., WA15 8PA. M.: Rabbi Joel Portnoy. Hon. Sec.: F. Greibach. ☎ 0161-980 8846.

Heaton Park Hebrew Cong., Ashdown, Middleton Rd., M8 6JX. M.: Rev. L. Olsberg. Admin.: K.D. Radivan. ☎ 0161-740 4766.

Higher Crumpsall & Higher Broughton, Bury Old Rd., Salford M7 4PX. ☎ 0161-740 1210. M.: Rabbi Arnold Saunders B.A.. ☎ 0161-692 5155. Sec.: Mrs. E. Somers. ☎ 0161-740 8155.

Higher Prestwich, 445 Bury Old Rd., Prestwich, M25 1QP. M.: Rev. H. Hillman. Sec.: Vacant. ☎ 0161-773 4800.

Hillock Hebrew Cong., Ribble Dr., Whitefield, M45. Sec.: R. Walker, 13 Mersey Close, Hillock, Whitefield, M45 8LB. ☎ 0161-766 1162.

Holy Law South Broughton Cong., Bury Old Rd., Prestwich, M25 0EX. Morn. and evg. services daily. M.: Rabbi Y. Chazan. ☎ 0161-792 6349/0161-721 4705. Admin.: Mrs P. Mann. ☎ 0161-740 1634. Fax 0161-720 6623.

Kahal Chassidim, 62 Singleton Rd., Salford M7 0LU. Sec.: D. Lipsidge. ☎ 0161-740-1629.

Machzikei Hadass, Syn. & Com. Office: 17 Northumberland St., Salford, M7 0FE. Org. Sec.: A. Vogel. ☎ 0161-792 1313.

Manchester Great & New Synagogue, Stenecourt, Holden Rd., Salford, M7 4LN. M.: Rev. Gabriel Brodie. ☎ 0161-792 8399.

Manchester Reform Synagogue, Jackson's Row, M2 5NH. ☎ 0161-834 0415 & 01514. M.: Rabbi Dr. Reuven Silverman. Sec.: N. J. Franks.

North Salford, 2 Vine St., Salford, M7 0NX. M.: Rabbi L. W. Rabinowitz. Hon. Sec.: D. Haffner. ☎ 0161-792 3278.

Ohel Torah, 132 Leicester Rd., Salford, M7 0EA. Sec.: P. Koppenheim, 5 Granville Av., Salford, M7 0HB. ☎ 0161-740 6678.

Prestwich Hebrew Cong., Bury New Rd., M25 9WN. M.: Rabbi Mordechai Ginsbury. Sec.: A. Frankel. ☎ 0161-773 1978, Fax 0161-773 7015.

Sale & District Hebrew Cong., 14 Hesketh Rd., Sale, M33 5AA. ☎ 0161-973

2172. M.: Rabbi Gershon Overlander. Hon. Sec.: M. J. Coppel. ☎ 0161-973 4054.
Sedgley Park (Shomrei Hadass), Park View Rd., Prestwich, M25 5FA. Sec.: G.
R. Marks. ☎ 0161-773 6092.
Sha'are Sedek Syn. & Talmud Torah, Old Lansdowne Rd., W. Didsbury, M20
8NZ. ☎ 0161-445 5731. M.: Rabbi S. Ellituv. ☎ 0161-434 6903.
Sha'arei Shalom, North Manchester Reform Cong., Elms St., Whitefield M45
8GQ. Hon. Sec.: Mrs. B. L. Tucker. ☎ 0161-796-6736.
South Manchester, Wilbraham Rd., Fallowfield, M14 6JS. M.: Rabbi Y. R.
Rubin. Admin.: S. L. Rydz. ☎ 0161-224 1366. Fax 0161-225 8033.
United Synagogue, Meade Hill Rd., M8 4LR. ☎ 0161-740 9586. Pres.: S.
Huller.
Whitefield Hebrew Cong., Park Lane, Whitefield, M45 7PB. ☎ 0161-766
3732. Fax 0161-767 9453. M.: Rabbi Jonathan Guttentag, B.A. Admin.: Mrs.
P. M. Deach.
Withington Cong. of Spanish & Portuguese Jews, 8 Queenston Rd., West
Didsbury, M20 2WZ. ☎ 0161-445 1943. Fax 0161-434 8094.
Yeshurun Hebrew Cong., Coniston Rd., Gatley, Cheshire, SK8 4AP. M.: Dr.
Alan Unterman. Admin.: Mrs. N. Shepherd. ☎ 0161-428 8242.
Beth Din & Kashrus Authority Offices, 435 Cheetham Hill Rd., M8 0PF. ☎
0161-740 9711. Fax 0161-721 4249. Rosh Beth Din: Dayan G. Krausz.
Admin.: J. Brodie.
Mikvaot: Com. Mikva (under the authority of the Manchester Beth Din),
Broom Holme, Tetlow Lane, Salford, M7 0BU. ☎ 0161-792 3970 during
opening times; Manchester & District Mikva (under the authority of
Machzikei Hadass), Sedgley Pk. Rd., Prestwich. ☎ 0161-773 1537 & 7403;
Naomi Greenberg South Manchester Mikva (under the authority of the
Manchester Beth Din), Shay Lane, Hale Barns, Altrincham, Cheshire. ☎ 0161-
904 8296.
Whitefield Hebrew Congregation Mikva, Park Lane, Whitefield M45 7PB. ☎
0161-796 1054.

Representative Organisations
Jewish Representative Council of Greater Manchester & Region, Jewish
Cultural Centre, Bury Old Rd., M8 6FY. ☎ 0161-720 8721. Affiliated to the
Council are 140 syns. and orgs. Pres.: Mr. Isidore Fromson.

Cultural & Educational Organisations
Central Library, St. Peter's Sq., M2 5PD. Large collection of Jewish books for
reference and loan, including books in Hebrew. ☎ 0161-234 1983/1984.
Contact the Social Sciences Library.
Jewish Cultural Centre, Bury Old Rd., M8 6FY. ☎ 0161-795 4000. Syn.; stu-
dent accom.; short-term accom.; library and Kosher restaurant.
Manchester Jewish Museum, 190 Cheetham Hill Rd., M8 8LW. ☎ 0161-834
9879 & 0161-832 7353. Mon.-Thurs., 10.30 a.m. to 4 p.m. Sundays, 10.30
a.m. to 5 p.m. Admission charge. Exhibitions, Heritage trails, Demonstration
& Talks. Calendar of events available on request. Educational visits for schools
and adult groups must be booked in advance. Admin: D. Rainger.
Manchester Central Board for Hebrew Education & Talmud Torah, Emanuel
Raffles Hse., 57 Leicester Rd., Salford M7 4DA. ☎/Fax 0161-708 9200.
Chairman S. Pine.

Welfare Organisations, Hospitals, etc.
Brookvale caring for people with special needs. Simister Lane, Prestwich, M25
2SF. Dir. of Services Mrs. L. Richmond,. ☎ 0161-653 1767. Fax 0161-655
3635. Short term care available.
Manchester Jewish Blind Society, Nicky Alliance Day Centre, 85 Middleton

Rd., M8 6JY. ☎ 0161-740 0111. Fax 0161-721-4273.
Jewish Social Services (Greater Manchester), (Est. 1867, Reg. Charity No. 220165), 12 Holland Rd., Higher Crumpsall, M8 4NP. ☎ 0161-795 0024. Chief Ex.: I. Lewis. Dir. of Services: Karen Rapaport.
Outreach, Manchester Jews' Benevolent Society, League of Jewish Women, Heathlands, Home for the Aged. Morris Feinmann Home for the Aged.

Student & Youth Organisations
Bnei Akiva (North of England), 72, Singleton Rd, Salford M7 4LU. ☎ 0161-740 1621. Fax 0161-740-8018. Email: bnei.akiva@ort.org
Habonim-Dror, Moadon Habonim, 11 Upper Park Rd., Salford, M7 0HY. ☎ 0161-795 9447. Fax 0161 740 1981.
Hillel House, Greenheys La., M15 6LR. ☎ 0161-226 1139 (Warden). ☎ 0161-266 1973 (Housekeeper). (K) Meals (under Manchester Beth Din). Inq. about accom. to Dr. S. Baigel, 4 Danesway, Prestwich M25 0FS. ☎/Fax 0161-740-2521. Chaplain: Rabbi Y.Y. Rubinstein, 97 Singleton Rd, Salford M7. ☎/Fax 0161-721-4066. Mobile 0831-253 136.
Jewish Scouts & Guides. 401st Manchester Scout Group and 5th Cheetham Guides & Brownies, H.Q., Willow Hill Rd., Crumpsall, Manchester 8. ☎ 0161 792 3431.
Group Scout Leader: Howard Balkind, 16 Vine St., Kersal, Salford, M7 0PG.
Lubavitch Community & Youth Centre, Lubavitch Hse., 62 Singleton Rd., Salford, M7 0LV. ☎/Fax 0161-740 9514.
University & Polytechnic Jewish Societies. Sec.: Hillel Hse., Greenheys La., M15 6LR.

Zionist Organisations
Zionist Central Council of Greater Manchester, Joseph Mamlock Hse., 142 Bury Old Rd., M8 4HE. ☎ 0161-740 8835. Here are the offices of the Joint Israel Appeal, Jewish National Fund ☎(for both: 0161-740 1825), Jewish Agency Aliya Dept. ☎ 0161-740 2864, and Women's Zionist Council (Wizo and Emunah). ☎ 0161-740 3367).

Sport
Whitefield Golf Club, Higher Lane, Whitefield, M25 7EZ. Sec.: J. Peatfield. ☎ 0161-766 2904.
Dunham Forest Golf and Country Club, Oldfield Lane, Altrincham, Cheshire WA4 4TY. Sec.: Mrs. S. Klaus. ☎ 0161-928 2605.

Newspaper
Jewish Telegraph, Telegraph Hse., 11 Park Hill, Bury Old Rd., Prestwich, M25 0HH. ☎ 0161-740 9321. Fax 0161-740-9325.

Booksellers
J. Goldberg, 11 Parkside Av., Salford, M7 0HB. ☎ 0161-740 0732.
B. Horowitz, 20 King Edward Bldgs., Bury Old Rd., M8. ☎ 0161-740 5897, & 2 Kings Rd., Prestwich, M25. ☎ 0161-773 4956.
Hyman's, Wilmslow Rd., Cheadle, Cheshire.
Jewish Book Centre (Terence Noyek), 25 Ashbourne Gr., Salford, M7 0DB. ☎ 0161-792 1253.

Hotel
(K) Fulda's Hotel, 144 Bury Old Rd., M7 4QY. ☎ 0161-740 4748. Fax 0161- 740 4551.

Restaurants
(K) Broadway Kosher Diner, 9 Kings Rd., Prestwich, M25 8LE. ☎ 0161-773 2909. Under Manchester Beth Din.

(K) J.S.Kosher Restaurant, 7 Kings Rd., Prestwich M25 0LE. ☎ 0161-798 7776.

Captain Restaurant, 85 Rochdale Rd. ☎ 0161-839 7198.

★ **Lapidus**, 21 Bury Old Rd., Prestwich, M25 8EQ. ☎ 0161-740 3095.

The Nose, 6 Lapwing Lane, West Didsbury. ☎ 0161-445 3653.

(V) Pie in the Sky, 160b Wellington Rd., Withington, M20 9UH. ☎ 0161-4452772.

Terrace Restaurant, Jewish Cultural Centre, Bury Old Road, M86 6FY.

(V) The Greenhouse, 331 Western St., Rusholme, M14 4AN. ☎ 0161-2240730.

Caterers

(K) Celia Clyne Catering Ltd., 54 Chapeltown St., Manchester. M1 2NN. ☎ 0161-273 8888. Fax 0161-273 8890.

(K) I & M Kosher Banqueting Caterers, 54 Brooklands Rd., Prestwich, Manchester M25 0ED. ☎ 0161-740 8624/766 1245 (Manchester Beth Din).

(K) Renee Hodari, 36 Brooklawn Dr., Withington, M20 9GZ.

(K) Simon's Catering, 105 Leicester Rd., Salford, 7.

Sheila Mendelson Catering, 81-87 Silverdale Rd., Gatley, Cheshire, SK8 4QR.

Delicatessen

(K) Deli King, Kings Rd., Prestwich, M25 8LQ. ☎ 0161-798 7370. fAX 0161-798 5654.

MARGATE (KENT)

Syn.: Godwin Rd., Cliftonville, CT9 2HA. Sec.: D. Kaye, 46 Eastchurch Rd., Cliftonville, CT9 3HY. ☎ 01843 223219.

MIDDLESBROUGH (CLEVELAND)

Syn.: Park Rd. S., TS5 6LE. Sec.: Mr. Broady. ☎ 01642 819034 (for details of services). J. Bloom. ☎ 01642-781363.

Restaurant: **(V)** Filberts, 47 Borough Rd., TS1 4AF. ☎ 01642-245455.

MILTON KEYNES

Milton Keynes & District Reform Synagogue, Services at Tinkers Bridge Meeting Place, Milton Keynes. Chairman: Stanley Cohen, 74 Corn Hill, Two Mile Ash, MK8 8JR. ☎ 01908 569661.

NEWARK (NOTTS)

Beth Shalom Holocaust Memorial Centre, Laxton, NG22 0PA. ☎ 01623-836627. Fax 01623-836647. Dir. S.D. Smith, J.M. Smith and Mrs M.H. Smith.

NEWCASTLE UPON TYNE (TYNE & WEAR)

The community was established before 1831, when a cemetery was acquired. (Jews have lived in Newcastle since 1775). There are about 1,200 Jews in the city today.

Synagogues & Religious Organisations

United Hebrew Congregation. Syn., Graham Park Rd., Gosforth, NE3 4BH. Daily morn. & evg. services throughout the year. Mikva on premises. M.: Rabbi Y.L. Black. Sec.: Mrs. P. Ashton, Lionel Jacobson Hse., address below. ☎ 0191 2840959.

Lionel Jacobson Hse., Graham Park Rd., Gosforth, NE3 4BH. Full communal facilities available inc. Kashrus Com., Hebrew Classes & Jewish Welfare Soc.

Newcastle Reform Syn. Services at The Croft, off Kenton Rd., Gosforth, NE3 4RF. ☎ 0191 2848621. M.: Rabbi F. Berry. ☎ 0191 285 2593.

Representative Organisation

Representative Council of North-East Jewry, 24 Adeline Gardens, Gosforth NE3 4JQ. Pres.: Barry Speker. Hon. Sec.: C. E. van der Velde. ☎ 0191 2851253. Publishes fortnightly 'The North-East Jewish Recorder'.

Miscellaneous

Bnei Akiva, Inf.: Miss. J. Lustman, 56 The Drive, Gosforth.
Hillel Hse., 29-31 Hawthorn Rd., Gosforth.
(K) Student meals available Fri. nights. Further inf. from G. Lurie, 32 St. Mary's Pl., NE1 7PS. ☎ 0191 2610577 or 2857928.
Bridge Club, c/o Mr. A. Deane. ☎ 0191-281 1992.
Newcastle Jewish Leisure Group,
Newcastle Maccabi —
Badminton, c/o Mr. S. Doberman.
Table Tennis, Tennis, c/o Mr. P. Mickler. ☎ 0191-285 5195.
North-East Jewish Youth Study Group. Inf. from D. Ross, 56 Southwood Gardens, Kenton, NE3 4LT. ☎ 0191 2854043.

Kosher Meat, Poultry & Groceries

(K) Zelda's Delicatessen, Unit 7 Kenton Park Shopping Centre NE3 4RU. ☎ 0191-2130013. Under Newcastle Kashrus Committee.

Restaurants

(V) Old School House, Kirkwhelpington, NE19 2RT. ☎ 01830-40226. B&B.
(V) The Red Herring, 3 Studley Terrace, Fenham, NE4 5AH. ☎ 0191-2723484.
(V) Veggies, 12 St Mary's Place, NE1 7PG.

NORTHAMPTON (NORTHANTS.)

Syn.: Overstone Rd., NN1 3JW. Sec.: A. Moss. ☎ 01604 33345. Services: Fri. night.
Cemetery: Towcester Road.

NORWICH (NORFOLK)

The present community was founded in 1813, Jews having been resident in Norwich during the Middle Ages, and connected with the woollen and worsted trade, for which the city was at that time famous. A resettlement of Jews is believed to have been completed by the middle of the eighteenth century. A syn. was built in 1848 and destroyed in an air raid in 1942. A temporary syn. opened in 1948. A new syn. was consecrated by the Chief Rabbi in 1969. The congregation serves a large area, having members in Ipswich, Gt. Yarmouth, Lowestoft and Cromer.
Syn.: 3a Earlham Rd., Norwich, NR2 3RA. Hon. Sec.: B. I. Levy. ☎ 01603-503 434.
Israel and Social Society, 3a Earlham Rd., Norwich. P.: B. Leveton; Hon Sec.: Maureen Leveton.
Progressive Jewish Community of East Anglia. Information from Hon. Sec.: Frimette Carr. ☎ 01603-714162. M. Rabbi F.D. Smith. ☎ 01923-820002.

Restaurants

(V) Eat Naturally, 11 Wensum St., NR3 1LA. ☎ 01603-660838.
(V) The Treehouse, 16 Dove St., NR2 1DE. ☎ 01603 625560.

NOTTINGHAM

Jews settled in Nottingham as early as mediaeval times, and centres of learning and worship are known to have existed in that period. The earliest known record of an established community dates from 1822 when a grant of land for burial purposes was made by the Corporation; in 1825 the then Chief Rabbi appointed the community's first shochet. The community grew apace as a result of the late 19th century pogroms in Eastern Europe and during the 20 years preceding and following World War II, growing to some 1,700 to 1,800 by the early 1950s. Today the known Jewish population is estimated at 1,000 about two-thirds of whom are members of the Orthodox Synagogue. The present synagogue was consecrated by Chief Rabbi Dr. Israel Brodie in 1954. (See also Newark).

Syn.: Shakespeare St., NG1 4FQ. M. Rabbi M. Perez; Sec.: ☎ 0115 9472004. For times of services, telephone Syn. Sec. Min: 0115 9624691.

Nottingham Progressive Jewish Cong. Syn.: Lloyd St., Sherwood, Nottingham, NG5 4BP. ☎ 0115 9624761. Chairman: B. Peters. ☎ 0115 978609.

★ Jewish Rest Home. Miriam Kaplowitch Hse., 470 Mansfield Rd., NG5 2EL. ☎ 0115 9622038 (Matron & Administrator), 0115 9624274 (residents).

Jewish Welfare Board. Ch.: Dr. M. Caplan. Hon. Sec.: Peter Seymour, 115 Selby Rd., West Bridgford, NG2 7BB. ☎ 0115 9-452895.

Jewish Women's Benevolent Society. Ch.: Mrs. D. Christie, 8 Croft Rd., Edwalton, NG12 4BW. ☎ 0115 9231105. Hon. Sec.: Mrs. H. Markson. ☎ 0115 9231177.

Students: Hillel House, 363 Derby Rd., Lenton, NG7 2DZ. Inq.: Sandra Flitterman (0115) 937 5403). Jewish & Israel Soc., University of Nottingham, University Pk., NG7 2RD.

Restaurants

(V) **Krisha Restaurant**, 144 Alfreton Rd., Redford, NG7 3NS. ☎ 0115 9708608.

(V) **Maxine's Salad Table**, 56 Upper Parliament St., NG1 2AG. ☎ 0115 9473622.

(V) **Rita's Cafe**, 15 Goosegate, Hockley, NG1 1FE. ☎ 0115 9481115.

(V) **The Vegetarian Pot**, 375 Alfreton Rd., Redford, NG7 5LT. ☎ 0115 9703333.

OXFORD (OXON.)

There was an important medieval com., and the present one dates from 1842. The Oxford Syn. and Jewish Centre, opened in 1974, serves both the city & the university. It is available for all forms of Jewish worship.

The Syn. and Jewish Centre is at 21 Richmond Rd., OX1 2JL. For inf. about services, ☎ 01865 553042.

Pres. of Cong.: Mrs P. Faust, 22 Feilden Gr., OX3 0DU. Sec. Mrs K. Tomlinson, 18 Belvedere Rd., OX4 2AZ. ☎ 01865 725129. Hon. Tr.: A. M. Curtis, 257 Woodstock Rd., OX2 7AE. ☎ 01865 515107.

(K) A kosher meals service operates during term time. Inq. to 01865 553042.

Organisations

L'Chaim Society, Albion House, Little Gate. ☎ 01865-794462.

Menorah Society, President Mrs J. Patterson, 35 Hayward Rd., OX2 8LH. ☎ 01865 59003.

For Jewish Youth activities, 21 Richmond Rd., Oxford, OX1 2JL. ☎ 01865 863210.

WIZO: Mrs M. Da Costa, Windrush, Hamels Lane, Boars Hill, OX15 5DJ. ☎ 01865 735240.

PETERBOROUGH (CAMBS.)

Hebrew Congregation (U.S.), 142 Cobden Av., PE1 2NU. Inq. to C. Conn, 22 Edinburgh Av., Werrington. ☎ 01733 571282.

Liberal Jewish Community (ULPS). Enquiries to Nat Gordon. ☎ 01933 461555.

PLYMOUTH (DEVON)

The cong. was founded in 1752 and a syn. erected ten years later. This is now the oldest Ashkenazi syn. building in England still used for its original purpose. It is a scheduled historical monument. In 1815 Plymouth was one of the four most important provincial centres in Anglo-Jewry.

Syn.: Catherine St., PL1 2AD. Sec.: Dr. P.I. Lee. ☎ 01822 612281. Services: Fri., 6 p.m. Sat., 9.30 a.m.

Cong. offers free use of minister's modern flat as holiday accom. in return for conducting Orthodox Fri. evg. & Sabbath morn. services. Inq.: Dr P.I. Lee. ☎ 01822 612281.

A Jewish collection of fiction & non-fiction books, mainly lending copies, has been integrated into the stock of the Plymouth Central Library, Drake Circus, PL4 8AL. It is known as the Holcenberg Collection.

Restaurant

(V) **Plymouth Arts Centre Vegetarian Restaurant**, 38 Looe St., PL4 0EB. ☎ 01752 660060.

PORTSMOUTH AND SOUTHSEA (HANTS.)

The Portsmouth com. was founded in 1746. Its first syn. was in Oyster Row, but the cong. removed to a building in White's Row, which it continued to occupy for almost two centuries. A new building was erected in 1936. The cemetery is in a street which was once known as Jews' Lane. It is the oldest in the Provinces still used for the interment of Jews.

Syn.: Synagogue Chambers, The Thicket, Southsea, PO5 2AA. ☎ 01705 821494. M.:

PRESTON (LANCS.)

Inf. from Hon. Sec. of com.: Dr. C. E. Nelson, 31 Avondale Rd., Southport, Merseyside.

RADLETT (HERTS)

Syns.: Radlett United Syn., P.O. Box 28, WD7 7PN; Radlett & Bushey Reform Syn., 118 Watling St., WD7 7AA. ☎ 0181 953 8889.

RAMSGATE (KENT)

Syn.: Montefiore Endowment, Hereson Rd.

Communications to Spanish & Portuguese Synagogue, 2 Ashworth Rd., London, W9 1JY. ☎ 0171-289 2573.

Visitors wishing to see the Montefiore Mausoleum and Synagogue should apply to A. G. G. Da Costa, 33 Luton Av., Broadstairs. ☎ 01843 862507.

Thanet and District Reform Synagogue, 293A Margate Rd., Ramsgate, Kent, CT12 6TA. ☎ 01843-851164. Services: Fri. 8.00pm, Sat. 11.00am.

READING (BERKS.)

Jewish settlement began in 1886. The orthodox synagogue was opened in 1900, and has been in continuous use ever since. This flourishes today as the centre of the Reading Hebrew Congregation, which has a growing membership of 160 families, and is the only Orthodox congregation in Berkshire. The Sir Hermann Gollancz Hall next to the synagogue is the venue of many social groups and the Congregation has a Cheder, a mother and toddler group, a Judaica shop, a kosher food shop, WIZO, a Ladies Guild and several social groups.

Synagogue, Goldsmid Rd., Reading, RG1 7YB. ☎ 01734 571018. M.: Hon. Sec.: Mrs. Louise Creme. ☎ 01734-571710.
University Jewish Society, c/o Reading Hillel House, 82 Basingstoke Rd., RG? ☎ 01734 873282.
Thames Valley Progressive Jewish Community, 6 Church St., Reading. Chairman: Ms D. Edelman. ☎ 01734 867769.

ROCHESTER (KENT)
Syn.: Magnus Memorial Synagogue, 366 High St., Rochester, ME1 1DJ. ☎ 01634-847665. (Grade 2, listed building, known as The Chatham Memorial Synagogue.) Inq.: H. Halpern, Boley Hill Hse., Boley Hill, Rochester, Kent, ME1 1TE. ☎ 01634 842405.

ROMFORD (GREATER LONDON)
Syn.: 25 Eastern Rd. Inq.: H. Lexton, 11 Mulberry Cl., Gidea Pk.

RUISLIP (GREATER LONDON)
Syn.: Shenley Av., Ruislip Manor, HA4 6BP. M.: Rev. D. Wolfson. ☎ 01895 632934. Inq. The Synagogue, Shenley Avenue, Ruislip Manor, Middx., HA4 6BT. ☎ 01895 622059.

ST. ALBANS (HERTS.)
Syn.: Oswald Rd., AL1 3AQ. ☎ 56 54872. Services, Fri. 8 p.m.
St. Alban's Masorti Syn. P.O. Box 23, St. Albans. Inq. Sec: A. Hoffman, ☎ 01727 760891.

ST. ANNES-ON-SEA (LANCS.)
Syn.: Orchard Rd., FY8 1PJ. ☎ 01253 721831. Services 7.30 a.m. and 8 p.m. M.: Rabbi N. Lew. President.: P. Davidson. ☎ 01253 723920.
Hon. Sec.: M. Brody. ☎ 01253 734722.
Ladies' Guild. Ch.: Mrs. E. Davidson. ☎ 01253-721831.
St. Annes and Fylde Jewish Literary Society & Friendship Club. Hon. Sec.: Mrs. Gene Kay, 15 Crestway, Newton Dr., Blackpool, FY3 8PA. ☎ 01253 392513.

Delicatessen
Safeway Food Store, St. Andrew's Rd., North St.;
The Lytham Delicatessen, 53 Warton St., FY8 2JE. ☎ 01253 735861.

SHEFFIELD (S. YORKS.)
The earliest records of the Sheffield cong. date from 1837, although it had already been in existence for some time before then.

Synagogues
Sheffield Jewish Congregation and Centre, Wilson Rd., S11 8RN. Daily services. M. Rabbi Golomb. ☎ 0114 266 3567. Hon. Sec.: Mrs. M. Shaw. ☎ 0114 2362217.
Sheffield & District Reform Jewish Cong. Services alternate Fri. evgs. Chairman: Dr J. Kinderlerer. ☎ 0114 2301054. Further inf.: ☎ 0114 2308433 or 2360970.
Jewish Centre ☎ 0114 2552296.
Communal inq. to Mrs. A. Spier. ☎ 0114 2360984.

SOLIHULL (W. MIDLANDS)
Syn.: Solihull & District Hebrew Cong., 3 Monastery Dr., St. Bernard's Rd., B91 3HN. M.: Rabbi Pink. Services Fri. evg., Sat., 9.45 a.m., Sun., 9 a.m.
Hon. Sec.: P. D. Fiddler. ☎ 0121-707 5199.
Jewish Social and Cultural Soc. Hon. Sec.: Mr. H. Kay, 964 Warwick Rd., B91 3HN.

Shirley Golf Course Ltd., Stratford Rd., Monkspath, Shirley, B90 4EW. ☎ 0121-744 6001. Sec.: A. J. Phillips.
Shirley Park Sports Club, Stratford Rd., Monkspath, Shirley, B90 4EW. Chairman: R. Gold. ☎ 0121-745 6190.

SOUTHAMPTON (HANTS.)
Syn.: Mordaunt Rd., The Inner Av., SO2 0GP. Services, Sat. morn., 10 a.m. Southampton & District Jewish Soc. Hon. Sec.: c/o Hillel Hse., address below. Residential accom. for students (8 rooms) is available at Hillel House, 5 Brookvale Rd., Portswood, SO2 1QN.
The Hartley library at the University of Southampton houses both the Parkes Library and the Anglo-Jewish Archives.

SOUTHEND AND WESTCLIFF (ESSEX)
Jews began settling in the Southend area in the late 19th century, mainly from the East End of London. The first temporary syn. was built in Station Rd., Westcliff, in 1906. Six years later, the present syn. was erected in Alexandra Rd., and has been in continuous use ever since.
In 1928, a breakaway group built its own syn. in Ceylon Rd., but later reunited with the Alexandra Rd. cong. When a new syn. was built in Finchley Rd., Westcliff, in 1968, the Ceylon Rd. building was turned into a youth centre. The Southend and Westcliff area's Jewish population is about 4,500.

Synagogues & Religious Organisations
Southend and Westcliff Hebrew Cong. Syn., Finchley Rd., Westcliff, SS0 8AD. M.: Also at 99 Alexandra Rd., Southend. Syn. office: Finchley Rd., Westcliff, SS0 8AD. Sec.: Mrs. R. Silver. ☎ 01702 344900.
Southend Reform Syn., 851 London Rd., Westcliff. ☎ 01702 75809. Services: Fri., 7.30 p.m. Sabbath, 10.30 a.m. Hon Sec.: Mrs. A. Klass, 22 Crowstone Av., Westcliff, SS0 8HU. ☎ 01702 338460.
Jewish Cemetery: Sutton Rd. (entrance Stock Rd.), Southend. Inq.: ☎ 01702 344900.

Representative Organisation
Southend & District Jewish Representative Council. Sec.: J. Barcan, 22 Second Ave., Westcliff-on-Sea, SS0 8HY. ☎ 01702 343192

Clubs, Organisations, etc.
Aid Society (Welfare Board). Chairman: Mrs. J. Berg, 5 Tower Court, Westcliff-on-Sea, Essex.
Ajex Sec.: J. Barcan, 22 Second Av., Westcliff, SS0 8HY. ☎ 01702 343192.
Ajex Club. Ch. H. Eichen Esq., 53 Hamlet Court Rd., Westcliff-on-Sea, Essex.
B'nai B'rith Unity Lodge. Chairman: M. Bloch, 43 Finchley Rd., Westcliff. ☎ 01702 341134. Women's Sec.: Mrs. E. Ross, 29 Albion Rd., Westcliff. ☎ 01702 347718. BBYO Ch.: David Cregor, 162 Lifstan Way, Thorpe Bay. ☎ 01702 68334.
Day Centre, Victoria Oppenheim Hse., 1 Cobham Rd., Westcliff, SS0 8EG. ☎ 01702 334655. Organiser: Mrs. Christine Carter.
Emunah, Chairman: Mrs. L. Sober, Emunah, 16 Crosby Rd., Westcliff-on-Sea, Essex.
Friends of Ravenswood. Chairman: J. Freeman Esq., 111 Hampton Gds., Southend-on-Sea, Essex.
Invicta Tennis Club, Crosby Rd., Westcliff, SS0 8LB. Hon. Captain: M. King, 16 Galton Rd., Westcliff, SS0 8LE. ☎ 01702 341604.
J.I.A., Chairman: S. Salt Esq., 157 Chalkwell Av., Westcliff-on-Sea, Essex.
J.L.G.B. Chairman: A. Kalms Esq., 6 Leitrim Av., Thorpe Bay, Essex.

Kosher Meals on Wheels. Sec.: Mrs. B. Franks, 90 Chalkwell Av., Westcliff-on-Sea, Essex.
Ladies Guild (Orthodox) Sec.: Mrs. G. Jay, 15 Seymour Rd., Westcliff-on-Sea, Essex.
Ladies Guild (Reform) Chairman: Mrs. R. Brenner, 12 The Drive, Westcliff-on-Sea, Essex.
Myers Communal Hall, Finchley Rd., Westcliff, SS0 8AD. ☎ 01702 345152.
Raymond House for the Aged, 7-9 Clifton Ter., Southend. ☎ 01702 340054 (residents), 01702 352956 (matron).
Shalom Club. Chairman: G. Kalms Esq., Flat 14, Tower Court, Westcliff Parade, Westcliff-on-Sea, Essex.
Southend Jewish Youth Centre, 38-40 Ceylon Rd., Westcliff, SS0 7HS. ☎ 01702 346545. Sec.: David Jay.
Thursday Friendship Club. Sec.: Mrs. M. Davis, 9 Britannia Rd., Westcliff.
Women's Zionist Society. Hon. Sec.: Mrs. J. Barnett, 22 Kings Rd., Westcliff, SS0 8LL. ☎ 01702 340731.
Young Marrieds Cultural & Social Group. Secs.: L. & F. Herlitz, 10 Cliff Rd., Leigh-on-Sea, SS9 1HJ. ☎ 01702 715676.
Zionist Society. Chairman: I. Burns, 6 Chadwick Rd., Westcliff. SS0 8LS. ☎ 01702 341776.

Bookseller
Dorothy Young, 21 Colchester Rd., Southend, SS2 6HW. ☎ 01702 331218 for appointment. Religious articles, Israeli giftware, etc., also stocked.

Hotels & Restaurants
★ Archery's Hotel, 27 Grosvenor Rd., Westcliff. Janice & Glen Archery. ☎ 01702 353323 or 334001.
★ Embassy Hotel (53), 35-41 Grosvenor Rd., Westcliff, SS0 8EP. ☎ 01702 335803 (reservations) & 341175 (visitors). Mark & Mildred Friedlander.
★ Redstone's Hotel (38), Pembury Rd., Westcliff, SS0 8DS. Redstone & family. ☎ 01702 348441.

Delicatessen
(K) Westcliff Kosher Bagel, Hamlet Court Road, Westcliff. ☎ 01702 435678. Licensed by Southend & Westcliff Kashut Commission.

SOUTHPORT (MERSEYSIDE)
Synagogues
Southport Hebrew Cong., Arnside Rd., PR9 0QX. ☎ 01704 532964. M.: Rabbi Mair Rogosnitzky. ☎ 01704 537606. Sec.: Mrs. Maureen Cohen. ☎ 01704 540247. Services twice daily, week-days and Sabbath. Mikva on premises.
New (Reform), Portland St., PR8 1LR. ☎ 01704 535950. M.: Rabbi Amanda Golby. ☎ 01704 66235.

Representative Organisations
Council of Christians and Jews. Hon. Sec.: Mrs. M. Roche, 4 Bells Cl., Lydiate, Merseyside. ☎ 0151-531 9551.
Jewish Representative Council. Pres.: Dr. Cyril Nelson, 31 Avondale Rd., PR9 0NH. ☎ 01704-538276.

Social & Welfare Organisations
Friendship Club. Ch.: Mrs. C. Cowan, 23 Warren St., Westcliffe Rd.

Homes

Jewish Convalescent & Aged Home, 81 Albert Rd., PR9 9LN. ☎ 01704 531975 (office), 01704 530207 (visitors).
(K) Sharon Rest Home, 111 Leyland Rd., PR9 0JL. ☎ 01704 531386 (office), 530170 residents. Mr. & Mrs. A. Sawitz. (Manchester Beth Din.)
(K) Southport Nursing & Care Home, 126 Leyland Rd., PR9 0JL. ☎ 01704 531386 (office), 543898 (Matron) 544116 (residents).(Manchester Beth Din.)

Meat & Delicatessen

Kosher Counter at Tesco, Town Lane, Kew, Southport.

STAINES (MIDDX.)

Includes Slough and Windsor Synagogue.
Syn.: Staines & District Synagogue, Westbrook Rd., South St., TW18 4PR. Hon. Sec.: Mrs. P. D. Fellman. ☎ 01784 254604.

STOKE ON TRENT (STAFFS.)

Syn.: Birch Ter., Hanley, ST1 3JN. ☎ 01782 616417.

SUNDERLAND (TYNE & WEAR)

Communal Rav: Rabbi S. Zahn, 11 The Oaks E., SR2 8EX. ☎ 0191 5650224.

Synagogues

Sunderland Hebrew Cong., Ryhope Rd., SR2 7EQ. Incorporating Sunderland Beth Hamedrash. Services twice daily. President: J. Sadlik. ☎ 0191 5227560. Sec.: T. Jackson. ☎ 0191 5658093.
Mikva: Contact Mrs. Zahn, ☎ 0191 5650224.

Education

Centre for Advanced Rabbinics (Kolel), 2 The Oaks W., SR2 8HZ. ☎ 0191 5671108.
Welfare North-East Joel Intract Memorial Home for Aged Jews, 6 Gray Rd., SR2 8JB. ☎ 0191 5144816 (office), 5656574 (residents).

SUTTON AND DISTRICT (SURREY)

(Covering Banstead, Belmont, Carshalton, Carshalton Beeches, Cheam, Croydon, Epsom, Hackbridge, Kingswood, Mitcham, Morden, Sutton, Wallington, Worcester Pk.)
Syn.: 14 Cedar Rd., Sutton, SM2 5DA. Hon. Sec.: Mrs T. Raphael. ☎ 0181 6429285.

SWINDON (WILTS)

Swindon Jewish Community. Vice Chairman: Mr. Martin Vandervelde, 4 Lakeside, Swindon, Wilts SN3 1QE. Inq: ☎ 01793 521910

TORQUAY (SOUTH DEVON)

(Covering also Brixham & Paignton.)
Syn.: Old Town Hall, Abbey Rd., Torquay, TQ1 1BB. Hon. Sec.: Anne Salter. ☎ 01803 607724. Services, first Sabbath of every month & festivals, 10.30 a.m. Inq. to Ernest Freed, 'Son Bou', 7 Broadstone Park Rd., Livermead, TQ2 6TY.

Restaurant

(V) Brookesby Hall Hotel (14), Hesketh Rd., Meadfoot Beach, TQ1 2LN. ☎ 01803 292194. B&B.

WALLINGFORD (OXON.)

Carmel College, Mongewell Pk., Wallingford, Oxon., OX10 8BT. ☎ 01491

837505. Boarding school for boys & girls, 11-18. Founder, the late Rabbi Kopul Rosen. Hd.: Philip Skelker, M.A. (Oxon.).
(**K**) Kosher meals available in term time (except on Shabbat), provided Bursar is telephoned in advance.

WATFORD (HERTS.)
(Covering also Carpenders Pk., Croxley Gn., Garston, King's Langley & Rickmansworth.)
Syn.: 16 Nascot Rd., WD1 3RE. M. Rabbi: D. Roselaar. ☎ 01923 222755. Sec.: M. Shrago. ☎ 01923 674737.

WELWYN GARDEN CITY (HERTS.)
(Affiliated to United Synagogue. Covering also Hatfield, Harpenden, Hertford, Letchworth, St. Albans & Stevenage.)
Syn. (with Ladies' Guild): Barn Close, Handside Lane, AL8 6ST. Hon. Sec.: Mr Hirschfield, 3 Newton Cl., Harpenden, Herts., AL5 1SP. ☎ 015827 62829.

WHITLEY BAY (TYNE & WEAR)
Syn.: 2 Oxford St. Visitors required for services. Hon. Sec.: M. A. Sonn, 2 Grasmere Cres., NE26 3TB. ☎ 01670 367053 (day), 0191-2521367 (night).

WOLVERHAMPTON (W. MIDLANDS)
Syn.: Fryer St., WV1 1HT (est. over 150 years ago). Membership 15 families. (Services, Fri. evg. & some Sabbath morns.) Sec.: H. Kronheim, 94 Wergs Rd., Tettenhall, WV6 8TH.

WORTHING (W. SUSSEX)
Tudor Guest House, 5 Windsor Rd., BN11 2LU. ☎ 01903 210265.

YORK
There is a memorial stone at Clifford's Tower, York Castle, marking the massacre of the city's Jewish community in 1190. Jews returned to York in later years, continuing to live in the city until the expulsion of 1290. There is a small community living in York today.
Contact: A. Burton, ☎ 01532-436786.

Restaurants
(**V**) 10 Melbourne St., Fishergate, YO1 5AQ. ☎ 01904-620082. B&B.
(**V**) **Mrs. Moore's**, 21 Park Gr., YO3 1LG. ☎ 01904-644790. B&B.
(**V**) **The Vegetarian Cafe**, Gillygate Whole Food Bakery, Miller's Yard, Gillygate YO3 7EB. ☎ 01904-610676.

CHANNEL ISLANDS

ALDERNEY
On the Corblets Rd. at Longy, there is a memorial to the victims of the Nazis during their occupation of the Channel Islands during the Second World War. It bears plaques in English, French, Hebrew and Russian.

JERSEY
There is a syn. in Route des Genets, St. Brelade. Services every Sab. morn. at 10.30 a.m. and on festivals. Hon. Sec.: Stephen Regal, c/o The Synagogue. Information: Mrs. D. Bloom, 3 Batisse de la Mielle, St. Brelade, Jersey. ☎ 01534 71644. Visiting M.: Rev. M. Weisman, 25 Enford St., London, W1H 2DD. ☎ 0171-724 7778. Fax 0171-706 1710. Mr. Weisman is also the visiting Min. for Guernsey.

A limited selection of kosher meat & poultry is sometimes available to order. Contact Mrs. Bloom.

ISLE OF MAN

There are more than 70 Jews on the island.

DOUGLAS

Hon. Ch. of Hebrew Cong.: J. Beech, 'Hilldene', 7 Links View, Onchan. ☎ 01624 24214. Visiting M.: Rev. M. Weisman, 25 Enford St., London, W1H 2DD. ☎ 0171-742 7778. Fax 0171-706 1710.

WALES

CARDIFF (S. GLAMORGAN)

Jews settled in Cardiff about the year 1787. The present community was founded in 1840.

Synagogues & Religious Organisations

Cardiff United Synagogue (Orthodox), Brandreth Rd., Penylan. Sec.: Mrs. S. C. Glavin. ☎ 01222 473728/491795.
Cardiff New Synagogue (constituent of the Reform Synagogues of Great Britain), Moira Ter., CF2 1EJ, opp. Howard Gdns. Sec.: Mrs R. Melcher, 5 Park Avenue, Whitechurch, CF4 7AL. ☎ 0122-614915.
Mikva, Wales Empire Pool Bldg., Wood St., CF1 1PP. ☎ 01222 382296.

Representative Organisation

Cardiff Jewish Representative Council. Sec.: Mrs. Judy Cotsen, 71 Cyncoed Rd., Cardiff CF2 6AB. ☎ 01222 484999.

Welfare Organisations

Penylan House, Jewish Retirement & Nursing Home, Penylan Rd., CF2 5YG. ☎ 01222 485327.
Cardiff Jewish Helpline. Chairman: Mr. A. Schwartz. Contact: ☎ 01222-750990.

Student & Youth Organisations, etc.

Cardiff Jewish Students' Assoc.: Hillel Hse. Address below.
Hillel Hse. 89, Crwys Rd., Cathays.
Self-catering accomm. Inq. to Mrs P. Freed, 210 Lake Rd. East, CF2 5NR. ☎ 0122-758614.
Jewish Students' Society, Inq. to Ch., c/o Hillel Hse., Address above. Inq. about student accom. to the Dir., Hillel Hse.
Cardiff Maccabi: Mr. S. Hamilton. ☎ 01222-747653.

Restaurant

(V) Munchies Wholefood Co-op, 60 Crwys Rd, Cathays, CF2 4NN. ☎ 01222-399677.

LLANDUDNO (GWYNEDD)

Syn.: 28 Church Walks, LL30 2HL. Hon. Sec.: B. Hyman, 9 Glyn Isaf, Llandudno Junction. ☎ 01492 572549. No resident minister, but visiting ministers during summer months; Friday night services held throughout the year, 6.16 p.m. (winter), 8 p.m. (summer).

NEWPORT (GWENT)

Newport Mon Hebrew Congregation, 3 Queens Hill Crescent, NP9 5HH. ☎ 01633-262308. Hon Sec. Mrs M. Sarano. ☎ 01633-262605.

SWANSEA (W. GLAMORGAN)

Syn.: Ffynone. All correspondence to Hon. Sec.: J. Arron, 17 Ffynone Drive, Swansea, SA1 6DB. ☎ 01792 473333.
Dr. N. H. Saunders (95 Cherry Gr., Sketty, Swansea, SA2 8AX. ☎ 01792 202106) and Dr. L. Mars (70 Gabalfa Rd., Sketty, Swansea, SA2 8NE. ☎ 01792 205263), are willing to help and advise students coming to University College.
Cemeteries at Oystermouth and Townhill.

Restaurant

(V) **Chris's Kitchen**, The Market, SA1 3PE. ☎ 01792-643455. 8.30-5.30, Mon-Sat.

SCOTLAND

Scottish Tourist Board, 19 Cockspur St., SW1Y 5BL. ☎ 0171-930-8661.

ABERDEEN (GRAMPIAN)

Syn.: 74 Dee St., AB1 2DS. ☎ 01224 582135. Inq. to Sec.: ☎ 01467 642726, or caretaker. Two-bedroomed flat available for long stay students.

Restaurant

(V) **Jaws Wholefood Cafe**, 5 West North St., AB1 3AT. ☎ 01224-645676. 10-3, Mon-Sat; 10-9 Thur-Fri.

DUNDEE

Syn.: St. Mary Pl., DD1 5RB. Inq. to Harold Gillis, 49 Meadowside, DD1 1EQ. ☎ 01382 223557.
Jewish Students' Society: c/o Sec., Students' Union, Dundee University.

DUNOON

Argyll & Bute Jewish Community. Enquiries Barry Kaye, Edgemont, 34 Argyll Rd., PA23 8ES. ☎/Fax 01369 705118.

EDINBURGH

The Town Council and Burgess Roll minutes of 1691 and 1717 record applications by Jews for permission to live and trade in Edinburgh. Local directories of the eighteenth century contain Jewish names.

There is some reason to believe that there was an organised Jewish com. in 1780 (but no cemetery) and in 1817 it removed to Richmond Court, where there was also for a time a rival cong. In 1795 the Town Council sold a plot of ground on the Calton Hill to Herman Lyon, a Jewish dentist, to provide a burial place for himself and his family. In 1816, a syn. was opened and a cemetery acquired. There is a Jewish cemetery dating from the middle of the nineteenth century at Sciennes Hse. Pl., E9 (behind the police station in Causewayside). In 1932, two smaller congs. merged to form a single large one with a 1,000-seat synagogue. Major alterations were carried out in 1980, creating a complex of syns., halls & classrooms within the existing shell.

Syn.: 4 Salisbury Rd., EH16 5AB. ☎ 0131-667 3144. Daily services 6.30 p.m.; Sat., 10 a.m.; Sun., 9 a.m. M.: Rabbi D. Sedley, 67 Newington Rd, EH9. ☎ 0131-667 9360. Hon. Sec.: W. Simpson, 3 Hallhead Rd., EH16 5QT. ☎ 0131-667 1521.

Kosher Products

(K) Kosher bread & bakery products under the supervision of the Edinburgh Hebrew Cong. obtainable from William Innes Wood, 84 E. Crosscauseway, EH8 9HQ. ☎ 0131-667 1406.

Kosher Meat
Kosher Meat: Regular deliveries from suppliers in Glasgow and Manchester. Further information from Hon. Sec. of Synagogue.

Restaurants
(V) **Anna Purna**, 45 St. Patrick Sq. ☎ 0131-662 1807.
(V) **Black Bo's**, Blackfriars St. ☎ 557-6136.
(V) **Henderson's**, 94 Hanover St., EH2 1DR. ☎ 0131-225 2131.
(V) **Kalpna Restaurant**, 2 St. Patrick Sq., EH8 9EZ. ☎ 0131-667-9890.
(V) **Pierre Lapin**, West Nicholson St. ☎ 668-4332.

GLASGOW
The Glasgow Jewish community dates back to 1823. It grew slowly during the nineteenth century. The oldest synagogue building is the Garnethill Synagogue, now also the home of the Scottish Jewish Archives, which opened in 1879. The community grew rapidly from 1891 with many Jews settling in the Gorbals where many synagogues were founded. In recent years the community has gradually spread southwards and is now mainly situated in the Giffnock and Newton Mearns areas. Details of the early history of Glasgow Jewry can be found in "Second City Jewry" by Dr. Kenneth Collins, published by the Scottish Jewish Archives, Garnethill Synagogue (£6.95).

Synagogues & Religious Organisations
Garnethill, 127 Hill St., G3 6UB. ☎ 0141-332 4151. M.: Aharon Soudry. Sec.: Mrs. R. Livingston.
Giffnock & Newlands, Maryville Av., Giffnock, G46 7NE. M.: Rabbi Phillip T. Greenberg, Rabbi A.M. Rubin; Sec.: Mrs. G. Gardner. ☎ 0141-638 6600.
Yeshiva Kollel. Director: Rabbi M. Bamberger. ☎ 0141-620 3156.
Glasgow New Synagogue (Reform), 147 Ayr Rd., Newton Mearns, G77 6RE. ☎ 0141-639 4083. Hon. Sec.: P. Kraven. ☎ 0141-639 1838.
Langside, 125 Niddrie Rd., G42 8QA. ☎ 0141-423 4062. M.: Rev. B. Kass. Hon. Sec.: N. Barnes. ☎ 0141-638-3908.
Lubavitch. Rabbi C. Jacobs, 8 Orchard Dr., G46. ☎ 0141-638 6116.
Netherlee & Clarkston, Clarkston Rd. at Randolph Dr., G44. Sec.: Mrs. V. R. Mann. ☎ 0141-637-8206. M.: Rabbi A. Jesner.
Newton Mearns, 14 Larchfield Court, G77 5BH. M.: Rev P. Copperman. ☎ 0141-639 4000. H. Sec.: H. Hyman. ☎ 0141-639 3399.
Queens Park, Falloch Rd., G42 9QX. M.: Rabbi M. Fletcher. Hon. Sec.: Mrs. G. Fox. ☎ 0141-632 1743.
Mikva: Giffnock & Newlands Syn. ☎ 0141-621 0021. Enq. Mrs C. Fletcher. ☎ 0141-620 3156.

Representative Organisation
Glasgow Jewish Representative Council, 222, Fenwick Rd., Giffnock, G46 6UE. Admin.:. ☎ 0141-620-1700. Fax 0141-638-2100.

Welfare Organisations
Glasgow Jewish Welfare Board, 49 Coplaw St., G42 7JE. ☎ 0141-423 8916.
Jewish Care Scotland (Est 1868). May Terrace, Griffnock, G46 6DL. ☎ 0141-620 1800. Fax 0141-620 1088. Chairman: A. Tankel. Dir.: Mrs E. Woldman.
Newark Lodge (formerly Jewish Old Age Home for Scotland), 41-43 Newark Dr., G41 4QA. ☎ 0141-423 8941. Nursing home for the elderly.

Student & Youth Organisations
Glasgow Jewish Students' Society, 3 Dalmeny Ave., G46.
Bnei Akivah. Contact Dr K. Collins. ☎ 0141-638 7462.
Habonim-Dror Youth Centre, 59 Barrhead Rd., Newton Mearns, G77. ☎ 0141-639-6128.

Jewish Lads' & Girls' Brigade. Youth organisation providing uniformed as well as sports and social activities. Commanding Officer: B/Captain Pamela Livingston, 90 Beechwood Av., Clarkston, G76 7XG. ☎ 0141-639 7194.
Maccabi & Youth Centre, May Ter., Giffnock, G46 6DL. Sec: Mrs F. Tuck. ☎ 0141-638 6177.
Northern Region Chaplaincy Board, Jewish Student House, 3 Dalmerry Ave., G46. Chairman: S. Woldman.

Zionist Organisations
WIZO. Sec.: Mrs. F. Warrens. ☎ 0141-639 4386.
Glasgow Zionist Organisation, Abraham Links Hse., 43 Queen Sq., G41 2BD.
Glasgow Israel Committee, 222 Fenwick Rd., Giffnock, G46 6UE. ☎ 0141-620-2194.
J.N.F. ☎ 0141-423 4089; J.I.A. ☎ 0141-423 8785; Youth & Hechalutz Dept, 222 Fenwick Rd., Giffnock, G46 6UE. ☎ 0141-638-8760.

Cultural Organisations
Jewish Resource Centre, 222 Fenwick Rd., Giffnock, G46 6UE. ☎ 0141-620 2194. Fax 0141-638 2100.
Scottish-Jewish Archives, Garnethill Syn., 125-7 Hill St., G3 6UB. ☎ 0141-332 4911.

Clubs, etc.
Bonnyton Golf Club, Eaglesham, G76 0QA. ☎ 0135 53 2781. Hon. Sec.: M. Wise.
Jewish Senior Citizens' Association. Inf. from: Mrs. B. Mann. ☎ 0141-644 3611.

Newspaper
Jewish Telegraph, 43 Queen Sq., G41 2BD. Tel/Fax 0141-423-9200.

Bookseller
J. & E. Levingstone, 47 & 55 Sinclair Dr., G42 9PT. ☎ 0141-649 2962. Religious requisites also stocked.
Well of Wisdom, Giffnock Syn. ☎ 0141-638 2030.

Hotel
Guest House (Bed and Breakfast), 26 St. Clair Av., Giffnock, G46 7QE. (Kosher but not supervised) ☎ 0141-638 3924.
Forres Guest House, 10 Forres Ave., Giffnock, G46 6L. ☎ 0141-638 5554.

Restaurants
(K) The Inn Plaice (fish only), Maccabi Youth Centre, May Terrace, Giffnock, G46. ☎ 0141-620 3233.
(K) Kaye's Restaurant (meat), 49 Coplaw St., G42 7JE. ☎ 0141-423 2711.

Kosher Food
(K) Giffnock Kosher Deli, 200 Fenwick Rd., Giffnock, G46. ☎ 0141-638 8267 & 632 2313.
★ Marilyn's Kosher Deli, 2 Burnfield Rd., Giffnock, G46 7QB. ☎ 0141-638 4383.
★ Michael Morrison & Son, 52 Sinclair Dr., G42 9PY. ☎ 0141-632 60191 & 0998.

ST. ANDREWS
Jewish Students' Soc., c/o Sec., Students' Union, St. Andrews University, KY16 9UY.

NORTHERN IRELAND

Northern Ireland Tourist Board, 11 Berkeley Sq., London W1X 5AD. Fax 0171-409 0487. Callers to: All Ireland Desk, British Travel Centre, 4-12 Lower Regent St., London SW1.

Vegetarian Society of Ulster, 66 Ravenhill Gdns, Belfast BT6 8QG. Tel: 01232 457888.

BELFAST

There were Jews living in Belfast in the year 1652, but the present community was founded in 1869.

Syn.: 49 Somerton Rd., BT15 3LH. ☎ 01232 777974. Services: Sat., Sun., Mon., & Thurs am; M.: Rev. E. Kohn. Nearest Mikva is in Dublin.

Pres. of Hebrew Cong.: Ronald Appleton, Q.C, 5 Fort Rd., Helens Bay, Co. Down. Sec.: Mrs. N. Simon, 42 Glandore Av. ☎ 779491.

Hebrew School, Wolfson Centre, 49 Somerton Rd., BT15 3LH. ☎ 01232 777974.

WIZO. Co-Ch.: Rose Moss, Nadia Lantin. Hon. Sec.: Margaret Black. ☎ 662859.

(K) Kosher meals can be obtained at the Jewish Com. Centre, 49 Somerton Rd., BT15 3LH. ☎ 01232 777974. Sunday 6.30 p.m.-9.30 p.m.

Delicatessen

Levey's (J. Glackin), 493 Antrim Rd., BT15 3BP. ☎ 01232 777462.

TRAVEL ABROAD
Travel Agents Specialising in Travel to Israel

Note: A full list of members (£20.00) can be obtained from the Assoc. of British Travel Agents, 55-57 Newman St., W1 4AH. ☎ 0171-637 2444.

Gee Travel Service (New York). 12 Stamford Hill, N16 6XZ. ☎ 0181 806 3434 Open Sundays. After hours 0181-800 1082. 24 hour airport ticketing service.

Goodmos Tours, Dunstan Hse., 14a St. Cross St., EC1N 8XA. ☎ 0171-430 2230. Fax 0171-405 5049. Telex 21676.

Longwood Holidays, 182 Longwood Gdns., Ilford, Essex, IG5 OEW. ☎ 0181-551 4494. Open Sun., 10 a.m. to 2 p.m.

Magic of Israel, 47 Shepherds Bush Green, W12 8PS. ☎ 0181-743-9000.

Peltours Ltd., Sovereign Hse., 11-19 Ballards La., N3 1UX. ☎ 0181-346 9144. Telex 24542 PELTOUR G. Fax 0181-343 0579; 240 Station Rd., Edgware, Middx., HA8 7AU. ☎ 0181-958 1144. Fax 0181 958 5515.

Sabra Travel Ltd., 9 Edgwarebury Lane, Edgware, Middx., HA8 8LH. ☎ 0181-958 3244-7.

Travelink Group Ltd., 3 Phoenix St., off Charing Cross Rd., WC2H 8PW. ☎ 0171-379 5959. Fax 0171-379 5222.

Goodmos Tours, 23 Leicester Rd., Salford, M7 OAS. ☎ 0161-792 7333.

ITS: Israel Travel Service, 546-550 Royal Exchange, Old Bank St., Manchester, M2 7EN. ☎ 0161-839 1111. Fax 0161-839 0000.

Peltours Ltd., 27-29 Church St., Manchester, M4 1QA. ☎ 0161-834 3721. Telex 667893 PELTOUR G. Fax 0161-832 9343.

Kosher Food on Flights

El Al (Israel Airlines), 185 Regent St., W1R 8EU. ☎ 0171-437 9255, & 231-232 Royal Exchange, Manchester, M2 7FF. ☎ 0161-832 4208.

El Al, the Israeli national airline, maintains its own fully equipped (K) kosher kitchens at London Heathrow airport (☎ 0181-897 6136).

The kitchens, which are under the direct supervision of the London Federation of Synagogues, have a Mashgiach (supervisor) on duty on a permanent basis. They supply every El Al flight out of London and also supply kosher meals to most other airlines, including British Airways. El Al also supplies glatt kosher, vegetarian and a range of dietetic meals.

Orthodox Jewish passengers on airlines other than El Al should see that their kosher food boxes are sealed with the official Federation Commission label.

Kosher food along with many other diets is increasingly being catered for by airlines. Passengers should confim their requirements with the airline at the time of ticket reservation; some airlines accept notice of 24 hours prior to departure. This facility is free. Note: Very often (e.g. London–Amsterdam, London–Paris) kosher food is not provided on short flights except for El Al.

(K) Kedassia meals supplied by Hermolis & Co. Ltd., 26a Abbey Manufacturing Estate, Mount Pleasant, Alperton, Middx., HA0 1OA ☎ 0181-810 4321. Fax 0181-810 4331, are available on request on most flights from the majority of British airports. Passengers should confirm with their airline that they require this facility, which is free.

KLM Royal Dutch Airlines have a kosher kitchen at Schiphol Airport, Amsterdam, Swissair have one at Zurich, and there is also one at Orly airport, Paris.

Kosher Food on Ships

Most shipping lines provide packaged kosher food on request. Intending passengers requiring this should obtain written confirmation well in advance.

Travel Guides
The following selection of travel guides may be of interest to readers:

Israel:
The best Jewish travel guide to Israel. New York: Israelowitz, 1994.
Culture shock!: Israel, by Dick Winter. London: Kuperard, 1992 (A guide to etiquette and customs series).
Customs and etiquette in Israel, D. Starr-Glass. Folkestone: Global, 1996.
Essential Jerusalem, Greer Fay Cashman. London: Automobile Association, 1991.
The heart of Jerusalem, by Arlynn Nellhan. London: John Muir Publication, 1988.
The Holy Land: the indispensable archaeological guide for travellers, 3rd ed., Jerome Murphy O'Connor, Oxford: OUP, 1992.
Israel, Automobile Association Basingstoke, 1996.
Israel, the complete guide with Biblical sites, Kibbutzim etc. Fodor, 1995.
Israel, including the West Bank and Gaza Strip, ed. George Melrod. 3rd edn, APA Publications, 1994.
Israel Direct '96: a complete guide to educational opportunities from the UK to Israel. London: Jewish Continuity, 1996.
Israel tourist and accommodation guide, 1993-94: B&B in Israel. Gedera: B B. Gilon Ltd., 1992.
Jerusalem, Kay Prag. London: A & C Black, 1989. (The Blue Guide).
Jerusalem, edited by Michael Shichor. 2nd ed. 1994 (Michaels guides)
Jerusalem, written by Norman Atkins. APA Publications, 1988.
Jewish Israel: a guide for Jews to the land of their fathers. London: Namlock Ltd., 1988.
Kibbutz volunteer, by John Bedford; revised by Victoria Pybus. Oxford: Vacation Work, 1990.
Lets go: the Budget guide to Israel and Egypt, by Lorraine Shang-Huei Chang. London: Pan Books, 1992.
The museums of Israel, by Nitza Rosovsky and Joy Ungerlieder-Mayerson. New York: Harry N. Abrams, 1989.

Jewish travel guides to other countries:
Guide to Jewish Europe - Western Europe, 8th edition. Brooklyn: Israelowitz Publishing, 1993.
Guide to Jewish Italy, by Annie Sacerdoti in collaboration with Luca Fiorentino; translated by Richard F. de Lossa. Brooklyn: Israelowitz Publishing, 1989.
Guide to kosher eating and accommodation in North America, by Judith Korey Charles and Cila Teich Gold. Cold Spring, N.Y.: Nightingale Resources, 1991.
Jewish heritage travel: a guide to Central and Eastern Europe, by Ruth Gruber. New York: Wylie, 1992.
Jewish sites and synagogues in Greece, by Nicholas P. Stavroulakis and Timothy J. DeVinney. Athens: Talos Press, 1992.
The Jewish Traveller, Hadassah Magazine's guide to the world's Jewish communities and sights, edited by Alan M. Tigay, Lanham, N.J, Jason Aronson, 1994.
Oscar Israelowitz's Guide to Jewish Canada and USA - Vol. 1: Eastern Provinces. Brooklyn: Israelowitz Publishing, 1990.
Oscar Israelowitz's Guide to Jewish New York City. Brooklyn: Israelowitz Publishing, 1990.
A travel guide to Jewish Europe, by Ben G. Frank. Gretna: Pelican Publishing Co., 1992.

N.B. Travel guides to many other places, in particular Central and Eastern Europe, have expanded their references to Jewish landmarks and many can be commended for detail.

Tours in Eastern Europe

LestAir Services promote Jewish Heritage Tours to the Czech Republic, Poland, Hungary, Byelorus, Latvia and Lithuania and can be contacted for detailed information and guidance. Ad.: 1 The Grove, Edgware, Middx HA8 9QA. ☎ 0181-958 9340.

Interom Tourism Ltd., ☎ 972-3-9246425. Fax. 972-3-5791720.

ISRAEL
(Total population 5,500,000. Jews 3,755,000).

Intending visitors to Israel should get in touch as early as possible with the nearest Israel Government Tourist Office, which will supply literature and detailed information about hotels, tours, and so on.

Israel Government Tourist Offices
The tourist offices listed below supply all relevant literature and information, but do not make bookings.

Austria: Offizielles Israelisches Verkehrsbuero, Rossauer Lande 41/12, A-1090 Wein. ☎ 0043-1-3108174. Fax 0043-1-3103917.

Canada: Israel Government Tourist Office, 180 Bloor Street West, Suite 700, Toronto, Ontario M5S 2V6. ☎ 416-964-3784. Fax 416-964-2420.

Germany: Staatliches Israelisches Verkehrsbureau, Bettinastr. 62 7th Floor, 6000 **Frankfurt/Main:** 1. ☎ 69-752084.   Fax 69-746249.   Staatliches Israelisches Verkehrsbureau, Kurfuerstendamm 202, 100 **Berlin:** 15. ☎ 30-8819685/ 8836759. Fax 30-8824093. Staatliches Israelisches Verkehrsbureau, Stollbergstr. 6, **Muenchen:** ☎ 892289568. Fax 89-2289569.

France: Office National Israelien de Tourisme, 14 rue de la Paix, Paris 75002. ☎ 0033-1-4261-0197/4261-0367. Fax 0033-1-49270946.

Holland: Israelisch Nationaal Verkeersbureau, Wiide Kapelsteeg 2 (hoek Rokin), 1012 NS Amsterdam. ☎ 0031-20-6249642/6249325. Fax 0031-206242751.

Hungary: Israeli Nagykovetsege Ykovetseg, 1026 Budapest 11, Fullank U.8. ☎ 1767-896/7 Fax 176-0534.

Italy: Uffizio Nazionale Israeliano del Turismo, Via Podgora 12/b, Milan 20122. ☎ 760-210-51. Fax 760-124-77.

Japan: Israel Government Tourist Office, Kojimachi Sanbancho Mansion #406, 9-1 Sanbancho, Chiyoda-Ku, Tokyo 102. ☎ 0081-3-32389081/2. Fax 0081-3-32389677.

South Africa: Israel Government Tourist Office, 5th Floor, Nedbank Gardens, 33 Bath Ave., Rosebank, P.O. Box 52560, Saxonwold 2132, Johannesburg. ☎ 7881700. Fax 4473104.

Spain: Oficina Nacional Israeli de Turismo, Gran via 69, Ofic 801, 28013 Madrid. ☎ 559-7903. Fax 542-6511.

Sweden: Israeliska Statens Turistbyra, Sveavagen 28-30, 4 tr., Box 7554, 10393 Stockholm 7. ☎ 0046-21 33 86/7. Fax 0046-8-217814.

Switzerland: Offizielles Israelisches Verkehrsbureau, Lintheschergasse 12, 8021 Zurich. ☎ 0041-211-2344/5. Fax 0041-1-2122036.

United Kingdom: Israel Government Tourist Office, 18 Great Marlborough St., London WlV 1AF. ☎ 0171-434 3651. Fax 0171-437 0527.

U.S.A.: Israel Government Tourist Office, 19th Floor, 350 Fifth Ave., New York, **New York** 10118. ☎ 001-212-5600738/5600600.   Fax 001-212-6294368. Israel Government Tourist Office, 5 South Wabash Av., **Chicago,** Illinois 60603. ☎ 001-312-7824306. Fax 312-782 1243. Israel Government Tourist Office, 6380 Wilshire Boulevard #1700, **Los Angeles,** California 90048. ☎ 001-213-6587462/6587240. Israel Government Tourist Office, 12700 Park Central Drive, Dallas, TX, 75251. ☎ 001-214-991-9098/7. Fax 001-214-3923521. Israel Government Tourist Office, 420 Lincoln Road Suite 745, **Miami Beach**, FLa 33139. ☎ 001-305-673-6862-3. Fax 001-305-6734486. Israel Government Tourist Office, 1100 Spring St., NW Suite 440, **Atlanta**, Ga. 30309. ☎ 001-404-875-9924. Fax 001-404-875-9926.

Note: Telephone numbers in Israel are being extended to 7 digits, taking effect from the end of 1996. Changes have not been systematically notified in the current process of updating the Guide.

The Ministry of Tourism publishes a "Best of Israel Guide" detailing shops participating the VAT refund scheme and recommended restaurants; and **Israel:** a visitors' companion.
Available: 6 Wilson St., Tel Aviv. Fax (03)-5562339.

HOW TO GET THERE

You can travel by sea or air, or a combination of both. Air France, Air Sinai, Alitalia, Austrian Airlines, British Airways, Cyprus Airways, El Al Israel Airlines, Iberia Airlines of Spain, KLM, Lufthansa, Olympic Airways, Sabena, SAS, South African Airways, Swissair, Tarom Romanian Airlines and T.W.A. maintain regular services to Israel.

If you are flying to South Africa by El Al, or to the Far East or Australia by British Airways, Air France, Alitalia (from Rome) or T.W.A., you can break your journey in Israel at no extra cost.

There are scheduled and charter flights to Israel from a number of European countries, including Britain, as well as from the United States.

There are no direct sea passenger services between Israel and Britain, but there are regular services between Israel and Greece and/or Italy. Many cruise liners also call at Israeli ports.

Student Travel to Israel

Throughout the long summer vacation student flights to Israel are operated by ISSTA (Israel Students' Tourist Association), in conjunction with various other national student travel bureaux. In London these are operated by the National Union of Students Travel Dept., 3 Endsleigh St., WC1. ☎ 0171-387 2184. ISSTA has offices in Haifa (28 Nordau St. ☎ (04) 660411), Jerusalem (5 Eliashar St. ☎ (02) 225258) and Tel Aviv (109 Ben Yehuda St. ☎ (03) 247164-5). WST Charters, Priory Hse., 6 Wright's La., W8 6TA. ☎ 0171-938 4362, also specialises in Israel holidays for students and young people.

Individual arrangements for working on a kibbutz for a minimum period of one month can be made for any time of the year, except July and August, through Hechalutz b'Anglia, the Jewish Agency, 741 High Rd., Finchley N12 OBQ. ☎ 0171-446 1477. Details of other kibbutz schemes are available from Kibbutz Representatives, 523 Finchley Rd., London, NW3 7BD. ☎ 0171-794 5692. Airlines and most shipping lines offer reductions to students.

Disabled Persons

Friends of Yad Sarah, 43 Hanevi'im Street, 95141 Jerusalem, Israel. ☎ 02-244242. Fax 02-244493. (Reg. Charity No. 294801). Yad Sarah, a volunteer operated home care organization, lends free, regular and hi-tech medical rehabilitative equipment and provides a spectrum of home care supportive services. Services available to tourists. Head offices, Jerusalem; 77 branches in Israel. UK Trustee: D.S. Davis, c/o Cohen Arnold & Co., 13-17 New Burlington Place, London W1X 21P. ☎ 0171-734 1362. Fax 0171-434 1117. In the U.S.: Friends of Yad Sarah, Inc., Room 1450, Parker Plaza, 400 Kelly Street, Fort Lee, NJ 07024. ☎ 201-944-7920.

Passports and Visas

Applications for British passports should be made to any of the five Passport Offices in London, Liverpool, Newport (Gwent), Peterborough and Glasgow. Those holding a British visitors passport (obtainable from a post office and valid for one year) will be allowed in provided they also carry with them a full passport that has expired within the past five years.
Holders of valid UK passports do not need a transit or visitor's visa for entry into Israel.

The Passports of UK subjects must conform with the following conditions: (a) country of residence must be stated in the passport as being in the United Kingdom, Northern Ireland, the Channel Islands or the Isle of Man; (b) national status should appear in the passport as "British citizen".

Other countries whose nationals do not require a transit or visitor's visa to Israel are: Austria, Bahamas, Barbados, Belgium, Bolivia, Colombia, Costa Rica, Denmark, Dominican Republic, Dutch Antilles, Ecuador, El Salvador, Fiji, Finland, France, Greece, Guatemala, Haiti, Holland, Hong Kong, Iceland, Jamaica, Japan, Lesotho, Liechtenstein, Luxembourg, Maldive Islands, Mauritius, Mexico, Norway, Paraguay, Philippines, Surinam, Swaziland, Sweden, Switzerland, Trinidad and Tobago.

Citizens of the following countries receive a visa **free of charge at the place of entry:** Argentina, Australia, Brazil, Canada, Central African Republic, Chile, Germany (if born after January 1, 1928), Italy, New Zealand, San Marino, South Africa, Spain, United States of America, Uruguay. Citizens of the Republic of Ireland also receive a visa at the place of entry, **but are required to pay the requisite fee.**

Citizens of the following countries receive a visa free of charge, but must apply for it **before departure** to any Israel diplomatic or Consular mission: Cyprus, Germany (if born before 1 January 1928), Yugoslavia. (Until further notice, Israel is represented in Yugoslavia by the Belgian Embassy.) Citizens of the following countries receive a visa on application to the mission and **must pay the prescribed fee:** Bermuda, Botswana, Burma, Cambodia, Cameroon, Chad, (People's Republic of) Congo, Dahomey, Egypt, Equatorial Guinea, Ethiopia, Gabon, Gambia, Ghana, Guinea, Guyana, Honduras, India, Ivory Coast, Kenya, (South) Korea, Laos, Liberia, Madagascar, Malawi, Mall, Malta, Nepal, Nicaragua, Niger, Nigeria, Panama, Peru, Portugal, Romania, Rwanda, Senegal, Sierra Leone, Singapore, Spain, Thailand, Togo, Turkey, Tanzania, Upper Volta, Venezuela, Vietnam, Zaire and Zambia.

Citizens of countries not listed above must apply for a visa to the nearest Israel diplomatic or Consular mission and pay the requisite fee. Israel visas, when necessary, can be obtained at all Israel Consulates. In London application should be made in person or by post to the Consulate of Israel, 2 Palace Green, London, W8 5QB. Office Hours, Mon. to Thurs., 10 a.m. to 12.30 p.m.; Fri., 10 a.m. to 12 noon. Inquiries to Visa Section. ☎ 0171-937 8050.

A visitor's visa is valid for a stay of three months from the date of arrival.

Health Regulations
There are no vaccination requirements for tourists entering Israel.

However, vaccination against smallpox is required by some countries from travellers returning from abroad, so it is advisable for visitors to check the health regulations of their own country and, if vaccination is required, to obtain it before departure. Tourists already in Israel wishing to obtain vaccination against smallpox, cholera and yellow fever can do so at any Ministry of Health district or sub-district office.

Customs & Currency Regulations
The red-green dual-channel customs clearance system operates at Ben Gurion airport, Lod. Tourists bringing any articles expressly specified in lists 1A and 1B below may leave the airport by the green channel after collecting their luggage. Tourists bringing in articles not mentioned in the lists, even if they are exempt from duty and intended for re-export, must take the red channel.

1A. Every tourist aged 17 or over may bring into Israel the following free of duty, provided they are for personal use and are brought in on the ship or aircraft on which the tourist arrives: Eau de cologne or perfume not exceeding 0.44 pint 1/4 litre); wine up to 3.55 pints (2 litres); other alcoholic beverages not exceeding 1.77 pints (I litre); tobacco or cigars not exceeding 250 grammes, or 250 cigarettes; gifts up to approximately NS150 in value c.i.f. (including assorted foodstuffs not exceeding 6.6 lb. or 3kg. in weight, but excluding typewriters, cameras, movie cameras, tape recorders and TV sets); clothing and footwear.

1B. The following items may also be brought in free of duty and the green channel taken, provided that they are appreciably used and are re-exported on departure: one pair of binoculars, cameras (1 still and 1 cine less than 16 mm.), tape recorder, typewriter, sports and camping equipment, radio, portable musical instruments, perambulator, bicycle, 10 plates or rolls of film for still cameras and 10 reels of cine film, 750 yards of recording tape or 2 cassettes, portable record player, personal jewellery in reasonable quantities.

The following items are subject to deposits, and tourists bringing in any of them should-take the red channel: hand-held and operated professional tools and instruments for personal use up to NS1,650 in value c.i.f., rowing - sailing, or motor-boat, scuba-diving equipment (portable and used), reasonable quantity of used records, portable used TV set, TV & video cameras. The deposits are refundable when the items are re-exported on departure.

Certain additional items are liable for flat-rate duty and, in some cases, VAT. Import duties and taxes are payable in full on such items as refrigerators, radiograms, washing machines and electric ovens and cookers.

Tourists may bring into Israel any amount of foreign currency, which need not be declared upon entry. Foreign currency can be exchanged only at banks.

There is no restriction on the amount of Israeli currency which can be brought into the country by tourists, but they are allowed to take out no more than 500 Shekels.

During each visit, tourists over 18 may reconvert into foreign currency Shekels up to a maximum of the equivalent of NS5,000. The maximum or tourists under 18 is the equivalent of NS2,000.

Tourists leaving Israel may change Shekels in their possession up to a maximum of the equivalent of £50. Tourists are permitted to pay for all services and purchases in freely exchangeable currencies, including Canadian and United States dollars, South African rands, pounds sterling, Australian dollars, Swiss and French francs, Danish and Swedish kroner, Norwegian kronor, Dutch florins, German marks, Belgian francs, Italian lire, Austrian schillings and Japanese yen.

However, where payment in foreign currency is not acceptable, payment must be made in Israeli currency. In all cases, change may be given in Israeli currency.

Rates of Exchange

The Israeli currency unit is the Shekel. There are coins and notes of various denominations. Rates of exchange are subject to fluctuation and vary from bank to bank.

Free Trade Zone

Eilat has been a free trade zone since 1985. Details of how this benefits tourists can be obtained from all Israel Government Tourist Offices.

Cars

Provided his foreign car registration is valid and he is in possession of a valid driving licence, a tourist may import his vehicle into Israel free of duty and taxes for a maximum period of one year, against a personal undertaking to re-export it when he leaves Israel or within a year, whichever is the shorter period. No customs document or deposit of duty is required. Once the vehicle has been re-exported, it (or a replacement) cannot be re-imported for at least three months, during which time the tourist concerned must have been outside Israel. A valid International Driving Licence is recognised and preferred, although a valid national driving licence is also accepted, provided it has been issued by a country maintaining diplomatic relations with Israel and recognising an Israeli driving licence.

Further information with regard to licences, as well as other information and legal and technical advice, are available free of charge to visiting motorists from the Automobile & Touring Club of Israel (MEMSI), whose offices are at the following addresses:
Head Office: 19 Derech Petach Tikva, Tel Aviv. Telegraphic address: Actail, Tel Aviv. ☎ (03) 622961. Address for correspondence: P.O.B. 36144, Tel Aviv. Office hours: Sun. to Thurs., 9 a.m.-3.30 p.m. - Fri. & eve of Holy-days and festivals, 9 a.m.-12 noon.
Beersheba: Beit Uniko. ☎ (057) 36264.
Eilat: c/o Yaela Office, New Commercial Centre. ☎ (07) 372166.
Haifa: 7 Shmaryahu Levin St. ☎ (04) 674343.
Jerusalem: 31 King George St. ☎ (02) 244828. Office hours: Sun. to Thurs., 8 a.m.-3.30 p.m. Fri. & eve of holidays, 8 a.m.-l p.m.
Netanya: c/o Shartours, 6 Shmuel Hanatziv St. ☎ (053) 31343-4.
Tiberias: c/o Shahak, 23 Yohanan Ben-Zakai St. ☎ (067) 90715.
The Automobile & Touring Club of Israel is affiliated to the Federation Internationale de l'Automobile and to the Alliance Internationale de Tourisme.
Third-party (Act) insurance is compulsory in Israel in respect of bodily injury to all third parties. Further information is available from Act Pool Insurance, 70 Ibn Gvirol St., P.O.B. 2622, Tel Aviv. ☎ 268146-8. Office hours: Sun. to Thurs., 8 a.m. to I p.m. Fri. & eve of holidays, 8 a.m. to 11 a.m.

Green Card
The following countries have so far signed Green Card agreements with Israel: Austria, Belgium, Britain, Bulgaria, Denmark, Finland, France, Greece, Holland, Iceland, Irish Republic, Italy, Luxembourg, Norway, Portugal, Romania, Spain, Sweden, Switzerland, Turkey, West Germany and Yugoslavia. Tourists wishing to bring their cars to Israel may acquire a Green Card from insurance companies in any of the above countries.
If "Israel" and the national identification letters, "IL", do not appear on the Green Card, it must be accompanied by an endorsement certifying that it is valid for Israel.
Without "Israel" and "IL" on the Green Card or endorsement, the card cannot be used in Israel, and insurance cover will have to be taken out at the port of arrival.
For further details concerning car insurance, consult your local Israel Government Tourist Office or travel agent before leaving for your visit.

Traffic Regulations
Traffic travels on the right and overtakes on the left. Drivers coming from the right have priority, unless indicated otherwise on the road signs, which are international.
Distances on road signs are always given in kilometres (1 km. is equal to 0.621 miles).
The speed limit is 50 km. (approx. 31 miles) per hour in built-up areas; 80-90 km. (approx. 50-56 miles) per hour on open roads.

All vehicles in Israel (including those of visiting motoristst) must be equipped with striped reflective strips. For private cars these strips must be 2" deep x 18" wide (5 cm. x 45cm.), and affixed to both the left and righthand sides of the rear bumper.

All motor-cycle and scooter riders, as well as pillion passengers, must wear safety helmets.

It is compulsory for drivers and front-seat passengers to wear safety belts on all journeys. Back-seat passengers must wear seat belts in post-1986 vehicles.

Climate

With a long Mediterranean coastline, Israel's climate is similar to that of the French and Italian Rivieras. It may also be compared to that of Florida and southern California. Winters are mild and summers warm.

There are differences not only in temperature, but also in rainfall between the northern and southern regions of the country, as well as between the hills and valleys. The rainless summer lasts from April to October. The winter season, November to March, is characterised by bright sunshine with occasional rain. During this period, Tiberias on the Sea of Galilee, Sdom on the Dead Sea and Eilat on the Red Sea, are all absolutely ideal for winter holidays.

Airport Tax

All passengers departing by air must pay an airport tax. This is equivalent to approximately £10.

Some General Information

Hotels and Motels

The Ministry of Tourism abolished the hotel star grading system in 1992. Instead, hotels are to be classified as a "Listed Hotel" according to minimum requirements covering the business licence, security and fire facilities. Regulations stipulate that prices should be quoted in Shekels and US Dollars.

All hotels in the following list are recommended by the Israel Ministry of Tourism. Most are members of the Israel Hotel Association, Head Office, 29 Hamered St., P.O.B. 50066, Tel Aviv, 68125. ☎ (03) 650131, Fax: (03) 5100197

Kashrut

Hotels marked (**K**) are kosher, which in Israel means under official rabbinical Supervision.

Kosher restaurants under rabbinical supervision display a kashrut certificate.

Hotel Rates

Rates vary slightly from resort to resort according to season.

Youth Hostels

(**K**) All hostels are kosher by Rabbinate.

There are 31 Youth Hostels in Israel for students, youth groups and adults, which are supervised by the Israel Youth Hostels Association (a member of the International Youth Hostels Federation). All hostels offer the standard facilities: dormitories, kosher dining rooms. Most hostels also have a Guest House section, with double and family rooms, and private facilities. Most are air-conditioned. Attractive travel packages are offered by the Youth Travel Bureau, P.O.B. 6001 Jerusalem 91060 Israel ☎ (02) 6558432.

The Israel Youth Hostels Association offices are at Convention Hall Bldg., P.O.B. 1075, Jerusalem, 91060. ☎ (02) 6558400.

Maccabiah 1997

The 15th Maccabiah will be held between 14th and 24th July 1997. Details from Maccabi World Union Kfar Maccabiah, Ramat Gan 52105.

Holiday Villages

Holiday villages are all situated on or near the sea-shore and offer water and other sports, as well as entertainment.

Camping

There are camping sites at Achziv and Lehmann, in Western Galilee; Tal, in Upper Galilee; Kibbutz Ein Gev, Kibbutz Haon, and Maagan, all on the Sea of Galilee; Kfar Hittim, 1¼ miles west of Tiberias; Harod, south of Nazareth; Kibbutz Neve Yam, south of Haifa, on the coast, and Moshav Dor, south of Neve Yam, also on the coast; Ashkelon; Ramat Rachel, 1¼ miles from the centre of Jerusalem, and Mevo Betar, 9 miles south-west of Jerusalem; Bet Zayit, in the Judean Hills; Neve Zohar and Ein Gedi, north of Sdom; Elat on the Red Sea; Ye'elim, nr. Yotvata, in the southern Negev, about 12 miles north of Elat.

All the above sites, which belong to the Israel Camping Union, P.O.B. 53, Naharia, ☎ (04) 925392 (London representative: Project 67, 36 Great Russell St., WC1B 3PP. (0171-636 1262), are easily accessible. They all have hot showers, toilets, drinking water, electricity, and a small restaurant or facilities for buying provisions. All except Tal, Haon, Kfar Hittim, Moshav Dor and Harod (which are open from April-October) are open all year round. There is also a camping village at Ein Gedi, on the Dead Sea. ☎ 84342-3. Open all year round.

Shopping, Bank & Office Hours

Shops and offices are open from Sun. to Thurs. inclusive, from 8a.m. to 1p.m. and from 4p.m. to 7p.m. Shopping hours on Fri. are from 8.30a.m. to 2p.m. In Haifa, most shops are closed on Tues. afternoons. Banks are open Sun., Tues., and Thurs. from 8.30 a.m. to 12.30 p.m. Branches of most banks are also open from 4 to 6p.m. On Mon. & Wed., they open from 8.30 a.m. to 12.30 p.m. only. On Fri. and the eve of Holy-days and festivals, they open at 8.30a.m. and close at 12 noon. Government offices are generally open to the public Sun. to Thurs. inclusive from 8a.m. to 1p.m.

TOURS

Regular scheduled tours, using air-conditioned coaches, are operated by Egged and other companies on week-days to all parts of the country, starting from Jerusalem, Tel Aviv and Haifa. Egged's intercity toll — free information number is 177022 5555.

Among the most important sites visited are the Western Wall; the Old City of Jerusalem; Mount Scopus; the Mount of Olives; Rachel's Tomb in Bethlehem; the Tomb of the Patriarchs (Cave of Machpela) in Hebron; Jericho, and the Dead Sea. Tours starting in Jerusalem also visit Beersheba, Masada, Sdom, Ein Gedi and Galilee.

From Tel Aviv, regular tours go south to the Dead Sea and Elat, and north to Galilee and the Golan Heights as far as Banias.

From Haifa, regular tours go north to Galilee, and south to all places visited by tours from Jerusalem and Tel Aviv.

Air tours, operated by Arkia, Israel's internal airline (Sde Dov airport, Tel Aviv. ☎ (03) 424266), cover all of Israel.

In addition a number of smaller companies operate flights and tours to all parts of the country on a charter basis.

It is now possible to fly to Cairo from Israel, as well as to enter Egypt by land. Full details are available from all Government Tourist Information Offices in Israel and Israel Government Tourist Offices abroad.

Information about coach and air tours inside Israel is available from all Government Tourist Information Offices in Israel.

Transport in Israel

Buses are the most popular means of transport, both for urban and inter-urban journeys.

The Israel Railway runs from Naharia in the north to Beersheba in the south, and fares are lower than on the buses. All passenger trains have a buffet car. Taxis are quick and convenient. All urban taxis have meters, which drivers must use.

Certain taxi companies operate a 'Sherut' service in and between the main cities on weekdays, and some independent taxi owners operate similar services seven days a week. Individual seats are sold at fixed prices, with up to seven people sharing a taxi. In some cities and towns, 'Sherut' taxis follow the main bus routes, charging slightly higher fares than the buses.

Self-drive cars and motor-cycles can also be hired.

Tourist Information Offices

Ministry of Tourism, 24 King George St., Jerusalem. ☎ (02) 6754811.
[Tourist coordinators for the Administered Territories: Allenby Bridge. Fax (02) 942294. Jerusalem Fax (02) 240571.]

Akko: Eljazar St. (opposite Mosque). ☎ (177) 0227764, (04) 991764.
Arad: Visitors' Centre (opposite Community Centre), 28 Elazar Ben Ya'ir St. ☎ (07) 9954409/9955866.
Ashdod: 4 Haim Moshe Shapira St., Rova Daled. ☎ (08) 640485/640090.
Ben Gurion International Airport (Min. of Tourism) ☎ (03) 971 1485.
Eilat: Arava Highway Corner, Yotam Rd. ☎ (07) 6372111/6374233. Fax (07) 6376763.
Ein Hamifratz: Kibbutz Ein Hamifratz, 25210. ☎ (04) 9852377.
Haifa: 18 Herzl Boulevard. ☎ (04) 666521/2/654692. Fax (04) 622075; 106 Sderot Hanassi. ☎ (04) 374010.
Jerusalem: 17 Jaffa Rd. ☎ (02) 258844; Jaffa Gate. ☎ (02) 280382/280457.
Mahanayim: Zomet Mahanayim. ☎ (06) 935016.
Nahariyya: 19 Ga'aton Boulevard, Municipal Square. ☎ (04) 9879800/9879811. Fax (04) 9922303.
Nazareth: Casanova St. (Min. of Tourism). ☎ (06) 570555/573003. Fax (06) 573078.
Netanya: Kikar ha'Atzmaut. ☎ (09) 827286.
Ramat Hanegev: Zomet Mashabay Sadeh. ☎ (07) 6557314.
Safed: 50 Jerusalem St. ☎ (06) 920961/920633.
Tel Aviv: Shop No. 6108, 6th Floor, New Central Bus Station. ☎ (03) 6395660. Fax (03) 639 5659.
Tiberias: HaBanim St., The Archaeological Park. ☎ (06) 725666.

Border Crossings
Jordan–Israel
Allenby Bridge. ☎ (02) 941 038.
Arava. ☎ (07) 6336811.
Jordan River. ☎ (06) 586410/586392. Fax (06) 586421.
Egypt–Israel
Rafiah (Rafah). ☎ (07) 6734080.
Taba. ☎ (07) 6372104/6373110.

Israel Embassy (UK) Travel Information:
http://www.israel-embassy.org.uk/london
Emergencies: Fire, ☎ 102; Medical and first aid, ☎ 101 (Magen David Adom); Police, ☎ 100. Note that the foregoing applies to Haifa, Jerusalem and Tel Aviv only.

Medical Equipment: Wheelchairs, oxygen cylinders and many other items are available on temporary loan free of charge from the Yad Sarah Organisation for the Free Loan of Medical Equipment in Haifa (4a Mapu St., Ahuza. ☎ (04) 245286), Jerusalem (49 Hane'viim St. ☎ (02) 244242 or 244047), Tel Aviv (14a Ruppin St. ☎ (03) 238974) and many other places.

Photographic Hints: Take along an adequate supply of cine film, since it is not readily available. Colour roll film, however, is obtainable.

No colour cine film can be processed in Israel, but you can develop Kodachrome colour roll film. Keep your film well protected against heat and direct sunlight. The light, both direct and reflected, is much stronger in Israel than in most countries of Europe and North America.

Tourists leaving Israel at Ben-Gurion airport are advised to ensure that their cameras are empty of film, in order to facilitate the checking of cameras before boarding.

Electrical Equipment: Israel's electrical current is 220 volts, A.C., single phase, 50 cycles. Your dealer will advise you further.

Radio: You can hear the news in English four times a day on Israel Radio at 576, 1170 and 1458 kHz: 7 a.m.; 1p.m.; 5 p.m.; 8 p.m. BBC. World Service at 1322 kHz.; 1400, 1700 and 2015 G.M.T. Voice of America at 1260 kHz: 5 to 6 a.m. and 8 to 9 a.m. 5 p.m. 5.30 p.m. 11 p.m.

It must be emphasised that only selected, albeit wide-ranging, information can be given here. Full details are available from Israel Government Tourist Offices and travel agents.

Average Temperature (Celsius)

	Jerusalem	Tel Aviv	Haifa	Tiberias	Eilat
January	12	15	14	17	17
March	16	18	17	17	22
May	22	22	21	26	29
July	23	24	25	30	35
September	23	26	26	30	32
November	16	19	19	21	21

Rainy Days

January	12	14	15	12	1
March	8	8	9	5	2
May	2	1	1	1	0
July	0	0	0	0	0
September	0	1	1	0	0
November	7	8	5	5	1

Thanks are due to Geoffrey D. Paul, former Editor of the "Jewish Chronicle", and who was formerly the paper's correspondent in Israel, for writing the introduction to the three main cities.

AFULA
Restaurants and cafes
(**K**) La Cabania, Ha'atzmaut Sqr. ☎ (06) 591638.
(**K**) San Remo, 4 Ha'atzmaut St. ☎ (06) 522458.

AKKO (ACRE)
Hotels
(**K**) **Argaman Motel**, Sea Shore. ☎ (04) 916691-7.
(**K**) **Palm Beach Club Hotel**, Sea Shore. ☎ (04) 9815815.

Restaurants and cafes
(V) Amirei Hagalil, Akko-Safed Rd. nr. Moshav Amirim, 20115. ☎ (06) 989815/6.
(K) Palm Beach. ☎ (04) 912891.
Youth hostel
Akko (Acre) (125). ☎ (4) 9911982; Fax (04) 9911982.

ARAD
Hotels
(K) **Arad**, 6 Hapalmach St. ☎ (07) 957040.
(K) **Margoa**, Mo'av St. ☎ (07) 951222; Fax (07) 957778.
(K) **Nof Arad**, Moav St. ☎ (07) 975056-8.
Restaurants and cafes
(K) Bulgaria, 112 Kesen Kayemet St. ☎ (057) 38504.
(K) Hahavaya, 32 Hapalmach St. ☎ (057) 952186.

ASHDOD
Hotel
(K) **Miami**, 12 Nordau St. ☎ (08) 522085.

ASHKELON
Hotels
(K) **Samson's Gardens**, 38 Hatamar St., Afridar. ☎ (051) 36641, 34666 and 711039.
(K) **Shulamit Gardens**, 11 Hatayassim St., Afridar Beach. ☎ (051) 711261.
Restaurants and cafes
(K) Rachel, 29/7 Chen St., Industrial Centre. ☎ (057) 959219.
Riko (K without supervision), 51 Ben-Yehuda St. ☎ (051) 24592.

BAT YAM
Hotel
(K) **Mediterranean Towers**, 2 Hayam St., 59303. ☎ (03) 555 3666

BEERSHEBA
Hotels
(K) **Arava**, 37 Ha'histadrut St. ☎ (07) 78792.
(K) **Aviv**, 40 Mordei Hagetaot St. ☎ (07) 78059.
(K) **Desert Inn**. ☎ (07) 424922.
(K) **Hanegev**, 26 Ha'atzmaut St. ☎ (07) 77026.
Restaurants and cafes
(K) Beit Halimon (Cafeteria), 18 Histadrut St. ☎ (07) 71095.
(K) Bulgarian, 112 Keren Kayemet St., ☎ (07) 623-8504.
(K) Ceparis, 1 Herzl St. ☎ (07) 32392.
(K) Chin Shin, 100 Herzl St. ☎ (07) 70983.
(K) Palm Trees Garden, 17 Hapoalim St. ☎ (07) 85997.

BIKAT BET KEREM
Holiday Village
(K) Manof Recreation Village. ☎ (04) 914583 & 914592.

B'NEI BERAK
Restaurants and cafes
(K) Chapanash, 6 Jabotinsky St.

CAESAREA
Hotel
(K) **Dan Caesarea Golf Hotel**. ☎ (06) 362266-8.
Restaurants and cafes
(K) Caesarean (Self-service), Paz petrol station. ☎ (06) 334609.

DEAD SEA
Hotels
(K) Carlton Galei Zohar, Ein Bokek. ☎ (057) 584311-4.
(K) Ein Bokek, 86930 Ein Bokek. ☎ (057) 584331-4.
(K) Hod, Ein Bokek. ☎ (057) 584644.
(K) Lot, Hotel, Dead Sea. ☎ (057) 584321-4; Fax (057) 584623.
(K) Moriah Gardens, Mobile Post Dead Sea. ☎ (057) 584351.
(K) Nirvana on the Dead Sea, Ein Bokek. ☎ (057) 584626.
(K) Radisson Moriah Plaza Dead Sea Spa Hotel, Mobile Post Dead Sea. ☎ (057) 6591591 Fax (057) 584238.
(K) Tsell Harim, Ein Bakek. ☎ (057) 584121-2.

EILAT
Hotels
(K) Americana Eilat, PO Box 27, North Beach. ☎ (07) 6333777.
(K) Caesar, North Beach. ☎ (07) 6333111.
(K) Caravan Sun Club, Coral Beach. ☎ (07) 6373145-7.
(K) Carlton Coral Sea, Coral Beach. ☎ (07) 6333555.
(K) Dalia, North Beach. ☎ (07) 6334004.
(K) Edomit, New Tourist Center. ☎ (07) 6379511.
(K) Etzion, Hatmarim St. ☎ (07) 6374131.
(K) Galei Eilat, P. O. Box 1866, North Beach. ☎ (07) 6367444; Fax: (07) 6330627.
(K) King Solomon's Palace, North Beach. ☎ (07) 6337111.
(K) Lagoona, North Beach. ☎ (07) 6333666.
(K) Marina Club all suite hotel, North Beach. ☎ (07) 6334191.
(K) Moriah Plaza Eilat, North Beach. ☎ (07) 6361111; Fax (07) 6334158.
(K) Neptune, P. O. Box 295, North Beach. ☎ (07) 6369369; Fax (07) 6333767.
(K) Queen of Sheba, North Beach. ☎ (07) 6334121.
(K) Red Rock, North Beach, 88102 P.O.B. 306. ☎ (07) 6373171.
(K) Shulamit Gardens, North Beach. ☎ (07) 6333999.
(K) Sport, North Beach. ☎ (07) 6333333.
(K) Paradise N.L., North Beach, 88000. ☎ (07) 6335050.
(K) Red Sea Sport N.L., Coral Beach. ☎ (07) 6373145-7.
(K) Sonesta Suites N.L., Harava Rd. ☎ (07) 6376222.

Restaurants and cafes
(K) Arizona, on main road to Tel Aviv. ☎ (07) 672710.
(K) Bar-B-Que, Hatemarim Blvd. ☎ (07) 673634 & 675793.
(K) Café Royal, King Solomon's Palace Hotel, North Beach. ☎ (07) 676111.
(K) Chinese Restaurant, Shulamit Gardens Hotel, North Beach. ☎ (07) 677515.
(K) Dolphin Baguette, Tourist Centre.
(K) Egged, Central Bus Station. ☎ (07) 675161.
(K) El Morocco, Tourist Centre. ☎ (07) 671296.
(K) Golden Lagoon, New Lagoona Hotel, North Beach. ☎ (07) 672176.
(K) Hakerem, Elot St. cnr. Hatemarim Blvd. ☎ (07) 674577.
(K) Halleluyah, Bldg. 9, Tourist Centre. ☎ (07) 675752.
(K) Metamei Teman, Hatemarim Blvd.
Mini Golf. ☎ (07) 674402.
(K) Neve Elat, Hatemarim Blvd.
Neviot, North Shore. ☎ (07) 6971081.
(K) Off the Wharf, King Solomon's Palace Hotel, North Beach. ☎ (07) 679111.
(K) Panorama, New Commercial Centre. ☎ (07) 671965.
There are three **(K)** tour boats at the marina: Pirate, ☎ (07) 676549; Sea Bird, ☎ (07) 76549; Orionia, ☎ (07) 672902.

EIN HATZEVA
Restaurants and cafes
(K) Pundak Ein Hatzeva, Arava Rd. ☎ (057) 81407.

EIN HOD
Restaurants and cafes
Ein Hod (K without supervision), Artists' Village. ☎ (06) 794209.

GALILEE
Hotels
(K) Ayelet Hashahar Kibbutz Guest House, Upper Galilee, 12200. ☎ (06) 932611.
(V) Sea View, P.O.B. 27, Rosh Pina. ☎ (06) 937014.
(K) Kfar Hittim N.L., DN. Galil Tachton. ☎ (06) 795921.
(K) Rakefet N.L., Gush Segev, Western Galilee. ☎ (04) 800403.
Youth Hostels
Karei Deshe (Tabgha): Yoram (280). ☎ (06) 720601; Fax (06) 724818. 11 miles north of Tiberias.

GOLAN HEIGHTS
Restaurants and cafes
(K) Hamat Gader. ☎ (06) 751039.

GUSH ETZION
Restaurants and cafes
(K) Moshav Elazar Restaurant. ☎ (02) 741191.

HAIFA
This city of sea and mountain is built on three levels, each with its distinctive and highly special character. Mount Carmel (Har Hacarmel), the top level, which offers some magnificent views, is mostly residential and recreational; Hadar Hacarmel, the central level, is also residential, but it also contains the city's main commercial district. The third level, the lowest, contains the port area, Israel's largest, and another business district. Over recent years the beach front to the south of the port has been attractively refurbished.
Like Jerusalem and Tel Aviv, Haifa has a university, and it is also the home of the Technion Israel's Institute of Technology. The city's theatre and symphony orchestra are well-known, and its array of unusual museums are worth a visit. They include the National Maritime Museum, the Grain Museum, the Mané Katz Museum and the Illegal Immigration Museum. In addition to being Israel's premier port and a major industrial centre, Haifa is also a tourist resort, with miles of bathing beaches and acres of woodland parks and well-tended gardens. It is also the scene of international flower shows, folklore-festivals, conventions and other events.
Useful Addresses
Syns.: Central, 60 Herzl St.; Eliahu Hanavi, 16 Sinai Blvd., Mount Carmel; Hechal Netanel (Sephardi), 43 Herzl St.; Moriah (Conservative), 7 Horeb St., Mount Carmel; Mount Carmel Central, 10 Sea Rd., Mount Carmel; Or Hadash Progressive Cong., Bet Rothschild, 142 Hanassi Blvd., Central Carmel.
Fri. evening services are also held at the Dan Carmel Hotel, Hanassi Blvd.
Central Bus Station: 2 Hagana Blvd. For bus inf. ☎ (04) 549121/131.
Railway Station: near Central Bus Station. ☎ (04) 564564.
Technion, Israel Institute of Technology: Campus, Neve Shaanan. Guided tours. Visitors' Centre. ☎ (04) 320664
University of Haifa: Mount Carmel. ☎ (04) 240097.

Main Post Office: 19 Palyam Blvd. ☎ (04) 640892.
Hadar Post Office & Philatelic Service: 22 Haneviim St.
Municipal Information Offices:
Municipality Bldg. ☎ (04) 645359; Central Bus Station, 2 Hagana Blvd. ☎
(04) 512208; 23 Haneviim St. ☎ (04) 663056; 119 Hanassi Blvd. ☎ (04)
383683.
Haifa Tourism Development Assoc.: 10 Ahad Ha'am St. ☎ (04) 671645-7.
Voluntary Tourist Service also at this address.
Municipal Theatre: 50 Pevsner St. ☎ (04) 670956.
'What's on in Haifa' 24-hour telephone service: ☎ (04) 640840.
Consulates
Austria, 12 Allenby Rd. ☎ (04) 522498; Belgium & Luxembourg, 104 Derech
Ha'atzmaut. ☎ (04) 533261; Costa Rica, 9 Disraeli St. ☎ (04) 241157;
Denmark, 53 Derech Ha'atzmaut. ☎ (04) 645428; Finland, 7 Hayovel St. ☎
(04) 338585; France, 37 Hagefen St. ☎ (04) 526281; Germany, 35
Hameginim Blvd. ☎ (04) 534112; Greece, 59 Derech Ha'atzmaut. ☎ (04)
522098; Guatemala, 43 Derech Ha'atzmaut. ☎ (04) 643232; Holland, 11
Givat Downes St. ☎ (04) 241962; Honduras, 37 Liberia St. ☎ (04) 255318;
Ivory Coast, 55 Hanamal St. ☎ (04) 670456; Madagascar, 31 Derech
Ha'atzmaut. ☎ (04) 645386; Norway, 20 Hanamal St. ☎ (04) 670141;
Panama, 5 Baerwald St. ☎ (04) 665265; Peru, 62 Sweden St. ☎ (04) 253304;
Spain, 3 Anilewitz St. ☎ (04) 510228; Sweden (also representing Liberia &
Hungary), 2 Khayat Sq. ☎ (04) 643162; U.S.A., 37 Derech Ha'atzmaut. ☎
(04) 672176; Uruguay, 67 Moriah St. ☎ (04) 245165.
Hotels
(K) **Dan Carmel**, 87 Hanassi Av. ☎ (04) 386211.
(K) **Dan Panorama**, 107 Hanassi Av. ☎ (04) 352222.
(K) **Dvir**, 124 Yefe Nof St. ☎ (04) 389131-7.
(K) **Nesher**, 53 Herzl St. ☎ (04) 640644.
(K) **Nof**, 101 Hanassi Av. ☎ (04) 354311.
(K) **Shulamit**, 15 Kiryat Sefer St., 34676. ☎ (04) 342811.
(K) **Yaarot Hacarmel**, Mt. Carmel. ☎ (04) 229144-9.
Restaurants and cafes
(K) Bankers' Tavern, 2 Habankim St. ☎ (04) 528439 (lunch only. Closed Sat.)
(K) Ben Ezra, 71 Hazayit St. ☎ (04) 842273.
(K) Chinese Restaurant of Nof, Nof Hotel, 101 Hanassi Blvd. ☎ (04) 38873.
(K) Egged, Central Bus Station. ☎ (04) 515221. (Self-service.)
(K) Gan Rimon, 10 Habroshim St. ☎ (04) 381392. (Lunch only.)
(K) Ha'atzmaut, 63 Derech Ha'atzmaut. ☎ (04) 523829.
(K) Hamber Burger, 61 Herzl St. ☎ (04) 666739.
(K) Mac David, 131 Hanassi Blvd. & 1 Balfour St. ☎ (04) 383684.
(K) Milky Pinky (Milk Bar), 28 Haneviim St. ☎ (04) 664166.
(K) Paznon, Hof Carmel. ☎ (04) 538181.
(K) Restaurant Hamidrachov, 10 Nordau St. ☎ (04) 662050.
(K) Rondo, Dan Carmel Hotel, 87 Hanassi Blvd. ☎ (04) 386211.
(K) Technion, Neve Shaanan. ☎ (04) 233011. (Self-service, lunch only.)
(K) The Chinese Restaurant of Nof, Nof Hotel, 101 Hanassi Blvd. ☎ (04)
388731.
(K) The Second Floor, 119 Hanassi Blvd. ☎ (04) 382020.
(K) Tsemed Hemed, Herbert Samuel Sq. ☎ (04) 242205.
Youth Hostels
Carmel (280). ☎ (04) 531944; Fax (04) 532516.
Shlomi (944). ☎ (04) 9808975. Hanita Forest.

HAMAT GADER
Restaurants and cafes
(K) Hamat Gader Restaurant, Golan Heights. ☎ (06) 751039.

HAON
Holiday Village
(K) Kibbutz Haon, Jordan Valley. ☎ (06) 757555-6.

HERZLIA
Useful address
English Speaking Residents Association, PO Box 3132, 46104. ☎ 580632.
Hotels
(K) **Dan Accadia**, Herzlia on Sea. ☎ (09) 556677; Fax (09) 571311.
(K) **Holiday Inn**, Crown Plaza, Herzliya. ☎ (09) 544444; Fax (09) 544675.
(K) **The Sharon**, Herzlia on Sea. ☎ (09) 575777; Fax (09) 572448.
(K) **Tadmor**, 38 Basel St. ☎ (09) 572321; Fax (09) 574560.
Restaurants and cafes
(K) **Dona Flor**, 22 Hagalim Blvd, Herzlia Pituach. ☎ (09) 509669.
(K) **La Cabana**, 60 Medinat Hayehudim St., ☎ (09) 55037.
(K) **Tadmor Hotel School**, 38 Basel St., 46660. ☎ (09) 9572321.

JAFFA
Restaurants and cafes
(K) **Emerald**, 4 Pasteur St. ☎ (03) 829595.

JERUSALEM
Despite her present-day accessibility, Jerusalem is a secret city. Your tourist coach or taxi will show you her face. But to find her heart, you must take to your feet, climbing her hills, strolling her streets and lanes, and pushing on beyond the seemingly closed gates which enclose a myriad life styles, To sense the mystery of Jerusalem, start with Mount Scopus just before dawn. Watch the red ball of a new day's sun ascend the mists from behind the Mountains of Moab and set afire the Judean Desert which laps at the city's skirts. Near sunset, look down again from near the same vantage point on the city itself, when the light catches the gold of the Dome of the Rock, scattering its rays across Jerusalem's many hills.

Now, with a new clarity, you catch the poignant imagery Jerusalem's contemporary poet-laureate, Yehuda Amihai, when he speaks of a "port city on the shores of eternity."

But Jerusalem is also a city of people, a collection of villages separated by faith and custom. Enter the Old City by Jaffa Gate and turn right on to Armenian Patriarchate Road, where you will find the Cathedral of St. James. Walk through the side gate and you are in a unique, hidden village community homes, shops, schools, playgrounds, churches, all are contained within the ancient and massive compound, where the gates close at 8.30 p.m., after which time no one may enter or leave.

The language here is Armenian. The children learn it in school, the people talk it in the streets and there is a fine printing press preparing Armenian Bibles and other literature for distribution to a community which, like the Jews, is scattered throughout the world.

By contrast, spend a Friday morning in Mea Shearim, the walled city of Ultra-Orthodoxy, where the ghetto way of life is maintained with fierce pride and where still live Jewish communities which deny the existence of the Jewish State and speak only Yiddish, Hebrew being retained as the holy language of prayer and study.

Friday all is abustle. A bescarfed housewife hurries to the slaughterer with a live chicken. Youngsters, their earlocks bouncing like coiled springs, scamper out of school in a babble of Yiddish (although, increasingly their language of conversation is Hebrew). Men, young and old, eyes averted from the passing tourists, hurry to the mikva, for here males as well as females take the ritual cleansing bath.

But also in Jerusalem, you must touch history, not the spurious history of this tomb or that stone, but the reality, say, of such as Hezekiah's Tunnel, hewn by the Judean king's workmen through the rock of Jerusalem nearly 2,700 years ago so that water would be available in the city in time of war. The tunnel, still a conduit for water through which intrepid Jerusalem explorers frequently wade for 600 yards of its winding course, starts close by the spring of Gihon in the Kidron Valley, on the edge of the ancient City of King David, south-west of the Old City, with its excavations.

As it has since the beginning of recorded time, the spring still gushes its waters at regular intervals throughout the day, and Arabs from the adjoining village of Silwan come there regularly with pots, jug and, an accommodation with the twentieth century, jerricans, to take their water from its flow.

Near by is the "Archaeological Garden" being created from the manifold finds in the two decades of excavation in the area adjoining the Temple Mount.

Jerusalem is also a city of today, and you feel this nowhere better than in one of the city's newer suburbs. Take a bus or taxi to Denmark Square in Bet Hakerem and ask to be put down outside the huge supermarket there. Sit awhile among the stone seats and sculptures in the square, watching the continuous parade of young mothers and children, and sprightly oldsters out for a stroll. You will find that you do not sit alone for long.

Jerusalem now has pavement cafes in the part of Ben-Yehuda Street which is now closed to traffic. There are also many stalls selling a variety of foods to be enjoyed as one strolls, and they are well patronised. When night falls, it does quite early as compared with the slow dusk of the West, it seems that most of the inhabitants have gone to bed.

Many have, because the day's early start, despite the traditional afternoon siesta, dampens any inclination for late nights. But there is a night-life of sorts.

Also, Israel being an immigrant country, there is an enormous variety of national and ethnic food available in numerous restaurants. These offer everything from kosher Chinese to kosher Argentine.

The Israel Philharmonic Orchestra provides frequent concerts at Binyanei Ha'Ooma, and tickets can be bought for performances by the fast-rising Israel Radio Symphony Orchestra, whose headquarters is in the superb Jerusalem Theatre (which also boasts a fine kosher dairy restaurant and bar, with entertainment from 10 p.m. into the small hours).

There are a couple of discotheques, but since these are apt to come and go, it is best to ask your taxi-driver what is in vogue. If you know some Hebrew, the leading companies from Tel Aviv perform one-night stands at both the Jerusalem Theatre and Bet Ha'am.

If your next stop is Tel Aviv, rent a car from one of the hire-it-here, leave-it-there agencies and drive yourself down. Don't take the main highway out of Jerusalem. Instead, travel one of the least known but most beautiful roads in the whole of Israel, the one that leaves Jerusalem by way of the magnificent village of Ein Karem (which contains, incidentally, a fine gallery of modern Israeli art and prints, run by a brother and sister from England specialising in excellent concerts of solo and small-group music) and cuts through the hills and forests, via Eshtaol, to bring you out on the old Jerusalem-Tel Aviv road.

Telephone Numbers

Changes announced include new prefixes as follows:
Existing numbers (02) and starting with 3, 6 or 8, new prefix 5
Existing numbers (02) and starting with 2, 4 or 7, new prefix 6

Useful addresses

The Jerusalem Marathon 1997 is scheduled for November. Details from (03) 296179; Fax (03) 296180.

There are 450 synagogues in Jerusalem. The following are the most representative and easily accessible: Yeshurun, 44 King George St. (Ashkenazi). Great adjoining Hechal Shlomo, 60 King George St.

Italian Synagogue, 29 Hillel St. (Italian rite). Baba Tamah Synagogue, 5 David St. (Bokharan).

Emet V'Emuna, Narkis St., Gan Rehavia. Har El (Progressive), 16 Shmuel Hanagid St.

Hebrew Union College (Reform), 13 King David St. Metivta Hagedola (Ashkenazi upstairs, Sephardi downstairs), 31 Jabotinsky St. Midrash Porat Yosef, Geula St., Mount Zion (Ashkenazi and Sephardi). President, 22 Ussishkin St., Rehavia.

Israel Movement for Progressive Judaism. ☎ (2) 6203484. Fax (02) 6203343. To place messages at the Western Wall use Fax (02) 61222.

Embassies:

Cost Rica, Clal Centre, 97 Jaffa Rd., 7th Floor, Room 714. ☎ (02) 244418; El Salvador, 16 Kovshei Katamon St. ☎ (02) 633575; Ivory Coast, 4 Elroy St., German Colony. ☎ (02) 632296.

Centre for Guiding of the City, 17 Jaffa Rd. ☎ (02) 241379 or 232251.

General Post Office, 23 Jaffa Rd.

Hebrew University, Mount Scopus, 91905. ☎ (02) 585111.

Ministry of Tourism, 24 King George St. ☎ (02) 237311.

Hotels

Boker Tov Jerusalem lists rooms available for tourists, Binyanei Ha'ooma. ☎ (02) 511270; Fax (02) 511272.

Good Morning Jerusalem, lists rooms and apartments for tourists. 9 Coresh St., 94146. ☎ (02) 6233459 Fax (02) 6259330.

(K) Ariel, 31 Hebron Rd. ☎ (02) 719222.

(K) Caesar, 208 Jaffa Rd. ☎ (02) 382156.

(K) Central, 6 Pines St. ☎ (02) 384111 Fax (02) 381480.

(K) Hyatt Regency Jerusalem, 32 Lehi St. ☎ (02) 5331234 Fax (02) 815947.

(K) Jerusalem Gate, 43 Yirmiyahu St. ☎ (02) 383101.

(K) Jerusalem Hilton, Givat Ram. ☎ (02) 536151.

(K) Jerusalem Renaissance, 6 Wolfson St., 91033; ☎ (02) 6528111.

(K) Jerusalem Tower, 23 Hillel St. ☎ (02) 209209.

(K) King David, 23 King David St. ☎ (02) 6208888. Fax (02) 6208880.

(K) Kings, 60 King George St. ☎ (02) 201-201; Fax (02) 201211.

(K) King Solomon, 32 King David St. ☎ (02) 695555.

(K) Knesset Tower, 4 Wolfson St. ☎ (02) 511111.

(K) Lev Yerushalayim, 18 King George St. ☎ (02) 300333.

(K) Mishkenot Sha'ananim Guesthouse, Yemin Moshe, ☎ (020) 254321

(K) Mount Zion, 17 Hebron Rd. ☎ (02) 724222.

(K) Palatin, 4 Agripas St. ☎ (02) 231141.

(K) Paradise, 4 Wolfson St.; ☎ (02) 6558888. Fax (02) 6512266.

(K) Radisson Moriah Plaza Jerusalem, 39 Keren Hayesod St. ☎ (02) 6695-695. Fax (02) 623241.

(K) Reich, 1 Hagai St., Bet Hakerem. ☎ (02) 523121.

(K) Ron, 44 Jaffa Rd. ☎ (02) 6223122. Fax (02) 6250707.

(K) Sheraton Jerusalem Plaza, 47 King George St. ☎ (02) 259111.

(K) Sonesta Jerusalem, 2 Wolfson St. ☎ (02) 528221.
(K) Windmill, 3 Mendele St. ☎ (02) 5663111.
(K) Zion, 4 Luntz St. ☎ (02) 232367.
(K) Zion, 10 Dorot Rishonim. ☎ (02) 259511.
(K) Zohar, 47 Leib Jaffe St. ☎ (02) 717557.
Holiday Village
(K) Youth Recreation Centre Holiday Village, Yefei Nof. Jerusalem Forest. ☎
(02) 416060.
Youth Hostels
Bayit Vegan: Louise Waterman-Wise (300). 8 Hapisgah St. ☎ (02) 423366 or
420990; Fax (02) 423362.
Bet Bernstein (80). 1 Keren Hayesod St. ☎ (02) 258286.
Bet Meir: Ramot Shapira (300). ☎ (02) 342691 or 343793; Fax (02) 342098.
12½ miles west of Jerusalem.
Bet Shmuel (240). 13 King David St. ☎ (02) 203466 or 203467; Fax (02)
203466.
Ein Karem (97). ☎ (02) 416282. 10 mins. from Louise Waterman-Wise Hostel
in Bayit Vegan.
Davidka (26), 67 HaNevi'im St., ☎ (02) 384555.
Jerusalem Forest (140). ☎ (02) 752911.
Kfar Etzion (273). ☎ (02) 9935133 or 9935233. 14 miles south of Jerusalem.
Groups only.
Moreshet Yahadut (75). ☎ (02) 288611. Old City.
Restaurants and cafes
(K) Abu Tor, 5 Ein Rogel St., Abu Tor. ☎ (02) 718088.
(K) Agam, 121 Agrippas St. ☎ (02) 222445.
(K) Alno (Coffee Shop), 15 Ben-Yehuda St. ☎ (02) 223821.
(K) Alumah, 8 Yavetz St. ☎ (02) 6255014.
(K) Ashafit, Jerusalem Theatre. ☎ (02) 630078.
(K) Au Sahara, 17 Jaffa Rd. ☎ (02) 233239.
(K) Backstage, Jerusalem Theatre, 20 Marcus St. ☎ (02) 669351.
(K) Bagel Nash (Coffee Shop), 14 Ben-Yehuda St. ☎ (02) 225027.
(K) Bangkok 15 Hebron Rd. ☎ (02) 713077.
(K) Beit Maskit (Dairy & Fish), 12 Harav Kook St. ☎ (02) 227941.
(K) Besograyim, 45 Ussishkin St. ☎ (02) 245353.
(K) Burger Ranch, 18 Shlomzion Hamalka St., ☎ (02) 222392, & 3 Lunz St.
☎ (02) 225935.
(K) Cactus, 36 Keren Hayesod St. ☎ (02) 667719.
(K) Café Center, Centre 1, Jaffa Rd. ☎ (02) 383507-8.
(K) Café Finzi, 11a Ben-Yehuda St. ☎ (02) 243436.
(K) Café Ha'uga, 2 Hasoreg St. ☎ (02) 244491.
(K) Café Max, 23 Ben-Yehuda St. ☎ (02) 233722.
(K) Café Navah, 44 Jaffa Rd. ☎ (02) 222861.
(K) Casa della Pasta, 7 King George St. ☎ (02) 244228.
(K) China Caan, 2 Lunz St. ☎ (02) 242464.
(K) Chung Ching, 122 Herzl Blvd., Bet Hakerem. ☎ (02) 525152.
(K) Citadel (Cafeteria), 14 Hativat Yerushalayim St. opp. David's Citadel. ☎
(02) 288887.
(K) Csardas, 11 Shlomzion Hamalka St. ☎ (02) 243186.
(K) Dagim Beni, 1 Mesilat Yesharim St. ☎ (02) 222403.
(K) Daglicataesse, 6 Ibn Shaprut St. ☎ 632657.
(K) The Derby, 2 Ben-Yehuda St. ☎ (02) 244454.
(K) El Gaucho, 22 Rivlin St. ☎ (02) 226665.
(K) El Marrakesh, 4 King David St. ☎ (02) 227577.

(K) Europa, 42 Jaffa Rd., at Zion Sq. ☎ (02) 228953.
(K) Feferberg's, 53 Jaffa Rd. ☎ (02) 254841.
(K) Fish Shlomo, 27 Salmon St. ☎ (02) 231631.
(K) Fonte Bella, 8 Rabbi Akiva St. ☎ (02) 248408.
(K) Four Seasons, 54 Haneviim St. ☎ (02) 222195.
(K) G.U.Y.'s Gallery, 12 Hebron Rd. ☎ (02) 672 511. Fax (02) 672 5166.
(K) Hahoma, 128 Hayehudim St., Jewish Quarter. ☎ (02) 271332.
(K) Hakerem, 21 King George St. ☎ (02) 222922.
(K) Hama'alot, 3 Hama'alot St. ☎ (02) 234235.
(K) Ha'uga, 2 Hasoreg St. ☎ (02) 244491.
(K) Heppner's Deli, 4 Lunz St. ☎ (02) 221703.
(K) Ima, 189 Agrippas St. ☎ (02) 246860.
(K) Jerusalem, 7 Hyrcanos St. ☎ (02) 222757.
(K) Jerusalem Skylight, Eilon Tower Hotel, 34 Ben-Yehuda St. ☎ (02) 233281.
(K) La Fondue, 37 Hillel St. ☎ (02) 224352.
(K) La Pasta, 16 Rivlin St. ☎ (02) 227687.
(K) Lee, 33 Hillel St. ☎ (02) 225955.
(K) Little Jerusalem, 59 Hanevi'im St. ☎ (02) 244377.
(K) Little Mama Mia (Self-service Dairy), 9 Dorot Rishonim St. ☎ (02) 232368.
(K) Mac David, 16 King George St.
(K) Mama Mia (Dairy), 38 King George St., 94262. (02) 248080.
(K) Marcel's Stage, 20 Marcus St. ☎ (02) 30078.
(K) Marina, President Hotel, 3 Ahad Ha'am St. ☎ (02) 31273.
(K) Michael's, 13 Maayan St., Ein Kerem. ☎ (02) 431840.
(K) Min Hamuchan, 19 Keren Kayemet St. ☎ (02) 639845.
(K) Monitin, 220 Jaffa Rd. ☎ (02) 380761.
(K) Navah (Coffee Shop), 44 Jaffa Rd. ☎ (02) 222861.
(K) Norman's Bar & Grill, 27 Emek Refaim St. ☎ (2) 5666603. Fax (02) 6731768.
(K) Of Course!, Zionist Confederation Hse., Emile Botta St. ☎ (02) 245206.
(K) Off the Square (Dairy), 6 Yoel Salamon St. ☎ (02) 6242549.
(K) Original Pie Shop, 4 Nachlat Shiva St.
(K) Palmachi, 13 Shammai St. ☎ (02) 234784.
(K) Pinat Hahumous, 14 Ben-Yehuda St. ☎ (02) 225027.
(K) Pizzeria Papi, 9 Ben-Hillel St. ☎ (02) 223914 & 234 Jaffa Rd. ☎ (02) 535881.
(K) Pizzeria Rimini, 43 Jaffa Rd., ☎ (02) 225534, 15 King George St. ☎ (02) 226505, & 7 Paran St., Ramat Eshkol.
(K) Pizzeria Trevi, 8 Leib Yaffe St. ☎ (02) 724136.
(K) Poire et Pomme, The Khan Theatre, 2 Remez Sq. ☎ (02) 719602.
(K) Primus (Dairy & Fish), 3 Yavetz St. ☎ (02) 246565.
(K) Rimon, 41 Lunz St. ☎ (02) 222772.
(K) Rondo, 41 King George St. ☎ (02) 242874.
(K) Savion Hut (Fish & Dairy), 12 Gaza St. ☎ (02) 632813.
(K) Shemesh, 21 Ben-Yehuda St. ☎ (02) 222418.
(K) Shipodei Hagefen, 74 Agrippas St. ☎ (02) 222 367.
(K) Shteisel, 11 Malchei Israel St. ☎ (02) 245775.
(K) Sinai Café, 6 Ben-Yehuda St. ☎ (02) 222627.
(K) Sova, 3 Histadrut St. ☎ (02) 222266.
(K) Tavlin, 16 Yoel Salamon St. ☎ (02) 243847.
(K) Tchung Tching, 122 Herzl Blvd. ☎ (02) 528152.
(K) Ten Li Chow, 8 Ramban St. ☎ (02) 665956.
(K) Villa B., 104 Shderot Herzl. ☎ (02) 439002.
(K,V) Village Green, 10 Ben Yehuda St., & 1 Bezalel St.

(K,V) Village Green, 10 Ben Yehuda St., & 1 Bezalel St.
(K) Ye Olde English Tea Room, 68 Jaffa Rd. ☎ (02) 376595.
(K) Yemenite Step, 12 Yoel Salamon St. ☎ (02) 240477.
(K) Yo-si Peking, 5 Shimon Ben-Shetach St. (226893.
(K) Zeze (Dairy), 11 Bezalel St. ☎ (02) 231761.

KATZRIN
Restaurants and cafes
(K) Lev Hagolan, 30 Dror St. ☎ (06) 9616643.
(K) Orcha, Commercial Centre. ☎ (06) 961440.

KIBBUTZ HOTELS
Kibbutz Hotels Chain. Head Office: 1 Smolanskin St., P.O.B. 3193, Tel Aviv 61031. ☎ (03) 5246161. Fax (03) 527 8088.
(K) Ayelet Hashahar, Upper Galilee, 12200. ☎ (06) 932611.
(K) Ein Gedi, Kibbutz Ein-Gedi. ☎ (07) 594222/(07) 594726.
(K) Gesher Haziv, Western Galilee. ☎ (04) 825715.
(K) Hagoshrim, Upper Galilee. ☎ (06) 956231.
Ha'on Camping Village, Sea of Galilee. ☎ (06) 757555-6.
(K) Kfar Blum, Upper Galilee. ☎ (06) 943666.
(K) Kfar Giladi, Upper Galilee. ☎ (06) 941414-5; Fax (06) 951248.
(K) Kiriat Anavim, Judea Hills. ☎ (02) 348999.
(K) Lavi, Lower Galilee, 15267. ☎ (06) 799450; Fax (06) 799399.
(K) Ma'ale Hachamisha, Judea Hills. ☎ (02) 342591.
(K) Mitzpeh Ramat Rachel, M.P. North Judea 90900. ☎ (02) 702555; Fax (02) 733155.

KFAR VITKIN
Youth Hostel
Emek Hefer (220). ☎ (09) 666032. 25 miles north of Tel Aviv.

KIBBUTZ HARDOF
Restaurants and cafes
(V) Vegetarian Restaurant. ☎ (04) 9865655.

KIBBUTZ YOTVATA
Restaurants and cafes
Dairy restaurant. ☎ (07) 357449.

KORAZIM
Holiday Village
(K) Amnon Bay Recreation Centre. ☎ (06) 934431.
Vered Hagalil Guest Farm. ☎ (06) 935785. Fax (06) 934964.

MAAGAN
Holiday Village
Maagan Holiday Village, Sea of Galilee. ☎ (06) 753753.

MAAYAN HAROD
Youth Hostel
Hankin (150). ☎ (06) 581660. 7 miles east of Afula.

METULA
Hotels
(K) Arazim. ☎ (06) 944143-5.
(K) Hamavri. ☎ (06) 940150.
(K) Sheleg Halevanon, P.O.B. 13. ☎ (06) 944015-7.

MITZPE RAMON
Restaurants and cafes
(K) Tzukit. ☎ (07) 88019.

MOSHAV SHORESH
Hotel
(K) Shoresh Apartment Hotel, Harey Yehuda. ☎ (02) 338338;
Fax (02) 340262

NAHARIA
Hotels
(K) Astar, 27 Gaaton Blvd. ☎ (04) 923431.
(K) Beit Hava, Shavei Zion, 25227. ☎ (04) 820391.
(K) Carlton, 23 Ha'gaaton Blvd. ☎ (04) 922211.
(K) Eden N.L., Meyasdim St. ☎ (04) 923246-7.
(K) Frank, 4 Haaliya St. ☎ (04) 920278.
(K) Kalman, 27 Jabotinsky St. ☎ (04) 920355 926539.
(K) Panorama, 6 Hamaapilim St. ☎ (04) 920555.
(K) Rosenblatt, 59 Weizmann St. ((04) 920069.
Restaurants and cafes
(K) Café Tsafon, 10 Gaaton Blvd. ☎ (04) 922567.

NAZARETH
Restaurants and cafes
(K) Iberia, Rassco Centre, Nazareth Elite. ☎ (06) 556314.
(K) Nof Nazareth, 23 Hacarmel St., Nazareth Elite. ☎ (06) 554366.

NEGEV
Youth Hostels
Arad: Blau-Weiss (180). ☎ (07) 957150. Centre of town.
Beersheba: Bet Yatziv (270). ☎ (07) 277444 or 271490. 79 Ha'atzmaut St.
Ein Gedi: Bet Sara (206). ☎ (07) 584165. 1½ miles north of Kibbutz Ein Gedi,
on Dead Sea.
Eilat (370). ☎ (07) 370088.
Masada: Isaac H. Taylor (150). ☎ (07) 584349. 28 miles from Arad.
Mitzpeh Ramon: Bet Noam (164). ☎ (07) 588443; Fax (07) 588074.

NETANYA
Useful addresses
There are more than 200 syns. & places of worship here. The following cater
to English-speakers:
Cong. Agudat Achim, 45 Jabotinsky St.
New Syn. of Netanya, 7 MacDonald St. ☎ (09) 627178.
Young Israel of N. Netanya, cnr. Shlomo Hamelech & Yehuda Hanassi Sts.
Netanya Assoc. for Tourism, 15 Herzl St. ☎ (09) 30583.
Ohel Shem Civic Auditorium, Cultural Centre, 4 Raziel St. ☎ (09) 336688.
Hotels
(K) Arches, 4 Remez St. ☎ (09) 823 322.
(K) Blue Bay, 37 Hamelachim St., 42228. ☎ (09) 603603; Fax (09) 337475.
(K) Gal Yam, 46 Dizengoff St. ☎ (09) 625033.
(K) Galei Hasharon, 42 Ussishkin St. 42273. ☎ (09) 825125.
(K) Galei Zans, 6 Ha'melachim St. ☎ (09) 621777.
(K) Galil, 18 Nice Blvd. ☎ (09) 624455.
(K) Ginot Yam, 9 David Hamelech St. ☎ (09) 341007.
(K) Goldar, 1 Usishkin St. ☎ (09) 338188.
(K) Grand Yahalom, 15 Gad Makhnes St. ☎ (09) 624888.
(K) Green Beach, P.O.B. 230. ☎ (09) 656166.

(K) Jeremy N.L., 11 Gad Machnes St. ☎ (09) 622651.
(K) King Koresh, 6 Harav Kook St. ☎ (09) 613555.
(K) King Solomon, 18 Hamaapilim St. ☎ (09) 338444.
(K) Margoa (new), 9 Gad Makhnes St. ☎ (09) 624434.
(K) Maxim, 8 King David St. ☎ (09) 621062.
(K) Metropol Grand, 17 Gad Makhnes St. ☎ (09) 624777.
(K) Orly, 20 Hamaapilim St., ☎ (09) 333091.
(K) Palace N.L., 33 Gad Machnes St. ☎ (09) 620222. Fax (09) 620224.
(K) Park, 7 David Hamelech St. ☎ (09) 623344.
(K) Residence, 18 Gad Machnes St. ☎ (09) 623777.
(K) The Seasons Hotel, 1 Nice Blvd. ☎ (09) 601555. Fax (09) 623022. Email: seasons@netmedia.net.il.
(K) Topaz, 25 King David St. ☎ (09) 624555.
Holiday Village
(K) Green Beach Holiday Village. ☎ (053) 44166 & 52422.
Restaurants and cafes
(K) Bagel Nash, 10 Ha'atzmaut Sq. ☎ (09) 616920.
(K) Hagozal, 95 Herzl St. ☎ (09) 335301.
(K) MacDavid, 7a Ha'atzmaut Sq. ☎ (09) 618711.
(K) Milky Way, 6 Herzl St. ☎ (09) 324638.
(K) Zli-Esh, 6 Shaar Hagai St. ☎ (09) 324295.

PETACH TIKVA
Youth Hostel
Yad Labanim (206). ☎ (03) 926666. Yahalom St. 7½ miles north-east of Tel Aviv.

RAANANA
Useful addresses
Syn.: Great, 103 Achuza; ☎ (09) 914006.
Cons, 8 Borochov. Mikva Herzl St.
Restaurants and cafes
(K) Dana, 198 Achuza ☎ (09) 901452.
(K) Lady D, 158 Achuza ☎ (09)-916517.
(K) Pica Aduma, 87 Achuza ☎ (09) 910508.
(K) Limosa 5 Eliazar Jaffe ☎ (09) 903407.

RAMAT GAN
Useful address
Bar-Ilan University. ☎ (03) 718111. Guided tours daily.
Holiday Village
(K) Kfar Hamaccabiah, Bernstein St. ☎ (03) 715715.

RAMAT YOHANAN
Youth Hostel
Yehuda Hatzair (180). ☎/Fax (04) 442976. 11 miles north-east of Haifa.

REHOVOT
Hotel
Margoa, 11 Moskowitz St. ☎ (08) 451303.
Restaurants and cafes
(K) Rehovot Chinese Restaurant, 202 Herzl St. ☎ (08) 471616.

RISHON-LE-ZION
Restaurants and cafes
(K) Gan Dror Yaacov Affendi Inn, 12 Tarmav St. ☎ (03) 942416.

ROSH HANIKRA
Youth Hostel
Rosh Hanikra (220). ☎ (04) 982516. Near the grottos.

ROSH PINA
Youth Hostel
Hovevei Hateva (90). ☎ (06) 937086. 16 miles north of Tiberias.

TEL AVIV
While Jerusalem is introvert, Tel Aviv is extrovert. It wears its noisy heart on its sleeve, and all you need do is to move with the crowds, pausing only for refreshment and to watch the passing scene from a Dizengoff Street cafe table.

The central sea-front has had to adapt, so as not to be over-shadowed by the huge new hotels which have gone up along the length of Hayarkon Street. But if you walk past the Dan Hotel in the direction of Jaffa, you can see the fine, recently laid-out sea-front parks and yachting marinas which have transformed this once dingy end of the city into a first class resort area.

Tel Aviv, say the Tel Avivians, has everything, which is true since Beth Hatefutsoth, the Nahum Goldmann Museum of the Diaspora, has been built and an art museum added to the city's offerings of theatre, music and cinema. It also has something else, which can bring a few hours' relief to sore-pressed parents – an amusement park in the Exhibition Grounds on the northern out-skirts of the city.

If you want to see Tel Aviv at its most colourful, an hour or two during the morn-ing at the Carmel Market will provide sufficient boisterous clamour until the evening, when the Yemenite quarter, with its narrow streets and exotic restau-rants, can offer another glimpse of a little-known face of Israel's largest city.

Useful addresses
Synagogues
Bilu, 122 Rothschild Blvd.
Great, 314 Dizengoff St.
Ihud Shivat Zion, 86 Ben-Yehuda St. (Central European rite).
Kedem (Progressive), 20 Carlebach St.
Main Synagogue, 110 Allenby Rd. (Ashkenazi).
Ohel Mis'ad, 5 Shadal St. (Sephardi).
Tiferet Zvi, Hermann Hacohen St.

Miscellaneous
Automobile Club & Touring Association, 20 Karekevet St., ☎ (03) 622961.
Hadassah Club for Overseas Visitors, 80 Hayarkon St. ☎ (03) 56039.
Israel, Britain & the Commonwealth Association, (IBCA), 44, Pinsher St., 63146. ☎ (03) 5262255.
The British Olim Society Ltd., 76 Ibn Gvirol St., P.O.Bx. 16266, 61162 Tel Aviv, Israel. ☎ (03) 6965244. Fax (03) 6967049.
The B.O.S. represents the Zionist Federations and Olim from Great Britain & Ireland, Australia, New Zealand, Scandinavia & Germany.
Magen David Adom Central Headquarters, 60 Yigal Alon St., 67062. ☎ (03) 6300222.
Ministry of Tourism (Tel Aviv & Central Region). ☎ (03) 223268 & 231263.
Moadon Haoleh, Club for English-Speaking Immigrants and Tourists, 109 Hayarkon St. ☎ (03) 236102.
Tel Aviv-Yafo Assoc. for Tourism, City Hall, Malchei Israel Sq., ☎ (03) 232581.
Tel Aviv Municipality, City Hall, Malchei Yisrael Sq. ☎ (03) 243311.
Tel Aviv University, Ramat Aviv. ☎ (03) 416111.
Z.O.A. (Zionist Organisation of America) House & Tourist Club, 1 Daniel Frisch St. ☎ (03) 259341.

Embassies

Argentina: 112 Hayarkon St., 2nd Floor. ☎ (03) 293411; Australia: 185 Hayarkon St. ☎ (03) 243152; Austria, 11 Herman Cohen St. ☎ (03) 246186; Belgium, 266 Hayarkon St. ☎ (03) 454164-6; Bolivia, 85 Ben-Gurion Blvd. ☎ (03) 230868; Brazil, 14 Heh Be'Iyar St., Hamedina Sq., 5th Floor. ☎ (03) 219292-4; Britain, 192 Hayarkon St. ☎ (03) 249171-8; Burma, 19 Yona St., Ramat Gan. ☎ (03) 783151; Canada, 220 Hayarkon St. ☎ (03) 228122-5; Chile, 54 Pincus St., 11th Floor. ☎ (03) 440414-5; Colombia, 52 Pincus St., 6th Floor. ☎ (03) 449616; Denmark, 23 Bnei Moshe St. ☎ (03) 440405-6; Dominican Republic, 32 Zamenhof St., Herzlia B. ☎ (052) 72422; Ecuador, Asia Hse., Room 231, 4 Weizmann St. ☎ (03) 258764; Egypt, 54 Basel St. ☎ (03) 224151; Finland, Bet Eliahu, 8th Floor, 2 Ibn Gvirol St. ☎ (03) 250527-8; France, 112 Herbert Samuel Blvd., ☎ (03) 245371-3; Germany, 16 Soutine St. ☎ (03) 243111-5; Greece (Diplomatic Representation), 35 King Saul Blvd. ☎ (03) 259704; Guatemala, 1 Bernstein Cohen St., Flat 10, Ramat Hasharon. ☎ (03) 490456; Haiti, Asia Hse., Room 230, 4 Weizmann St. ☎ (03) 252084; Holland, Asia Hse, 4 Weizmann St. ☎ (03) 257337-9; Italy, Asia Hse., 4 Weizmann St. ☎ (03) 264223-5; Japan, Asia Hse., 4 Weizmann St. ☎ (03) 257292-4; Liberia, 119 Rothschild Blvd. ☎ 247507; Mexico, 14 Heh Be'Iyar St., Hamedina Sq. ☎ (03) 210266; Norway, 10 Heh Be'Iyar St., Hamedina Sq. ☎ (03) 295207-8; Panama, 28 Heh Be'Iyar St., Hamedina Sq. ☎ (03) 253158; Peru, 52 Pincus St., 8th Floor. ☎ (03) 454065; Philippines Republic, 12 Heh Be'Iyar St., 4th floor, Hamedina Sq. ☎ (03) 258143; Poland (Interest Section), 2 Isaac Ramba St., Ramat Gan. ☎ (03) 7520555.
Romania, 24 Adam Hacohen St. ☎ (03) 247379; South Africa, 2 Kaplan St., 9th Floor. ☎ (03) 256147; Sweden, Asia Hse., 4 Weizmann St. ☎ (03) 258111. Switzerland, 228 Hayarkon St. ☎ (03) 244121-2; Turkey (Legation), 34 Amos St. ☎ (03) 454155-6; United States, 71 Hayarkon St. ☎ (03) 654338; Uruguay, 52 Pincus St., 2nd Floor. ☎ (03) 440411; Venezuela, 2 Kaufman St. ☎ (03) 656287; Zaire, 1 Rachel St. ☎ 222002.

Hotels

(K) Adiv, 5 Mendele St. ((03) 5229141.
(K) Ambassador, 56 Herbert Samuel. ☎ (03) 5103993.
(K) Ami, 152 Hayarkon St. ☎ (03) 5249141-5.
(K) Armon Hayarkon, 268 Hayarkon St. ☎ (03) 455271-3.
(K) Avia, B. G. International Airport Area. ☎ (03) 5360221. Fax (03) 5360036.
(K) Basel, 156 Hayarkon St. ☎ (03) 244161.
(K) Bell, 12 Allenby St. ☎ (03) 5177011.

(K) Carlton Tel Aviv, 10 Eliezer Peri St. ☎ (03) 5201818; Fax (03) 5271043.
(K) City, 9 Mapu St. ☎ (03) 5246253.
(K) Dan Panorama, 10 Y. Kaufman St.. ☎ (03) 5190190.
(K) Dan Tel Aviv, 99 Hayarkon St. ☎ (03) 5202525; Fax (03) 524 9755.
(K) Deborah, 87 Ben-Yehuda St. ☎ (03) 5448282.
(K) Florida, 164 Hayarkon St. ☎ (03) 5242184.
(K) Grand Beach, 250 Hayarkon St. ☎ (03) 5466555.
(K) Maxim, 86 Hayarkon St. ☎ (03) 5173721-5; Fax (03) 5173726.
(K) Metropolitan,11-16 Trumpeldor St. ☎ (03) 5192727.
(K) Monopol N.l. on the promenade, 4 Allenby St. ☎ (03) 655906.
(K) Moriah Plaza Tel Aviv, 155 Hayarkon St. ☎ (03) 5271515.
(K) Ora N.L., 35 Ben Yehuda St. ☎ (03) 650941.
(K) Ramada Continental, 121 Hayarkon St. ☎ (03) 5272626.
(K) Ramat Aviv, 151 Derech Namir. ☎ (03) 6990777; Fax (03) 699-0997.
(K) Shalom, 216 Hayarkon St. ☎ (03) 5243277.
(K) Sheraton Tel Aviv, 115 Hayarkon St. ((03) 5211111.
(K) Tal, 287 Hayarkon St. ☎ (03) 5442281.
(K) Tel Aviv Hilton, Independence Park, 63405. ☎ (03) 5202222.
(K) Tayelet N.L. On the promenade, 6 Allenby St. ☎ (03) 5105845.
(K) Wagshal, 13 Meltzer St., Bnei, Brak. ☎ (03) 784536, 785052.
(K) Wiznitz, 16 Damesek Eliezer St., Bnei-Brak. ☎ (03) 777141-3.
(K) Yamit Towers, 79 Hayarkon St. ☎ (03) 5171111.
Restaurants and cafes
(K) Ambassador Grill Room, Diplomat Hotel, 45 Hayarkon St. ☎ (03)294422.
(K) Asia House, 4 Weizmann St. ☎ (03) 210717.
(K) Bagel Nash, 72 Ibn Gvirol St. ☎ (03) 261348; 38
(K) China Palace, 102 Hayarkon St. ☎ (03) 224455.
(K) Dag Bareshet, 196 Dizengoff St. ☎ (03) 232919.
(K) Dagim Beni, 192 Ben-Yehuda. ☎ (03) 237784.
(K) Delicatesse, 53 Shenkin St. ☎ (03) 201651.
(K) El Gaucho, 90 Hayarkon St. ☎ (03) 220166 & 2 Shaul Hamelech Blvd. ☎ (03) 250079.
(K) Fish 'n' Chips, 196 Dizengoff St. ☎ (03) 232919.
(K) Galit, 3 Wingate St., Yad Eliahu, 67611. ☎ (03) 338032.
(K) Gamliel (Pninat Hakerem), 47 Hakovshim St. ☎ (03) 658779.
(K) Ganei Hatarucha, Rokach Blvd. ☎ (03) 422171.
(K) Habikta, Shalom Tower.
(K) Ha Blintzes Ha Hungari, 94 Dizengoff Circle.
(K) Hamakom, 1 Lilienblum St. Tel (03) 5101823.
(K) Ha Pinna, 317 Hayarkon St. ☎ (03) 443864.
(K) Herli, 114 Yehuda Halevy St. ☎ (03) 282059.
(K) Holyland, 49 Bograshov St. ☎ (03) 287382.
(K) Hungarian Blintzes, 35 Yirmiyahu St. ☎ (03) 6050674 (Dairy).
(K) King Donald Ben-Yehuda, 59 Ben Yehuda St. Tel (03) 246752.
(K) Lool, 39 Ben-Yehuda St. cnr. Bograshov.
(K) Marina Chinese, Marina Hotel, Namir Sq. ☎ (03) 282244.
(K) Naknikiot, 4 Dizengoff Circle. ☎ (03) 280939.
(K) Natalie Blintzes, Dizengoff Centre. ☎ (03) 289252.
(K) New York, 164 Dizengoff St. ☎ (03) 225966.
(K) Passage to India, 1 Yordei Hasira St. ☎ (03) 441438.
(K) Pizza Pino, 169 Ben Yehuda St. ☎ (03) 239582.
(K) Pninat Hakerem, 47 Hakovshim St. ☎ (03) 658779.
(K) Princess of the Nile, 18 Hatsorfim St. ☎ (03) 814266.
(K) Rickshaw Kosher, 163 Ben-Yehuda St. ☎ (03) 227813.
(K) Shaul's Inn, 11 Elyashiv St., Kerem Hatemanim. ☎ (03) 653303.

(K) Shmulik Cohen, 146 Herzl St. ☎ (03) 810222.
(K) Sinima, 65 Dizengoff St. Dizengoff Centre. ☎ (03) 200484.
(K) Twelve Tribes, Sheraton Hotel, Hayarkon St. ☎ (03) 286222.
(K) Zion Exclusive, 28 Peduim St. ☎ (03) 658714.
Youth Hostel
Tel Aviv (300). ☎ (03) 5441748 or 5460719; Fax (03) 5441030.
32 Bnei Dan St.

TIBERIAS
Hotels
(K) Ariston, 19 Herzl Blvd. ☎ (06) 790244.
(K) Astoria, 13 Ohel Ya'akov St. ☎ (06) 722351-2.
(K) Caesar, ☎ (06) 732333.
(K) Carmel Jordan River, Habanim St. ☎ (06) 6714444.
(K) Daphna, Ussiskin St. ☎ (06) 792261-4.
(K) Eshel, Tabur Haaretz St. ☎ (06) 90562.
(K) Gai Beach, Derech Hamerchatzaot ☎ (06) 790790.
(K) Galei Kinnereth, 1 Kaplan St. ☎ (06) 6728888.
(K) Galilee, Elhadef St. P.O.B. 616.☎ (06) 791166-8.
(K) Ganei Hamat, Habanim St. nr. Hot Springs. ☎ (06) 792890.
(K) Golan, 14 Achad Ha'am St. ☎ (06) 791901-4.
(K) Hawai, P.O.B. 366 Migdal. ☎ (06) 790202, 720549, 720568.
(K) Kinar, N.E. Sea of Galilee. ☎ (06) 732670.
(K) Moriah Plaza Tiberias, Habanim St. ☎ (06) 792233.
(K) Quiet Beach, Gdud Barak St. ☎ (06) 790125.
(K) Ramot-Resort Hotel, Sea of Galilee. ☎ (06) 732636.
(K) Tzameret Inn, Plus 2000 St. ☎ (06) 794951.
(K) Washington, 13 Seidel St. ☎ (06) 791861-3.
Restaurants and cafes
(K) Gan Esther, Hadishon St. ☎ (06) 729946.
(K) Hamat Gader Restaurant, ☎ (06) 751049.
(K) Lido Kinneret, Gdud Barak St. ☎ (06) 721538.
(K) Pagoda, Lido Beach, P.O.B. 253, 14102. ☎ (06) 725513.
(K) Quiet Beach, Gedud Barak St. ☎ (06) 790125.
(K) Sironit Beach, Hamerchazaot Rd. ☎ (06) 721449.
Youth Hostels
Taiber (144). ☎ (06) 750050; Fax (06) 7551628. 2½ miles south of Tiberias.
Yosef Meyouhas (248). ☎ (06) 721775 or 790350.
Hayarden St., cnr. Alhadif St.

WESTERN NEGEV
Youth Hostel
Hevel Katif: Hadarom (220). ☎ (07) 847597; Fax (07) 847680.
For more detailed information, apply either to the Israel Youth Hostels
Association or to the nearest Israel Government Tourist Office.

ZEFAT
Hotels
(K) David, Mr. Canaan. ☎ (06) 920062.
(K) Nof Hagalil, Mt. Canaan. ☎ (06) 921595.
(K) Pisgah, Mr. Canaan. ☎ (06) 920105.
(K) Rimon Inn, Artists Colony. ☎ (06) 920665-6.
(K) Ron, Hativat Yiftah St. ☎ (06) 972590.
Youth Hostel
Bet Benyamin (104). ☎ (06) 921086; Fax (06) 973514. In southern part of town.

ZICHRON YA'ACOV
Hotel
(K) Barons' Heights & Terraces N.L., P.O.B. 332. ☎ (06) 300333; Fax (06) 300310.

Some Interesting Visits
There are guided tours of the Knesset (Parliament) on Sun. and Thurs. between 8.30a.m. and 2.30p.m. Further inf. from Knesset P.R. Dept. ☎ (02) 554111.

On Saturday mornings at 10 a.m. the Jerusalem municipality organises a free walking tour to various points of interest. Details from Tourist Information Offices.

The Quartercentre in the Jewish Quarter contains a memorial site for the fighters of the War of Independence in 1948, an exhibition of photographs taken during the conquest of the quarter in 1948, and a sight and sound presentation about the quarter.

A visit to Hechal Shlomo, the Supreme Religious Centre in King George St., Jerusalem, is a 'must'. This magnificent building houses the Chief Rabbinate, the Central Rabbinical Library and the Supreme Rabbinical Court, as well as a museum. Adjoining it is the outstanding Great Synagogue, inaugurated in August, 1982, which is dedicated to the memory of the six million victims of the Holocaust and all who fell in the founding and defence of the State of Israel. Services, Fri. evg. & Sat. morn. Visits are by appointment only. Further inf. ☎ (02) 635212.

The Holyland Hotel model of ancient Jerusalem at the time of the Second Temple is worth seeing.

Bayit Lepletot Girls' Town is worth a visit. Inf. from 1 Beharan St., nr. Strauss St., Jerusalem. ☎ (02) 227986 or 228581.

Visitors are welcome at the Mother & Baby Convalescent Home, 22 Hapisga St., Bayit Vegan, Jerusalem. ☎ (02) 22581 or 284056.

Free tours of the Jewish Quarter and free accom. in the American P'eylim Student Union hostel in the quarter, at 10 Shoarim St., ☎ (02) 532131, as well as Shabbat hospitality with either a Chasidic family in Mea Shearim or a modern Orthodox family in the Jewish Quarter, are offered to Jewish students by Jeffrey Seidel. Jewish students are also offered free acccom. at the Jerusalem Jewish Youth Centre in the quarter, at 9 Shonei Halachot St. ☎ (02) 285623.

On Friday nights local youth groups entertain visitors with songs and dances of Israel at Z.O.A. House in Tel Aviv.

Israel Nature Trails, the touring section of the Society for the Protection of Nature in Israel, offers guided tours on set dates throughout the year. All start in Tel Aviv and most can be joined in Jerusalem. Full inf. from the Society, 13 Helen Hamalka St., P.O. Box 930, Jerusalem. ☎ (02) 249567.

Every Wednesday at 9.30 a.m. there is a free walking tour of Jaffa, organised by the Tel Aviv-Yafo Tourism Assoc. The tour, which takes about 2½ hours, starts in Clock Square near Yefet St., in the centre of Jaffa.

The Zoological Centre in Ramat Gan (☎ (03) 744991 & 762586) combines a safari park and a conventional zoo.

Thursday is market day in Beersheba. Beduin come into the town from all parts of the Negev and hold a market.

In Haifa, there is an Oneg Shabbat at the Dan Carmel Hotel every Friday night at 9 p.m.

On Sundays, Mondays, Tuesdays, Thursdays and Saturdays at 9.30 a.m., there are guided tours of Mount Carmel, Druse villages, Kibbutz Bet Oren and Ein Hod artists' colony. On Wednesdays at 9.30 a.m., there are guided tours of the Bahai shrine and gardens, Druse villages, Muchraka, the Moslem village of Kababir, the Carmelite monastery and Elijah's Cave. For bookings and further inf., ☎ (04) 674342.

There is a first-class, modern golf course at Caesarea, with its ancient ruins, situated on the Mediterranean. Caesarea Golf & Country Club Ltd., Or Akiva. ☎ (063) 88174.

Culture and the Arts

Music: The Israel Philharmonic Orchestra gives subscription concerts and special concerts throughout the year, both in the main cities and towns and smaller centres. There are also a number of chamber music ensembles, choirs and music-lovers' associations. In Jerusalem there is a Spring Festival of the performing arts in April and May.

Theatre: The Habimah, Ohel and Chamber Theatre companies have their headquarters in Tel Aviv, but frequently tour other towns and rural centres. There is also a Haifa Theatre.

Art: There are several permanent and many special art exhibitions in the three main cities and in quite a number of smaller centres such as Safed and Ein Hod, which have attracted artists' colonies.

See: **The Museums of Israel**, by Nitra Rosovsky and Joy Ungerleider – Mayerson. New York: Harry N. Abrams, 1989; **In and About Jerusalem: A Guide to Art, Tradition and Leisure in Jerusalem**, by Colin Hamburger. Jerusalem 1993.

Museums and Exhibitions

Haifa: Edible Oil Museum, Shemen Factory, 2 Tovim St. ☎ (04) 670491; Haifa Museum includes Museums of Ancient Art, Modern Art, Music & Ethnology, 26 Shabetai Levy St. ☎ (04) 523255; Reuben & Edith Hecht Museum, Haifa University, 31905. ☎ (04) 257773; Israel Railways Museum, Haifa Railway Station (East); National Maritime Museum, 198 Allenby Rd., 31447. ☎ (04) 536622, 34455, ☎ (04) 371833.

Moshe Shtekelis Museum of Pre-History, 124 Hatishbi St., Entrance from Gan Ha'em; Tikotin Museum of Japanese Art, 89 Hanassi Blvd., Mount Carmel; Mané Katz Museum, 89 Panorama Rd.; Museum of Clandestine Immigration & Naval Museum, 204 Allenby Rd.; Bet Pinchas Biological Institute, 124 Hatishbi St., includes Nature Museum, Zoo and Botanical Garden.

Dagon Grain Museum, Plumer Sq.; Technoda, National Museum of Science and Technology, opp. 15 Balfour St. ☎ (04) 671372.

Jerusalem: Ammunition Hill Memorial & Museum, Ramat Eshkol. ☎ (02) 828442; Bible Lands Museum, 25 Granot St. ☎ (02)-611066.

Herzl Museum, Herzl Blvd., Mount Herzl; Israel Museum, Hakirya, includes Bezalel National Museum, Samuel Bronfman Biblical & Archaeological Museum, Shrine of the Book, & the Rockefeller Museum in East Jerusalem; L.A. Mayer Memorial Institute of Islamic Art, 2 Hapalmach St.; Museum of the History of Jerusalem, Tower of David, Jaffa Gate. ☎ (02) 283273; Museum of Musical Instruments, Rubin Academy of Music, 7 Smolenskin St.; Museum of Natural History, 6 Mohilever St.; Nahon Museum of Italian Jewish Art, 22 Hillel St., 94581. ☎ (02) 241610.

Old Yishuv Court Museum, 6 Or Hachayim St., Jewish Quarter, Old City; Shocken Institute, 6 Balfour St.; Sir Isaac & Lady Wolfson Museum, Hechal Shlomo, 58 King George St.; S.Y. Agnon's House, 16 Klausner St., Talpiot. Tel/Fax (02) 716498.

Siebenberg House Archaeological Museum, 6 Hagittit St., Jewish Quarter. ☎ (02) 282341; Tourjeman Post Museum, 1 Hel Hahandassa St. ☎ 281278; Yad Vashem, Martyrs' & Heroes' Remembrance Authority, Har Hazikaron, P.O.B. 3447, 91034. ☎ (02) 751611; Fax (02) 433511.

Yad Vashem Art Museum, same address.

Tel Aviv: Bet Bialik, 22 Bialik St.; Bet Eliahu-Bet Hahagana, 23 Rothschild Blvd., 65122. ☎ (03) 5608624.

Goldmann Museum of the Diaspora (Beth Hatefutsoth), Klausner St., Ramat Aviv; Haaretz Museum includes eight smaller museums at Ramat Aviv, as well as the Israel Theatre Museum, 17 Ben-Gurion Blvd., Antiquities Museum, 10 Mifratz Shlomo St., & Tel Aviv History Museum, 27 Bialik St.; Independence Hall Museum and Bet Hatanach, 16 Rothschild Blvd.; Jabotinsky Institute, 38 King George St.; Tel Aviv Museum of Art, 27 Shaul Hamelech Blvd., 64283. ☎ (03) 6957361. Includes Helena Rubinstein Pavilion, 7 Tarsat St.

Other Museums:

Akko Municipal Museum, Old City; Kibbutz Ashdot Yaakov; Avihail, Bet Hagedudim (History of Jewish Brigade); Kibbutz Ayelet Hashahar; Beersheba, Negev Museum, Ha'atzmaut St., cnr. of Herzl St. & Man in the Desert Museum, 5 miles north-east of the city; Bet Shean Museum, 1 Dalet St.; Kibbutz Dan, Bet Ussishkin; Kibbutz Degania Alef, Bet Gordon; Dimona Municipal Museum; Kibbutz Ein Harod, Bet Sturman & Art Institute; Elat, Museum of Modern Art, Hativat Hanegev St.; Hadera, Khan Museum, 74 Hagiborim St.; Kibbutz Hanita, Tower & Stockade Period Museum; Kibbutz Hazorea, Wilfrid Israel House of Oriental Art; Kibbutz Kfar Etzion, Gush Etzion Museum; Kibbutz Kfar Giladi, Bet Hashomer; Katzrin (Golan Heights), Golan Archaeological Museum; Kibbutz Kfar Menachem; Kibbutz Lohamei Hagetaot, Ghetto Fighters', Holocaust & Resistance Museum; Kibbutz Maabarot; Kibbutz Maayan Baruch; Midreshet Ruppin; Naharia Municipal Museum, Hagaaton Blvd.; Netanya Museum of Biology & Archaeology; Neve Zohar (Dead Sea area), Bet Hayotser; Kibbutz Nir David; Kibbutz Palmachim; Petach Tikva, Bet Yad Labanim, 30 Arlosorov St.; Ramat Gan, Bet Emmanuel Museum, 18 Chibat Zion St., & Pierre Gildesgame Maccabi Museum, Kfar Hamaccabiah; Safed, Bet Hameiri Institute (History & Heritage of Safed); Safed, Israel Bible Museum; Safed, Museum of Printing Art, Artists' Colony; Tel Hai; Tiberias; Tiberias Hot Springs Lehmann Museum, Hammat Tiberias National Park; Kibbutz Yad Mordechai; Kibbutz Yifat; Zichron Yaakov, Nili Museum & Aaronson House, 40 Hameyasdim St.

Nature Reserves

The National Parks and Nature Reserves Law was passed in 1963 and established a Nature Reserves Authority. There are some 300 nature reserves in Israel although not all have attained official recognition. The recognised reserves occupy 741,000 acres. Visitors to reserves must adhere to a strict code of behaviour. Advance reservation and entrance fees are required at most of the reserves.

The following are the major reserves:

Metulla: Nahal Ayoun (HaTanur) Reserve; ☎ 011-972-6-951519; Tel Dan: ☎ 011-972-6-951579;
Nahal Hermon (Banias) Reserve. ☎ 011-972-6-950272;
Huleh Reserve. ☎ 011-972-6-937069;
Gamla. ☎ 011-972-6-762040;
Ein Afeq. ☎ 011-972-4-704992;
Nahal Mearot. ☎ 011-972-4-841750;
Soreq Caves. ☎ 011-972-2-911117;
Ein Gedi Reserve. ☎ 011-972-57-84285;
Arad Visitors' Centre. ☎ 011-972-07-959333. Fax (07) 955052.
Ramon Crater. ☎ 011-972-07-88691;
Yotvata Hai Bar Visitors' Center. ☎ 011-972-59-76018;
Coral Beach Reserve. ☎ 011-972-59-76829.

UNITED STATES OF AMERICA

Though there had been individual Jewish settlers before 1654 in the territory which is now the United States, it was not until that year that Jewish immigrants arrived in group at New Amsterdam – 23 of them, who probably came from Brazil by way of Cuba and Jamaica. The story of the growth of Jewry in the U.S.A is the story of successive waves of immigration resulting from persecution in Russia, Germany and other countries. Today the Jewish population has grown to 5,950,000, of whom some 2,500,000 live in greater New York. For general information about the American Jewish Community contact: UJA-Federation Resource Line, 130 E. 59th St., N.Y.C. 10022.

Representative Organisations

American Jewish Committee: 165 E. 56th St., 10022. ☎ (212) 751-4000. Offices in thirty communities across the USA.
Israel H.Q.: P. O. Box 37068, Jerusalem 91370.
American Jewish Congress: Stephen Wise Congress House, 15 E. 84th St., 10028. ☎ (212) 879-4500.
Anti-Defamation League of B'nai B'rith: 823 United Nations Plaza, 10017. ☎ (212) 490-2525.
B'nai B'rith International, Headquarters: 1640 Rhode Island Av. N.W., Washington, D.C., 20036. ☎ (202) 857-6600.
Conference of Presidents of Major American Jewish Organisations: 515 Park Av., 10022. ☎ (212) 752-1616.
Council of Jewish Federations, 730 Broadway, 10003. ☎ (212) 475-5000.
Jewish War Veterans of the U.S.A.: 1811 "R" St. N.W., Washington, D.C. 20009. ☎ (202) 265-6280.
National Conference on Soviet Jewry: 10 E. 40th St., Suite 907, 10016. ☎ (212) 679-6122.
National Conference of Synagogue Youth, 333 Seventh Ave, 10001-5072. ☎ (212) 563-5400. Fax (212) 613-8333.
National Council of Jewish Women: 15 E. 26th St., 10019. ☎ (212) 532-1740.
National Jewish Community Relations Advisory Council: 443 Park Av. S., 11th Floor, 10016. ☎ (212) 684-6950.
North American Jewish Students' Network: 15 E. 26th St., 10110.
World Jewish Congress: 501 Madison Av., 17th Floor, 10022. ☎ (212) 755-5770.

Cultural & Scientific Organisations

American Academy for Jewish Research: 3080 Broadway, 10027.
American Jewish Historical Society: 1 Thornton Rd., Waltham, Mass., 02154. ☎ (617) 891-8110. Fax (617) 899-9208.
Assoc. of Orthodox Jewish Scientists: 1373 Coney Island Av., 11219. ☎ (718) 338-8592.
Histadruth Ivrith of America: 1841 Broadway, 10023. ☎ (212) 581-5151.
Jewish Book Council: 15 E. 26th St., 10010. ☎ (212) 532-4949.
Jewish Information & Referral Service: 130 E. 59th St., 10022. ☎ (212) 753-2288.
Jewish Museum: 1109 Fifth Av., 10028.
Jewish Publication Society of America: 1930 Chestnut St., Philadelphia, Pa., 19103. ☎ (215) 564-5925. (New York: 60 E. 42nd St., 10017.)
Memorial Foundation for Jewish Culture: 15 E. 26th St., 10010. ☎ (212) 679-4074.
National Foundation for Jewish Culture, 330 Seventh Av., NY 10001. ☎ (212)

629-0500; Fax (212) 290-0508. Publishes a list of Jewish theatres in North America.
Yivo Institute for Jewish Research: 555 West 57th St., 10019. ☎ (212) 535-6700. (Temporary address 1995-96).

Overseas Aid Organisations
American Jewish Joint Distribution Committee: 711 Third Av., 10017.
American Ort Federation: 817 Broadway, 10003. ☎ (212) 677-4400.
United Hias Service: 333 7th Av., 1000.
United Jewish Appeal: National Office, 1290 Av. of the Americas, 10104. ☎ (212) 757-1500.

Religious, Educational Organisations, Etc
Agudath Israel World Org.: 84 William St., 10273. ☎ (212) 797-9600. The org. will provide free of charge a list of people in most major US cities who can provide reliable inf. about local kashrut.

American Assoc. of Rabbis: 350 5th Av., Suite 3308, 10001. ☎ (212) 244-3350.
American Fed. of Jewish Fighters, Camp Inmates & Nazi Victims: 823 United Nations Plaza, 10017. ☎ (212) 697-5670.
American Sephardi Fed.: 8 W. 40th St., Suite 1203, 10018. ☎ (212) 730-1210.
Central Conference of American Rabbis (Reform): 21 E. 40th St., 10016. ☎ (212) 684-4990.
Central Sephardic Jewish Community of America: 8 W. 70th St., 10023. ☎ (212) 787-2850.
Council for Jewish Education: 114 Fifth Av., 10011. ☎ (212) 575-5656.
Federation of Reconstructionist Congregations & Havurot, 270 W. 89th St., 10024. ☎ (212) 496-2960.
Hillel Foundations: 1640 Rhode Island Av. N.W., Washington, D.C., 20036. ☎ (202) 857-6576. Fax (202) 857-6693.
Jewish Ministers' Cantors' Assoc.: 3 W. 16th St., 10011. ☎ (212) 675-6601.
Lubavitch Movement: 770 Eastern Parkway, Brooklyn, 11213. ☎ (718) 221-0500. Fax (718) 221-0985.
National Council of Young Israel: 3 W. 16th St., 10011. ☎ (212) 929-1525. Can provide a world-wide list of branch synagogues.
National Jewish Committee on Scouting: 1325 Walnut Hill La., Irving, Texas, 75062. ☎ (214) 659-2059.
National Jewish Girl Scout Committee: 327 Lexington Av., 10016. ☎ (212) 686-8670.
Rabbinical Alliance of America (Igud Harabonim) (Orthodox): 156 Fifth Av., Suite 807, 10010. ☎ (212) 242-6420.
Rabbinical Assembly (Conservative): 3080 Broadway, 10027. ☎ (212) 678-8060.
Rabbinical Council of America (Orthodox): 275 7th Av., 10001. ☎ (212) 807-7888.
Synagogue Council of America: 327 Lexington Av., 10016. ☎ (212) 686-8670.
Union of American Hebrew Congregations (Reform): 838 Fifth Av., 10021. ☎ (212) 249-0100.
Union of Orthodox Jewish Congregations of America: 333 Seventh Ave., 10001. ☎ (212) 563-4000. Fax (212) 613-8333.
Union of Orthodox Rabbis of the U.S. and Canada: 235 E. Broadway Av., 10002. ☎ (212) 964-6337.
Union of Sephardic Congregations: 8 W. 70th St., 10023. ☎ (212) 873 0300.
United Synagogue of America (Conservative): 155 Fifth Av., 10010. ☎ (212) 533-7800.

World Council of Synagogues (Conservative): 155 Fifth Av., 10010. ☎ (212) 533-7800.

World Union for Progressive Judaism: 838 Fifth Av., 10021. ☎ (212) 249-0100, Ext 502. Fax (212) 517-3940.

World Union of Jewish Students: 15 E. 26th St., 10010.

Welfare Organisations

Baron de Hirsch Fund: 386 Park Av. S., 10016. ☎ (212) 532-7088.

City of Hope National Medical Center & Beckman Research Institute: 208 W. 8th St., Los Angeles, 90014. ☎ (310) 626-4611. (New York Office: 250 W. 57th St., 10019.)

Jewish Braille Institute of America: 110 E. 30th St., 10016. ☎ (212) 889-2525.

Jewish Welfare Board: 15 E. 26th St., 10010. ☎ (212) 532-4949.

Zionist Organisations

America-Israel Friendship League: 134 E. 39th St., 10016. ☎ (212) 679-4822.

America-Israel Cultural Foundation: 485 Madison Av., 10022. ☎ (212) 751-2700.

American Israel Public Affairs Committee: 444 N. Capitol St. N.W., Suite 412, Washington, D.C., 20001.

American Red Magen David for Israel: 888 7th Av., 10019. ☎ (212) 757-1627.

American Zionist Federation: 515 Park Av., 10022.

Emuna Women of America: 370 7th Av., 10001. ☎ (212) 564-9045.

Hadassah (Woman's Zionist Org. of America): 50 W. 58th St., 10019. ☎ (212) 355-7900.

Jewish National Fund of America: 42 E. 69th St., 10021. ☎ (212) 879-9300.

Religious Zionists of America: 25 W. 26th St., 10010. ☎ (212) 889-5260.

State of Israel Bonds Org.: 215 Park Av. S., 10003. ☎ (212) 677-9650.

United Israel Appeal: 515 Park Av., 10022. ☎ (212) 688-0800.

World Confederation of United Zionists: 30E. 60th St., 10022. ☎ (212) 371-1452.

World Zionist Organisation — American Section: 515 Park Av., 10022. ☎ (212) 752-0600.

Zionist Org. of America: 4 E. 34th St., 10016. ☎ (212) 481-1500.

Israel Consulate-General: 800 Second Av., 10017.

Local Synagogues and Organisations

NOTES: The letter (O) after the name of a syn. means that the practice is Orthodox (akin to the Minhag of the United Synagogue in Britain). (C) stands for Conservative (corresponding roughly to the ritual of the W. London Syn. of British Jews). (R) stands for Reform (the form of worship is similar to that of the Liberal Jewish movement in Britain).

There is no unified Jewish ecclesiastical control in America. A Chief Rabbinate, such as Anglo-Jewry has, is unknown.

Kashrut: There is little official supervision of kashrut, so the standard of observance at kosher hotels and restaurants is by no means uniform. Travellers should always check with a local rabbi or religious organisation.

It should be pointed out here that space limitations and other difficulties make it impossible to list every synagogue in the U.S.A., and in many cases the choice is unavoidably an arbitrary one. However, we should be glad to receive details from users of the Guide of any omissions they consider to be particularly glaring.

The Jewish Community Councils and similar bodies in the larger centers generally publish an annual directory of local Jewish organisations which are invaluable. 'Yellow Pages' in telephone directories can also prove useful in supplementing information given here.

B'nai B'rith lodge members, members of Friends of the Hebrew University, Zionist organisations and similar bodies with wide international membership can rely on local contact organisations in the many Jewish centres in North America and should refer to their home organisation for specific details.

Kosher Restaurants

There is a kosher restaurant guide accessible on the networks at: www. shamash.org/kosher/krestquery.html.

ALABAMA

BIRMINGHAM

Birmingham Jewish Fed., 3966 Montclair Rd., 35213. ☎ (205) 879 0416.
Fax (205) 803-1526.
Com. Center: 3960 Montclair Rd., 35213.
The Hess Library is at the same address.
Jewish Family Service, 3940 Montclair Rd. ☎ 9205) 879-3438.
Syn.: Knesseth Israel (O), 3225 Montevallo Rd., 35223, ☎ (205) 879-1464;
Beth-El (C), 2179 Highland Av., 35205; Emanu-El (R), 2100 Highland Av.,
35205.
Mikva: 3225 Montevallo Rd., 35213 and 2179 Highland Av., 35255.
Delicatessen: Browdy's, 2607 Cahaba Rd., 35223. ☎ (205) 879-6411.
Visitors requiring information about kashrut, temporary accommodation, etc.,
should contact Rabbi Meir Rosenberg, of Knesseth Israel.

HUNTSVILLE

Syn.: Etz Chayim (C), 7705 Bailey Cove Rd. S.E., 35802.

MOBILE

Syn.: Spring Hill Av. Temple (R), 1769 Spring Hill Av., 36607.

MONTGOMERY

Jewish Fed., P.O. Box 20058, 36120. ☎ (205) 277-5820.
Syn.: Etz Ahayem (Sephardi, O), 725 Augusta Rd., 36111; Agudath Israel (C)
3525 Cloverdale Rd., 36111. Mikva attached; Beth Or (R), 2246 Narrow
Lane, 36106.
There is a Jewish chapel at Maxwell Air Force base. The Jewish chaplain can
be contacted at Bldg. 833, Chaplain's School, at the base.

ALASKA

ANCHORAGE

Syn.: Beth Sholom (R), 7525 E. Northern Lights Blvd., 99504. ☎ (907) 338-
1836. Fax (907) 357-4013. Website:http//Alaska.Not/Sholom. This is the only
synagogue in Alaska and it has the only Jewish pre-school in the state.
There is also an Orthodox minyan called Cong. Shomerei Ohr. Inf. from 1210
E26th, 99508. ☎ (907) 279-1200.

ARIZONA

MESA

Syn.: Beth Sholom Cong. (C), 316 Le Seuer St., 85204. ☎ (602) 964-1981.

PHOENIX

Jewish Fed. of Greater Phoenix, 32 W. Coolidge, Suite 200, 85013. ☎ (602)
274-1800. Publishes 'Shalom Arizona'.

Synagogues:

Chabad-Lubavitch Center (O), 2110 E, Lincoln Dr., 85020.☎ (602) 944-
2753; Cong. Beth Joseph (O), 515 E. Bethany Home Rd., 85012. ☎ (602)
277-7479; Cong. Beth El (C), 1118 W. Glendale, 85021. ☎ (944 3359) (944-
2464); Temple Beth Ami (R), 4545 N. 36th St., No. 211, 85018. ☎ (602) 956-
0805; Temple Beth Israel (R), 3310 N. 10th Av., 85013, whose building also
houses the Plotkin Judaica Museum. ☎ (602) 264 4428.
Temple Chai (R), 4645 E. Marilyn Av., 85032. ☎ (602) 971-1234.
Congregation Shaarei Tzedek (O); P: Marty Miller, 7608 N. 18th Avenue,

continued from *Arizona*

85021 (944-1133); Temple Kol ami (R), 15030 N. 64th St. 204 85254 ☎ (602) 951 9660.
Valley of the Sun Jewish Community Center, 1718 W. Maryland Av., 85015.
☎ (602) 249-1832
Tri-Cities Jewish Community Center 1965 E. Hermosa Temp, AZ 85282 ☎ (602) 897-0588.
Greater Phoenix Jewish News, 1625 E. Northern 106, 85020, ☎ (602) 870-9470.

Restaurants and Delis:
Laura's Kitchen, 4818 N. 7th St., 85015. ☎ (602) 285-1515; J.J's Kosher, 1331 E. Northern Av., 85015. ☎ (602) 371-0999; Segal's Kosher R., 4818, N. 7th St., 85014. Visitors requiring information about kashrut should contact Rabbi David Rebibo, Phoenix Hebrew Academy, 515 E. Bethany Home Rd., 85012. ☎ (602) 277-7479.

SCOTTSDALE
Syn.: Beth Emeth of Scottsdale (C), 5406 E. Virginia Av., 85254. ☎ (602) 947-4604; Har Zion (C), 5929 E. Lincoln Dr., 85253. ☎ (602) 991-0720.
Temple Solel, (R), 6805 E. MacDonald Dr., 85253. ☎ (602) 991-7414.
Beth Joshua Congregation (C), 6230 E. Shea Blvd., 85254 ☎ (991-5404).

SIERRA VISTA
Syn.: Temple Kol Hamidbar, 228 North Canyon Dr., ☎ 458-8637 (Answer machine, summer only).

SOLOMONSVILLE
The town was founded by Isador E. Solomon, a friend of the Indians, in 1876.
Beth Sholom of Mesa (C), 316 LeSeuer St., Mesa 85204 ☎ (964-1981).
Har Zion - Conservative, 5929 E. Lincoln Drive, Paradise Valley 85253 ☎ (991-0720).

SUN CITY AND SUN CITY WEST
Syn.: Beth Emeth of Sun City (C), 13702 Meeker Blvd., Sun City West, 85373. ☎ (602) 584-1953; Beth Shalom of Sun City (R), 12202 101st Av., Sun City, 85351. ☎ (602) 977-3240.

TEMPE
Syn.: Chabad-Lubavitch Center (O), 23 W. 9th St., 85281. ☎ (602) 966-5163; Temple Emanuel (R), 5801 S. Rural Rd., 85283. ☎ (602) 838-1414.
Tri-City Jewish Com. Center, 1965 E. Hermosa Dr., 85282. ☎ (602) 897-0588.

TUCSON
Jewish Fed. of Southern Arizona, 3822 E. River Rd., 85718. ☎ (602) 577-9393.
Syn.: Cong. Chofetz Chayim (O), 5150 E. 5th St., 85711; Young Israel (O), 2443 E. 4th St., 85719; Anshei Israel (C), 5550 E. 5th St., 85711; Cong. Bet Shalom (C), 3881 E. River Rd., 85718; Temple Emanuel (R), 225 N. County Club Rd., 85716.

Kosher Meat and Delicatessen:
Feig's Kosher Foods, 5071 E. 5th St., 85711.

ARKANSAS
EL DORADO
Syn.: Beth Israel (R), 1130 E. Main St.

continued from *Arkansas*

HELENA
Syn.: Temple Beth-El (R), 406 Perry St., 72342. Founded 1875.

HOT SPRINGS
Syn.: House of Israel (R), 300 Quapaw St., 71901.Hot Springs is known for its curative waters. The Leo Levi Memorial Hospital (for joint disorders, such as arthritis) was founded by B'nai B'rith, as was the adjacent Levi Towers, a senior citizen housing project.

LITTLE ROCK
Jewish Fed. of Arkansas, 2821 Kavanaugh, Garden Level., 72205 3868.
☎ (501) 663-3571; Fax (501) 663 7286.
Syn.: Agudath Achim (O), 7901 W. 5th St., 72205.
Mikva & Hebrew School on premises. The only Orthodox syn. in the State of Arkansas open all year round; B'nai Israel (R), 3700 Rodney Parham Rd., 72212., open all year.
Kosher Bakery: André's, 11121 Rodney Parham Rd., 72212.

CALIFORNIA
As the general population of California continues to increase — it now stands at 30,000,000 – the Jewish community has grown to 915,000.
Places of worship abound, from Eureka in the north to San Diego in the south, just a few miles from the Mexican border, but the major part of the community lives and prospers in the Los Angeles metropolitan area. There is an increasing number of truly kosher restaurants and, in addition, 'kosher-style' delicatessens are everywhere. The hungry traveller should bear in mind that English-style 'salt beef' is 'corned beef' in the United States, but most popular European dishes are readily available.
Noah's Bagels Cafes in California are now kosher. Locations available from ☎ (510) 352-6624. Email: noah@noahs.com

ALAMEDA
Syn.: Temple Israel (R), 3183 Mecartney Rd., 94501.

ANAHEIM
Syn: Temple Beth Emet (C), 1770 W. Cerritos Av., 92804. ☎ (714) 772-4720.

ARCADIA
Syn.: Cong. Shaarei Torah (C), 550 S. 2nd Av., 91006. ☎ (818) 445-0810.

ARLETA
Syn.: Temple Beth Solomon of the Deaf (R), 13580 Osborne St., 91331. ☎ (818) 899-2202 or 896-6721 (TDD).

BAKERSFIELD
Syn.: B'nai Jacob (C), 600 17th St., 93301; Temple Beth El (R), 2906 Loma Linda Dr., 93305.

BERKELEY
Syn.: Beth Israel (O), 1630 Bancroft Way, 94703; Chabad Hse. (O), Chabad Hse., 2643 College Av., 94704; Temple Beth El (R), 2301 Vine St., 94708.
Netivot Shalom (C) has services on Sat. morning at the Berkeley-Richmond Jewish Community Center at 1414 Walnut St.
Mikvah Taharas Israel, 2520 Warring St., 94707. ☎ (510) 848-7221.
Hillel Foundation, 2736 Bancroft Way, 94704. ☎ (510) 845-7793. Traditional egalitarian services on Fri. evening.

continued from *California*

Judah L. Magnes Museum — Jewish Museum of the West, 2911 Russell St., 94705, is among the largest institutions of its kind west of New York. It includes the Western Jewish History Center & the Blumenthal Library. ☎ (510) 549 6950; Fax (510) 849 3650. Open Sun-Thurs 10-4.
Lehrhaus Judaica, 2736 Bancroft Way, 94704.
(See also under Oakland.)

BEVERLY HILLS
Note: Beverly Hills, Hollywood and Los Angeles are contiguous communities and in many cases have overlapping bodies.
Syns.: Beth Jacob (O), 9030 Olympic Blvd., 90211; Young Israel of Beverly Hills (O), 8701 W. Pico Blvd., 90211; Temple Emanuel (R), 8844 Burton Way, 90211.

BURLINGAME
Syn.: Peninsula Temple Sholom (R), 1655 Sebastian Dr. 94010. ☎ (415) 697 2266; Fax (415) 697 2544.

CARMEL
Cong. Beth Israel (R), 5716 Carmel Valley Rd., 93923. ☎ (408) 624-2015.

CASTRO VALLEY
Syn.: Shir Ami (R), 4529 Malabar Av., 94546. ☎ (415) 537-1787.

COSTA MESA
Jewish Federation of Orange County, 250 E. Baker St., 92626. ☎ (714) 755-5555. Fax (714) 755-0307.
(K) The Kosher Bite Deli, 23595 Moulton Pkwy, Laguna Hills, 92653. ☎ (714) 770-1818.

DALY CITY
Syn.: B'nai Israel (C), 1575 Annie St., 94015. ☎ (415) 756-5430.

DAVIS
Syn.: Davis Jewish Fellowship (R), 1821 Oak Av., 95616.

DOWNEY
Syn.: Temple Ner Tamid (R), 10629 Lakewood Blvd., Downey 90241. Rabbi R. Ettleston, ☎ (310) 861-9276.

EUREKA
Syn.: Beth El (R), Hodgson & T Sts., P. O. Box 442, 95502. ☎ (707) 444 2846.

FREMONT
Syn.: Temple Beth Torah (R), 42000 Paseo Padre Pkwy., 94539. ☎ (415) 656-7141.

FRESNO
Jewish Fed. Office: 1340, W. Herndon, Suite 103, 93711.
Syn.: Beth Jacob (C), 406 W. Shields Av., 93705; Temple Beth Israel (R), 6622 N. Maroa Av., 93704. This syn. has its own etrog tree, planted from a sprig brought to the United States from the Holy Land.
Chabad House (O) 6735 N. ILA, 93711.

GARDENA
Syn.: Southwest Temple Beth Torah (C), 14725 S. Gramercy Pl., 90249.

GREATER EAST BAY
(See Oakland).

continued from *California*

HOLLYWOOD
Syn.: Young Israel of Los Angeles (O), 660 N. Spaulding Av., 90036;
Hollywood Temple Beth El (C), 137 N. Crescent Heights Blvd., Los Angeles
90046; Temple Israel (R), 7300 Hollywood Blvd., Los Angeles 90046.
Kosher Information Bureau, 15365 Magnolia Blvd., Sherman Oaks, 91403. ☎
(818) 762-3197.

LAFAYETTE
Syn.: Temple Isaiah (R), 3800 Mt. Diablo Blvd., 94549. ☎ (415) 283-8575.

LAKEWOOD
Syn.: Beth Zion-Sinai (C), 6440 Del Amo Blvd., 90713. ☎ (310) 429-0715.

LONG BEACH AREA
Jewish Fed. of Greater Long Beach & W. Orange County, 3801 E. Willow St.,
90815. ☎ (310) 426-7601.
Synagogues:
Cong. Lubavitch (O), 3981 Atlantic Av., 90807; Beth Shalom (C), 3635 Elm
Av., 90807; Cong. Shalom of Leisure World (C), 1661 Golden Rain Rd.,
Northwood Clubhouse No. 3, Seal Beach 90740; Adat Chaverim (C) P.O. Box
662, Los Alamitos 90720; Temple Beth Zion Sinai (C), 6440 Del Amo Blvd.,
90713; Temple Israel (R), 338 E. 3rd St., 90812.; Temple Beth David (R) 6100
Hefley St., Westminster; Young Israel (O), 4134 Atlantic, 90807.
Mikva: 3847 Atlantic Av., 90807.
Newspaper: Jewish Community Chronicle, 3801 E. Willow St., 90815 1791.
Edr.Ms H. Ellis.

LOS ALAMITOS
Fairfax Kosher Market & Bakery, 11196-98 Los Alamitos Blvd., 90720 ☎
(714) 828-4492.

LOS ALTOS HILLS
Syn.: Congregation Beth Am (R), 26790 Arastradero Rd., 94022. ☎ (415)
493-4661.

LOS ANGELES
Los Angeles is America's, and the world's second largest Jewish metropolis,
with a Jewish population of 600,000.
Fairfax Av. and Beverly Blvd. together form the crossroads of traditional
Jewish life while a growing Orthodox enclave Centers around Pico and
Robertson Blvds. Fairfax Av. is lined with Jewish book and gift shops, deli-
catessens and restaurants, and all kinds of small stores.
The most complete selection of books of Jewish interest can probably be found
at House of David, 9020 W. Olympic Blvd., Beverly Hills, 90211. ☎ (310) 276
9414.
The Skirball Museum of Hebrew Union College has an outstanding collection
of Jewish ceremonial art and archaeological artifacts, a photographic record of
destroyed Jewish landmarks in Europe and changing exhibitions.
The Jewish Studies Collection at the University of California, Los Angeles
(UCLA), is the largest of its kind in the western United States, with 180,000
volumes of Judaica and Hebraica. Other major libraries are at the Jewish
Community Building, University of Judaism, University of Southern California
(USC) and the Frances-Henry Library of the Hebrew Union College. The
Wiesenthal Center is a major repository of Holocaust literature.
There are three Jewish weeklies: the 'L.A. Jewish Times', the 'Heritage-

continued from *California*

Southwest Jewish Press,' and the 'Jewish Journal' all published on Fri. 'Jewish News' appears monthly. Others include: Jewish calendar magazine, Yisrael Shelanu, Jewish news and Israel today.
Jewish Fed.-Council of Greater Los Angeles, 6505 Wilshire Blvd., 90048. ☎ (310) 852 7758. Fax (310) 852 8723.
At same address: Bd. of Rabbis of Southern California. Exec. P.: Rabbi Paul Dubin. ☎ (310) 852-1234.
Com. Bldgs.: Los Angeles: Jewish Com. Bldg., 6505 Wilshire Blvd., 90048; West Side Com. Center, 5870 W. Olympic Blvd., 90036. This address also houses the Jewish Centers Assoc. of Los Angeles; and includes a 'hands-on' museum for children.
Hollywood: Los Feliz Center, 1110 Bates Av., 90029; Bay Cities Center, 2601 Santa Monica Blvd., Santa Monica, 90404; South Bay Center, 22401 Palos Verdes Blvd., Torrance 90505; Valley Cities Center, 13164 Burbank Av., Van Nuys, 91401; W.V.J.C.C., 22622 Vanowen, West Hills.
There is a statue of the American Jewish pioneer, Haym Salomon, in the W. Wilshire Recreation Center.

Synagogues:
B'nai David Congregation (O), 8906 W. Pico Blvd., 90035; Breed St. Shule (O), 247 N. Breed St., 90033. This syn. is of historical interest; Chabad House (O), 741 Gayley Av., W. Los Angeles, 90025; Etz Jacob (O), 7659 Beverly Blvd., 90036; Kahal Joseph (Sephardi, O), 10505 Santa Monica Blvd. 90025; Magen David (Sephardi, O), 322 N. Foothill, Beverly Hills, 90210; Mogen David (O), 9717 W. Pico Blvd., 90035; Ohel David (O), 7967 Beverly Blvd.; Ohev Shalom (O), 525 S.Fairfax Av., 90036; Temple Tifereth Israel (Sephardi, O), 10500 Wilshire Blvd., 90024; Young Israel of Hancock Pk. (O), 140 S. La Brea Blvd., 90036; Adat Shalom (C), 3030 Westwood Blvd., 90034; Beth Am (C), 1039 S. La Cienega Blvd., 90035; Sinai Temple (C), 10400 Wilshire Blvd., 90024; Leo Baeck Temple (R), 1300 N. Sepulveda Blvd., 90049; Stephen S. Wise Temple (R), 15500 Stephen S. Wise Dr., Bel Air, 90024; Temple Akiba (R), 5249 S. Sepulveda Blvd., Culver City 90230.
Temple Isaiah (R), 10345 W. Pico Blvd., 90064; University Syn. (R), 11960 Sunset Blvd., 90049; Wilshire Blvd. Temple (R), 3663 Wilshire Blvd., 90010; Kehillath Israel (Reconstructionist), 16019 Sunset Blvd., Pacific Palisades, 90272. Beth Chayim Chadishim (R), 6000 W. Pico Blvd, 90035.
Los Angeles Mikva; 9548 W. Pico Blvd., 90035.

Institutions of Learning:
Hebrew Union College (R), 3077 University Av., 90007; Kollel Bais Avrohom (O), 7466 Beverly Blvd.; Yeshiva Gedolah of Los Angeles (O), 5822 W. 3rd St.; Yeshivah Ohr Elchanon Chabad (O), 808 N. Alta Vista Blvd.; University of Judaism (C), 15600 Mulholland Dr., 90024; Yeshiva University of Los Angeles (O), 9760 W. Pico Blvd., 90035.
The Simon Wiesenthal Center, ☎ (310) 553-9036, is on Yeshiva University campus.
Museum of Tolerance, (Beit Hashoah), 9786 West Pico Blvd. (corner of Pico and Roxbury Drive), 90035. ☎ (310) 553 9036. Fax. (310) 553 4521. Opened in 1993.
Cedars-Sinai Medical Center, 8700 Beverly Blvd., 90048.
Israel Consulate & Govt. Tourist Office: 6380 Wilshire Blvd., 90048.

Kosher Information Bureau: ☎ (818) 762-3197; Fax (818) 980-6908; and
Kashrut Authorities:
Rabbinical Council of California, Att: Rabbi A. Union, 1122 S. Robertson

continued from *California*

Blvd., Los Angeles, CA 90035. ☎ (310) 271-4160. Fax (310) 271-7147.
Board of Rabbis, 6505 Wilshire Blvd., Suite #511, Los Angeles, CA 90048. ☎ (310) 852-7710; Rabbi Bukspan, 6407 Orange St., Los Angeles, CA 90048. ☎ (310) 653-5083.
Note: The RCC is undergoing an upgrading of enforcement of kosher standards. They now claim that all their non-deli meat restaurants use glatt kosher meat exclusively. All restaurants labeled 'Mahadrin' have permanent, on-site kosher supervision. All information supplied and updated as a community service by Rabbi Aaron Simkin ☎ (818) 368-8881.

Hotels with ability to do kosher affairs
– must request kosher supervision.
Bel Air Hotel, West Los Angeles (RCC); Radisson Bel Air Summit, ☎ (310) 476-6571 (RCC); Beverly Grand, ☎ (310) 939-1653 (RCC); Beverly Hilton, Beverley Hills, ☎ (310) 274-7777; Beverly Wilshire, Beverly Hills, ☎ (310) 275-4282 (RCC); Century Plaza, Century City, ☎ (310) 277-2000 (RCC); Four Seasons, LA (RCC) ☎ (310); Hyatt (Airport), Inglewood, ☎ (231) 670-9000 (RCC); La Bel Age, ☎ (310) 854-1111 (RCC); Marriott-Century City, ☎ (310) 277-2777 (RCC); Marriott-Woodland Hills, ☎ (818) 887-4800 (RCC); Ramada-Airport, ☎ (310) 337-2800 (RCC); Sheraton Grand, ☎ (310) 617-1133 (RCC); Universal City Hilton, Universal City, ☎ (310) 617-0666 (RCC); Radisson Hotel, Sherman Oaks, ☎ (818) 981-5400; Westin Boneventure, ☎ (310) 624-1000 (RCC).

Kosher Restaurants & Delicatessens:
Fairfax-La Brea Area: B&B Bagels, 7113 Beverly Blvd., ☎ (310) 933-8844; Berookhim Royal Catering, 324 Marguerita Ave., ☎ (310) 458-9993; Beverly/Fairfax & Downtown; East Side Kosher, 7231 Beverly Blvd., ☎ (310) 936-1653; Cedars-Sinai Cafeteria, 8700 Beverly Blvd., ☎ (310) 855-4541; Dizengoff Restaurant, 8103 Beverly Blvd., ☎ (310) 651-4465 (RCC); Elite Cuisine, 7119 Beverly Blvd., ☎ (310) 930-1303 (RCC); Fish Grill, 7226 Beverly Blvd., ☎ (310) 937-7162; Grill Express, 501 N. Fairfax Av., LA, (310) 655-0649; Judy's, 129 N. Labrea Av., ☎ (310) 934-7667 (RCC-Mehadrin); La Gondola Ristorante, 6405 Wilshire Blvd., ☎ (310) 852-1915; Mosaique, 8146 W. Third St., ☎ (310) 951-1133; Ole's, 7912 Beverly Blvd., ☎ (310) 937-7154; Pico Kosher Deli, 8826 W. Pico Blvd., ☎ 310) 273-9381 (RCC); Pizza Mayven, 140 N. La Brea Area ☎ (310) 857-0353; Pizza World, 365 S. Fairfax Ave., ☎ (310) 653-2896; Rfib Tickler, 533 N. Fairfax Ave., ☎ (310) 655-6333; Simone, 8706 W. Pico Blvd., ☎ (310) 657-5552 (RCC-Mehadrin); Simon's La Glatt, 446 N. Fairfax, ☎ (310) 658 7730; Shula & Esther, 5519 N. Fairfax Ave., ☎ (310) 951 9651.
Kosher Food Services: PS Food Services/World Class Travel 9760 W. Pico Blvd, 90035. ☎ (310) 553 8889. Fax (310) 553 8989 (See inside back cover).
Pico Robertson Area: Berookhim Royal Catering, 6170 Wilbur Ave., ☎ (310) 458-9993; Chick'N Chow, 9301 W. Pico Blvd., ☎ (310) 274-5595; Coffee Brake, 1507 s. Robertson Blvd., ☎ (310) 277-6741; Elat Burger, 9340 W. Pico Blvd., ☎ (310) 278-4692; The Fishing Well, W. Pico Blvd., ☎ (310) 859-9429 (RCC); Glatt Hut, 9303 W. Pico Blvd., ☎ (310) 246-1900; Grill at the Beverly Carlton, 9400 W. Olympic, ☎ (310) 282-0945; Habayit Restaurant, 11921 W. Pico Blvd., ☎ (310) 488-9877; Haifa Restaurant, 8717 W. Pico Blvd., ☎ (310) 550-2704; I'm a Deli, 8930 W. Pico Blvd., ☎ (310) 274-3452; Kosher Pizza Nosh, 8644 W. Pico Blvd., ☎ (310) 276-8708; Micheline's, 2627 S. LaCienega Blvd., ☎ (310) 204-5334 (RCC Mehadrin); Milk N'Honey Fine Dining, 8837 W. Pico Blvd., ☎ (310) 858-8850; The Milky Way, 9108 W. Pico Blvd., ☎ (310) 859-0004; Nagila Pizza, 9216 W. Pico Blvd., ☎ (310) 550-7735; Pat's, 9233 W. Pico Blvd., ☎ (310) 205-8707; Pizza Mayven, 140 N. Labrea Av., ☎

continued from *California*

(310) 847-0353; Rimini Restaurant, 9400 W. Olympic Blvd., ☎ (310) 552-1056; Royal Palate Foods, 960 E. Hyde Park Blvd., ☎ (310) 330-7710; Simon's Gourmet Glatt Caterers, 10505 S. Monica Blvd., ☎ (310) 474-4011; Tami's Fish House, 553 B, Fairfax Av., ☎ (310) 655-7953; Westside Grille, 9411 W. Pico Blvd., ☎ (310) 843-9829.
LA. Downtown: New York Sandwich, 600 W. 9th St., ☎ (310) 623-4623; Sharon's II, 306 E. 9th St., ☎ (310) 622-1010.
See also Beverly Hills, Hollywood, San Fernando Valley and Venice (Cali.).

MODESTO
Syn.: Congregation Beth Shalom (C), 1705 Sherwood Av., 95350. ☎ (209) 522 5613.

NAPA
Syn.: Cong. Beth Sholom (R), 1455 Elm St., 94559. ☎ (707) 253-7305. Services Friday 7.30 p.m. Saturday 10 a.m.

OAKLAND (Greater East Bay)
Jewish Fed. of the Greater East Bay: 401 Grand Av., #500, Oakland 94610.
Museum: Judah L. Magnes Memorial Museum, 2911 Russell St., Berkeley 94705.

Synagogues:
Temple Israel (R), 3183 Mecartney, Alameda 94501; Beth El (R), 2301 Vine, Berkeley 94708; Beth Israel (O), 1630 Bancroft, Berkeley 94704; Netivot Shalom (C), PO Box 12761, Berkeley 94701; Kehilla (Renewal), PO Box 3063, Berkeley, 94703; Aquarian Minyan (JR), c/o Goldfarb, 2020 Essex, Berkeley 94703; Chabad (O), 2643 College Av., Berkeley 94704; Shir Ami (R), 4529 Malabar Av., Castro Valley 94546; Beth Torah (R), 42000 Paseo Padre Parkway, Fremont 94538; Beth Emek (R), PO Box 722, Livermore 94550; Beth Abraham (C), 327 MacArthur Blvd., Oakland 94610; Beth Jacob (O) 3778 Park Blvd., Oakland 94610; Mikvah, ☎ (510) 482-1147.
Temple Sinai (R), 2808 Summit, Oakland 94609; Beth Sholom (C), 642 Dolores, San Leandro 94577; Temple Isaiah (R), 3800 Mt Diablo Blvd., Lafayette 94549; Beth Chaim (I), PO Box 23632, Pleasant Hill 94523; Beth Hillel (R), 801 Park Central, Richmond 94803; B'nai Shalom (C), 74 Eckley Lane, Walnut Creek 94596; B'nai Tikvah (R), 25 Hillcroft Way, Walnut Creek 94596; B'nai Israel of Rossmoor (I), c/o Fred Rau, 2601 Ptarmigan #3, Walnut Creek 94595.
Mikva: Beth Jacob, address as above.
Jewish Com. Centers: Berkeley/Richmond JCC, 1414 Walnut St., Berkeley 94709; Contra Costa JCC, 2071 Tice Valley Blvd., Walnut Creek 94595.
Kosher Delicatessen: Oakland Kosher Foods, 3256 Grand Av., Oakland 94610; Holy Land Restaurant, 677 Rand Av., Oakland 94610. ☎ (510) 272-0535. Glatt kosher.

PALM DESERT
Syn.: Temple Sinai (R), 43-435 Monterey Av., 92260. ☎ (619) 568-9699.

PALM SPRINGS
Jewish Fed. of Palm Springs Desert Area, 611 S. Palm Canyon Dr., 92264. ☎ (619) 325-7281.
Syn.: Temple Isaiah & Jewish Com Center (C), 332 W. Alejo Rd., 92262.
Desert Syn. (O), 1068 N. Palm Canyon Dr., Ca. 92262. ☎ (619) 327-4848.
(K) New York Sandwich, 125 E. Tahquitz. ☎ (619) 323-7883 (Dairy).

continued from *California*

PALO ALTO
Syn.: Cong. Chabad (O), 3070 Louis Rd., 94308. ☎ (415) 429 8444.
Palo Alto Orthodox Minyan (O), 260 Sheridan Av., 94306. ☎ (415) 326-5001; Kol Emeth (C), 4175 Manuela Av., 94306. ☎ (415) 948-7498.
The Albert L. Schultz Com. Center is at 655 Arastradero Rd., 94306. ☎ (415) 493 9400.

Delicatessen, etc.
(K) Mollie Stone's Markets, 164 South California Avenue. ☎ (415) 323-8361.
(V) Garden Fresh, 1245 W. El Camino Road, Mt. View, 94040. ☎ (415) 961-7795.

PASADENA
Syn.: Jewish Temple & Center (C): 1434 N. Altadena Dr., 91107. Rabbi Gilbert Kollin. ☎ (818) 798 1161.

POMONA
Syn.: Temple Beth Israel (R), 3033 N. Towne Av., 91767. ☎ (714) 626-1277.

RICHMOND
Syn.: Temple Beth Hillel (R), 801 Park Central, 94803. ☎ (51) 223 2560.

RIVERSIDE
Syn.: Temple Beth El (R), 2675 Central Av., 92506. ☎ (909) 684 4511.

ROHNERT PARK
Syn.: Sonama County Syn. Center (Reconstructionist), 4627 Snyder La., 94928. ☎ (707) 664-8622.

SACRAMENTO
Jewish Fed. of Sacramento, 2351 Wyda Way, 95825. ☎ (916) 486-0906.
Syn.: Kenesset Israel Torah Center (O), 1024 Morse Av., 95864. ☎ (916) 481-1159; Mosaic Law (C), 2300 Sierra Blvd., 95825 ☎ (916) 488-1122.; Beth Shalom (R), 4746 El Camino Av., 95608 ☎ (916) 485-4478.
B'nai Israel (R), 3600 Riverside Blvd., 95818. ☎ (916) 446-4861.
Sunrise Jewish Congregation, 8741 Auburn Folsom Blvd., Granite Bay, 95746. ☎ (916) 791-8975.
Congregation Bet Haverim-Davis 1821 Oak Av., 95616, ☎ (916) 758-0842.
Com. Center: Same address & ☎ as Jewish Fed. below.
Restaurant: (K) Farah's Catering & Fine Foods, 2319 El Camino Av., 95821. ☎ (916) 971-9500.
Bob's Butcher Block & Deli, 6436 Fair Oaks Blvd., Carmichael, 95608.

SALINAS
Syn.: Temple Beth El (R), 1212 S. Riker St., 93901. ☎ (408) 424-9151.

SAN BERNARDINO
Syn.: Emanu El (R), 3512 N. 'E' St., 92405. ☎ 886-4818.
The Congregation, established in 1851, is the oldest in Southern California.
The city's central library is named in honour of Rabbi Norman F. Feldheym, who was the rabbi of Temple Emanu-El from 1937 to 1971.
The 'Home of Eternity' cemetery, at 8th St. & Sierra Way, presented by the Mormons, is one of the oldest Jewish cemeteries in the western U.S.A. Here lies buried Wolf Cohn, believed for many years to have been the first Jew to be scalped by the Red Indians. He was in fact shot dead in 1862 by a drunken man described by a contemporary San Bernardino newspaper as "a noted desperado".

continued from *California*

SAN DIEGO AREA

United Jewish Fed. of San Diego County, 4797 Mercury St., 92111-2101. ☎ (619) 571-3444. Fax (619) 571-0701. Publishes a Jewish Directory.

Synagogues

Beth Jacob Cong. (O), 4855 College Av., 92115. ☎ (619) 287-9890; Beth Eliyahu Torah Center. (O), 5012 Central Av., Bonita, 91902. ☎ (619) 472 2144; Chabad Hse. (O), 6115 Montezuma Rd., 92115. ☎ (619) 265-7700; Chabad of La Costa (O), 1980 La Costa Av., Carlsbad, 92009. ☎ (619) 943 8891; Chabad of La Jolla (O), 3232 Governor Dr., Suite N, 92122. ☎ (619) 455-1670; Chabad of Rancho Bernardo (O), 16934 Old Espola Rd., Poway, 92064. ☎ (619) 451-0455; Cong. Adat Yeshurun (O), 8950 Villa La Jolla Dr., Suite 1224, La Jolla, 92037. ☎ (619) 535-1196; Young Israel of San Diego (O), 7290 Navajo Rd., Suite 102, Ca 92119. ☎ (619) 589-1447. Cong. Adat Ami (C), 123 Camino de la Reina, Suite N100, 92108. ☎ (619) 220-8888. Cong. Beth Am (C), 525 Stevens Av., Solana Beach, 92075. ☎ (619) 481-8454; Cong. Beth El (C), 8660 Gilman Dr., La Jolla, 92037. ☎ (619) 452-1734; Cong. Beth Tefilah (C), 4967 69th St., 92115. ☎ (619) 463-0391; Cong. Ner Tamid (C) 16981 Via Tazon, Suite G. 92127. ☎ (619) 592 9141; Temple Beth Sholom (C), 208 Madrona St., Chula Vista, 91910. ☎ (619) 420-6040; Temple Judea (C), 1527 Roma Dr., Vista, 92083. ☎ (619) 724-8318; Tifereth Israel (C), 6660 Cowles Mountain Blvd., 92119. ☎ (619) 697-6001; Cong. Beth Israel (R), 2512 3rd Av., 92103. ☎ (619) 239-0149; Cong. Etz Chaim (R), PO Box 1138 Ramona 92065. ☎ (619) 789 8117; Temple Adat Shalom (R), 15905 Pomerado Rd., Poway, 92064. ☎ (619) 451-1200; Temple Emanu-El (R), 6299 Capri Dr., 92120. ☎ (619) 286-2555; Temple Solel (R), 552 S. El Camino Real, Encinitas, 92024. ☎ (619) 436-0654; Cong. Dor Hadash (Rec), 4858 Ronson Ct., Suite A., 92111. ☎ (619) 268-3674.

Com. Centers: Lawrence Family Jewish Com. Ctr., Central Office, 4201 Eastgate Mall, La Jolla, 92037. ☎ (619) 457-3161; 4126 Executive Dr., La Jolla, 92037. ☎ (619) 457-3030; 552 S. El Camino Real, Encinitas, 92024 (North County branch). ☎ (619) 944-0640.

San Diego Hebrew Homes, 4075 54th St., 92105. ☎ (619) 582 5168; Seacrest Village, 211 Saxony Rd., Encinitas 92024. ☎ (619) 632 0081.

Jewish Campus Centers, 5742 Montezuma Rd., 92115. ☎ (619) 583-6080.

Balboa Park, the largest public park in San Diego, includes the House of Pacific Relations, which comprises 30 cottages for various ethnic groups. These include the Cottage of Israel, which mounts exhibitions throughout the year, portraying the history & traditions of the Jewish people, & of biblical and modern Israel. Open Sun. 1.30 p.m. to 4.30 p.m., except on Holy-days & major festivals.

Newspapers

'Heritage', 3443 Camino Del Rio S., Suite 315, 92108. ☎ (619) 282-7177; 'San Diego Jewish Times', 4731 Palm Ave., La Niesa 91941. ☎ (619) 463-5515.

Restaurants, etc.

City Delicatessen, 6th Av. & University Av., 92103. ☎ (619) 295-2747; Croce's Restaurant-Jazz Bar, 802 5th Av. (at "F" St.), 92101. ☎ (619) 233-4355; D.Z. Akin's Deli, 6930 Alvarado Rd., 92120. ☎ (619) 265-0218; **(K)** **(K)** Eva's Fresh and Natural, 6717 El Cajon Blvd., 92115. ☎ (619) 462-5018; Lang's, 6165 El Cajon Blvd., 92115. ☎ (619) 287-7306; **(K)** Mossarella's Vegetarian Restaurant & Pizerria, 6366 El Cajon Blvd., 92115, ☎ (619) 583

continued from *California*

1636; **(K)** Western Glatt Kosher & N.Y. Deli, 7739 Fay Av., La Jolla, 92037. ☎ (619) 454-6328.

SAN FERNANDO VALLEY

The Adat Ari El Synagogue is at 5540 Laurel Canyon Blvd., N. Hollywood, 91607. In the David Familian Chapel at the syn. are eleven beautiful stained-glass windows, designed by Mischa Kallis, depicting significant dates in the religious calendar.

Other synagogues in the Valley (which is about 12 miles from Hollywood) include:

Chabad Hse. (O), 4917 Hayvenhurst, Encino, 91346; Shaarey Zedek (O), 12800 Chandler Blvd., N. Hollywood, 91607; 7401 Shoup Av., Canoga Park; Beth Meier Cong. (C), 11725 Moorpark, Studio City; Ner Maarev Temple (C), 5180 Yarmouth Av., Encino, 91316; Temple Aliyah (C), 24400 Aliyah Way, Woodland Hills, 91367; Shomrei Torah (C) at Valley Circle, West Hills. ☎ (818) 346-0811; Temple B'nai Hayim (C), 4302 Van Nuys Blvd., Sherman Oaks; Temple Emanu-El (C), 1302 N. Glenoaks Av., Burbank, 91504; Temple Ramat Zion (C), 17655 Devonshire Av., Northridge; Valley Beth Shalom (C), 15739 Ventura Blvd., Encino, 91316; Beth Emet (R), 320 E. Magnolia Blvd., Burbank, 91502; Temple Ahavat Shalom (R), 11261 Chimineas Av., Northridge; Temple Judea (R), 5429 Lindley Av., Tarzana.
Shir Chadash (R) 17000 Ventura Blvd., Encino.
Mikva: Teichman Mikvah Soc., 12800 Chandler Blvd., N. Hollywood, 91607. ☎ (818) 506-0996.
Aish Hatorah College of Jewish Studies, 6348 Whitsett Av., N. Hollywood, 91607.
Emek Hebrew Academy, 12753 Chandler Blvd., N. Hollywood, 91607.
The Kashrus Information Bureau, Rabbinic Administrator, Rabbi Eliezer Eidlitz, is also at the above address. ☎ (818) 762-3197

Jewish Community Centers:

North Valley Center, 16601 Rinaldi St., Granada Hills, 91344; Valley Cities Center, 13164 Burbank Blvd., Van Nuys, 91401; West Valley Center, 22622 Vanowen St., West Hills, 91307.

All the restaurants & delicatessens listed below are under rabbinical supervision.

Kosher Restaurants:

(K) Apropo Falafel, 6800 Reseda Blvd., ☎ (818) 881-6608; **(K)** Carvel's Ice Cream, 25948 McBean Parkway, Valencia (805) 259-1450 (KOF-K); **(K)** Continental Kosher Bakery, 12419 Burbank Blvd., ☎ (818) 762-5005; **(K)** Drexler's Kosher Restaurant, 12519 Burbank Blvd., N. Hollywood, (818) 984-1160; **(K)** Falafel Village, 16060 Ventura Bl., ☎ (818) 783 1012; **(K)** Falafel Express, 5577 Reseda Bl., ☎ (818) 345 5660; **(K)** Flora Falafel, 12450 Burbank Blvd., No. Hollywood, (818) 766-6567 (RCC); **(K)** Golan, 6361 Woodman Av., Van Nuys, (818) 989-5423 (RCC-Mehadrin); **(K)** Hadar, 12514 Burbank Blvd., N. Hollywood, (818) 762-1155; **(K)** La Pizza, 12515 Burbank Blvd., N. Hollywood, (818) 760-8198; **(K)** Orly Dairy Restaurnt + Pizza, 12454 Magnolia Blvd., ☎ (818) 508-5570; **(K)** Pacific Kosher Pizza, 12460 Oxnard, ☎ (818) 760-0087; **(K)** Sam's Kosher Bakery, 12450 Burbank, ☎ (818) 769-8352; **(K)** Sharon's Kosher Restaurant, 18608 1/2 Ventura Blvd., Tarzana, ☎ (818) 344-7472; **(K)** Sportsman's Lodge, Sherman Oaks, (818) 984-0202; **(K)** Tiberias, 18046 Ventura Blvd., Encino, (818) 343-3705; **(K)** Ventura Kosher Market, 18357 Ventura Blvd., ☎ (818) 881-3777.

continued from *California*

SAN FRANCISCO
Jewish Com. Fed. of San Francisco, the Peninsula, Marin & Sonoma Counties, 121 Steuart St., 94105. ☎ (415) 777-0411. Fax (415) 495-6635. Publishes 'Resource guide to the Bay Area' and 'Resource guide to Jewish life in Northern California'.

Marin Jewish Community Center, 200 N. San Pedro Road, San Rafael, 94903. ☎ 479-2000.

Albert L. Schultz Jewish Community Center, 655 Arastradero Road, Palo Alto, 94306. ☎ 493-9400.

Jewish Com. Museum; same address as Jewish Com. Fed. ☎ 543-8880

Jewish Com. Information & Referral, same address as Jewish Com. Fed. ☎ (415) 777-4545.

San Francisco Jewish Com. Center: 3200 California St., 94118. ☎ 346-6040

Brotherhood Way Com. Center, 655 Brotherhood Way, 94132. ☎ 334-7474

Peninsula Com. Center, 2440 Carlmont Dr., Belmont, 94002. ☎ 591-4438.

Jewish Family & Children's Service Agency, 1600 Scott St., 94115 ☎ 564-8860.

Synagogues:
Adath Israel (O), 1851 Noriega St., 94122. ☎ 564-5665; Anshey Sfard (O), 1500 Clement St., 94118. ☎ 752-4979; Chabad House (O), 11 Tillman Pl., 94108. ☎ 956-8644; Chevra Thilim (O), 751 25th Av., 94121. ☎ 752-2866; Keneseth Israel (O), Suite 203 655 Sutter Street, 94102. ☎ 771-3420. A downtown synagogue offering meals over Shabbat.

Magain David (Sephardi, O), 351 4th Av., 94118. ☎ 752-9095; Torat Emeth (O), 768 27th Av., 94121. ☎ 386-1830; Beth Sholom (C), 14th Av. & Clement St., 94118. ☎ 221-8736; B'nai Emunah (C), 3595 Taraval St. 94116 ☎ 664-7373; Ner Tamid (C), 1250 Quintara St., 94116. ☎ 661-3383; Beth Israel-Judea (C-R), 625 Brotherhood Way, 94132. ☎ 586-8833.

Young Israel (O), 1806-A Noriega St., 94122. ☎ 752-7333; Sha'ar Zahav (R), 220 Danvers St. 94114 ☎ 861-6932; Sherith Israel (R), 2266 California St., 94118. ☎ 346-1720; Emanu-El (R), Arguello Blvd. & Lake St., 94118. ☎ 751-2535.

Mikva, 3355 Sacramento St., 94118. ☎ (415) 921-4070.

Board of Rabbis of Northern California, 121 Steuart St., Suite 403, 94105. ☎ 788-3630

Bureau of Jewish Education & Jewish Com. Library, 639 14th Av., 94118. ☎ 751-6983

Hillel Foundation, 33 Banbury St., 94132. ☎ 334 4440

Holocaust Library & Research Center, 601 14th Av., 94118. ☎ 751-6040

Jewish Home for Aged, 302 Silver Av., 94112.

Mt. Zion Hospital, 1600 Divisadero St., 94115.

Kosher Delicatessen, Meat & Poultry:
Tel Aviv Strictly Kosher Meats, 2495 Irving St., 94122, ☎ (415) 661-7588. Under supervision of Orthodox Rabbinical Council. Kosher meals are available at the Kosher Nutrition Kitchen, Montefiore Senior Center, 3200 California Av., and through Gourmet Kosher Meals, cooked and prepared in the kitchens of Cong. Adath Israei (O), 1851 Noriega St., 94122. Further inf. about Kosher meals etc. from Board of Rabbis of Northern California.

Kosher Meat Israel & Cohen Kosher Meats, 5621 Geary Blvd., 94121, ☎ 752-3064; Grill Middle Eastern Cuisine, 430 Geary St., ☎ (415) 749-0201.

Jacob Kosher Meats, 2435 Noriega St., 94122. ☎ 564-7482.

Jerusalem, 420 Geary (at Mason), 94108. ☎ 776-2683. Under Rabbinic supervision of Cong. Thilim.

continued from *California*

Lotus Garden, 532 Grant Av., 94108. ☎ (415) 397-0130.
This is It (Middle Eastern cuisine), 430 Geary St., 94210. ☎ (415) 749-0201.

SAN JOSE
Jewish Fed. of Greater San Jose, 14855 Oka Rd., Los Gatos 95030. ☎ (408) 358-3033; Fax (408) 356 0733.

Synagogues:
Ahavas Torah (O), 1537-A Meridian Av., 95125, ☎ (408) 266 2342; Almaden Valley Torah Center (O), 1281 Juli Lynn Dr., 95120, ☎ (408) 997 9117; Congregation Am Echad (O), 1504 Meridian Av., 95125, ☎ (408) 267 2591; Congregation Beth David (C), 19700 Prospect Rd., Saratoga, 95070, ☎ (408) 257 3333; Congregation Emeth (C), P. O. Box 1430, Gilroy, 95021, ☎ (408) 847 4111; Congregation Sinai (Traditional), 1532 Willowbrae Av., 95125, ☎ (408) 264 8542; Congregation Shir Hadash (R), 16555 Shannon Road, Los Gatos, 95032, ☎ (408) 358 1751; Temple Beth Sholom (R), 2270 Unit D, Canoas Garden Av., 95153, ☎ (408) 978 5566; Temple Emanu-El (R), 1010 University Av., 95126, ☎ (408) 292 0939.
Com. Center, 14855 Oka Rd., Los Gatos, 95030. ☎ (408) 358-3636.
Alef Bet Judaica, 14103-0 Winchester Blvd, Los Gatos, 95030. ☎ (408) 370 1818.

Kosher Delicatessen
(K) Willow Glen Kosher Deli, 1185 Lincoln Av., 95125. ☎ (408) 297-6604. Under Rabinical supervision.
(V) White Lotus, 80 North Market St., ☎ (408) 977-0540.

SAN RAFAEL (Marin County)
Syn.: Rodef Sholom (R), 170 N. San Pedro Rd., 94903.

SANTA BARBARA
Syn.: Young Israel of Santa Barbara (O), 1826C Cliff Dr., 93109. ☎ (805) 966-4565.
Cong. B'nai B'rith (R), 900 San Antonio Creek Rd., 93111.

SANTA MONICA
Syn.: Chabad Hse. (O), 1428 17th St., 90404; Beth Sholom (R), 1827 California Av., 90403.

SANTA ROSA
Syn.: Com. Center, Beth Ami (C), 4676 Mayette Av., 95405. ☎ (707) 545-4334. Dairy kitchen on premises; Shomrei Torah (R), Services at United Methodist Church, 1717 Yulupa Av., 95405. ☎ (707) 578-5519.

SARATOGA
Syn.: Cong. Beth David (C), 19700 Prospect Rd. at Scully, 95070-3352. ☎ (408) 257-3333.

STOCKTON
Stockton is one of the oldest communities west of the Mississippi River, founded in the days of the California Gold Rush. Temple Israel was founded as Congregation Ryhim Ahoovim in 1850 and erected its first building in 1855.
Syn, Temple Israel (R), 5105 N. El Dorado St., 95207.

SUNNYVALE
School: S. Peninsula Hebrew Day School, 1030 Astoria Dr., 94087. Kashrut & com. inf. from the Principal, Rabbi Yitchak Young.

continued from *California*

THOUSAND OAKS
Syn.: Temple Etz Chaim (C), 1080 E. Janss Rd., 91360. Hebrew School on premises. Kosher catering. Inf. from Rabbi Shimon Paskow. ☎ (805) 497-6891; Fax (805) 497 0086. Synagogue contains unique artistic Aron Kodesh & Holocaust memorial.

TIBURON
Syn.: Cong. Kol Shofar (C), 215 Blackfield Dr., Tiburon 94920. ☎ (415) 388-1818.

TUSTIN
Syn.: Cong. B'nai Israel (C), 655 S. "B" St., 92680. ☎ (714) 259-0655.

VALLEJO
Syn.; Cong. B'nai Israel (unaffiliated), 1256 Nebraska St., 94590 ☎ (707) 642-6526.

VENICE
Syn.: Pacific Jewish Center Syn. (O), 505 Ocean Front Walk, 90291. ☎ (310) 392-8749; Pacific Jewish Center (O), 720 Rose Av., 90291. ☎ (310) 392-8749. The Center has a mikva and an elementary day school with summer camp facilities for visitors. It also offers a full range of kosher food, bakery products and meat, as well as accom.; Mishkon Tephilo (C), 206 Main St., 90291.

VENTURA
Syn.: Ventura County Jewish Council-Temple Beth Torah (R), 7620 Foothill Rd., 93004. ☎ (805) 647-4181.
Jewish Community Centre, 259 Callens Road, ☎ (805) 658-7441.

WALNUT CREEK
Syn.: Cong. B'nai Shalom (C), 74 Eckley Lane, 94595; Cong. B'nai Tikvah (R), 25 Hillcroft Way, 94595.
Contra Costa Jewish Com. Center (C), 2071 Tice Valley Blvd., 94595.

WHITTIER
Syn.: Beth Shalom Syn. Center (C), 14564 E. Hawes St., 90604. ☎ (310) 914-8744.

COLORADO
BOULDER
Synagogues:
Congregation Har Hashem (R), 3950 Baseline Road, 80303. ☎ (303) 499 7077; Congregation Bonai Shalom (C), 1527 Cherryvale Rd., 80303, ☎ (303) 442 6605. Call for home hospitality. Services Friday evening, Saturday morning 9.30 a.m., All Holidays; Jewish Renewal Community of Boulder (R), 5001 Pennsylvania, 80303, ☎ (303) 271 3541. Meets third Friday each month; Lubavitch of Boulder County (O), 4900 Sioux Dr., 80303, ☎ (303) 494 1638. Call for home hospitality.
Hillel Foundation, University of Colorado. Dir.: Cynthia Fisher. 2795 Colorado Av., ☎ (303) 442 6571.

COLORADO SPRINGS
Syn.: Chabad Hse. (O), 3465 Nonchalant Circle, 80909. ☎ 596-7330; Temple Shalom (C-R), 1523 E. Monument St., 80909.
Reform services are held on Fri. evg. & Conservative services on Sat. morn. ☎ 634-5311. There is a Jewish chapel at the U.S. Air Force Academy.

continued from *Colorado*

DENVER
Allied Jewish Fed. of Colorado, 300 S. Dahlia St., 80222. ☎ (303) 321-3399
Fax (303) 322-8328.
Robert E. Loup, Jewish Community Centre, 350 S. Dahlia St., 80222. ☎ (303)
399-2660.

Synagogues:
Bais Medrash Kehillas Yaakov (O), 295 S. Locust St., 80222. ☎ (303) 377-
1200; B.M.H. Cong. (T), 560 S. Monaco Pkwy., 80222; E. Denver Syn. (O),
198 S. Holly, 80222. ☎ 322-7943; Hebrew Educational Alliance (C), 6445
East Ohio #200, 80224. ☎ (303) 331-6950; Zera Israel (O), 3934 W. 14th Av.
at Perry, 80204 ☎ (303) 825-5919; Rodef Shalom (C), 450 S. Kearney, 80224;
Cong. Temple Emanuel (R), 51 Grape St., 80220; Temple Micah (R), 2600
Leyden St., 80207; Temple Sinai (R), 3509 S. Glencoe St., 80237. ☎ (303)
359-1827; Colorado Jewish Reconstructionist Fed. (Rec.), 6445 E. Ohio,
80224. ☎ (303) 388-4441; Zera Abraham Congregation (O), 1560 Winona
Ct., 80204. ☎ (303) 825-7517.
Mikveh, 1404 Quitman, 80204. ☎ (303) 893-5315.
Vaad Hakashrus, 1350 Vrain, 80204. ☎ ((303) 595-9349.
Rocky Mountain Rabbinic Council c/o B'nai Havarah, 6445 East Ohio Ave.,
80224. ☎ (303) 388-4441.
Synagogue Council of Greater Denver, PO Box 102732, 80250. ☎ (303) 759
8484.
Com. Center, 4800 E. Alameda Av., 80222 (the Com. Center also operates a
kosher children's camp); Jewish Family & Children's Service, 1335 S.
Colorado Blvd., Building C-800, 80222. ☎ (303) 759-4890; Rose Medical
Center, 4567 E. 9th Av., 80220.
Newspaper: Intermountain Jewish News (weekly), 1275 Sherman Ave.,
80203. ☎ (303) 861-2234. Fax (303) 832-6942.
Kosher Delicatessen: B & J's Utica Grocery & Deli, 4500 W. Colfax Av., 80204.
Shomer Shabbat; Steinberg's Kosher Grocery, 4017 W. Colfax Av., 80204. ☎
(303) 534-0314. Glatt kosher. Under supervision of Denver Vaad Hakashrus.

Kosher Restaurants:
East-Side Kosher Deli, Inc., 5475 Leetsdale Dr., 80222. ☎ (303) 322-9862;
Elegance by Andrew, 745 Quebec St., 80220. ☎ (303) 322-9862; Johnny's
Pizza, 9345, Monaca Pkwy, ☎ (303) 399-6666; Mediterranean Cafe, 2817 E.
3rd Av., 80206. ☎ (303) 399-2940.

LITTLETON
Syn.: Beth Shalom (C), 2280 E. Noble Pl., 80121. ☎ (303) 794-6643.

PUEBLO
Syn.: United Hebrew Cong. (C), 106 W. 15th St., 81003; Temple Emanuel (R),
1325 Grand Av., 81003.

CONNECTICUT

BRANFORD
Jewish Center, Svea Av., 06405.

BRIDGEPORT
Jewish Fed. of Greater Bridgeport, 4200 Park Av., 06604. ☎ (203) 372-6504.
Serving Bridgeport, Easton, Fairfield, Monroe, Shelton, Stratford and
Trumball.
Bridgeport Va'ad, 1571 Stratfield Rd, Fairfield, 06432. ☎ (203) 372-6529.

continued from *Connecticut*

Synagogues:

Agudas Achim (O), 85 Arlington St. 06606; Ahavath Achim (O), 1571 Stratfield Rd., Fairfield, 06432; Bikur Cholim (O), Park & Capitol Avs., 06604; Shaare Torah Adath Israel (O), 3050 Main St., 06606; B'nai Torah (C), 5700 Main St., Trumbull, 06611; Cong. Beth El (C), 1200 Fairfield Woods Rd., Fairfield, 06430; Rodeph Sholom (C), 2385 Park Av., 06604; Temple B'nai Israel (R), 2710 Park Av., 06604; Cong. Shirei Shalom (Rec), P.O. Box 372, Monroe, 06468.

Mikveh Israel, 1326 Stratfield Rd., Fairfield, 06432.

Com. Center: 4200 Park Av., 06604. ☎ (203) 372-6567.

Jewish Family Service, 2370 Park Ave, 06604. ☎ (203) 366-5438.

Seymour Hollander Housing for Elderly, 4190 Park Ave, 06604. ☎ (203) 374-7868.

Jewish Home for the Elderly, 175 Jefferson St., Fairfield 060432. ☎ (203) 374-9461.

Restaurant: 'Cafe Shalom' and catering by Abel c/o Community Center, ☎ 203-372-6567.

Radio: WVOF Radio, c/o Fairfield University, Fairfield 06430. ☎ (203) 254-4111. Jewish public affairs show on Sundays at 7pm on 88.5FM.

Newspaper: Bridgeport Jewish Ledger c/o Jewish Federation, ☎ (203) 372-6504.

DANBURY

Syn.: Cong. B'nai Israel (C), 193 Clapboard Ridge Rd., Danbury 068111. ☎ (203) 792-6161; United Jewish Center (R), 141 Deer Hill Av., Danbury 06810. ☎ (203) 748-3355.

The Jewish Fed. 105 Newtown Rd., 06810. ☎ (203) 792-6353. Fax (203) 748-5099. Publishes a monthly newspaper.

DERBY

Syn.: Beth Israel Syn. Center (C), 300 Elizabeth St., 06418, ☎ (203) 734-3361.

HAMDEN

Syn.: Beth Sholom (C), 1809 Whitney Av., 06517, ☎ (203) 288-7748; Temple Mishkan Israel (R), 785 Ridge Rd., 06514.

Kosher Restaurant & Delicatessen: Abel's, 2100 Dixwell Av., 06514. Under rabbinical supervision.

HARTFORD

Jewish Fed. of Greater Hartford, 333 Bloomfield Av., W. Hartford, 06117. ☎ (203) 232 4483. Publishes 'All things Jewish', an independent resource guide to Connecticut.

Kashrut Commission, 162 Brewster Rd., West Hartford, 06117, ☎ (203) 563-4017.

Synagogues:

Agudas Achim (O), 1244 N. Main St., W. Hartford, 06117; Beth David (O), 20 Dover Rd., W. Hartford, 06119, ☎ (203) 236-1241; Chabad House of Greater Hartford (O), 798 Farmington Av., W. Hartford, 06119; Teferes Israel (O), 27 Brown St., Bloomfield, 06002; United Synagogue of Greater Hartford, (O), 840 N. Main St., W. Hartford, 06117; Young Israel of Hartford (O), 1137 Troutbrook Dr., W. Hartford, 06119; Young Israel of West Hartford (O), 2240 Albany Av., W. Hartford, 06117; Beth El (C), 2626 Albany Av., W. Hartford 06117; Beth Tefilah (C), 465 Oak St., E. Hartford, 06118; B'nai Sholom (C), 26 Church St., Newington, 06111; Temple Emanuel (C), 160 Mohegan Dr.,

continued from *Connecticut*

W. Hartford, 06117; Beth Israel (R), 701 Farmington Av., W. Hartford, 06119; Temple Sinai (R), 41 W. Hartford Rd., Newington, 06011.
Mikva: 61 N. Main St., W. Hartford, 06119.
Com. Center: 335 Bloomfield Av., W. Hartford, 06117.
Hebrew Academy, 53 Gabb Rd., Bloomfield, 06002.
Bookshop: Israel Gift Shop/Hebrew Book Store, 262 S. Whitney St., 06105. ☎ (203) 232-3984.
For kosher meal & Shabbat arrangements, contact Chabad Hse. above.

MANCHESTER
Syn.: Temple Beth Sholom (C), 400 Middle Turnpike E., 06040. ☎ (860) 643 9563.

MERIDEN
Syn.: B'nai Abraham (C), 127 E. Main St., 06450.

MIDDLETOWN
Syn.: Adath Israel (C), 48 Church St., 06457.

NEW BRITAIN
Syn.: Tephereth Israel (O), 76 Winter St., 06051; B'nai Israel (C), 265 W. Main St., 06051.

NEW HAVEN
Jewish Fed. of Greater New Haven, 360 Amity Rd., Woodbridge Ct. 06525. ☎ (203) 387-2424.
Syn.: Beth-Hamedrosh Westville (O), 74 West Prospect St., 06515, ☎ (203) 389-9513.
Young Israel of New Haven (O), 292 Norton St., 06511, ☎ (203) 776-4212.
Beth-El Keser Israel (C), 85 Harrison St., 06515, ☎ (203) 389-2108.
Mikva: 86 Hubinger St., 06511. ☎ (203) 387-2184.
Com. Center, 360 Amity Rd., Woodbridge, Ct. 06525. ☎ (203) 387-2522.
Jewish Historical Society of New Haven, 169 Davenport Ave.,, 06519. ☎ (203) 787-3183.
Yale University has a large collection of Judaica, housed in the Sterling Memorial Library. ☎ (203) 432-2798.
Kosher Snacks and Delicatessen
(K) Fox's Deli, and (K) Westville Kosher Bakery, 1460 Whalley Av., 06515, ☎ (203) 387-2214, ☎ (203) 397-0839.
Zackey's, 1304 Whalley Av., 06515. ☎ (203) 387-2454.
(K) Westville Kosher Meat Market, 95 Amity Rd., 06525. ☎ (203) 389 1723.

NEW LONDON
Jewish Fed. of Eastern Conn., 28 Channing St., 06320. ☎ (203) 442-8062.
Syn.: Ahavath Chesed (O), 590 Montauk Av., 06320 ☎ (203) 442 3234; Cong. Beth El (C), 660 Ocean Av., 06320.

NORWALK
Jewish Fed. of Greater Norwalk, Shorehaven Rd., E. Norwalk, 06855. ☎ (203) 853-3440.
Syn.: Beth Israel (O), 40 King St., 06851; Beth El (C), 109 E. Av., 06851. This synagogue contains a number of religious frescoes painted by Raymond Katz; Temple Shalom (R), Richards Av., 06850.

NORWICH
Syn.: Brothers of Joseph (O), Broad & Washington Avs., 06360. Mikva attached. ☎ (203) 887-3777.

continued from *Connecticut*

Beth Jacob (C), 400 New London Turnpike, 06360.

ORANGE
Syn.: Or Shalom (C), 205 Old Grassy Hill Rd., 06477, ☎ (203) 799-2341; Temple Emanuel (R), 150 Derby Av., 06477.

STAMFORD
United Jewish Fed., 1035 Newfield Av., 06905. ☎ (203) 321-1373.
All things Jewish (magazine) 39, Regent Court, 06907. ☎ (203) 322-2840.
Syn.: Agudath Shalom (O), 301 Strawberry Hill Av., 06902. ☎ (203) 358 2200; Young Israel of Stamford (O), 69 Oaklawn Av., 06905; Beth El (C), 350 Roxbury Rd., 06902; Temple Sinai (R), 434 Lakeside Dr., 06903.
Kosher Delicatessen: Nosherye, JCC Bldg., 1035 Newfield Av., 06905.

WALLINGFORD
Syn.: Beth Israel Cong. (C), 22 N. Orchard St., 06492, ☎ (203) 269-5983.

WATERBURY
Jewish Fed. of Greater Waterbury, 73 Main St., South Woodbury, 06798. ☎ (203) 263-5121.
Syn.: Beth El (C), 359 Cooke St., 06710; Temple Israel (R), 100 Williamson Dr., 06710.

WEST HAVEN
Syn.: Sinai (C), 426 Washington Av, 06517.

WESTPORT
Syn.: Temple Israel (R), 14 Coleytown Rd., 06880.

WILLIMANTIC
Syn.: B'nai Israel (C),·345 Jackson St., 06226.

WOODBRIDGE
Syn.: B'nai Jacob (C), 75 Rimmon Rd., 06525. ☎ 389 2111.
Center Cafe and Jewish Library, 360 Amity Rd., 06525. ☎ (203) 387-2424.

DELAWARE

DOVER
Syn.: Cong. Beth Sholom of Dover, P.O. Box 223, Dover, DE 19903.

NEWARK
Syn.: Temple Beth El, 101 Possum Pk. Rd., Newark De19711.

WILMINGTON
Syn.: Adas Kodesh Shel Emeth (O), Washington Blvd. & Torah Dr., 19802; Beth Shalom (C), 18th St. and Baynard Blvd., 19802; Beth Emeth (R), 300 W. Lea Blvd., 19802.
Jewish Com Center, 101 Garden of Eden Road. Wilmington, 19803 ☎ (302) 478-5660. Fax (302) 478 6068.

DISTRICT OF COLUMBIA
WASHINGTON
Communal & Cultural Organisations
Jewish Com. Council of Greater Washington. Publishes a Directory of Jewish Organisations in Greater Washington.

continued from *District of Columbia*

American Israel Public Affairs Committee, Suite 412, 500 N. Capitol St. N.W., 20001.
A memorial to Oscar S. Straus, the first Jew to serve in the U.S. Cabinet, is in front of the Commerce Dept. Bldg., 1st St. & Constitution Av.
The Samuel Gomperts Memorial, corner 10th St. & Massachusetts Av. of the American Federation of Labour. He was English-born.
George Washington University B'nai B'rith Hillel Foundation, 2300 "H" St., 20037. ☎ (202) 296-8873.
Hirshhorn Museum & Sculpture garden, Independence Av. & 8th St. S.W. Joseph Hirshhorn, a Jewish immigrant from Latvia, donated his collection of modern art to the American people. The museum contains more than 4,000 paintings and 2,000 pieces of sculpture.
Jewish Historical Society of Greater Washington, 701 3rd St. N.W., 20001-2624. ☎ (202) 789-0900.
Maintains the Lillian & Albert Small Jewish Museum, 3rd & "G" Sts. N.W., 20008. Housed in Washington's oldest synagogue building, Adas Israel, built 1876.
Jewish War Veterans, USA National Memorial 1811 R. St. N.W, 20009. ☎ (202) 265-6280.
The Library of Congress has a large collection of Judaica.
The Natural History Building of the Smithsonian Institute, 10th & Constitution Avs. N.W., 20001, contains a collection of Jewish ritual articles.
The National Portrait Gallery, "F" St. between 7th & 8th Sts., houses more than 100,000 portraits, including Albert Einstein, Mrs. Golda Meir and George Gershwin.
The National Archives, Pennsylvania Av. at 8th St. N.W., contain historical Jewish documents.
The Isaac Polack Building, 2109 Pennsylvania Av. N.W., built in 1796, was the home of the first Jew to settle in Washington.
In the John F. Kennedy Center, 2700 "F" St. N.W., is an Israeli lounge donated by the people of Israel.
B'nai B'rith Museum, Klutznick Exhibit Hall, 1640 Rhode Island Av. N.W., 20036. There is a bookshop on the premises.
United States Holocaust Memorial Museum. Details from 2000L Street NW, #717, DC 20036-4907. ☎ (202) 822-6464.
Newspaper:'The Jewish Week', 1910 "K" St. N.W., 20006.
Israel Embassy, 3514 International Dr. N.W., 20008.

Synagogues:
Beth Sholom (O), 13th St. & Eastern Av. N.W., 20012; Kesher Israel (O), 2801 "N" St. N.W., 20007. (333-4808; Ohev Sholom Talmud Torah (O), 1600 Jonquil St. N.W., 20012; Adas Israel (C), 2850 Quebec St. N.W., 20008; Tifereth Israel (C), 7701 16th St. N.W., 20012; Temple Micah (R), 600 "M" St. S.W., 20024; Temple Sinai (R), 3100 Military Rd. N.W., 20015; Washington Hebrew Cong. (R), 3935 Macomb St. N.W., 20016.
Rabbinical Council of Greater Washington, 7826 Eastern Av. N.W., 20012 will provide inf. about kashrut.
For details of the Eruv in Georgetown area, call 338-ERUV.

Restaurants
Hunan Deli, 2300 "H" St., NW: Wednesday Evening Dinner, Lunch Mon-Friday 202-833-1018.
Hunan Gourmet, 350 Fortune Terrace (7 Locks Plaza), Potomac Md 301-424-0192.
Nuthouse, 11419 Georgia Av., Wheaton Md. 20901. ☎ (301) 942-5900.

continued from *District of Columbia*

Royal Dragon 4840 Boiling Brook, Parkway Rockville Md 301-468-1922.
Wooden Shoe Bakery, Silver Springs. 301-942-9330.
Shalom Meat Market, 2307 University Blvd West, Silver Spring. MD 301-946-6500.
Shaul & Hershel Meat Market, Silver Spring. 301-949-8477 (Delivers to G W Hillel every Wednesday).
Katz Supermarket, 4860 Boiling Brook Parkway, Rockville MD 301-468-0400.
Wasseman & Lemberger, 610 Reistertown Rd., Baltimore, MD 301-486-4191 (Will Deliver to DC on Monday).
Nut House Pizza 301-942-5900.
Posins Bakery & Deli, 5756 Georgia Av., NW 202-726-4424. Bakery is under Conservative Hashgacha.
Potomac Wines and Spirits, 3057 M St., NW WDC ☎ (202) 333-2847.
St James Preffered Residence, 950 24th St NW WDC ☎ (202)457-0500 (Gives discount to Kesher Israel Guests).
Note: The Greater Washington area includes a number of locations in Maryland and Virginia. See notes at the end of the entries for those States.

FLORIDA

It started with three Sephardic Jews from Louisiana who established businesses in Pensacola in 1763. By 1896 Jewish settlers arrived in the Miami area. The United States entry into WWII dramatically changed Florida. Tourist facilities were converted to accommodate troops. The post war population including the Jewish population, exploded. From fewer than 25,000 Jews in 1940 it grew to a present state population of over 740,000.

BELLE GLADE
Syn.: Temple Beth Sholom (C), 224 N.W. Av. "G", 33430. ☎ 996-3886.

BOCA RATON
Jewish Federation of South Palm Beach County, The Richard and Carole Siemens Jewish Campus of the Jewish Federation of South Palm Beach County, 9901 Donna Klein Blvd., 33428-1788. ☎ (407) 852-3100; Adolph and Rose Lewis Jewish Community Centre, 9801 Donna Klein Blvd., 33428-1788. ☎ (407) 852-3200; Donna Klein Jewish Academy, 9701 Donna Klein Blvd., 33428-1788. ☎ (407) 852-3300; Ruth Rales Jewish Family Service, 21300 Ruth & Baron Coleman Blvd., 33428. ☎ (407) 852-3333.

Synagogues:
Beth Ami Congregation (C), 1401 N.W. 4th Ave. 33432, ☎ (407) 347-0031; B'nai Torah Congregation (C), 6261 S.W. 18th St., 33433, ☎ (407) 392-8566; Boca Raton Synagogue (O), 7900 Montoya Circle, 33433, ☎ (407) 394-5732; Chabad Lubavitch (O), West Boca Raton, 9070 Kimberly Blvd. #53, 33434, ☎ (407) 994-6257; Chabad Lubavitch (O), Central Boca Raton, 5030 Champion Blvd., D-6 33496, ☎ (407) 994-6257; Congregation Beth Ada (H), S. Fla. Ctr. For Humanistic Judaism, P.O. Box 2579, 33427, ☎ (407) 477-0585; Congregation Beth Tikvah of W. Boca Raton (C), ☎ (407) 392-7877; Congregation B'nai Israel (R), 2200 Yamato Road 33431, ☎ (407) 241-8118; Congregation Kol Ami (recon.), P.O. Box 811564, 33481, ☎ (407) 392-0696; Congregation Torah Ohr (O), 19146 Lyons Road 33434, ☎ (407) 479-4049; Temple Beth El (R), 333 S.W. Forth Ave., 33432, ☎ (407) 391-8900; Temple Beth Shalom (C), 19140 Lyons Road, 33434, ☎ (407) 483-5557; Temple Emanuel of Boca Raton (Jewish Renewal), 19557 Lyons Road, 33434, ☎ (407) 852-8578; Youth Israel (O), 7040 W. Palmeto Park Rd., Suite 2-287, 33433, ☎ (407) 391-3235.

continued from *Florida*

Jewish Association of Residential Care, 9901 Donna Klein Blvd., 33428-1788. ☎ (407) 852-3174.

Kosher Restaurants:
The Cafe, Cultural Arts Bldg. on the Richard and Carole Siemens Jewish Campus 33428, ☎ (407) 852-3204; Deli Maven, 8208 Glades Rd., 33434, ☎ (407) 477-7008; Eliat Cafe, Delmar Shopping Village, 7158 N. Beracasa Way, 33433, 368-6880; Falafel Armon, 22767 State Road 7, 33428, ☎ (407) 477-0633; Orchids Garden, 9045 La Fontana Blvd. #B-9, 33434, ☎ (407) 482-3831.

CLEARWATER
Jewish Fed. of Pinellas County, 13191 Starkey Rd, Suite 8, 34643-1438. ☎ (813) 530-3223. Fax (813) 531-0221.
Syn.: Young Israel of Clearwater (O), 2385 Tampa Rd, Suites 1 & 2, Palm Harbor, 34684. ☎ (813) 789-0408; Beth Shalom (C), 1325 S. Belcher Rd., 34624. ☎ (813) 531-1418; B'nai Israel (R), 1685 S. Belcher Rd., 34624. ☎ (813) 531-5829; Temple Ahavat Shalom (R), 1575 Curlew Rd., Palm Harbor, 34683. ☎ (813) 785-8811.
Golda Meir Center, 302 S. Jupiter Av., 34623. ☎ (813) 461-0222.
Kent Jewish Com. Center, 1955 Virginia St., 34623. ☎ (813) 736-1494.
Gulf Coast Jewish Family Service, 14041 Icot Blvd., 34620. ☎ (813) 538-7460.

DAYTONA BEACH
Jewish Fed. of Volusia & Flagler Counties, 733 S. Nova Rd., Ormond Beach, 32174. ☎ (407) 672-0294.
Syn.: Temple Israel (C), 1400 S. Peninsula Dr., 32118. ☎ (904) 252-3097; Temple Beth El (R), 579 N. Nova Rd., Ormond Beach, 32174. ☎ (904) 677-2484.

DELRAY BEACH
Syn; Anshei Emuna (O), 16189 Carter Rd., 33445. ☎ 499-9229; Temple Anshei Shalom of W. Delray (C), Oriole Jewish Center, 7099 W. Atlantic Av., 33446. ☎ 495-1300; Temple Emeth (C), 5780 W. Atlantic Av., 33446. ☎ 498-3536; Temple Sinai (R), 2475 W. Atlantic Av., 33445. ☎ 276-6161.
Restaurant: (K) Mandarin, 5046 West Atlantic Ave., FL 33 484 (Pines Plaza) ☎ (407) 496-6278
Meat Market: (K) Oriole Kosher Market, 7345 West Atlantic Ave., 33446.

FORT LAUDERDALE AREA
Jewish Fed. of Greater Fort Lauderdale, 8358 W. Oakland Pk. Blvd., 33321. ☎ (305) 748-8400, Fax (305) 748-6332.

Synagogues:
Chabad Lubavitch Community Syn. (O), 9791 W. Sample Rd., Coral Springs, 33065. ☎ (305) 344-4855; Cong. Migdal David (O), 8575 W. McNab Rd., Tamarac, 33321. ☎ (305) 726-3583; Syn. of Inverrary Chabad (O), 4561 N. University Dr., Lauderhill, 33351. ☎ (305) 748-1777; Temple Ohel B'nai Raphael (O), 4351 W. Oakland Pk. Blvd., Lauderdale Lakes, 33313. ☎ (305) 733-7684; Young Israel of Deerfield Beach (O), 1880 W. Hillsboro Blvd., Deerfield Beach, 33441. ☎ (305) 421-1367; Beth Am (C), 9730 Stirling Rd., Hollywood, 33024. ☎ (305) 431-5100; Beth Am (C), 7205 Royal Palm Blvd., Margate, 33063. ☎ (305) 974-8650; Beth Israel (C), 7100 W. Oakland Pk. Blvd., Sunrise, 33313. ☎ (305) 742-4040; Beth Israel of Deerfield Beach (C), 200 S. Century Blvd., Deerfield Beach, 33441. ☎ (305) 421-7060; B'nai Moshe (C), 1434 S.E. 3rd St., Pompano Beach, 33060. ☎ (305) 942-5380;

continued from *Florida*

Cong. Beth Hillel of Margate (C), 7640 Margate Blvd., Margate, 33063. ☎ (305) 974-3090; Cong. Beth Tefilah (C), 6435 W. Commercial Blvd., Tamarac, 33319. ☎ (305) 722-7607; Conservative Syn. of Coconut Creek (C), Lyons Plaza, 1447 Lyons Rd., Coconut Creek, 33063. ☎ (305) 975-4666; Hebrew Cong. of Lauderhill (C), 2048 N.W. 49th Av., Lauderhill, 33313. ☎ (305) 733-9560; Tamarac Jewish Center (C), 9101 N.W. 57th St., Tamarac, 33321. ☎ (305) 721-7660; Temple Sha'aray Tzedek (C), 4099 Pine Island Rd., Sunrise, 33321. ☎ (305) 741-0295; Temple Sholom (C), 132 S.E. 11th Av., Pompano Beach, 33060. ☎ (305) 942-6410; Temple Bet Chavarim, 10444 W. Atlantic Blvd., Coral Springs, 33071. (475-8045; Temple Bet Tikvah (R) 3000 N. University Dr., Sunrise, 33322. ☎ (305) 741-8088; Temple Beth Orr (R), 2151 Riverside Dr., Coral Springs, 33065. ☎ (305) 753-3232; Temple B'nai Shalom of Deerfield Beach (R), Menorah Chapels, 2305 W. Hillsboro Blvd., Deerfield Beach, 33441. ☎ (305) 426-532; Temple Emanu-El (R), 3245 W. Oakland Pk. Blvd., Lauderdale Lakes, 33311. ☎ (305) 731-2310; Temple Kol Ami (R), 8200 Peters Rd., Plantation, 33324. ☎ (305) 472-1988; Ramat Shalom (Reconstructionist), 11301 W. Broward Blvd., Plantation, 33325. ☎ (305) 472-3600.

Kosher Restaurants:
East Side Kosher Restaurant & Deli, 6846 W. Atlantic Blvd., Margate, 33063; David Shai King, 5599 N. University Dr., Lauderhill, 33321. ☎ (305) 572-6522; Kosher Cafe (Victor), 5485 N. University Dr., Lauderhill, 33321. ☎ (305) 572-6522.

FORT MYERS
Syn.: Temple Beth El (R), 16225 Winkler Rd Ext., Ft Myers, 33908. ☎ (941) 433-0018.

FORT PIERCE
Syn.: Temple Beth-El Israel(R), 4600 Oleander Av., 34982; P. O. Box 12128, 34979-2128. ☎ (407) 461-7428.

HOLLYWOOD AND VICINITY
Jewish Fed. of South Broward, 2719 Hollywood Blvd., Hollywood, FL 33020. ☎ (305) 921-8810.
David Posnack Jewish Community Center, 5850 S. Pine Island Rd., Davie, FL 33328. ☎ (305) 434-0499.

Synagogues:
B'nai Aviv (C), 200 Bonaventure Blvd., Weston; B'nai Sephardim (Seph), 3670 Stirling Rd., Ft. Lauderdale; Century Pines Jewish Center (C), 13400 S.W. 10 St., Pembroke Pines; Chabad Ocean Syn. (O), 4000 S. Ocean Dr., Hallandale; Chabad of Southwest Broward (L), 11251 Taft St., Pembroke Pines; Congregation Ahavat Shalom (O), 315 Madison St., Hollywood; Cong. Levi Yitzchok-Lubavitch (L), 1295 E. Hallandale Beach Blvd., Hallandale; Hallandale Jewish Center (C), 416 N.E. 8 Av., Hallandale; Hollywood Community Syn. (L), 4441-51 Sheridan St., Hollywood; Temple Adath Or (New Age), 11450 S.W. 16 St., Davie; Temple Beth Ahm Israel (C), 9730 Stirling Rd., Hollywood;Temple Beth El (R), 1351 S. 14 Av., Hollywood; Temple Beth Emet (R), 10801 Pembroke Rd., Pembroke Pines; Temple Beth Shalom (C), 1400 N. 46 Av., Hollywood; Temple Judea of Carriage Hills (C), 6734 Stirling Rd., Hollywood; Temple Sinai (C), 1201 Johnson St., Hollywood; Temple Solel (R), 5100 Sheridan St., Hollywood; Young Israel of Hollywood/Ft. Lauderdale (O), 3291 Stirling Rd., Ft. Lauderdale; Young Israel of Pembroke Pines (O), 13400 S.W. 10 St., Pembroke Pines.

continued from *Florida*

Jewish Family Service of Broward County, 6100 Hollywood Blvd., Suite 410, Hollywood, FL 33024. ☎ (305) 966-0956.
Joseph Meyerhoff Senior Center, 3081 Taft St., Hollywood, FL 33021. ☎ (305) 966-9805.
South Broward Central Agency for Jewish Education, 3081 Taft St., Hollywood, FL33021. ☎ (305) 964-9040.
Newspaper: The Jewish Community Advocate of South Broward, 2719 Hollywood Blvd., Hollywood, FL 33020. ☎ (305) 922-8603.

Restaurants
Pita Plus, 5650 Stirling Rd., Hollywood, FL 33021. ☎ (305) 985-8028; Jerusalem Pizza II, 5650 Stirling Rd., Hollywood, FL 33021. ☎ (305) 964-6811.

JACKSONVILLE
Jacksonville Jewish Fed., 8505 San Jose Blvd., 32217. ☎ (904) 448-5000.
Jewish Community Alliance, 8505 San Jose Blvd., 32217. ☎ (904) 730-2100.
Jewish Family & Community Services, 3601 Cardinal Point Dr., 32257. ☎ (904) 448-1933.
Syn.: Etz Chaim (O), 10167 San Jose Blvd., 32257. Mikva on premises. ☎ (904) 262-3565; Beth Shalom (C), 4072 Sunbeam Rd., 32257. ☎ (904) 268-0404; Jewish Center (C), 3662 Crown Point Rd., 32257. ☎ (904) 292-1000; Cong. Ahavath Chesed (R), 8727 San Jose Blvd, 32217. ☎ (904) 733-7078.
River Garden Hebrew Home for Aged, 11401 Old St. Augustine Rd., 32258. ☎ (904) 260-1818.
Kosher Nutrition Center, 5846 Mt. Carmel Terr., 32216. ☎ (904) 737-9075.

KEY WEST
Syn.: Cong. B'nai Zion (C), 750 United St., 33040-3251. Rabbi. Louis Dimpson. ☎ (305) 294-3437.
Chabad House, 418 Eaton St., 33040.

LAKELAND
Syn.: Temple Emanuel (C), 600 Lake Hollingsworth Dr., 33803. ☎ (813) 682-8616.

MIAMI, MIAMI BEACH AND VICINITY
South-Eastern Florida, often called the state's Gold Coast, is the only tropical area in the United States, and is visited yearly by millions of tourists, winter as well as summer. Comprising three counties — Dade, Broward & Palm Beach – with several dozen cities, it is actually a megalopolis with 695,000 Jews, the second largest concentration of Jews in the United States after Metropolitan New York. The best known cities in this area are Miami & Miami Beach, in Dade County, whose population includes 163,000 Jews. The center of Jewish population in South Florida is shifting northwards and is now near Oakland Park Boulevard in Broward County (Fort Lauderdale) with 29% (163,000) of the Jewish population living in Dade County (Miami), 41% (284,000) in Broward County (Hollywood/Fort Lauderdale), and 30% (209,000) in Palm Beach. Currently South Florida is the second largest Jewish community in the United States. Syns. are listed below according to where they are situated. Other institutions are listed after the syns.
Other Gold Coast communities include Boca Raton, Fort Lauderdale, Hallandale, Hollywood, Miramar, Pompano Beach and West Palm Beach.

Institutions, Organisations & Services
Greater Miami Jewish Federation, 4200 Biscayne Blvd., 33137. ☎ (305) 576-

continued from *Florida*

4000 Fax (305) 573-8115. Publishes Resource Directory of Jewish Life in Dade County and Kosher listings.
American Jewish Committee: 3000 Biscayne Blvd., 33137.
American Jewish Congress: 420 Lincoln Rd., Suite 601, Miami Beach 33139.
Anti-Defamation League: 150 S.E. Second Av., 33132.
B'nai B'rith: 3107 W. Hallandale Beach Blvd., Suite 105, Hallandale, 33009, Miami. ☎ (305) 667-5964.
Central Agency for Jewish Education: 4200 Biscayne Blvd., 33137. There are about 25 Jewish afternoon & week-end schools in the Greater Miami area.
Florida Hillel Council (serving students at all colleges in Florida), University of Miami, 1100 Stanford Dr., 33146.
Florida Lubavitch Headquarters, 1140 Alton Rd., Miami Beach, 33139. ☎ (305) 673 5664.
Hadassah: 4200 Biscayne Blvd., Miami, 33137 & 300 71 St., Miami Beach, 33140.
Rabbinical Association of Greater Miami, 4200 Biscayne Blvd., 33137. ☎ (305) 576-4000.
Jewish Community Centers: N. Dade, 18900 N.E. 25th Av., N. Miami Beach, 33180; S. Dade, 11155 S.W. 112 Av., Miami, 33176; Senior Adult Center, 610 Espanola Way, Miami Beach, 33139.
Jewish Family Service: 1790 S.W. 27th Av., 33145.
Jewish Home for Aged: 151 N.E. 52nd St., 33137
Jewish Library of Greater Miami: 3950 Biscayne Blvd., 33137.
Jewish National Fund: 420 Lincoln Rd., Miami Beach, 33139.
Jewish Vocational Service: 735 N.E. 125th St., 33161.
Mount Sinai Hospital: 4300 Alton Rd., Miami Beach, 33140.
Museums: **Jewish Museum of Florida**, 301 Washington Av., Miami Beach. 33139-6965.
☎ (305) 672 5044; Temple Emanu-El, 1701 Washington Av., Miami Beach, 33139; Temple Israel, 137 N.E. 19th St., Miami, 33132; Beth David, 2625 SW Ave., 33129.
National Council of Jewish Women: 12944 W. Dixie Highway, N. Miami, 33161.
Women's American ORT: 1990 NE 163rd St., #102, North Miami Beach, 33162.
Most national Jewish orgs. have branches in the Greater Miami area.
Local Jewish tours: (Jewish Travel and Education Network-JTEN), M. Heller, ☎ (305) 931-1782.

Beth Raphael (C), 1545 Jefferson Av., 33139. ☎ (305) 538-4112.
This syn. is dedicated to the six million martyrs of the Holocaust. On an outside marble wall, a large six-light menorah burns every night in their memory. Six hundred names, representing each city, have been inscribed on the marble. There is also a notable Holocaust Memorial at Dade Av., and Meridian Av.;

Temple Beth Sholom (R), 4144 Chase Av., 33140. ☎ (305) 538-7231. Has a beautiful landscaped Biblical Garden containing plants of the Bible, and a year-round art gallery.

Mikvaot

B'nai Israel & Greater Miami Youth Synagogue Mikveh, 16260 S.W. 288th St., Naranja, 33033. ☎ (305) 264 6488.
Boca Raton Synagogue Mikveh, 7900 Montoya Circle South, Boca Raton, 33433. ☎ (305) 538-0070.
Congregation Adas Dej Mikveh, 225 37th St., Miami Beach, 33140. ☎ (305) 538-0070.

continued from *Florida*

Daughters of Israel, 2530 Pinetree Drive, 33140. ☎ (305) 672-3500.
Rabbi Meisel's Mikveh (for men only), Washington Av. & 2nd St., Miami Beach, 33139. ☎ (305) 673 4641.
Miami Beach Mikveh, 2530 Pinetree Dr., Miami Beach, 33140. ☎ (305) 672 3500.
Mikveh Blima of North Dade, Inc., 1054 N.E. Miami Gardens Dr., North Miami Beach, 33179. ☎ (305) 949 9650.
Mikveh/Young Israel of Hollywood & Ft. Lauderdale, 3291 Sterling Rd., Ft. Lauderdale, 33312. ☎ (305) 966 7877.
Shul of Bal Harbour Mikvah, 9500 Collins Ave., Surfside, 33154. ☎ (305) 868 1411.

Kosher Hotels

Crown Hotel, 4041 Collins Av., 33140, is under the supervision of the Union of Orthodox Jewish Congregations of America.
The following hotels are under local kashrut supervision: Embassy, 1051 N. Miami Beach Blvd., 33168. ☎ (305) 538-7550; Saxony, 3201 Collins Av., 33140. ☎ (305) 538-6811; Sans Souci Hotel, 31st St., & Collins Av., 33140. ☎ (305) 531-8261; Sasson Ocean Resort, 2001 Collins Ave., 33139. ☎ (305) 531-0761; Sherry Frontenac, 6565 Collins Av., 33141. ☎ (305) 866-1637.
Some of the hotels are open all year round. The others close for varying lengths of time between the end of Pesach and November 20.
Some other leading Miami hotels, which are not kosher but offer kosher catering and passover facilities (visitors must check), are:
Alexander, 5225 Collins Av., 33140; Carriage House, 5401 Collins Av., 33140; Doral, 4833 Collins Av., 33140; Eden Roc, 4525 Collins Av., 33140; Fontainebleau-Hilton, 4441 Collins Av., 33140; Harbor House Hotel Apartments, 10275 Collins Av., 33154; Marco Polo, 19201 Collins Av., 33160; Sea View, 9909 Collins Av., 33154; Shawnee Miami Beach Resort, 4343 Collins Av., 33140; Sheraton Bal Harbor, 9701 Collins Av., 33154.

Kosher Restaurants

The following restaurants are under local kashrut supervision:
Aviva's Kitchen, 16355 W. Dixie Hwy., N. Miami Beach, 33160. ☎ (305) 944 7313.
Bagel Time, 3915 Alton Rd., Miami Beach, 33140. ☎ (305) 538 0300.
Beethoven Restaurant, Sasson Hotel, 2001 Collins Av., Miami Beach, 33139. ☎ (305) 531 0761.
China Kikor Tel Aviv, 5005 Collins Av., Miami Beach, 33140. ☎ (305) 866 3316.
Crown Buffet & Dairy Bar, Crown Hotel, 4041 Collins Av., Miami Beach, 33140. ☎ (305) 531 5771 or (800) 541 6874.
Embassy Peking Tower Suite, 4101 Pine Tree Dr. (in Tower 41), Miami Beach, 33160. ☎ (305) 538 7550.
Gitty's Hungarian Kitchen, 6565 Collins Av. (Sherry Frontenac Hotel), Miami Beach, 33141. ☎ (305) 865 4893.
Jerusalem Pizza, 761 N.E. 167th St., North Miami Beach, 33162. ☎ (305) 653 6662.
Jerusalem Peking, 4299 Collins Av., Miami Beach, 33140. ☎ (305) 532 2263.
The Noshery (Dairy) (seasonal), Located in the Saxony Hotel, 3201 Collins Av., Miami Beach, 331340. ☎ (305) 538 6811.
Ocean Terrace Restaurant & Grille, Crown Hotel, 4041 Collins Av., Miami Beach, 33140. ☎ (305) 531 5771.
Pinati Restaurant, 2520 Miami Gardens Dr., N. Miami Beach, 33180. ☎ (305) 931 8086.
Pita King, 343 East Flagler, Miami, 33131. ☎ (305) 358 0386

continued from *Florida*

Pita Plus, 20103 Biscayne Blvd., North Miami Beach, 33180. ☎ (305) 935 0761.
Sarah's Kosher Pizza, 2214 N.E. 123 St., North Miami, 33181. ☎ (305) 891 3312. 1127 N.E. 163 St., North Miami Beach, 33162. ☎ (305) 948 7777.
Shalom Haifa, 1330 N.E. 163 St., North Miami Beach, 33162. ☎ (305) 945 2884.
Shemtov Kosher Pizza, 514 - 41st St., Miami Beach, 33140. ☎ (305) 538 2123.
South Beach Pita, 1448 Washington Av., Miami Beach, 33139. ☎ (305) 534 3706.
Wing Wan II, 1640 N.E. 164 St., North Miami Beach, 33162. ☎ (305) 945 3585.
Yonnie's Kosher Pizza, 19802 W. Dixie Hwy., North Miami Beach, 33180. ☎ (305) 932-1961.

A printed booklet 'South Florida guide to kosher living', listing all kosher hotels, restaurants, bakeries, butchers, bookstores, nursing homes, etc. in Dade, Broward and Palm Beach Counties is available from: Information and Referral Service, Greater Miami Jewish Federation, 4200 Biscayne Blvd., Miami, FL 33137. ☎ (305) 576-4000.

ORLANDO
Jewish Fed. of Greater Orlando, 851 N. Maitland Av., Maitland FL 32751, P.O.B. 1508, Maitland FL 32794-1508 ☎ (407) 645-5933.

Synagogues:
Cong. Ahavas Yisroel (O), 708 Lake Howell Rd., Maitland, 32741; Cong. Beth Shalom (C), 13th & Center Sts., Leesburg, 32748. ☎ (904) 742-0238 or 787-3946; Cong. Ohev Shalom (C), 5015 Goddard Av., 32804. ☎ (407) 298-4650; Cong. Shalom Aleichem, (C) P.O. Box 424211, Kissimmee, 34742-4211.
Temple Israel (C), 4917 Eli St., 32804. ☎ (407) 647-3055; Cong. Shalom (Williamsburg), (C) c/o Sydney Ansell, 11821 Soccer Lane, 32821-7952.
Cong. of Liberal Judaism (R), 928 Malone Dr., 32810. ☎ (407) 645-0444; Southwest Orlando Jewish Cong (C), 11200, S. Apopka-Vineland Rd., 32836.

Restaurants
Some Disney World restaurants stock kosher meals and some of the larger hotels will order them on request.
Kinneret Kitchens, 517 South Delaney, ☎ (407) 422 7205. Senior Citizens dining room. Meals: d, Mon. - Fri. at 5 p.m. Call at least 24 hours in advance to reserve a meal.
The Lower East Side (Glatt **K**), at Catalonia Inn Hotel. ☎ (467) 648-4830.
Amira's Catering and Specialty - 1351 E. Altamonte, Altamonte Springs. ☎ (407) 767 7577. Cold cuts, side dishes, frozen meals, groceries.
Kosher Korner, 8464 Palm Pkwy, 32836. ☎ (407) 238-9968. Complete kosher grocery and takeout. Packaged frozen Glatt meat. Will deliver to hotels.
Market Place Deli, Hyatt Orlando, 6375 W. Irlo Bronson Hwy., ☎ (407) 396 1234. Has frozen kosher food only.

PALM CITY
Syn.: Treasure Coast Jewish Center-Cong. Beth Abraham (C), 3998 S.W. Leighton Farms Av., 34990. ☎ 287-8833.

PENSACOLA
Syn.: B'nai Israel (C), 1829 N. 9th Av., 32503; Beth El (R), 800 N. Palafox St., 32501.

continued from *Florida*

ROCKLEDGE
Jewish Federation of Brevard, 108A Barton Av., 32955. ☎ (407) 636-1824.

ST. AUGUSTINE
Syn.: First Sons of Israel (O), 161 Cordova St., 32084.

ST. PETERSBURG
Syn.: Beth Chai (C); Beth Shalom (C), 1844 54th St. S., 33707; B'nai Israel
(C), 301 59th St. N., 33710; Beth-El (R), 400 Pasadena Av. S., 33707. ☎ (813)
347-6136.
J. Com. Center: 5001 Duhme Rd., Madeira Beach, 33708. ☎ (813) 392-3424.
Menorah Center, 250 58th St. N., 33710.
Jo-El's Specialty Foods, 2619 23rd Av. N., 33713. (321-3847. Under rabbinical supervision.

SARASOTA
Sarasota-Manatee Jewish Fed., 580 S. McIntosh Rd., 34232-1959. ☎ (813)
371-4546.

Synagogues:
Beth Sholom (C), 1050 S. Tuttle Av., 34237. ☎ (813) 955-8121; Chabad
Lubavitch of Sarasota & Manatee Counties, 7119 S. Tamiami Tr., Suite L,
34231. ☎ (813) 925-0770;
Temple Emanu-El (R), 151 S. McIntosh Rd., 34232. ☎ (813) 371-2788; Temple
Beth El, 2209 — 75th St. W., Bradenton 34209. ☎ (813) 792-0870; Temple
Beth El/North Port (C), P.O. Box 7195, North Port 34287. ☎ (813) 426-9048.
Temple Beth Israel (R), 567 Bay Isles Rd., Longboat Key, 34228. ☎ (813) 383-
3428; Venice Jewish Community Center, P.O. Box 62, Venice 34284. ☎ (813)
484-2022.

SURFSIDE
Syn.: The Shul, 9540 Collins Av., 33154. ☎ (305) 868 1411.
The Shul of Bal Harbor, Bay Harbor & Surfside.

TAMPA
Tampa Jewish Federation, 13009 Community Campus Dr., 33625-4000.
☎ (813) 960-1840; (813) 264-9000. Fax (813) 265-8450.

Synagogues:
Bais Tefilah (O), 14908 Pennington Rd., 33624. ☎ (813) 963-2317. Mikva,
Orthodox pre-school on premises.
Hebrew Academy (O), 14908 Penington Rd., 33624. ☎ (813) 963-0706;
Young Israel of Tampa (O), 3721 W. Tacon St., 33629. ☎ (813) 832-3018; Kol
Ami (C), 3919 Moran Rd., 33618. ☎ (813) 962-6338; Rodeph Sholom (C),
2713 Bayshore Blvd., 33629. ☎ (813) 837-1911; Temple David (C), 2001
Swann Av., 33606. ☎ (813) 254-1771; Schaarai Zedek (R), 3303 Swann Av.,
33609. ☎ (813) 876-2377.

VERO BEACH
Syn.: Temple Beth Shalom (R), 365 43rd Av., 32968. ☎ (407) 569-4700.

WEST PALM BEACH AND VICINITY
Jewish Federation of Palm Beach County, 4601 Community Dr., W. Palm
Beach, FL 33417. ☎ (407) 478-0700.

Synagogues:
Chabad House, (O) 4800 23rd St. North, 33407. ☎ (407) 640-8111. Aitz

continued from *Florida*

Chaim (O), 2518 N. Haverhill Rd., W. Palm Beach, 33417. ☎ (407) 686-5055; Boynton Beach Jewish Center-Beth Kodesh (C), 501 N.E. 26th Av., Boynton Beach, 33435. ☎ (407) 586-9428; Cong. Anshei Sholom (C), 5348 Grove St., W. Palm Beach, 33417. ☎ (407) 684-3212; Golden Lakes Temple (C), 1470 Golden Lakes Blvd., W. Palm Beach, 33411. ☎ (407) 689-9430; Beth Tikvah, Lake Worth Jewish Center (C), 4550 Jog Rd., Lake Worth, 33467. ☎ (407) 967-3600; Temple Beth David (C), 4657 Hood Rd., Palm Beach Gardens, 33418. ☎ (407) 694-2350; Temple Beth El (C), 2815 N. Flagler Dr., W. Palm Beach, 33407. ☎ (407) 833-0339; Temple Beth Sholom (C), 224 N.W. Avenue 'G', Belle Glade, 33430. ☎ (407) 996-3886; Temple Beth Zion (C), 129 Sparrow Dr., Royal Palm Beach, 33411. ☎ (407) 798-8888; Temple B'nai Jacob (C), 2177 S. Congress Av., W. Palm Beach, 33406. ☎ (407) 433-5957; Temple Emanu-El (C), 190 N. County Rd., Palm Beach, 33480. ☎ (407) 832-0804; Temple Torah (C), 9776D, S. Military Trail, Boynton Beach, 33436. ☎ (407) 369-1112; Reform Temple of Boynton Beach (R), P.O. Box 3791, Boynton Beach, 33424. ☎ (407) 732-0824; Temple Beth Am (R), 759 Parkway St., Jupiter, 33477. ☎ (407) 747-1109; Temple Beth Torah (R), 900 Big Blue Trace, W. Palm Beach, 33414. ☎ (407) 793-2700; Temple Israel (R), 1901 N. Flagler Dr., W. Palm Beach, 33407. ☎ (407) 833-8421; Temple Judea (R), 100 Chillingworth Dr., W. Palm Beach, 33419. ☎ (407) 471-1526.
Jewish Com. Center of the Palm Beaches, 3151 N. Military Trail, 33409. ☎ (407) 689-7700.
Jewish Family & Children's Service, 4605 Community Dr., W. Palm Beach, FL 33417. ☎ (407) 684-1991.
Commission for Jewish Education, 4603 Community Dr., W. Palm Beach, FL 33417. ☎ (407) 640-0700.

GEORGIA

ATHENS
Syn.: Cong. Children of Israel (R), Dudley Dr., 30606. ☎ (404) 549-4192.

ATLANTA
Jewish Fed., 1753 Peachtree Rd., NE 30309. ☎ (404) 873-1661. Fax (404) 874-7043. Publishes an annual community guide.
The Atlanta Jewish Times, 1575 Northside Drive, 30318. ☎ (404) 352-2400. Fax: (404) 355-9388.
Zachor Holocaust Center, 1745 Peachtree Rd. NE, 30309. ☎ (404) 873-1661.
Emory Hillel House, 1531 Clifton Rd., 30329. ☎ (404) 634-6664; Hillel Atlanta (Federation), Drawer 'A', Emory University, 30322. ☎ (404) 727-6490.
Israel Consulate; 1100 Spring St., Suite 440, 30309. ☎ (404) 875-7851.

Synagogues:
Anshe S'fard (O), 1324 North Highland Av., 30306. ☎ (404) 874-4513; Beth Jacob (O), 1855 La Vista Rd., 30329. ☎ (404) 633-0551. Mikva on premises; Beth Tefillah (Observant), 5065 Highpoint Rd., 30342. ☎ (404) 843-2464; Cong. Or Ve Shalom (Sephardi), 1681 N. Druid Hills Rd., 30319. ☎ (404) 633-1737; Shearith Israel(T), 1180 University Dr., NE, 30306. ☎ (404) 873-1743; Ahavath Achim (C), 600 Peachtree Battle Av., 30327. ☎ (404) 355-5222; Beth Shalom (C), 5303 Winters Chapel Rd., 30360 ☎ (404) 399-5300; Etz Chaim (C), 1190 Indian Hills Pkwy., Marietta, 30068. ☎ (404) 973-0137; Beth David (R), 1885 McGee Rd., Snellville, 30278. ☎ (404) 978-3916; Beth Tikvah (R), 9955 Coleman Rd., Roswell, 30075. ☎ (404) 642-0434; B'nai Israel (R), PO Box 383, Riverdale, 30274. ☎ (404) 471-3586; Kehillat Chaim Cong. (R), 10200 Woodstock Rd., Roswell, 30075. ☎ (404) 641-8630;

continued from *Georgia*

Temple Emanu-El (R), 1580 Spalding Dr., Dunwoody, 30338. ☎ (404) 395-1340; Kol Emeth (R), 1415 Old Canton Rd., Marietta, 30062. ☎ (404) 973-3533; Temple Sinai (R), 5645 Dupree Dr., 30327. ☎ (404) 252-3073; The Temple (R), 1589 Peachtree Rd. N.W., 30367. ☎ (404) 873-1731. (The sanctuary is designed along the lines of the Biblical Temple.) Ner Hamizrach (Iranian) P. O. Box 95242, 30347. ☎ (404) 315 9020. Chabad Center, 5065 Highpoint Rd., 30342. ☎ (404) 843-2464.
Com. Center: 1745 Peachtree Rd., 30309. ☎ (404) 875-7881. Zaban branch, 5342 Tilly Mill Rd., Dunwoody, 30338. ☎ (404) 396-3250. 2509

Kosher Restaurant & Meat
Quality Kosher, 2153 Briarcliff Rd., 30329. ☎ (404) 636-1114.
Visitors requiring kosher & Shomer Shabbat bed & breakfast accom. should contact Bed & Breakfast Atlanta, 1801 Piedmont Av. (Suite 208), 30324. ☎ (404) 875-0525. Fax (404) 875-9672.

AUGUSTA
Syn.: Adas Yeshuron (O), 935 Johns Rd., Walton Way, 30904.

Delicatessen
Strauss, 965 Broad St., 30902; Sunshine Bakery, 1209 Broad St., 30902; Parti-Pal, Daniel Village, 30904.

COLUMBUS
Syn.: Shearith Israel (C), 2550 Wynnton Rd., 31906; Temple Israel (R), 1617 Wildwood Av., 31906.

MACON
Syn.: Sherah Israel (C), 1st & Plum Sts., 31201; Beth Israel (R), 892 Cherry St., 31201.

SAVANNAH
Syn.: B'nai B'rith Jacob (O), 5444 Abercorn St., 31405; Agudath Achim (C), 9 Lee Blvd., 31405; Mickve Israel (R), Bull & Gordon Sts., 31401. (This is the oldest synagogue in Georgia, having been founded before 1790.)
Jewish Fed., 5111 Abercorn St., 31405. ☎ (912) 355-8111.
The Com. Center is in the same building.
One of the oldest Jewish cemeteries in North America is to be found in Savannah.
Visitors requiring inf. about kashrut, temporary accommodation, etc., should contact Rabbi Avigdor Slatus, 5444 Abercorn St., 31405.

HAWAII
HILO
Syn.: Temple Beth Aloha (unaffiliated), P.O.B. 1538, 96720. ☎ (808) 969-4153.

HONOLULU
Jewish Fed. of Hawaii, 44 Hora Lane, 96813. ☎ (808) 941-2424.
Syn.: Chabad of Hawai (O), 4851 Kahala Av. ☎ (808) 735-8161; Cong. Sof Ma'arav (C), 2500 Pali Highway, 96817. ☎ (808) 373-1331 or 923-5726; Temple Emanu-El (R & Trad.), 2550 Pali Highway, 96817. ☎ (808) 595-7521. Kosher food available at Foodland Supermarket Beretania, cnr. Kalakana; and, 'Down to Earth' on King's St. nr. University Av.
Bed & Breakfast, 3242 Kaohinani Dr., 96817. ☎ (808) 595-7533. Fax (808) 595-2030. Contact Mary Lee Bridges.

continued from *Hawaii*

KONA
Syn.: Kona Beth Shalom (R), Kailua-Kona. ☎ 322-9144.

MAUI
Syn.: Maui Cong. Probably now closed.

PEARL HARBOR
There are combined military-civilian congs. in Pearl Harbor, on the island of Guam and on Kwajalein Atoll. Details from the Jewish Chaplain at Pearl Harbor, c/o Aloha Jewish Chapel (Military), Makalapa Gate. ☎ 471-0050.

WAIKIKI
Syn.: Chabad, Alana Hotel, Park Plaza, 1956 Ala Moana Blvd. ☎ 735-8161.

IDAHO
BOISE
Syn.: Ahavath-Beth Israel (C), 1102 State St., 83702.

ILLINOIS
CHAMPAIGN-URBANA
Syn.: Sinai Temple (R), 3104 Windsor Rd., Champaign, 61821. ☎ (217) 352-8140.
Champaign-Urbana Jewish Fed., 503 E. John St., Champaign, 61820. ☎ (217) 367-9872.

CHICAGO
Chicagoland (Greater Chicago) consists of the City of Chicago and the collar counties of Cook, Dupage, Kane, Lake and McHenry Counties. The Jewish community is spread throughout Chicagoland, with the main concentrations being in West Rodgers Park (City of Chicago), Skokie (Cook County), Buffalo Grove and Highland Park (Lake County). The entry is in the process of revision with the assistance of Mr Michael Anisfeld.
There are three basic divisions in Chicagoland: (a) *City of Chicago* (telephone area codes starting 312), includes West Rogers Park and the Devon Avenue areas; (b) *North and Northwest Suburbs* (includes Cook, Lake and McHenry counties, telephone area codes are 815 or 847), includes Buffalo Grove, Deerfield, Evanston, Highland Park, Northbrook and Skokie; (c) *South and West Suburbs* (includes DuPage and Kane counties, telephone area codes are 630 or 708), includes Flossmoor and Olympia Fields.
Greater Chicago, has a Jewish population of about 261,000. For a History of the Jews of Chicago see I. Cutter, 'The Jews of Chicago: from Shtetl to Suburbs'.

Organisations
Jewish Fed. of Metropolitan Chicago, 1 S. Franklin St., 60606. ☎ (312) 346-6700.
B'nai B'rith Council: 9933 N. Lawler St., Skokie, 60076.
Chicago Board of Rabbis (Orthodox, Conservative, Reform, Rec.): 1 S. Franklin St., 60606.
Chicago Mikva Assoc.: 3110 W. Touhy Av., 60645.
Chicago Rabbinical Council (Orthodox): 3525 W. Peterson Av., 60659. ☎ (312) 588 1600. Inf. about kashrut and allied matters may be obtained from the Council, which issues an annual directory; also Dinei Tora and Religious Divorces (Gittin).

continued from *Illinois*

The Ark, 6450 N. California, 60645, is a privately-run Orthodox org. providing free legal, medical and welfare advice.
Jewish United Fund of Metropolitan Chicago, 1 S. Franklin St., 60606. ☎ (312) 346-6700.

Synagogues:

Adas B'nai Israel (O), 6200 N. Kimball Av., 60659; Adas Yeschurun (O), 2949 W. Touhy Av., 60645; Anshe Mizrach (O), 627 W. Patterson Av., 60613; Anshe Motele (O), 6520 N. California Av., 60645; Anshe Sholom B'nai Israel (O), 540 W. Melrose Av., 60657; Beth Itzchok of West Rogers Park (O), 6716 N. Whipple St., 60645; Beth Sholom Ahavas Achim (O), 5665 N. Jersey St., 60659; Bnei Ruven (O), 6350 N. Whipple St., 60659; Chabad Hse. (O), 2014 Orrington Av., Evanston, 60201; Chesed L'Avrohom Nachlas David (O), 6342 N. Troy St., 60659; Cong. Yehuda Moshe (O), 4721 W. Touhy Av., Lincolnwood, 60646; Persian/Iran Hebrew Cong. (O), 3820 Main St., Skokie, 60076; Sephardic Congregation (O), 1819 W. Howard St., Evanston, 60202; Kehilath Jacob Beth Samuel (O), 3701 W. Devon Av., 60659; Lev Someach (O), 5555 N. Bernard St., 60625; Mishne Ugmoro (O), 6045 N. California Av., 60659; Or Torah, (O), 3738 W. Dempster St., Skokie, 60076; Poalie Zedek West Rogers Park (O), 2801 W. Albion St., 60645; Shaarei Torah Anshei Maariv (O), 2756 W. Morse Av., 60645; Warsaw Bikur Cholim (O), 3541 W. Peterson Av., 60659; A.G. Beth Israel (T), 3635 W. Devon Av., 60659; Agudas Achim-Bickur Cholim (Trad.), 8927 S. Houston Av., 60617; Agudath Jacob (T), 633 Howard St., Evanston, 60202; Beth Sholom of Rogers Park (T), 1233 W. Pratt Blvd., 60626; B'nai Shalom (T), 701 Aptakisic Rd., Buffalo Grove, 60090; Chicago Loop Syn. (T), 16 S. Clark St., 60603; Ezras Israel (T), 7001 N. California Av., 60645; K.I. N.S. of West Rogers Park (T), 2800 W. North Shore Av., 60645; Lake Shore Drive Syn. (T), 70 E. Elm St., 60611; Lawn Manor-Beth Jacob (T), 6601 S. Kedzie St., 60629; Lincolnwood Jewish Cong. (T), 7117 N. Crawford Av., Lincolnwood, 60646; Mikro Kodesh Anshe Tiktin (T), 2832 W. Foster Av., 60625; Or Chodash (T), 2356 Hassel Rd., Hoffman Estates, 60195; Skokie Central Traditional Cong. (T), 4040 Main St., Skokie, 60076; Skokie Valley Traditional Syn. (T), 8825 E. Prairie Rd., Skokie, 60076; Agudas Achim N. Shore Cong. (C), 5029 N. Kenmore Av., 60640; Am Echad (C), 160 Westwood Dr., Park Forest, 60466; Am Yisrael (C), 4 Happ Rd., Northfield, 60093; Anshe Emet (C), 3760 N. Pine Gr., 60613; Beth Hillel Cong. of Wilmette (C), 3220 Big Tree Lane, Wilmette, 60091; Beth Judea of Buffalo Grove (C), P.O. Box 62, Buffalo Grove, 60092; Beth Shalom Cong. of Northbrook (C), 3433 Walters Av., Northbrook, 60062; B'nai Emunah (C), 9131 Niles Center Rd., Skokie, 60076; B'nai Israel Cong. of Proviso (C), 10216 Kitchener St., Westchester, 60153; B'nai Jacob Cong. of West Rogers Park (C), 6200 N. Artesian St., 60659; B'nai Tikvah (C), 1558 Wilmot Rd., Deerfield, 60015; B'nai Zion (C), 6759 N. Greenview Av., 60626; Central Syn. of the South Side Hebrew Cong. (C), 30 E. Cedar St., 60611; Cong. Mishpaha-Our Family (C), Congregation Hse., 760 Checker Dr., Buffalo Grove, 60090; Etz Chaim Cong. of DuPage County (C), 1710 S. Highland Av., Lombard, 60148; Ezra-Habonim (C), 2620 W. Touhy Av., 60645; Kol Emeth (C), 5130 W. Touhy Av., Skokie, 60077; Maine Township Jewish Cong. (C), 8809 Ballard Rd., Des Plaines, 60016; Mikdosh El Hagro Hebrew Center (C), 303 Dodge St., Evanston, 60202; Moriah Cong. (C), 200 Hyacinth St., Deerfield, 60015; Ner Tamid Cong. of North Town (C), 2754 W. Rosemont Av., 60659; North Sheridan Hebrew Cong. Adath Israel (C), 6301 N. Sheridan Rd., 60660; North Suburban Syn. Beth El (C), 1175 Sheridan Rd., Highland Park, 60035; Northwest Suburban Jewish Cong. (C), 7800 W. Lyons Rd., Morton Grove, 60053; Rodfei Zedek (C), 5200 S. Hyde Pk. Blvd., 60615;

continued from *Illinois*

Shaare Tikvah (C), 5800 N. Kimball Av., 60659; West Suburban Temple Har-Zion (C), 1040 N. Harlem Av., River Forest, 60305; Am Chai (R), 504 Iverson St., Schaumburg, 60172; Am Shalom (R), 614 Sheridan Rd., Glencoe, 60022; Anshe Shalom (R), 20820 Western Av., Olympia Fields, 60461; Beth El (R), 3050 W. Touhy Av., 60645; Beth Emet (R), 1224 Dempster St., Evanston, 60202; Beth Israel (R), 3601 Dempster, Skokie, 60076; Beth Sholom (R), 1 Dogwood Av., Park Forest, 60466; Beth Tikvah (R), 300 Hillcrest Blvd., Hoffman Estates, 60172; B'nai Jehoshua Beth Elohim (R), 901 Milwaukee Av., Glenview, 60025; B'nai Torah (R), 2789 Oak St., Highland Park, 60035; B'nai Yehuda (R), 1424 W. 183rd St., Homewood, 60430; Chicago Sinai Cong. (R), 5350 S. Shore Dr., 60615; Emanuel Cong. (R), 5959 N. Sheridan Rd., 60660; K.A.M. Isaiah Israel Cong. (R), 1100 Hyde Pk. Blvd., 60615; Kol Ami (R), 845 N. Michigan Av., 60611; Lakeside Cong. for Reform Judaism (R), 1221 County Line Rd., Highland Park, 60035; North Shore Cong. Israel (R), 1185 Sheridan Rd., Glencoe, 60022; Oak Park Temple (R), 1235 N. Harlem Av., Oak Park, 60302; Or Shalom (R), 21 Hawthorne Pkwy., Vernon Hills, 60061; Solel Cong. (R), 1301 Clavey Rd., Highland Park, 60035; Temple Jeremiah (R), 937 Happ Rd., Northfield, 60093; Temple Judea Mizpah (R), 8610 Niles Center Rd., Skokie, 60076; Temple Menorah (R), 2800 W. Sherwin St., 60645; Temple Shalom (R), 3480 N. Lake Shore Dr., 60657; Jewish Reconstructionist Cong. (Rec), 303 Dodge, Evanston, 60202; Niles Township Jewish Cong. (C-Rec), 4500 Dempster St., Skokie, 60076; Beth Or (Humanist-Rec), 2075 Deerfield Rd., Deerfield, 60015; Bene Shalom of the Hebrew Assoc. of the Deaf (Independent), 4435 Oakton St., Skokie, 60076; Etz Chaim Cong. of Des Plaines, 335 Bellaire Av., Des Plaines, 60016.

Community Centers:

Florence G. Heller Center, 524 W. Melrose Av., 60657; Bernard Horwich Center, 3003 W. Touhy Av., 60645; Hyde Park Center, 1100 E. Hyde Park Blvd., 60615; Mayer Kaplan Center, 5050 W. Church St., Skokie, 60076; North Suburban Center, 633 Skokie Hwy. #407, Northbrook, 60062; Northwest Suburban Center, 1250 Radcliffe Rd., Buffalo Gr., 60090; Anita M. Stone Center, 3400 W. 196th St., Flossmoor, 60422; Russian Jewish Cultural Center, 3003 W. Touhy Av., 60645.
Hebrew Theological College-Jewish University of America, 7135 N. Carpenter Rd., Skokie, 60076.
Spertus College of Judaica, 618 S. Michigan Av., 60605. The Maurice Spertus Museum of Judaica and the Asher Library are housed at the College. (922-9012. Fax 922-6406.
Yeshivot: Brisk Yeshiva, 2961 W. Peterson Av., 60659; Telshe Yeshiva (Rabbinical College of Telshe-Chicago Inc.), 3535 W. Foster Av., 60625.
Hebrew Theological College, 7135 Carpenter Rd., Skokie, IL 60077.
Israel Consulate, 111 E. Wacker Dr., 60601.

Newspapers

The Sentinel, 175 W. Jackson, 1927, 60604.
JUF News, 1 Ben Gurion Way.

Booksellers

Chicago Hebrew Book Store, 2942 W. Devon Av., 60645; Hamakor Judaica, 4150 Dempster, Skokie; Rosenblum, 2906 W. Devon Av., 60659; Spertus College Museum Store, 618 S. Michigan Av., 60605.

Kosher Restaurants and Carryouts:

Slice of Life (Dairy), 4120 W. Dempster Av., Skokie, 60076; Dunkin' Donuts

continued from *Illinois*

(Dairy), 3132 W. Devon Av., 60659; Bugsy Schwartz, 3355W. Dempster, Skokie. Falafel King (Glatt), 4507 W. Oakton St., Skokie, 60076; Jerusalem Café, 3014 W. Devon Av., 60659. ☎ (312) 262-0515; Ken's Diner, 3353 W. Dempster St., Skokie; King Solomon, 3445 W. Dempster St., Skokie; Kosher Gourmet (Glatt), 3553 W. Dempster Av., Skokie, 60076; Kosher Karry (Glatt), 2828 W. Devon Av., 60659; Mi Tsu Yun, 3010 W. Devon Ave.; Tel Aviv Kosher Pizza & Dairy Restaurant, 6349 N. California Av., 60659; Adis, 2700 W. Pratt, 60645; Kosher City, 3353 Dempster Av., Skokie, 60076.

Kosher Meat & Delicatessen
Hungarian Kosher Foods, 4020 Oakton St., Skokie, 60076; Miller's Meat Market, 2725 W. Devon Av., 60659; New York Kosher Sausage Corp., 2900 W. Devon Av., 60659; Romanian Kosher Sausage Co., 7200 N. Clark St., 60626; Selig's Kosher Delicatessen, 209 Skokie Valley Rd., Crossroads Shopping Center, Highland Park, 60035; Tel Aviv Kosher Deli & Supermarket, 4956 W. Dempster Av., 60077.

DECATUR
Syn.: B'nai Abraham (R), 1326 West Eldorado St., 62522. ☎ (217) 429-5740. Fax (217) 429-3766.

JOLIET
Syn.: 250 N. Midland Av. at Campbell St., 60435.

PEORIA
Jewish Fed., Town Hall Bldg., 5901 N. Prospect Rd., 61614. ☎ (309) 689-0063.
Syn.: Agudas Achim (O), 5614 N. University, 61604. ☎ (309) 692-4848.
Anshai Emeth (R), 5614 N. University St., 61614. ☎ (309) 691-3323.
Bradley University Hillel, 1410 W. Fredonia, Peoria, IL 61606. ☎ (309) 676-0682.

ROCK ISLAND
Jewish Fed. of the Quad Cities, 209 18th St., 61201.
Syn.: Tri-City Jewish Center (C), 2715 30th St., 61201. See also Davenport, Iowa.

ROCKFORD
Jewish Fed., 1500 Parkview Av., 61107. ☎ (815) 399-5497.
Syn.: Ohave Sholom (C), 3730 Guildford Rd., 61107; Temple Beth El (R), 1203 Comanche Dr., 61107. ☎ (815) 398-5020.

SPRINGFIELD
Jewish Fed., 730 E. Vine St., Room 205, 62703. ☎ (217) 528-3446.
Syn.: Temple Israel (C), 1140 West Governor St., 62704; B'rith Sholom (R), 1004 S. 4th St., 62703.

INDIANA
BLOOMINGTON
Cong Beth Shalom (R), 3750 E. Third., 47401. ☎ (812) 334-2440.
Chabad House (O), 516 E. Seventh St., 47408. ☎ (812) 332-6784.
Hillel Centre, 730 E. Third St. 47401. ☎ (812) 336-3824. Fax (812) 339-1949. Email: Hillel@Indiana.edu.
Jewish Studies Program of Indiana University, Goodbody Hall, #308, Indiana

continued from *Indiana*

EAST CHICAGO
Syn.: B'nai Israel (O), 3517 Hemlock St., 46312; Beth Sholom (C), 4508 Baring Av., 46312.

EVANSVILLE
Syn.: Adath Israel (C), 3600 E. Washington Av., 47715; Washington Av. Tempe (R), 100 Washington Av., 47714.

FORT WAYNE
Jewish Fed.: 227 E. Washington Blvd., 46802. ☎ (219) 422-8566. Fax (219) 422 8567.
Syn.: B'nai Jacob (C), 7227 Bittersweet Moors Dr., 46804. ☎ (219) 672-8459. Achduth Vesholom (R), 5200 Old Mill Rd., 46807. ☎ (219) 744-4245.

GARY
Syn.: Temple Israel (R), 601 N. Montgomery St., 46403. ☎ (219) 938-5232

HAMMOND
Syn.: Beth Israel (C), 7105 Hohman Av., 46324; Temple Beth-El (R), 6947 Hohman Av., 46324.

INDIANAPOLIS
Jewish Fed. of Greater Indianapolis, 6705 Hoover Rd., 46260. ☎ (?).
Syn.: B'nai Torah (O), 6510 Hoover Rd., 46260. ☎ (317) 253-5253.
Etz Chaim (Sephardi, O), 826 W. 64th St., 46260. ☎ (317) 251-6220.
Shaarey Tefilla Cong. (C), 5879 Central Av., 46220. ☎ (317) 253-4591; Beth-El Zedeck (C), 600 W. 70th St., 46260. ☎ (317) 253-3441.
Indianapolis Hebrew Cong. (R), 6501 N. Meridian St., 46260. ☎ (317) 255-6647.
Anglo-Jewish visitors are invited to get in touch with the Exec. Vice-Pres., Bureau of Jewish Education, 6711 Hoover Rd., 46260. ☎ (317) 255-3124.
Hooverwood Home for Aged, 7001 Hoover Rd., 46260. ☎ (317) 251-2261.
Jewish Com. Center, 6701 Hoover Rd., 46260. ☎ (317) 251-9467.
Jewish Com. Relations Council, 1100 W. 42nd St., 46208. ☎ (317) 926-2935.

LAFAYETTE
Syn.: Sons of Abraham (O), 661 N. 7th St., 47906; Temple Israel (R), 620 Cumberland St., 47901.
Kosher frankfurters & salamis are available at the Jewel Food Store, which will also order kosher frozen foods on request. The store also stocks Pesach goods.

MICHIGAN CITY
Syn.: Sinai Temple (R), 2800 S. Franklin St., 46360. ☎ (219) 874-4477.

MUNCIE
Syn.: Temple Beth El (R), 525 W. Jackson St., (cnr. Council St.), 47305. ☎ (317) 288-4662.

NORTH WEST INDIANA
Jewish Fed. of North West Indiana, 2939 Jewett St., Highland 46322. ☎ (219) 972-2251. (Gary, Hammond, Michigan City, Valparaiso and Whiting.)

SOUTH BEND
Jewish Fed. of St. Joseph Valley, 105 Jefferson Center, Suite 804, 46601. ☎ (219) 233-1164. Fax 219-288-4103.
Syn.: Hebrew Orthodox Cong. (O), 3207 S. High St., 46614; Sinai (C), 1102 E. Lasalle St., 46617; Beth-El (R), 305 W. Madison St., 46601. ☎ (219) 234-4402.

continued from *Indiana*

E. Lasalle St., 46617; Beth-El (R), 305 W. Madison St., 46601. ☎ (219) 234-4402.
Visitors requiring information about kashrut, temporary accommodation, etc., should contact Rabbi Y. Gettinger, at the Hebrew Orthodox Cong., address above, ☎ (219) 291-4239 or 291-6100, or Michael Lerman, (1-800 348-2529. For mikva appointments, ☎ (219) 291-6240.

TERRE HAUTE
Syn.: United Hebrew Cong. (R), 540 S. 6th St., 47807.
Kosher Meat & Sandwiches: 410 W. Western Av., 47807.

VALPARAISO
Syn: Temple Israel (C), P.O. Box 2051, 46383.

WHITING
Syn.: B'nai Judah (O), 116th St. & Davis Av., 46394.

IOWA
CEDAR RAPIDS
Syn.: Temple Judah, 3221 Lindsay La. S.E., 52403. ☎ (319) 362-1261.

DAVENPORT
Syn.: Temple Emanuel (R), 12th St. and Mississippi Av., 52803. Davenport is part of the Rock Island, Illinois, area, which is divided by the Mississippi River. See Rock Island entry. (p. 129).

DES MOINES
Jewish Fed. of Greater Des Moines, 910 Polk Blvd., 50312. ☎ (515) 277-6321. Also at this address: Jewish Community Relations Com. & Jewish Family Services.
Syn.: Beth El Jacob (O), 954 Cummins Pkwy., 50312; Tifereth Israel (C), 924 Polk Blvd., 50312; B'nai Jeshurun (R), 51st & Grand, 50312; Chabad, ☎ (515) 277-1718.
Bureau for Jewish Education: 924 Polk Blvd., 50312.
Iowa Jewish Senior Life Center, 900 Polk Blvd., 50312.
Kosher Food: Pickle Barrel, 1241 6th Av., 50314; The Nosh, 800 First St., W. Des Moines, 50265.

DUBUQUE
Syn.: Beth El, 475 W. Locust St., 52001.

FORT DODGE
Syn.: Beth El (C), 501 N. 12th St., 50501. ☎ (515) 573-8925 (office), (515) 573-6000.

IOWA CITY
Syn.: Agudas Achim (C & R), 602 E. Washington St., 52240. ☎ (319) 337-3813.

SIOUX CITY
Jewish Fed.: 525 14th St., 51105. ☎ (712) 258-0618.
Syn.: United Orthodox (O), 14th & Nebraska Sts., 51105; Beth Sholom (C), 815, 38th St., 51105.
Kosher Meat & Food: Sam's Food Market, 1911 Grandview, 51104.

KANSAS
OVERLAND PARK
Syn.: Beth Israel Abraham & Voliner (O), 9900 Antioch, 66212.

continued from *Kansas*

Chabad House, 6201 Indiana Creek Dr., 66207.
Young Israel (O), 8716 Woodward, 66212; Kehilath Israel (Traditional.
Generally Orthodox ritual, but mixed seating), 10501 Conser Av., 66212. The
largest traditional congregational synagogue in the USA.
Day School: Hyman Brand Hebrew Academy of Greater Kansas City, 5801 W.
115th St, Suite 102.
Central Agency for Jewish Education, 5801 W. 115th St., Suite 104, 66211.
Weekly newspaper: 'Kansas City Jewish Chronicle', 7375 W. 107th St., 66204.

PRAIRIE VILLAGE
Syn.: Ohev Sholom (C), 5311 W. 75th St., 66208. (Orthodox rite but mixed
seating).
Butcher: Jacobsons Strictly Kosher Foods, 5200 W95th St., Prairie Village, Ka
66207.
Note: The institutions and organisations in Overland Park and Prairie Village
form part of the community of Metropolitan Kansas City, Missouri (which see
p.149).

TOPEKA
Syn.: Beth Sholom (R), 4200 Munson St., 66604.
Topeka Lawrence Jewish Fed., 4200 Munson Av., 66604.

WICHITA
Syn.: Hebrew Cong. (O), 1850 N. Woodlawn, 67208; Temple Emanu-El (R),
7011 E. Central St., 67206.
Grocers: Dillon's, 21st St. & Rock Rd., & 13th St. & Woodlawn St.;
Foodbarn Woodlawn & Central Sts., 67208; The Bread Lady, 20205 Rock
Rd., #80, 2607.

KENTUCKY
The University of Kentucky Press published "The Synagogues of Kentucky:
architecture and history" by Lee Shai Weissbach, in 1995. (ISBN 0-8131-
1912-X).

LEXINGTON
Central Kentucky Jewish Fed., 340 Romany Rd., Ky 40502. ☎ (606) 268-
0672/0775.
Syn.: Lexington Havurah (C), P.O.B. 54958, 40551; Ohavay Zion (C), 2048
Edgewater Ct., 40502; Adath Israel (R), 124 N. Ashland Av., 40502.

LOUISVILLE
Jewish Com. Fed., 3630 Dutchman's Lane, 40205.
Syn.: Anshei Sfard (O), 3700 Dutchman's Lane, 40205. Mikva attached;
Keneseth Israel (T), 2531 Taylorsville Rd., 40205; Adath Jeshurun (C), 2401
Woodbourne Av., 40205; Temple Shalom (R), 4615 Lowe Rd., 40205; The
Temple (R), 5101 Brownsboro Rd., 40241.
The Com. Center is at 3600 Dutchman's Lane, 40205.
Central Agency of Jewish Education, 3595 Dutchmans Lane, 40205.
Hillel, Interfaith Center, University of Louisville, 40292. Contains the Banks-
Kaplan Jewish Affairs Library.
Jewish Family & Vocational Service, 3640 Dutchman's La., 40205.
Jewish Hospital, 217 E. Chestnut St., 40202.
Shalom Tower, 3650 Dutchman's Lane, 40205.

PADUCAH
Syn.: Temple Israel (R), 330 Joe Clifton Dr., 42001.

LOUISIANA

ALEXANDRIA
Syn.: B'nai Israel (C), 1907 Vance St., 71301; Gemiluth Chassodim (R), 2021 Turner St., 71301.
Jewish Welfare Fed., 2815 Hill St., 71301.
Library: Meyer Kaplan Memorial Library (Judaica), c/o B'nai Israel.
Kosher food: By arrangement, from Dr. and Mrs. B. Kaplan, 100 Park Place, 71301. ☎ (318) 445 9367.

BATON ROUGE
Jewish Fed. of Greater Baton Rouge, P.O.B. 80827, 70898. ☎ (504) 291-5895.
Syn.: B'nai Israel (R), 3354 Kleinert Av., 70806; Beth Shalom Syn. (R), 9111 Jefferson Highway, 70809.

LAFAYETTE
Syn.: Temple Rodef Sholom (R), 603 Lee Av., 70501.
There is a very fine Judaica library at the University of Southwestern Louisiana.

NEW ORLEANS
Jewish Fed. of Greater New Orleans, 3500 N. Causeway Blvd., #1240, Metairie, 70002. ☎ (504) 828-2125. Fax (504) 828-2827.

Synagogues:
Anshe Sfard (O), 2230 Carondelet St., 70130; ☎ (504) 522-4714.
Beth Israel (O), 7000 Canal Blvd., 70124. ☎ (504) 283-4366. (Mikva attached).
Chabad Hse. (O), 7037 Freret St., 70118. ☎ (504) 866-5342; Chevra Thilim (C), 4429 S. Claiborne Av., 70125. ☎ (504) 895-7987; Chabad Center (O), 4141 W. Esplanade Av., Metairie, 70002. ☎ (504) 454-2910; Tikvat Shalom (C), 3737 W. Esplanade Av., Metairie, 70002. ☎ (504) 889-1144; Gates of Prayer (R), 4000 W. Esplanade Av., Metairie, 70002. ☎ (504) 885-2600; Temple Sinai (R), 6227 St. Charles Av., 70118. ☎ (504) 861-3693; Touro (R), 1501 General Pershing Av., 70115. ☎ (504) 895-4843 (the oldest in the Mississippi Valley).
Jewish Com. Center, Uptown 5342 St. Charles Av., 70115. ☎ (504) 987-0143; Metairie, 6121 W. Esplanade Av., 70003. ☎ (504) 887 5158.
Hillel Foundation, 912 Broadway St., 70118. ☎ (504) 866-7060. Near the Tulane University Campus.
Newspaper: 'The Jewish News' (as Jewish Federation). Community newspaper.
Touro Infirmary, 1401 Foucher St., 70115. ☎ (504) 897-8246. Glatt Kosher meals available.

Accommodation and Restaurants
The Pontchartrain Grand Heritage Hotel, 2031 St Charles Ave., 70140. ☎ (504) 524-0581. Res. 1-800-777-6193. Kosher food available on request.
Visitors wishing Glatt kosher b&b in New Orleans should contact Dr. & Mrs. Saul Kahn, 4000 Clifford Dr., Metairie, 70002. ☎ (504) 831-2230 or 833-1352. Fax 834-6563 We keep glatt kosher. 'Having guests from all over the world enriches our lives.'
(K) Casablanca, 3030 Seven Ave., Metairie, 70002-4826. ☎ (504) 888-2209.
Grocery Kosher Cajun Deli and Grocery, 3520 N. Hullen St., Metairie, 70002. ☎ (504) 888 2010.

continued from *Louisiana*

SHREVEPORT

Jewish Fed., 2032 Line Av., 71104. ☎ (318) 221-4129.
Syn.: Agudath Achim (C), 9401 Village Green Dr., 71115. ☎ (318) 797-6401;
B'nai Zion (R), 245 Southfield Rd., 71105.

MAINE

AUBURN

Syn.: Cong. Beth Abraham (C), Main St. & Laurel Av., 04210. ☎ (207) 783-1302; Temple Shalom (C), 74 Bradman St., 04210. See also Lewiston, below.

BANGOR

Syn.: Beth Abraham (O), 145 York St., 04401; Cong. Beth Israel (C), 144 York St., 04401.
(K) The Bagel Shop, 1 Main St., Bangor, Maine 04451. ☎ (207) 947-1654.

LEWISTON

Lewiston-Auburn Jewish Fed., 74 Bradman St., 04210. ☎ (207) 786-4201.

OLD ORCHARD BEACH

Syn.: Beth Israel (O), 49 E. Grand Av., 04064. ☎ (207) 934-2973. Daily minyan, May 28 to Yom Kippur. Shabbat & Yomtov minyan all year round.
For kashrut inf. contact: Eber Weinstein, 187 E. Grand Av., 04064. ☎ (207) 934-7522; Eddie Hakim, ☎ (207) 934-7223, or Harold Goodkovski. ☎ (207) 934-4210.

PORTLAND

Jewish Fed.-Com. Council of Southern Maine, 57 Ashmont St., 04103. ☎ (207) 773-7254.
Syn.: Etz Chaim (O), 267 Congress St., 04101; Shaarey Tphiloh (O), 76 Noyes St., 04103; Mikva & Hebrew Day School on premises; Beth El (C), 400 Deering Av., 04103. ☎ (207) 774-2649.
Cong. Bet Ha'am (R), 158 North St., 04101. ☎ (207) 879-0028.
Jewish Com. Center, 57 Ashmont St., 04103. ☎ (207) 772-1959.
Cedars Nursing Care Center, 630 Ocean Avenue, 04103. Jewish Home for Aged/Kosher Kitchen.
Penny Wise Super Market, 182 Ocean Avenue, 04130. Kosher butcher & take-out deli.
Smith Street Cemetery, Smith Street, South Portland, ME0 4106. Established 1860. Key available at Jewish Federation Office.

MARYLAND

ANNAPOLIS

Syn.: Kneseth Israel (O), 1125 Spa Rd., 21403. ☎ (410) 263-3924; Cong. Kol Ami (C), 1909 Hidden Meadow La., 21401; Temple Beth Sholom (R), 1461 Baltimore-Annapolis Blvd., 21012.
There is a kosher kitchen at Kneseth Israel.
There is now a Jewish Chapel at the US Naval Academy, and midshipmen usually worship there.

BALTIMORE

The city's Jewish community, numbering some 93,000, is one of the most cohesive and dynamic in the whole of the United States.
Baltimore is the home town of the late Henrietta Szold. There is a street named after her.

continued from *Maryland*

Associated Jewish Community Fed. of Baltimore, 101 W. Mount Royal Av., 21201. ☎ (410) 727-4828.
There are at least 50 syns in the Baltimore metropolitan area, but only the most important are listed below.
Syn.: Agudath Israel (O), 6202 Park Heights Av., 21215; Beth Jacob (O), 5713 Park Heights Av., 21215; Beth Tfiloh (O), 3300 Old Court Rd., 21208; Shomrei Emunah (O), 6221 Greenspring Av., 21209; Suburban Orthodox (O), 7504 Seven Mile Lane, 21208; Beth El (C), 8101 Park Heights Av., 21208; Beth Israel (C), 3706 Crondall Lane, Owings Mills, 21117; Chizuk Amuno (C), 8100 Stevenson Rd., 21208; Baltimore Hebrew Cong. (R), 7401 Park Heights Av., 21208; Har Sinai (R), 6300 Park Heights Av., 21215; Oheb Shalom (R), 7310 Park Heights Av., 21208.
Baltimore Jewish Council, 5750 Park Heights Av., 21215. ☎ 542 4850.
Only one Jewish historical institution in the United States includes two historic syns. (Lloyd St. & B'nai Israel), a museum and a research Center — the Jewish Heritage Center, at 15 Lloyd St., 21202 (732-6400), which is run by the Jewish Historical Society of Maryland. The Lloyd St. Syn., built in 1845, is the third oldest syn. building in the US. B'nai Israel, built in 1876, is the oldest syn. in continuous use in Baltimore.
At Gay and Water Sts. is the community's Holocaust Memorial, maintained by the Baltimore Jewish Council.
Mikva of Baltimore, Inc., 3207 Clarks Lane, Baltimore, MD 21225. ☎ 664-5834.
Jewish Com. Centers: 5700 Park Heights Av., 21215. ☎ 542-4900; 3506 Gwynnbrook Av., Owings Mills, 21117. ☎ 356-5200.
Baltimore Hebrew University, 5800 Park Heights Av., 21215. ☎ 578-6900.
Council on Jewish Education, 5800 Park Heights Av., 21215. ☎ 578-6943.
Meyerhoff Library, 5800 Park Heights Av., 21215. ☎ 578-6936.
Ner Israel Rabbinical College, Mount Wilson Lane, 21208 ☎ 484-7200, claims to be the largest yeshiva campus anywhere.
Jewish Historical Society of Maryland: 15 Lloyd St., 21202. ☎ 732 6400.
Sinai Hospital:Greenspring & Belvedere Avs., 21202. ☎ 578-5678.

Kosher Restaurants:
Chapps Kosher Chinese, Pomona Sq. Shopping Center, 1700 Reisterstown Rd., 21208; Kosher Bite, 6309 Reisterstown Rd., 21215; Royal Restaurant, 7006 Reisterstown Rd., 21208; Tov Pizza, 6313 Reisterstown Rd., 21208.
Kosher Delicatessens and Take out: Knish Shop, 508 Reisterstown Rd., 21208; Liebes, 607 Reisterstown Rd., Pikesville, MD 21208. ☎ 653-1977; Danielle's, 401 Reisterstown Rd., 21208.

Kosher Supermarkets
Mirakle Market, 6836 Reisterstown Rd., 21215. ☎ 358-3443.
Seven Mile Market, 4000 Seven Mile La., Pikesville, 21208. ☎ 653-2000.
Shlomo Meat & Fish, 4030 Falstaff Rd., 21215. ☎ 358-9633.
Wasserman & Lemberger, 7006-D, Reisterstown Rd., 21208. ☎ 486-4191.

Bakeries
Goldman's Kosher Bakery 6848 Reisterstown Rd., 21215; Pariser's Kosher Bakery, 6711 Reisterstown Rd., 21215; Schmell & Azman Kosher Bakery, 21215.

For all kashrut inf., contact: Orthodox Jewish Council Vaad Hakashrut, 11 Warren Rd., Baltimore, MD 21208. ☎ 484-4110.

Jewish Info. Service is open from 10.00 am to 2 pm daily at 5750 Park Heights Av., 21215. ☎ (410) 466-4636. For help about almost anything.

continued from *Maryland*

BETHESDA
United Jewish Appeal-Fed. of Greater Washington, 7900 Wisconsin Av., 20814. ☎ (301) 652-6480.
Syns.: Beth El of Montgomery County (C), 8215 Old Georgetown Rd., 20814; Bethesda Jewish Cong. (unaffiliated), 6601 Bradley Blvd., 20817.

BOWIE
Syn.: Nevey Shalom (C), 12218 Torah Lane, 20715 (corner of Rt 450 & Trinity Drive). ☎ (301) 262-4020.
Temple Solel (R), 2901 Mitchelville Rd., 20716. ☎ (301) 249-2424.

CHEVY CHASE
Syn.: Ohr Kodesh (C), 8402 Freyman Dr., 20815. ☎ 589-3880.
Temple Shalom (R), 8401 Grubb Rd., 20815. ☎ 587-2273..

CUMBERLAND
Syn.: Beth Jacob (C), 11 Columbia St., 21502; B'Er Chayim (R), 107 Union St., 21502.
Kosher Dairy Restaurant, Delicatessen & Bakery
The Bagel Shop, 1 Main St., 04401. ☎ (207) 947-1654. Also take out. Closed Sats. Under rabbinical supervision.

GAITHERSBURG
Syn.: Kehilat Shalom (C), 9915 Apple Ridge Rd., 20879. ☎ (301) 869-7699. Fax (301) 977-7870.

GREENBELT
Syn.: Mishkan Torah (C), Westway and Ridge Rd., 20770. ☎ (301) 474-4223.

HAGERSTOWN
Syn.: B'nai Abraham (R), 53 E. Baltimore St., 21740. ☎ (301) 733-5039.
Celebrity Deli, 36 N. Potomac St., 21740. ☎ (301) 714-1768.

HYATSVILLE
Beth Torah Cong. (C), 6700 Adelphi Rd., 20782. ☎ 927-5525.

KENSINGTON
Syn.: Temple Emanuel (R), 10101 Connecticut Av., 20895. ☎ (301) 942-2000. Fax (301) 942-9488.

LAUREL
Syn.: Oseh Shalom (Rec), 8604 Briarwood Dr., 20708. ☎ 498-5151.

LEXINGTON PARK
Syn.: Beth Israel (C), Bunker Hill Dr., 20650. ☎ 862-2021.

OLNEY
Syn.: B'nai Shalom (C), 18401 Burtfield Dr., 20832. ☎ 774-0879.

POCOMOKE
Syn.: Temple Israel (C), 3rd St., 21851.

POTOMAC
Syn.: Beth Sholom of Potomac (O), 11825 Seven Locks Rd., 20854. ☎ 279-7010; Har Shalom (C), 11510 Falls Rd., 20854. ☎ 299-7087.

continued from *Maryland*

Restaurant: (**K**) Hunan Gourmet, 350 Fortune Terrace. ☎ 424-0191.

ROCKVILLE
Syn.: Beth Tikvah (C), 2200 Baltimore Rd., 20853; B'nai Israel (C), 6301 Montrose Rd., 20852; Mogen David Sephardic Cong (O), 11418 Old Georgetown Rd., 20852, ☎ (301) 770-6818.
Temple Beth Ami (R), 800 Hurley Av., 20850. ☎ 340-6818.
Jewish Com. Center of Greater Washington & Hebrew Home, 6125 Montrose Rd., 20852.

Kosher Restaurants:
Katz's Kafe, 4860 Boiling Brook Pkwy, ☎ (301) 468-0400.
Moshe Dragon Glatt Kosher Chinese Restaurant, 4840 Boiling Brook Pkwy. ☎ 468-1922. Under Supervision of Rabbinical Council of Washington.

SALISBURY
Syn.: Beth Israel (C), Camden Av. & Wicomico St., 21801.

SILVER SPRING AND WHEATON
Syn.: Silver Spring Jewish Center (O), 1401 Arcola Av., 20902. ☎ 649-4425. Mikva on premises; South-East Hebrew Cong. (O), 10900 Lockwood Dr., 20902; Woodside Syn. Ahavas Torah (O), 9001 Georgia Av., 20910; Young Israel Shomrai Emunah (O), 1132 Arcola Av., 20902; Har Tzeon-Agudath Achim (C), 1840 University Blvd. W., 20902; Shaare Tefila (C), 11120 Lockwood Dr., 20901; Temple Israel (C), 420 University Blvd. E., 20901. ☎ 439-3600.
Mikva: 8901 Georgia Av., 20907.
Orthodox Rabbinical Assoc., 1401 Arcola Av., 20902.
The Hebrew Sheltering Society has premises where people visiting the Washington area who are unable to afford a hotel can stay for up to three nights. This 'guest house' is at 11524 Daffodil La., 20902. In addition, if space is available, people wishing to stay within walking distance of a syn. on Shabbat or Yom Tov only can be accommodated. (The Silver Spring Jewish Center is only one short block away.) For further inf., ☎ 649-3141, 649-4425 or 649-2799 (Rabbi Herzel Kranz).

Bookshops
Lisbon's Hebrew Book Store & Giftshop, 2305 University Blvd. W., Wheaton, 20902; The Jewish Bookstore, 11250 Georgia Av., 20902.

Kosher Dairy Restaurants
The Nut House, 11419 Georgia Av., Wheaton, 20902. ☎ 942-5900; Under the supervision of the Rabbinical Council of Greater Washington.

Bakeries
Virtuoso, 11203A Lockwood Av., 50901. ☎ 593-6034; The Wooden Shoe Pastry Shop, 11301 Georgia Av., 20902.
Meat & Delicatessen: Shalom, 2307 University Blvd., 20902.

TEMPLE HILLS
Syn.: Shaare Tikva (C), 5405 Old Temple Hills Rd., 20748. ☎ 894-4303.

Note: Bethesda, Bowie, Chevy Chase, Gaithersburg, Greenbelt, Hyattsville, Kensington, Laurel, Lexington Park, Olney, Potomac, Rockville, Silver Spring & Wheaton and Temple Hills are all part of Greater Washington, D.C.

MASSACHUSETTS

ACTON
Syn.: Beth Elohim (Independent), 10 Hennessey Dr., 07120. ☎ (508) 263-3061.

AMHERST
Jewish Community, 724 Main St., 01002. ☎ (413) 256-0160.

ANDOVER
Temple Emanuel (R), 7 Haggett's Pond Rd., 01810. ☎ (508) 470-1356.

ATHOL
Syn.: Temple Israel (Ind), 107 Walnut St., 01331. ☎ (508) 249-9481.

ATTLEBORO
Syn.: Agudas Achim Cong. (R), Kelly & Toner Blvds., 02703. ☎ (508) 222-2243.

AYER
Syn.: Cong. Anshey Sholom (Ind), Cambridge St., 01432. ☎ (508) 772-0896.

BELMONT
Syn.: Beth El Temple Center (R), 2 Concord Av., 02178. ☎ (617) 484-6668.

BEVERLY
Syn.: B'nai Abraham (C), 200 E. Lothrop St., 01915. ☎ (508) 927-3211.

BOSTON AREA (GREATER BOSTON)
Greater Boston includes some 69 cities and towns in the contiguous area. Its Jewish population is now concentrated in Brookline, Newton and Sharon (which see), and not in Boston proper.
Jewish Com. Relations Council of Greater Boston, 1 Lincoln Plaza, Suite 308, 02111. ☎ (617) 330-9600, represents 34 community organisations in the area. Brandeis University in Waltham, Massachusetts, est. 1948, ☎ (617) 8918110, is the second university in the U.S.A. under Jewish auspices. It is a secular institution. The American Jewish Historical Society library on the Brandeis campus contains the largest collection of American Hebraica in the world.
The Public Library has a number of Sargent paintings of the Prophets and many other items of Jewish interest, as well as one of the largest collections of Anglo-Judaica in the country. Boston University has a library containing many items of Jewish interest.
For inf. about the many syns. and kosher restaurants in other parts of the Greater Boston area, contact the **Synagogue Council of Massachusetts**, 1320 Center St., Newton Center, 02159. ☎ (617) 244 6506. Fax (617) 964-7055. Email: syncouncil@aol.com. Publisher an annual Directory.
Vaad Harabonim of Massachusetts, 177 Tremont St., 02111. ☎ (617) 426-2139. The Kashruth Commission, which is at the same address, provides inf. about kosher restaurants, accom. and products. Also at 177 Tremont St. are the Rabbinical Council of New England & the Rabbinical Court.

Synagogues:
Chabad House (O), 491 Commonwealth Av., 02215. ☎ (617) 523-0453; The Boston Synagogue at Charles River Park (O), 55 Martha Rd., 02114. ☎ (617) 523-0453; Cong. Kadimah-Toras Moshe (O), 113 Washington St., Brighton,

continued from *Massachusetts*

02135. ☎ (617) 254-1333; Lubavitch Shul of Brighton (O), 239 Chestnut Hill Av., Brighton, 02135. ☎ (617) 782-8340; Zvhiller Beis Medrash (O), 15 School St., 02108. ☎ (617) 227-8200. Hillel B'nai Torah (C), 120 Corey St., W. Roxbury, 02132. ☎ (617) 323-0486; Temple B'nai Moshe (C), 1845 Commonwealth Av., Brighton, 02135. ☎ (617) 254-3620; Temple Israel (R), Plymouth St. & Longwood Av., 02115. ☎ (617) 566-3960.
Mikva: Daughters of Israel, 101 Washington St., Brighton, 02135.
Combined Jewish Philanthropies of Greater Boston 1, Lincoln Plaza, 02111. ☎ (617) 330-9500.
Vilna Center for Jewish Heritage, 1 Financial Center, 40th Floor, 02111. The Center aims to restore the sole surviving synagogue in the Beacon Hill area.
Newspapers: 'The Jewish Advocate' and the 'Boston Jewish Times', 15 School St., 02108. ☎ (617) 367-9100. Fax (617) 367-9310. Publishes a "Jewish guide to Boston and New England".

Restaurants
Milk St. Café, 50 Milk St. ☎ (617)-542-FOOD. Dairy foods only. Under rabbinical supervision; The Park at Post Office Sq. ☎ (617)-350-PARK. Rabbinically supervised kosher meals are available (by previous arrangement) at the Hillel Foundation, Boston University. ☎ (617) 266-3882.

BRAINTREE
Syn.: Temple Bnai Shalom (C), 41 Storrs Av., 02184. ☎ (617) 843-3687.

BROCKTON
Syn.: Agudath Achim (O), 144 Belmont Av., 02401. ☎ (508) 583-0717; Beth Emunah (C), Pearl & Torrey Sts., 02401. ☎ (508) 583-5810; Temple Israel (R), 184 W. Elm St., 02401. ☎ (508) 587-4130.
The Jewish Com. Center is in Stoughton, see p.000.

BROOKLINE
Syn.: Beth David (O), 64 Corey Rd., 02146. ☎ (617) 232-2349; Beth Pinchas (Bostoner Rebbe) (O), 1710 Beacon St., 02146. ☎ (617) 734-5100; Chai Odom (O), 77 Englewood Av., 02146. ☎ (617) 734-5359; Young Israel of Brookline (O), 62 Green St., 02146. ☎ (617) 734-0276; Beth Zion (C), 1566 Beacon St., 02146. ☎ (617) 566-8171; Kehillath Israel (C), 384 Harvard St., 02146. ☎ (617) 277-9155; Ohabei Shalom (R), 1187 Beacon St., 02146. ☎ (617) 277-6610; Temple Sinai (R), Charles St. & Sewall Av., Coolidge Cnr., 02146. ☎ (617) 277-5888; Sfardic Cong. of New England, 151 Salisbury Rd., 02146. ☎ (617) 964-1526.
New England Hebrew Academy, 9 Prestcott St., 02146.
Yeshiva: Maimonides,Philbrick Rd. at Boylston St., 02146.
The Hebrew College at 43 Hawes St., 02146, ☎ (617) 232-8710, is the only institution of higher Jewish learning in the six New England States. Its library contains more than 100,000 volumes of Hebraica & Judaica, manuscripts, etc. It has a kosher cafeteria.

Kosher Restaurants
Rubin's, 500 Harvard St., 02146. ☎ (617) 731-8787. Shalom Hunan, 92 Harvard St., 02146. ☎ (617) 731 9760. The foregoing are under the supervision of the Vaad Harabonim.
Cafe Shiraz, 1030 Commonwealth Av., 02146. ☎ (617) 566-8888.
Rami's, 324 Harvard St. ☎ (617) 738-3577; Ruth's Kitchen, 401 Harvard St. ☎ (617) 734-9810.

continued from *Massachusetts*

Victor's Pizza, 1364 Beacon St., 02146. ☎ (617) 730-9903.

Harvard St. is the Jewish commercial Center, with art & bookshops, as well as many kosher butcher's shops & bakeries.

BURLINGTON
Syn.: Temple Shalom Emeth (R), 14-16 Lexington St., 01803. ☎ (617) 272-2351.

CAMBRIDGE
Syn.: Temple Beth Shalom of Cambridge (C), 8 Tremont St., 02139. ☎ (617) 864-6388.
Kosher meals are obtainable (by previous arrangement) at Hillel Hse., Harvard University, 52 Mt. Auburn St., 02138; Hillel Hse., Massachusetts Institute of Technology, 312 Memorial Dr., 02139; all the foregoing are under rabbinical supervision.

CANTON
Syn.: Beth Abraham (C), 1301 Washington St., 02021. ☎ (617) 828-5250; Temple Beth David of the South Shore (R), 256 Randolph St., 02021. ☎ (617) 828-2275.

CHELMSFORD
Syn.: Cong. Shalom (R), Richardson Rd., 01824. ☎ (508) 251-8091.

CHELSEA
Syn.: Agudas Shalom (O), 145 Walnut St., 02150. ☎ (617) 884-8668; Cong. Ahavas Achim Anshe Sfard (O), 57 County Rd., 02150 ☎ (617) 889 2016; Cong. Shaare Zion (O), 76 Orange St., 02150. ☎ (617) 884-0498; Shomrei Linas Hazedek (O), 140 Shurtleff St., 02150. ☎ (617) 884-9443; Temple Emmanuel (Ind.), Carey Av. & Tudor St., 02150. ☎ (617) 884-9699.

CHESTNUT HILL
Syn.: Cong. Lubavitvch (O), 100 Woodcliff Rd., 02167. ☎ (617) 469-9007; Temple Emeth (C), 194 Grove St., 02167. ☎ (617) 469-9400; Mishkan Tefila (C), 300 Hammond Pond Pkwy., 02167. ☎ (617) 332-7770. This is the oldest Conservative cong. in New England.

CLINTON
Syn.: Shaarei Zedeck, (Ind), Water St., 01510. ☎ (508) 365-3320.

EAST FALMOUTH
Syn.: Falmouth Jewish Cong. (R), 7 Hatchville Rd., 02536. ☎ (508) 540-0602.

EASTON
Syn.: Temple Chayai Shalom (T), 9 Mechanic St., 02356. ☎ (508) 238-4896.

EVERETT
Syn.: Tifereth Israel (T), 34 Malden St., 02149. ☎ (617) 387-0200.

FALL RIVER
Syn.: Adas Israel (O), 1647 Robeson St., 02720. ☎ (508) 674-9761; Beth El (C), 385 High St., 02720. ☎ (508) 674-3529.
Fall River Jewish Com. Council, Room 327, 56 N. Main St., 02720.

FITCHBURG
Syn.: Agudas Achim (Ind.), 40 Boutelle St., 01420. ☎ (508) 342-7704.

continued from *Massachusetts*

FRAMINGHAM
Combined Jewish Philanthropies, Metrowest Office and Metrowest J.C.C., 76 Salem End Rd., 01701. ☎ (508) 879-3300. Fax (508) 879-5856.
Syn.: Chabad Hse. (O), 74 Joseph Rd., 01701. ☎ (508) 877-8888; Beth Sholom (C), Pamela Rd., 01701. ☎ (508) 877-2540; Beth Am (R), 300 Pleasant St., 01701. ☎ (508) 872-8300.

GLOUCESTER
Syn.: Ahavath Achim (C), 86 Middle St., 01930. ☎ (508) 281-0739.

GREENFIELD
Syn.: Temple Israel (C), 27 Pierce St., 01301. ☎ (413) 773-5884. Rabbi Louis A. Reser.

HAVERHILL
Syn.: Anshe Sholom (O), 427 Main St., 01830. ☎ (508) 372-2276; Temple Emanu-El (R), 514 Main St., 01830. ☎ (508) 373-3861.

HINGHAM
Syn.: Cong. Sha'aray Shalom (R), 1112 Main St., 02043. ☎ (617) 749-8103.

HOLBROOK
Syn.: Temple Beth Sholom (C), 95 Plymouth St., 02343. ☎ (617) 767-4922.

HOLLISTON
Temple Beth Torah (C), 2162 Washington St., 01746. ☎ (508) 429-6268.

HOLYOKE
Syn.: Rodphey Sholom (O), 1800 Northampton St., 01040. ☎ (413) 534-5262; Sons of Zion (C), 378 Maple St., 01040. ☎ (413) 534-3369.

HULL
Syn.: Temple Beth Sholom (C), 600 Nantasket Av., 02045. ☎ (617) 925-0091. Temple Israel of Nantasket (C), 3 Hadassah Way, 02045. ☎ (617) 925-0289 (Summer only).

HYANNIS
Syn.: Cape Cod Syn. (R), 145 Winter St., 02601. ☎ (508) 775-2988.

HYDE PARK
Syn.: Temple Adas Hadrath Israel (C), 28 Arlington St., 02136. ☎ (617) 364-2661.

LAWRENCE
Jewish Com. Council of Greater Lawrence, 580 Haverhill St., 01841. ☎ (617) 686-4157.
Syn.: Anshai Sholum (O), 411 Hampshire St., 01843. ☎ (508) 683-4544;

LEOMINSTER
Syn.: Cong. Agudat Achim (C), 268 Washington St., 01453. ☎ (508) 534-6121.

LEXINGTON
Syn.: Chabad Center (O), 9 Burlington St., 02173. ☎ (617) 863-8656; Temple Emunah (C), 9, Piper Rd., 02173. ☎ (617) 861-0300; Temple Isaiah (R), 55 Lincoln St., 02173. ☎ (617) 862-7160.

LOWELL
Syn.: Montefiore Synagogue (O), 460 Westford St., 01851. ☎ (508) 459-

continued from *Massachusetts*

9400; Temple Beth El (C), 105 Princeton Blvd., 01851. ☎ (508) 453-7744; Temple Emanuel of Merrimack Valley (R), 101 W. Forest St., 01851. ☎ (508) 454-1372.

Mikvah, 48 Academy Dr. ☎ (508) 970-2008.

Willow Manor Nursing Home, 30 Princeton Blvd., 01851. ☎ (508) 454-8086. Under supervision of Vaad Hakashrus of Massachusetts.

Kosher Restaurants
The Very Victorian Sherman-Berry House, B&B.
Donut Shack. Contact Montefiore Synagogue for information.

LYNN
Syn.: Ahabat Shalom (O), 151 Ocean St., 01902. (Houses the Eliot Feuerstein Library). ☎ (617) 593 9255; Anshai Sfard (O), 150 S. Common St., 01905. ☎ (617) 599-7131; Chevra Tehilim (O), 12 Breed St., 01902. ☎ (617) 598-2964.

North Shore Jewish Historical Society, 31 Exchange St., 01901.

MALDEN
Syn.: Beth Israel (O), 10 Dexter St., 02148. ☎ (617) 322-5686; Young Israel (O), 45 Holyoke St., 02148. ☎ (617) 322-5686; Ezrath Israel (C), 245 Bryant St., 02148. ☎ (617) 322-7205; Tifereth Israel (R), 539 Salem St., 02148. ☎ (617) 322-2794; Cong. Agudas Achim (T), 160 Harvard St., 02148. ☎ (617) 322-9380.

MARBLEHEAD
Jewish Fed. of the North Shore, 4 Community Rd., 01945. ☎ (617) 598-1810. Syn.: Orthodox Cong. of the North Shore (O), 17 Seaview Av., 01945. ☎ (617) 631-4925; Temple Sinai (C), 1 Community Rd., 01945. ☎ (617) 631-2244; Temple Emanu-El (R), 393 Atlantic Av., 01945. ☎ (617) 631-9300. N. Shore Com. Center, 4 Community Rd., 01945. Houses the Eli & Bessie Cohen Library.

MARLBORO
Syn.: Temple Emanuel (C), 150 Berlin Rd., 01752. ☎ (508) 485-7565 or (508) 562-5105.

MEDFORD
Syn.: Temple Shalom (C), 475 Winthrop St., 02155. ☎ (617) 396-3262.

MELROSE
Syn.: Temple Beth Shalom (R), 21 E. Foster St., 02176. ☎ (617) 665-4520.

MILFORD
Syn.: Beth Shalom (C), 49 Pine St., 01757. ☎ (508) 473-1590.

MILLIS
Syn.: Cong. Ael Chunon (C), 334 Village St., 02054. ☎ (508) 376-5984.

MILTON
Syn.: B'nai Jacob (O), 100 Blue Hill Pkwy., 02187. ☎ (617) 698-0698; Temple Shalom (C), 180 Blue Hill Av., 02186. ☎ (617) 698-3394.

NATICK
Syn.: Chabad Lubavitch Center (O), 2 East Mill St., 01760. ☎ (508) 650-1499; Temple Israel (C), 145 Hartford St., 01760.

NEEDHAM
Syn.: Temple Aliyah (C), 1664 Central Av., 02192. ☎ (617) 444-8522. Fax

continued from *Massachusetts*

(617) 449-7066; Temple Beth Shalom (R), Highland & Webster Sts., Needham Heights, 02194. ☎ (617) 777-0077.

NEW BEDFORD
Jewish Fed. of Greater New Bedford, 467 Hawthorn St., N. Dartmouth, 02747. ☎ (508) 997-7471.
Syn.: Ahavath Achim (O), 385 County St., 02740. ☎ (508) 994-1760; Tifereth Israel (C), 145 Brownell Av., 02740. ☎ (508) 997-3171.

NEWBURYPORT
Syn.: Cong. Ahavas Achim, Washington & Olive Sts., 09150. ☎ (508) 462-2461.

NEWTON
Jewish Com. Center of Greater Boston, 333 Nahanton St., 02159. ☎ (617) 558-6522. Kosher Snack bar supervised by Orthodox Rabbinical Council of Massachusetts. ☎ (617) 558-6475.

Synagogues:
Syn. Council of Massachusetts, 1320 Center St., Newton Center, 02159. ☎ (617) 244-6506.
Cong. Agudas Achim-Anshe Sfard (O), 168 Adams St., 02160. Cong. Beth El-Atereth Israel (O), 561 Ward St., 02159. ☎ (617) 244-7233; Cong. Shaarei Tefillah (O), 35 Morseland Av., 02159. ☎ (617) 527-7637; Mishkan Tefila (C), the oldest Conservative cong. in New England, is "located in two cities which overlap" – Newton & Chestnut Hill, Mass., which see; Temple Emanuel (C), 385 Ward St., 02159 ☎ (617) 332-5770; Temple Reyim (C), 1860 Washington St., 02166. ☎ (617) 527-2410; Beth Avodah (R), 45 Puddingstone La., 02159. ☎ (617) 527-0045; Temple Shalom (R), 175 Temple St., 02165. ☎ (617) 332-9550; Shir Hadash (Rec.), 1320 Center St., 02159. ☎ (617) 965-6862; Dorshei Tzedek (Rec.), 67 Chester St., 02161. ☎ (617) 965-0330; Zvhiller Beis Medrash (O), Cong. Bnai Jacob, 955 Beacon Street, ☎ (617) 227-8200.
Bakery: Tuler's Bakery, 551 Commonwealth Ave., 02159. ☎ (617) 964-5653.

NORTH ADAMS
Syn.: Cong. Beth Israel (C), 265 Church St., 01247. ☎ (413) 663-5830.

NORTHAMPTON
Syn.: B'nai Israel (C), 253 Prospect St., 01060. ☎ (413) 584-3593.
Hillel Foundation, Smith College, Elm St. & Round Hill Rd., 01060. ☎ (413) 584-2700.

NORWOOD
Syn.: Temple Shaare Tefilah (C), 556 Nichols St., 02062. ☎ (617) 762-8670.

ONSET
Syn.: Beth Israel (O), cnr. of Onset Av. & Locust St., P. O. Box 24, Onset, 02558. Services three times daily from last Sat. in June to Labour Day. Services are also held on the High Holy-days. Efficiency apts, available near syn. Further inf. from Burt Parker, ☎ (508) 295 9185.
Bridge View Hotel, 12 S. Water St., 02558, welcomes Jewish guests. Self-catering flatlets available. Kosher meat and other products available. ☎ (508) 295-9820. Self-catering flatlets also available at Bay View Motel, 181 Onset Av., 02558. ☎ (508) 295-5937. Rooms available also at the Onset Pointe Inn, 9 Eagle Way, 02558. ☎ (508) 295-8442. 1-800-35-Onset. Breakfast included

PEABODY
Syn.: Temple Ner Tamid (C), 368 Lowell St., 01960. ☎ (508) 532-1293; Beth

continued from *Massachusetts*

Shalom (R), 489 Lowell St., 01960. ☎ (508) 535-2100; Cong. Sons of Israel (T), Park & Spring Sts., 01960. ☎ (508) 531-7576; Cong. Tifereth Israel (Ind), Pierpont St., 01960. ☎ (508) 531-8135.

PITTSFIELD (Berkshires)

Jewish Fed. of the Berkshires, 235 East St., 01201. ☎ (413) 442-4360. Syn.: Ahavath Sholom Cong. (O), 177 Robbins Av., 01201. ☎ (413) 442-6609; Knesset Israel (C), 16 Colt Rd., 01201. ☎ (413) 445-4872; Anshe Amunim (R), 26 Broad St., 01201. ☎ (413) 442-5910.
Ahavath Sholom Synagogue (O), North St., Great Barrington, MA 01230. ☎ (413) 528-4197.
Hevreh (C), Box 912, Great Barrington, MA 01230. ☎ (413) 298-3394.

PLYMOUTH

Syn.: Cong. Beth Jacob (R), 8 Pleasant St., 02361. ☎ (508) 746-1575.
Comm. Center at Brewster, P. O. Box 3284, 02361. ☎ (508) 746-1575.
Holocaust Memorial Monument, at Beth Jacob Cemetery, 1km west of Plymouth Center.

QUINCY

Syn.: Adas Shalom (C), 435 Adams St., 02169. ☎ (617) 471-1818; Temple Beth El (C), 1001 Hancock St., 02169. ☎ (617) 479-4309; Beth Israel (O), 33 Grafton St., 02169. ☎ (617) 472-6796.

RANDOLPH

Syn.: Young Israel — Kehillath Jacob of Mattapan & Randolph (O), 374 N. Main St., 02368. ☎ (617) 986 6461; Temple Beth Am (C), 871 N. Main St., 02368. ☎ (617) 963-0440.
Bookshop: Davidson's Hebrew Book Store, 1106 N. Main St., 02368.

REVERE

Syn.: Ahavas Achim Anshei Sfard (O), 89 Walnut Av., 02151. ☎ (617) 289-1026; Tifereth Israel (O), 43 Nahant Av., 02151. ☎ (617) 284-9255; B'nai Israel (Independent), 1 Wave Av., 02151. ☎ (617) 284-8388.
Com. Center, Shirley Av., 02151.
Kosher Meat and Take-Away: Myer's Kosher Kitchen, 168 Shirley Av., 02151.

SALEM

Syn.: Temple Shalom (C), 287 Lafayette St., 01970. ☎ (508) 741-4880.

SHARON

Synagogues:
Chabad Center (O), 101 Worcester Rd., 02067. ☎ (617) 784-8167; Young Israel of Sharon (O), 9 Dunbar St., 02067. ☎ (617) 784-6112. Mikva on premises, operated by Mikveh Org. of the S. Shore, Chevrat Nashim; Adath Sharon (C), 18 Harding St., 02067. ☎ (617) 784-2517; Temple Israel (C), 125 Pond St., 02067. ☎ (617) 784-3986; Temple Sinai (R), 100 Ames St., 02067. ☎ (617) 784-6081.
Eruv maintained by Sharon County Eruv Society. ☎ (617) 784-6112.

SOMERVILLE

Syn.: B'nai Brith of Somerville (Independent), 201 Central St., 02145. ☎ (617) 625-0333.

SPRINGFIELD AND LONGMEADOW

Jewish Fed. of Greater Springfield, 1160 Dickinson St., 01108. ☎ (413) 737-

continued from *Massachusetts*

4313. The Com. Center is at the same address. Kosher Coffee Corner (closed in Summer).

Synagogues:
Beth Israel (O), 1280 Williams St., Longmeadow, 01106. ☎ (413) 567-3210; Cong. Kodimoh (O), 124 Sumner Av., 01108, the largest Orthodox cong. in New England. ☎ (413) 781-0171; Kesser Israel (O), 19 Oakland St., 01108. ☎ (413) 732-8492; Lubavitcher Yeshiva Syn. (O), 1148 Converse St., Longmeadow, 01106. ☎ (413) 567-8665; B'nai Jacob (C), 2 Eunice Dr., Longmeadow, 01106. ☎ (413) 567-3163; Temple Beth El (C), 979 Dickinson St., 01108. ☎ (413) 733-4149; Temple Sinai (R), 1100 Dickinson St., 01108. ☎ (413) 736-3619.
Mikveh Assoc., 1138 Converse St., Longmeadow, 01106.
Kosher Meat: Waldbaum's Food Mart, 355 Belmont Ave., 01108. ☎ (413) 732-3866.

STOUGHTON
Syn.: Cong. Ahavath Torah (C), 1179 Central St., 02072. ☎ (617) 344-8733. Striar Jewish Com. Center on the Fireman Campus, 445 Central St., 02072. ☎ (617) 341-2016.
(K) Green Manor Café, JCC Campus, 445 Central St. (341-2016.

SUDBURY
Syn.: Cong. Beth El (R), Hudson Rd., 01776. ☎ (508) 443-9622; Cong. B'nai Torah (Independent), Woodside Rd., 01776. ☎ (508) 443-2082.

SWAMPSCOTT
Syn.: Beth El (C), 55 Atlantic Av., 01907. ☎ (617) 599-8005; Temple Israel (C), 837 Humphrey St., 01907. ☎ (617) 595-6635.
Kosher Bakery: Newman's, 252 Humphrey St., 01907.

VINEYARD HAVEN
Syn.: Martha's Vineyard Hebrew Center, Center St., 02568. ☎ (508) 693-0745.

WAKEFIELD
Syn: Temple Emmanuel (C), 120 Chestnut St., 01880. ☎ (617) 245-1886.

WALTHAM
Syn.: Beth Israel (C), 25 Harvard St., 02154. ☎ (617) 894-5146.
American Jewish Historical Society (Brandeis University campus), 2 Thornton Rd., 02154. ☎ (617) 891-8110. Fax (617) 899-9208.

WAYLAND
Syn.: Temple Shir Tikva (R), 141 Boston Post Rd., 01778. ☎ (508) 358-5312.

WELLESLEY HILLS
Syn.: Beth Elohim (R), 10 Bethel Rd., Wellesley Hills, 02181. ☎ (617) 235-8419.

WESTBORO
Syn.: B'nai Shalom (R), 117 E. Main St., P. O. Box 1019, 01581-6019 ☎ (508) 366-7191.

WESTWOOD
Syn.: Beth David, 40 Pond St., 02090. ☎ (617) 769-5270.

WINCHESTER
Syn.: Temple Shir Tikvah (R), P. O. Box 373, 01890. ☎ (617) 792-1188.

continued from *Massachusetts*

WINTHROP

Syn.: Tifereth Abraham (O), 283 Shirley St., 02152. ☎ (617) 846-5063; Tifereth Israel (O), 93 Veterans' Rd., 02152. ☎ (617) 846-1390.

WORCESTER

Jewish Federation, 633 Salisbury St., 01609. ☎ (508) 756-1543.

Synagogues:

Cong. Beth Judah Young Israel of Worcester (O), 889 Pleasant St., 01602. ☎ (508) 754-3681; Shaarai Torah East (O), 32 Providence St., 01604. ☎ (508) 756-3276; Shaarai Torah West (O), 835 Pleasant St., 01602. ☎ (508) 791-0013; Yeshiva Syn. Chabad, Tifereth Israel, Sons of Jacob (O), 22 Newton Av., 01602. ☎ (508) 752-0904; Beth Israel (C), Jamesbury Dr., 01609. ☎ (508) 756-6204; Temple Emanuel (R), 280 May St., 01602. ☎ (508) 755-2519; Temple Sinai (R), 661 Salisbury St., 01609. ☎ (508) 755-2519.

Mikva, Huntley St., 01602. ☎ (508) 755-1257.

Com. Center, 633 Salisbury St., 01609. ☎ (508) 756-7109.

Jewish Home for Aged, 629 Salisbury St., 01609. ☎ (508) 798-8653.

For inf. about kashrut, temporary accom., etc. visitors should contact Rabbi Reuven Fischer, 69 S. Flagg St., 01602, Ch., Agudath Israel of America Hachnosas Orchim Committee, or Rabbi Hershel Fogelman, 22 Newton Av., ☎ (617) 752-5791.

Kosher food is available on a daily basis at the "kosher kitchen" of Clark University, Main St., 01610.

MICHIGAN

ANN ARBOR

Jewish Federation/UJA, 2939 Birch Hollow Dr., 48108.

Syn.: B'nai B'rith Hillel Foundation (O,C,R), 1429 Hill St., 48104; Chabad House (O), 715 Hill St., 48104. Mikva on premises; The Orthodox Minyan (O), 1429 Hill St., 48104; Beth Israel Cong. (C), 2000 Washtenaw St., 48104; The Conservative Minyan, (C), 1429 Hill St., 48104; Temple Beth Emeth (R), 2309 Packard St., 48104; The Reform Havurah (R), 1429 Hill St., 48104.

B'nai B'rith Hillel Foundation, University of Michigan. Office: 1429 Hill St., 48104.

Com. Center, 2935 Birch Hollow Dr., 48108.

Hebrew Day School of Ann Arbor, 2935 Birch Hollow Dr., 48108.

BENTON HARBOR (ST. JOSEPH)

Syn.: Temple B'nai Shalom (C), 2050 Broadway, 49022.

DETROIT

Organisations

Jewish Federation of Metr. Detroit, Telegraph Rd., Bloomfield Hills, 48303.

B'nai B'rith Hillel Foundations, Wayne State University, 667 Charles Grosberg Religious Center, 48202. Hot lunch, sandwiches, salads, soups served during academic year (Sept.—April).

Jewish Com. Center of Metropolitan Detroit: 6600 W. Maple Rd., W. Bloomfield, 48322. ☎ (810) 661-1000. Fax (810) 661-3680.

Council of Orthodox Rabbis of Detroit (Vaad Harabonim): 17071 W. Ten Mile Rd., Southfield, 48075. ☎ (313) 559-5005/06.

Kosher restaurant: Center branch: Jimmy Prentis Morris Bldg., 15110 W. Ten Mile Rd., Oak Park, 48237. ☎ (810) 967-4030.

continued from *Michigan*

Synagogues:

Bais Chabad of Farmington Hills (O), 32000 Middlebelt Rd., Farmington Hills, 48018; Bais Chabad of W. Bloomfield (O), 5595 W. Maple Rd., W. Bloomfield, 48322; Beth Jacob-Mogain Abraham (O), 15751 W. Lincoln Dr., Southfield, 48076; Beth Tefilo Emanuel Tikvah (O), 24225 Greenfield Rd., Southfield, 48075; B'nai Israel-Beth Yehuda (O), 15400 W. Ten Mile Road, Oak Park, 48237; B'nai Jacob (O), 15230 Lincoln Rd., Oak Park, 48237; B'nai Zion (O), 15250 W. Nine Mile Rd., Oak Park, 48237; Dovid Ben Nuchim (O), 14800 W. Lincoln Rd., Oak Park, 48237; Mishkan Israel, Nusach H'Ari, Lubavitch Center (O), 14000 W. Nine Mile Rd., Oak Park, 48237; Shaarey Shomayim (O), 15100 W. Ten Mile Rd., Oak Park, 48237; Shomrey Emunah (O), 25451 Southfield Rd., Southfield, 48075; Shomrey Emunah Ohel Moed (O), 6191 Farmington Rd., W. Bloomfield, 48322; Young Israel of Greenfield (O), 15140 W. Ten Mile Rd., Oak Park, 48237; Young Israel of Oak Woods (O), 24061 Coolidge Av., Oak Park, 48237; Young Israel of Southfield (O), 27705 Lahser Rd., Southfield, 48034; B'nai David Cong. (T), 24350 Southfield Rd., Southfield, 48075; Adat Shalom (C), 29901 Middlebelt Rd., Farmington Hills, 48018; Beth Abraham Hillel Moses (C), 5075 W. Maple Rd., W. Bloomfield, 48322; Beth Achim (C), 21100 W. Twelve Mile Rd., Southfield, 48076; Beth Isaac (C), 2730 Edsel Dr., Trenton, 48143; Beth Shalom (C), 14601 W. Lincoln Rd., Oak Park, 48237; B'nai Israel (C), 4200 Walnut Lake Rd., W. Bloomfield, 48033; B'nai Moshe (C), 6800 Drake Rd., W. Bloomfield, 48322; Downtown Synagogue (C), 1457 Griswold, 48226; Livonia Jewish Cong. (C), 31840 W. Seven Mile Rd., Livonia, 48152; Shaarey Zedek (C), 27375 Bell Rd., Southfield, 48034; Cong. Shir Tikvah, 3633 W. Big Beaver Rd., Troy, 48084. ☎ (313) 643-6520; Temple Beth El (R), 7400 Telegraph Rd., Bloomfield Hills, 48301. ☎ (810) 851-1100; Temple Beth Jacob (R), 79 Elizabeth Lake Rd., Pontiac, 48053; Temple Emanu-El (R), 14450 W. Ten Mile Rd., Oak Park, 48237; Temple Israel (R), 5725 Walnut Lake Rd., W. Bloomfield, 48033; Temple Kol Ami (R), 5085 Walnut Lake Rd., W. Bloomfield, 48033; Temple Shir Shalom (R), 5642 Maple Rd., W. Bloomfield, 48322. ☎ (313) 737-8700; The Birmingham Temple (Humanistic), 28611 Twelve Mile Rd., Farmington Hills, 48018; T'chiyah Cong. (Unaffiliated), 1404 Nicolet Pl., 48207.

Holocaust Memorial Center, 6602 W. Maple Rd., W. Bloomfield, 48322-3005. ☎ (810) 661-0840. Fax (810) 661-4240. First institution of its kind in USA.

Newspaper: Jewish News, Franklin Rd., Southfield, 48034.

Homes for Aged: 26051 Lahser Rd., Southfield, Maple, W. B. 48034.
Borman Hall, 19100 W. Seven Mile Rd., 48219; Fleischman Residence, 6710 W. Maple, West Bloomfield, 48322.

Machon L'Torah (The Jewish Network of Michigan) W. 10 Mile Rd. 48237.
Sinai Hospital, 6767 W. Outer Dr., 48235.

Kosher Restaurants: Mertz's Cafe Katon, 23055 Coolidge Rd., Oak Park, 48237. ☎ (313) 547-3581; Sarah's Glatt Kosher Deli, 15600 W. Ten Mile Rd., Southfield, 48075. ☎ (313) 443-2425; Sperber's Kosher Karry-Out, 25250 W. Ten Mile Rd., Oak Park, 48237. ☎ (313) 443-2425.

For inf. about kosher food contact the Council of Orthodox Rabbis at the address above.

EAST LANSING

Syn.: Shaarey Zedek (C & R), 1924 Coolidge Rd., 48823.
B'nai B'rith Hillel Foundation, Michigan State University. Office: 402 Linden

continued from *Michigan*

St., 48823. ☎ (517) 332-1916. Fax (517) 332-4142. Kosher meals available during academic year.

FARMINGTON HILLS
Lubavitch Foundation, 28555 Middlebelt Rd., 48334-4129. ☎ (313) 737-7000. Fax (313) 737-4808.

FLINT
Flint Jewish Fed., 619 Wallenberg St., 48502. ☎ (810) 767-5922.
Syn.: Cong. Beth Israel (C), 5240 Calkins Rd., 48532. ☎ (810) 732-6310; Temple Beth El (R), 501 S. Ballenger Highway, 48532. ☎ (810) 232-3138.
Jewish Family & Social Services, 619 Wallenberg St., 48502. ☎ (810) 767-5922.
Chabad House, 5385 Calkins, Flint, MI 48532. ☎ (810) 230-0770.

GRAND RAPIDS
Syn.: Chabad Hse. of Western Michigan (O), 2615 Michigan St. N.E., 49506; Cong. Ahavas Israel (C), 2727 Michigan St. N.E., 49506; Temple Emanuel (R), 1715 E. Fulton St., 49503.
Jewish Com. Fund of Grand Rapids, 2609 Berwyck St. S.E., 49506. ☎ (616) 956-9365.

JACKSON
Syn.: Temple Beth Israel (R), 801 W. Michigan Av., 49202.

KALAMAZOO
Syn. Cong. of Moses (C), 2501 Stadium Dr., 49008.

LANSING
Syn.: Kehillat Israel (Rec), 2014 Forest Rd., 48910. ☎ (517) 882-0049.

SAGINAW
Syn.: Temple B'nai Israel (C), 1424 S. Washington Av., 48601; Cong. Beth El (R), c/o Leo A. Kahan, 100 S. Washington Av., 48607.

SOUTH HAVEN
Syn.: First Hebrew Cong. (O), 249 Broadway, 49090. ☎ (616) 637-1603.

MINNESOTA
DULUTH
Jewish Fed. & Com. Council, 1602 E. 2nd St., 55812. ☎ (218) 724-8857.
Syn.: Adas Israel (O), 302 E. 3rd St., 55802; Temple Israel (C-R), 1602 E. 2nd St., 55812.

MINNEAPOLIS
Jewish Com. Center of Greater Minneapolis: 4330 Cedar Lake Rd. S., 55416.

Synagogues:
Kenesseth Israel (O), 4330 W. 28th St., 55416. Mikva on premises. ☎ (612) 920-2183; Adath Jeshurun (C), 34th St. & Dupont Av. S., 55408; Beth El (C), 5224 W. 26th St., 55416; B'nai Emet (C), 3115 Ottawa Av. S., 55416; Gemilus Chesed (O), 28th St. & Rhode Island Av., 55426;
Bet Shalom (R), 201 9th Av. N., Hopkins, 55343; Temple Israel (R), 24th St. & Emerson Av. S., 55405.
Kosher Restaurant: Knollwood Place, 3630 Phillips Pkwy, St. Louis Park, 55426. ☎ 993-1833.

continued from *Minnesota*

ROCHESTER

Among other services, the Lubavitch Bais Chaya Moussia Hospitality Center, 730 2nd St. S.W., 55902, ☎ (507) 288-7500, provides Shabbat dinners, hospital visitations, Judaica lending library. Mikvah.

ST. PAUL

Syn.: Adath Israel (O), 2337 Edgcumbe Rd., 55116; Beth Jacob (C), Highway 110 & Hunter La., 55118; Temple of Aaron (C), 616 S. Mississippi River Blvd., 55116.
Temple Mount Zion (R), 1300 Summit Av., 55105.
Com. Center: 1375 St. Paul Av., 55116.
United Jewish Fund & Council: 790 S. Cleveland Av., Suite 201, 55116. ☎ (612) 690-1707.
Kosher Grocery: L'chaim, 655 Snelling Av., 55116.
Kosher Restaurant: Old City Cafe, 1571 Grand Ave. ☎ 699-5347.

MISSISSIPPI

GREENVILLE

Syn.: Hebrew Union Cong. (R), 504 Main St., 38701.

GREENWOOD

Syn.: Ahavath Rayim (O), Market & George Sts., P.O. Box 1235, 38935-1235. ☎ 453-7537.

NATCHEZ

Syn.: B'nai Israel (R), Washington & S. Commerce Sts., P.O.B. 2081, 39120 (oldest synagogue in Mississippi).

TUPELO

Syn.: B'nai Israel (C), Marshall & Hamlin Sts., 38801.

MISSOURI

KANSAS CITY

(N.B. Please consult also, under Kansas, Overland Park and Prairie Village, since Kansas City spans both Missouri and Kansas).
Jewish Fed. of Greater Kansas City, 5801 W. 115th St., Suite 201, Overland Park, Kansas, 66211.
Syn.: Beth Shalom (C), 9400 Wornall Rd., 64114;
B'nai Jehudah (R), 712 E. 69th St., 64131; New Reform Temple (R), 7100 Main St., 64114.
Beth Torah (R), 9401 Nall, Suite 200, Shawvee Mission, Kansas 66207 .
Com. Center: 5801 W. 115th St., Suite 101, Overland Park, Kansas 66211; The Jewish Com. Foundation, (Suite 202) & Jewish Family & Children Services, (Suite 103), are also at the foregoing address; Jewish Vocational Service, 1608 Baltimore Av. Kansas City, MO 64108; Menorah Medical Center, 4949 Rockhill Rd. Kansas City, MO 64110; Shalom Geriatric Center, 7801 Holmes Av., Kansas City, MO 64131.
The Harry S. Truman Library, 24 Highway & Delaware, Independence, Mo., 64050, contains the silver Ark & Torah scroll presented to ex-President Harry Truman by Israel's first President, Dr. Chaim Weizmann.
Restaurant : **(K)** Sensations, 1148 W. 103 St., 64114.
Weekly newspaper: "Kansas City Jewish Chronicle", 7375 W. 107th St., Overland Park, Kansas, 66204.

continued from *Missouri*

ST. LOUIS

Jewish Fed.: 12 Millstone Campus Dr., 63146. ☎ (314) 432-0020. Fax (314) 432-1277.

The Brodsky Jewish Com. Library is also at this address.

The Vaad Hoeir (United Orthodox Jewish Community of St. Louis), 4 Millstone Campus, 63141, ☎ (314) 569-2770, is the recognised Orthodox religious authority for the city. Any inquiries concerning kashrut, etc., should be addressed to the Executive Director.

Synagogues:

Agudas Israel (O), 8202 Delmar Blvd., 63124; Bais Abraham (O), 6910 Delmar Blvd., 63130; Beth Hamedrosh Hagodol (O), 1227 North & South Rd., 63130; Chesed Shel Emeth (O), 700 North & South Rd., 63130; Nusach Hari B'nai Zion (O), 8630 Olive Blvd., 63132; Tpheris Israel Chevra Kadisha (O), 14550 Ladue Rd., Chesterfield, 63017; Young Israel (O), 8101 Delmar Rd., 63130; B'nai Amoona (C), 324 S. Mason Rd., 63141; B'rith Sholom Kneseth Israel (C), 1107 Linden St., 63117; Shaare Zedek (C), 829 N. Hanley Rd., 63130; B'nai El (R), 11411 Highway 40, 63131; Shaare Emeth (R), 11645 Ladue Rd., 63141; Temple Emanuel (R), 12166 Conway Rd., 63141; Temple Israel (R), 10675 Ladue Rd., 63141; Traditional Cong., 12437 Ladue Rd., 63141.

Mikva: 4 Millstone Campus, 63146. ☎ (314) 569-2770.

Com. Center: 2 Millstone Campus Dr., 63146. ☎ (314) 432-5700.

The following establishments are under the supervision of the Vaad Hoeir and are strictly kosher:

Hotels & Banquet Facilities

Adam's Mark Hotel, 4th & Chestnut. ☎ 241-7400; Airport Marriott Hotel, I-70 at Airport, ☎ 423-9700; Frontenac — Hilton Hotel, 1335 S. Lindbergh. ☎ 993-1100; Hyatt Regency, 1 St. Louis Union Station. ☎ 231-1234; The Ritz Carlton, One Ritz Carlton Dr., ☎ 863-6300.

Caterers

Simon Kohn's Kosher Meat & Deli, 10424 Old Olive. ☎ 569-0727; Lazy Suzan Imaginative Catering, 110 Millwell Dr., ☎ 291-6050; Sol's Kosher Meat Market, 8627 Olive. ☎ 993-9977.

Bakery

Schnucks Nancy Ann Bakery, Olive & Mason. ☎ 434-7323.

Dining

NoBull Cafe, 10477 Old Olive. ☎ 991-9533; Diamant's, 618 North & South Rd. ☎ 712-9624; Simon Kohn's, 10424 Old Olive. ☎ 569-0727; Sol's, 8627 Olive. ☎ 993-9977; The Jewish Hospital, 216 S. Kingshighway. ☎ 454-7150.

Butchers

Diamant's Kosher Meat Market, 618 North & South Rd., ☎ 721-9624. S. Kohn's, 10424 Old Olive St. Rd., ☎ 569-0727; Sol's, 8627 Olive. ☎ 993-9977.

The Jewish Tercentenary monument and flagpole are in Forest Park.

MONTANA

BILLINGS

Syn.: Cong. Beth Aaron, 1148 N. Broadway, Billings, 59101. ☎ (406) 248-6412.

GREAT FALLS

Syn.: Aitz Chaim (R), P.O.B. 6192, Great Falls, 59406. ☎ (406) 542-9521.

continued from *Montana*

MISSOULA
Syn.: Har Shalom, P.O.B. 7581, Missoula, 59807. ☎ (406) 523-5671.

NEBRASKA
LINCOLN
Syn.: Tifereth Israel (C), 3219 Sheridan Blvd., 68502; South St. Temple B'nai Jeshurun (R), 20th & South Sts, 68502.

OMAHA
Jewish Fed. of Omaha, 333 S. 132nd St., 68154. ☎ (402) 334-8200.
Syn.: Beth Israel (O), 1502 N. 52nd St. 68104; Beth El (C), 14506 California St., Omaha 68154,
Bnai Israel, P.O.B. 24161, 68124.
Temple Israel (R), 7023 Cass St., 68132.
Com. Mikva: 323 S. 132nd St., 68154.
Jewish Community Center, 333 S. 132 St., 68154.
Friedel Jewish Academy, 335 S. 132nd St., 68154.
Rose Blumkin Jewish Home for Aged, 323 S. 132nd St., 68154.

NEVADA
LAS VEGAS
For additional info. call: Mrs. Beverly Eisen, Community Relations Dir. (702) 732-0556.

Synagogues:
Cong. Shaarei Tefilla (O), 1331 S. Maryland Pkwy., 89104. ☎ (702) 384-3565; Temple Beth Sholom (C), 1600 E. Oakey Blvd., 89104. ☎ (702) 384-5070; Temple Emanu-El (C), 4925 So. Torrey Pines Dr., ☎ (702) 363-8722; Cong. Ner Tamid (R), 2761 E. Emerson Av., 89105. ☎ (702) 733-6292; Temple Beth Am (R), 4765 Brussels Av., 89121. ☎ (702) 456-7014; Chabad of Southern Nev. (0) 1254 Vista Drive, ☎ (702) 259-0770; Or-Bamidbar (O) Sefardic 2959 E. Emerson Av., 89121. ☎ (702) 361-1175; Bet Knesset Bamidbar of Sun City (C), 8813 Marble Dr., 89134. ☎ (702) 254-5973; Adat Ari El (R), 2800 W. Sahara, Bldg. 4-B, 89102. ☎ (702) 221-6064.

Kosher Food: Casba Glatt Kosher, 2845 Las Vegas Blvd., ☎ (702) 791-3344; Sara's Place, 4972 S. Maryland, ☎ (702) 736-32304; Jerusalem Kosher Restaurant & Deli, 1305 Vegas Valley, 89109. ☎ (702) 791-3668; Rafi's Place, 6135 West Sahara, 89102. ☎ (702) 253-0033.

RENO
Syn.: Temple Emanu-El (C), 1031 Manzanita La., at Lakeside Dr., 89509. ☎ (702) 825-5600.

NEW HAMPSHIRE
BETHLEHEM
Syn.: Machzikei Hadas (O), Lewis Hill Rd, 03574 (summer only); Bethlehem Hebrew Cong. (C), Strawberry Hill, 03574.
Kosher Hotels: Arlington (summer only); Pinewood Motel

MANCHESTER
Jewish Fed. of Greater Manchester, 698 Beech St., 03104. ☎ (603) 627-7679.
Publishes "The Reporter". Fax (603) 627-7963.

continued from *New Hampshire*

Lists further communities in Amherst, Concord, Derry, Dover, Durham, Hanover, Keene, Laconia and Nashua.
Syn.: Temple Israel (C), 66 Salmon St., 03104. ☎ (603) 622-6171; Adath Yeshurun (R), 152 Prospect St., 03104. ☎ (603) 669-5650; Lubavitch, 7 Camelot Place, 03104. ☎ (603) 647-0204.

PORTSMOUTH
Syn.: Temple Israel, 200 State St., 03801. ☎ (603) 436 5301.
The Curator of the Historic Waterfront Neighbourhood reports the creation of a Jewish (Russian immigrants) home at Strawberry Banke. ☎ (603) 433-1100. Fax (603) 433-1115.

NEW JERSEY

ABERDEEN
Syn.: Bet Tefilah (O), 479 Lloyd Rd., Matawan, 07747. ☎ 583-6262.

ATLANTIC CITY
Syn.: Rodef Shalom (O), 3833 Atlantic Av., 08401; Beth El (C), 500 N. Jerome Av., Margate, 08402; Beth Judah (C), 6725 Ventnor Av., Ventnor, 08406; Chelsea Hebrew Cong. (C), 4001 Atlantic Av., 08401; Community Syn. (C), Maryland & Pacific Avs., 08401; Beth Israel (R), 2501 Shore Rd., Northfield, 08225; Temple Emeth Shalom (R), 8501 Ventnor Av., Margate, 08402.
Fed. of Jewish Agencies of Atlantic County.

BAYONNE
Syn.: Ohab Sholom (O), 1016-1022 Av. "C", 07002; Ohav Zedek (O), 912 Av. "C", 07002; Uptown Syn. (O), 49th St. & Av. "C", 07002; Temple Emanuel (C), 735 Kennedy Blvd., 07002; Temple Beth Am (R), 111 Av. "B", 07002.
Jewish Com. Center, 1050 Kennedy Blvd., 07002. ☎ (201) 436-6900.

BELMAR
Syn.: Sons of Israel Cong. (O), P.O.B. 298, 07719.
Hotel: New Irvington, 112 12th Av., 07719.

BRADLEY BEACH
Syn.: Cong. Agudath Achim (O), 301 McCabe Av., 07720.

BRIDGETON
Syn.: Cong. Beth Abraham (C), 330 Fayette St., 08302.
Jewish Fed. of Cumberland County. See entry for Vineland, New Jersey.

BURLINGTON
Syn.: B'nai Israel (C), 212 High St., 08016.

CARMEL
Syn.: Temple Beth Hillel, 08332.

CARTERET
Com. Center, 44 Noe St., 07008.

CHERRY HILL
Jewish Fed. of Southern New Jersey, 2393 W. Marlton Pike, 08002. ☎ (609) 665-6100.
Syn.: Beth Shalom (C), 1901 Kresson Rd., 08003.
Sons of Israel (O), 720 Cooper Landing Rd., 08002. Mikva on premises, ☎ (609) 667-9700; Cong. M'kor Shalon (R), 850 Evesham Rd.; Temple Emanuel (R), 1101 Springdale Rd.; Beth El (C), 2901 W. Chapel Av., 08002; Cong.

continued from *New Jersey*

Beth Tikva (C), 115 Evesboro-Medford Rd., Marlton.
Com. Center: 2395 W. Marlton Pike, 08002.
Newspaper: "The Jewish Community Voice", 2393 W. Marlton Pike, 08002.
Restaurant: David's Harp, 1603 Kings Highway, (609) 795-3633.
Kosher Bakery: Pastry Palace, State Highway 70, 08034. ☎ 429-3606.
Kosher Meat: Cherry Hill Kosher Market, 907 W. Marlton Pike, 08002.

CINNAMINSON
Syn.: Temple Sinai (C), New Albany Rd. & Route 130, 08077.

CLARK
Syn.: Temple Beth O'r (C), 111 Valley Rd., 07066. ☎ 381-8403.

CLIFTON
Jewish Fed. of Greater Clifton-Passaic, 199 Scoles Av., 07012. ☎ (201) 777-7031. Fax (201) 777-6701.
Syn.: Clifton Jewish Center (C), 18 Delaware St., 07011; Beth Sholom (R), 733 Passaic Av., 07012.
Jewish Family Services, 199 Scoles Av., 07012. ☎ (201) 777-7638
YM-YWHA, 199 Scoles Av., 07012. ☎ (201) 779-2980.
Newspaper: "Jewish Com. News", 199 Scoles Av., 07012.

COLONIA
Syn.: Ohev Shalom (C), 220 Temple Way, 07067. ☎ (908) 388 7222.

CRANBURY
Syn.: Jewish Cong. of Concordia, c/o Club House, 08512. ☎ (609) 655 8136.

CRANFORD
Syn.: Temple Beth El (C), 338 Walnut Av., 07016. Contact Rabbi Hoffberg for kosher hospitality. ☎ (201) 276-9231
Solomon Schechter Day School of Essex & Union, 721 Orange Av., 07016. ☎ 272-3400.

DEAL
Syn.: (O) 128 Norwood Ave., 07723. ☎ (908) 531-3200; Ohel Yaacob (O), 4-6 Ocean Ave., 07723. ☎ (908) 531-0217
Bookstore: Nathan's Judaica Bookstore, 256 Norwood Ave., 07723. ☎ (908) 531-8657
Restaurants: (K) Deal Gardens, ☎ (908) 531-4887; (K) J II Pizza, 106 Norwood Ave, 07723. ☎ (908) 531-7936; (K) Lhangmao, 214 Roosevelt Ave., Oakhurst, 07755.

EAST BRUNSWICK
Syn.: Young Israel of E. Brunswick (O), 193 Dunham Corner Rd., 08816. ☎ (908) 254-1860; E. Brunswick Jewish Center (C), 511 Ryders La., 08816. ☎ (908) 257-7070; Temple B'nai Shalom (R), Old Stage Rd. & Fern Rd., 08816. ☎ (908) 251-4300.
Jewish Family Service of Southern Middlesex, 517 Ryders La., 08816. ☎ (908). 257-4100.
Butcher: East Brunswick Kosher Meats, 1020, State Highway 18, 08816. ☎ (908) 257-0007.

EDISON
Jewish Fed. of Greater Middlesex County, 230 Old Bridge Turnpike, South River, 08882. ☎ (908) 432-7711. Fax (908) 432-0292.

continued from New Jersey

Jewish Com. Center of Middlesex County, 1775 Oak Tree Rd., 08820.
Syn.: Beth El (C), 91 Jefferson Blvd., 08817.
Ohr Torah (O), 2 Harrison St., 08817. ☎ (908) 572-0526; or 572-7181; ;
Temple Emanu-El. ☎ (908) 549-4442. (R), 100 James St., 08820.
Chabad House (O), 8 Sicard St., New Brunswick, NJ 08901. ☎ (908) 828-9191.
Jewish Family Service of Northern Middlesex, 10 Franklin Av., 08837. ☎
(908) 738-5225.
Butcher.: Edison Kosher Meats, State Highway 27, and Evergreen Rd., ☎
(201) 549-3707.

ELIZABETH
Syn.: Adath Israel (O), 1391 North Av., 07208; Adath Jeshurun (O), 200 Murray
St. 07202. ☎ (908) 355-6723; Bais Yitzchok Chevrah Thilim (O), 153 Bellevue
St., 07202. ☎ (980) 354-4789; Elmora Hebrew Center (O), 420 West End Av.,
07202. ☎ (980) 353-1740; Jewish Educational Center (O), 330 Elmora Av.,
07208; Jewish Education Center (Adath Israel) (O), 1391 North Av., 07208;
Temple Beth El of Elizabeth (R), 737 N. Broad St., 07208. ☎ (908) 354-3021.
Inf. about kosher food, temporary accom., etc. can be obtained from Rabbi
Elazar Teitz, 35 North Av., 07208.
Mikva: 35 North Ave, 07208. ☎ (908) 352-5048.

Kosher Establishments
Kosher Express (packaged and cooked foods), 155 Elmora Ave., 07202;
Jerusalem Restaurant (pizza and dairy), 150 Elmora Ave., 07202;
New Kosher Special, 163 Elmora Ave., 07202. ☎ (908) 353-1818.
Superior Deli and Restaurant, 140 Elmora Ave., 07202;
Dunkin' Donuts, 186 Elmora Ave., 07202.

ENGLEWOOD
Syn.: Ahavath Torah (O), 240 Broad Av., 07631. ☎ (201) 568-1315. Fax (201)
568-2991.
Shomrei Emunah (O), 89 Huguenot Av., 07631; Temple Emanu-El (C), 147
Tenafly Rd., 07631. ☎ (201) 567-1300.
Mikva at 89 Huguenot Av. ☎ (201) 567-1143.
Kosher Bakery & Restaurant: Dairy Menagerie & Caterers, 10 S. Dean St.,
07631. ☎ (201) 569-2704.
J.C. Pizza and Felafel, 24 W. Palisade Ave., 07631. ☎ (201) 569-5546

FAIR LAWN
Syn.: Ahavat Achim (O), 18-19 Saddle River Rd., 07410; Cong. United
Brotherhood (O), 8-09 Plaza Rd., 07410; Shomrei Torah (O), 19-19 Morlot
Av., 07410; Beth Sholom (C), 40-25 Fair Lawn Av., 07410; B'nai Israel (C),
Pine Av. & 30th St., 07410; Fair Lawn Jewish Center (C), 10-10 Norma Av.,
07410; Temple Avoda (R), 10-10 Plaza Rd. 07410.

Restaurants
Kosher Nosh Deli Restaurant, 894 Prospect Av., Glen Rock, 07140. ☎ (201)
445-1186.
Plaza Pizza, 14-20 Plaza Rd., 07410. ☎ (201) 796-3113. Dairy only. Under
rabbinical supervision.
Sandwiches, etc.: River Road Hot Bagels, 13-38 River Rd., 07410. ☎ (201)
791-5646. Under rabbinical supervision.

Kosher Groceries, Meat, etc.
Ben-David International Foods Emporium, 24-28 Fair Lawn Av., 07410. ☎
(201) 794-7740; Harold's Kosher Meat Market, 19-11 Fair Lawn Av., 07410.

continued from *New Jersey*

☎ (201) 796-0003; New Royal Bake Shop, 19-09 Fair Lawn Av., 07410. ☎ (201) 796-6565; Petak Bros. Kosher Deli, 19-03 Fair Lawn Av., 07410. ☎ (201) 797-5010.
Meat Restaurant :Fair Lawn Glatt Kosher Deli & Israeli Restaurant, 14-20 Plaza Rd., Fair Lawn, N.J. 07410 ☎ (201) 703-0088.
Sandwiches: Hot Bagels, 6-07 Saddle River Rd., Fair Lawn, N. J. 07410. ☎ (201) 796-9625.
Please note that in both stores, only the bagels are Kosher under Rabbinical Supervision.

FREEHOLD
Syn.: Agudath Achim (O), Broad & Stokes Sts., 07728.
Congregation Agudath Achim (O), Freehold Jewish Center, Broad & Stokes St., Freehold, 07728.

HACKENSACK
Syn.: Temple Beth El (C), 280 Summit Av., 07601.
Jewish Fed. of Com. Services of Bergen County, 170 State St., 07601.

HADDONFIELD
Kosher Butcher: Sarah's Kosher Kitchen, 63 Ellis Rd.

HIGHLAND PARK
Syn.: Cong. Ahavas Achim (O), PO Box 4242. ☎ (908) 247-0532; Cong. Etz Ahaim (O, Sephardi), 230 Dennison St., 08904. ☎ (908) 247-3839; Cong. Ohav Emeth (O), 415 Raritan Av., 08904. ☎ (908) 247-3038; Highland Park Conservative Temple & Center (C), 201 S. 3rd Av. 08904. ☎ (908) 545-6482.
Park Mikva, 112 S. 1st Av., 08904.
Y.M.-Y.W.H.A. of Raritan Valley, 2 S. Adelaide Av., 08904. ☎ (908) 249-2221.
Bookshop: Highland Park Sefarim & Judaica, 227 Raritan Ave.
Kosher food stores under rabbinical supervision: B & E Kosher Meat Market, 76 Raritan Av., ☎ (908) 846-3444; Berkley Bakery, 405 Raritan Av., 08904; Dan's Deli & Meat Market, 515 Raritan Av., 08904; Kosher Catch, 239 Raritan Ave., ☎ (908) 572-9052; Mystic Gourmet, 229 Raritan Rd., 08904.

HILLSIDE
Syn.: Cong. Sinai Torath Chaim (O), 1531 Maple Av., 07205. ☎ 923-9500.
Cong. Shomrei Torah Ohel Yosef Yitzchok (C), 910 Salem Av., 07205. ☎ 289-0770.

HOBOKEN
Syn.: United Synagogue of Hoboken (C), 830 Hudson St. (Office) & 115 Park Av., 07030. ☎ (201) 659-2614. Fax (201) 659-7944.

JAMES BURG
Syn.: Rossmoor Jewish Cong. Rossmoor Meeting Room, 08831. ☎ (609) 655-0439.

JERSEY CITY
Syn.: Agudath Shalom (O), 2456 Kennedy Blvd., cnr. Gifford Av., 07304; Mount Sinai (O), 128 Sherman Av., 07307; Mount Zion (O), 233 Webster Av., 07307; Rogosin Yeshiva Synagogue (O), 25 Cottage St., 07306; Sons of Israel (O), 294 Grove St., 07302; B'nai Jacob (C), 176 W. Side Av., 07305; Temple Beth-El (R), 71 Bentley Av., 07304.

continued from *New Jersey*

LAKEWOOD

Ocean County Jewish Fed., 301 Madison Av., 08701. ☎ (201) 363-0530.
Syn.: Lakewood Yeshiva (O), Private Way & 6th St., 08701; Sons of Israel (O),
Madison Av. & 6th St., 08701; Ahavat Shalom (C), Forest Av. & 11th St.,
08701; Beth Am (R), Madison Av. & Carey St., 08701.
Hotel: Capitol Hotel (Kosher).
Restaurant: Kosher Experience, Kennedy Blvd., 08701. Closed on Sabbath &
all Holy-days & festivals. Under supervision of manager, Rabbi Chumsky.
Delicatessen: R. & S. Kosher, 416 Clifton Av., 08701. Closed on Sabbath &
all Holy-days & festivals. Meat only. Under supervision of Vaad Hakashruth
of Lakewood.

LINDEN

Syn.: Cong. Anshe Chesed (O), 100 Orchard Ter. at St. George Av., 07036. (
486-8616.
Mekor Chayim Suburban Jewish Center (C), Deerfield Rd. & Academy Ter.,
07036. ☎ 925-2283.

LIVINGSTON

Syn.: Synagogue of the Suburban Torah Center, 85 W. Mt. Pleasant Av.,
Livingston, New Jersey 07039. ☎ (201) 994-0122/2620.

Restaurants

(**K**) Metro Glatt/Delancey St., 515 S. Livingston Av., Livingston, New Jersey
07029. ☎ (201) 992-9189; (**K**) Jerusalem Restaurant & Pizzeria (Dairy), 16
East Mt. Pleasant Av., Livingston, New Jersey 07039. ☎ (908) 289-0291.
(**K**) Super Duper Bagels, 498 S. Livingston Av., Livingston, New Jersey 07039.
☎ (201) 533-1703.

METUCHEN

Syn.: Neve Shalom (C), 250 Grove Av., 08840. ☎ 548 2238.

MILLVILLE

Syn.: Beth Hillel (C), 3rd Av. & Oak St., 08332.
Jewish Fed. of Cumberland County. See entry for Vineland, New Jersey.

MORRISTOWN

Syn.: Cong. Ahavath Yisrael (O), 9 Cutler St., 07960. ☎ (201) 267-4184. The
syn. operates a kosher food buying service for the community, dealing only in
strictly kosher products. Further inf. from Baila Mandel, ☎ (201) 267-4184;
Rabbinical College of America (O), 226 Sussex Av., 07960. ☎ (201) 267-9404.
Morristown Jewish Center (C), 177 Speedwell Av., 07960. ☎ (201) 538-9292;
Temple B'nai Or (R), Overlook Rd., 07960.

NEW BRUNSWICK

Syn: Chabad Hse. Friends of Lubavitch (O), 8 Sicard St., 08901. ☎ (908) 828-
9191; Anshe Emeth Memorial Temple (R), 222 Livingston Av., 08901. ☎
(908) 545-6484; Cong. Poile Zedek (unaffiliated), 145 Neilson St., 08901. ☎
(908) 545-6123.
B'nai B'rith Hillel Foundation, Rutgers University, Clifton Av. & Ryders La.,
08901. ☎ (908) 545-2407. Fax (908) 932-1063.

NEWARK AND DISTRICT

(Essex, Morris, Sussex, Warren and parts of Union and Hudson Counties)

continued from *New Jersey*

Organisations

United Jewish Fed. of Metrowest, 901 Route 10, Whippany, NJ 07981. ☎ (201) 884-4800; Fax (201) 884-7361.
Beth Israel Medical Center: 201 Lyons Av., 07112.
Mikvaot: Mikvah of Essex County, 717 Pleasant Valley Way, West Orange 07052; Sarah Esther Rosenhaus Mikvah Institute, 93 Lake Rd., Morristown, 07960.
Newspaper: "The Metrowest Jewish News," 901 Route 10, Whippany, NJ 07981. ☎ (201) 887-3900; is published weekly. It is owned by the United Jewish Fed. of Metrowest.
Booksellers: Rabbi L. Sky, Hebrew Book Store, 1923 Springfield Av., Maplewood 07040. ☎ (201) 763-4244-5.

Synagogues:

Agudath Israel (O), 1125 Stuyvesant Av., Irvington, 07111; Ahavas Achim B'nai Israel (C), 706 Nye Av., Irvington, 07111; Ahavas Sholom (O), 145 Broadway, 07104; Ahavath Zion (O), 421 Boyden Av., Maplewood, 07040; Ahawas Achim B'nai Jacob and David (O), 700 Pleasant Valley Way, W. Orange, 07052; Anshe Lubowitz (O), 74 Mill Rd., Irvington, 07111; Beth Ephraim-B'nai Zion (O), 520 Prospect St., Maplewood, 07040; Cong. Ahavat Torah (O), 1180 Route 46, Colony Plaza, Parsippany, 07054; Chabad Center of North West N.J. (O), 23-25 Pawnee Av., Rockaway, 07866; Cong. Israel of Springfield (O), 339 Mountain Av., Springfield, 07081; Federation Plaza (O), 750 Northfield Av., W. Orange, 07052; Daughters of Israel Geriatric Center (O), 1155 Pleasant Valley Way, W. Orange, 07052; Hillside Jewish Center (O), 1538 Summit Av., Hillside, 07205; Lev Israel (O), 1548 Summit Av., Hillside, 07205; Mount Sinai Cong. (O), 250 Mt. Vernon Pl., Newark, 07106; Sinai Torath Chaim (O), 1531 Maple Av., Hillside, 07205; Suburban Torah Center (O), 85 W. Mount Pleasant Av., Livingston, 07039; Young Israel (O), 1 Henderson Dr., W. Caldwell, 07006; Young Israel of W. Orange (O), 567-569 Pleasant Valley Way, W. Orange, 07052; Adat Israel Cong. (C), 200 Overlook Rd., Boonton, 07005; Adath Shalom (C), 18 Thompson Av., Dover, 07801; Agudath Israel (C), 20 Academy Rd., Caldwell, 07006; Ahavath Achim (C), 122-139 Academy St., Belleville, 07109; Ahavath Achim B'nai Israel (C), 706 Nye Av., Irvington, 07111; Beth Ahm (C), 60 Temple Drive, Springfield, 07081; Beth El (C), 222 Irvington Av., S. Orange, 07079; Beth Shalom (C), 193 E. Mount Pleasant Av., Livingston, 07039; B'nai Abraham (C), 300 E. Northfield Rd., Livingston, 07039; B'nai Israel (C), 160 Millburn Av., Millburn, 07041; B'nai Israel (C), 192 Center St., Nutley, 07110; B'nai Israel of Kearny & North Arlington (C), 780 Kearny Av., Kearny, 07032; Cong. Beth Ahm of W. Essex (C), Box 329, 56 Grove Av., Verona, 07044; Jewish Center of Sussex County (C), 13 Washington St., Box 334, Newton, 07860; B'nai Shalom Jewish Center of W. Orange (C), 300 Pleasant Valley Way, W. Orange, 07052; Jewish Com. Center of Summit (C), 67 Kent Pl. Blvd., Summit, 07901; Lake Hiawatha Jewish Center (C), 140 Lincoln Av., Lake Hiawatha, 07034; Oheb Shalom-Beth Torah (C), 170-180 Scotland Rd., S. Orange, 07079; Pine Brook Jewish Center (C), 174 Changebridge Rd., Montville, 07045; Shomrei Emunah (C), 67 Park St., Montclair, 07042; Suburban Jewish Center of Morris County (C), 165 Ridgedale Av., Florham Park, 07932; Temple Ner Tamid (C&R), 936 Broad St., Bloomfield, 07003; Temple Hatikvah (C), Pleasant Hill Rd., Flanders, 07836; White Meadow Temple (C), White Meadow Rd., Rockaway, 07866; B'nai Jeshurun (R), 1025 S. Orange Av., Short Hills, 07078; Shaarey Shalom (R), 78 S. Springfield Av., Springfield, 07081; Sharey Tefilo-Israel (R), 432 Scotland Rd., S. Orange, 07079; Temple

continued from *New Jersey*

Beth Ahm (R), 879 S. Beverwick Rd., Parsippany, 07054; Temple Emanu-El of W. Essex (R), 264 W. Northfield Rd., Livingston, 07039; Temple Shalom of Sussex County (R), Oak St., Franklin; Temple Shalom (R), 215 S. Hillside Av., Succasunna, 07876; Temple Sholom of W. Essex (R), 760 Pompton Av., Cedar Grove, 07009; Temple Sinai (R), 208 Summit Av., Summit, 07901; B'nai Keshet (Rec.), Church St. and Trinity Place, Montclair, 07042.

Restaurants

Arlington Kosher Deli, Restaurant & Caterers, Arlington Shopping Center, 744 Route 46W, Parsippany, NJ 07054. ☎ (201) 335-9400; David's Deco-Tessen, 555 Passaic Av., West Caldwell, NJ 07006. ☎ (201) 808-3354. Fax (201) 808-5806; (K) Gourmet Galaxy, 659 Eagle Rock Av., West Orange, NJ 07052. ☎ (201) 736-0060; (K) Jerusalem West, 16 E. Mt. Pleasant Av., Livingston, NJ 07039. ☎ (201) 533-1424; (K) Metro Glatt/Delancey Street, 515 Livingston Av., Livingston, NJ 07039. ☎ (201) 992-9189. Fax (201) 992-6430 (for take-out); Pleasantdale Kosher Meat, 470 Pleasant Valley Way, West Orange, NJ 07052. ☎ (201) 731-3216; (K) Reuben's Deli Delite, 500 Pleasant Valley Way, West Orange, NJ 07052. ☎ (201) 731-6351; Zayda's Super Value, Meat Market & Deli, 309 Irvington Av., South Orange, NJ 07079. ☎ (201) 762-1812.

NORTH BRUNSWICK

Syn.: Cong. B'nai Tikvah (C), 1001 Finnegans Lane 08902. ☎ (908) 297-0696.

PARLIN

Syn.: Ohav Shalom (C), 3018 Bordertown Av., 08859. ☎ (201) 727-4334.

PASSAIC

Jewish Fed. of Greater Clifton-Passaic. See entry for Clifton, New Jersey.
Syn.: Adas Israel (O), 565 Broadway, 07055; Aguda Israel (O), 5 Main Av., 07055. ☎ (201) 614-0196. Bais Torah U'Tfila (O), 263 Pennington Av., 07055. ☎ (201) 470-0222; Tifereth (O), 180 Passaic Av., 07055; Young Israel of Passaic-Clifton (O), 200 Brook Av., 07055; Ahavas Israel (T), 181 Van Houten Av., 07055; Temple Emanuel (C), 181 Lafayette Av., 07055.
Beth Israel Hospital: 70 Parker Av., 07055. ☎ (201) 365-5000. Kosher restaurant on premises.
Hillel Academy, 565 Broadway, 07055.
Yeshiva: Talmudic Research Center, 35 Ascension St., 07055.
Rituarium: Mikvah Yisroel, 242 High St., 07055.
Kosher Restaurant: Jerusalem II Pizza of Passaic, 224 Brook Av., 07055.
Kosher Meat: Brook Kosher, 222 Brook Av., 07055.
Food: B&Y Kosher Korner Inc., 200 Main Av., 07055. ☎ (201) 777-1120; (K) China Pagoda, 227 Main Ave., ☎ (201) 777-4900.

PATERSON

Syn.: Temple Emanuel (C), 151 E. 33rd St., 07514.

PERTH AMBOY

Syn.: Shaarey Tefiloh (O), 15 Market St., 08861. ☎ 826-2977; Beth Mordechai (C), 224 High St., 08861. ☎ 442-2431.
Y.M.H.A., 316 Madison Av., 08861. ☎ 442-0365.

PISCATAWAY

Syn.: Cong. B'nai Shalom (R), 25 Netherwood Av., 08854. ☎ (908) 885-9444.

continued from *New Jersey*

PLAINFIELD
Syn.: United Orthodox Synagogue (O), 526 W. 7th St., 07060; Beth El (C), 225 E. 7th St., 07060. ☎ (201) 755-0043; Temple Sholom (R), 815 W. 7th St., 07063. ☎ (201) 756-6447.

PRINCETON
Syn.: Jewish Center (T), 435 Nassau St., 08540. ☎ (609) 921-0100. Fax (609) 921-7531.

RAHWAY
Syn.: Temple Beth Torah (C), 1389 Bryant St., 07065. ☎ 576-8432.

RANDOLPH
Syn.: Mount Freedom Jewish Center (O), 1209 Sussex Turnpike, 07970.

RIVER EDGE
Syn.: Temple Sholom (R), 385 Howland Av., 07661.
United Jewish Community of Bergen County, 111 Kinderkamack Rd., 07661. ☎ (201) 488-6800.

ROSELLE
Jewish Federation of Central New Jersey, 843 St.Georges Av., 07203. ☎ (908) 298-8200. Fax (908) 298-8220. Also publishes "Shalom Book", a guide to Jewish Life in the area.

RUMSON
Syn.: Cong. B'nai Israel (C), Hance & Ridge Rds., 07760. ☎ 842-1800.

SCOTCH PLAINS
Jewish Com. Center of Central New Jersey, 1391 Martine Av., 07076. ☎ 889-1830.
Syn.: Temple Israel Fanwood (C), 1920 Cliffwood St., 07076. ☎ 889-1830.

SOMERSET
Syn.: Temple Beth El (C) 1495 Amwell Rd., 08873. ☎ (201) 873-2325.

SOUTH RIVER
Syn.: Cong. Anshe Emeth (Trad.), 88 Main St., 08882. ☎ (201) 257-4190. (See also Edison)

SPOTSWOOD
Syn.: Monroe Township Jewish Center (R), 11 Cornell Av., 08884. ☎ (201) 251-1119.

TEANECK
Syn.: Bnai Yeshurun (O), 641 W. Englewood Av., 07666. ☎ (201) 836-8916; Cong. Beth Aaron (O), 950 Queen Anne Rd., 07666; Roemer Syn. (O), Whittier School, W. Englewood Av., 07666; Beth Sholom (C), Rugby Rd. & Rutland Av., 07666; Jewish Center of Teaneck (C), 70 Sterling Place, 07666. ☎ (201) 833-0515.
Beth Am (R), 510 Claremont Av., 07666; Rinat Yisrael (O), 389 W. Englewood Av., 07666; Temple Emeth (R), 1666 Windsor Rd., 07666.
Mikveh: 1726 Windsor Rd., 07666. ☎ (201) 837-8220.
Kosher Foods: Glatt Express, 1600 Queen Anne Rd., 07666. ☎ (201) 837-8110.; Hot Bagels, 513 Cedar La., 07666. ☎ (201) 836-9705.; Maadan, 446 Cedar La., 0766. ☎ (201) 692-0192.
Restaurants
Fliegels, 456 Cedar Lane. ☎ (201) 692-8060.

continued from *New Jersey*

Noah's Ark, 493 Cedar La., 07666. ☎ (201) 692-1200; Hunan Teaneck, 515 Cedar La., 07666. ☎ (201) 692-0099; Jerusalem Pizza (Dairy), 496 Cedar La., 07666. ☎ (201) 836-2120 or 836-2165; Grill Express, 540 Cedar La., 07666. ☎ 836-4115; Shelly's Dairy, 482 Cedar Lane, ☎ (201) 692-0001. Santoro's, 439 Cedar La., 07666. ☎ (201) 836-9505.
All the foregoing are under orthodox rabbinical supervision.
Bakery: Butterflake, 448 Cedar Lane. ☎ (201) 836-3516.
Bookstore: Zoldan's Judaica Center, 406 Cedar Lane. ☎ (201) 907-0034.

TRENTON
Jewish Fed. of Mercer & Bucks Counties, 999 Lower Ferry Rd., 08628. ☎ (609) 883-5000.
Jewish Comm. Center, 999 Lower Ferry Rd., 08628. ☎ (609) 883-9550.
Syn.: People of Truth (Anshe Emes) (O), 1201 W. State St., 08618; Workers of Truth (O), 832 W. State St., 08618. ☎ (609) 396-2231; Adath Israel (C), 1958 Lawrenceville Rd, Lawrenceville, N. J. 08648; Ahavath Israel (C), 1130 Lower Ferry Rd., 08618; Cong. Brothers of Israel (C), 499 Greenwood Av., 08609; Har Sinai (R), 491 Bellevue Av., 08618. ☎ (609) 392 7143; Temple Micah (Rec), P. O. Box 6355, Lawrenceville, 08648. ☎ (609) 921-1128.

UNION
Jewish Fed. of Central New Jersey, Green La., 07083. ☎ (201) 351-5060.
Syn: Beth Shalom (C), 2046 Vauxhall Rd., 07083; Temple Israel (C), 2372 Morris Av., 07083. ☎ (201) 686-2120.
YM-YWHA of Union County, Green La., 07083. ☎ (201) 289-8112.

VINELAND
More than 1,000 families were settled in the Vineland area after being liberated from Nazi concentration camps in Europe. Some 60 years earlier, the area was the site of many farm settlements founded at the end of the last century with aid from Baron de Hirsch.
Jewish Fed. of Cumberland County, 629 Wood St., Suite 202-204, 08360. ☎ (609) 696-4445. Also serves the Bridgeton & Cumberland County areas.
Syn: Ahavas Achim (O), 618 Plum St., 08360; Sons of Jacob (O), 321 Grape St., 08360; Beth Israel (C), 1015 E. Park Av., 08360.

WARREN
Jewish Fed. of Central New Jersey, Suburban Services Office, 150 Mt. Bethel Rd., 07059 ☎ (908) 647-0232. Fax (908) 647-3115.
Syn.: Mountain Jewish Com. Center (R), 104 Mt. Horeb Rd., 07060. ☎ 356-8777.

WAYNE
Jewish Fed. of N. Jersey, 1 Pike Dr., 07470. ☎ (201) 595-0555.
Syn.: Shomrei Torah (C), 30 Hinchman Av., 07470; Temple Beth Tikvah (R), 950 Preakness Av., 07470.
YM-YWHA, 1 Pike Dr., 07470.

WEST NEW YORK
Syn.: Congregation Shaare Zedek (O); 5308 Palisade Av., 07093.

WESTFIELD
Syn.: Temple Emanu-El (R), 756 E. Broad St., 07090. ☎ (908) 232-6770. Fax (908) 233-3959.

WILLINGBORO
Syn.: Adath Emanu-El (R), 299 John F. Kennedy Way, 08046.

continued from *New Jersey*

WOODBRIDGE
Syn.: Adath Israel (C), 424 Amboy Av., 07095. ☎ 634-9601.

NEW MEXICO
ALBUQUERQUE
Jewish Fed. of Greater Albuquerque: 5520 Wyoming Blvd. N.E., 87109. ☎ (505) 821-3214. Fax (505) 821-3351.
Publishes a monthly community newspaper 'The Link'. Visitors requiring kosher meals should contact the JFGA, ☎ (505) 821-3214.
Syn.: B'nai Israel (C), 4401 Indian School Rd. N.E., 87110. ☎ (505) 266-0155; Cong. Albert (R), 3800 Louisiana Blvd., N.E., 87110. ☎ (505) 883-1818; Chabad, 4000 San Pedro Dr. NE, 87110. ☎ (505) 880-1181; Nahalat Shalom (R), 295 La Plata N.W. Albuquerque, 87107. ☎ (505) 343-8227. Rio Rancho Jewish Center (C/R), 2009 Grande Blvd., 87124. ☎ (505) 892-8511.

LAS CRUCES
Syn.: Temple Beth El, Parker Rd. at Melendres, Las Cruces.

LOS ALAMOS
Syn.: Jewish Center, 2400 Canyon Rd., 87544. ☎ (505) 662-2440.

RIO RANCHO
Syn.: Rio Rancho Jewish Center, 2009 Grande Blvd., Rio Rancho, 87124. ☎ (505) 892-8511.

SANTA FE
Syn.: Pardes Yisroel (O). ☎ (505) 986-2091; 205 E. Barcelona Rd., 98501. for inf. about home hospitality, Shabbos, Mikva, Kosher catering, (986-2091. Rabbi Weinbaum, 983-8065; Temple Beth Shalom (C) & (R), 205 E. Barcelona Rd., 87501. ☎ (505) 982-1376. (R) & (C) also held here. Rabbi Bentley, 983-7446.
Kosher Food: Kaunes Food Town, Wild Oats, Market Place.

NEW YORK STATE
Work on revising the sections on New York State and New York City is in progress.
New York City may be a world metropolis, but the other places in New York State these are America. Indeed, New York State, which stretches from New York City to the Canadian border, possesses within its 50,000 square miles a superb array of natural features.
Apart from New York City and its suburbs, with its 2 1/2 million Jews (probably 90 per cent of the Jewish population of New York State), numerous upstate cities and towns, like Buffalo, Rochester, Binghamton, Syracuse, Utica, Schenectady and many more, have flourishing Jewish communities. At least 25 of them have communities numbering several thousand or more. Actually, the Dutch first colonised New York, which was then known as New Amsterdam, and they ruled it until, September, 1664, when four British warships took possession of the Dutch colony for King Charles II who made a present of it to his brother, James, Duke of York, and it was hastily renamed and became the Province of New York.
The first group of Jews had reached New Amsterdam from Recife in 1654, and some of them made their way northwards soon afterwards, including

continued from *New York State*

Asser Levy, who began dealing in real estate up in Albany, now the state capital. He also traded up and down the Hudson River, as did Jacob de Lucena in 1678, who reached as far north as Kingston. By 1760, Jews had settled on Long Island, which today has a Jewish population of some 450,000 and about 150 synagogues. Jews came to Westchester a century later, in 1860, and Westchester County now boasts a Jewish population of more than 135,000. In Newburgh, Jewish merchants set up a trading post in 1777, but it was not until 1848 that a Jewish community was established there.

The first Jewish community in the State outside New York City is no longer in existence. It was in the lush hills of Ulster County, now in the Center of the Catskills resort area, and was founded by twelve families and called Sholom. The oldest existing com. above New York City is Albany, where Congregation Beth El (now merged into Beth Emeth) was founded in 1838.

It was in Albany that Benjamin N. Cardozo served as Chief Justice of the State before becoming an Associate Justice of the U.S. Supreme Court. The law school at Yeshiva University in New York City is named after him. The late Herbert H. Lehman presided over the State as Governor from 1933 to 1942, and his brother, Irving, was Chief Judge from 1939 to 1942.

The State Capitol building had as co-architect Leopold Eidlitz. In the cornerstone are a prayer and a mezuza from the Albany Jewish community.

To the south and south-west of Albany is the famous Catskills resort area. Covering two counties, and known as the "Borscht Belt" or "Circuit", it is about two hours from New York City by car, bus or door-to-door limousine service. From Memorial Day (the last weekend in May) to Labour Day (the last weekend in September), tens of thousands flock to the Catskills for their holidays, to fill scores of hotels ranging from the luxurious to the simple, and clusters of rented cottages known as bungalows or retreats (which used also to be known as "kuchaleins" - meaning, roughly: "Do your own cooking"), many owned by Orthodox groups, including Chasidim belonging to the various sects.

On a summer's day in the Catskills, it is a common occurrence to see groups of bearded young men with side-curls, dressed in black hats and long black coats, walking along the edge of a country road and hoping to catch a ride into the nearest town or hamlet.

Some of the bigger hotels now remain open throughout the year, offering golf on some of the finest courses in the land, indoor and outdoor bathing pools, and skiing when there is snow (and in some places, which have "snow machines," even when there is no snow).

All the larger Jewish hotels and many of the smaller ones have special services for Passover and the High Holy-days, presenting the finest chazanim and choirs obtainable.

Entertainment is the key word as far as the Catskills are concerned. No star is too big or expensive for the larger hotels, and some of the most famous American Jewish entertainers - people like the late Danny Kaye and Jerry Lewis — got their first break in the Catskills. All this had its beginnings in a Jewish relief project during the first great wave of East European immigration in the last two decades of the past century, when Jewish agencies made it possible for newcomers to leave the East Side of New York City and start small farms in the area. Some became successful farmers, others — most of the others — had to take in boarders to make a living. Boarding houses became small hotels and small hotels large ones. These are listed in the gazetteer.

On the periphery of the Catskills are two villages founded by Chasidim New Square at Spring Valley, a misspelling by a county official of "Skvir" from which this sect stems, and Monsey, two miles away. They are worth a visit. Both New Square and Monsey are, of course, run on strictly Orthodox lines, so all commercial activities and traffic cease before Shabbat comes in on Friday afternoon or evening.

There is an International Synagogue at Kennedy Airport in New York, with a museum which includes contributions from every Jewish community in the world.

ALBANY
Syn.: Beth Abraham-Jacob, 380 Whitehall Rd., 12208. ☎ (518) 489-5819 or (518) 489-5179 (O); Shomray Torah (O), 463 New Scotland Av., 12208; Chabad-Lubavitch Center of the Capital District (O), 122 S. Main Av., 12208. ☎ (518) 482-5781; Daughters of Sarah Nursing Home (T, R), Washington Av. Extension, 12208. ☎ (518) 456-7831; Traditional service, Sat. 9.15 a.m. Reform service, Fri. 3 p.m.; Ohav Shalom (C), New Krumkill Rd., 12208. ☎ (518) 489-4706; Temple Israel (C), 600 New Scotland Av., 12208. ☎ (518) 438-7858; Beth Emeth (R), 100 Academy Rd., 12208. ☎ (518) 436-9761. (At this 160-year-old congregation, Rabbi Isaac Mayer Wise, founder of American Reform Judaism, served when he first arrived in the United States); B'nai Sholom (R), 420 Whitehall Rd., 12208. ☎ (518) 482-5283.
Mikva: Bnos Israel of the Capital District, 190 Elm St., 12202.
Com. Center, 340 Whitehall Rd., 12208. ☎ (518) 438-6651.
Jewish Family Services, 930 Madison Av., 12208. ☎ (518) 482-8856.
Shabbos House, State University of New York, 67 Fuller Rd. ☎ (518) 438-4227.
Restaurants: Dahlia Vegetarian & Dairy Restaurant, 858 Madison Av. between Ontario & Partridge Sts., 12203. ☎ (518) 482-0931. Under supervision of Vaad Hakashruth.
Price Chopper Market, 1892 Central Av., 12205. ☎ (518) 456-2970. Full service kosher department. Under supervision of Vaad Hakashruth.

AMSTERDAM
Syn.: Cong. Sons of Israel (C), 355 Guy Pk. Av., 12010. ☎ (518) 842-8691.

BEACON
Hebrew Alliance: 55 Fishkill Av., 12508. ☎ (914) 831-2012.

BINGHAMTON
Jewish Fed. of Broome County, 500 Clubhouse Rd., Vestal 13850. ☎ (607) 724-2332. Fax (607) 724-2311.
The Jewish Fed. publishes the weekly "Reporter", ☎ (607) 724-2360, at the same address. Email: TReporter@AOL.com
Syn.: Beth David (O), 39 Riverside Dr., 13905. ☎ (607) 722-1793. Mikva on the premises; Temple Israel (C), Deerfield Pl., Vestal, 13850. ☎ (607) 723-7461; Temple Concord (R), 9 Riverside Dr., 13905. ☎ (607) 723-7355.
Com. Center: 500 Clubhouse Rd., 13903. ☎ (607) 724-2417. Fax (607) 824-2311. Email: JCC13850@AOL.com

BUFFALO
Jewish Fed. of Greater Buffalo: 787 Delaware Av., 14209. ☎ (716) 886-7750. Fax (716) 886-1367. Publishes 'Shalom Buffalo: a guide to Jewish Buffalo'.
Synagogues:
B'nai Shalom (O), 1675 N. Forest Rd., 14221. ☎ (716) 689-8203.
Beth Abraham (O), 1073 Elmwood Av., 14222. ☎ (716) 874-4786.
Chabad Hse. (O), 3292 Main St., 14214 & 2501 N. Forest Rd., 14068. ☎ (716) 688-1642.

continued from *New York State*

Saranac Syn. (O), 85 Saranac Av., 14216. ☎ (716) 837-0989.
Young Israel of Greater Buffalo (O), 105 Maple Rd., Williamsville, 14221. ☎ (716) 634-0212.
Kehilat Shalom (T), 700 Sweet Home Rd., 14226. ☎ (716) 885-6650.
Beth El (C), 2360 Eggert Rd., Tonawanda, 14223. ☎ (716) 836-3762.
Hillel Foundation (C), 40 Capen Blvd., 14214. ☎ (716) 838-3232.
Shaarey Zedek (C), 621 Getzville Rd., 14226. ☎ (716) 838-3232.
Beth Am (R), 4660 Sheridan Dr., 14221. ☎ (716) 633-8877.
Beth Shalom (R), Union & Center Sts., Hamburg; Beth Zion (R), 805 Delaware Av., 14209. ☎ (716) 886-7150.
Cong. Havurah (R), 6320 Main St., 14221. ☎ (716) 874-3517.
Temple Sinai (Rec), 50 Alberta Dr., 14226. ☎ (716) 834-0708.
Mikva: 1248 Kenmore Av., 14216. ☎ (716) 875-8451.
Jewish Community Center of Greater Buffalo: 787 Delaware Av., 14209 & 2640 N. Forest Rd., Getzville, 14068. ☎ (716) 688-4033 & 886-3145.
Buffalo Jewish Review, 15 Mohawk St., 14203. ☎ (716) 854-2192.

CLIFTON PARK
Syn.: Beth Shalom (C), Clifton Pk. Center Rd., 12065. ☎ 371-0608.

DELMAR
Delmar Chabad Center (O), 109 Elsmere Av., 12054. ☎ 439-8280; Reconstructionist Havurah of the Capital District (Rec.), 98 Meadowland St., 12054. ☎ 439-5870.

ELLENVILLE
Syn.: Ezrath Israel (O), Rabbi Herman Eisner Sq., 12428. ☎ (914) 647-4450.
Mikva at same address, ☎ (914) 647-4472 (e), 647-6846 (d).

ELMIRA
Syn.: Shomray Hadath (O), Cobbles Pk., 14905; B'nai Israel (R), Water & Guinnip Sts., 14905.
Com. Center & Jewish Young Men's & Women's Assoc.: 115 E. Church St., 14901.

FALLSBURG AND SOUTH FALLSBURG
Kosher Hotel: The Pines Resort Hotel, S. Fallsburg, 12779.

FLEISCHMANNS
(K) Glatt Kosher Hotel: Oppenheimer's Regis, 12430. ☎ (914) 254-5080.
Under supervision of Rabbinate of K'hal Adas Jeshurun, New York City.

GENEVA
Syn.: Temple Beth El (R), 755 South Main St., 14456. ☎ (315) 789 2945.

GILBOA
Catskill Mountain "Dude Ranch Vacations" Near: Howe Caverns, Cooperstown, Catskill Game Farm.
Golden Acres Farm & Ranch. 1-800-252-7787, 1-800-847-2251 Rabbinical Supervision, Services.

GLENS FALLS
Syn.: Shaarey Tefila (C), 68 Bay St., 12801. ☎ 792-4945; Temple Beth El (R), 3 Marion Av., 12801. ☎ 792-4364.

GLOVERSVILLE
Syn.: Knesseth Israel (C), 34 E. Fulton St., 12078. ☎ 725-0649.
Com. Center: 28 E. Fulton St., 12078.

continued from *New York State*

GREENFIELD PARK
Kosher Hotel: Tamarack Lodge, 12435.

HAVERSTRAW
Syn.: Cong. Sons of Jacob (O), 37 Clove Av., 10927.

HUDSON
Syn.: Anshe Emeth (C), 240 Jolsen Blvd., 12534. ☎ 828-9040.
The Rose Kline Memorial Judaica Collection is housed in the library of the Daughters of the American Revolution.

HYDE PARK
There are many items of Jewish interest in the Franklin D. Roosevelt Memorial Library.

ITHACA
Syn.: Temple Beth El (C), 402 N. Tioga St., 14850.

KIAMESHA LAKE
Kosher Hotel: Concord, 12751. ☎ (914) 794-4000. Fax (914) 794-7471.

LAKE PLACID
Syn.: 30 Saranac Av. (T), P. O. Box 521, 12946-0521. ☎ (518) 523-3876, (518) 891-3458.

LATHAM
United Jewish Fed. of Northeastern New York, 800 New Loudon Rd., 12110. ☎ 783-7800. (Covers Albany, Colens Falls, Saratoga, Schenectady and Troy).

LOCH SHELDRAKE
Kosher Hotel: Brown's, 12759.

LONG ISLAND
Organisations
Conference of Jewish Orgs. of Nassau County, North Shore Atrium, 6900 Jericho Turnpike, Syosset, 11791. ☎ (516) 364-4477. Publishes 'Directory of Jewish Services in Nassau County'.
Suffolk Jewish Communal Planning Council, 74 Hauppauge Rd., Commack, 11725. ☎ (516) 462-5826.
Long Island Board of Rabbis (O, C & R), 330 Central Av., Deer Park, 11729. ☎ (516) 667-7695; Long Island Commission of Rabbis (O), 1300 Jericho Turnpike, New Hyde Park, 11040. ☎ (718) 343-5993.
Mikvaot: 26 Old Mill Rd., Great Neck, 11023. ☎ (516) 487-2726; Sharf Manor, 274 W. Broadway, Long Beach, 11561. ☎ (516) 431-7758; 3397 Park Av., Oceanside, 11572. ☎ (516) 766-3242; 775 Hempstead Av., W. Hempstead, 11552. ☎ (516) 489-9358; Peninsula Blvd., Hewlett, 11557. ☎ (516) 569-5514.
Newspapers: "Long Island Jewish Week", 98 Cutter Mill Rd., Great Neck, 11020. ☎ (516) 773-3679; "Long Island Jewish World", 115 Middle Neck Rd., Great Neck, 11021. ☎ (516) 829-400.
Bookshop: Theodore S. Cinnamon, 420 Jerusalem Av., Hicksville, 11801. ☎ (516) 935-7480.

Kosher Restaurants
Ben's, 933 Atlantic Av., Baldwin. ☎ (516) 868-2072; 140 Wheatley Plaza, Greenvale. ☎ (516) 621-3340; 135 Alexander Av., Lake Grove. ☎ (516) 979-

continued from *New York State*

8770. All under rabbinical supervision; Hunki's Kosher Pizza & Felafel, 338 Hempstead Av., W. Hempstead. ☎ (516) 538-6655; Jacob's Ladder (Glatt), 83 Spruce St., Cedarhurst. ☎ (516) 569-3373; King David, 550 Central Av., Cedarhurst. ☎ (516) 569-2920; Pastrami 'N Friends, 110A Commack Rd., Commack, 11725. ☎ (516) 499-9537; Te'Avone, 64 Manetto Hall Rd., Plainview, 11803. ☎ (516) 822 4545.

For all kashrut information, contact the Long Island Commission of Rabbis, address above.

MIDDLETOWN
Com. Center: 13 Linden Av., 10940.

MONROE
Syn.: Cong. Eitz Chaim (C), County Route, 105, 10950. ☎ (914) 783-7424.; Monroe Temple of Liberal Judaism (R), 314 N. Main St., 10950.

MONSEY
See New York State and Spring Valley & Monsey entries.

MONTICELLO
Syn.: Tifereth Israel (O), 18 Landfield Av., 12701. ☎ 794-8470 (daily services); Temple Sholom (R), Port Jervis & Dillon Rds., 12701. (Daily services). Mikva, 16 North St., 12701. ☎ 794-6757.
Kosher Hotel: Kutsher's Country Club, 12701. (Daily Services).

MOUNT VERNON
Syn.: Brothers of Israel (O), 116 Crary Av., 10550; Fleetwood (O), 11 E. Broad St., 10552.
Y.M.H.A. & Y.W.H.A.: 30 Oakley Av., 10550.

NASSAU
Jewish Fed. of Greater Orange County, 360 Powell Av., 12550. ☎ (914) 562-7860.
Syn.: Route 20, Albany St. ☎ 477-6691.

NEW CITY
Chabad Lubavitch of Rockland, 315 North Main St., 10956. ☎ (914) 634-0951.
Syn.: New City Jewish Center (C), 47 Old Schoolhouse Rd., 10956. ☎ (914) 634-3619.
Temple Beth Sholom (R), 228 New Hempstead Rd., 10956.

Kosher Restaurants and Delis
Steve's Deli-Bake, 179 South Main Street, 10956. ☎ (914) 634-8749.
M & S Kosher Meats, 191A South Main Street, 10956. ☎ (914) 638-9494.

NEW ROCHELLE
Syn.: Anshe Shalom (O), 50 North Av., 10805. ☎ (914) 632-2426.
Young Israel (O), 1228 North Av., 10804; Bethel (C), Northfield Rd.; Temple Israel (R), 1000 Pine Brook Blvd., 10804.

NEW SQUARE
See note on New York State.

NEW YORK CITY

The entry is in progress of revision with the assistance of Mr Jack Goldfarb.
"Shtetl on the Hudson" is what some call this towering Manhattan Island.
Some "shtetl", you might say.

There are more Jews here than in any other city in the world and more than
in any country except Israel, Russia, and the rest of the U.S. itself. Nobody
knows the true Jewish population figures in the U.S.A. Best estimates say that
1.1 million Jews live in New York City's five boroughs, and 750,000 or so in
its immediate suburbs.

The headquarters of practically every national Jewish organisation in the
United States is located in New York City, otherwise known as the unofficial
capital of Jewish America.

It is probably the only city in the world where Yiddish words have entered the
everyday vocabulary of its non-Jewish residents - kibbitz, gannef, kosher ("that
deal doesn't smell kosher to me"), shlemiel, shlepp ("I shlepped my feet off
looking for a job"), shnook, megilla ("he spouted a whole megilla at me") and,
of course, goy.

This city, the largest urban Jewish community in history, opens its arms to the
Jewish traveller, who will have no problem whatsoever in finding a minyan at
practically any hour; eating in a kosher restaurant; attending a Jewish lecture;
going to play with or about Jews; or browsing in a Jewish bookstore.

There are streets named after David Ben-Gurion, the Prophet Isaiah, Natan
Sharansky, Golda Meir, Richard Tucker and Jacob H. Schiff. A huge modern
convention Center commemorates the name of the late Senator Jacob K.
Javits, and the late Solomon R. Guggenheim has given his name to a magnificent museum. Such commemorative buildings abound throughout the city.

As for food, there is kosher Chinese, kosher Moroccan, kosher Italian, kosher
Romanian. It's all here, and easy to find.

There are many Jewish neighbourhoods: the Lower East Side, Borough Park,
Williamsburg, and even what they now call the "Fourth City of Israel", which
is Forest Hills in the borough of Queens, because so many Israelis live there.
There is also Riverdale, as well as the Upper West Side and, in its own affluent way, the Upper East Side.

But Jews do not live only in Jewish neighbourhoods; they live everywhere in
the Greater New York region, including Nassau, Suffolk, Rockland and
Westchester counties – the greatest concentration of Jews in one metropolitan
area in the world.

For over 300 years, Jews have emigrated to New York from their countries of
origin. They still do. Hungarian Jews came here after the Hungarian
Revolution. Cuban Jews arrived here after Castro took over. Egyptian, Syrian,
Russian, and Iranian Jews have settled here. And there are probably several
hundred thousand former Israelis who live, work, study and raise families in
the New York area. They help keep alive a number of home-grown Hebrew
newspapers, as well as ones flown in daily from the Jewish State. They also
keep the Israeli felafel restaurants churning out countless orders.

It all began one day early in September, 1654, when 23 Sephardi and
Ashkenazi Jews aboard the French privateer, "St. Catherine", docked in New
York harbour after a tortuous journey from Recife, Brazil. The story is well-
known: "Governor" Stuyvesant tried to keep them out; the Jews protested to
the Dutch West Indies Company, and it overruled him and allowed the Jews

continued from *New York City*

to settle. They have been coming ever since, first in trickles and then a deluge between 1880 and 1924, when more than two million Jews reached the shores of the land they called "the goldene medineh".

About one third of all American Jews live in and around New York City. One supposes this is because New York City is still the financial, commercial, intellectual and art capital of the United States. Perhaps it is also because this is "where the action is."

Jews feel at home here. Their impact and contributions are meaningful.

The minute you land in N.Y.C., whether by train, boat, bus, car, or airline, you will feel the vibrancy of a great, throbbing metropolis which is constantly on the go. One thing is for certain: despite the hectic pace here, Jews will take time out to greet you. After all, they have been doing it for each layer of Jewish immigrants, as well as for thousands of visitors. As the sign says: "Welcome!" The Central Synagogue (Reform) at 652 Lexington Av., 10022, is the city's oldest Jewish house of worship on an original site, and has been designated an official "Landmark of New York." It is a fine example of Moorish-style architecture, and seats 1,300 people. B'nai Jeshurun (Conservative) over which Rabbi Dr. Israel Goldstein presided for more than 40 years, is at 270 W. 89th St., 10024, and is the oldest Ashkenazi congregation in New York (1825). On the roof of the Wall St. Synagogue (Orthodox) at 47 Beekman St., 10038, is a replica of the first synagogue in America. The synagogue operates a kosher luncheon club to which Stock Exchange brokers and insurance company executives belong. Services are held four times daily, seven days a week.

Nearest to the United Nations is the Sutton Place Synagogue (Conservative) at 225 E. 51st St., 10022. A very popular Orthodox synagogue particularly with the young, stylish, upscale set is the Lincoln Square Synagogue, 200 Amsterdam Av., 10023. It houses a remarkable singles scene. Also to be mentioned is the congregation Kehilath Jacob on W. 79th Street in Manhattan which is presided over by the famous Rabbi Schlomo Carlebach, the singing Rabbi.

Among Ashkenazi synagogues where visitors may say Kaddish are the Millinery Center Synagogue, 1025 Av. of the Americas (near 38th St.), 10018; B'nai Jeshurun, 270 W. 89th St., 10024; the Jewish Center, 131 W. 86th St., 10024); Sutton Place Synagogue, 225 E. 51st St., 10022; Park East Synagogue, 16 E. 67th St., 10021, and the Fifth Av. Synagogue, 5 E. 62nd St., 10021.

The Synagogue of the Society for the Advancement of Judaism at 15 W. 86th St., 10024, belongs to the Reconstructionist Foundation established by the late Rabbi Dr. Mordecai M. Kaplan. Women as well as men are called to the Torah. Worth noting are murals depicting the rebirth of Israel.

The Ethiopian Hebrew Congregation, 1 W. 123rd St., 10027, in Harlem, is one of several synagogues in which Black Jews worship.

Also worth a visit is Cong. Kehilath Jeshurun (Orthodox), at 125 E. 85th St.

Synagogues

There are several thousand Orthodox, Conservative, Reform, Reconstructionist and traditional synagogues, chavurot and shtiblech in the city, but only a few can be listed here, for obvious reasons.

Complete lists of synagogues in New York City — and throughout the country, for that matter — are available from the following national organisations, whose addresses appear at the beginning of the United States section: Union of Orthodox Jewish Congregations of America; National Council of Young Israel (Orthodox); United Synagogue of America (Conservative); Union of

continued from *New York City*

American Hebrew Congregations (Reform); Federation of Reconstructionist Congregations & Havurot.

Below is a selection of what N.Y.C. has to offer.

First, Shearith Israel (the Spanish and Portuguese Synagogue), Central Park W. and 70th St., 10023, one of the oldest congregations in America, stemming from the 23 refugees from the Inquisition in Brazil who landed in New Amsterdam in 1654. The present building has religious appurtenances dating to the early days of the congregation, and its small chapel is a gem of the colonial period.

The impressive Temple Emanu-El (Reform), the city's (and the world's) largest Jewish house of worship, is on Fifth Av. and 65th St., 10021. Dating from 1929, the building can seat more than 2,000 people. The congregation itself was founded in 1848. The beautiful Fifth Av. Synagogue (Orthodox) at 5 E. 62nd St., 10021, was, until early in 1967, presided over by Rabbi Dr. I. Jakobovits, subsequently Chief Rabbi of Britain and the Commonwealth.

At 163 E. 67th St. is the Park East Synagogue, which is presided over by the father-and-son team of Rabbis Arthur & Marc Schneier. Founded in 1890, it has been designated an historic landmark. The Stephen Wise Free Synagogue (Reform) is at 30 W. 68th St., 10023. Its religious decorations were designed by a Jewish artist, A. Raymond Katz.

The most modern synagogue is the windowless Reform Temple Shaaray Tefila at 250 E. 79th St., 10021. The largest German Jewish congregations are Kahal Adath Jeshurun Synagogue (Orthodox) at 90 Bennett Av., 10033, in the Washington Heights section, and Habonim Congregation at 44 W. 66th St., 10023.

Among the synagogues most worth visiting is the Park Av. Synagogue (Conservative) at 50 E. 87th St., 10128, where the spiritual leader is Rabbi David H. Lincoln. The rabbi emeritus is Rabbi Judah Nadich. Ansche Chesed, at 251 W. 100th St. and West End Av., 10025, is where B'nai B'rith was founded more than a century ago.

Libraries and Museums

The Jewish Museum, under the auspices of the Theological Seminary of America, at Fifth Av. and 92nd St., 10028, is one of the outstanding museums in the city and a "must" not only for Jews, but for all interested in art. The permanent display consists of one of the finest collections of Jewish ritual and ceremonial art in the world, along with notable paintings and sculptures.

The Yivo Institute for Jewish Research, 555 West 57th Street, ☎ (212) 246-6080, has a large collection of original documents on Jewish life, along with some 300,000 volumes, and thousands of photographs, music sheets, gramophone records, etc. Visitors welcome. The Jewish Division of the New York Public Library, Fifth Av. at 42nd St., 10017, has 125,000 volumes of Judaica and Hebraica, along with extensive microfilm and bound files of Jewish publications, one of the finest collections in existence.

In 1973, Yeshiva University opened a museum at its main Center in Amsterdam Av. at 185th St., 10033. The museum's salient feature is a permanent display of scale-model synagogues.

The library of the Jewish Theological Seminary of America, housing what is believed to be the greatest collection of Judaica and Hebraica in the world, is in the Seminary building at 3080 Broadway at 122nd St., 10027. Rare manuscripts, including a work in the hand of Maimonides, as well as Cairo Geniza fragments, may be seen on application to the librarian. Other libraries of note:

continued from *New York City*

the New York University Library of Judaica and Hebraica has a stunning collection of priceless items; the Butler Library of Columbia University, Broadway at 116th St., 10027, has some 6,000 Hebrew books and pamphlets, plus 1,000 manuscripts and a Hebrew psalter printed at Cambridge University in 1685 and used by Samuel Johnson at the graduation of the first candidates for bachelor's degrees at King's College; the Levi Yitzhak Library is at 305 Kingston Av., Brooklyn, 11213.

The House of Living Judaism, the Center of the Reform movement in the U.S.A., at 5th Av. and 65th St., frequently shows paintings and ritual objects. The twelve marble pillars symbolising the Twelve Tribes, in the lobby, the sculptures and the paintings, make a visit to this fine building well worth while.

The Leo Baeck Institute, 129 E. 73rd St., 10021, has vast collections of books, manuscripts, letters and photographs of German Jewish authors, scientists, rabbis & communual leaders, as well as an art collection of the Jews of Germany.

The Chasidic Art Institute is at 375 Kingston Av., Brooklyn.

Institutes of Learning

Yeshiva University, with its main Center at 500 W. 185th St., 10033, is America's oldest and largest university under Jewish auspices, and celebrated its centenary in 1985. It has an enrolment of 7,000 male and female students. At the main Center are the undergraduate schools for men — Yeshiva College, Isaac Bruer College of Hebraic Studies, and the James Striar School of General Jewish Studies; four graduate schools — the Mazer School of Talmudic Studies, the Bernard Revel Graduate School, the Wurzweiler School of Social Work and the Harry Fischel School for Higher Jewish Studies. The mid-town Center, 245 Lexington Av. (at 35th St.), 10016, houses the undergraduate schools for women — Stern College for Women, the Teachers' Institute for Women and the School for Jewish Graduate Education. At 2540 Amsterdam Av., 10033, is the Rabbi Isaac Elchanan Theological Seminary. At the Brookdale Center, 55 Fifth Av. (at 12th St.), 10003, is the Benjamin N. Cardozo School of Law.

The Bronx Center, at Eastchester Rd. & Morris Pk. Av., 10461, is the home of the Albert Einstein College of Medicine, the Sue Golding Graduate Division of Medical Sciences, the Belfer Institute for Advanced Biomedical Studies, the Camp David Institute for International Health and the Ferkauf Graduate School of Psychology.

Kosher meals may be obtained at the cafeterias of the main, mid-town and Bronx Centers.

The Jewish Theological Seminary of America (Conservative), 3080 Broadway at 122nd St., 10027, stands in the academic Center of Morningside Heights, neighbour to the Union Theological Seminary and Columbia University. The seminary, dedicated to Sabato Morais, its founder, and Solomon Schechter, under whose guidance it became one of the great Jewish institutions of the world, is well worth the trip up town for its library. Its cafeteria is open for luncheon and dinner, and there are services in its synagogues daily, open to all. The buildings house all the various components of the Conservative movement in America, as well as the World Council of Synagogues.

Hebrew Union College-Jewish Institute of Religion (Reform), New York branch, is at 1 W. 4th St., 10012. The main seminary is in Cincinnati, Ohio. Open to the public are ancient manuscripts and books, as well as the collection of personal letters, speeches, articles and other writings in the hand of Rabbi Dr. Stephen S. Wise.

continued from *New York City*

Touro College, 30 W. 44th St., has courses in Jewish studies, in addition to undergraduate and graduate curricula.

In the Williamsburg and other sections of Brooklyn are grouped many Chasidic institutions including the Lubavitch movement's headquarters at 770 Eastern Parkway, 11211. The Satmarer Synagogue at 152 Rodney St., 11211, has a regular Saturday attendance of some 4,000.

Special Points of Interest

On a plaque on the Statue of Liberty, the focal point of New York harbour, was the poem "The New Colossus" – "Give me your tired, your poor, your huddled masses yearning to breathe free ..." by the Jewish poetess, Emma Lazarus. The plaque is now in the museum at the base of this huge statue. In Battery Park, near where the ferry to the Statue of Liberty takes on its passengers, is a plaque commemorating the spot where the first 23 Jews landed in 1654.

Also in Battery Park are the remains of "Castle Garden," the first entry place of the wave of Jewish immigration beginning in the 1880s. It was replaced by Ellis Island, now abandoned, which can be seen from the Park.

The Lower East Side, the cradle of the American Jewish community, which once had a Jewish population of more than 11/2 million, is no longer wholly Jewish, as it once was when Jews came there in the stream of mass immigration from Eastern Europe between 1881 and the beginning of the First World War. Now their tenements are for the most part peopled by other groups of immigrants like Hispanics and Asians, as well as by Blacks, who have created a diverse area of small shops, push carts and open markets. In addition, an effort is under way to bring affluent young adults into the neighbourhood. The Lower East Side is increasingly favoured as a good place to live by employees of the large financial institutions in nearby Wall Street.

However, there is still enough to see to make a "Jewish tour" of the section worthwhile, especially on a Thursday afternoon, for Jews from all over the city still come to the Lower East Side then to lay in their week's supply of fresh meat, live carp, black bread and chalot.

Sunday morning is also a good time to take a walk along Essex, Delancey, E. Broadway, Canal and Hester Sts. There are dozens of stores, large and small, stacked with Jewish books in various languages, as well as yarmulkas, talitot, tefilin, prayer books and other Jewish articles, religious as well as general. Stavsky's, at 147 Essex St., 10002, is typical of these stores, and also sells records and tapes.

For browsers, the J. Levine Co. "department store" of Jewish items, 5 W. 30th St., 10001 between Broadway & 5th Av. is well worth a visit Levine's, into its fourth generation, also has a mid-town store at 5 W 30th St 1001, between Broadway and 5th Av. Zelig Blumenthal, 13 Essex St., 10002, has a wide variety of religious items.

Side by side with the bookstores and the stores selling religious items are delis, kosher restaurants, old-fashioned luncheonettes and old synogogues like Beth Hamidrash Hagodol, on Norfolk St., still in the building it acquired in 1888, and the Eldridge St. Synagogue, a National Historic Landmark. Also worth seeing are the Bialystoker Synagogue, 7 Willett St., and the First Roumanian American Congregation at 89 Rivington St.

Stop in at Shapiro's Wine Company at 124 Rivington St., which has been in business since 1899. Call (212) 475-7383 for free tours.

When you reach 39 Essex St., say "Shalom" to Leibel Bistritsky, who has a wonderful kosher food and provision store, and even holds a daily minyan.

continued from *New York City*

Of course, many old-time institutions are gone or have moved. The "Jewish Forward" building used to be located at 175 East Broadway. This famous newspaper has moved to 45 East 33rd Street, and its former location is now a church. Another important Yiddish newspaper is the "Algemeiner Journal", 404 Park Avenue S.

Another colourful shopping area is Orchard Street, New York City's Petticoat Lane, with dozens of outdoor stalls and racks. Most of the owners are Jewish, but they employ many Hispanic salesmen, who hawk their wares in Spanish. In the neighbourhood is the Henry Street Settlement, founded by the Jewish pioneer in social work, Lilian Wald, and along 2nd Av. are what is left of the Jewish theatres. Also in the neighbourhood, in Chatham Sq., is what remains of the first Jewish cemetery in America. For a tour, call the sexton or clerk of Shearith Israel. Another old cemetery is on 21st St., near Avenue of the Americas. The Educational Alliance, the settlement-house that did so much to Americanise the many thousands of Jewish immigrants at the turn of the century, is at East Broadway and Jefferson St. The area is dotted with yeshivas and synagogues too numerous to mention individually.

Williamsburg, which had become the Center of Chasidic life in America, if not in the world, is now beginning to lose some rebbes and their flocks, as they move away into suburban areas where they can lead their cloistered lives undisturbed by the world around them. One such village is New Square. A trip into Williamsburg is recommended. There, along Bedford Av., one can see the kaftanecy sect going about its business. The area is crowded with synagogues and shtiblech.

Boro Park, also in Brooklyn, is almost totally inhabited by Chasidic Jews. On Sundays one can see husbands escorting their wives and children along the streets. The shops are open, of course, and sell all kinds of Chinese, Hungarian, Turkish and Greek kosher food.

Crown Heights, another part of Brooklyn, is the "spill-over" from Williamsburg, and a fair number of Chasidic sects are now to be found there. One of the most colourful sights is the diamond Center on 47th St., 10036, between 5th Avenue & Avenue of the Americas (6th Av.). Many Chasidim are in the diamond business, and they can be seen trading with each other in what amounts to an open-air market. Deals are sealed with a handshake and the words "Mazzel brocha," a "contract" binding throughout the world.

Three-quarters of the diamonds entering the United States pass through this single block.

The Jewish Conciliation Board at 225 Broadway, 10007, is presided over by a rabbi, a judge and a businessman. Disputes arising over synagogue matters are among the cases heard.

For entertainment, and art, there is the Y.M.H.A. & Y.W.H.A. at 92nd St. and Lexington Av., which has a kosher cafeteria. The 92nd St. Y. is one of the premier venues in New York (perhaps the nation) in a wide range of cultural fields including poetry. Indeed, the 'Y's poetry Center is one of the nation's most prestigious forums for poets' reading. The various Jewish lecture series attract many of the most important figures of the day. Some of its cultural activities are suspended during the summer, but call (212) 427-6000 to see what is on. The Jewish Theatre for Children puts on plays at 154 W. 93rd St. on Sunday afternoons from November until March.

The Abraham Goodman House-Hebrew Arts School, 129 W. 67th St., 10023, has an art gallery and houses the Merkin concert hall, which puts on many Jewish music programmes. The school also organises walking tours.

continued from *New York City*

Productions are also staged by the Jewish Repertory Theatre, at the Midtown YMHA, 344 E. 14th St. ☎ (212) 505-2667 or 674-7200 for information.

Borough Synagogues
There are literally thousands of synagogues in the five boroughs of New York and suburbs. The following list contains a few of the more representative ones.

MANHATTAN
Orthodox
Beth Hillel of Washington Heights, 571 W. 182nd St., 10033. ☎ (212) 568-3933.
Emunath Israel, 236 W. 23rd St., 10011. ☎ (212) 675-2819.
Fifth Avenue, 5 E. 62nd St., 10021. ☎ (212) 838-2122.
First Rumanian American (East Side), 89 Rivington St., 10002. ☎ (212) 673-2835.
Fur Center, 230 W. 29th St., 10001. ☎ (212) 594-9480.
Garment Center, 205 W. 40th St., 10018. ☎ (212) 391-6966.
Jewish Center, 131 W. 86th St., 10024. ☎ (212) 724-2700.
K'hal Adath Jeshurun, 90 Bennet Av., 10033. ☎ (212) 923-3614.
Kehillath Jacob (Carlebach Shul), 305 W. 79th St., 10024.
Kehilath Jeshurun (and Remaz School), 125 E. 85th St., 10028. ☎ (212) 427-1000.
Lincoln Square, 200 Amsterdam Av., 10023. ☎ 212) 874-6100.
Ohab Zedek, 118 W. 95th St., 10025. ☎ (212) 749-5150.
Park East Syn., 163 E. 67th St., 10021. ☎ (212) 737-6900.
Radio City, 30 W. 47th St., 10036. ☎ (212) 819-0839.
Ramath Orah, 550 W. 110th St., 10025. ☎ (212) 222-2470.
Shearith Israel (Sephardi), Central Park W. & 70th St., 10023. ☎ (212) 873-0300.
Wall Street, 47 Beekman St., 10038. ☎ (212) 227-7800. ☎ (212) 227-7800.
West Side Institutional Synagogue, 122 W. 76th St., 10023. ☎ (212) 877-7652.
Young Israel of West Side, 210 W. 91st St., 10024. ☎ (212) 787-7513.

Park Avenue Synagogue
Rabbi Emeritus Judah Nadich   *Senior Rabbi* David H Lincoln
Rabbi Elana Zaiman   *Rabbi* Kenneth A Stern
Cantor David Lefkowitz   *Asst. Cantor* Yaacov Ephron
Executive Director Barrie Modlin

Services

Mornings	*Evenings*
Daily: 7.15am	Daily: 5.45pm
Sundays &Holidays: 9.00am	Fridays: 6.15pm
Sabbath & Festivals : 9.15am	

50 East 87th Street, New York, NY 10128
Tel. (212) 369 2600 Fax. (212) 410 7879

Conservative
B'nai Jeshurun, 270 W. 89th St., 10024. ☎ (212) 787-7600.
Little Syn., 155 East 22 St., 10003. ☎ (212) 475-7081.
Millinery Center, 1025 Av. of the Americas, nr. 38th St., 10018. ☎ (212) 921-1580.

continued from *New York City*

Park Avenue, 50 E. 87th St., 10028. ☎ (212) 369-2600.
Shaare Zedek, 212 W. 93rd St., 10025. ☎ (212) 874-7005.
Sutton Place, 225 E. 51st St., 10022. ☎ (212) 593-3300.
Temple Ansche Chesed, W. End Av. & 100th St., 10025. ☎ (212) 865-0600.

Reform
Central, 123 E. 55th St., 10022. ☎ (212) 838-5122.
East End, 398 2nd Av., 10010. ☎ (212) 254-8518.
Metropolitan, 10 Park Av., 10016. ☎ (212) 679-8580.
Rodeph Sholom, 7 W. 83rd St., 10024. ☎ (212) 362-8800.
Shaaray Tefila, 270 E. 79th St., 10021. ☎ (212) 535-8008.
Stephen Wise Free Synagogue, 30 W. 68th St., 10023. ☎ (212) 877-4150.
Temple Emanu-El, 5th Av. at 65th St., 10021. ☎ (212) 744-1400.
Temple Israel, 112 E. 75th St., 10021. ☎ (212) 249-5000.

Reconstructionist
Society for the Advancement of Judaism, 15 W. 86th St., 10024. ☎ (212) 724-7000.

THE BRONX
Orthodox
Concourse Center, 2315 Grand Concourse, 10468.
Kingsbridge Heights Jewish Center, 124 Eames Pl., 10468. ☎ (718) 549-4120.
Riverdale Jewish Center, 237th St. & Independence Av., 10471. ☎ (718) 548-1850.

Conservative
Jacob H. Schiff, 2510 Valentine Av., 10458.
Conservative Synagogue of Riverdale, 250th St. & Henry Hudson Parkway, 10471. ☎ (718) 543-8400.
Pelham Parkway, 900 Pelham Parkway S. ☎ (718) 792-6450.

Reform
Riverdale Temple, 246th St. & Independence Av., 10471. ☎ (718) 548-3800.

BROOKLYN
Orthodox
Agudath Israel of Boro Park, 4511 14th Av., 11219. ☎ (718) 438-6508.
Ahi Ezer, 2433 Ocean Parkway, 11223. ☎ (718) 648-6100.
Beth Medrash Hagadol of Boro Park (of the Infants' Home of Brooklyn), 1358 56th St., 11219.
Cong. Ahaba ve Ahva of Ocean Parkway (Egyptian), 1801 Ocean Parkway, 11223. ☎ (718) 998-0283.
Kingsway Jewish Center, 2902 Kings Highway, 11229. ☎ (718) 258-3344.
Prospect Park, 1604 Av. "R" & E. 16th St.
Shromrei Emunah, 5202 14th Av., 11219.
United Lubavitcher, 770 Eastern Parkway, 11213.
Young Israel of Flatbush, Coney Island Av. & Avenue I, 11230.
Vaad Harabbanim of Flatbush, 1575 Coney Island Ave., 11230. ☎ (718) 951-8585. Fax (718) 951-8510. Beth Din, ☎ (718) 951-6292. Publishes Directory for Kashrut, Mikvaoth, etc.

Conservative
Beth-El, Manhattan Beach, 111 West End Av., 11235.
Brooklyn Jewish Center, 667 Eastern Parkway, 11213. ☎ (718) 493-880.

continued from *New York City*

East Midwood Jewish Center, 1625 Ocean Av., 11230. ☎ (718) 338-3800.
Flatbush and Shaare Torah Jewish Center (Cong. Ahavath Achim), Church Av. & Ocean Parkway, 11218. ☎ (718) 871-5200.
Temple Emanuel of Boro Park, 1364 49th St., 11201.

Reform
Beth Elohim, 8th Av. & Garfield Pl., 11215.
Progressive Syn., 1395 Ocean Av., 11230.
Union Temple of Brooklyn, 17 Eastern Parkway, 11238. ☎ (718) 638-7600.

QUEENS
The Borough of Queens is a wide area of suburban coms., all with their own congs. A call to the Union of Orthodox Jewish Congs., the United Syn. of America (Conservative), or the Union of American Hebrew Congs. (Reform) will elicit the name and location of the synagogue of your choice.

Orthodox
Beth El, 30-85 35th St., Astoria, 11102.
Kneseth Israel, 728 Empire Av. (cnr. Sage St.), Far Rockaway, 11691.
Queens Jewish Center, 66-05 108th St., Forest Hills, 11375.☎ (718) 830-9024.
Shaaray Tefila, 1295 Central Av., Far Rockaway, 1691.
Tifereth Israel, 88th & 32nd Ave., Jackson Heights, 11369. (Nr. La Guardia).
Young Israel of Kew Gardens Hills, 70-11, 150th St., Kew Gardens Hills. ☎ (718) 261-9723.

Conservative
Forest Hills Jewish Center, 106-06 Queens Blvd., 11375. ☎ (718) 263-7000.
Gates of Prayer, 38-20 Parsons Blvd., 11354.
Hillcrest Jewish Center, 183-02 Union Turnpike, Jamaica, 11366. ☎ (718) 380-4145.
Hollis Hills Jewish Center, 210-10 Union Turnpike, Flushing, 11364. ☎ (718) 776-3500.
Jackson Heights Jewish Center, 34-25 82nd St., Jackson Heights, 11372. ☎ (718) 429-1150.
Jewish Center, 182-69 Wexford Ter., Jamaica, 11432.
Rego Park Jewish Center, 97-30 Queens Blvd., 11374.

Reform
Free Synagogue, 41-60 Kissena Blvd., Flushing, 11355. ☎ (718) 961-0030.
Temple Isaiah, 75-24 Grand Central Parkway, Forest Hills, 11375. ☎ (718) 544-2800.
Temple Israel, 188-15 McLaughlin Av., Jamaica, 11423. ☎ (718) 776-4400.

STATEN ISLAND
Orthodox
Agudath Achim Anshe Chesed, 641 Delafield Av., 10310.
Young Israel of Staten Island (O), 835 Forest Hill Rd. ☎ (718) 494-6700.

Conservative
B'nai Israel, 45 Twombly Av., 10306.
Temple Emanu-El, 984 Post Av., 10302. ☎ (718) 442-5966.

Reform
Temple Israel, 315 Forest Av., 10310. ☎ (718) 727-2231.

continued from *New York City*

Restaurants, Hotels, Etc.

There is a kashrut law in New York State which makes it a punishable fraud to advertise or sell non-kosher food as kosher. The law is administered by the Kosher Law Enforcement Section of the State Department of Agriculture under the supervision of Rabbi Shulem Rubin, a respected Orthodox rabbi.

There are heavy penalties on "a person who, with intent to defraud, sells or exposes for sale in any hotel, restaurant or other places where food products are sold . . . food or food products . . . and falsely represents the same to be kosher . . . or as having been prepared under . . . the Orthodox Hebrew religious requirements . . . or sells or exposes for sale in the same place of business both kosher and non-kosher . . . food or food products . . . and who fails to indicate on his window signs and all display advertising in block letters at least four inches in height 'Kosher and non-kosher food sold here'," etc.

The Union of Orthodox Jewish Congregations issues "The Kosher Directory" listing kosher food products supervised and recommended by them and bearing their U-in-a-circle insignia. The directory, for which a charge is made, is available from the UOJC at 333 7th Av., New York City, N.Y., 10018. ☎ (718) 563-4000. Other reliable kashrut insignia include the Circle K trademark of Organised Kashrus Laboratories, P.O. Box 218, Brooklyn. ☎ 851-6428.

The Crown Palace Hotel, in Brooklyn at 570-600 Crown St., ☎ (718) 604-1777 is glatt kosher.

It should be noted at this point that packaged kosher food, cooked and uncooked, is available in most supermarkets, so one need not go hungry, even if there is no restaurant near by, although Manhattan has enough kosher restaurants to eat in for months, and a good variety too.

You can get kosher Won-Ton soup, couscous, hot pastrami and corned (salt) beef sandwiches, gefilte fish, felafel, hummus, tehina and much, much more. The 'Dining Guide' of the Jewish Press can give current information. ☎ (718) 330-1100.

Other kosher places (in Manhattan, unless otherwise stated) include:

Abigael's (glatt kosher), 9 East 37 St. ☎ (212) 725-0130.
Adelman's, 1906 Kings Highway, Brooklyn. ☎ (718) 336-4915.
Ben's Best Deli Restaurant, 96-40 Queens Blvd., Rego Pk, Queens. ☎ (718) 897-1700.
Berso (glatt kosher), 64-20 108th St., Forest Hills, Queens. ☎ (718) 275-9793.
Bombay Kitchen, 113–25 Queens Blvd., Forest Hills, Queens. ☎ (718) 263-4733.
Cafe Classico, 35 West 57th St. ☎ (212) 355-5411. Glatt kosher.
Cafe Masada, 1239 First Ave. ☎ (212) 988-0950.
Cafe Roma, 175 W. 90th St., ☎ (212) 875-8972.
Cafeteria (glatt kosher), Crown Palace Hotel, 570-600 Crown St., Brooklyn, 11213. ☎ (718) 604-1777.
Catchet Restaurant, 815 Kings Highway, Midwood, Brooklyn. ☎ (718) 336-8600.
Chaap-a-Nosh (glatt kosher), 1426 Elm Av., Brooklyn. ☎ (718) 627-0072.
Chick Chack Chicken, 121 University place. ☎ (212) 228-3100.
Club Rafael, 116-29 Queens Blvd., Forest Hills, Queens. ☎ (718) 268-3308.
Colbeh, 43 West 39 St. ☎ (212) 354-8181.
Deli Glatt, 152 Fulton St. ☎ (212) 349-3622.
Deli Kasbah, 251 W. 85th St. ☎ (212) 496-1500.
Deli Kasbah II, 2553 Amsterdam Av. ☎ (212) 568-4600.
Deli Master, 184-02 Horace Harding Expwy., Fresh Meadows, Queens. ☎ (718) 353-3030.

continued from *New York City*

Deniz, 400 East 57th, 10022. ☎ (212) 486-2255.
Dougie's BBQ, 222 West 72nd St., 10023. ☎ (212) 724-2222. Glatt kosher.
Edna's Restaurant & Deli (glatt kosher), 125 Church Av., Brooklyn, 11202. ☎
(718) 438-8207.
Empire Kosher Roaster, 100-19 Queens Blvd., Forest Hills. ☎ (718) 997-
7315.
Galil Restaurant (glatt kosher), 1252 Lexington Av. ☎ (212) 439-9886.
Glatt Dynasty (glatt kosher), 1042 2nd Av. ☎ (212) 888-9119.
Gottlieb's (glatt kosher), 352 Roebling St., Brooklyn. ☎ (718) 384-9037.
Grand Deli Corp, 399 Grand St. ☎ (212) 477-5200.
Jasa Senior Center (Seniors only), 27-35 Crescent St., Astoria, Queens. ☎
(718) 728-9200.
Jasmine, 11 East 30 St. ☎ (212) 251-8884.
Jay and Lloyd's Kosher Deli, 2718 Av. 'U', Brooklyn. ☎ (718) 891-5298.
Jerusalem Pita (glatt kosher), 212 E. 45th St. ☎ (212) 922-0009.
Jerusalem Steak House, 533 Kings Highway, Brooklyn, 11223. ☎ 336-5115.
Jewish Theological Seminary of America cafeteria, 3080 Broadway at 122nd
St., 10027. ☎ (212) 678-8000.
Joseph's Cafe, 50 West 72 St. ☎ (212) 721-1943.
Kosher Delight (glatt kosher), 1359 Broadway (37th St.). ☎ (212) 563-3366;
1223 Av. "J" (E. 13th St.), Flatbush. ☎ (718) 377-6873.
Kosher Hut, 709 Kings Hwy., Brooklyn. ☎ (718) 376-8996.
Kosher International Restaurant, JF Kennedy Airport, Arrivals Bldg., Queens.
☎ (718) 656-1757.
Kosher Tea Room (glatt kosher), 193 Second Av. ☎ (212) 677-2947.
La Bagel, 263 1st Av. ☎ (212) 388-9292.
La Casa Verde, 811 Kings Highway, Brooklyn, 11223. ☎ 339-9733.
La Fontana (glatt kosher), 309 E. 83 St. ☎ (212) 734-6343.
Le Marais (glatt kosher), 150 W. 46th St. ☎ (212) 869-0900.
Lelot Tel Aviv, 1910 Coney Island Ave., Brooklyn, 11223. ☎ 934-6786
Levana Restaurant (glatt kosher), 141 W. 69th St. ☎ (212) 877-8457.
Lou G. Siegel's (glatt kosher), 209 W. 38th St., 10018. ☎ (212) 921-4433.
Madras Mahal, 104 Lexington Av. ☎ (212) 684-4010.
Mr. Broadway, 1372 Broadway. ☎ 921-2152.
On The Way, 69-54 Main St., Flushing, Queens. ☎ (718) 544-6262.
Pastrami King, 124-24 Queens Blvd., Kew Gardens, Queens. ☎ (718) 263-1717.
Pita Express (glatt kosher), 261 1st Av. (15th St.) ☎ (212) 533-1956.
Pita Express (glatt kosher), 1470 2nd Av. (77th St.) ☎ (212) 249-1300.
Ratner's, 138 Delancey St., 10002. ☎ (212) 677-5588.
Second Avenue Delicatessen-Restaurant, 156 2nd Av., cnr. 10th St. ☎ (212)
677-0606.
Shalom Hunan, 1619 Avenue M, Brooklyn. ☎ (718) 382-6000.
Shang-Chai (glatt kosher), 2189 Flatbush Av., Brooklyn, 11234. ☎ (212) 377-
6100.
Siegel's Kosher Deli & Restaurant, 1646 2nd Av. ☎ (212) 288-3632.
Tevere '84' (glatt kosher), 155 E. 84th St. ☎ (212) 744-0210.
Village Crown (glatt kosher), 96 3rd Av. ☎ (212) 674-2061.
What's Cooking, Manhattan, 18 E. 41st St. ☎ (212) 725-6096.
Wok Mavin, 97-20A 64th Ave., Rego Park. ☎ (718) 897-2888.
Yeshiva University: Main Center, 500 W. 185th St., 10033. ☎ (212) 960-5248;
Mid-town Center, 245 Lexington Av. at 35th St., 10016. ☎ (212) 340-7712;
Bronx Center, Eastchester Rd. & Morris Pk. Av., 10461. ☎ (718) 430-2131.
Yun-Kee (glatt kosher), 1424 Elm Av., cnr. E. 15th St. & Av. "M", Brooklyn.
☎ (718) 627-0072.

continued from *New York City*

Dairy Restaurants

All-American Health Bar, 24 E. 42nd St. ☎ (212) 370-4525.
American Cafe Health Bar, 160 Broadway. ☎ (212) 732-1426.
Cafe I II III, 2 Park Av. ☎ (212) 685-7117.
Diamond Dairy Luncheonette, 4 W. 47th St., 10036, in the diamond Center. ☎ (212) 719-2694.
Great American Health Bar, 821 Third Av. ☎ (212) 758-0883.
Great American Health Bar, 35 W. 57th St. ☎ (212) 355-5177.
Vegetarian Heaven, 364 W. 58th St. ☎ (212) 956-4678.
Vege-Vege II, 544 3rd Av. ☎ (212) 679-4710.
Vegetable Garden, 15 E. 40th St. ☎ (212) 545-7444.
Vegetable Garden 2, 175 Madison Av. ☎ (212) 545-7666.
The following, although not listed as kosher, may have a special interest for Jewish tourists because of their menus, atmosphere or clientele:
Carnegie Deli, 854 7th Av., 10019. ☎ (212) 757-2245. Very popular with entertainment & Broadway people.
Jasa, 27-35 Crescent St., Queens 11102
Knish-Knosh, 101-02 Queens Blvd., Queens 11375. ☎ (718) 897-5554.
Sammy's Restaurant, 157 Chrystie St. ☎ (212) 673-0330.
Stage Delicatessen, 834 7th Av., 10019. ☎ (212) 245-7850. Popular with television & entertainment people.

NEWBURGH

This is the nearest Jewish com. to West Point, the United States Military Academy, which is worth a visit.
Syns.: Agudas Israel (O), 290 North St., 12550; Temple Beth Jacob, Gidney & Fullerton Avs., 12550. ☎ (914) 562-5604. Kosher food available by advance arrangement.
Nearby, at Marlboro is the Gomez Mill House, Millhouse Rd., Marlboro, N.Y. 12542. ☎ (914) 236-3126, the oldest extant Jewish residence in North America, maintained as a museum.

NIAGARA FALLS

Jewish Fed. of Niagara Falls, c/o Beth Israel. ☎ (716) 284-4575.
Syns.: Beth Israel (C), College & Madison Avs., 14305. ☎ (716) 285-9894; Beth El (R), 720 Ashland Av., 14301. ☎ (716) 282-2717.

ORANGEBURG

Syn.: Orangetown Jewish Center (C), Independence Av., 10962.

PEEKSKIL

Syn.: First Hebrew Cong., 1821 E. Main St., 10566. ☎ (914) 739-0500.

PORT CHESTER

Syn.: Kneses Tifereth Israel (C), 575 King St., 10573. ☎ (914) 939-1004.

POUGHKEEPSIE

Syn.: Shomre Israel (O), 18 Park Av., 12603; Temple Beth El (C), 118 Grand Av., 12603; Vassar Temple (R), 140 Hooker Av., 12601.
Jewish Community Center of Dutchess County 110. Grand Av., 12603. ☎ (914) 471-0430.

ROCHESTER

Jewish Com. Fed., 441 E. Av., 14607. ☎ (716) 461-0490.
Jewish Com. Center of Greater Rochester, 1200 Edgewood Av., 14618. ☎ (716) 461-2000.

continued from *New York State*

Synagogues:

Beth Hakneses Hachodosh (O), 19 N. St. Regis Dr., 14618; Beth Sholom (O), 1161 Monroe Av., 14618; B'nai Israel-Ahavas Achim (O), 692 Joseph Av., 14621; Light of Israel (O), 206 Norton St.; Talmudical Institute of Upstate New York (O), 759 Park Av.; Beth Hamedrash-Beth Israel (C), 1369 East Av., 14610; Temple Beth Am (C), 3249 E. Henrietta Rd., Henrietta, 14467; Temple Beth David (C), 3200 St. Paul Blvd., 14617; Temple Beth El (C), 139 S. Winton Rd., 14610; B'rith Kodesh (R), 2131 Elmwood Av., 14618; Temple Emanu-El (R), 2956 St. Paul Blvd., 14617; Temple Sinai (R), 363 Penfield Rd., 14625.

Temple b'rith Kodesh (R), 2131 Elmwood Av., 14618; Etz. Chaim Synagogue (R), P.O. Box 522, Pittsford, 14534.

Newspaper: "Jewish Ledger," 2525 Brighton-Henrietta Town Line Rd., 14623.

(K) Kosher Delicatessen: Brownstein's Deli and Bakery, 1862 Monroe Av., 14618; Fox's Kosher Restaurant and Delicatessen, 3450 Winton Place, 14623; **(K)** Brighton Donuts, Monroe Ave., ☎ (716) 271-6940.

(K) Jewish Home of Rochester Cafeteria, 2021 S. Winton Rd., 14618.

SARATOGA SPRINGS

Syn.: Orthodox Minyan (O), 510½ Broadway, 12866. ☎ (518) 587-8980.

Cong. Mikveh Israel (O), 26 Lafayette St., 12866. ☎ (518) 584-6338. Services in July-August.

Shaare Tfille (C), 260 Broadway, 12866. ☎ (518) 584-2370; Temple Sinai (R), 509 Broadway, 12866. ☎ (518) 584-8730.

SCARSDALE

Syn.: Magen David Sephardic Cong., 1225 Weaver St., 10583. ☎ (914) 633-3728.

SCHENECTADY

Syn.: Beth Israel (O), 2195 Eastern Parkway, 12309. ☎ (518) 377-3700; Gates of Heaven (R), 852 Ashmore Av., 12309. ☎ (518) 374-8173; Agudat Achim (C), 2117 Union St., 12309. ☎ (518) 393-9211.

Com. Center.: 2565 Balltown Rd., 12309. ☎ 377-8803.

Jewish Family Services, 246 Union St., 12305. ☎ 372-3716.

SPRING GLEN

Syn.: Beth Israel (O), Main St., Monsey, 10952; Beth Rochel (O), 210 Maple Av., Monsey, 10952; B'nai Jeshurun (O), Park Lane, Monsey, 10952; Community Syn. (O), W. Maple Av., Monsey, 10952; Kehilath Israel (O), Old Nyack Turnpike, Spring Valley, 10977; Yeshiva Wiznitz (O), Phyllis Ter., Monsey, 10952; Young Israel (O), 23 N. Union Rd., Spring Valley, 10977; Com. Center (C), 250 N. Main St., Spring Valley, 10977; Monsey Jewish Center (C), 101 Route 306, Monsey, 10952; Ramat Shalom (C), Lomond Av., Spring Valley, 10977; Shaare Tfiloh (C), 972 S. Main St., Spring Valley, 10977; Temple Beth El (R), 415 Viola Rd., Spring Valley, 10977.

Kosher Hotels

Davidman's Homowack Hotel, 12483 ☎ (914) 647-6800. Glatt kosher. Under the supervision of the Union of Orthodox Jewish Congregations. Fax 914-647-4908; Toll Free number from US and Canada 800-243-4567.

Mendel & Margalit Zuber, 32 Blauvelt Rd., Monsey, 10952, write: "Anyone wishing to spend a Shabbat or Yomtov with us is more than welcome. We are Lubavitch Chasidim, glatt kosher". ☎ (914) 425-6213.

continued from *New York State*

Gartner's Inn, Hungry Hollow Rd., Spring Valley, 10977. ☎ 356-0875.

Kosher Restaurants & Delicatessen

Heshey's Kosher Pizza, 33½ Maple Av., 10977; GPG Deli, Main St., 10977;
Crest Hill Deli, 279 Main St., 10977; K & G Deli, 31 S. Central Av., 10977.
All in Spring Valley.
Mehadrin Restaurant, 82 Route 59, Monsey, 10952.
New Square, the village of the Skvirer Chasidim, is near by.

SYRACUSE

Syn.: Young Israel (O), 4313 E. Genesee St., Dewitt, 13214.☎ (315) 446-6194.
Temple Beth El (Modern Orth.), 3528 E. Genesee St., 12306. ☎ (315) 446-5858.
Adath Yeshurun (C), 450 Kimber Rd., 13224. ☎ (315) 445-0002.
Beth Sholom (C), 5205 Jamesville Rd., Dewitt, 13214. ☎ (315) 446-9570.
Ner Tamid (C), 5061 W. Taft Rd., N. Syracuse. ☎ (315) 458-2022.
Society of Concord (R), 910 Madison St., 13210. ☎ (315) 475-9952.
Com. Center: P.O.B. 29, 5655 Thompson Rd., Dewitt, 13214. ☎ (315) 445-2360.

TROY

Syn.: Beth Tephila (O), 82 River St., 12180. ☎ 272-3182; Troy Chabad Center
(O), 2306 15th St., 12180. Mikva on premises. ☎ (518) 274-5572; Temple
Beth El (C), 411 Hoosick St., 12180. ☎ 272-6113; Berith Sholom (R), 167 3rd
St., 12180. ☎ 272-8872.
Com. Center: 2500 21st St., 12180.

UTICA

Jewish Community Federation of the Mohawk Valley, 2310 Oneida St.,
13501. ☎ (315) 733-2343. Fax (315) 733-2346.
Syn.: Cong. Zvi Jacob (O), 112 Memorial Pkwy., 13501; Temple Beth El (C),
1607 Genesee St., 13501; Temple Emanu-El (C), 2710 Genesee St., 13502.
Com. Center, 2310 Oneida St., 13501.

WEST POINT

Site of the U.S. Military Academy, most of it on land originally owned by
Eleazer Levy, a New York businessman. There are some points of Jewish interest in the area including a Jewish Chaplaincy offering services on Friday
nights. (See also Newburgh, above).

WHITE PLAINS

Syn.: Hebrew Institute of White Plains (O), 20 Greenridge Av., 10605; Temple
Israel (C), Old Mamaroneck Rd. at Miles Av., 10605; Bet Am Shalom (Rec.),
295 Soundview Av., 10606.
Jewish Comm. Center (R), 252 Soundview Av.; Young Israel, 2 Gedney Way.
☎ (914) 683-YIWP.

WOODBOURNE

Kosher Hotel: Chalet Vim, 12788. Glatt kosher.

WOODRIDGE

Kosher Hotel: The Lake House Hotel, 12789. ☎ (914) 434-7800 or (212)
740-8686. Glatt kosher. Cholov Yisroel products only. Open Pesach to Succot.

YONKERS

Syn.: Rosh Pinah (O), Riverdale Av., 10705; Sons of Israel (O), 105 Radford
Av., 10705; Agudas Achim (C), 21 Hudson St., 10701; Lincoln Park Center

continued from *New York State*

(C), 323 Central Park Av., 10704; Temple Emanu-El (R), 306 Rumsey Rd., 10705.
Com. Center: 122 South Broadway, 10701.

NORTH CAROLINA

ASHEVILLE
Syn.: Cong. Beth Israel (C), 229 Murdoch Av., 28804; Beth Ha-Tephila (R), 43 N. Liberty St., 28801.

CHARLOTTE
Jewish Fed., 5007 Providence Rd., 28226. ☎ (704) 366-5007. Other orgs. at the same address include the Com. Center, the Hebrew Academy & Social Services, and the Speizman Jewish Library.
Syn.: Chabad Hse. (O), 6619 Sardir Rd., 28270. ☎ 366-3984. Mikva on premises.
Temple Israel (C), 4901 Providence Rd. ☎ 362-2796; Temple Beth El (R), 5101 Providence Rd., 28207. ☎ 366-1948.

Charlotte Yiddish Institute at Shalom Park.
Charlotte Jewish News. ☎ 366-5007.

Kosher Food
The Kosher Meat & Delicatessen, Amity Gardens Center, 3824 E. Independence Blvd. ☎ 563-8288.
Shalom Park Sandwich Shoppe, 5007 Providence Rd. ☎ 366-5007

DURHAM
Durham-Chapel Hill Jewish Fed. & Com. Council, 205 Mt. Bolus Rd., Chapel Hill, 27514. ☎ (919) 967-6916.
Syn: Beth El (C), Watts St., 27701; Judea (R), 2115 Cornwallis Rd., 27705. An (O) kehilla has taken over the smaller sanctuary at Beth-El. It also has a mikva & nursery school. Inf. about Beth El from Leon Dworsky, 1100 Leon St., Apt. 28, 27705, & about Judea from Rabbi John Friedman. ☎ (919) 489-7062.
The B'nai B'rith Hillel House at Chapel Hill serves kosher meals by previous arrangement.

FAYETTEVILLE
Syn.: Beth Israel Cong. (C), 2204 Morganton Rd., 28303. ☎ (919) 484-6462.

FORT BRAGG
U.S. Army Jewish Chapel, adjoining Chaplain's Activities Center. Rabbi's duty ☎ (919) 396-7574.

GREENSBORO
Jewish Fed., 713a N. Greene St., 27401. ☎ (910) 272-3189.
Jewish Family Service at same address.. ☎ (910)-272-5388.
Syn.: Beth David (C), 804 Winview Dr., 27410. ☎ (910) 294-0006; Temple Emanuel (R), 713 N. Greene St., 27401. ☎ (910) 275-6316.

HENDERSONVILLE
Syn.: Agudas Israel Cong., (C), 328 N. King St., P.O.B. 668, 28793.

RALEIGH
Wake County Jewish Federation, 3900 Merton Drive, Raleigh NC 27609. ☎ (919) 751-5459.
Syn.: Cong. Sha'arei Israel (O), 7400 Falls of the Neuse Rd., 27615. ☎ (919) 847-8986. Mikva, pre-school & primary school on premises; Distributor of

continued from *North Carolina*

kosher meat & poultry; Beth Meyer Syn. (C), 504 Newton Rd., 27615. ☎ (919) 848-1420; Temple Beth Or (R), 5315 Creedmoor Rd., 27612. Preschool. ☎ (919) 781-4895.

WILMINGTON
Syn.: B'nai Israel (C), 2601 Chestnut St. 28401.

WINSTON-SALEM
Syn.: Beth Jacob (C), 1833 Academy St., 27101; Temple Emanuel (R), 201 Oakwood Dr., 27103. ☎ 722-6640.
Jewish Com. Council, P.O.B. 15441, 27113. ☎ (919) 725-9091.
Blumenthal Jewish Home for the Aging, 7870 Fair Oaks Dr., Clemmons, 27012. Kosher meals available for visitors. ☎ 766-6401.

NORTH DAKOTA
FARGO
Syn.: Fargo Hebrew Cong., (O), 901 S. 9th St., 58103; Temple Beth El (R), 809 11th Av. S., 58103.

OHIO
AKRON
Jewish Com. Fed., 750 White Pond Dr., 44320. ☎ (216) 869-2424.
Syn.: Ansbe Sfard, Revere Rd. (O), Revere Av. & Smith Rd., 44320; Beth El (C), 464 S. Hawkins Av., 44320; Temple Israel (R), 133 Merriman Rd., 44303.
Com. Center, 750 White Pond Dr., 44320.
Jerome Lippman Jewish Com. Day School, 750 White Pond Dr., 44320.

CANTON
Jewish Com. Fed., 2631 Harvard Av. N.W., 44709. ☎ (216) 452-6444.
Syn.: Agudas Achim (O), 2508 Market St. N., 44704; Shaaray Torah (C), 423 30th St. N.W., 44709; Temple Israel (R), 333 25th St. N.W., 44709.
Com. Center, 2631 Harvard Av., N.W. 44709. ☎ (216) 453-0132.

CINCINNATI
Jewish Fed.: 1811 Losantiville, Suite 320, 45237. ☎ (513) 351-3800.
Beth Adam Cincinnati Cong. for Humanistic Judaism, 1720 Section Rd., Apt. 107, 45237.
Com. Center: 1580 Summit Rd., 45237. ☎ (513) 761-7500.
Hillel Jewish Students' Center, 2615 Clifton Av., 45220. ☎ (513) 221-6728.
Homes for Aged: Glen Manor, 6969 Glenmeadow Dr., 45237. ☎ (513) 351-7007.
Orthodox Home, 1171 Towne St., 45216.
Jewish Com. Relations Council, 4380 Malsbary Rd., 11300, 45242. ☎ (513) 891-5248.
Jewish Hospital, 3200 Burnet Av., 45229.
Details of schools, afternoon Hebrew schools, etc. are available from: Bureau of Jewish Education, 1580 Summit Rd., 45237.
The Hebrew Union College-Jewish Institute of Religion, at 3101 Clifton Av., 45220, is the oldest and largest Jewish theological seminary in America for training Reform rabbis. Its library is one of the largest Jewish libraries in the world. It also has a gallery of art and artifacts, housing a collection of Jewish objets d'art, religious and ceremonial appurtenances, rare books and manuscripts.
The University of Cincinnati has a Department of Judaic Studies.

continued from *Ohio*

Synagogues:
Syn.: Chabad Hse. (O), 1636 Summit Rd., 45237. ☎ (513) 821-5100;
Golf Manor Syn. (O), 6442 Stover Av., 45237. ☎ (513) 531-6654;
Kehelath B'nai Israel (O), 1546 Beaverton Ave., 45237. Mikva on premises. ☎
(513) 761-5260.
Kneseth Israel (O), 1515 Section Rd., 45237. ☎ (513) 948-2209.
New Hope Cong. (O), 1625 Crest Hill, 45237. ☎ (513) 821-6274.
N. Avondale Syn. (O), 3870 Reading Rd., 45229. ☎ (513) 281-3243.
Ohav Sholom Cong. (C), 1834 Section Rd., 45237. ☎ (513) 531-4676.
Orthodox Jewish Home for Aged (O), 1171 Towne St., 45216. ☎ (513) 242-
1360.
Roselawn Syn. (O), 7600 Reading Rd., 45237. ☎ (513) 761-7755.
Adath Israel (C), 3201 E. Galbraith Rd., 45236. ☎ (513) 793-1800.
B'nai Tzedek (C), 1580 Summit Rd., 45237. ☎ (513) 821-0941.
Downtown Syn. (C), 36 E. 4th St., 7th Floor, 45202. ☎ (513) 241-3576.
Northern Hills Syn. (C), 715 Fleming Rd., 45231. ☎ (513) 731-6038.
Sephardic Beth Sholom Cong. (C), P.O. Box 37431, 45222. ☎ (513) 793-
6936.
Hebrew Union College Chapel (R), 3101 Clifton Av., 45220. ☎ (513) 221-
1875.
Isaac M. Wise Temple (R), 8329 Ridge Rd., 45236. ☎ (513) 793-2556.
Plum St. Temple (R), 8th & Plum Sts., 45202.
Rockdale Temple (R), 8501 Ridge Rd., 45236. ☎ (513) 891-9900.
Temple Sholom (R), 3100 Longmeadow, 45236. ☎ (513) 791-1330.
Valley Temple (R), 145 Springfield Pike, 45215. ☎ (513) 761-3555.

The Chestnut St. Cemetery, Chestnut St. & Central Av., is the oldest Jewish
cemetery west of the Alleghany Mountains. It was founded in 1821.
Newspaper: "American Israelite", 906 Main St., 45202. Oldest Anglo-Jewish
weekly in the United States.
Kosher Bakery: Golf Manor, 2200 Losantiville Av. (All parve. Closed Sat.)

Kosher Food
Bilkers, 7648 Reading Rd., 45237. ☎ (513)
Hot Bagels Factory, 7617 Reading Rd., 45237 & 477 E. Kemper Rd., 45246.
Also available at Com. Center & Jewish Hospital (addresses above).

Kosher Meat
Toron's Meat, 1436 Section Rd., 45237; Pilder's Kosher Foods, 7601 Reading
Rd., 45237.

CLEVELAND
Jewish Com. Fed. of Cleveland, 1750 Euclid Av., 44115. ☎ (216) 566-9200.
Synagogues:
Syn.: Beth El (O), 15808 Chagrin Blvd., 44120. ☎ 991-6044; Chabad House
of Cleveland (O), 4481 University Pkwy., 4418; Green Road Syn., (O), 2437
Green Road Syn., 44122; Beth Hamidrosh Hagodol-Heights Jewish Center
(O), 14270 Cedar Rd., 44121. ☎ 382-1958; Kehillat Yaakov-Warrensville
Center Syn. (O), 1508 Warrensville Center Rd., 44121; Sinai Syn. (O), 3246
De Sota Av., 44118; Oheb Zedek-Taylor Rd. (O), 1970 S. Taylor Road Syn.,
44118; Torah U'Tefilah (O), 1861 S. Taylor Road Syn., 44118; Young Israel of
Cleveland (O), 14141 Cedar Rd., 44121; Young Israel of Beechwood (O),
2120 S. Green Rd., 44121. Zemach Zedek (O), 1922 Lee Rd., 44118;
Zichron Chaim (O), 2203 S. Green Rd., 44122. ☎ 291-5000; Oer Chodesh

continued from *Ohio*

Anshe Sfard (O), 3466 Washington Blvd., 44118; Beth Am Community Temple (C), 3557 Washington Blvd., Cleveland Heights, 44118; Bethaynu (C), 27900 Gates Mills Blvd., 44124; Cong. Shaarey Tikvah (C), 26811 Fairmount Blvd, 44124; Beth Israel-The West Temple (R), 14308 Triskett Rd., 44111; Chevrei Tikva (R), (Outreach to Gay/Lesbian), P.O. Box 18120, Cleveland, 44118. ☎ 932-551; Suburban Temple (R), 22401 Chagrin Blvd., 44122; Temple Emanu El (R), 2200 S. Green Rd., 44121; Temple Israel (R), 1732 Lander Rd., 44124.
Mikvaot: 1774 Lee Rd., 44118; Lubavitch, 2479 S. Green Rd.
Cleveland Hillel Foundation, 11291 Euclid Av., 44106.
Jewish Education Center, 2030 S. Taylor Rd., 44118.
Jewish Com. Centers: 3505 Mayfield Rd., 44118; and 26001 S. Woodland Rd., 44122.
Menorah Park Center for the Aging 27100 Cedar Rd., 44122.
Montefiore Home, David Myers Parkway, 44122.
Mt. Sinai Medical Center, One Mt. Sinai Dr. 44106
Newspaper: "Cleveland Jewish News", 3645 Warrensville Center Rd., Suite 230, 44122.

Places of Jewish interest
The Temple Museum of Religious Art Library, Abba Hillel Silver Archives (Jewish art objects, religious & ceremonial treasures, rare books and manuscripts) University Circle at Silver Park, 441062; the collection of Jewish art & sculpture, Park Synagogue, 3300 Mayfield Rd., 44118;

Restaurants
Empire Kosher Kitchen, 2234 Warrensville Center Rd. ☎ 691-0006; Yacov's Restaurant, 13969 Cedar Rd., 44118; Kinneret Kosher Restaurant, 1869 S. Taylor Rd., 44118; Peking Kosher Chinese Restaurant, 1841 S. Taylor Rd., 44118.
Academy Party Center, 4182 Mayfield Rd., 44121; Del: Cellar, Hillel Bldg.-CWRU, 11291 Euclid Av., 44106.

COLUMBUS
Jewish Fed., 1175 College Av., 43209. ☎ (614) 237-7686.
Syn.: Agudas Achim (O), 2767 E. Broad St., 43209; Ahavas Sholom (O), 2568 E. Broad St., 43209; Cong. Beth Jacob (O), 1223 College Av., 43209. Mikva on premises; Schottenstein Chabad House (O), 207 E. 15th St., 43201; Tifereth Israel (C), 1354 E. Broad St., 43205; Beth Shalom (R), 3100 E. Broad St., 43209; Beth Tikvah (R), 6121 Olentangy River Rd., 43085; Temple Israel (R), 5419 E. Broad St., 43213.
Leo Yassenoff Jewish Center, 1125 College Av., 43209. ☎ 231-2731.
Jewish Family Service, 2831 E. Main St., 43209. ☎ 231-1890.
Columbus Torah Academy, 181 Noe-Bixby Rd., 43213. ☎ 864-0299.
Wexler Jewish Student Center (B'nai Brith Hillel Foundation), OSU, 46 E. 16th Av., 43201. ☎ 294-4797.
Kosher Delicatessen: Bexley Kosher Market, 3012 E. Broad St., 43209. ☎ 231-3653.
Sammy's New York Bagels, 40 N. James Rd., 43213. ☎ 237-2444.
Kosher Buckeye, 2942 E. Broad St., 43209. ☎ 235-8070.

DAYTON
Jewish Fed. of Greater Dayton, Jesse Philips Bldg., 4501 Denlinger Rd., 45426. ☎ (513) 854-4150. Fax (513) 854-2850. Includes Dayton Jewish Community Center, ☎ (513) 854-4014, Com. Relations Council, ☎ (513) 854-4150 and Jewish Family Service. ☎ (513) 854-2944.

continued from *Ohio*

Syn.: Shomrei Emunah (O), 1706 Salem Av., 45406. ☎ (513) 274-6941.
Beth Jacob (T), 7020 N. Main St., 45415. ☎ (513) 274-2149.
Beth Abraham (C), 1306 Salem Av., 45406. ☎ (513) 275-7403.
Temple Beth Or (R), 5275 Marshall Rd., 45429. ☎ (513) 435-3400.
Temple Israel (R), One Riverbend, 45406. ☎ (513) 496-0500.
Mikva: 556 Kenwood Av., 45406.
Jewish Home for Aged: Covenant Hse., 4911 Covenant Hse. Dr., 45426. ☎ (513) 837-2651.
Apartments for Elderly & Handicapped, Covenant Manor, 4951 Covenant Hse. Dr., 45426. ☎ (513) 854-4596.
Monthly **Newspaper**: "Dayton Jewish Advocate", 4501, Denlinger Rd., 45426.
Bakery: Rinaldo's Bake Shoppe, 910 W. Fairview Av. ☎ (513) 274-1311.

LORAIN
Syn.: Agudath B'nai Israel (C), 1715 Meister Rd., 44053.

TOLEDO
Syn.: Cong. Etz Chayim (O), 3853 Woodley Rd., Toledo, Oh 43606; B'nai Israel (C), 2727 Kenwood Blvd.,   Toledo, Oh 43606; The Temple-Congregation Shomer Emunim, 6453 Sylvania Av., Sylvania, 43560.

YOUNGSTOWN AREA
Syn.: Children of Israel (O), 3970 1/3 Logan Way, 44505. Mikva on premises; Beth Israel Temple Center (C), 2138 E. Market St., Warren, 44482; Ohev Tzedek-Shaarei Torah (C), 5245 Glenwood Av., 44512; Temple Beth Israel (R), 840 Highland Rd., Sharon, PA 16146; Temple El Emeth (C), 3970 Logan Way, 44505; Rodef Sholom (R), Elm St. & Woodbine Av., 44505.
Youngstown Area Jewish Fed., 505 Gypsy La., 44501. ☎ (216) 746-3251.

OKLAHOMA
OKLAHOMA CITY
Jewish Fed. of Greater Oklahoma City, 3022 N.W. Expressway, Suite 116, 73112. ☎ (405) 949-0111.
Syn.: Emanuel Synagogue (C), 900 N.W. 47th St., 73106; Temple B'nai Israel (R), 4901 N. Pennsylvania Av., 73112.
B'nai B'rith Hillel Foundation, 494 Elm St., Norman.
Bakery: Ingrid's Kitchen, 2309 N.W. 36th St., 73112.

TULSA
Jewish Fed., 2021 E. 71st St., 74136. ☎ (918) 495-1100. Publishes monthly newspaper 'Tulsa Jewish Review'.
Syn.: B'nai Emunah (C), 1719 S. Owasso Av., 74120; Temple Israel (R), 2004 E. 22nd Pl., 74114.
Com. Center, 2021 E. 71st St. 74136. ☎ (918) 495-1111.
Heritage Academy (day school) is also at this address.
Chabad House, Lubavitch of Oklahoma, 6622 S. Utica Av., ☎ (918) 492-4499/493-7006. Exec. Dir. Rabbi Yehuda Weg. Hospitality for travellers.
The Gershon & Rebecca Fenster Museum of Jewish Art, 1223 E. 17th Pl., 74120, is the only independent Jewish Museum in the South-West. It is well worth a visit.
Tulsa Jewish Retirement & Health Care Center, 2025 E71 St., 74136.

OREGON
ASHLAND
Temple Emek Shalom-Rogue Valley Jewish Com. (R), P.O. Box 1092, 97520.
☎ (541) 488-2909.

EUGENE
Syn.: Beth Israel (C), 42 W 25th Ave., 97405. ☎ (503) 485-7218.

PORTLAND
Jewish Fed. of Portland, 6651 S.W. Capitol Highway, 97219. ☎ (503) 245-6219. Fax (503) 245-6603. Publishes 'Shalom Portland' a newcomers guide.
Syn.: Ahavath Achim (Sephardi, O), 3225 S.W. Barbur Blvd., 97201; Kesser Israel (O), 136 S.W. Meade St., 97201; Shaare Torah (T), 920 N.W. 25th Av., 97209; Neveh Shalom (C), 2900 S.W. Peaceful Lane, 97201; Beth Israel (R), 1931 N.W. Flanders St., 97209; Chabad, 14355 Scholls Ferry Rd., 97007; Gesher, 10701 SW 25th Av., 97219; Havurah Shalom, 6651 SW Capitol Hwy, 97219.
Mikva: Ritualarium, 1425 S.W. Harrison St., 97201. ☎ (503) 224-3409.
Mittleman Jewish Com. Center, (Kosher restaurant), 6651 S.W. Capitol Highway, 97219. ☎ (503) 244-0111.
Kosher meat & foodstuffs obtainable from Albertson's, 5415 SW Beaverton-Hillsdale Hwy, 97221. ☎ (503) 246-1713.

SALEM
Syn.: Beth Shalom (Rec), 1795 Broadway NE, 97303. ☎ (503) 362-5004.

PENNSYLVANIA
ALLENTOWN
Jewish Fed., 702 N. 22nd. St., 18104. ☎ (610) 821-5500.
The Com. Center and Jewish family service are at the same address. ☎ (610) 435-3571.
Syn.: Agudas Achim (O), 625 N. Second St., 18102. ☎ (610) 432-4414; Sons of Israel (O), 2715 Tilghman St., 18104. ☎ (610) 433-6089; Beth-El (C), 1702 Hamilton St., 18104. ☎ (610) 435-3521; Keneseth Israel (R), 2227 Chew St., 18104. ☎ (610) 435-9074; Am Haskalah (Rec), Ott & Walnut Sts., 18104. ☎ (610) 435-6512.
Mikva: 1834 Whitehall St., 18104. ☎ (610) 776-7948.
Glatt Kosher Restaurant: Com. Center, 702 N. 22nd St., 18104. Since opening hours vary according to season, it is advisable to ☎ (610) 435-3571.
(K) Abe's Place, 1741 Allen St., 18104. ☎ (610) 435-1735.

ALTOONA
Syn.: Agudath Achim (C), 1306 17th St., 16601; Temple Beth Israel (R), 3004 Union Av., 16602.
Com. Center, 1308 17th St., 16601.

BETHLEHEM
Syn.: Agudath Achim (O), 1555 Linwood St., 18017; Cong. Brith Sholom (C), Macada & Jacksonville Rds., 18017.

BLUE BELL
Syn.: Tiferet Bet Israel (C), 1920 Skippack Pike, 19422. ☎ (610) 275-8797.

EASTON
Syn.: B'nai Abraham (C), 16th & Bushkill Sts., 18042. Established 1888;

continued from *Pennsylvania*

Covenant of Peace (R), 15th & Northampton Sts., 18042. Established in 1839.
The cemetery in 7th St., 18042, has graves with tombstone inscriptions dating from the early 18th century.

ERIE
Syn.: Brith Sholom Jewish Center (C), 3207 State St., 16508; Anshe Hesed (R), 10th & Liberty Sts., 16502.
Jewish Com. Council, Suite 405, Professional Building, 161 Peach St., 16501.
☎ (814) 455-4474. Fax (814) 455-4475.

HARRISBURG
United Jewish Com. of Greater Harrisburg, 100 Vaughn St., 17110. ☎ (717) 236-9555.
Syn.: Kesher Israel (O), 2945 N. Front St., 17110; Beth El (C), 2637 N. Front St., 17110; Chisuk Emuna (C), 5th & Division Sts., 17110; Ohev Sholom (R), 2345 N. Front St., 17110.
Kosher Self-Service Snack Bar: J.C.C., 100 Vaughn, 17110.
Bakeries Giant Food Store and Weis Market on Linglestown Road.
Quality Kosher 7th Division St., 17110.
Norman Gras Catering, 3000 Green St., 17110-1234. Glatt kosher.

HAZLETON
Syn.: Agudas Israel (C), 77 N. Pine St., 18201; Beth Israel (R), 98 N. Church St., 18201.
Jewish Com. Council, 99 N. Laurel St., 18201. ☎ (717) 454-3528.

JOHNSTOWN
United Jewish Fed., 700 Indiana St., 15905. ☎ (814) 536-0647.
Syn.: Beth Sholom Cong. (C), 700 Indiana St., 15905.
Grandview Cemetery contains the graves of Jews who died in the famous Johnstown flood of 1889. Approximately 22 perished.

LANCASTER
Jewish Fed., 2120 Oregon Pike, 17601. ☎ (717) 597-7354.
Syn.: Degel Israel (O), 1120 Columbia Av., 17603; Beth El (C), 25 N. Lime St., 17602; Temple Shaarai Shomayim (R), N. Duke & James Sts., 17602.
Jewish Community Center, 2120 Oregon Pike, 17601.

LEVITTOWN
Named after its builder, William Levitt, Levittown is one of the largest planned towns in the U.S.A.
Syns.: Cong. Beth El (C), 21 Penn Valley Rd., Fallsington, 19054. ☎ (215) 945-9500; Temple Shalom (R), Edgeley Rd., off Mill Creek Pkwy. 19057. ☎ (215) 945-4154.

MCKEESPORT
Syn.: Gemilas Chesed (O), 1400 Summit St., White Oak 15131. Rabbi Irvin Chinn. ☎ (412) 678-9859; Tree of Life-Sfard (C), Cypress Av., 15131; B'nai Israel (R), 536 Shaw Av., 15132.

PHILADELPHIA
(Thanks are due to Lewis Bokser for the information about Philadelphia).

There is a large Jewish com. in Greater Philadelphia (250,000). In the city Center on Spruce St., between 8th & 9th Sts., opposite the Pennsylvania

continued from *Philadelphia*

Hospital, is Mikveh Israel Cemetery, founded in 1738, which is a national shrine. Buried there are Haym Salomon, who gave his fortune to help the Revolutionary War and was never repaid; he was featured on a postage stamp some years ago; Rebecca Gratz, and Aaron Levy, who founded the city of Aaronsburg in Pennsylvania.

In the city Center, at Broad & Pine, are the Y.M. & Y.W.H.A., said to be the second oldest in the country; the Rosenbach Museum, 2010 Delancy St.; the Jewish Publication Society, 1930 Chestnut St., 19103; the headquarters of the Jewish Federation of Greater Philadelphia, 226 S. 16th St., 19102.

The old Mikveh Israel Synagogue (Sephardi), established in 1740, is located near Independence Hall in Commerce St., between 4th and 5th Sts. (just north of Market St.). A number of members are Afro-American or Black. Between 1828 & 1972, the cong. had only three ministers, one of them, the Rev. Leon Elmaleh, serving for 75 years (1897 until 1972). It contains many religious and personal memorabilia of early Jewish settlers in America. Many of these pioneers became mayors and governors of the cities and States in which they settled. There are guided tours of the synagogue for visitors. Attached to the synagogue is the National Jewish Museum.

At the Balch Institute, 18 S. 7th St., can be found the Philadelphia Jewish Archives, which collect congregational, organisational, family and personal records.

Rodeph Shalom, originally Orthodox and now Reform, is the second oldest synagogue in the city and is at Broad & Mt. Vernon Sts.

The Chapel of the Four Chaplains at the S.E. corner of Broad & Berks Sts., on the campus of Temple University, is a memorial to the Rev. Clark V. Poling, the Rev. George Fox, John P. Washington and Rabbi Alexander D. Goode, who turned their lifejackets over to sailors who had none when their troopship was sunk in the Second World War.

A complex near the Olney Av. station of the Broad St. Subway, beginning at Old York Rd. and Tabor Rd., and extending south about half a mile, contains the Albert Einstein Medical Center, the Willowcrest-Bamberger Post-Hospital Care Nursing Home, the York Houses, which are high-rise apartments for retired or semi-retired persons, and the Philadelphia Geriatric Center with its Home for the Aged. At 7601 Old York Rd., 19027, is Gratz College, a school for Hebrew studies at the high school and advanced levels.

The Center for Judaic Studies (formerly Dropsie University with its 150,000 volume library), which offers post-doctoral courses, is at 420 Walnut St.

The Samuel Fleisher Memorial (formerly the Graphic Sketch Club) is at 719 Catherine St. It has a museum and sanctuary devoted to all monotheistic religions.

The Golden Slipper Home for the Aged, founded by the late Mrs. David Bokser, is at Bustleton Av. & Glendale.

Many sections of the Free Library, on Parkway, are gifts of Jews, such as the Fleisher Collection, said to be the largest collection of classical and symphonic music in the world, and the Rosenbach Collection of children's books. At the N.W. end of Parkway is the Art Museum, in front of which is the Phillips Fountain, named after Henry M. Phillips, who bequeathed large sums for works of art. A statue of Moses is to be seen in the western part of Fairmount Park.

A sculptured memorial to the six million martyrs of the Holocaust stands at 16th St. & Benjamin Franklin Parkway. A huge sculpture by Jacques Lipshitz can be found in the patio of the Municipal Service Bldg., at 15th St. and John Kennedy Blvd., opposite City Hall.

continued from *Philadelphia*

Jewish Federation of Greater Philadelphia, 226 S. 16th St., 19102. ☎ (215) 893-5821. Publishes 'Guide to Jewish Philadelphia'.

Synagogues

Board of Rabbis, 1616 Walnut St., 19103. ☎ (215) 985-1818.

Beth Zion/Beth Israel, (C), 18th & Spruce Sts., 19103, is in the city Center. Society Hill (C), 418 Spruce St., 19106; B'nai Abraham (O), 6th & Lombard Sts., 19147.

On Old York Rd., about a mile above City Line, is Beth Sholom (C), designed by the late Frank Lloyd Wright. Keneseth Israel (R) is immediately above at Old York Rd., & Township Line, 19141, while Adath Jeshurun (C), is at Ashbourne & Old York Rd., 19117.

On the way to Chestnut Hill are Germantown Jewish Center (C), Lincoln Dr. & Ellet St., 19119; Beth Tikvah (C), 1001 Paper Mill Rd., 19118; Temple Sinai (C), Limekiln Park & Dillon Rd., Dresher, 19025; and Beth Or (R), Penllyn Pk. & Dager Rd., Spring House, 19477.

In N.E. Phila. are Temple Sholom (C), Large St. & Roosevelt Blvd., 19149; Temple Menorah (C), 4301 Tyson Ave., 19135; Beth Emeth (C). Bustleton & Unruh, 19149; Ahavath Torah (O), 7525 Loretto Av. 19111; Oxford Circle Jewish Com. Center (C), 1009 Unruh Sts., 19111; Ner Zedek (C), Bustleton & Oakmont Sts., 19152; Aitz Chaim (O), 7600 Summerdale Av. 19111; Beth Ami (C), 9201 Old Bustleton Av., 19115; B'nai Israel-Ohev Zedek (O), 8201 Castor Av., 19152; B'nai Jacob Dershu Tov (O), 1147 Gilham St. 19111; Young Israel (O), 6427 Large St. 19149; Beth Torah (R), 608 Welsh Rd. 19115; Shaare Shamayim (O), 9768 Verree Rd., 19115.

Politz Hebrew Academy Elementary School is at Old Bustleton Av..

Adath Zion (C), Penway & Friendship St., 19111.

In W. Phila. are Beth T'fillah (C), 7630 Woodbine Av., 19151; Beth Hamedrosh of Overbrook Park (O), 7505 Brookhaven Rd. 19151; Lenas Hazedek (O), 2749 Cranston Rd. 19131.

Near by, above City Line, are Adath Israel (C), Old Lancaster Rd. & Highland Av., Merion, 19066.

Lower Merion (O), 123 Old Lancaster Ave., Cynwyd 19006; Beth Hillel (C), Remington Rd., Wynnewood, 19096.

In the suburbs west of the city are Temple Israel of Upper Darby (C), Bywood & Walnut. 19082; Beth El (C), 715 Paxon Hollow Rd., Broomall, 19104; Temple Sholom (R), 55 N. Church Lane, Broomall, 19008; Beth Israel (FRCH), Gayley Ter. Media, 19063; B'nai Aaron (C), 560 Mill Rd., Havertown, 19083; Beth Am Israel (C), 1301 Hagys Ford Rd., Penn Valley 19072; Beth Elohim (R), 410 Montgomery Av., Wynnewood, 19096; Kesher Israel (C), 1000 Pottstown Pike, West Chester, 19380, West Chester and Brith Achim (R), 481 S. Gulph Rd., King of Prussia, 19046; Beth Chaim (C), 350 E. Street Rd., Feasterville, 19047; Ohev Shalom (C), 944 Second St. Pike, Richboro, 18954; Shir Ami (R), 101 Richboro Rd., Newtown, 18940.

Mikvaot: Ahavat Torah, 7525 Loretto Av. 19111; Lower Merion Syn., 123 Old Lancaster Ave., Cynwyd 19006; Torah Academy, 742 Argyle Rd., Wynnewood, 19096.

Cultural Organisations

National Museum of American Jewish History, 55 North 5th St., 19106. ☎ (215) 923-3811. Fax (215) 923-0763.

Jewish Publication Society of America, 1930 Chestnut St., 19103. ☎ (215) 564-5925.

Newspapers: Jewish Exponent, 226 S. 16th St., 19102. ☎ (215) 893-5700;

continued from *Philadelphia*

Jewish Times, 103a Tomlinson Rd, Huntington Valley, 19006. ☎ (215) 938-1177.

Kosher Meat Supply:
Algon Kosher Meat Market, 6834 Bustleton Ave., 19149. ☎ (215) 338-8282.
Best Value Kosher Meats Inc., 8564 Bustleton Ave., 19152. ☎ (215) 342-1902.
Bustleton Kosher Meat Market, 6834 Bustleton Ave., 19149. ☎ (215) 332-0100.
Glendale Kosher Meat Market Inc., 19152. ☎ (215) 725 4100.
Main Line Kosher Meats, 7562 Haverford Ave., 19151. ☎ (215) 877 3222.
Rhawnhurst Kosher Meat Market, 8261 Bustleton Ave., 19152. ☎ (215) 742-5287.
Wallace's Krewstown Kosher Meat Market, 8919 Krewstown Rd, 19115. ☎ (215) 464-7800 or (215) 247-6613.

Restaurants
Hillel Hse. of Univ. of Pennsylvania, 202 S. 36th St., serves lunches & dinners during the academic year. Prior booking necessary;
Dragon Inn Glatt Kosher Chinese Restaurant, 7628 Castor Av., 19152.
Tiberias Chinese & American, 7638 Castor Av., 19152.
King David, 130 South 11th St., 19107. ☎ (215) 829-8101.
Maccabeam Restaurant 128 S. 12th St. Pa 19107; ☎ (215) 922-5922. Glatt kosher.
Singapore, 1029 Race St., ☎ (215) 922-3288.
The Waterwheel (glatt kosher), 1526 Samson St.

PITTSBURGH
Thanks are due to Edie B. Naveh, Director of the Pittsburgh Community Relations Committee of the United Jewish Federation, for the following information.

There are about 45,000 Jews in Pittsburgh, a significant number in the Squirrel Hill area (where an Eruv is in operation), which also houses the majority of Jewish institutions. There are smaller coms. in East Liberty, Stanton Heights, Oakland and the South Hills and East and North Hills areas round Pittsburgh.

Organisations
United Jewish Fed. of Greater Pittsburgh building, 234 McKee Pl., 15213, ☎ (412) 681-8000, Fax (412) 681-8804, houses all administrative offices of the Fed. & the Com. Relations Committee.
Mikva: 2326 Shady Av., 15217. ☎ (412) 422-7110.
Com. Center: 5738 Forbes Av., 15217. ☎ (412) 521-8010.
Newspaper: The "Pittsburgh Jewish Chronicle" is at 5600 Baum Blvd. ☎ (412) 687-1000.
Anathan House, 1620 Murray Av., 15217, is the headquarters of the Pittsburgh branch of the National Council of Jewish Women.
Montefiore Hospital, a leading research and teaching hospital and nurses' training school, 3459 5th Av., 15213, has a kosher kitchen.
(K) Riverview Center for Jewish Seniors, provides intermediate and skilled nursing care, Brown's Hill Rd., 15217. ☎ (412) 521-5900.
Holocaust Center of the United Jewish Federation, 242 McKee Pl., 15213. ☎ (412) 682-7111; serves as a living memorial by providing educational resources, sponsoring community activities, housing archives and cultural materials related to the Holocaust.
Jewish Education Institute, 6401 Forbes Av., 15217. Tel. (412) 521-1100; offers resources in Jewish education to synagogue schools, day schools, and other community organisations.

continued from *Pittsburg*

Bookseller: Pinsker's, 2028 Murray Av., 15217.☎ (412) 421-3033.

Synagogues:
Adath Israel (O), 3257 Ward St., 15213; Adath Jeshurun (O), 5643 E. Liberty Blvd., 15224; Beth Hamedrash Hagodol (O), 1230 Colwell St., 15219; B'nai Emunoh (O), 4315 Murray Av., 15217; B'nai Zion (O), 6404 Forbes Av., 15217; Bohnei Yisroel (O), 6401 Forbes Av., 15217; Kether Torah (O), 5706 Bartlett St., 15217; Kneseth Israel (O), 1112 N. Negley Av., 15206; Machsikei Hadas (O), 814 N. Negley Av., 15206; Poale Zedeck (O), Phillips & Shady Avs., 15217; Shaare Tefillah (O), 5741 Bartlett St., 15217; Shaare Torah (O), 2319 Murray Av., 15217; Shaare Zedeck (O), 5751 Bartlett St., 15217; Torath Chaim (O), 728 N. Negley Av., 15206; Ahavath Achim (C), Lydia & Chestnut Sts., Carnegie, 15106; Beth El of South Hills (C), 1900 Cochran Rd., 15220; Beth Shalom (C), Beacon & Shady Avs., 15217; B'nai Israel (C), 327 N. Negley Av., 15206; New Light (C), 1700 Beechwood Blvd., 15217; Parkway Jewish Center (C), 300 Princeton Dr., Pittsburgh, 15235; Tree of Life (C), Wilkins & Shady Avs., 15217; Rodef Shalom (R), 4905 5th Av., 15213; Temple David (R), 4415 Northern Pike, Monroeville, 15146; Temple Emanuel (R), 1250 Bower Hill Rd., South Hills, 15243; Temple Sinai (R), 5505 Forbes Av., 15217; Dor Hadash (Rec.), 6401 Forbes Av., 15217.

Kosher Restaurants:
King David's, 2020 Murray Av., 15217. ☎ (412) 422-3370; Yaacov's, 2109 Murray Av., 15217. ☎ (412) 421-7208.

Kosher Meat, Poultry, etc:
Brauner's Emporium, 2023 Murray Av., 15217; Greenberg's Kosher Poultry, 2223 Murray Av.; Koshermart, 2121 Murray Av.; Pastries Unlimited, 4743 Liberty Av., & 2119 Murray Av.; Prime Kosher, 1916 Murray Av. All the above are under rabbinical supervision.

POTTSTOWN
Syn.: Cong. Mercy & Truth (C), 575 N. Keim St., 19464.

READING
Jewish Fed., 1700 City Line St., 19604. ☎ (610) 921-2766.
Syn.: Shomrei Habrith (O), 2320 Hampden Blvd., 19604; Kesher Zion (C), Eckert & Perkiomen Sts., 19602; Oheb Sholom (R), 13th & Perkiomen Sts., 19604.
Com. Center, 1700 City Line St., 19604. ☎ (610) 921-0624.

SCRANTON
Scranton-Lackawanna Jewish Fed., 601 Jefferson Av., 18510. ☎ (717) 961-2300. Fax (717) 346-6147.
The Com. Center is at the same address. ☎ (717) 346-6595.
Syn.: Beth Shalom (O), Clay Av. at Vine St., 18510; Cong. Machzikeh Hadas (O), cnr. Monroe and Olive., 18510; Ohev Zedek (O), 1432 Mulberry St., 18510; Temple Israel (C), Gibson St. & Monroe Av., 18510; Temple Hesed (R), Lake Scranton, 18505.
Jewish Family Service, 615 Jefferson Av., 18510.
Jewish Home, 1101 Vine St., 18510.
Yeshivath Beth Moshe, 930 Hickory St., 18505.

SHARON
Syn.: Temple Beth Israel (R), 840 Highland Av., 16146.

continued from *Pittsburg*

WALLINGFORD

Syn.: Ohev Shalom (C), 2 Chester Rd., 19086. The syn. vestibule contains 12 stained glass panes (designed & executed by Rose Isaacson) each depicting a Jewish holiday.
Another work in glass by Rose Isaacson is on display in the vestibule. Depicting Jeremiah crying out to God, it is a memorial to the Six Million murdered in the Holocaust.

WILKES-BARRE

Jewish Fed. of Greater Wilkes-Barre & Comm. Center, 60 S. River St., 18702. ☎ (717) 822-4146/(717) 824-4646. Fax (717) 824-5966.
Syn.: Ohav Zedek (O), 242 S. Franklin St., 18702; Temple Israel (C), 236 S. River St., 18702; B'nai B'rith (R), 408 Wyoming Av., Kingston, 18704; United Orthodox Syn. (O), 13 S. Welles St., 18702.

WILLIAMSPORT

Syn.: Ohev Sholom (O & C), Cherry & Belmont Sts., 17701; Beth Ha-Sholom (R), 425 Center St., 17701.

RHODE ISLAND

BARRINGTON

Syn.: Temple Habonim (R), 165 New Meadow Rd., 02806.

BRISTOL

Syn.: United Brothers Syn. (C), 215 High St., 02809.

CRANSTON

Syn.: Temple Torat Yisrael (C), 330 Park Av., 02905; Temple Sinai (R), 30 Hagan Av. 02920.

MIDDLETOWN

Syn.: Temple Shalom (C), 223 Valley Rd., 02842. ☎ (401) 846-9002.

NARRAGANSETT

Syn.: Cong. Beth David (C), Kingstown Rd., 02882.

NEWPORT

Syn.: Touro (Sephardi, O), 85 Touro St., 02840. ☎ (401) 847-4794. The synagogue, designed by Peter Harrison and dedicated in 1763, is one of the finest examples of 18th Century Colonial architecture. It has been declared a national site by the U.S. Government. The Jewish cemetery, the 2nd oldest in the U.S., dates back to 1677 and was immortalised in Longfellow's poem "The Jewish Cemetery of Newport". Judah Touro is buried there.
Com. Center: Touro St.

PAWTUCKET

Syn.: Ohawe Shalom, East Av., 02860.

PROVIDENCE

Jewish Fed. of Rhode Island, 130 Sessions St., 02906. ☎ (401) 421-4111. Publishes 'L'Chaim' magazine with communal listings, etc.
Syn.: Beth Sholom (O), 275 Camp Av., 02906; Cong. Sons of Jacob (O), 24 Douglas Av., 02908; Mishkon Tfiloh (O), 203 Summit Av., 02906; Shaare Zedek (O), 688 Broad St., 02907; Temple Emanu-El (C), 99 Taft Av., 02906; Beth El (R), 70 Orchard Av., 02906.
Mikva: 401 Elmgrove Ave., 02906.

continued from *Rhode Island*

Jewish Com. Center of Rhode Island: 401 Elmgrove Av., 02906. ☎ (401) 861-8800. The Center houses the Rhode Island Holocaust Memorial Museum, the state memorial to the victims of the Holocaust. Many survivors now living in Rhode Island have donated memorabilia & personal mementoes. There is also a garden of remembrance. For further details, contact the Center.

The Rhode Island Jewish Historical Association in Providence has a vast amount of material regarding Colonial Jewry. ☎ (401) 863-2805.

Vaad Hakashrut. ☎ (401) 331-9393.

Kosher meals are available at Brown University Hillel, 80 Brown St., 02912.

WARWICK
Syn.: Temple Am David (C), 40 Gardiner St., 02888.

WESTERLY
Syn.: Cong. Shaare Zedek (O), Union St., 02891.

WOONSOCKET
Syn.: B'nai Israel (C), 224 Prospect St., 02895.

SOUTH CAROLINA
CHARLESTON
Jewish Fed. & Com. Center, 1645 Raoul Wallenberg Blvd., P. O. Box 31298, 29417. ☎ (803) 571-6565. Fax (803) 556-6206.

Syn.: B'rith Sholom (O) & Mikvah, 182 Rutledge Av., 29403. ☎ (803) 577-6599; Emanu-El (C), 5 Windsor Dr., 29407. ☎ (803) 571-3264; Beth Elohim (R), 86 Hasell St., 29401. ☎ (803) 723-1090.

Beth Elohim dates from 1749. It is the birthplace of Reform Judaism in the United States, the second oldest syn. bldg. in the country, and the oldest surviving Reform syn. in the world. It has been designated a national historic landmark. A museum is housed in the administration bldg. next door.

B'rith Sholom celebrated its 140th anniversary in 1995 being one of the oldest continuously operating Ashkenazi synagogues in the USA.

The cemetery in Coming St. is the largest and oldest in the South, and contains graves of Revolutionary War soldiers. In City Hall Park, there is a plaque honouring Francis Salvador, the first Jew to hold public office in the Colonies and to die in the Revolution.

Sherman House (Old Age House), 1635 Raoul Wallenberg Blvd., 29407. ☎ (803) 763-2242.

Addlestone Hebrew Academy (Day School), 1639 Raoul Wallenberg Blvd., 29407. ☎ (803) 571-1105.

Kosher bread and baked goods
Nathan's Deli, 1836 Ashley River Rd., 29407. ☎ (803) 556-3354.

Great Harvest Bread Co., 975 Savannah Hwy., 29407. ☎ (803) 763-2055.

Ashley Bakery, 1662 Savannah Hwy., 29407. ☎ (803) 763-4125.

Kosher restaurants
West Side Market and Deli, 1300 Savannah Hwy., 29407. ☎ (803) 763-9988.

COLUMBIA
Columbia Jewish Fed.: 4540 Trenholm Rd., Cola, 29206. ☎ (803) 787-2023.

Syn.: Beth Shalom (C), 5827 N. Trenholm Rd., 29206; Tree of Life (R), 6719 Trenholm Rd., Cola, 29206. ☎ (803) 787-0580.

Chabad, 4540 N. Trenholm Rd., 29206.

Com. Center; 4540 Trenholm Rd., 29206.

continued from *South Carolina*

Delicatessen: Groucho's, Five Points, 29205.

GEORGETOWN
Although there are now very few Jews in Georgetown, and there is no synagogue, there is a very old Jewish cemetery, which is maintained by the city.

MYRTLE BEACH
Syn.: Beth El (O), 401 Hwy 17 N., 56th Av., 29577. ☎ 449-3140.
Chabad Lubavitch (O), 2803 N. Oak St. ☎ 626-6403.

SOUTH DAKOTA
ABERDEEN
Syn.: B'nai Isaac (C), 202 N. Kline St., 57401. ☎ 225-3404 or 225-7360.

DEADWOOD
The cemetery here contains a number of graves of Jewish pioneers of the Gold Rush days.

RAPID CITY
Syn.: Syn. of the Hills (R), P.O. Box 2320, 57709. ☎ (605) 394-3310.
Affiliated with UAHC. Services sporadic.

TENNESSEE
CHATTANOOGA
Jewish Comm. **Federation**: 5326 Lynnland Terrace, 37411. ☎ (423) 894-1317. Fax (423) 894-1319.
Syn.: Beth Sholom (O), 20 Pisgah Av., 37411. ☎ (423) 894-0801.
B'nai Zion (C), 114 McBrien Rd., 37411. ☎ (423) 894-8900.
Mizpah Cong. (R), 923 McCallie Av., 37403. ☎ (423) 264-9771.
Siskin Museum of Religious Artefacts, One Siskin Plaza, 37403. ☎ (423) 634-1700.

MEMPHIS
Jewish Fed. & Comm. Center, 6560 Poplar Av., 38138. ☎ (901) 767-7100/761-0810.
Syn.: Anshei Sephard-Beth El Emeth (O), 120 E. Yates Rd. N., 38117; Baron Hirsch Cong. (O), 369 Winter Oak La., 38119. Mikvah on premises.
Baron Hirsch East Educational Center (O), 5631 Shady Gr. Rd., 38117; Beth Sholom (C), 482 S. Mendenhall Av., 38117; Temple Israel (R), 1376 E. Massey Rd.
Kosher Delicatessen: Rubenstein's, 4965 Summer Av., 38122. (Under rabbinical supervision. Closed Shabbat).
Kosher Restaurants: M.I. Gottlieb's, 5062 Park Av., 38119. (Under rabbinical supervision. Closed Shabbat); Jon's Place, 764 Mt. Moriah, 38117. ☎ (901) 378-0600 (under rabbinical supervision. Closed Shabbat).
Kosher Bakery: Carl's Bakery, 1688 Jackson Av., 38107. (Under rabbinical supervision. Closed Shabbat).

NASHVILLE
Jewish Fed. of Nashville & Middle Tennessee, 801 Percy Warner Blvd., 37205.
☎ (615) 356-3242. Fax (615) 352-0056.
Syn.: Sherith Israel (O), 3600 West End Av., 37205. ☎ (615) 292-6614. Mikva on premises; West End Synagogue (C), 3814 West End Av., 37205. ☎ (615) 269-4592.
The Temple (R), 5015 Harding Rd., 37205. ☎ (615) 352-7620.

continued from *Tennessee*

Com. Center, 801 Percy Warner Blvd., 37205. ☎ (615) 356-7170. Fax (615) 352-0056.

TEXAS
AMARILLO
Syn.: Temple B'nai Israel (R), 4316 Albert St., 79106. ☎ (806) 352-7191.

AUSTIN
Jewish Fed. of Austin (and Comm. Center), 11713 Jollyville Rd., 78759. ☎ (512) 331-1144. Fax (512) 331 7059.
Syn.: Chabad Hse. (O), 2101 Nueces Av., 78705. Mikva on premises. ☎ (512) 499-8202; Agudas Achim (C), 4300 Bull Creek Rd., 78731; Cong. Beth El (C), 8902 Mesa Dr., 78759. ☎ (512) 346-1776; Temple Beth Israel (R), 3901 Shoal Creek Blvd., 78756. ☎ (512) 454-6806.
Hillel, 2105 San Antonio St., 78705. ☎ (512) 476-0125.

BEAUMONT
Syn.: Temple Emanuel (R), 1120 Broadway, 77704. ☎ (409) 832-6131.

CORPUS CHRISTI
Syn.: B'nai Israel (C), 3434 Fort Worth Av., 78411; Temple Beth El (R), 4402 Saratoga St., 78413.
Com. Council, 750 Everhart Rd., 78411. ☎ (512) 855-6239.

DALLAS
Jewish Fed. of Greater Dallas & Comm. Center, 7800 Northaven Rd., Suite A, Dallas, Texas 75230. ☎ (214) 369-3313. Fax (214) 369-8943. The Center houses the Dallas Memorial Center for Holocaust Studies and the Dallas Jewish Historical Society.
Va'ad Hakashrus, 7800 Northaven Rd., Suite A, 75230. ☎ (214) 750-8223.

Synagogues:
Cong. Beth El Binah, P.O. Box 64460, Dallas, TX 75206; Cong. Anshai Emet (C), 1301 Custer Rd., #810, Plano, TX 75075; Cong. Beth Emunah (C), 206B S. Jefferson, Irving, TX 75060; Cong. Beth Torah (C), 720 Lookout, Richardson, TX 75080; Cong. Ner Tamid (R), 4018 Marsh Ridge, Carrollton, TX 75007; Cong. Ohev Shalom (O), 6959 Arapaho #575, Dallas, TX 75248; Cong. Shaare Tefilla (O), 6131 Churchill Way, Dallas, TX 75230; Cong. Shearith Israel (C), 9401 Douglas, Dallas, TX 75225; Cong. Tiferet Israel (T), 10909 Hillcrest, Dallas, TX 75230; Forest Lane Shul (O), 7008 Forest Lane, Dallas, TX 75230; Temple Emanu-El (R), 8500 Hillcrest, Dallas, TX 75225; Temple Shalom (R), 6930 Alpha, Dallas, TX 75240; Young Israel of Dallas (O), 1456 Preston Forest Sq. #145, Dallas, Texas 75230.
Mikvah: Cong. Tiferet Israel. ☎ (214) 397-3428 for appointment.
Rabbinic Association of Greater Dallas, 6930 Alpha, ☎ (214) 661-1810.
Newspaper: Texas Jewish Post (weekly), 11333 N. Central Expressway, Dallas, Texas 75230.

Kosher Establishments:
Adolphus Hotel, 1321 Commerce St., 75202. ☎ (214) 742-8200. Fax (214) 651-3563.
The Grand Kempinski Hotel, 15201 Dallas Parkway, 75248. ☎ (214) 386-6000. Fax (214) 404-1848.
Fairmont Hotel, 1717 N. Akard St., 75201. ☎ (214) 720-5261.

continued from *Texas*

Sheraton Park Central, 12720 Merit Dr., 75240. ☎ (214) 385-3000.t
The Southland Centre,
The Westin Hotel, 13340 Dallas Parkway. ☎ (214) 934-9494.
Afghan Gourmet Bakery, 13920 Josey Lane, Farmers Branch, 75234. ☎ (214) 247-9835.
Cakes of Elegance, 9205 Skillman, 75243. ☎ (214) 343-2253.
Deco's by Arthur Dairy Restaurant, 1418 Preston Forest Square, 75230. ☎ (214) 788-2808.
(K) Kosher Meat & Delicatessen: Kosher Link, 7517 Campbell Rd., Dallas, Texas 75230. ☎ (214) 248-3773. Under supervision of Vaad Hakashrus.
Highland Park Bakery, 3125 Ross Av., 75220. ☎ (214) 330-7097.
Minyards, 714 Preston Forest Shopping Center, 75230.
Neiman-Marcus Bakery, North Park. Location only. Closed Saturdays. ☎ (214) 363-8311.
Strictly Cheesecake, 8139 Forest Lane, Suite 117, Forest Central Village, 75243. ☎ (214) 783-6545.
Tom Thumb Bakery & Kosher Deli, 11920 Preston Rd., 75230. ☎ (214) 392-2501; Forest Lane only open 24 hours. Most Tom Thumb and Albertson grocery stores in North Dallas have a small kosher section for dried goods.

EL PASO
Jewish Fed., 405 Wallenberg Dr., 79912. ☎ (915) 584-4437.
Syn.: B'nai Zion (C), 805 Cherry Hill La., 79912. Mikva on premises; Mount Sinai (R), 4408 N. Stanton St. 79902.
Chabad House, 6505 Westwind 79912.
Jewish Com Center. 405 Wallenberg Dr 79912 (915) 584 4437.
Jewish Family and Childrens Service 401 Wallenberg Dr 79912 (915) 581 3256
El Paso Holocaust Museum and Study Center 401 Wallenberg Dr 79912 for information call 484-4437.
Chai Manor Housing for the elderly 406 Wallenberg 79912 833-1588.
Kosher delicatessen, etc: Alex's, 1000 Wyoming St., 79902; Kahn's Bakery & Sweet Shop, 918 N. Oregon St., 79901. Both the foregoing are under rabbinical supervision.

FORT WORTH
Syn: Ahavat Shalom (C), 4050 South Hulen, 76109. ☎ (817) 731-4721.

HOUSTON
Jewish Fed. of Greater Houston, 5603 S. Braeswood Blvd., 77096. ☎ (713) 729-7000.

Synagogues:
Beth Rambam (O), 11333 Braesridge Blvd., 77071; Chabad Lubavitch Center (O), 10900 Fondren Rd., 77096. Mikva on premises; United Orthodox Syns. (O), 4221 S. Braeswood Blvd., 77096. Mikva on premises; Young Israel (O), 7823 Ludington, 77071; Beth Am (C), 1431 Brittmore Rd., 77043; Beth Yeshurun (C), 4525 Beechnut St., 77096; B'rith Shalom (C), 4610 Bellaire Blvd., 77401; Cong. Shaar Hashalom (C), 16020 El Camino Real, 77062; Beth Israel (R), 5600 N. Braeswood Blvd., 77096; Emanu-El (R), 1500 Sunset Blvd., 77005; Jewish Community North (R), 18519 Klein Church Rd., Spring, 77039; Cong. for Reform Judaism (R), 801 Bering Dr., 77057; Temple Sinai (R), 783 Country Pl., 77079; K'nesseth Israel (Unaffiliated), cnr. Sterling & Commerce Sts., Baytown.
Com. Center, 5601 S. Braeswood Blvd., 77096.
Kosher Restaurants: Com. Center Snack Bar, 5601 S. Braeswood Blvd., 77096;

continued from *Texas*

Drumsticks, 10202 S. Main St., 77025; Nosher, 2 Braeswood Sq., 77096; Simon's Gourmet Kosher Foods, 5411 Braeswood, 7549; Wonderful Vegetarian Chinese, 7549 Westheimer. The foregoing are under rabbinical supervision.

LUBBOCK
Syn.: Congregation Shaareth Israel, 6928 83rd St., 79424. (Mailing Address: P.O. Box 93594, 79493-3594). ☎ (806) 794-7517.
Restaurnt: (V) Souper Salad, 6703 Slide Rd. ☎ (806) 794-0997.
Kosher Food: The major supermarkets (Albertson's United) can special order some kosher meats (e.g. Empire chicken) with a week's notice. Call Albetson's ☎ (806) 794-6761; United ☎ (906) 791-0220. Lowe's Supermarket at 82th and Slide stocks matzos and whitefish. All three chains have good selections for Passover.

SAN ANTONIO
Jewish Fed., 8434 Ahern Dr., 78216. ☎ (512) 341-8234.
Syn.: Rodfei Sholom (O), 3003 Sholom Dr 78230. Mikva on premises. Rabbi's ☎ (512) 492-4277; Agudas Achim (C), 1201 Donaldson Av., 78228; Beth El (R), 211 Belknap Pl., 78212.
Jewish Comm. Center, 103 West Rampart, 78216.
Holocaust Museum, 8434 Ahern Dr., 78216.
There is an exhibit dealing with Texan Jewish history at the Institute of Texan Cultures, Hemisphere Plaza (in the downtown-Riverfront area).
Kosher food & delicatessen available from Delicious Food, 7460 Callaghan Rd., 78229. ☎ (512) 366-1844.

WACO
Syn.: Agudath Jacob (C), 4925 Hillcrest Dr., 76710; Rodef Sholom (R), 1717 N. New Rd., 76707.

UTAH
OGDEN
Cong. Brith Sholem, 2750 Grant Av., Ogden, 84401. ☎ (801) 782-3453.

SALT LAKE CITY
United Jewish Federation of Utah, 2416 E. 1700 St. S., 84108. ☎ (801) 581-0102.
The Com. Center is at the same address (801) 581-0098.
Syn.: Chavurah B'Yachad (Rec.), 509 E. Northmont Way, Salt Lake, 84103. ☎ (801) 364-7060; Kol Ami, 2425 E. Heritage Way, Salt Lake, 84109. ☎ (801) 484-1501.

VERMONT
BURLINGTON
Syn.: Ahavath Gerim (O), cnr. Archibald & Hyde Sts., 05401; Ohavi Zedek (C), 188 N. Prospect St., 05401; Temple Sinai (R), 500 Swift St., 05401.

VIRGINIA
Note: Alexandria, Arlington, Fairfax, Falls Church and Reston are all part of Greater Washington, D.C.

ALEXANDRIA
Syn.: Agudas Achim (C), 2908 Valley Dr., 22302; Beth El Hebrew Cong. (R), 3830 Seminary Rd., 22304.

continued from *Virginia*

ARLINGTON

Syn.: Arlington-Fairfax Jewish Cong. (C), 2920 Arlington Blvd., Arlington 22204.
☎ (703) 979-4466. Daily Minyan and Shabbat services. Rabbi: Dr. Marvin I. Bash.
(Includes the areas known as Crystal City, Rosslyn, and Skyline).

CHARLOTTESVILLE

Syn.: Temple Beth Israel (R), 301 E. Jefferson St., 22902. ☎ (804) 295-6382.
The Hillel Jewish Center at The University of Virginia, 1824 University Circle,
22903. ☎ (804) 295-4963.

DANVILLE

Syn.: Temple Beth Sholom (R), Sutherlin Av. This bldg. is 95 years old, one of
the oldest syns. in the South. Fri. evg. and holiday services.

FAIRFAX

Syn.: Cong. Olam Tikvah (C), 3800 Glenbrook Rd., 22031, two miles from
Beltway Exit 6W. ☎ (703) 425-1880.

FALLS CHURCH

Syn.: Temple Rodef Shalom (R), 2100 Westmoreland St., 22043. ☎ 532-2217.

HAMPTON

See Virginia Peninsula.

NEWPORT NEWS

See Virginia Peninsula.

NORFOLK

United Jewish Fed. of Tidewater, 7300 Newport Av., 23505. ☎ (804) 489-
8040. Fax (804) 489-8230. This bldg. also houses the Com. Center. Publishes
'UJF Virginia News' (bi-weekly) and 'Renewal Magazine' (quarterly).
Syn.: B'nai Israel Cong. (O) and Va'ad Hakashrut, 420 Spotswood Av., 23517.
☎ (804) 627-7358.
Beth El (C), 422 Shirley Av., 23517. ☎ (804) 625-7821.
Temple Israel (C), 7255 Granby St., 23505. ☎ (804) 489-4550.
Ohef Sholom (R), Stockley Gdns. at Raleigh Av., 23507. ☎ (804) 625-4295.
The Commodore Levy Chapel, Frazier Hall, Bldg. C-7 (inside Gate 2),
Norfolk U.S. Navy Station is the U.S. Navy's oldest syn. Services are open to
civilians. Inq. to the Jewish Chaplain.
Communal Mikva. Inq. to B'nai Israel. ☎ (804) 444-7361.
Kosher Meat: The Kosher Place, 738 W. 22nd St.
Hotel: Omni International, Waterside Dr., 23510. ☎ (804) 622-6664. Va'ad
supervision.

RICHMOND

The Richmond com. is the sixth oldest in the United States.
Jewish Com. Fed., 5403 Monument Av., 23226. ☎ (804) 288-0045.
Syn.: Keneseth Beth Israel (O), 6300 Patterson Av., 23226; Young Israel-Kol
Emes (O), 4811 Patterson Av., 23226. Mikva on premises; Beth El (C), 3330
Grove Av., 23221; Beth Ahabah (R), 1117 W. Franklin St., 23220. The syn.
also houses Jewish archives which are of great historical interest; Or Ami (R),
9400 N. Huguenot Rd., 23235; Or Atid (C), 501 Parham Rd., 23229.
Com. Center, 5403 Monument Av., 23226. ☎ (804) 288-6091.

continued from *Virginia*

Places of interest include the cemetery for the Jewish soldiers of the Civil War. Chabad-Lubavitch of the Virginias, 212 Gaskins Rd., 23233. ☎ (804) 740-2000. Kosher facilities and rooms for Shabbat and holidays.

VIRGINIA BEACH
Syn.: Chabad Lubavitch (O), 533 Gleneagle Dr. 23462. ☎ (804) 499-0507. Kehillat Bet Hamidrash (C), 952 Indian Lakes Blvd 23464. ☎ (804) 495-8510. Temple Emanuel (C), 25th St., 23451. Beth Chaverim (R), 3820 Stoneshore Rd., 23452-7965. ☎ (757) 463-3226.

VIRGINIA PENINSULA
United Jewish Community of the Virginia Peninsula, 2700 Spring Rd., Newport News, 23606. ☎ (804) 930-1422. Syn.: Adath Jeshurun (O), 12646 Nettles Dr., Newport News, 23606. Mikva on premises; B'nai Israel (T), 3116 Kecoughtan Rd., Hampton, 23661; Rodef Shalom (C) 318 Whealton Rd., Hampton, 23666; Temple Sinai (R), 11620 Warwick Blvd., Newport News, 23601. Kosher Bakery: Brenner's Warwick Bakery, 240 31st St., Newport News, 23607. Under supervision of Va'ad Hakashrut.

WASHINGTON
ABERDEEN
Syn: Temple Beth Israel (C), 1219 Spur St., 98520. ☎ (360) 533-3784.

SEATTLE
Organisations
Jewish Fed. of Greater Seattle, 2031 3rd. Av., 98121. ☎ (206) 443-5400. The Jewish Fed. publishes "The Jewish Transcript", at the same address. The Washington Association of Jewish Communities also shares the same address. Va'ad Harabanim, 6500 52nd Av. S., 98118. Inq. concerning kashrut, etc., should be addressed to the Board. B'nai B'rith Hillel Foundation, University of Washington, 4745 17th Av. N.E., 98105. ☎ 527-1997. The University library has a Jewish archives section dealing with the Seattle com. Com. Center, 3801 E. Mercer Way, Mercer Island, 98040. ☎ (206) 232-7115. A Holocaust memorial with a bronze sculpture by Gizel Berman has been dedicated here. Northend Com. Center. 8606 35th Ave NE (206) 526 8073 Jewish Family Service, . 1601-16th Av., 98122. Jewish books and religious articles are obtainable from: B'nai B'rith Hillel Foundation and the following syns.: Beth Am, Beth Shalom, Bikur Cholim Machzikay Hadath, Bikur Holim, Ezra Bessaroth, Herzl-Ner Tamid, Temple de Hirsch-Sinai. (For addresses, see above.) The Jewish com. in the Seattle area numbers some 30,000 (27,000 Ashkenazi & 3,000 Sephardi), and makes up just over one per cent of the total population.

Synagogues:
Bikur Cholim Machzikay Hadath (O), 5145 S. Morgan St., 98118. ☎ (206) 721-0970; Bikur Holim (Sephardi, O), 6500 52nd Av. S., 98118. ☎ (206) 723-3028; Chabad Hse. (O), 4541 19th Av. N.E., 98105. ☎ (206) 527-1411; Ezra Bessaroth (Sephardi, O), 5217 S. Brandon St., 98118. ☎ (206) 722-5500; Yeshiva Gedola of Greater Seattle (O), 5220 20th Av. N.E., 98105. ☎ (206) 527-1100; Cong. Shaarei Tefilah-Lubavitch (T), 6803 40th St. N.E., 98115. ☎

continued from *Washington*

(206) 523-1323; Emanuel Cong. (Traditional, but with mixed seating), 3412 65th Av. N.E., 98115. ☎ (206) 525-1055; Cong. Beth Shalom (C), 6800 35th Av. N.E., 98115. ☎ (206) 524-0075; Herzl-Ner Tamid (C), 3700 E. Mercer Way, Mercer Island, 98040. ☎ (206) 232-8555; Beth Am (R), 8015 27th Av. N.E., 98115. ☎ (206) 525-0915; B'nai Torah (R), 6195 92nd Av. S.E., Mercer Island, 98040. ☎ (206) 232-7243; Temple de Hirsch-Sinai (R), 1511 E. Pike St., 98122. ☎ (206) 323-8486.

Congregation Tikuah Chadarhah (Gay-Lesbian). ☎ 328-2590.

Southland Jewish Center (0) 236-2386.

South King County Community Synagogue (Liberal) (206) 722-2822.

Kosher hotels

The Va'ad Harabanim supervises the catering at the following hotels:
Bellevue Hilton, 100 112th St. N.E., Bellevue, 98004. ☎ (206) 455-3330; Four Seasons Olympic Hotel, 4th & University Sts. ☎ (206) 621-1700; Red Lion Inn, 18740 Pacific Highway S. ☎ (206) 246-8600; Red Lion Inn, Bellevue. ☎ (206) 455-1300; Seattle Hilton, 8th & University Sts. ☎ (206) 624-0500; Seattle Sheraton. ☎ (206) 621-0900; Westin Hotel, 5th & Westlake Sts. ☎ (206) 728-1000.

Stouffer Madison, 6th & Madison, Tel (206) 583 0300

The following supply kosher food:

Bagel Deli, 340 15th Av. E., ☎ (206) 322-2471 & 1309 N.E. 43rd St. ☎ (206) 634-3770; Betayawone, 113 Blanchard, 98121. ☎ (206) 448-5597; Brenner Brothers Bakery, 12000 N.E. Redmond Rd., Bellevue. ☎ (206) 454-0600; Kosher Delight, 801 South King St., 98101. ☎ (206) 623-0801; Park Deli, 5011 S. Dawson St., Seward Park 98118. ☎ 206-722-NOSH; Varon's Kosher Meats, 3931 M.L. King Way S., 98108. ☎ (206) 723-0240, and 5011 South Dawson, ☎ (206) 722-6674.

SPOKANE

Syn.: Temple Beth Shalom (C), 1322 E. 30th St., 99203. ☎ (509) 747-3304. Jewish Com. Council, North 221 Wall, Suite 500, Spokane, Wa 99201. ☎ (509) 838-4261

There are also Jewish communities in other towns in the State: Bainbridge Island, Bellingham, Edmonds, Fort Lewis, Kent, Pullman, Tacoma and Yakima.

WEST VIRGINIA
HUNTINGDON
Syn.: B'nai Sholom (C & R), 949 10th Av., 25701. ☎ (304) 522-2980.

WISCONSIN
MADISON
Madison Jewish Com. Council, 6434 Enterprise Lane, 53179. ☎ (608) 278-1808.
Syn.: Chabad Hse (O), 1722 Regent St., 53705; Beth Israel Center (C), 1406 Mound St., 53711; Beth El (R), 2702 Arbor Dr., 53711.
Hillel Foundation, 611 Langdon St., 53703.

MILWAUKEE
Milwaukee Jewish Fed., 1360 N. Prospect Av., 53202. ☎ (414) 271-8338. Fax 271-7081. Publishes Directory and Wisconsin Jewish Chronicle. ☎ (414) 271-2992.

Synagogues:
Agudas Achim (O), 5820 W. Burleigh Av., 53210; Anshai Lebowitz (O), 3100 N. 52nd St., 53216; Beth Jehudah (O), 2700 N. 54th St., 53210; Chabad Hse. (O), 3109 N. Lake Dr., 53211; Lake Park Syn. (O), 3207 Hackett Av., 53211; Anshe-Sfard-Kehillat Torah (O), 6717 N. Green Bay Av., 53209; Temple Menorah (C), 9363 N. 76th Street, 53223
Milwaukee Jewish Home Chapel (O), 1414 N. Prospect Av., 53202; Beth El Ner Tamid (C), 2909 W. Mequon Rd., 53092; Beth Israel (C), 6880 N. Green Bay Av., 53209; Cong. Shalom (R), 7630 N. Santa Monica Blvd., 53217; Cong. Sinai (R), 8223 N. Port Washington Rd., 53217; Emanu-El B'ne Jeshurun (R), 2419 E. Kenwood Blvd., 53211; Chabad of North Shore (O), 2233 W. Mequon Rd., Mequon, WI 53092.
Com. Center: 6255 N. Santa Monica Blvd., 53217.
Milwaukee Assoc. for Jewish Education, 6401 N. Santa Monica Blvd., 53217. ☎ (414) 962-8860.
Milwaukee Jewish Council, 1360 N. Prospect Av., 53202. ☎ (414) 276-7920. Fax 276-7902.
Sinai-Samaritan Medical Center, Sinai Campus, 945 N. 12th St., 53233. ☎ (414) 345-3400.
Wisconsin Council of Congregation Rabbis, 6880 N. Green Bay Rd., 53217. ☎ (414) 352-7310.

SHEBOYGAN
Syn.: Temple Beth El (T), 1007 North Av., 53083.

WYOMING
CASPER
Syn.: Temple Beth El, 4105 S. Poplar, P.O.B. 3534, Casper, 82602. ☎ (307) 237-2330.

CHEYENNE
Syn.: Mt. Sinai, 2610 Pioneer Av., Cheyenne, 82001. ☎ (307) 634-3052.

continued from *Wyoming*

GREEN RIVER
Syn.: Congregation Beth Israel, P.O.B. 648, Green River, WY, 82935. ☎ (307) 875-4194.

LARAMIE
Syn.: Laramie J.C.C., P.O.B. 202, Laramie, 82070. ☎ (307) 745-8813.

NATIONAL TOURIST OFFICES IN THE UK

Australian Tourist Commission, Gemini Hse., 10-18 Putney Hill, SW15 6AA. ☎ 0181-780 2227.

Bahamas Tourist Office, Bahamas Hse., 3 The Billings, Walnut Close, Guildford, Surrey GU1 4UL. ☎ 148-344-8900. Fax 148-344-8990.

Belgian Tourist Office, 29 Princes St., W1R 7RG. ☎ 0891-887799 (premium rate line). Fax 0171-629 0454.

Bermuda Tourism, 1 Battersea Church Rd., SW11 3LY. ☎ 0171-734 8813. Fax 0171-352 6501.

Bulgarian National Tourist Office, 18 Princes St., W1R 7RE. ☎ 0171-499 6988.

Cedok Travel Ltd, 53-54 Haymarket, SW1Y 4RP. ☎ 0171-839 4414. Fax 0171-839 0204.

Cyprus Tourism Organisation, 213 Regent St., W1R 8DA. ☎ 0171-734 9822. Fax 0171-287-6534.

Danish Tourist Board, 55 Sloane St., SW1X 9SY. ☎ 0171-259 5959.

Egyptian State Tourist Office, 170 Piccadilly, W1V 9DD. ☎ 0171-493 5282.

Finnish Tourist Board, 3rd Floor, 30-35 Pall Mall, SW1Y 5LP. ☎ 0171-930 5871. Fax 0171-321 0696.

French Government Tourist Office, 178 Piccadilly, W1V 0AL. ☎ 0891-244 123 (premium rate line). Written inquiries dealt with promptly (but £1 in stamps requested for post & packing for bulky literature).

Gibraltar Information Bureau, Arundel Gt. Court, 179 Strand, WC2R 1EH. ☎ 0171-836 0777. Fax 0171-240 6612. Web site: http://www.gibraltar.gi

Greece — National Tourist Organisation of Greece, 4 Conduit St., W1R 0DJ. ☎ 0171-734 5997-9.

Holland — Netherlands Board of Tourism, P.O. Box 523, SW1E 6NT. ☎ 0891-717777 (premium rate line).

Hong Kong Tourist Association, 125 Pall Mall, SW1Y 5EA. ☎ 0171-930 4775 Fax 0171-930 4777. Web site: http://www.hkta.org

India — Government of India Tourist Office, 7 Cork St., W1X 1LN. ☎ 0171-437 3677. Fax 0171-494 1048.

Ireland — Irish Tourist Board, 150 New Bond St., W1Y 0AQ. ☎ 0171-493 3201.

Israel Government Tourist Office, 18 Gt. Marlborough St., W1V 1AF. ☎ 0171-434 3651. Fax 0171-437 0527.

Italian State Tourist Board (ENIT), 1 Princes St., W1R 8AY. ☎ 0171-408 1254. Fax 0171-493 6695.

Jamaica Tourist Board, 1-2, Prince Consort Rd, SW7 2BZ. ☎ 0171-224 0505. Fax 0171-224 0551.

Japan National Tourist Organisation, 167 Regent St., W1R 7FD. ☎ 0171-734 9638.

Luxembourg Tourist Office, 122/124 Regent St., W1R 5FE. ☎ 0171-434 2800. Fax 0171-734 1205.

Malta Tourist Office, 36-38 Piccadilly, W1V 0PP. ☎ 0171-292 4900. Fax 0171-734 1880.

Mexico Ministry of Tourism Office, 60-61 Trafalgar Sq., 3rd Floor, WC2N 5DS. ☎ 0171-734 1058.

Moroccan National Tourist Office, 205 Regent St., W1R 7DE. ☎ 0171-437 0073. Fax 0171-734 8172.

Northern Ireland Tourist Board, 11 Berkeley St., W1X 5AD. Tourist inf.: ☎ 0171-355 5040. Fax 0171-409 0487; and All Ireland Desk, British Travel Centre, 4-12 Lower Regent St., SW1Y 4PQ.

Norwegian Tourist Board, 5-11 Lower Regent St., SW1Y 4LR. ☎ 0171-839 6255.

Portuguese National Tourist Office, 22/25a Sackville St., W1X 1DE. ☎ 0171-494 1441. Fax 0171-494 1868. Telex 265653.

Romanian National Tourist Office, 83A, Marylebone High St., W1M 3DE. ☎ 0171-224 3692.

Russia & the former Soviet Union, Intourist Travel Ltd., 219 Marsh Wall, E14 9PD. ☎ 0171-538 8600. Fax 0171-538 5967; Suite 2F, Central Buildings, 211 Deansgate, Manchester, M3 3NW. ☎ 0161-834 0230. Fax 0161-831 7865; 29 St. Vincent Pl., Glasgow G1 2DT. ☎ 0141-204-5809. Fax 0141-204-5807.

Scottish Tourist Board, Tourist Information Centre (Relocating late 1996).

South African Tourism Board, 5/6 Alt Grove, London SW19 4DZ. ☎ 0181-944 6646.

Spanish National Tourist Office, 57-58 St. James's St., SW1A 1LD. ☎ 0171-499 0901. Brochures only ☎ 0891-669920.

Swedish Travel & Tourism Council, 73 Welbeck St., W1M 8AN. ☎ 0171-487 3135.

Switzerland Tourism, Swiss Centre, Swiss Court, New Coventry St., W1V 8EE. ☎ 0171-734 1921.

Turkish Information Office, 1st Floor, 170-173 Piccadilly, W1V 9DD. ☎ 0171-629 7771. Fax 0171-491 0773.

United States Travel & Tourism Administration, P.O. Box 1EN, London W1A 1EN. ☎ 0171-495 4466 (Consumer & Trade Inf. Service). Please note that they no longer have a walk-in facility.

Visit Canada Centre, 62/65 Trafalgar Sq., WC2N 5DY. ☎ 0891-715000 (premium rate line).

Yugoslav National Tourist Office, 143 Regent St., W1R 8AE. ☎ 0171-439 0399.

OTHER COUNTRIES

AFGHANISTAN

From a peak of some 40,000 a century ago, Afghanistan's Jewish population has dwindled to about 120 today. Most are of Persian origin. There are some 12 families in Kabul, the capital, and five or six in Herat. All of them, in both cities, are strictly Orthodox. There is one rabbi/shochet in the country. Jewish settlement in Afghanistan goes back much further than the last century. There were Jews in the country 800 years ago, although little is known of their history until about 120 years ago. In recent years, many have emigrated to Israel.

KABUL

The syn. is on the 2nd floor of a building in Charshi Torabazein St.

ALBANIA

Jews have lived in Albania since Roman times. Remnants of an ancient syagogue have been found in Dardania, northern Albania. Sephardic Jews came during the Inquisition. Shabbetai Zevi, the false Messiah, died in exile near the town of Berat in 1676, and an annual fair is held on his assumed burial site. Most of the modern Jews of Albania, numbering about 350, emigrated to Israel in the Spring of 1991, arriving on the last day of the Gulf War. Their World War II history then became known: 99% of the Albanian Jews survived the Nazi Occupation by being protected and hidden by Moslems and Christians. Today only a handful of Jews are left in the country, but there are active branches of the Albanian-Israel Friendship Society in Tirana and other cities. Mr. Refik Veseli, President, will be glad to provide information. His address: Rruga "Barrikatave" 226. Tirana. Telephone: 22611.

ALGERIA

There are approximately 200–300 Jews in Algeria today. Most live in Algiers, and there are a few families in Blida, Constantine and Oran. Algiers is the headquarters of the Algerian Consistoire. In 1962, when Algeria became independent, the community numbered 130,000. Of this total almost a quarter — 30,000 — lived in Algiers. By 1968, only some 2,000 Jews remained in the country, and their number has continued to dwindle over the years.

ALGIERS

Association Consistoriale Israélite d'Alger, 6 rue Hassena Ahmed (formerly rue de Suffren). ☎ (213) 262-85-72. Pres.: Roger Said.
Fédération des Communautés Isráelites d'Algérie. Same address & ☎ as above. Syn.: 6 rue Hassena Ahmed.

BLIDA

Consistoire d'Algérie, 29 rue des Martyrs. ☎ 3492657. Pres.: Roger Said.

ARGENTINA

The Argentine community, which includes about 50,000 Sephardim, is estimated to total about 250,000. About a fifth live in rural areas. It is by far the largest in Latin America. The Ashkenazi majority come from East European stock. Immigration from Russia and other East European countries began in 1889.
Greater Buenos Aires, the capital, has some 160,000 Jews. There are important communities in 11 provincial centres: Rosario (15,000), Cordoba (10,000), Santa Fé (5,000), La Plata (4,000), Bahia Blanca (4,000), Mendoza (4,000), Mar del Plata (4,000), Parana (3,000), Resistencia (2,000), Corrientes

(1,500), and Salta (1,500). Altogether there are about 90 Jewish communities in Argentina, including a number of families in the former colonies set up by the Jewish Colonization Association (J.C.A.), who live on the land or from economic activities linked with agriculture. Several of these colonies were in the provinces of Buenos Aires, Santa Fé, La Pampa and Entre Rios. The three most important Jewish colonies are: Moisesville (where 20 per cent of the total population of 3,000 are Jews) in the province of Santa Fé, Rivera (with a Jewish population of 1,000 — half the total) in La Pampa, and General Roca (1,000 Jews) in Rio Negro, in the south.

BUENOS AIRES
Synagogues & Religious Organisations
The number of synagogues in Buenos Aires, where there is a minyan at least on Friday night and Saturday morning, is nearing fifty (their addresses can be obtained by inquiring from one of the community centres below). A list of the most important synagogues follows.
Congregacion Israelita de la Republica Argentina (the oldest Argentine Synagogue) Libertad 785. ☎ 476-2474/371-8929 (Centro).
Asociacion Shuva Israel Paso 557. ☎ 962 6255 (Once).

Ashkenazi
Orthodox: Adat Iereim, Argerich 380; Ahabat Israel, Serrano 69; Anshei Galitzia, Jose Evaristo Uriburu 234; Baron Hirsh, Billinghurst 664. ☎ 862-2624; Bet Jabad Lubavitch, Agüero 1164. ☎ 963-1221; Bet Jabad Lubavitch Belgrano, 11 de Septiembre 858. ☎ 772-5324; Bet Rajel, Ecuador 522. ☎ 862-2701; Brit Abraham, Antezana 145. ☎ 855-6567; Etz Jaim, Julian Alvarez 745. ☎ 772-5324; Ezra, Azcuenaga 778; Floresta Norte, Cervantes 1034; Jebrat Mishnaiot, Tucuman 2186; Shomrei Shabat, Sarmiento 2309; Sinagoga Israelita Lituana, Jose Evaristo Uriburu 348. ☎ 952-7968; Tefilat Moshe, Manuel Artigas 5779; Torah Vaaboda, Julian Alvarez 667. ☎ 854-0462; Zijron Le David, Azcuenaga 736. ☎ 953-0200.
Beit Jabad Villa Crespo, Serrano 69.

Sephardi
Orthodox: Aderet Eliahu, Ruy Diaz de Guzman 647. ☎ 302-9306; Agudat Dodim, Avellaneda 2874. ☎ 611-0056; Akedat Itzjak, Anchorena 829; Bajurim Tiferet Israel, Helguera 611. ☎ 611-3376; Comunidad Israelita, Camargo 870. ☎ 854-1952 or 0287; Etz Hajaim, Pueyrredon 645; Etz Jaim, Carlos Calvo 1164. ☎ 302-6290; Israelita, Monroe 5640. ☎ 51-6722; Jaike Grimberg, Campana 460. ☎ 672-2347; Jerusalem, Tucuman 2153; Kehal Jaredim, Helguera 270. ☎ 612-0410; Maguen Abraham, Helguera 547; Od Yosef Jai, Tucuman 3326. ☎ 963-2349; Ohel Abraham, Campana 560; Or Misraj, Ciudad de la Paz 2555. ☎ 784-5945; Or Torah, Brandsen 1444. ☎ 21-3426; Shaar Hashamaim, Viamonte 2342; Shaare Tefila, Paso 733. ☎ 962-2865; Shaare Tzion, Helguera 453. ☎ 612-9484; Shalom, Olleros 2876. ☎ 552-2720; Shebet Ajim, Pinzon 1261. ☎ 28-5261; Shuba Israel, Ecuador 627. ☎ 862-0562; Sinagoga Rabino Eliahu Freue, Canalejas 3465; Sinagoga Rabino Shaul Setton Dabbah, Boulogne sur Mer 833; Sinagoga Rabino Zeev Gringberg, Canalejas 3047. ☎ 611-3366; Sinagoga Saban Lavalle 2656; Sucath David, Paso 724. ☎ 962-1091; Yeshurun, Republica de la India 3035. ☎ 802-9310; Yesod Hadat, Lavalle 2449. ☎ 961-1615.

Conservative
Templo La Paz (Chalom) Olleros 2876. ☎ 552-6730.
The following three syns. make no distinction between Ashkenazi & Sephardi – Conservative: Comunidad Bet El, Sucre 3338. ☎ 552-2365; Colegio

Wolfson, Comunidad Or-El, Amenabar 2972. ☎ 544-5461.
Comundad Jerusalem, 24 de Noviembre 1434. ☎ 93.0012/0907; (P.Patricios);
Beit Hilel, Araoz 2854. ☎ 804-2286; (Palermo); Dor Jadash, Murillo 649. ☎
854-4467; (V. Crespo); Or Jadash, Varela 850. ☎ 612-1171/(Flores);
Congregacion Hebrea de San Martin, Tucuman 130 (San Martin).

Reform
Templo Emanu-El, Tronador 1455. ☎ 552-4343.

German
Orthodox: Ajdut Yisroel, Moldes 2449. ☎ 783-2831.
Conservative: Nueva Comunidad Israelita, Arcos 2319. ☎ 781-0281.
Progressive: Asociación Religiosa Lamroth Hakol, Caseros 1450 (Florida);
Benei Tikva, Vidal 2049. ☎ 795-0380.
All the Conservative syns. are affiliated to the World Council of Synagogues;
all Reform & Liberal syns. to the World Council for Progressive Judaism, and
all except the Orthodox syns. to the Latin American Rabbinical Seminary (see
below).

Mikvaot: Bogotá 3015 (Flores); Ecuador 731 (Once); Helguera 270; Larrea
734 (Once); Moldes 2449. (Belgrano); José Hernandez 1750 (Belgrano).
The Orthodox Ashkenazi Chief Rabbi of Argentina is Rabbi Shlomo Benhamu
Anidjar. The Central Rabbinate of the Vaad Hakehillot (Orthodox) is at
Ecuador 1110. ☎ 961-2944.
Latin American Rabbinical Seminary (Seminario Rabínico Latinoamericano)
(Conservative), Dean: D. Feinstein. Rabbinical Director: Rabbi Sergio Spolsky,
José Hernandez 1750. ☎ 783-2009 & 783-6175.
High School for Jewish Studies, Ayacucho 632.
Michlalat Madaei Hayahadut, Ayacucho 632.

Representative Organisations
AMIA (Central Ashkenazi community). Pasteur 633. ☎ 953-9777 & 2862.
Pres.: Luis Perelmuter. Sec: Morris Azar.
Asociacion Israelita Sefaradi Argentina (AISA), Paso 493. ☎ 952-4707
B'nai B'rith. Office for Latin America: Talcahuano 438, 3rd Floor. ☎ 40-1087.
Office for Argentina: Juncal 2573. Tel 80-4625.
DAIA (Political representative body of Argentine Jewry).
Pasteur 633, Fifth Floor. ☎ 953-5380 & 5394. Pres.: Dr. Ruben Beraja. Sec.:
Edgardo Gorenberg.
ECSA (Central Sephardi body) Larrea 674, Fourth Floor.
Latin American Jewish Congress. Fax 963-7056. Larrea 744, 1030. ☎ 961-
4534. Pres.: Benno Milnitzky. Dir.: M. Tenenbaum.
Vaad Hakehillot, Pasteur 633, Second Floor.

Cultural Organisations, Libraries, etc.
Asoc. Judeo de Cultura y Educación, Mendoza 1470. ☎ 782-7806.
Latin American Rabbinical Seminary Library, José Hernandez 1750. ☎ 783-
2009. 781-4057.
Museo Judio (Jewish Museum) de Buenos Aires, Libertad 769. ☎ 45-2474.
ORT, Monta–eses 2845. ☎ 782-7571. Fax 782-8583.
Sociedad Hebraica Argentino (with library, art gallery, etc.), Sarmiento 2233.
☎ 952-5570.
YIVO Library, Pasteur 633, Third Floor. ☎ 951-6624.

Homes for Aged
Agudat Dodim, Avellaneda 2735.
Hajnasat Orjim, Valentin Gomez 2952.

Kehal Yereim, Argerich 630.
Hogar Adolfo Hirsch, Gaspar Campos 2975. (San Miguel).
Hospital: Hospital Israelita Terrada 1164. ☎ 581-8172.

Sports & other Clubs
C.A.S.A. (Sephardi), Av. Del Libertador General San Martin 77, Vicente Lopez. ☎ 791-8460.
Hacoaj, Estado de Israel 4156. ☎ 862-8081.
Maccabi, Tucuman 3135. ☎ 963-8785.

Zionist Organisations
Argentine Zionist Org. & Jewish Agency, Cangallo 2471. ☎ 952-2450. Pres.: Alberto Astrovsky.
B'nei Akiva, Azcuenaga 736. ☎ 953-0200.
Instituto Cultural Argentina Israel, Paraguay 1535. ☎ 813-9205 & 812-4657.
Fund for Argentine-Israeli Agricultural Co-operation, Corrientes 2194.
OSFA (Argentine WIZO), Larrea 1225. ☎ 821-6347.

Israel Embassy: Av. de Mayo 701. ☎ 342-1465.

Newspapers: 'La Voz Judia', 'Nueva Sion', 'Die Presse', 'Comunidades', 'Kesher Kehilari', 'Mundo Israelita'.

Booksellers
Agudat Dodim, Bogota 2973. ☎ 613-7900.
Ediciones del Seminario Rabínico Latinoamericano, José Hernandez 1750. ☎ 783-2009.
Editorial Yehuda, Lavalle 2168, Oficina 37.
Kehot Lubavitch Sudamerica, San Luis 3281.
E. Milberg, Lavalle 2223. ☎ 951-1979.
Otzar Hatora, Viamonte 2712. ☎ 865-7208. Fax 962-7931.
Libreria Editorial Sigal. Corrientes 2854. ☎ 865-7208. Fax 962-7931.

Kosher Restaurants, etc.
(K) Bar Helueni, Tucuman 2620. ☎ 961-0541;
(K) Gueula (Pizzeria), San Luis 2539. ☎ 962-5249.
(K) Hambra Aranguren 3192. ☎ 613-9828.
(K) Kosher Nic, Paso 2607.
(K) Restaurant Maadanim, Nazca 544. ☎ 611-9686.
(K) Restaurant Sucath David, Tucuman 2349. ☎ 952-8878.
(V) Giardino Lavalle 835.

Meat & Groceries
There are 20 kosher butchers' shops as well as 18 kosher grocery shops & supermarkets.

Other Principal Communal Centres
Avellaneda (Greater Buenos Aires), H. Yrigoyen 987.
Bahia Blanca, Buenos Aires Prov., Las Heras 40; Bet Jabad Lubavitch, Chiclana 763. ☎ (091) 36582; Espana 42. ☎ 39040 (Cons).
Catamarca, Catamarca Prov., Salta 842.
Ceres, Santa Fé Prov., Teodoro Herzl 50.
Cipoletti, Neuquen Prov., Irigoyen 161.
Ciudadela, Buenos Aires Prov., Alianza 310.
Concepción del Uruguay, Entre Rios Prov., Ameghino 132.
Concordia, Entre Rios Prov., Entre Rios 478; Agudat Israel (Seph), Andrade 138; Bet Jabad Entre Rios 212. ☎ (045) 211934.

Cordoba, Cordoba Prov., Centro Union Israelita de Cordoba, Alvear 254.
Corrientes, Corrientes Prov., San Martin 1493.
Formosa, Formosa Prov., Rivadavia 1246.
General Roca, Rio Negro Prov., Chacabuco 446.
Jujuy, Jujuy Prov., Belgrano 865.
Lanus, Buenos Aires Prov., Sitio de Montevideo 1021. ☎ 241-0551.
Lomas de Zamora (Greater Buenos Aires),
Gorriti 333; Anshei Emuna, Boedo 693. ☎ 243-5480.
Mar Del Plata, Buenos Aires Prov., Sociedad Union Israelita Marplatense,
Espana 1853; Sinagoga Gabriel, Tres de Febrero 2451; Bet Abraham, Falucho 1539.
Kosher Restaurant: **(K)** Sucath David, Bogota 2165. (Summer only).
Mendoza, Mendoza Prov., Av. Espana 1930.
Miramar, Buenos Aires Prov., Calle 27 entre 14 y 16 (Seph).
Moisesville, Santa Fé Prov. (There are apparently 4 synagogues and a Jewish
population of 300).
Parana, Entre Rios Prov., 9 de Julio 391.
La Plata, Buenos Aires Prov., Calle 11 1426; Beit Chabad, Calle 50, no. 463.
☎ (021) 258304.
Posadas, Misiones Prov., Rivadavia 199.
Resistencia, Chaco Prov., Ameghino 355.
Rio Cuarto, Cordoba Prov., Belgrano 462.
La Rioja, La Rioja Prov., 9 de Julio 175.
Rivera, Buenos Aires Prov.
Rosario, Santa Fé Prov., Paraguay 1152; Bet Jabad Lubavitch, Maipu 1428. ☎
(041) 67440; Shebet Ajim, Donnego 1160; Etz Hajaim, Catamarca 2032. ☎
(041) 251-341.
Salta, Salta Prov., Caseros 945.
San Juan, San Juan Prov., Cordoba 939.
San Luis, San Luis Prov., Pedernera 1049.
Santa Fé, Santa Fé Prov., 4 de Enero 2539.
Santiago del Estero, Santiago del Estero Prov., La Plata 146.
Tigre, Buenos Aires Prov., Maraboto 535.
Tucuman, Tucuman Prov., Las Piedras 980; 9 de Julio 625 (Sephardi). ☎ (081)
220734; Bet Obadia (Lubavitch), Lamadrid 752. ☎ (081) 311-257. Las
Piedras 980 (Cons).
Villa Angela, Chaco Prov., Rivadavia 81.
Villaguay, Entre Rios Prov., Balcarce 654.
Zapala, Neuquen Prov., Calle Julio Argentino Roca.
Zarate, Buenos Aires Prov., L. N. Alem 115.

AUSTRALIA

Jews have lived in Australia since 1788. Sixteen known Jews, and possibly others, arrived on the first fleet of convict ships in 1788, although it was not until
the 1820s that the first regular, organised worship began. In 1832, the
Government recognised the establishment of the congregation in Sydney. It
was also in Sydney that the first syn. in Australia was built — in 1844. Jews
rose to prominence in political, commercial and cultural life in 19th-century
Australia. In more recent times, there have been two Jewish Governors-
General, as well as a Jewish Chief Justice and Commander-in-Chief of the
armed forces (in the First World War).

However, the country's Jewish population has always been small, never reaching 0.6 per cent of its total population. Only because of waves of immigration
at crucial periods has Jewish life remained viable. Today, Australian Jewry
totals some 100,000. There are about 40,000 in Melbourne, 35,000 in Sydney,

with smaller communities in the federal capital, Canberra, as well as Perth, Brisbane and Adelaide.

General inf. from the Australian Tourist Commission, Gemini Hse., 10-18 Putney Hill, SW15 6AA. ☎ 081-780 1424.

Note: Some information is given about kosher hotels, restaurants, etc., but as these details are liable to change, visitors should consult the ministers of synagogues about accommodation and meals.

AUSTRALIAN CAPITAL TERRITORY
CANBERRA
The A.C.T. Jewish Com. syn. & office are at the National Jewish Memorial Centre, cnr. Canberra Av. & National Circuit, Forrest, 2603. ☎ 295-1052. Fax. 295-8608. Postal address: P.O. Box 3105, Manuka 2603.

Israel Embassy, 6 Turrana St., Yarralumla, 2600. ☎ 73-1309.

NEW SOUTH WALES
NEWCASTLE
Syn.: 122 Tyrrell St., P. O. Box 5222D, 2302. ☎ (049) 26-2820. Sec.: Dr. L. Fredman

SYDNEY
Representative Organisations
B'nai B'rith, P.O. Box 443, Kings Cross, 2011. ☎ 556-1079. Fax. 597-2758.
National Council of Jewish Women, 111 Queen St., Woollahra, 2025. ☎ 363-0257. Fax. 362-4092.
N.S.W. Association of Jewish Ex-Servicemen & Women, 146 Darlinghurst Rd., Darlinghurst. ☎ 361-5539.
N.S.W. Jewish Board of Deputies, 146 Darlinghurst Rd., Darlinghurst, 2010. ☎ 360-1600. Fax. 331-4712.
N.S.W. Association of Sephardim, 40-42 Fletcher St., Bondi Junction. ☎ 389-3385.

Synagogues & Religious Organisations
Adath Yisroel, 243 Old South Head Rd., Bondi. ☎ 300-9447.
Central, 15 Bon-Accord Av., Bondi Junction. ☎ 389-5622.
Coogee, 121 Brook St., Coogee. ☎ 315-8291.
Cremorne & District, 12a Yeo St., Neutral Bay. ☎ 908-1853.
Great, Elizabeth St. Offices: 166 Castlereagh St. ☎ 267-2477. Fax. 264-8871. Houses the Rabbi L. A. Falk Memorial Library, and the A. M. Rosenblum Jewish Museum.
Illawarra, 502 Railway Parade, Allawah. ☎ 587-5643.
Kehillat Masada, 9-15 Links Rd., St. Ives. ☎ 988-4417.
Machzike Hatorah, 54 Roscoe St., Bondi. ☎ 365-1812.
Maroubra (K.M.H.C.), 635 Anzac Pde., Maroubra. ☎ 344-6095.
Mizrachi, 339 Old South Head Rd., Bondi. ☎ 30-2031.
North Shore, 15a Treatts Rd., Lindfield. ☎ 416-3710.
North Shore Temple Emanuel (Liberal), 28 Chatswood Av., Chatswood. ☎ 419-7011.
Parramatta, 116 Victoria Rd., Paramatta. ☎ 683-5381.
Sephardi, 40-42 Fletcher St., Bondi Junction. ☎ 389-3355. Fax 369-2143.
Shearit Yisrael, 146 Darlinghurst Rd., Darlinghurst. ☎ 365-8770.
South Head & District, 666 Old South Head Rd., Rose Bay. ☎ 371-7300.
Strathfield & District, 19 Florence St., Strathfield. ☎ 642-3550.
Western Suburbs, 20 George St., Newtown. ☎ 349-3319.

continued from *New South Wales*

Temple Emanuel (Liberal), 7 Ocean St., Woollahra, 2025. ☎ 328-7833.
Yeshiva, 36 Flood St., Bondi. ☎ 387-3822.
Beth Din, 166 Castlereagh St. ☎ 267-2477. Fax. 264-8871.
Mikva, 117 Glenayr Av., Bondi. ☎ 30-2509.
Kashrut Authority: Rabbi M. D. Gutnick, POB 206, Bondi 2026. ☎ 369-4286.
Publishes a Kosher products directory.

Cultural & Educational Organisations
Australian Jewish Genealogical Society, P.O. Box 154, Northbridge, 2063. ☎ 331-2582.
Australian Jewish Historical Society, 166 Castlereagh St. ☎ 267-2477, 261-8407.
Moriah College, Queens Park Rd., Bondi Junction, 2022. ☎ 387-3555.
N.S.W. Board of Jewish Education, (BJE), 134 Old South Head Rd., Bondi Junction. ☎ 369-1551.
Shalom College, University of New South Wales, Sydney, 2052. ☎ 663-1366. This is a Jewish residential college and the central address of the Jewish student movement in New South Wales. Accom. for travellers available on occasion. **(K)** Kitchen and dining facilities. Inq. to Dr. Hilton Immerman.
Sydney Jewish Museum, 148 Darlinghurst Rd., Darlinghurst. ☎ 360-7999.
Yeshiva College, 32 Flood St., Bondi. ☎ 387-3822.

Welfare Organisations, Hospitals, etc.
Jewish Community Services (ex-Australian Jewish Welfare Society), 146 Darlinghurst Rd., Darlinghurst. ☎ 331-5184. Fax. 360-5574.
Sir Moses Montefiore Jewish Home, 120 High St., Hunters Hill. ☎ 816-1333.
Wolper Jewish Hospital, 8 Trelawney St., Woollahra. ☎ 328-6077.

Sporting & Social Clubs
Hakoah Club, 61-67 Hall St., Bondi. Tel 30-3344. (Kosher restaurant open on Tues. and Wed. only.)
NSW Maccabi Inc. 146 Darlinghurst Rd., Darlinghurst, 2010. ☎ 360-5100. Fax. 332-4207.

Zionist Organisations
State Zionist Council of N.S.W., 146 Darlinghurst Rd., Darlinghurst, 2010. ☎ 360-6300.
WIZO State Council of N.S.W., 53 Edgecliff Rd., Bondi Junction. ☎ 387-3666.
Israel Consulate-General, 37 York St. ☎ 264-7933. Fax. 290-2259.

Newspaper: 'Australian Jewish Times', 146 Darlinghurst Rd., Darlinghurst, 2010. ☎ 360-5100. Fax 332-4207

Booksellers, etc.
Gold's Book & Gift Co., 166 O'Brien St., Bondi, 2026. ☎ 300-0495.
Geniza Book Shop, 4/38 Waiora Av., Bondi, 2026. ☎ 365-5783.
Shalom Gifts, 323 Pacific Highway, Lindfield. ☎ 416-7076.

Restaurants
(K) Avivim, 49 Hall St., Bondi. ☎ 308-302.
(K) Eze Moses Deli, 113 Brighton Blvd., Bondi Beach. ☎ 301-242.
(K) Grandma Moses Deli, 511 Old South Head Rd., Rose Bay. ☎ 371-0874.
(K) Lewis' Continental Kosher Kitchen, 2 Curlewis St., Bondi. ☎ 30-1833.
(K) Savion, 38 Wairoa Av., Bondi. ☎ 306-357.
(V) Stuff It Kosher Vegetarian, 379 Old South Head Rd., Bondi. ☎ 30-4016.
(K) Tibby's, 2d Campbell Parade, Bondi Beach. ☎ 305-051.

continued from *New South Wales*

For information about tours of Jewish Sydney, contact the Great Syn., ☎ 167-2477 or Karl Maehrischel, ☎ 328-7604.

QUEENSLAND
BRISBANE
Organisations
Queensland Jewish Board of Deputies. Pres.: Laurie Rosenblum, 27 Berkeley St., Holland Park, 4121. Tel/Fax. 397-4878.
State Zionist Council, 144 Adelaide St., 4000. ☎ 229-4462.
Jewish Communal Centre, 2 Moxom Rd., Burbank, 4156. ☎ 349-9749.
Queensland Jewish Help in Need Society, 87 Ascot Ter., Toowona. ☎ 870-9504.
Brisbane Jewish Women's Guild, 42 Morningview St., Chapel Hill. ☎ 359-8626. Exec. Dir.: 878-2796.
Wizo State Council. ☎ (07) 395-0735.
Catering service available.
Fellowship of Jewish Doctors. ☎ 371-8977.
Maccabi, ☎ (07) 367-1151.
National Council of Jewish Women, 24 Ceratonia St., Sunny Banks Hill, 4109. ☎ 345-9509.
Queensland Union of Jewish Students, 51 Bunora Av., Ferny Hills, 4055. ☎ 351-2090.

Syns.: Brisbane Hebrew Cong., 98 Margaret St., 4000. ☎ 229-3412 Sec. 397-1213; Givat Zion (South Brisbane Hebrew Cong. & Mikvah), 43 Bunya St., Greenslopes; ☎ 848-5886; Temple Shalom,13 Koolatah St., Camp Hill, 4152. ☎ 398-8843.

Religious Groups: Brisbane Chevra Kadisha, 242 Kingsford Smith Drive, Hamilton 4007. ☎ 262-6564 (h). Pres.: Lance Philips.
Chabad House of Queensland, 43 Cedar St., Greenslopes, 4120. ☎ 848-5886 or 018-73-2879. Contact: Ken Thomas.
Queensland Mikvah, 46 Bunya St., Greenslopes, 4120. ☎ 848-5886. Contact: J. Thomas.

(K) Brumby's Bakery, 408 Milton Rd., Auchenflower 4066. ☎ 371-8744.

GOLD COAST
Syn.: Gold Coast Hebrew Cong., 34 Hamilton Av., Surfers' Paradise, 4215. ☎ (075) 701-851; Temple Shalom, 25 Via Roma Dve, Isle of Capri 4217. ☎ (075) 70-1716.
Chevra Kadisha. ☎ (075) 97-2239.
Organisations
Association of Jewish Organisations, 31, Ranock Av., Benown Waters, 4217. ☎ 97-2222.
Maccabi Gold Coast, 108 Pappas Way, Carrara 4211. ☎ 942-261.
Goldstein's Bakery, PO Box 147, Ashmore City, 4214. ☎ 39-3133.

SOUTH AUSTRALIA
ADELAIDE
Syns.: Adelaide Hebrew Cong. (O), 13 Flemington St., Glenside SA 5065. ☎ (08) 338 2922. Fax. (08) 3790142. Mail to: PO Box 320, Glenside SA 5065 and Mikva.

continued from *South Australia*

Progressive Jewish Congregation, Beit Shalom, 41 Hackney Rd., Hackney, 5069. ☎ 362-8281.
South Australian Zionist Council & Habonim, 13, Flemington St., 5065. ☎ 379-0144.
National Council of Jewish Women, PO Box 10, Glenside 5089. ☎ 337-2369.
B'nai Brith, 4 Giles St., Dernan Court, 5057. ☎ 337-5767. Friends of the Hebrew University, 218 Brougham Pk., North Adelaide, 5006. ☎ 267-1081.
Massada College, 13 Flemington St., Glenside 5065. ☎ (08) 3382800.
(K) Kosher products & Judaica available from Kosher Imports, c/o Hebrew Congregation.

Kosher Bakeries
Bagel Boys, Goodwood Road, 5034.
Bakers Delight, Frewville Shopping Centre, Green Osmond Road.

TASMANIA
HOBART
Syn.: Argyle St., P.O. B. 128B, 7001. Sec.: Miss A. Rauner. ☎ 28-4097. The synagogue is the oldest in Australia, having been consecrated in July, 1845. Open Sat., 10 a.m. and every second. Fri. in the month at 6.15 p.m. Other days by arrangement.
Chabad House, 93 Lord St., Sandy Bay, 7005. ☎ 237116. Mrs P. Clark. Contact in advance for Shabbat meals, etc.

LAUNCESTON
The syn. in St. John St. is the second oldest in Australia, founded in 1846. Inf. from the Pres., Dr. C. Meyerowitz. ☎ (004) 27-0270. Hon. Tr.: Mrs. B. Sandor, P.O. Box 66, 7250. ☎ 431143. There is also a Chabad Hse. ☎ 34-0705.

VICTORIA
BALLARAT
Syn.: 211 Drummond Street North, 3350. ☎ 32-6330.
GEELONG
Syn.: Yarra St.

MELBOURNE
Representative Organisations
Executive Council of Australian Jewry, GPO Box 5402 CC, 3001. ☎ 9828-8570. Fax. 982-88584.
Jewish Community Council of Victoria, 306 Hawthorn Rd., South Caulfield, 3162. Tel/Fax. 9272-5560. Contact: Helen Brustman.
Australasian Union of Jewish Students (Melbourne Branch), 306 Hawthorne Rd., South Caulfield.
B'nai B'rith, 99 Hotham St., E. St. Kilda, 3183. ☎ 9527-5169 offers a hospitality service to all Jewish visitors to Melbourne. Corr. to 15 Leaburn Av., Caulfield, Vic. 3162.
Mizrachi Hospitality Committee, 81 Balaclava Rd., Caulfield, 3161. ☎ 9525-9166. Fax 9527-5665.
National Council of Jewish Women, 54 Westbury St., Balaclava, 3183. ☎ 9527-3299.
Victorian Jewish Board of Deputies, 401 Swanston St., 3000. ☎ 967-5341.

continued from *Victoria*

Synagogues & Religious Organisations

Adass Israel (O), 16-24 Glen Eira Av., Ripponlea, 3182. ☎ 9568-3344.
Kashrut services, & Mikva.
Bentleigh Progressive, 549 Centre Rd., 3204. ☎ 9563-9208.
Bet Hatikva Syn. (I), 233 Nepean Highway, Gardenvale, 3185. ☎ 9576-9755.
Brighton (O), 134 Marriage Rd., E. Brighton, 3186. ☎ 9592-9179.
Brunswick Talmud Torah, 32 Lord St., E. Brunswick, 3057.
Burwood Hebrew Cong. (O), 38 Harrison Av., 3125. ☎ 9808-3120.
Caulfield Hebrew Cong. (O) 9572 Inkerman Rd., Caulfield, 3161. ☎ 9525-9492.
E. Melbourne, 488 Albert St., E. Melbourne, 3002. ☎ 9662-1372.
Elwood Talmud Torah Cong. (O), 39 Dickens St., Elwood, 3184. ☎ 9531-1547.
Kew (O), 53 Walpole St., Kew, 3101. ☎ 9853-9243.
Leo Baeck Centre (L), 33 Harp Rd., E. Kew, 3102. ☎ 9819-7160.
Melbourne Hebrew Cong. (O), cnr. Toorak & St. Kilda Rds., S. Yarra, 3141.
☎ 9866-2255.
Mizrachi, 81 Balaclava Rd., Caulfield, 3161. ☎ 9527-5680.
Moorabbin & District (O), 960 Nepean Highway, Moorabbin, 3189. ☎ 9553-3845.
North-Eastern Jewish War Memorial Centre, 6 High St., Doncaster, 3108. ☎
9857-8084.
St. Kilda (O), 12 Charnwood Gr., St. Kilda, 3182. ☎ 9537-1433.
Sassoon Yehuda-Sephardi Syn., 73 Darling Rd., E. Malvern, 3145. ☎ 9529-1818.
Sephardic Syn. Cong. Rambam, (O), 90 Hotham St., East St. Kilda 3183. ☎
9527-328.S.
S. Caulfield (O), 47 Leopold St., S. Caulfield, 3162. ☎ 9578-5922.
Southern Jewish Com. Centre, 139-141 Marriage Rd., E. Brighton, 3187. ☎
9578-5637.
Southern Liberal Cong., 549 Centre Rd., Bentleigh, 3204. ☎ 9557-6933.
Temple Beth Israel (L), 76 Alma Rd., St. Kilda, 3182. ☎ 9510-1488.
Yeshiva Shule (O), 92 Hotham St., E. St. Kilda, 3183. ☎ 9525-9535.
Melbourne Beth Din, Syn. Chambers, 572 Inkerman Rd., N. Caulfield, 3161.
☎ 9527-8337.
Association of Rabbis and Ministers of Australia & New Zealand, c/o 12
Charnwood Grove, St. Kilda, 3182. ☎ 9537-1433. Fax 9525-3759.
Council of Orthodox Synagogues of Victoria, c/o Jetset House, 5 Queens Rd.,
3000. ☎ 9828-8000.
Rabbinical Council of Victoria, 6 High St., Doncaster, 3180. ☎ 9531-1547.
Victorian Union for Progressive Judaism, 78 Alma Rd., St. Kilda, 3182. ☎
9510-1488. Fax. 9521-1229.

Cultural & Educational Organisations, etc.

Australian Jewish Historical Society, PO Box 255, Camberwell 3124. ☎ 9882-2600.
Australian Institute of Jewish Affairs, POB 5402CC, 3001 ☎ 9828-8570. Fax
982-88584.
Beth Rivkah Ladies' College, 14-20 Balaclava Rd., E. St. Kilda, 3183. ☎ 9527-3768.
Bialik College, 6 Shakespeare Gr., Hawthorne, 3122. ☎ 9818-5525, & 9429
Auburn Rd., E. Hawthorn, 3123. ☎ 920-7982.
Jewish Holocaust Centre, 29 Mackinnon Rd. ☎ 9578-7148.
Jewish Museum of Australia, 26 Alma Road, St. Kilda 3182, P.O. Box 117. ☎
9543-0083. Fax 9534-0844.
Kadimah Jewish Cultural Centre & National Library, 7 Selwyn St.,
Elsternwick, 3185. ☎ 9523-9817.

continued from *Victoria*

Makor Library, 306 Hawthorn Rd., South Caulfield 3162. ☎ (03) 9272-5611. Fax (03) 9272-5540.

Welfare Organisations
Jewish Community Services, 25 Alma Rd., St. Kilda, 3182. ☎ 9325-4000.
Melbourne Hebrew Memorial Hospital, 95-107 High St. Rd., Ashwood, 3147. ☎ 9277-1255.
Montefiore Homes for the Aged, 619 St. Kilda Rd., 3004. ☎ 9510-8556 (with Synagogue).

Zionist Organisations
Australia-Israel Chamber of Commerce (Victoria Division), 4th Floor, 416 Gore St., Fitzroy. ☎ 941-2153.
Betar, 14 Dickens St., Elwood. ☎ 994-3165.
Bnei Akiva, 81 Balaclava Rd., Caulfield, 3162. ☎ 9527-6067.
Habonim, 1 Sinclair St. Elsternwick, 3185. ☎ 9528-1256.
Hashomer Hatzair, 214 Inkerman St., E. St. Kilda, 3182. ☎ 9534-1091.
State Zionist Council of Victoria, 306 Hawthorn Rd., Caulfield, 3162. The following organisations are at the same address: Australia-Israel Publications, J.N.F., Magen David Adom, United Israel Appeal, WIZO, Zionist Fed. of Australia. ☎ 9272-5644. Fax. 9272-5640.

Booksellers, etc.
M. & L. Balberyszki, 98 Acland St., St. Kilda.☎ 9534-6003.
Chevrat Serarim Chabad Book Co-op., 92 Hotham St., E. St. Kilda, 3183. ☎ 9527-4177.
Gold's Book & Gift Co., 36 William St., Balaclava, 3183. ☎ 9527-8775.
Mazeltov Bookshop, 275 Cantalo St., East St. Kilda, 3183. ☎ 9527-3462.
Weekly Newspaper. 'Jewish News', P. O. Box 1000, South Cantfield. ☎ 41-7591.

Hotels
(K) **Kimberley Gardens**, 441 Inkerman St., Caulfield, 3183. ☎ (03) 9526 3888. Fax. (03) 9525-9691.
(K) **St Moritz**, 14 The Esplanade, St. Kilda Beach, 3182. ☎ 9525-5522.

Restaurants
(K) **Bessa Foods**, 57 Kooyong Rd., Caulfield, 3162. ☎ 9509-2387. Fax 9509-2387.
(K) **Big K Bakers**, 320 Carlisle St., Balaclava, 3183. ☎ 9527-4582.

continued from *Victoria*

Blusztein's Corner Store, 636 Inkerman St., Caulfield North, 3162. ☎ 9527-5349.
(K) Dairy Bell Ice Cream, 60 Belgrave Rd., Malvern East, 3145. ☎ 9571-9211. Fax 572-2865.
(K) E & S Delicatessen, 74 Kooyong Rd., Caulfield, 3161. ☎ 9576-0804.
Gefen Liquor Store, 144 Chapel St., Balaclava, 3183. ☎ 9531-5032.
(K) Glicks Cakes and Bagels, 330a Carlisle St., Balaclava, 3183. ☎ 9527-2198.
(K) The Golden Choice, 285A Carlisle Street, Balaclava, 3183. ☎ 9527-5768.
(K) Haolam Kosher Take-Away and Catering, Shop 5, 320 Carlisle St., Balaclava, 3182. ☎ 9527-7255.
(K) Haymishe Cookies, Shop 4, 320 Carlisle St., Balaclava, 3183. ☎ 9527-7116.
(K) Kemps Deli, 209 High St., Kew, 3101. ☎ 9861-8157.
(K) Kraus, 62 Glen Eira Rd., Elsternwick, 3185. ☎ 9523-8463. Fax 9523-0595.
(K) Manshari, 219 Carlisle St., Balaclava. ☎ 9525-9789.
Milecki's Balaclava Health Food, 227 Carlisle St., Balaclava, 3183. ☎ 9527-3350.
(K) Old Carlton Deli, 25 Village Av., Doncaster, 3108. ☎ 9816-3023.
Rishon Foods Pty. Ltd., 23 Williams St., Balaclava, 3183. ☎ 9527-5142.
(K) Rutti's Pizza, 241 Carlisle St., Balaclava, 3183. ☎ 9525-9939.
(K) Sheli Coffee Shop – Restaurant, Vegetarian - Diary, 306 Hawthorn Road, Caulfield, 3162. ☎ 9272-5607.
(K) Singer's Cnr Balaclava and Hawthorn Rd., Caulfield 3161. ☎ 9528 2544.
(K) The Olive Branch, 441 Inkerman Rd., East St. Kilda. ☎ 9526 3865. Proprietor: M. Khoen.
Tempo Beverages, 391 Inkerman St., St. Kilda, 3183. ☎ 9527-5021.

Butchers

(K) Chedva Kosher Butchers, 257 Carlisle St., Balaclava. ☎ 9527-3795.
(K) Continental Kosher Butchers, 155 Glenferrie Rd., Malvern, 3144. ☎ 9509-9822.
(K) Eatmore Kosher Poultry, 85 Acland St., St. Kilda, 3182. ☎ 9534-1145. Fax 534-2931.
(K) Melbourne Kosher Butchers, 251 Inkerman St., East St. Kilda, 3182. ☎ 9525-4230.
Ripponlea Fish Supply, 49 Glen Eira Rd., Ripponlea, 3182. ☎ 9528-5625.
(K) Smorgasbord Chicken Centre, 253 Carlisle St., Balaclava, 3182. ☎ 9525-8252.
Solomon Kosher Butcher, 140-144 Glen Eira Road, Elsternwick, 3185. ☎ 9532-8855.
Solomon Kosher Chicken, 328A Carlisle Street, Balaclava, 3183. ☎ 9527-3284.
Tasmanian Pacific Fish Supply, 29 Glen Eira Rd., Ripponlea, 3182. ☎ 9528-3851.
(K) Weislitzer Kosher Butcher Shop, 280 Carlisle St., Balaclava. ☎ 9534-5591.

WESTERN AUSTRALIA
PERTH
Representative Organisation

Council of Western Australian Jewry Inc. Pres.: Doron Ur, J.P., P.O. Box 763, Morley, 6062.
Welfare Organisation: Welfare Society. Pres.: Mr. L. Cohen, 44 Noranda Av., Noranda, 6062.

continued from *Western Australia*

Synagogues & Religious Organisations

Northern Suburbs Congregation. 4 Vernon St., Noranda, 6062. Rev. Ch. Davidowitz. ☎ 275 5932.

Perth Hebrew Cong., Freedman Rd., Menora. 6050, ☎ 271-0539

Temple David (Liberal), 34 Clifton Cres., Mt. Lawley, 6050. ☎ 271-1485

Chabad House (Lubavitch), 396 Alexander Drive, Dianella 6062. ☎ 275-4912.

Jewish Centre, Woodrow Ave., Mt. Yokine, 6060. ☎ 276-8572.

Zionist Organisations

Jewish National Fund, Jewish Centre, 61 Woodrow Av., Mount Yokine, 6060. M.D.A. as J.N.F.

National Council of Jewish Women (affiliated I.C.J.W). Mrs. E. Braune, same address as J.N.F.

West Australian Zionist Council & Habonim. Same address as J.N.F.

WIZO. Pres.: Mrs. A. Segler, 51 Armadale Cres., Mt. Lawley, 6050.

Other organisations

Fellowship of Jewish Doctors of W.A. Hon. Sec.: Dr. B. M. Saker, Roy. Perth Hospital. ☎ (09) 224 3094.

Sport

Maccabi (same as J.N.F.)

Students W.A. Jewish students society.

Seniors. Jewish Seniors Club, Mrs. R. Trobe, O.A.M., 1/24 Broomhall Way, Noranda. 6062. ☎ 375-1492

Aged Home: Maurice Zeffert Home, 91 Woodrow Av., Yokine 6060.

AUSTRIA

Nazi Germany's annexation and occupation of Austria in 1938 marked the beginning of the end for an ancient and numerous community. There were some 200,000 Jews in Austria at that time — 180,000 of them in Vienna — with a documented history going back to 906 C.E., although there were Jewish settlers in the area several hundred years earlier.

As the centuries passed, Austrian Jewry's fortunes waxed and waned, protection alternating with persecution, which reached a peak in 1420, after a charge of ritual murder had been levelled against the Jews. Almost the entire Jewish population of Austria was burnt to death, forcibly baptised or expelled.

Those who remained were harried and hounded until at the beginning of the 17th century, Jews were allowed to settle in an area outside the walls, only to be driven away from this second ghetto by Leopold I in 1670. Rich Jews were subsequently granted permission to return to the city in order to better the financial situation of the Empire. They were to live under considerable disabilities until 1867, when they were accorded full rights.

From then onwards, until 1938, the Austrian Jewish community flourished, despite the endemic antisemitism which, as in so many other European countries, was a feature of life in Austria. Between 1938 and 1940 about 120,000 Jews managed to leave. Some 60,000 men, women and children were killed in Nazi death camps. Today, there are about 12,000 Jews in Austria, 10,000 of them in Vienna.

BADEN

Syn.: Grabengasse 14. Services, Sat morn. from May to Sept. ☎ 2236-26383.

The Jewish cemetery, containing some 3,000 graves, is at Halsriegelstr. 30. ☎ (2252) 85405.

EDLACH
A memorial to Dr. Theodor Herzl, erected by the Viennese Jewish com., can be seen in the garden of the local sanatorium, where the founder of the Zionist movement died in 1904.

EISENSTADT (BURGENLAND)
The restored private syn. of Samson Wertheimer, Habsburg court Jew & Chief Rabbi of Hungary (1658-1724) is now part of the Austrian Jewish Museum, which is at Unterbergstr. 6. ☎ 026 821 5145. The museum is open daily except Mon. from 10 a.m. to 5 p.m.

The Eruv Arch, spanning Unterbergstr., is at the end near the Esterhazy Palace. The road chain was used in former times to prevent vehicular traffic on Shabbat and Yomtov.

Old & New Cemeteries. The old cemetery, closed around 1875, contains the grave of R. Meir b. Isak (Mram Asch), d. 1744, which is to this day the scene of pilgrimages, particularly on the anniversary of his death.

Keys of the cemeteries are with the porter of the local hospital, which adjoins the old cemetery.

GRAZ
Com. Centre: Synagogenplatz 1. ☎ 912468. President Consul: Kurt Brühl

INNSBRUCK
Com. Centre: Zollerstr. 1. ☎ 586892. Pres.: Dr. Esther Fritsch.

KOBERSDORF (BURGENLAND)
The keys of the cemetery on the Lampelberg are with Mr. Piniel, Waldgasse 25 (one of the two houses to the left of the cemetery) & Mr. Grässing, Haydngasse 4. The syn. is being rebuilt.

LINZ
Com. Centre: Bethlehemstr. 26. ☎ 779805. Pres.: Georg Wotzasek.

SALZBURG
Syn. & Mikva: Lasserstr. 8, 5020. M. Rabbi D. Nussbaum.
Com. Centre: at same address. ☎(0662) 875-665. Pres.: Marco Feingold.

SEMMERING
Kosher Boarding Houses (July 17th-August 24th) **(K)** Hotel Alpenhof, Spital/Semmering. ☎ 0663-808 439 (H. Steiner).

VIENNA
Synagogues & Religious Organisations
The Chief Rabbi of Vienna is Rabbi Paul Chaim Eisenberg. ☎ 53104-17.
Syn.: Seitenstettengasse 4, 1010. Built in 1824-1826 and partly destroyed during the Nazi period, this beautiful syn. was restored by the com. in 1988. Guides to syn. available from Jewish Com. Centre, Seitenstettengasse 2. ☎ 53-1-04. For inf. about guided tours, contact the Com. Offices, Seitenstettengasse 4, 1010. ☎ 53104.
The Vienna Tourist Board publishes a guide, with map, of 'Jewish Vienna: heritage and mission'. ☎ 513-8892. Fax 513-4015.
Prayer rooms: Agudas Yisroel, Grünangergasse 1, 1010. ☎ 512-83-31; Tempelgasse 3, Vienna 1020. ☎ 24-92-62. Rabbi David Grünfeld; Machsike

Haddas, Desider Friedmann-Platz, 1010. Rabbi Chayim Stern. ☎ 2141347; Misrachi, Judenplatz 8, 1010. ☎ 535-41-53, Rabbi Yosef Pardes; Ohel Moshe, Lilienbrunngasse 19. ☎ 26-88-64, 1020. Rabbi Abraham Yonah Schwartz (see also Other Orgs.); Agudas Yeshurun, Riemergasse 9, 1010; Thora Etz Chayim, Grosse Schiffgasse 8, 1020. ☎ 2145206; Shomre Haddas, Glasergasse 17, 1090; Sephardi Centre, Tempelgasse 7, 1020. Rabbi I. Niazov and Rabbi A. Michaelsvili.

Mikvaot: Agudas Yisroel, Tempelgasse 3, 1020. ☎ 24-92-62; Machsike Haddas, Fleischmarkt 22, 1010. ☎ 512-52-62.

Cemeteries

The Vienna central cemetery in the Simmering district, Vienna 1110, has a Jewish section (Gate 4) and there is an older Jewish part at Gate 1. ☎ 76-62-52. Those wishing to visit the Währinger cemetery, Semperstr. 64a, Vienna 1180, and the Floridsdorfer cemetery, Ruthnergasse 28, 1210, must first obtain a permit from the Com. Centre.

The Rossauer cemetery, Seegasse 9, 1090, the oldest Jewish cemetery in Vienna, which dates from the 16th century, has been restored, after having been devastated by the Nazis. It is open daily from 8 a.m. to 3 p.m. Access is via the front entrance of the municipal home for the aged at Seegasse 9-11, but a permit must be obtained beforehand from the Com. Centre. ☎ 53104-32.

Youth Organisations

Dachverband der jüdischen Jugend Österreichs, Vienna 1090, Währinger Strasse 24. ☎ 34 54 99; Jewish Students Organisation, 1090, Währinger Strasse 24. ☎ 34 54 99; Bnei-Akiva, Judenplatz 8, 1010, ☎ 5354153; Hashomer-Hatzair, 1010, Desider Friedmann-Platz 1 ☎ 5337499.

Other Organisations

B'nai B'rith, Taubstummengasse 17, 1040. ☎ 65-22-383. Pres.: Dr Ariel Muzicant.

Com. Centre, Seitenstettengasse 4, 1010. ☎ 53-1-04. Pres.: Paul Grosz. Admin. Dr A. Hodik.

Documentation Centre of Austrian Resistance Movement, Old City Hall, Wipplingerstr. 8, 1010. ☎ 534-36-332. Dir.: Dr. Wolfgang Neugebauer.

Documentation Centre of Union of Jewish Victims of the Nazis, Salztorgasse 6, Vienna 1010. ☎ 533-91-31. Dir.: Simon Wiesenthal.

Home for Aged, Bauernfeldgasse 4, 1190. ☎ 36-16-55.

Jewish Student Assoc., Währingerstr. 24, 1090. ☎ 34-54-99.

Jewish Welcome Service, Stephansplatz 10, 1010. ☎ 5338891. Fax 5334098. Dir.: Dr. Leon Zelman.

Mauthausen memorial site. Those wishing to visit the site should contact the Jewish Welcome Service or ☎ 072 38/24 39.

Jewish Museum of the City of Vienna, Dorotheergasse 11, A-1010. ☎ 535-0431. Fax 535-0424. Hours: Sun - Fri 10-6; Thurs to 9 p.m. Cafeteria & Bookshop.

Ohel Moshe Hilfs- & Versorgungsverein. Head office: Lilienbrunngasse 19, 1020. ☎ 26-88-64.

Com. Rabbi: Rabbi Avraham Yona Schwartz. ☎ 216-3695. Mikva on premises. **(K)** Guest rooms on premises. Up to 7 nights' accom. for Orthodox travellers with free breakfast.

Vaad Hakashrut, Karmelitergasse 13, 1020. ☎ 33-73-64.

Sigmund Freud Museum, Berggasse 19, 1090. ☎ 3191596.

Tourist Inf. Centre, Kärntner Str. 38 ☎ 313 8892. Open daily, 9 a.m. to 7 p.m.

Zionist Organisations and Israel Embassy

Israel Embassy, Anton-Frank-Gasse 20, 1180. ☎ 470 47 41.
Jewish Agency, Stubenring 4. ☎ 5123636.
Keren Kayemet & Keren Hayesod. Desider Friedmann-Platz 1. ☎ 5127705.
WIZO. Desider Friedmann-Platz 1. ☎ 5127705.
Zionist Fed. of Austria, Desider Friedmann-Platz 1.

Kosher restaurants

Arche Noah (under supervision of Rabbi Grünfeld, Agudas Yisroel),
Seitenstettengasse 2/Judengasse, 1010. ☎ 533 13 74; Tuv-Taam (café, restaurant) Shalom Bernholtz, 1020, Franz-Hochedlinger-Gasse 23. ☎ 216 08 68.

Kosher Butchers

Rebenwurzel (under the supervision of Rabbi Chayim Stern, Machsike
Haddas) Singerstrasse 24, 1010 ☎ 216-66-40; B. Ainhorn (under the supervision of Rabbi Grünfeld, Agudas Yisroel), Stadtgutgasse 7, 1020. Grosse
Pfarrgasse 6. ☎ 2145621.

Kosher bakery and wine

Engländer (under the supervision of Rabbi Abraham Yonah Schwartz, Ohel
Moshe) Vienna 1020, Hollandstrasse 7. ☎ 214 56 17.
Kosher supermarket: Kosher Supermarket and Shutnes Laboratory (under the
supervision of Rabbi Abraham Yonah Schwartz, Ohel Moshe) Vienna 1020,
Hollandstrasse 10. ☎ 26 96 75.
Vinothek Gross, Tabor Str. 15, 1020. ☎ 212-6299. Liechtenstein Str. 32,
1090. ☎/Fax 317-5277.

Books and religious articles

Chabad-Simcha-Center, Vienna 1020, Hollandstrasse 10. ☎ 216 29 24;
Bookshop 'Chai' Vienna 1020, Lessinggasse 5. ☎ 216 46 21. Bookshop at the
Jewish Museum. ☎ 512-5361.

BAHAMAS

The Jewish population of these islands, formerly a British colony, is put at
round around 100. However, it is estimated that at least 350,000 of the 3 million tourists who visit the Bahamas every year are Jewish. In Nassau, the capital, on New Providence Island, there are a number of Jewish residents. The
only active syn. is the Luis de Torres Synagogue, E. Sunrise Highway, P.O.B.
F41761, Freeport, Grand Bahama Island (☎ 373-2008). Services are held fairly regularly. The Pres. of the cong. is Jack Turner. ☎ 373-1041.
Hon. Consul-General of Israel: Ralph D. Seligman. ☎ 36-24421.
Geoff Hurst is happy to make arrangements for tourists. ☎/Fax 373-4025.
Email: hurst-gr@gbonline.win.net
The Jewish cemetery, a walled-off section of the public cemetery, is at the corner of Shirley St. and Lovers' Lane, Nassau.
Most major hotels can make special arrangements with regard to kosher food.
General inf. from Bahamas Tourist Office, 3 The Billings, Walnut Tree Close,
Guildford, Surrey GU1 4UL. ☎ 148-344 8900. Fax. 148-344-8990.

BARBADOS

A Jewish com. was formed on the island of Barbados by refugees from Brazil
after its reconquest by the Portuguese in about 1650. In 1802 all political disabilities of the Jews were removed, although this was not confirmed by
Parliament until 1820.

Nevertheless, Barbados was the first British possession to grant full political emancipation to its Jews. The island gained its independence in 1966, remaining a member of the British Commonwealth. A syn. bldg. in Bridgetown, dating from 1833 (although parts are much older, going back to 1654), remains from the days of the original Jewish population. In 1929, the syn. bldg. was sold, because only one Jew still remained on the island, and turned into offices. The syn. and the cemetery in Synagogue Lane which surrounds it and is still in use, are in process of restoration and repair after years of neglect. The restoration of the synagogue is now 95% completed and the original clock and chanuka lamp among other items have been returned from the museum. What is most urgently needed now is the restoration of the tombstones in the adjoining cemetery whose condition has deteriorated. In the 1930s and 1940s Jews returned to Barbados, there were more than 30 European Jewish families on the island in the 1940s, only about 20 remain today.

Services are held Fri. evgs. at 7 p.m. at 'True Blue,' Rockley New Rd., Christ Church, during the summer, and at the Syn. in winter.

Synagogue Restoration Project, P.O.B. 256, Bridgetown. ☎ (809) 432-0840.

Local inq. to Henry Altman, 'Sea Shell,' Gibbes Beach, St. Peter. ☎ 422-2664.

Barbados Jewish Community, P.O.B. 651, Bridgetown. ☎ 809-427-0703. Fax. 809-436-8807.

Caribbean Jewish Congress, P.O.B. 1331, Bridgetown. ☎ 809-436-8163.

BELGIUM

Belgian Jewry, like the communities of other European countries, achieved religious equality nearly 160 years ago — in 1831, when Belgium became a kingdom and religious equality was made part of the fundamental law of the State.

By the late 1930s, there were 100,000 Jews in Belgium, including refugees from Nazi Germany, but their respite from persecution was a short one. When Hitler's armies invaded Belgium in 1940 and swept on to occupy the whole of Western Europe as far as the Spanish border, few Belgian Jews managed to escape to safety. After introducing their racialist legislation, the Nazis began rounding up the Jews and deported 25,000 of them to concentration camps.

The names of the 23,838 who did not return after the end of the Second World War are engraved on the national monument to the Jewish Martyrs of Belgium. This stands in the Anderlecht district of Brussels.

There are about 40,000 Jews in Belgium today, most of them in Antwerp and Brussels.

General inf. from the Belgian Tourist Office, 29 Princes St., W1R 7RG. ☎ 071-629 0230. Fax. 071-629 0454.

ANTWERP
Synagogues & Religious Organisations
Machsike Hadass (Israelitische Orthodoxe Gemeente), Jacob Jacobsstr. 22. ☎ 233-55-67.

Rabbinate: Jacob Jacobstr. 22. ☎ 232-00-21. Rabbi Ch. Kreiswirth. Private address: Quinten Matsijslei 35, ☎ 234 31 48 Dayan E. Sternbuch. ☎ 233-71-94; Dayan T. Weiss. ☎ 230-21-63.

Main Syn.: Oostenstr., 43. Annexe: Jacob Jacobsstr. 22.

Shomre Hadass (Israelitische Gemeente), Terliststr. 35. ☎ 232-01-87.

Rabbinate: Terliststr. 35. ☎ 226-05-54. Dayan J. Kohen. ☎ 230-35-81. Rabbi D. Lieberman, Belgiëlei 194. ☎ 239-18-83.

Mikvaot: Machsike Hadass, Steenbokstr. 22. ☎ 239-75-88; Shomre Hadass, Van Diepenbeeckstr. 42. ☎ 239-09-65.

Representative Organisation
B'nai B'rith, Nervierstr.14. ☎ 239-39-11.

Cultural & Educational Organisations, etc.
Plantin-Moretus Museum, Vrijdagmarkt (near Groenplaats). ☎ 233-06-88.
Open daily (except Mon.). Contains examples of early Jewish printing, such as the famous Polyglot Bible.
Romi Goldmuntz Centre, Nervliersstr. 12. ☎ 239-39-11.

Student and Youth Organisations
Agudath Israel, Lamoriniérestr. 67. ☎ 230-85-13.
Bne Akiva, Consciencestr. 22. ☎ 230-22-19.
Hashomer Hatsair, Lamoriniérestr. 202. ☎ 239-61-01.
Hanoar Hatsioni, Gretry St. 12. ☎ 2813422.

Sport & Miscellaneous Organisations
Antwerp Tourist & Inq. Office, Suikerrui 19. ☎ 232-01-03.
Royal Maccabi Sports Club, Pelikaanstr 92, B53 ☎ 226 1708. 10-12. ☎ 239-56-73.

Diamond Exchanges:
Beurs voor Diamanthandel, Pelikaanstr. 78; Diamantclub, Pelikaanstr. 62; Diamantkring, Pelikaanstr. 86; Nieuwe Kring, Hovenierstr. 2; Vrije Diamanthandel, Pelikaanstr. 70.
Fed. of Jewish Women's Assoc. Mrs. Zucker, Beukenlaan 10b. ☎ 828-38-76.

Welfare Organisations, Hospital, etc.
Jewish Welfare Org., Jacob Jacobstr. 2. ☎ 232-38-90.
Home for the Aged and Geriatric Centre. Marialei 6-8. ☎ 218-93-99.
Apfelbaum-Laub Home, Marialei 2-4.

Zionist Organisations
Keren Hayesod, Schupstr. 1. ☎ 232-97-74.
Keren Kayemet, Hoveniersstr. 12. ☎ 231-26-28.
Mizrachi, Isabellalei 65. ☎ 230-21-12.
WIZO, Gretrystr. 53. ☎ 239-05-71.
Zionist Federation, Schupstr. 1. ☎ 232-97-74.

Booksellers
Epstein, Van den Nestlei 7. ☎ 232-75-62; I. Menczer, Simonstr. 40. ☎ 232-30-26; N. Seletsky, Lange Kievitstr. 70. ☎ 232-69-66; Stauber, Van Leriusstr. 3. ☎ 231-80-31.
Newspaper: 'Belgisch Israelitisch Weekblad,' Pelikaanstr. 106-108. ☎ 233-70-43.

Restaurants
(K) Blue Lagoon, Lange Herentalsestr. 70.
(K) Dresdner, Simonstr. 10. ☎ 232-54-55.
Falafel Behi, Lange Leemstr. 188 ☎ 218 8211; Lange Herentalstr. 60. ☎ 234-2632.
(K) Gelkop (Diamantkring), Van Leriusstr. 28. ☎ 233-07-
(K) Jacob, Lange Kievitstr. 49. ☎ 233-11-24.
(K) Sam (Diamantbeurs), Pelikaanstr. 28. ☎ 233-92-89.
(K) Snack Bar Hoffy's, Lange Kievitstr. 52. ☎ 234-35-35.
(K) Snack Bar, Romi Goldmuntz Centre, Nervliersstr. 12. ☎ 239-39-11.

Kosher Meat, Poultry, etc.
Butchers:
(K) Berkowitz, Isabellalei 9. ☎ 218-51-11.

(K) Fruchter Simonstr. 22. ☎ 233-18-11; (K) Kosher King, Lange Kievitstr. 40. ☎ 233-67-49. and Isabellalei 7, ☎ 239-41-89
(K) Moszkowitz, Lange Kievitstr. 47. ☎ 232-14-85.
Poulterers:
(K) Farkas, Lange Kievitstr. 66; ☎ 232-13-85; (K) Mandelovics, Isabellalei 96. ☎ 218-47-79; (K) Weingarten, Lange Kievitstr. 124. ☎ 233-28-28.
Bakers:
(K) Gottesfeld, Mercatorstr. 20. ☎ 230-00-03; (K) Grosz, Pelikaanstr. 130. ☎ 233-91-10;
(K) Kleinblatt, Provinciestr. 206. ☎ 233-75-13 & 226-00-18; (K) Steinmetz, Lange Kievitstr. 64. ☎ 234-09-47.
Dairies:
(K) Herzl & Gold, Korte Kievitstr. 38. ☎ 232-23-65; Stark, Mercatorstr. 24. ☎ 230-25-20; (K) Super Discount, Belgielei 104-108. ☎ 239-06-66.
Col-Bo, B.U.B.A. Jacob Jacobsstr. 40. 40. ☎ 2341212.
Grosz-Modern Terlinststr. 28. ☎ 2324626.

ARLON
Syn.: Rue St. Jean (est. 1863). Sec.: J. C. Jacob, 11 rue des Martyrs 6700. ☎ 063-217985.
A monument has been erected in the new Jewish cemetery to the memory of the Jews of Arlon deported and massacred by the Nazis.

BRUSSELS
National Monument to the Jewish Martyrs of Belgium
This monument commemorates the Jews of Belgium who were deported to concentration camps and killed by the Nazis during the Second World War. The names of all 23,838 are engraved on the monument, which has been erected in the Brussels district of Anderlecht, at the corner of rue Emile Carpentier and rue Goujons. The square in which the monument stands has been renamed 'Square of the Jewish Martyrs'.

Religious Organisations
Consistoire Central Israélite de Belgique. Pres.: Professor A. Georges Schnek. Sec.: 2 Rue Joseph Dupont, 1000. ☎ 512-21-90. Fax 512-35-78
Communauté Israélite de Bruxelles. Rabbi Albert Guigui. ☎ 512-43-34 & 512-92-37. Sec.: 2 rue Joseph Dupont. ☎ 512-43-34 & 512-92-37.
Machsike Hadass (Communauté Israélite Orthodoxe de Bruxelles). 67a rue de la Clinique. ☎ 524-14-86. Rabbi Chaikin.

Synagogues
Adath Israel, 126 rue Rogier, Schaerbeek. ☎ 241-16-64.
Ahavat Reim, 73 rue de Thy, St.-Gilles. Sec.: ☎ 648-38-37.
Beth Hamidrash, rue du Chapeau, Anderlecht. ☎ 524-14-86.
Beth Israel, 74 Av. Stalingrad.
Beth Israel, 33 Houzeau de Lehaie, Molenbeek.
Beth Itshak, 115 Av. du Roi, 1060. ☎ 538-33-74 & 520-13-59.
Communauté Israélite de Bruxelles, 32 rue dé la Régence.
Maale, 11 Av. de Messidor. ☎ 344-60-94.
Or Hahayim, 77 rue P. Decoster, 1190. ☎ 344-23-42.
Machsiké Hadass (Communauté Israélite Orthodoxe de Bruxelles). Rabbi I. Chaikin. ☎ 522-07-17. Sec.: 67a rue de la Clinique. ☎ 521-12-89.
Syn. & Beth Hamidrash: 67a rue de la Clinique. (Mikva on premises. ☎ 537-14-39.)
Sephard Cong. of Brussels (Communauté) Sepharadite de Bruxelles). Syn. & Sec.: 47 rue du Pavaillon, 1030. ☎ 215-05-25.
Liberal Syn. (Member of World Union for Progressive Judaism), 96 Av. Kersbeek. ☎ 332-25-28. Rabbi Abraham Dahan.
Beth Din (Machsike Hadass). 67a rue de la Clinique. ☎ 522-07-17.

Representative Organisations
B'nai B'rith, 319 Av. Brugmann, 1180 Bruxelles.
Centre Communautaire Laïc Juif, 52 rue Hotel des Monnaies. ☎ 537-82-16.
Jewish Restaurant on premises open daily for lunch and Friday eve.
Comité de Coordination des Organisations Juives de Belgique, 68 Av.
Ducpétiaux. ☎ 537-16-91.
Fédération Nationale des Anciens Combattants et Résistants Juifs Armés de
Belgique, 2 Av. Albert. ☎ 345-69-28.
Union des Anciens Résistants Juifs de Belgique, 148 Chaussée d'Ixells.
Union des Déportés, 68 Av. Ducpétiaux. ☎ 538-98-66.
World Jewish Congress (Belgian Section), 84 rue de Stassart, 1050.

Cultural & Educational Organisations, Schools, etc.
Amis Belges de l'Universite Hebraique de Jerusalem, 319 Ave Brugmann -
1180 Bruxelles.
Athenée Maïmonide, 67 Blvd. Poincaré. ☎ 523-63-36.
Athénée Ganenu, 3 rue Melkriek, 1180. ☎ 376-11-76.
Beth Aviv, 123 Av. Moliére, 1180. ☎ 347-37-19.
Beth Chabad, 87 Av. du Roi. ☎ 537-11-58.
Centre National des Hautes Etudes Juives, 17 Ave F. Roosevelt. ☎ 650.33.48.
La Maison de la Culture Juive, 77 rue P. Decoster, 1190. ☎ 343-62-24.
Yeshiva des Etudiants de Bruxelles, 94 rue de la Source, 1060.
Yessodé Hatorah, 67a rue de la Clinique.

Student, Youth & Sports Organisations
Jewish Students' Union, 27 rue de Hellenes, 1050. ☎ 649-08-08.
Centre Ben Gurion, 89 Chaussée de Vleurgat. ☎ 648-18-59. ((K) restaurant on
premises. Open daily from noon to 2.30 p.m. and 6 p.m. to 9 p.m. except Fri.
evg. and Sat. afternoon.
Maccabi, 89 Chaussée de Vleurgat. ☎ 648-18-59.

Welfare Organisations, Hospitals, Homes, etc.
Centrale d'Oeuvres Sociales Juives (combined welfare and fund-raising org.),
91 Av. H. Jaspar, 1060. ☎ 538-80-36.
Home for Aged, 31-35 rue de la Glaciére. ☎ 537-46-99.
Service Social Juif, 66-68 Av. Ducpétiaux. ☎ 538-81-80.
United Hias Service, 42 rue de Livourne.

Zionist Organisations
Bnei Akiva, 262 rue des Alliés, 1190. ☎ 343-78-13.
Hanoar Hatzioni, 234 Chaussée d'Alsemberg.
Keren Kayemet, Ave Maraix 19A - 1050 Bruxelles. ☎ 513-92-32.
Mizrachi, 2 Av. Rogier. ☎ 215-36-97.
Org. of Gen. Zionists & Independents, 168 Av. du Roi, 1060 Bruxelles.
Pioneer Women, Na'amat, 89 Ch. de Vleurgat, 1050.
Poale Zion, 118 Av. Albert. ☎ 537-42-99.
Union of General Zionists, 11 Av. du Polo.
WIZO, 48 Av. Brugmann. ☎ 343-38-61.
Zionist Fed. of Belgium, 66 Av. Ducpétiaux. ☎ 538-56-29.
Zionist Revisionists, 1 Blvd. de la Révision. ☎ 521-95-50.
Museum 74 Ave de Stalengrad 1000. ☎ 512-19.63.
Israel Embassy and Consular Section, 40 Av. de l'Observatoire. ☎ 373-55-00

Booksellers
Colbo, 121 rue du Brabant. ☎ 217-26-20
Menorah, 12 Ave J. Voldens, 1060. ☎ 537.50.73.

Newspapers and Periodicals
'Centrale' (monthly), 91 Av. Henri Jaspar. ☎ 538-80-36 & "Kehilatenou" (monthly), 2 rue Joseph Dupont. ☎ 512-43-34.
'La Tribune Sioniste' (fortnightly), 68 Av. Ducpétiaux.
'Regards' (fortnightly), 52 rue Hotel des Monnaies. ☎ 538.49.08. Fax. 537.55.65.
(The 'Jewish Chronicle' is obtainable from W. H. Smith & Son, 71-75 Blvd. Adolphe Max.)
Kosher Bakery: Bornstein, 62 rue de Suéde, St. Gilles. ☎ 537-16-79.
Kosher Butcher: Lanxner, 37 Av. Jean Volders. ☎ 537-06-08 & 121 rue de Brabant. ☎ 217-26-20.

CHARLEROI
Com. Centre: 56 rue Pige-au-Croly. Sec.: M. Weinberg, 65 rue van der Velde, 6300 Marchiennes.

GHENT
The com. is a very small one and there is no permanent syn. However, services are held on the High Holy-days. Jacques Bloch, Veldstr. 60, ☎ (09) 225-70-85, the treas. of the com., will be happy to meet Anglo-Jewish visitors.

KNOKKE
Syn.: 30 Van Bunnenlaan. ☎ (050) 61-103-72.
Kosher Restaurant:
(K) **Maison Steinmetz,** Piers de Raveschootlaan 129, 8300. ☎ (050) 61-0265, (Open July-August).

LIÈGE
Syn.: 19 rue L. Frédéricq, 4020. ☎ (041) 436106.
Com. Centre: 12 Quai Marcellis, 4020.
Musée Serge Kruglanski at 19 rue L. Frédéricq. ☎ (041) 438043.

MONS
Nearby, at Casteau the International Chapel of NATO's Supreme Headquarters Allied Powers Europe, includes a small Jewish Community (est. 1951) that holds regular services. Further inf. SHAPE, 7010, Belgium. ☎ 44.58.08 or 44.48.09.

OSTEND
Syn.: Van Maastrichtplein 3. Inf.: Sec. Liliane Wulfowicz: Parklaan 21, B-8400. ☎ (059) 80-24-05. Services during July and August. Sukkot at Hotel Royal Astor, Hertsstraat 15. ☎ 803773.

BERMUDA
There is a small but active Jewish community in Bermuda. High Holy-day services are normally held at the U.S. Naval Air Station chapel. There is also a Sabbath service on the first Fri. of each month in the Unity Foundation Room, 75 Reid St. Further inf. is available from the Jewish Com. of Bermuda, P.O. Box HM 1793, Hamilton, HM HX or the Jewish Community Voicemail ☎ 291-1785. Contact Diana Lynn, 17 Biological Lane, Ferry Reach, GE01. ☎ 297-2267. Fax 297-8143. Email dlynn@bbst.edu
General inf. from Bermuda Tourism, 1 Battersea Church Rd., SW11 3LY. ☎ 0171-734 8813. Fax. 0171-352-6501.

BOLIVIA

Although there have been Jews in Latin America for many centuries, they are comparative newcomers to Bolivia, which received its first Jewish immigrants only in 1905. They remained a mere handful until the 1920s, when some Russian Jews made their way to the country. After 1935, German Jewish refugees, began to arrive in Bolivia. Also from Rumania and mostly from Poland. Today some 640 Jews live there, mostly in the capital of La Paz (about 430), Cochabamba (120) and Santa Cruz (85), Tarija and other cities (5).

COCHABAMBA
Syn.: Calle Junin y Calle Colombia, Casilla 349.
Asociación Israelita de Cochabamba, P.O.B. 349 Calle Valdivieso.

LA PAZ
Syns.: Circulo Israelita de Bolivia, Casilla 1545 Calle Landaeta 346, P.O.B. 1545. Services Sat. morn. only. Pres.: Renè Doefler Elias. ☎ 32-5925. Fax 591-234-2738.
Comunidad Israelita Synagogue, Calle Canada Strongest 1846, P.O.B. 2198, is affiliated to the Circulo. Fri. evg. services are held. There is a Jewish school at this address. Circulo Israelita, P.O.B. 1545 is the representative body of Bolivian Jewry. All La Paz organisations are affiliated to it.
Two Homes for Aged: Calle Rosendo Gutierrez 307, and Calle Diaz Romero 1765.
Information office for Israeli tourist. Centro Shalom, Calle Canada Stronguest 1846, La Paz Country Club, Quinta J.K.G. Obrajes. Calle 1, esquina calle Hector Ormachea Castilla 1545 – La Paz.

SANTA CRUZ
Centro Cruceño P.O.B. 469.
WIZO, Casilla 3409.

BOSNIA HERCEGOVINA

The state of the Jewish Community remains in doubt following the civil war amongst the former Yugoslav republics.

SARAJEVO
Syn.: Dobrovoljacka St. 83, by the river bank near Princip Bridge. The head of the Jewish com. will be glad to show the treasures of the Jewish Museum, including priceless Jewish relics of the Spanish Inquisition. Pres.: Ivica Chereshnes. ☎ 272-142; Fax 271-851.
There is an historic Jewish cemetery (Kovacici, Nevesinjska St.) in the town. On a hill called Vrace, not far from the centre of the town, is a monument to the 7,000 Jews from the area who fell victim to the Nazis.
Jewish Museum: Marshall Tito St. 98. ☎ 535 688.

BRAZIL

Marranos from Portugal and, later, Sephardim from Holland were the first Jews to settle in Brazil about 400 years ago. Their early history was bedevilled by the struggle for power in this vast country between the Portuguese and Dutch, as well as by the Inquisition, which the Portuguese revived when they were on top, and which was abolished when the Dutch gained the upper hand.
Finally, in 1822, Brazil declared her independence of Portugal. Some Marranos reverted to open Judaism when liberty of worship was proclaimed, and in the years that followed, European Jews, mainly Ashkenazim, began to immigrate. Communities grew up in Rio de Janeiro, Recife, Bahia, Sao Paulo

and elsewhere and continued to grow, especially after the First World War, in the 1930s and again after the Second World War.

Today, Brazil's Jewish population numbers about 175,000. All save about 25,000 live in Rio and Sao Paulo. The overwhelming majority, some 140,000, are Ashkenazim.

AMAZONAS STATE

MANAUS
Social Centre: Grupo Kadima, Rua Ramos Ferreira 596.

BAHIA STATE

SALVADOR
Syn.: Rua Alvaro Tiberio 60. Com. Centre & Zionist Org. at same address. ☎ 3-4283.

BRASILIA FEDERAL DISTRICT
Syn. & Com. Centre: ACIB, Entrequadras Norte 305-306 Lote A. ☎ 23-2984. Embassy of Israel: Av. das Nacoes Sul, Lote 38. ☎ 244-7675, 7875, 5886 & 4886.

MINAS GERAIS STATE

BELO HORIZONTE
Syns.: Avenne Leonardo Malchez 630, Centro.
Mikva: Rua Grande do Norte 477. ☎ 2210690.
Com. Centres & Clubs:
Uniao Israelita de Belo Horizonte, Rua Pernambuco 326. ☎ 2246013; Associacao Israelita Brasileira, Rua Rio Grande do Norte 477. ☎ 2210690. Comunidade Religiosa Israelita Mineira, Rua Rio Grande do Norte 477.

PARA STATE

BELEM
Syns.: Shaar Hashamaim, Rua Alcipreste Manoel Theodoro 842; Eshel Avraham, Travessa Campos Sales 733.
Com. Centre: Travessa Dr. Moraes 37.

PARANA STATE
CURITIBA
Syn.: Francisco Frischman (Orthodox), Rua Cruz Machado 126. M.: Rabbi David Ben-Hayon.
Com. Centre and S. Guelman School, Rua Nilo Pecanha 664. ☎ 23-3734.

PERNAMBUCO STATE

RECIFE
Syn.: Rua Martins Junior 29.
Com. Centre: Rua da Gloria 215.

RIO DE JANEIRO STATE

CAMPOS
Com. Centre: Rua 13 de Maio 52.

NITEROI
Centro Israelita: Rua Visconde do Uruguai 255, 24030.
Sociedade Hebraica, Rua Alvares de Azevedo 185. Icarai, 24220.

PETROPOLIS
Machane Israel Yeshiva, Rua Duarte da Silveira 1246, 25600. ☎ 42-4952.
Sinagoga Israelita Brasileira, Rua Aureliano Coutinho 48, 25600.

GREATER RIO DE JANEIRO
Representative Organisations
B'nai B'rith, Do Flamengo 66, BLBS 904.
Bene Herzl (Sephardi), Rua Barata Ribeiro 489.
Rabinado do Rio de Janeiro, Rua Pompeu Loureiro, 40. Fax 236-0249.
Federação Israelita do Rio de Janeiro, Rua Buenos Aires 68.
Organição Israelita do Estado do Rio de Janeiro, Rua México 90/5. ☎ 532-0925.

Synagogues & Religious Organisations
Agudat Israel, Rua Nascimento Silva 109, Ipanema 22421.
Associacao Religiosa Israelita (Liberal), Rua General Severiano 170, Botafogo, 22290. ☎ 2269666 & 2379283.
Beth Aaron, Rua Gago Coutinho 63, Laranjeiras, 22221.
Beth El, Rua Barata Ribero 489, Copacabana, 22040.
Chevre Kedishe (Orthodox), Rua Barao de Iguatemi 306. ☎ 248-8716.
Conselho das Congregacoes Sefaraditas, Rua Barata Ribeiro 489. ☎ 2576193.
Grande Templo Israelita, Rua Tenente Possolo 8, Centro, 20230. ☎ 2323656.
Kehilat Moriah (Orthodox), Rua Pompeu Loureiro 48. ☎ 2353110.
Kehilat Yaakov, Rua Capelao Alvares da Silva 15, Copacabana, 22041. Mikva on premises.
Monte Sinai (Orthodox), Rua Sao Francisco Xavier Tijuca, 20550.
Sidon, Rua Conde Bonfim 521.
Sinagoga Beirutense, Rua Carvalho Alvim 467.
Templo Sidon, Av. Rio Branco 156-3110, Centro, 20040.
Templo Uniao Israel, Rua Jose Higino 375 & 381, Tijuca, 20520.
Uniao Israelita Shel Guemilut Hassadim (Orthodox, Sephardi), Rua Rodrigo de Brito 37. ☎ 2264885.
Jewish Cemetery: Av. Presidente Vargas 583/2006, Centro 20071.

Cultural Organisations, Clubs, etc.
Biblioteca Sholem Aleichem, Rua São Clemente 155, Botafogo, 22260. ☎ 2267740.
Biblioteca Bialik, Rua Fernando Osorio 16, Flamengo, 22230. ☎ 205-1946.
Biblioteca Theodor Herzl, Av. Copacabana 807, Salas 1005-6, Copacabana 22050.
Centro de Cultura Yiddish, Av. Copacabana 69010° andar.
Hebraica Club, Rua das Laranjeiras 346, Laranjeiras. 22240. ☎ 2458722.
Instituto Israelita Brasileiro de Cultura e Educação, Rua das Laranjeiras 405, Laranjeiras, 22240.
Jewish Museum, Rua Mexico 90-1°, Andar.
Monte Sinai Club, Rua Sao Francisco Xavier 104, Tijuca, 20550. ☎ 248-8448.

Welfare Organisations, Hospitals, etc.
Communal Fund (Funds Comunitario), Rua Buenos Aires 68.
Children's Home: Rua Jose Higino 240. ☎ 2380080, 2586162.
Homes for Aged: Av. Geremario Dantas 278 (Jacarepagua). Office: Rua

Uruguaiana 10. ☎ 252 6887; Rua Santa Alexandrina 464. ☎ 2737045 & 2737196.
Hospital Israelita, Rua Lucio de Mendonca 56, Maracana, 20270. ☎ 2282128.

Zionist Organisations
Naamat-Pioneiras, Rua Fernando Osorio 16, Flamengo, 22230.
Israel Consulate, Av. Copacabana 680. ☎ 255-5432.
Org. Sionista Unificada, Rua Décio Vilares 258. ☎ 456-2850.
United Zionist Org. of Rio, Rua Décio Vilares 258, Copacabana, 22041. ☎ 2562850.
WIZO, Praia do Flamengo 278, Sala 92, Copacabana, 22041.
Restaurant: **(K)** Shalom, Rua Pompeu Loureiro 40 (Copacabana). ☎ 2360249.

RIO GRANDE DO SUL STATE

ERECHIM
Syn.: Av. Pedro Pinto de Souza 131.

PASSO FUNDO
Syn.: Rua General Osório 1049.

PELOTAS
Syn.: Rua Santos Dumont 303.

PORTO ALEGRE
(Jewish population about 15,000.)
Syns. & Com. Centres: Centro Israelita Porto Alegrense, Rua Henrique Dias 73. ☎ 228-1935; Linath Ha-Tzedek, Rua Bento Figueredo 55. ☎ 332-1065; Poilisher Farband, Rua João Telles 329. ☎ 226-0379; União Israelita Porto Alegrense, Rua Barros Cassal 750. ☎ 2246515; Beit Chabad, Rua Felipe Camarão, 748. ☎ 330-7078; All the foregoing are Orthodox with daily services. The Centro Hebraico Riograndense (Sephardi), Rua Cel. Machado 1008 has services on Sabbaths only, as does SIBRA (Liberal), Mariante 772. ☎ 3318133.
City Rabbinate: Rua Henrique Dias 73. ☎ 219649. Rabbi Efraim F. Ginsberg & Rabbi Saul Farber.
Mikva: Rua Francisco Ferrer 170.

Clubs, Organisations, etc.
B'nai B'rith: Rua João Telles 329. ☎ 247126.
Club Campestre: Av. Coronel Marcos 1345. ☎ 249-2235.
Federação Israelita do Rio Grande do Sul. Same address as B'nai B'rith. ☎ 226-0379.
Gremio Esportiva Israelita: Av. Protasio Alves 3435. ☎ 3318435.
Home for Aged: Lar Dos Velhos. Rua Leopoldo Bettiol 501. C.P. 5043. ☎ 334-8400.
Organizacao Sionista Unificada, Rua Francisco Ferrer 170. ☎ 312296.
WIZO and Pioneiras, Rua João Teller, 329. ☎ 226-0379.
Associação Israelita – Avenida Protásio Alves, 3435, João Telles, 508. ☎ 334-8435 and 226-3248.
ECIBRAS (Entidades Communitárias Israelita Brasileira – Lar da Criança Anne Frank) – as WIZO.
Instituto Cultural Judaico Marc Chagall – Projeto Memória – Rua Dom Pedro II, 1220/ sala 216; ☎ 343-5748; Museu Judaico (Jewish Museum) – Rua João Telles, 329. ☎ 226-0379.

Youth Organisations
Habonim Dror – Rua Felipe Camarão, 487.
Chazit Hanoar – Rua Mariante, 772.

Betar – Rua João Telles, 508.
(K) Kosher Butcher: Rua Fernandes Vieira 518. ☎ 250441.

SANTA MARIA
Location of first Jewish settlement in Brazil, established by Jewish Colonization Assoc.

SAO PAULO STATE
CAMPINAS
Syn. & Com. Centre: Beth Yacob, Rua Barreto Leme 1203. ☎ 0192-314908.

MOGI DAS CRUZES
Jewish Soc.: Rua Dep. Deodato Wertheimer 421. ☎ 469-2505.

SANTO ANDRE
Syn. & Com. Centre: Rua Siqueira Campos 780. ☎ 449-1568.
School, Rua Onze de Junho 172. ☎ 449-1568.

SANTOS
Syn.: Rua Campos Sales 137.
Club: Rua Cons. Neblas 254. ☎ 32-9016.

SAO CAETANO DO SUL
Syn.: Rua Para 61. ☎ 442-3514.

SAO PAULO
Synagogues & Religious Organisations
Beit Chabad, Rabbi Shabsi Alpern, Rua Chabad 54/60. ☎ 852-4794 & 282-1819.
Centro Judaico Religioso de Sao Paulo (Orthodox). Office hours: 9 a.m. to 1 p.m. weekdays. ☎ 220-5642. Rabbi Elyahu B. Valt. ☎ 64-90-54 (home).
Comunidade Israelita Ortodoxa de Sao Paulo, Hitachdut Kehilot Hacharedim, Rua Haddock Lobo 1279. ☎ 282-1562 & 852-9710. This com. has two syns.: Beit Itzchok, Rua Haddock Lobo 1279. ☎ 881-3804; Adas Yereim, Rua Tocantins 86. M.: Rabbi M.A. Iliovitz, Rua Haddock Lobo 1091. ☎ 282-1562 & 852-9710.
Comunidade Israelita Sefaradi, Rua da Abolicao 457. ☎ 36-9982.
Syn.: Templo do Rito Portugues. Same address & ☎ M.: Rabbi J. Kadoch.
Comunidade Ortodoxa Israelita e K'hal Machzikei Hadass, Rabbi E. B. Valt. Rua Padre Joao Manuel 727. ☎ 282-6762.
Congregacao Israelita Paulista (Liberal), Rua Antonio Carlos 653. ☎ 256-7811
Congregacao K'hal Chasidim, Rabbi Joel Beer (Ratzferter Rebbe), Rua Mamore 597. ☎ 220-1735.
Congregacao Mekor Haim (Sephardi), Rua Sao Vicente de Paula 254. ☎ 67-2029. M.: Rabbi Itzhak Dichi.
Congregacao Monte Sinai (Sephardi), Rua Piaui 624. ☎ 66-5303.
Congregacao Tiferet Lubavitch, Rabbi Jacob Begun, Rua Alagoas 726, Higienopolis. ☎ 66 7783.
Sinagoga Beth Jacob, Rua Artur de Azevedo 1781.
Sinagoga Beth Yacov (Syrian & Lebanese), Rabbi Efraim Laniado, Rua Bela Cintra 801. ☎ 256-3115 & 258-7931.
Sinagoga Centro Israelita (Orthodox), Rua Newton Prado 76. ☎ 220-0185.
Sinagoga e Talmud Torah (Orthodox), Rua Tocantins 296. ☎ 220-0225.
Sinagoga Israelita Bras (Sephardi), Rua Odorico Mendes 174. ☎ 279-3145.
Sinagoga Israelita do Bom Retiro, Rua da Graca 160.
Sinagoga Israelita Paulista (Hungarian), Rua Augusta 259. ☎ 256-5970.
Templo Beth-El (Ashkenazi), Rua Avanhandava 137-Esquina Rua Martinho Prado 128. ☎ 256-8671 & 256-1246.

Mikvaot: Bom Retiro, Rua Tenente Pena 310; Rua Haddock Lobo 1279. ☎ 881-3804; Rua Padre Joao Manoel 727. ☎ 282-6762; Rua Mamore 597.

Communal Organisations, etc.
B'nai B'rith, Rua Cacapava 105. ☎ 282-5589 & 853-4804.
Com. Centre & Syn.: Rua Teixeira Mendes 54. ☎ 278-8919.
Federacao Israelita do Estado de Sao Paulo, Av. Paulista 726, 2nd Floor. ☎ 288-6411.
Instituto de Cultura Hebraica, Rua Bela Cintra 1233. ☎ 881-8185.

Hospitals
Albert Einstein, Rua Albert Einstein. ☎ 240-3322.
Linat Hatzedek, Rua Rodolfo Miranda 287. ☎ 227-8011.

Zionist Organisations
All the Zionist orgs. are at Rua Correa Mello 75. ☎ 221-9233 & 220-4133.
Israel Consulate, Rua Luis Coelho 308, 7th Floor. ☎ 257-2111 & 257-2814.

Booksellers
Oitzer Haseforim, Al. Lorena 1178. ☎ 64-6404.
Weltman's, Rua Ribeiro de Lima 604. ☎ 220-5079.

Newspapers, etc.
'O Hebreu' (Portuguese monthly), Rua Mamoré 570. ☎ 220-1717.
'Resenha Judaica' (Portuguese fortnightly), Rua Antonio Carlos 582. ☎ 258-2066.
'Revista Shalom' (Portuguese monthly), Rua da Graca 201. ☎ 220-0265.

Travel Agencies
Monumento Viagens E Turisma Ltda., Rua Augusta, 2516/111. ☎ 2824499. Fax. 2824707.
Vértice, Rua Sâo Bento 545, 10° And. ☎ 36-6341. Fax 34-6530.

Restaurants
* Buffet Mosaico, Rua Hungria 1000. ☎ 815-6788 & 815-6980.

Bakery & Catering
* Mazal Tov, Rua Peixoto Gomide 1724. ☎ 645-208 & 282-0761, & Rua da Graça 68. ☎ 223-1045.

Butchers
(K) Samuel Gaida, Rua da Consolocao 3297. ☎ 852-4773. Under supervision of Rabbi M. A. Iliovitz.
(K) Mehadrin, Rua Guarani 206. ☎ 227-9141. Under supervision of Rabbi M. A. Iliovitz.
(K) Tifereth, Rua Martinico Prado 389. ☎ 825-1042 & 826-8588. Under supervision of Rabbi Elyahu B. Valt.

SOROCABA
Syn. & Com. Centre: Rua Dom Pedro II 56. ☎ 31-3168.

BULGARIA
Bulgarian Jewry dates from the 2nd century C.E. when, after the Byzantine conquest, Greek Jews established a congregation in Serdica (now Sofia). After the establishment of the Bulgarian State in 681, Jewish settlement in the country increased, and during the reign of King Ivan Alexander (1331-1371) the Jewish com. flourished. His Queen was Theodora, a former Jewess whose original name was Sarah.

Rabbi Shalom of Nitra founded the first rabbinical school in Vidin, in 1370. His successor, Rabbi Dosa Ajevani, became famous for his commentary on Rashi. In the middle of the 15th century, Ashkenazi Jews driven out of Bavaria settled in Bulgaria and built a synagogue in Sofia. More than 30,000 Jews, expelled from Spain, arrived at the end of the 15th century, among them Joseph Caro, the codifier of the Shulchan Aruch. By the end of the 16th century Bulgaria's Sephardi Jews had assimilated the Ashkenazi and other groups.

By the beginning of the Second World War in 1939, there were about 50,000 Jews in Bulgaria. Since 1948, about 45,000 have emigrated to Israel; and today's Jewish population is about 5,000, of whom 3,200 live in Sofia. The others are scattered throughout the rest of the country. It is worth noting that few Jews became victims of the Nazis during the German occupation of Bulgaria in the Second World War, even though the Bulgarian Government was allied to Nazi Germany, thanks to the support of the Bulgarian population.

In the town museum of Nikopol there is a room dedicated to Joseph Caro.

General Inf. from Bulgarian National Tourist Office, 18 Princes St., W1R 7RE. ☎ 0171-499 6988.

PAZARDJIK
Comm. Centre: Asson Zlatarov St. 26. ☎ (034) 28-364.

PLOVDIV
Syn.: Tsar Kalojan St. 15 (in the courtyard of a large apartment complex).
Library & House of Culture: Vladimir Zaimov St. 20. ☎ (032) 761-376.

RUSSE
Synagogue and Comm.Centre: Ivan Vazov Sq. 4. ☎ (082) 270-540.

SOFIA
Social & Cultural Org. of Bulgarian Jews: Shalom, Alexander Stambolisky St. 50. ☎ (02) 870-163.
Publishes a periodical, 'Evreiski Vesti', & a yearbook. It also maintains a museum devoted to 'The Rescue of Bulgarian Jews, 1941-1944'. At the same address are the offices of El Al, the Joint and the Jewish Agency.
Syn. & Central Jewish Religious Council: Ekzarh Josef St. 16. Pres.: Yosif Levy. Above the synagogue is a museum dedicated to the history of Bulgarian Jewry.
Take a tram (Nos. 2, 10 or 14) to the last stop for a large Jewish cemetery in the Orlandovtzi suburb.

BURMA
(see Union of Myanmar)

BYELORUS
BARANOVICHI
Syn.: 39 Svobodnaya St.

BOBRUISK
Syn.: Engels St.

BORISOV
Syn.: Trud St.

BREST
Syn.: Narodnaya St.

GOMEL
Syn.: 13 Sennaya St.
MINSK
Syns.: 22 Kropotkin St. ☎ (017-2) 55-82-70; Kommunisticheskaya St.
MOGHILEV
Syn.: 1 2nd Krutoy La.
ORSHA
Syn.: Nogrin St.
RECHITSA
Syn.: 120 Lunacharsky St.

CANADA

Jews played some part in the British military occupation of Canada and a number settled in Montreal at an early date. But in the ten years following the conquest of Quebec in 1759, there were only ten Jews in Canada. A century later, this figure had grown to 1,250. At the end of the 19th century, large-scale emigration began from Eastern Europe, and many emigrants chose to settle in Canada. Today, the Jewish population is about 356,500. Chief centres are Montreal, Toronto and Vancouver.
General inf. from Tourism Canada, Canada Hse., Trafalgar Sq., SW1Y 5BJ. ☎ 0171-930 8540.

ALBERTA

CALGARY
Synagogues
House of Jacob (O), 1613 92nd Av. S.W., T2V 5C9. ☎ (403) 259-3230; Beth Tzedec (C), 1325 Glenmore Trail S.W., T2Y 4Y8. ☎ (403) 255-8688; Temple B'nai Tikvah (R), Calgary Jewish Centre, 1607 90th Av. S.W., T2V 4V7. ☎ (403) 252-1654.
Organisations
Calgary Rabbinical Council. ☎ (403)-253-8600 Fax (403) 253-7915.
Calgary Jewish Community Council, 1607 90th Av. S.W. ☎ (403) 253-8600. Fax (403) 253-7915.
The Com. Centre is at the same address. The Council issues a booklet 'Keeping Kosher in Calgary'.
B'nai Brith Canada, Western Region, 10655 Southport Rd. S.W., Suite, 1400, T2W 4Y1. ☎ (403) 225-5256. Fax (403) 278-0176.
Jewish Free Press, Box 72113, 16900 90th Av. S.W., T2V 5H9. ☎ (403) 252-9423. Fax (403) 255-5640.
Kosher Food
(K) Karen's Café, Calgary Jewish Centre, 1607 90th Av. S.W. Sun.-Thurs., 10.00 a.m. to 7.00 p.m.; Fri. 10.00 a.m. to 1.00 p.m. ☎ (403) 255-5311.
(K) Schaier's Meat & Kosher Deli, 2515 90th Av. S.W. ☎ (403) 251-2552.
(K) Susan's Kosher Bakery, ☎ (403) 238 5300.
(K) Wolf's Kosher World & Deli, 42, 180-94 Av. S.E. Sun.-Thurs 10.00 a.m. to 8.00 p.m., Fri. 10.00 a.m. to 2.00 p.m. ☎ (403) 253-3354.

EDMONTON
Syns.: Beth Israel, 10205 119th St., T5K 1Z3. ☎ (403) 482-2840; Beth Shalom, 11916 Jasper Av., T5K 0N9. ☎ (403) 488-6333; Temple Beth Ora (R), 7200, 156th St., T5R 1X3. ☎ (403) 487-4817.

continued from *Alberta*

For additional inf., contact Miriam Cooper, **Edmonton Jewish Federation,** 7200 156th St., T5R 1X3. ☎ (403) 487-0585. Fax. (403) 481-1854.

Newspapers:
Edmonton Jewish Life, 10342-147 St. T5J 1K2. ☎ (403) 488-7276. Fax (403) 487-4342.
Edmonton Jewish News, #330, 10036 Jasper Ave. T5J 2W2. ☎ (403) 421-7966. Fax (403) 424-3951.

Kosher Food
(K) Andy's Valleyview IGA, 9106 142 St. ☎ (403) 483 1525.
(K) Hello Deli, 10725-124 St. ☎ 454-8527.
(K) King David Pizza, 1195, 8770-170 St., West Edmonton Mall. ☎ (403) 486-9020.
(K) Kosher Mart, 14804 Stony Plain Rd., T5N 3S5. ☎ (403) 453-3988.
(K) Kosher Restaurant at Jewish Community Centre, 7200-156 St, T5R 1X3. ☎ (403) 444-4460.

LETHBRIDGE
Syn.: Beth Israel (O), 914 15th St. S., T1J 3A5. ☎ (403) 327-8621.

MEDICINE HAT
Syn.: Sons of Abraham (O), 540 5th St. S.E., T1A 1S6. ☎ (403) 526-3880.

BRITISH COLUMBIA

KELOWHA
Syn: Beth Shalom (T), 108 North Glenmore Rd. ☎ (604) 862-2305.

RICHMOND
Syns.: Eitz Chaim (O), 8080 Francis Rd., V6Y 1A4. ☎ (604) 275-0007; Beth Tikvah (C), 9711 Geal Rd., V7E 1R4. ☎ (604) 271-6262.
Orthodox Rabbinical Council of B.C. (604)-275-0042. Fax (604) 277-2225.
Richmond Jewish Day School, P.O. Box. 36523, Richmond V7C 5M4. ☎ (604) 275-3393.
Kosher Deli: Golda's, 101, 10151 No3 Rd., V6A 4R6. ☎ (604) 2241-5632.

SURREY – WHITE ROCK
Syn: Chabad (O) 210-6950 Nicholson Rd., Delta V4A 1Z7. ☎ (604) 596-9030; Jewish Comm. of Lower Fraser Valley (O), 1349 Johnston Rd., White Rock, V4B 3Z3. ☎ (604) 535-3251.

VANCOUVER
Vancouver, has a Jewish population of 25,000. The Jewish presence in B.C. is comparatively recent with the first Jews arriving on the heels of the news of the Cariboo gold rush of 1858. They were followed some thirty-five years later by European Jews escaping from religious and economic persecution. Jews have continued to come to B.C., mainly to Vancouver, from Europe, the Orient, Israel, South America and South Africa forming a sophisticated and international community. Many Jews have moved to Vancouver from eastern Canada and the Prairie Provinces.

Information on many smaller cities in the Province with Jewish communities can be obtained from Shalom Vancouver.

Synagogues
Beth Hamidrash Cong. (S), 3231 Heather St. V5Z 3K4. ☎ (604) 872-4222.

continued from *British Columbia*

Congregation Beth Israel (C), 4350 Oak St., V6H 2N4 ☎ (604) 731-4161.
Har-El Cong. (C). 1735 Inglewood Av., West Vancouver, V7V 1Y8. ☎ (604) 922-8245.
Chabad-Lubavitch Centre (O), 5750 Oak St., V6M 2V9. ☎ (604) 266-1313.
Louis Brier Chapel (O), 1055 West 41st Av., V6M 1W9. ☎ (604) 261-9376.
Schara Tzedeck Cong. (O), 3476 Oak St., V6H 2L8. ☎ (604) 736-7607.
Or Shalom (T), 710 E. 10th Av., V5T 2A7. ☎ (604) 872-1614.
Temple Shalom (R), 7190 Oak St., V6P 3Z9. ☎ (604) 266-7190.

Other Organisations
Shalom Vancouver - Jewish Information, Referral & Welcome Service for new-comers and visitors, 950 West 41st Av., V5Z 2N7. ☎ (604) 257-5111.
Publishes a 'Guide to Jewish life in British Columbia'. Coordinator: Janet Kolof.
Canadian Jewish Congress (Pacific Region), 950 West 41st Av., V5Z 2N7. ☎ (604) 257-5101. Exec. Dir.: Erwin Nest.
Jewish Community Centre of Greater Vancouver. 950 West 41st Av., V5Z 2N7. ☎ (604) 257-5111. Exec. Dir.: Gerry Zipursky.
Jewish Federation of Greater Vancouver. 950 West 41st Av., V5Z 2N7. ☎ (604) 257-5100. Exec. Director Drew Staffenberg.
Hillel House/Network, University of British Columbia. ☎ (604) 224-4748 & 224 2512. Exec Dir : Zack Kaye.
Louis Brier Home and Hospital: 1055 West 41st Av. V6M 1W9 ☎ (604) 261-9376. Only Jewish facility of its kind in B.C. Admin: Ken Levitt.

Accommodation
Mrs. Louise Houta, 638 West 17th Av., V5Z 1T8. ☎ (604) 872-3887, can provide accom. close to the syn., transport, shopping, etc.
Shulamit Mass, 5434 Manson St., VSZ 3H1. ☎ (604) 266-8965.

Kosher Food
Aviv, 3710 Oak St. ☎ (604) 736-5888.
Cafe Mercaz, Jewish Community Centre, 950 West 41st Av., V5Z 2N7. ☎ (604) 266-9111.
Leon's Kosher Korner, 3710 Oak St. ☎ (604) 736-6348.
Sabra Bakery, 3842 Oak St., V6H 2M5. ☎ (604) 733-4912.
Butcher shop, Bakery: Kosher Food under supervision of Orthodox Rabbinical Council of B.C. ☎ (604) 275-0042. Rabbi Mordechai Feurstein, Rabbinic Administrator, Fax (604) 277-2225.
For vegetarian restaurants contact Shalom Vancouver, 950 West 41st Av., ☎ (604) 266-9111.

Newspaper: Jewish Western Bulletin, 3268 Heather St., Vancouver V5Z 3K5. ☎ (604) 879-6575. Fax (604) 879-6573.

VICTORIA
Syn.: Cong. Emanu-El (C), 1461 Blanshard St., V8W 2J3. ☎ (604) 382-0615. Fax (604) 380-3553. Email: emanuel@islandnet.com. Admin. Michael Goldberg. M. Rabbi V. Reinstein.

MANITOBA
WINNIPEG
Synagogues & Religious Organisations
Ashkenazi Congregation (O), 297 Burrows Av., R2W 1Z7. ☎ (204) 589-1517.

continued from *Manitoba*

Bnay Abraham (O), 235 Enniskillen Av., R2V 0H6. ☎ (204) 339-9297. Fax 339-9298.

Chavurat Tefila (O), 459 Hartford Av., R2V 0X7. ☎ (204) 338-9451.

Chevra Mishnayes (O), 700 Jefferson Av., R2V 0P6. ☎ (204) 338-8503.

Herzlia-Adas Yeshurun (O), 620 Brock St. at Fleet Av., R3N 0Z4. ☎ (204) 489-6262 or 489-6668. Fax 489-5899.

Lubavitch Centre. (O), 2095 Sinclair St., R2V 3K2. ☎ (204) 339-4756.

Talmud Torah-Beth Jacob (O), 427 Matheson Av., R2W 0E1. ☎ (204) 589-5345.

Beth Israel (C), 1007 Sinclair St., R2V 3J5. ☎ (204) 582-2353. Fax 338-9907.

Rosh Pina (C), 123 Matheson Av. E., R2W 0C3. ☎ (204) 589-6306. Fax 582-0246.

Shaarey Zedek (C), 561 Wellington Cres., R3M 0A5. ☎ (204) 452-3711. Fax 474-1184.

Temple Shalom (R), 1077 Grant Av., R3M 1Y6. ☎ (204) 453-1625. Fax 452-0997.

Mikveh Chabad-Lubavitch, 455 Hartford Av., R2V 0W9. ☎ (204) 339-4761.

Vaad Ha'Ir, 370 Hargrave St., R3B 2K1. ☎(204) 949-9180. Fax (204) 956-0609.

The Vaad Ha'ir will be pleased to give inf. about kashrut.

Representative Organisations

B'nai B'rith Canada, Mid-West Region, 2nd Floor, 370 Hargrave Av., R3B 2K1. ☎ (204) 942-2597. Fax (204) 956-2819.

National Council of Jewish Women, 1588 Main St., R2V 1Y3. ☎ (204) 339-7291. Fax 334-3779.

Winnipeg Jewish Community Council/Canadian Jewish Congress, 200-370 Hargrave St., R3B 2K1. ☎ (204) 943-0406. Fax. (204) 956-0609.

Y.M.H.A. Jewish Com. Centre, 370 Hargrave St., R3B 2K1. ☎ (204) 947-0601. Fax. (204) 942-4537.

Cultural & Educational Organisations, etc.

B'nai Brith Jewish Community Camp, c/o YMHA Jewish Community Centre, 370 Hargrave St., R3B 2K1, ☎ (204) 947-0601. Fax. (204) 942-4537.

B'nai Brith Youth Organisation. c/o YMHA, 370 Hargrave St., R3B 2K1. ☎ (204) 943-0406, Ext. 251 0r 252.

Camp Massad, 25-370 Hargrave St., R3B 2K1. ☎ (204) 943-2815.

Jewish Historical Society of Western Canada, 404 -365 Hargrave St., R3B 2K3. ☎ (204) 942-4822. Fax 942-9299.

Jewish Public Library, 1725 Main St., R2V 1Z4. ☎ (204) 338-4048.

Jewish Student Assoc. Co-ordinator, c/o Y.M.H.A., 370 Hargrave St., R3B 2K1. ☎ (204) 947-0601.

Joseph Wolinsky Collegiate Institute, 437 Matheson Av., R2W 0E1. ☎ (204) 589-3075. Fax 589-3075.

Sarah Sommer Chai Folk Ensemble, c/o 370 Hargrave St., R3B 2K1, ☎ (204) 956-1765.

Winnipeg Board of Jewish Education, 200-370 Hargrave St., R3B 2K1. ☎ (204) 949-1482. Fax. (204) 956-0609.

Winnipeg Jewish Theatre, 504-365 Hargrave St., R3B 2K3. ☎ (204) 943-3222. Fax 949-1739.

YMHA Jewish Community Centre Day Camp (Summers Only), 370 Hargrave St., R3B 2K1. ☎ (204) 947-0601, Ext. 227. Fax 942-4537.

Welfare Organisations, Homes, etc.

Jewish Child & Family Service, 666 St. James St., Unit #3, R3G 3J6. ☎ (204) 949-6860. Fax 949-6879.

continued from *Manitoba*

Sharon Home for Aged, 146 Magnus Av., R2W 2B4. ☎ (204) 586-9781. Fax 589-7560.

Zionist Organisations

Canadian Zionist Federation, Mid-West Region, 25-370 Hargrave St., R3B 2K1. ☎ (204) 943-6494. Fax 956-0609.

Hadassah-WIZO Council of Winnipeg, 205-309 Hargrave St., R3B 2J8. ☎ (204) 942-8201. Fax 589-5251.

Histadrut-Amal, 1727 Main St., R2V 1Z4. ☎ (204) 339-5755.

J.N.F., 401-365 Hargrave St., R3B 2K3. ☎ (204) 947-0207. Fax 947-5449.

Naamat Winnipeg, 1727 Main St., R2V 1Z4. ☎ (204) 334-3637.

State of Israel Bonds, #606, 283 Portage Av., R3B 2B5. ☎ (204) 942-2291. Fax 942-4584.

Local Offices of Israeli Universities

Canadian Associates of Ben-Gurion University, 213A, 153 Lombard Ave., R3B 0T4. ☎ (204) 942-7347.

Canadian Friends of the Hebrew University, Suite 880, 167 Lombard Av., R3B 0V3. ☎ (204) 942-3085. Fax 943-6211.

Canadian Technion Society, P.O. Box 24004, 1853 Grant Ave., R3N 2B1. ☎ (204) 896-3372.

Miscellaneous

Combined Jewish Appeal, 370 Hargrave St., #200, R3B 2K1. ☎ (204) 943-0406. Fax 956-0609.

Jewish Women International, 207-2211 McPhillips St., R2V 3M5. ☎ 338-8229.

Glendale Country Club, 400 Augier Av., R3K 1S4. ☎ (204) 832-1306.

Gwen Secter Creative Living Centre, 1588 Main St., R2V 1Y3. ☎ (204) 339-1701. Fax 334-3779.

Jewish Foundation of Manitoba (Endowments), same add. ☎ (204) 958-4499. Fax 958-4497.

Winnipeg Women's ORT, 646 Portage Ave., R3C 0C6. ☎ (204) 489-9140.

Jewish Media

Jewish Post & News, 117 Hutchings St., R2X 2V4. ☎ (204) 694-3332. Fax. (204) 694-3916.

Jewish Radio Hour Weekly— Sundays, at 1.30 p.m.

Yiddish TV, Channel 11.

Kosher Restaurants

(**K**) Y.M.H.A. Jewish Com. Centre, 370 Hargrave St., R3B 2K1. ☎ (204) 946-5257.

(**K**) 'Desserts Plus' — 1595 Main St., R2V 1Y2. ☎ (204) 339-1957.

(**K**) Gwen Secter Creative Living Centre, 1588 Main St., R2V 1Y3. ☎ (204) 339-1701.

Kosher Bakeries

(**K**) City Bread, 238 Dufferin Av., R2W 2X6. ☎ (204) 586-8409; (**K**) Gunn's, 247 Selkirk Av., R2W 2L5. ☎ (204) 582-2364; (**K**) Miracle Bakery, 1385 Main St., R2W 3T9. ☎ (204) 586-6140.

(**K**) Goodies' Bake Shop, 2 Donald St., R3L 0K5. ☎ 489-5526/949-2480.

(**K**) Hearthstone Bakery, 605 Erin St., R3G 2W1. ☎ (204) 779-8627.

Kosher Butchers

(**K**) Acme Produce, 525 Jarvis St. ☎ (204) 589-6454; (**K**) Omnitsky's, 1428 Main St., R2W 3V4. ☎ (204) 586-8271; (**K**) Tuxedo Quality Foods, 1853

continued from *Manitoba*

Grant Av., R3N 1Z2. ☎ (204) 987-3830.

Kosher Food
Bathurst Street Market, 1570 Main St., R2W 5J8. ☎ (204) 338-4911.

NEW BRUNSWICK
FREDERICTON
Syn.: Sgoolai Israel (O), Westmoreland St. E3B 3L7. ☎ (506) 454-9698.
Mikva on premises.

MONCTON
Syn.: Tiferes Israel (O), 56 Steadman St., E1C 4P4. ☎ (506) 858-0258. Mikva
on premises.

SAINT JOHN
Syn.: Shaarei Zedek (C), 76 Carleton St., E2L 2Z4. ☎ (506) 657-4790.
Com. Centre. ☎ (506) 657-4790.
Jewish Historical Museum, 29 Wellington Row, E2L 3H4. ☎ (506) 633-1833.

NEWFOUNDLAND
ST. JOHN'S
Syn.: Hebrew Congregation of Newfoundland & Labrador (Beth El) (C), 122-
126 Elizabeth Av., P.O. Box 724, AIC 5L4. ☎ (709) 737-6548. Fax (709) 737-
6995.

NOVA SCOTIA
GLACE BAY
Syn.: Sons of Israel (O), 1 Prince St., B1A 3C8. ☎ (902) 849-8605.

HALIFAX
Syns.: Beth Israel (O), 1480 Oxford St., B3H 3Y8. ☎ (902) 422-1301. Mikva
on premises; Shaar Shalom (C), 1981 Oxford St., B3H 4A4. ☎ (902) 423
5848.
Atlantic Jewish Council, 1515 S. Park St., Suite 304, B3J 2L2. ☎ (902) 422-
7491. Also at this address: Canadian Jewish Congress; Canadian Zionist Fed.;
United Israel Appeal; ORT; Young Judea; B'nai B'rith; Hadassah; Jewish
National Fund; Atlantic Provinces Jewish Student Federation; Chabad-
Lubavitch.
Newspaper: Shalom Magazine, 1515 S. Park St., Suite 305, B3J 2L2. ☎ (902)
422-7491. Fax (902) 425-3722.

SYDNEY
Syn.: Temple Sons of Israel (C), P.O. Box 311, Whitney Av., B1P 6H2. ☎ (902)
564-4650.

YARMOUTH
Details of Jewish Community from R. & V. Indiq, 13 Parade St., B5A 3A5.

ONTARIO
BELLEVILLE
Syn.: Sons of Jacob (C), 211 Victoria Av., K8N 2C2. ☎ (613) 962-1433.

BRANTFORD
Syn.: Beth David (O), 50 Waterloo St., N3T 3R8. ☎ (519) 752-8950.

continued from *Ontario*

CHATHAM
Syn.: Children of Jacob (C), 29 Water St. N7M 3H4. ☎ (519) 352-3544.

CORNWALL
Syn.: Beth-El (C), 321 Amelia St., K6H 3P4. ☎ (613) 932-6373.

GUELPH
Syn.: Beth Isaiah (T), 47 Surrey St. W., N1H 3R5. ☎ (519) 836-4338.

HAMILTON
Synagogues
Adas Israel (O), 125 Cline Av. S., L8S 1X1. ☎ (905) 528-0039.
Beth Jacob (C), 375 Aberdeen Av., L8P 2R7. ☎ (905) 522-1351.
Anshe Sholom (R), 215 Cline Av. N., L8S 4A1. ☎ (905) 528-0121.

Hamilton Jewish Federation, Exec. Dir., 1030 Lower Lions Club Rd., P.O. Box 7258 Ancaster, L9G 3N6. ☎ (905) 648-0605. Fax. (905) 648-8350.
Newspaper: Hamilton Jewish News, PO Box 7528, Ancaster, L9G 3N6. ☎ (905) 648-0605. Fax (905) 648-8388.
Kosher Foods:
Hamilton Kosher Meats, 889 King St. W., L8S 1K5.
Westdale Deli, 893 King Street West, L8S 1K5. ☎ (905) 529-2605.

KINGSTON
Syns.: Beth Israel (O), 116 Centre St., K7L 4E6. ☎ (613) 542-5012.
Temple Iyr Hamelech (R), 331 Union St. W., K7L 2R3. V(613) 789-7022.
B'nai B'rith Hillel Foundation, 26 Barrie St. ☎ (613) 542-1120.

KITCHENER
Syn.: Beth Jacob (T), 161 Stirling Av. S., N2G 3N8. ☎ (519) 743-8422;
Temple Shalom (R) 116 Queen St. N., N2H 2H7. ☎ (519) 743-0401.

LONDON
Communal inq. to Exec. Dir., **Jewish Com. Council**, 536 Huron St. ☎ (519) 673-3310. Email: ljf@icis.on.ca
Syns.: Beth Tefilah (O), 1210 Adelaide St. N., N5Y 4T6. ☎ (519) 433-7081.
Mikva on premises; Cong. Or Shalom (C), 534 Huron St., N5Y 4J5. ☎ (519) 438-3081. Fax (519) 439-2994; Temple Israel (R), 651, Windermere Rd., N5X 2P1. ☎ (519) 858-4400.
Newspaper: London Jewish Community News, 536 Huron St., N5Y 4J5. ☎ (519) 673-3310. Fax (519) 673 1161.
Kosher frozen meat, prepared foods & selected groceries available, at local A&P and IGA Loeb Stores.

MISSISSAUGA
Syn.: Solel Cong. (R), 2399 Folkway Dr., L5L 2M6. ☎ (905) 820-5915.

NIAGARA FALLS
Syn.: B'nai Jacob (C), 5328 Ferry St., L2G 1R7. ☎ (905) 354 3934.

NORTH BAY
Syn.: Sons of Jacob (O), 302 McIntyre St. W., P1B 2Z1. ☎ (705) 474-2170.

OAKVILLE
Syn.: Shaarei-Beth El (R), 186 Morrison Rd., L6L 4J4. ☎ (905) 845-0837.

continued from *Ontario*

OSHAWA
Syn.: Beth Zion (O), 144 King St. E., L1H 1B6. ☎ (905) 723-2353.

OTTAWA
Representative Organisations
B'nai B'rith Canada, National Capital Region, 151 Chapel St., K1N 7Y2. ☎ (613) 789-4922. Fax (613) 789-1325.
Canadian Jewish Congress - National Capital District at Ottawa Jewish Community Council, Com. Centre, 151 Chapel St., K1N 7Y2. ☎ (613) 789-1818. Fax 789-3494. Exec. Dir. Ann Lynn Lipton.
Jewish Social Services Agency. ☎ (613) 235 6000.
Jewish Students' Union. ☎ (613) 232-7306.
Vaad Ha'ir (Jewish Com. Council), 151 Chapel St. ☎ (613) 232-7306. Exec. Dir.: Gerry Koffman and Vaad Hakashruth (Fax (613) 563-4593).
Israel Embassy, Suite 601, 410 Laurier Av. W., K1R 7T3. (613) ☎ 237-6450.

Synagogues & Religious Organisations
Adath Shalom Cong. (O), ☎ 613-228-0574.
Beth Shalom (O), 151 Chapel St., K1N 7Y2. ☎ (613) 789-3501.
Beth Shalom West (O), 15 Chartwell Av., Nepean, K2G 4K3. ☎ (613) 723-1800.
Chabad Hse., 25 Esquimault Av., K2H 6Z5. ☎ (613) 820-9484.
Machzikei Hadas (O), 2310 Virginia Dr., K1N 6S2. ☎ (613) 521-9700.
Young Israel of Ottawa (O), 627 Kirkwood Av., K1Z 5X5. ☎ (613) 722-8394.
Agudath Israel (C), 1400 Coldrey Av., K1Z 7P9. ☎ (613) 728-3501.
Temple Israel (R), 1301 Prince of Wales Dr., K2C 1N2. ☎ (613) 224-1802.
Newspaper: Ottawa Jewish Bulletin & Review. ☎ (613) 789-7306. Fax (613) 789-4593.
Club: Rideau View Golf & Country Club, Pres.: D. Molot, 185 Metcalfe St., Manotick. ☎ (613) 692-4112.

Kosher Meals
JCC Drop-In-Diner, 151 Chapel St. ☎ (613) 789-1818. Tuesdays 12.00-1.30 p.m.

Kosher Meat, etc.
(K) United Kosher Meat & Deli Ltd., 378 Richmond Rd. ☎ (613) 722-6556. (Meals & sandwiches available on week-days.)
(K) Kosher bread & other products are available from Rideau Bakery, 384 Rideau St. ☎ (613) 234-1019, & 1666 Bank St. ☎ (613) 737-3355.

OWEN SOUND
Beth Ezekiel (C), 3531 Bay Shore Rd., N4K 5N3. ☎ (519) 376-8774.

PEMBROKE
Syn.: Beth Israel, 322 William St., K8A 1P3. ☎ (613) 732-7811.

PETERBOROUGH
Syn.: Beth Israel (C), Waller St. ☎ (705) 745-8398.

ST. CATHARINE'S
Syns.: B'nai Israel (T), 190 Church St., L2R 4C4. ☎ (905) 685-6767. Fax (905) 685-3100; Temple Tikvah (R), 83 Church St., P.O.B. 484., L2R 3C7. ☎ (905) 682-4191.
Com. Centre, Newman Memorial Bldg. ☎ (905) 685-6767.

SUDBURY
Syn.: Shaar Hashomayim (O), 158 John St., P3E 1P4. ☎ (705) 673-0831.

continued from *Ontario*

THORNHILL

Syn.: Beth Avraham Yaakov of Tor (O), 613 Clark Av. W. L4J 3E3. ☎ (905) 886-3810; Chabad Lubavitch Com. Centre (O), 770 Chabad Gate, L4J 3V9. ☎ (905) 731-7000; Chabad Lubavitch of Markham, 135 Holm Cres., L3T 5J4. ☎ (905) 881-2012; B'nai Shalom N. (C), 275 Arnold Av., L4J 1C3. ☎ (905) 731-2797; Shaar Shalom (C), 2 Simonston Blvd., L3T 4L1. ☎ (905) 889-4975; Temple Har Zion (R), 7360 Bayview Av., L3T 2R7. ☎ (905) 889-2252; Temple Kol Ami (R), 36 Atkinson Av., L4J 9C9. ☎ (905) 709-1895. Bookseller: Israel's The Judaica Centre, 441 Clark Av. W., L4J 6W7. ☎ (905) 881-1010.

THUNDER BAY

Syn.: Shaarey Shomayim (O), 627 Gray St. P7E 2E4. ☎ (416) 622 4867.

TORONTO

Representative Organisations

B'nai B'rith, 15 Hove St., Downsview, M3H 4Y8. ☎ (416) 633-6224. Fax (416) 630-2159.

Canadian Council of Reform Judaism, 36 Atkinson Av., Thornhill, L4J 8C9. ☎ (905) 709-2275. Exec. Dir.: Rabbi Daniel K. Gottlieb.

Canadian Jewish Congress (Ontario Region), 4600 Bathurst St., North York, M2R 3V2. ☎ (416) 635-2883. Fax (416) 635-1408. Exec. Dir.: Manuel Prutschi. Also at this address: Jewish Federation of Greater Toronto, ☎ (416) 635-2883. Exec. Dir.: A. G. Reitzes; Rabbinical Vaad Hakashrut, ☎ (416) 635-9550. Exec. Dir.: Rabbi M. Levin (All enquiries re Kashrut here); National Council of Jewish Women of Canada, 4700 Bathurst St. National Office: 1111 Finch Av. W. ☎ (416) 633-5100.

Council of Jewish Feds., ☎ (416) 635-2883 Ext 168.

Synagogues & Religious Organisations

Orthodox: Agudath Israel, 129 McGilvray Av., M5M 2Y7. (416) 789-5514; Anshei Minsk, 12 St. Andrew's St., M5T 1K6. ☎ (416) 593-9892; Associated Hebrew Schools Chapel, 3636 Bathurst St., M6A 2E3. ☎ (416) 789-7471; Associated Hebrew Schools Chapel, 252 Finch Av. W., M2R 1M9. ☎ (416) 223-4845; Baycrest Centre Syn., 3560 Bathurst St., M6A 2E1. ☎ (416) 789-5131; Beach Hebrew Institute Syn., 109 Kenilworth Av., M4L 3S4. ☎ (416) 967-6379; Beth Abraham, 55 Ameer Av., M6A 2Z1. ☎ (416) 789-5131; Beth Jacob V'Anshe Drildz, 147 Overbrook Pl., Downsview, M3H 4R1. ☎ (416) 638-5955; Beth Lida Forest Hill Syn., 22 Gilgorm Rd., M5N 2M5. ☎ (416) 489-2550; B'nai Akiva Yeshiva Cong., 159 Almore Av., M3H 2M9. ☎ (416) 630-6772; Chevra Shass, 3545 Bathurst St., M6A 2C7. ☎ (416) 781-7126; Cong. Bais Moshe, 81 Bannockburn Av., M6M 2M9. ☎ (416) 781-6421; Cong. B'nai Torah, 465 Patricia Av., Willowdale, M2R 2N1. ☎ (416) 226-3700; Chasedei Bobov, 3703 Bathurst St., M6H 2E8. ☎ (416) 789-0971; JEP/OHR Somayach Centre of Jewish Learning, 2939 Bathurst St., M6B 2B2. ☎ (416) 785-5899; Kehillat Shaarei Torah, 2640 Bayview Av., Willowdale, M2L 1B7. ☎ (416) 229-2600; Keser Torah, 3387 Bathurst St., M6A 2B8; Kielcer Cong., 2941 Bathurst St., M6B 3B2. ☎ (416) 783-0522; Kiever Cong., 25 Bellevue Av., M6P 1W2. ☎ (416) 593-9702; Kol Yaakov Anshei Emes, 20 Brunswick Av., M5S 2L7. ☎ (416) 635-8478;

Kolel Averichim, 515 Coldstream Av., M6B 2K7. ☎ (416) 789-1853; Clanton Park, 11 Lowesmoor Av., Downsview, M3H 3H6. ☎ (416) 633-4193; Magen David Sephardic Cong., 10 McAllister Rd., Downsview, M3H 2M9. ☎ (416) 636-0865; Minyan Avreichem, 2919 Bathurst St., M6B 3B1. ☎ (416) 789-

continued from *Toronto*

4731; Minyan Sepharad, 475 Patricia Av., Willowdale, M2R 2N1. ☎ (416) 226-3145; Mishkan Avraham, 45 Canyon Av., Downsview, M3H 3S4. ☎ (416) 630-772; Moriah, 65 Waterloo Av., Downsview, M3H 3Y1. ☎ (416) 636-9707; Or Haemet Sephardic School, 37 Southbourne Av., Downsview, M3H 1A4. ☎ (416) 635-9881; Petah Tikva Anshe Castilla, 20 Danby Av., Downsview, M3H 2J3. ☎ (416) 636-4719; Shaarei Shomayim Cong., 470 Glencairn Av., M5N 1V8. ☎ (416) 789-3213; Shaare Tefillah, 3600 Bathurst St., M6A 2C9. ☎ (416) 787-1631; Shaarei Zion Assoc. Hebrew, 6100 Leslie St., Willowdale, M2H 3J1. ☎ (416) 494-7666; Shomer Israel Cong., 60 Rockford Rd., Willowdale, M2R 3A7. ☎ (416) 665-4815; Shomrei Shabboth Chevra Mishnayoth, 583 Glengrove Av. W., M6B 2H5. ☎ (416) 782-8849; Tiferet Israel, 756 Sheppard Av. W., Downsview, M3H 2S8. ☎ (416) 635-7435; Torath Emeth Jewish Centre, 1 Viewmount Av., M6B 1T2. ☎ (416) 782-9621; Yavneh Zion, 788 Marlee Av., M6B 3J9. ☎ (416) 781-1611; Yeshiva Limudei Hashem Cong., 517 Glengarry Av., M5M 1G2. ☎ (416) 783-2494; Yeshiva Torath Chaim, 475 Lawrence Av., W., M5M 1C6. ☎ (416) 781-6941; Zichron Shneur, 2801-3 Bathurst St., M6B 3A4. ☎ (416) 781-0136.

Conservative: Adath Israel, 37 Southbourne Av., M3H 1A4. ☎ (416) 635-5340; Beth David B'nai Israel Beth Am, 55 Yeomans Rd., Downsview, M3H 3J7. ☎ (416) 633-5500; Beth Emeth Bais Yehuda, 100 Elder St., Downsview, M3H 5G7. ☎ (416) 633-3838; Beth Sholom, 1445 Eglinton Av. W., M6C 2E6. ☎ (416) 783-6103; Beth Tikvah, 3080 Bayview Av., Willowdale, M2N 5L3. ☎ (416) 221-3433; Beth Torah, 47 Glenbrook Av., M6B 2L7. ☎ (416) 782-4495; Beth Tzedec, 1700 Bathurst St., M5P 3K3. ☎ (416) 781-3511; Beit Rayim, 9711 Bayview Av., Richmond Hill, L4J 9X7. ☎ (905) 764-2949.

Reform: Baycrest Terrace Reform Cong., 55 Ameer Av., M6A 2Z1. ☎ (416) 789-5131; Holy Blossom Temple, 1950 Bathurst St., M5P 3K9. ☎ (416) 789-3291; Temple Emanu-El, 120 Old Colony Rd., Willowdale, M2L 2K2. ☎ (416) 449-3872; Temple Sinai, 210 Wilson Av., M5M 3B1. ☎ (416) 487-4161; Or Hadash, 1110 Stellar Dr., Unit 10, Newmarket, L37 7B7. ☎ (905) 764-2949.

Other: Adath Sholom, 864 Sheppard Av. W., Downsview, M3H 2T5. ☎ (416) 635-0131; Bernard Betel Centre, 1003 Steeles Av. W., Willowdale M2R 3T6. ☎ (416) 225-2112; Beth Knesseth Anshei Stashov, Slipia, 11 Sultana Av., M6A 1S9. ☎ (416) 661-8323; Beth Radom Cong., 18 Reiner Rd., Downsview, M3H 2K9. ☎ (41) 636-3451; Cong. Beth Habonim, 12 Hollaman Rd., M6B 3B8. ☎ (416) 782-5125; Darchei Noam (Rec), 15 Hove St., Downsview, M3H 4YB. ☎ (416) 638-4783; First Narayever Egalitarian Minyan, 187-189 Brunswick Av., M5S 2M4. ☎ (416) 487-4951; Knesseth Israel, 52 Maria St., M6P 1W2. ☎ (416) 967-1019; Lodzer Centre Holocaust Cong., 12 Heaton St., Downsview, M3H 4Y6. ☎ (416) 636-6665; Pride of Israel Temple, 59 Lissom Cres., Willowdale, M2R 2P2. ☎ (416) 661-0505.

Cultural & Educational Organisations

Board of Jewish Education, 4600 Bathurst St., Willowdale, M2R 3V2. ☎ (416) 633-7770. Exec. Dir.: Rabbi I. Witty.

Holocaust Education & Memorial Centre, 4600 Bathurst St., Willowdale, M2R 3V2. ☎ (416) 635-2883.

Jewish Inf. Service, 4600 Bathurst St., Suite 345, Willowdale, M2R 3V2. ☎ (416) 635-5600. Fax (416) 631-5715. Publishes a 'Jewish Communtiy of Services Directory for Greater Toronto'.

Jewish Public Library. See entry above.

Welfare Organisations, Hospitals, etc.

Jewish Assistance Services, 4600 Bathurst St., Willowdale, M2R 3V2. ☎ (416) 635-1217.

continued from *Toronto*

Jewish Family & Child Service, 4600 Bathurst St., Willowdale, M2R 3V2. ☎ (416) 638-7800.
Baycrest Centre for Geriatric Care, 3560 Bathurst St. ☎ 789-5131.
Jewish Immigrant Aid Services, 4600 Bathurst St., Willowdale, M2R 3V2. ☎ (416) 630-6481.
Mount Sinai Hospital, 600 University Av., M5G 1X5.

Student & Youth Organisations
Jewish Students Union (at the University of Toronto), 604 Spadina Av. ☎ (416) 923-9861.
Jewish Camp Council, 3995 Bathurst St., #200, M3H 5U3. ☎ (416) 630 1180.
Bathurst Jewish Centre, 4588 Bathurst St., Willowdale. ☎ (416) 636-1880. Also at 750 Spadina Av. ☎ (416) 924-6211.
York University Jewish Student Federation, Room 442, York University, 4700 Keele St., Downsview. ☎ (416) 736-5178.

Zionist Organisations
Borochov Centre, 272 Codsell Av., Downsview, M3H 3X2. ☎ (416) 636-4021.
Canadian Zionist Fed., 3995 Bathurst St., Suite 300, M3H 5U3. ☎ (416) 663-3988.
Hadassah, 638 "A" Sheppard Av. West. ☎ (416) 630-8373.
Hapoel Hamizrachi, 3101 Bathurst St., #503, M5A 2A6.
Hashomer Hatzair, 181 Cocksfield Av., Downsview.
Jewish National Fund, 4600 Bathurst St., M2R 3V2. ☎ (416) 638-7200.
Labour Zionist Movement & Histadrut Campaign, 272 Codsell Av., Downsview
Toronto Zionist Council, 788 Marlee Av. ☎ (416) 781-3571.
United Israel Appeal of Canada, 4600 Bathurst St., Willowdale, M2R 3V2. ☎ (416) 636-7655. Exec. Dir.: S. Ain.
United Jewish Appeal. Same address as above. ☎ (416) 635-2883.
Israel Consulate, 180 Bloor St., W., Suite 700. ☎ (416) 961-1126.

Newspapers
Canadian Jewish News, 10 Gateway Blvd., Suite 420, Don Mills, M3C 3A1. ☎ (416) 422-2331. Fax (416) 422-3790.
Jewish Tribune, 15 Hove St., Downsview, M3H 4Y8. ☎ (416) 633-6227. Fax (416) 630-2159.
Shefner Communications Group publish "Ha Mekomon" a semi-monthly Hebrew newspaper, and "Jewish Life" (monthly). 2828, Bathurst St., Suite 604, M6B 3A7. ☎ (416) 782-3017. Fax. (416) 782-9981.

Booksellers, etc.
Israel's, The Judaica Centre, 897 Eglinton Av. W., M6C 2C1. ☎ (416) 256-2858. Also, 441 Clark Av., Thornhill, Ont. ☎ (905) 881-1010.
Miriam's, 3007 Bathurst St. ☎ (416) 781-8261.
Negev Importing Co. Ltd., 3509 Bathurst St., M6A 2C5. ☎ (416) 781-9356.
Pardes Hebrew Book Shop, 4119 Bathurst St. ☎ (416) 633-7113.
Zucker's Books & Art, 3453 Bathurst St.

Restaurants & Delicatessen
(K) Bagels Galore (dairy, take-out), First Canadian Pl., M5X 1E1. ☎ (416) 363-4233.
(K) Brooklyn Pizza, (dairy) 3028 Bathurst St., M6B 3B6. ☎ (416) 256-1477.
(K) Cafe Sheli (dairy) 441 Clark Av. W., L4J 6W8. ☎ (416) 905 886-7450.
(K) Chicken Nest, 3038 Bathurst St., M6B 4K2. ☎ (416) 787-6378.
(K) Dairy Treats Cafe, (dairy) 3522 Bathurst St., M6A 2C6. ☎ (416) 787-0309

continued from *Toronto*

(K) Hakerem, 1045 Steeles Av. W., Willowdale, M2R 2S9. ☎ (416) 736-7227.
(K) King David Pizza North, (dairy) 7000 Bathurst St., Thornhill, L4J 7L1. ☎ (905) 669-0660.
(K) King David Pizza, (dairy) 3020 Bathurst St., M6B 2B6. ☎ (416) 781-1326.
(K) King Solomon's Table, 3710 Chesswood Dr., Downs, M3J 2W4. ☎ (416) 630-0666.
(K) Kosher Facilities, York University, 4700 Keele St., Downsview, M3Y 1P3. ☎ (416) 736-5965.
(K) Kosher Hut, 3428 Bathurst St., M6A 2C2. ☎ (416) 787-7999.
(K) Marky's Delicatessen, 280 Wilson Av., Downsview. ☎ (416) 638-1081.
(K) Marky's Delicatessen (North), 7330 Yonge St., Thornhill, L4J 1V8. ☎ (905) 731-4800.
(K) Mati's Fallafel House (dairy products only), 3430 Bathurst St., M6A 1C2. ☎ (416) 783-9505.
(K) Milk'n Honey (dairy), 3457 Bathurst St., Downsview, M6A 2C5. ☎ (416) 789-7651
(K) My Zaidy's Cafe, (dairy) 7241 Bathurst St., Thornhill, L4J 6J8. ☎ (905) 731-3831.
(K) My Zaidy's Pizza (North), (dairy) 441 Clark Av., Thornhill, L4J 6W8. ☎ (905) 731-3029.
(K) My Zaidy's Pizza, 3456 Bathurst St., Downsview. ☎ (416) 789-0785.
(K) Not Just Yoghurt (dairy), 800 Steeles Av. W., Thornhill, L4J 7L2. ☎ (905) 738-1322.
(K) Tovli Pizza , 5792 Bathurst St., Willowdale, M2R 1Z1. ☎ (416) 650-9800.
(K) Wok'n'Deli, 441 Clarke Av. W., Thornhill, L4J 6W7. ☎ (905) 882-0809.

WINDSOR

Syns.: Shaar Hashomayim (O), 115 Giles Blvd. E., N9A 4C1. ☎ (519) 256-3123; Shaarey Zedek (O), 610 Giles Blvd. E., N9A 4E2. ☎ (519) 252-1594; Cong. Beth-El (R), 2525 Mark Av., N9E 2W2. ☎ (519) 969-2422.
Jewish Com. Council, 1641 Ouellette Av. Ont. N8X 1K9. Exec. Dir.: Steven Brownstein. ☎ (519) 973-1772.
Windsor Jewish Community Bulletin, Fax (519) 973-1774.

QUEBEC
MONTREAL
Representative Organisations
B'nai B'rith, 6900 Decarie Blvd., Suite 219, HBW 2W8. ☎ (514) 733-5377. Fax (514) 342-9632.
Canadian Jewish Congress National Headquarters, Samuel Bronfman Hse., 1590 Dr. Penfield Av., H3G 1C5. ☎ (514) 931-7531. Fax (514) 931-3281. Publishes National Synagogue Directory.
Federation CJA, 5151, ch. de la Côte Ste-Catherine, Montreal H3W 1M6. ☎ (514) 735-3541.
Operates Jewish Information & Referral Service (JIRS) (737-2221).
Jewish Com. Council, 5491 Victoria Av., Suite 117, H3W 2P9. ☎ (514) 739-6363.
National Council of Jewish Women, Room 102, 5775 Victoria Av., H3W 2R3. ☎ (514) 733-7589.

Synagogues & Religious Organisations
Orthodox: Adath Israel Poale Zedek Cong., 223 Harrow Cres., Hampstead, H3X 2X7. ☎ (514) 482-4252.

continued from *Quebec*

Anshei Ozeroff, 5380 Bourret St., H3X 1J2. ☎ (514) 738-2012.
Beth Hamedrash Hagadol, 4605 Mackenzie St., H3W 1B2. ☎ (514) 733-5356.
Beth Hazichoron, 3910 de Courtrai Av., H3S 1C1. ☎ (514) 733-8007.
Beth Hillel, 6230 Coolbrook Av., H3X 2M8. ☎ (515) 731-8707.
Beth Israel Beth Aaron Cong., 6800 Mackle Rd., Côte St. Luc, H4W 1A4. ☎ (514) 487-1323.
Beth Tikvah, 136 Westpark Blvd., Dollard des Ormeaux, H9A 2K2. ☎ (514) 683-5610.
Beth Zion, 5740 Hudson Av., Côte St. Luc, H4W 2K5. ☎ (514) 489-8411.
Chabad House, 3429 Peel St., H3A 1W7. ☎ (514) 288-3130.
Chevra Kadisha, 5237 Clanranald Av., H3X 2S5. ☎ (514) 482-3366.
Chevra Mishnais Jacob Joseph, 715 du Sablon Av., Chomedey, H7W 4H5. ☎ (514) 681-5844.
Chevra Shas Shevet Achim, 5855 Lavoie St., H3W 2K1. ☎ (514) 731-3231.
Chevra Thillim-Pinsker Kinyan Torah, 1904 Van Horne Av., H3S 1N7. ☎ (514) 737-6206.
Cong. Beth Ora, 2600 Badeaux St., Ville St. Laurent, H4M 1M5. ☎ (514) 748-6559.
Shomrim Laboker, 5150 Plamondon Av., H3W 1G1. ☎ (514) 731-6831.
Tifereth Beth David Jerusalem, 6519 Baily Rd., Cote St. Luc, H4V 1A1. ☎ (514) 489-3841.
Young Israel of Chomedey, 1025 Elizabeth Blvd., H7W 3J7. ☎ (514) 681-2571.
Young Israel of Montreal, 6235 Hillsdale Rd., H3S 2M8. ☎ (514) 737-6589.
Young Israel of Val Royal, 2855 Victor Dore, Ville St. Laurent, H3M 1T1. ☎ (514) 334-4610.
Zichron Kedoshim, 5215 Westbury Av., H3W 2W4. ☎ (514) 735-2113.

Orthodox Sephardi:
Beth Menouha, Adath Yeshurun, 5855 Lavoie St., H3W 2K1. ☎ (514) 739-7142.
Beth Yossef, 6235 Hillsdale Rd., H3S 2M8. ☎ (514) 737-6589.
Centre Communautaire Juif-YMHA, 5480 Westbury Av., H3W 3G2. ☎ (514) 735-5565.
Communauté Sépharade de Chomedey 4880 Du Souvenier, Chomedey, H7W 1C9. ☎ 514-682-2467.
Communauté Sépharade de Laval, 4860 Notre Dame Blvd., Chomedey, H7W 1V4. ☎ (514) 682-6606.
Communauté Sépharade Petah Tikvah, 2650 St. Louis St., Ville St. Laurent, H4M 1P8. ☎ (514) 744-3434.
Em Habanim, 6655 Côte des Neiges, H3S 2B4, ☎ (514) 731-0534.
Hekhal Shalom, 825 Gratton St., Ville St. Laurent, H4M 2G4. ☎ (514) 747-4530.
Kol Yehouda, 6501 Baily Rd., Côte St. Luc, H4V 1A1. ☎ (514) 481-4859.
Maghen David, 4691 Van Horne Av., H3W 1H8. ☎ (514) 731-1960.
Ohel Yaacov, 3541 Van Horne Av., H3S 1R7. ☎ (514) 733-3212.
Or Hahayim, 5700 Einstein Av., Cote St. Luc, H4W 1V3. ☎ (514) 489-1301.
Rabbinat Sépharade du Quebec, 5850 Victoria Av., H3W 2R5. ☎ (514) 738-1004.
Spanish & Portuguese Syn., 4894 St. Kevin Av., H3W 1P2. ☎ (514) 737-3695.
Traditional: Shaar Hashomayim, 450 Kensington Av., Westmount, H3Y 3A2. ☎ (514) 937-9471.
Conservative: Beth El, 1000 Lucerne Rd., Mount Royal, H3R 2H9. ☎ (514) 738-4766.

continued from *Quebec*

Shaare Zedek, 5305 Rosedale Av., H4V 2H7. ☎ (514) 484-1122.
Shaare Zion, 5575 Cote St. Luc Rd., H3X 2C9. ☎ (514) 481-7727.
Reform: Temple Emanu-El Beth Shalom, 4100 Sherbrooke St. W., Westmount, H3Z 1A5. ☎ (514) 937-3575.
Reconstructionist: Cong. Dorshei Emet, 18 Cleve Rd., Hampstead, H3X 1A6. ☎ (514) 486-9400.

Cultural & Educational Organisations
Golden Age Association, 5700 Westbury, H3W 3E8. ☎ 739-4731.
Jewish Education Council of Montreal, 5151 Chemin de la Côte Ste.-Catherine, H3W 1M6. ☎ (514) 345-2610, will provide full inf. about schools.
Jewish Public Library, 5151 Côte St. Catherine Rd., H3W 1M6. ☎ (514) 345-2627. There are branches in other parts of Montreal.
Saidye Bronfman Centre, 5170 Côte St. Catherine Rd., H3W 1M7. ☎ (514) 739-2301.
Montreal Holocaust Memorial Center, 5151 Côte St., Catherine Rd., H3W 1M6. ☎ (514) 735-2386.

Welfare Organisations, Hospitals, etc.
Federation CJA, 5151 Côte St. Catherine Rd., H3W 1M6. ☎ (514) 735-3541.
Jewish Rehabilitation Hospital, 3205 Alton Goldbloom Place, Chomedey, H7V 1R2. ☎ (514) 688-9550.
Jewish Family Services Social Service Centre, 5250 Decarie Blvd. H3X 2H9 ☎ (514) 485-1112.
Jewish General Hospital, 3755 Côte St. Catherine Rd, H3T 1E2. ☎ (514) 340-8222.
Jewish Hospital of Hope, 5725 Victoria, H3W 3H6.
Jewish Immigrant Aid Services of Canada, 5151 Côte St. Catherine Rd. H3W 1M6. ☎ (514) 342-9351.
Maimonides Hospital & Home for the Aged, 5795 Caldwell, Côte St. Luc. H4W 1W3. ☎ (514) 483-2121.

Student & Youth Organisations
Association of Young Jewish Adults. ☎ (514) 342-0289.
B'nai B'rith Hillel Foundation, 3460 Stanley St. H3A 1R8. ☎ (514) 845-9171.
B'nai B'rith Youth Org., 6900 Decarie Blvd., H3X 2T8. ☎ (514) 733-8221.
Y.M. & Y.W.H.A., 5500 Westbury Av., H3W 2W8. ☎ (514) 737-6551.
Federation CJA.Young Adult Division., 5151 Côte St. Catherine Rd., H3W 1M6. ☎ (514) 735-3541.

Zionist Organisations
Bnei Akiva, 5250, Decarie Blvd., (Suite 550), H3X 2H9. ☎ (514) 486-9526.
Hadassah-WIZO Org., 1310 Greene Av. Westmount, H3Z 2B8. ☎ (514) 937-9431.
Jewish National Fund, 1980 Sherbrooke St. W., Suite 500, H3H 2M7. ☎ (514) 934-0313.
Mizrachi Hapoel-Hamizrachi Org. of Canada, 5250 Decarie Blvd., H3X 2H9. ☎ (514) 483-3660.
Canadian Zionist Fed., 5250 Decarie Blvd., Suite 550, H3X 2H9. ☎ (514) 486-9526.
Kotel, 6414 Victoria Av., H3W 2S6. ☎ (514) 739-4142.
Israel Consulate-General, Suite 2620, 1155 René Lévesque Blvd., West, H3B 4J5. ☎ (514) 393-9372.
Newspaper : Canadian Jewish News, 6900 Decarie Blvd., #341, H3X 2T8. ☎ (514) 735-2612.

continued from *Quebec*

Booksellers, etc.

Kotel, 6414 Victoria Av., H3W 2S6. ☎ (514) 739-4142.
Rabbi J. Rodal's Hebrew Book Store & Gift Shop, 5689 Van Horne Av., H3W 1H8. ☎ (514) 733-1876.
Victoria Gift Shop, 5875 Victoria Av. H3W 2R6. ☎ (514) 738-1414.

Restaurants

(K) B'nai B'rith Hillel Foundation, 3460 Stanley St. ☎ 845-9171.
(K) Chabad Hse., 3429 Peel St. ☎ (514) 842-6616.
(K) Ernie & Elie's Place, 6900 Decarie Blvd., H3X 2T8. ☎ (514) 344-4444.
(K) El Morocco II, 3450 Drummond St. ☎ (514) 844-6888 & 844-0203.
(K) Foxy's, 5987A Victoria Av. ☎ (514) 739-8777.
(K) Golden Age Cafeteria, 5700 Westbury Av., H3W 3EB. ☎ (514) 739-4731.
(K) Golden Spoon (Cuiller d'or) 5217 Decarie Blvd. ☎ (514) 481-3431.
(K) Kotel 1422 Stanley St., H3W 3E8. ☎ (514) 739-4731.
(K) Kotel Restaurant, 3429 Peel. ☎ (514) 987-9875.
(K) L'Elysée Dame, 70 Notre Dame. ☎ (514) 842-6016.
(K) La Casa Linga, 5095 Queen Mary, H3W 1X4. ☎ (514) 737-2272. (Dairy).
(K) Le Passeport, 5071 Queen Mary, H3W 1X4. ☎ (514) 733-4768. (Meat).
(K) Odelia Snack Bar, 5897A Victoria Av. ☎ (514) 733-0984.
(K) Pizza Pita, 5710 Victoria Av. ☎ (514) 731-7482; 2145 St.Louis, Ville St. Laurent.
(K) Y.M.H.A. Cafeteria, 5500 Westbury Av. ☎ (514) 737-8704.
All the kosher establishments listed here are under the supervision of the Jewish Community Council of Montreal. In addition the Council supervises some 31 butchers, as well as bakeries, caterers, etc.
Visitors requiring additional inf. about kosher establishments, food, etc., should contact the Exec. Dir., Jewish Community Council (Vaad Ha'ir), Room 117, 5491 Victoria Av. ☎ (514) 739-6363. Fax (514) 739-7024.

QUEBEC CITY

Syn.: Beth Israel Ohev Sholom, 20 Cremazie St. E., G1R 1Y2. ☎ (418) 523-7346.

STE. AGATHE-DES-MONTS

Syn.: House of Israel Cong., 31 Albert St., J8C 1Z6. ☎ (819) 326-4320.
Mount Sinai Hospital, 5690 Cavendish Blvd., Cote St. Luc, Quebec H4W 1S7.

SASKATCHEWAN

MOOSE JAW

Syn.: Moose Jaw Hebrew Com. (C), 937 Henry St., S6H 3H1. ☎ (306) 692-1644.

REGINA

Syn.: Beth Jacob (O), 4715 McTavish St., S4S 6H2. ☎ (306) 757-8643. Fax (306) 352-3499; Temple Beth Tikvah (R), Box 33048, Cathedral Post Office, S4T 7X2. ☎ (306) 761-2218.

SASKATOON

Syn.: Agudas Israel (C), 715 McKinnon Av., S7H 2G2. ☎ (306) 343-7023; Rabbi ☎ (306) 343-6960. Fax (306) 343-1244. Rabbi R. Pavey, formerly of Southend-on-Sea, will be pleased to welcome visitors.

CANARY ISLANDS
(See Spain)

CAYMAN ISLANDS

There are approx. 40 members of the Jewish Com. in the 3 Cayman Islands, nearly all living on Grand Cayman. They are joined by about 30 others who are regular visitors. Services in private homes. Cont. Harvey DeSouza, P.O. Box 72, Grand Cayman, Cayman Islands, British West Indies.

CHILE

The Jewish population is 22,000, of whom the great majority live in Santiago, the capital, and its environs. There are some Jewish families in Antafugasta, Arica, Chuquicamata, Concepción and Puerto Montt.

ARICA
Sociedad Israelita Dr Herzl, Casilla 501.

CONCEPCIÓN
Communidad Israelita, 111. Religious leader: Americo Grünwald.

IQUIQUE
Comunidad Israelita, Playa Ligade 3263, Playa Brava.

LA SERENA
Com. Centre, Cordovez 652.

RANCAGUA
Comunidad Israelita, Casilla 890

SANTIAGO
Communal Headquarters (Comite Representativo de las Entidades Judias de Chile), Miguel Claro 196. ☎ 2358669.
Synagogues
Bicur Joilim (O), Av. Matte 624.
Comunidad Israelita de Santiago (Ashk) Rabbi Eduardo Wainsgortín, Serrano 214-218. ☎ 639387.
Jafets Jayim (O) (Rabbi Itzhak Shaked), Miguel Claro 196.
Maguen David (Seph), Av. R. Lyon 812.
Maze (Hungarian), Pedro Bannen 0166. ☎ 2742536.
Sociedad Cultural Israelita B'ne Jisroel (German), Portugal 810. ☎ 221993. (Rabbi Efraim Rosenzweig)
Jabad Lubavitch. Rabbi Menashe Perman, E. Yanez, Gloria 62 (Las Condes). ☎ 228-2240.
Homes for Aged: Hogar Israelita de Ancianos Abrahamy Malvina Wainstein, Francisco de Villagra 325, Los Guindos; Cisroco Maipu 525.
Maccabi, Av. las Condes 8361.
WIZO, M. Montt 207.
Zionist Offices: Federacion Sionista de Chile, Merced 136. ☎ 382248.

Israel Embassy, San Sebastian 2812, Casilla 1224. ☎ 2461570.

Restaurant
La Idishe Mama, M. Montt 1273 (Esquina Bilbao). ☎ 2098131.

TEMUCO
Comunidad Israelita, General Cruz 355.

VALDIVIA
Com. Centre. Arauco 136 E.

VALPARAISO
Comunidad Israelita, Rabbi Dr. L Cogan. Alvarez 490, Vina del Mar. ☎ 680373.

COLOMBIA
(Jewish population approx. 8,000)

BARANQUILLA
Centro Israelita Filantropico, Carrera 43, No. 85-95, Apartado Aereo 2537. ☎ 342310 & 351197. ☎ 344514. Pres.: Jaime Eisenband.
Comunidad Hebrea Sefaradita, Carrera 55 No. 74-71. Apartado Aereo 51351. ☎ 340054 & 340050. Rabbi Meir Botton. Pres.: Eli Suez.
School: Colegio Hebreo Union, Carrera 43 No. 85-95. Apartado Aereo 3656. ☎ 354369. Pres.: Victor Levy.

BOGOTA
Synagogues
Asociacion Israelita Montefiore (German), Carrera 20 No. 37-54. ☎ 245-5264. Pres.: Abraham Bibliowicz.
Centro Israelita de Bogota (Ashkenazi), Transversal 29, No. 126-31. ☎ 274-9069. Rabbi Alfredo Goldschmidt. Pres.: Dr. Leon Birbragher.
(K) Kosher meals available by prior arrangement with Rabbi Goldschmidt. ☎ 218-2500.
Congregacion Adath Israel, Carrera 7a, No. 94-20. ☎ 257-1660 & 257-1680. Mikva on premises. Rabbi Alfredo Goldschmidt. Pres.: Benjamin Korc.
Comunidad Hebrea Sefaradi, Calle 79, No. 9-66. ☎ 256-2629 & 249-0372. Mikva on premises. Rabbi Abraham Benchimol. Pres.: David Cohen.
Jabad (Chabad) House, Calle 92, No. 10, Apt. 405. ☎ 36408. Rabbi Joshua Rosenfeld. Calle 92, No. 10-49/400. ☎ 257-4920.
Colegio Colombo Hebreo, Diag. 154 No. 46-65. Apartado Aereo 51775. ☎ 671-1303 & 4991.
Confederación de Asociacones Judias de Colombia, Transversal 29, No. 126-31. ☎ 274-9069. Pres.: Leon Birbragher.
Union Rabinica Colombiana, (Orthodox). Same address as Confederación above. ☎ 274-9069 or 218-2500. Ch.: Rabbi Alfredo Goldschmidt.
Jewish Monthly: 'Menorah', Apartado Aereo 9081. Dir.: Eliecer Celnik.
Israel Embassy, Calle 35, No. 7-25, Edificio Caxdax. ☎ 245-6603 & 245-6712.

CALI
The Jewish population totals some 2,000.
Union Federal Hebrea. Pres.: Julio Werthaimer. Apartado Aereo 8918 Cali. ☎ 443-1814. Fax 444-5544. Rabbi: Ioseph Benchimol. ☎ 665-5419. Fax 665-5419. An umbrella organisation co-ordinating all Jewish activities in Cali.
Centro Israelita de Beneficiencia (Sephardi), Calle 44A, Av. 5a Norte Esquina. Apartado Aereo 77, Cali. ☎ 664-1379. Fax 665-5419. Pres.: Salomon Levy.
Sociedad Hebrea de Socoros (Ashekenazi), Av. 9a Norte #10-15. Apartado Aereo 011652 Cali. ☎ 668-8518. Fax 668-8521. Pres.: Ezequiel Birman.
Union Cultural Israelita (German), Apartado Aereo 5552. Cali. ☎ 668-9830. Fax 661-6857. Pres.: Daniel Feldsberg.
Jewish Country Club, Asociaccion Campestre Shalom, Av. la Maria, Pance, Cali. ☎ 555-1166. Fax 555-1749.

MEDELLIN

Union Israelita de Beneficencia, Carrera 43B No. 15-150, Apartado Aereo 4702. ☎ 668560. Pres.: Dr. Benjamin Rabinowich.
Jewish Day School: Colegio Hebreo Teodoro Herzl, Apartado Aereo 4378. ☎ 366697 & 366717. Pres.: Dr. Arturo Yanovich.

COMMONWEALTH OF INDEPENDENT STATES
(i.e. Remnant of the former U.S.S.R.)

A selection of information provided by the Commission on Jewish Education in the Republics of the former Soviet Union has been used as a first step in increasing coverage of these areas now that Jewish communal life is beginning to burgeon again.

Note: The break up of the Soviet Union into its separate republics signalled by the resistance to the attempted coup of August 1991 far outruns our capacity to retain contact with appropriate authorities and to give current information under new headings such as Latvia, Georgia etc.

The latest Soviet census, taken in 1989, gave the Jewish population of the U.S.S.R. as 1,450.000 Emigration and Aliyah in the past five years has hastened the lowering of this figure.

In Moscow alone there were estimated to be about 250,000 Jews.

The list of synagogues given below is complete as far as can be ascertained. It must be pointed out, however, that not all the cities and towns where a synagogue is listed are open to tourists, and even where they are, the synagogue is often difficult to find. Intending visitors must check with Intourist which areas may be visited. The Intourist London Office is at 219 Marsh Wall, Isle of Dogs, E14 9PD. ☎ 0171-538 8600.

ALMA-ATA (KAZAKHSTAN)
Syn.: Tashkentskaya St., 1a 480057. ☎ (327-2) 30-68-98.

ANDIZHAN (UZBEKISTAN)
Syn.: 7 Sovetskaya St.

ASTRAKHAN (RUSSIA)
Syn.: 30 Babushkin St.

BAKU (AZERBAIJAN)
Syns.: Mountain Jews: Dmitrova St. 39, 370014. ☎ (892-2) 32-88-67; Ashkenazi: Pervomoskaya St., 271. ☎ (892-2) 94-15-71.

BIROBIDJAN (RUSSIA)
Syn.: 9 Chapaev St., Khabarovsk Krai.

BISHKEK, formerly Frunze (KIRGHIZIA)
Syn.: 193 Karpinsky St.

BUKHARA (UZBEKISTAN)
Syn.: 20 Tsentralnaya St.

BUYNAKSK (DAGHESTAN)
Syn.: Narodov Vostoka St.

CHIMKENT (KAZAKHSTAN)
Syn.: Svobody St., 47th La. (Sephardi).

DERBENT (DAGHESTAN)
Syn.: 94 Tagi-Zade St.

DUSHANBE (TADZHIKISTAN)
Syns.: Bokharan: Nazyina Khikmeta St. 26; Ashkenazi: Proletarsky St.

IRKUTSK (RUSSIA)
Syn.: 17 Karl Liebknecht St.

KATTA-KURGAN (UZBEKISTAN)
Syn.: 1 Karl Marx Alley.

KERMINE (UZBEKISTAN)
Syn.: 36 Narimanov St.

KLINTSY (BRYANSK)
Syn.: 82 Lermontov St.

KOKAND (UZBEKISTAN)
Syn.: Dekabristov St., Fergan Oblast.

KUBA (AZERBAIJAN)
Syn.: 46 Kolkhoznaya St.

KUIBYSHEV (RUSSIA)
Syn.: 84 Chapaev St.

KURSK (RUSSIA)
Syn.: 3 Bolshevitskaya St.

MAKHACHKALA (DAGHESTAN)
Syn.: 111 Yermoshkin St.

MALAKHOVKA (MOSCOW)
Syn.: 2nd Korenyovsky La., Moscow Oblast.

MARGELAN (UZBEKISTAN)
Syn.: Turtkulskaya St., Fergan Oblast.

MOSCOW (RUSSIA)
Syns.: Central, 8 Arkhipova St., off B. Khmelnitsky Str. ☎ (095) 924-24-24; Mar'ina Roshcha, at 5a Viacheslavsky Lane. ☎ (095) 289-23-25; Chabad Center, Poliakoff Syn., Bolshaya Brennaya 6. ☎ (095) 202-7696. Fax (095) 202-7645. Dir.: Rabbi B. S. Cunin.
Jewish Museum at the Poliakoff Synagogue.
(K) Shamir 'Hamburger' Restaurant (Parev) (also called 'Vege-Burger'), 12 Krasnoprudnaya St., ☎ 007-0950264-9592.

NALCHIK (RUSSIA)
Syn.: 73 Rabochaya St., cnr. Osetinskaya.

NAVOY (UZBEKISTAN)
Syn.: 36 Narimanov St.

NOVOSIBIRSK (RUSSIA)
Syns.: 23 Luchezarnaya St.; Sad Dzerzhinskov.

ORDZHONIKIDZE (RUSSIA)
Syn.: Revolutsiya St.

PENZA (RUSSIA)
Syn.: 15 Krasnaya St.

PERM (RUSSIA)
Syns.: Pushkin St.; Kuibyshev St.

ROSTOV-ON-DON (RUSSIA)
Syn.: 18 Gazetnaya La.

SACHKHERE
Syns.: 145 Sovetskaya St.; 105 Tsereteli St.

ST. PETERSBURG (RUSSIA)
Syns.: 2 Lermontovsky Prospekt. ☎ (812) 114-11-53. (This is the second street past the Kirov Opera & Ballet Theatre.) Mikva on these premises. Adv. booking req. ☎ 007-812-1138974.
(K) Dining Room at Shamir School on Ligovskiy Prospekt, 161-8. ☎ (812) 116-10-03.
Organisations
St. Petersburg Jewish Assoc., Ryleev St. 29-31, a/b103. ☎ (812) 272-41-13.
Jewish Tourist & Research Center, Stachek 212-46, 198262. ☎ (812) 184-12-48. Fax (812) 310-6148.

SAMARKAND (UZBEKISTAN)
Syns.: 34 Khudzumskaya St.; 45 Respublikanskaya St.; 5 Denauskaya St.

SARATOV (RUSSIA)
Syns.: Posadskov St.; 2 Kirpichnaya St.

SHAKHRISABZ (TADZIKISTAN)
Syn.: 23 Bainal Minal St.

SVERDLOVSK (RUSSIA)
Syns.: 18/2 Kirov St.; 14 Kuibyshev St.

TASHKENT (UZBEKISTAN)
Syns.: Sephardi, 3 Sagban St. ☎ (371-2) 40-07-68; Gorbunova St. 62. ☎ (371)-2) 53-54-47; Ashkenazi, 77 Chempianov St.; 9 Chkalov St.

TULA (RUSSIA)
Syn.: 15 Veresaevskaya St.

CORSICA
(See France)

COSTA RICA
(Jewish population 2,500)

SAN JOSE
Centro Israelita Sionista de Costa Rica, Calle 22 y 22. ☎ 233-9222. Fax. 233-5801. Apartado Postal 1473-1000.
Israel Embassy, Calle 2, Avenidas 2 y 4. ☎ 21-60-11 & 21-64-44. Apartado Postal 5147.

CROATIA
(Former constituent republic of Yugoslavia)
It is not known how far the Jewish communities have survived the civil strife

accompanying the break up of the Yugoslav Federation. There are nine centres of the Jewish population of about 2500.

DUBROVNIK

Syn.: Zudioska St. 3 (St. of the Jews). This is the second oldest synagogue in Europe and is located in a very narrow street off the main street — the Stradun or Placa. The Jewish com. office is in the same building. Zudioska St. is the third turning on the right from the town clock tower.

There are 30 Jews in the city. Tourists help to make up a minyan in the syn on Fri. Evg. & high holidays.

OSIJEK

Comunity building in Brace Radica St. 13, with objects from the synagogue destroyed during the Second World War. ☎ 24 926. The community numbers about 150 members. No regular services. Two cemeteries. A monument, Mother with child by Neumann. A former building of the second pre-war synagogue in Cvjetkova St. exists as a Pentecostal church. There is a plaque at the site of the destroyed synagogue in Županijska St.

RIJEKA

The synagogue in Filipovica St., 9, P.O. Box 65. ☎ 425-156 is well maintained. Pres.: Josip Engel. The community numbers about 150. Services on Jewish holidays.

SPLIT

The syn. at Split is one of the few in Yugoslavia to have survived the wartime occupation. The Jewish com. numbers about 200. Inf. from com. offices, Zidovski prolaz 1. ☎ 45-672. Pres.: Eduard Tauber. There is a Jewish cemetery established in 1578.

ZAGREB

Com. Headquarters, Palmoticeva St. 16, P.O.B. 986. ☎ 434-619. Fax 434-638. Pres.: Ognjen Kraus. Sec. Gen.: Dunja Spracj.

Publishes 'Voice of the Jewish communities of Croatia'. Edr. V. Kovač. Email: JCZ@OLEH.SRCE.HR

Before the war Zagreb had 11,000 Jews. Now there are about 1,500. Despite this decimation, there is a very active com. life. The old people are well looked after, in a fine home for the aged built to the order of the Fed. of Jewish Com. in Yugoslavia. Pres.: Paula Novak. Bukovacka str. 55. Tel 210-026.

There is an impressive monument in the Mirogoj Cemetery to the Jewish victims of the Second World War. There is a plaque on the spot of the pre-war Central Synagogue in Zagreb in Praska St., 7. Services in the communal building there on Friday eves and Holy Days.

CUBA

(Population less than 1,000 of whom the majority are in Havana)

Havana has a fine Conservative syn. and modern com. centre at Patronado de la Casa de la Comunidad Hebrea de Cuba, Calle 13 e I, Vedado. ☎ 32-8953. There is also an Orthodox Beth Hamedrash (Hadath Israel) at Calle Picota 52, Habana Vieja. ☎ 61-34-95. The United Hebrew Congregation (Reform), is at Av. de los Presidentes 502. The Jewish cemetery is at Guanabacoa.

The synagogue in Santiago de Cuba was recently re-dedicated and the community numbers 85.

CYPRUS

The Jewish population is about 25. There are cemeteries at Margo (near Nicosia) and at Larnaca (disused). The Margo cemetery is in the Turkish-occu-

pied part of the island, and access is barred to residents of the Greek part.
General inf. from Cyprus Tourism Organisation, 213 Regent St., W1R 8DA.
☎ 071-734 9822 & 2593.
Committee of the Jewish Com. of Cyprus. Nicosia: c/o Mrs Z. Yeshurun,
P.O.B. 4784. ☎ 02-427982.
Israel Embassy, 44 Archbishop Makarios Av., Nicosia.

CZECH REPUBLIC

The beautiful buildings of the ancient Jewish quarter of Old Prague are a monument to what was once a great and flourishing Jewish community. The Jews of Prague have been in the Czech capital for close on 1,000 years and elsewhere in Bohemia almost as long. Between the 16th and 18th centuries, Prague Jewry enjoyed its 'golden age.' One of the largest and most important communities in Europe, the Prague community lived in an extensive and self-contained Jewish quarter (Judenstadt).

Its ancient synagogues, two with regular religious services, two belonging to the Jewish com. in Prague, the others forming part of the Jewish Museum, its scholars, its Hebrew printing press, its Jewish craft guilds, its communal institutions, lent added lustre to an already illustrious part of the Jewish people.

In 1745, however, the Jews were exiled from Prague and allowed to return only three years later, on payment of exorbitant taxes. Full equality was granted to Prague Jews in 1848, and the ghetto later abolished.

When the Republic of Czechoslovakia was formed in 1918, after the First World War, it became the first country in the world to recognise Jewish nationality. By 1935, there were an estimated 150,000 Jews in Slovakia, 120,000 (including 40,000 refugees from Nazi Germany) in Bohemia and Moravia, and 105,000 in Ruthenia (now part of the Ukraine).

The German occupation in 1939 spelt the end for the 375,000 Jews of Czechoslovakia. Some managed to emigrate, but many were rounded up by the Nazis and killed in concentration camps. The names of all 77,297 Bohemian and Moravian Jews who died in the camps were engraved on the inside walls of the famous old Pinkas Synagogue in Prague's Jewish quarter. (The syn., now part of the Jewish Museum, is being rebuilt). By 1968, the 25,000 Jews still in Czechoslovakia in 1945, the end of the Second World War, had dwindled to 18,000 or so. According to the Federation of Jewish Communities in the Czech Republic, there are some 10,000 Jews in Czechoslovakia today, of whom 6,000 live in the Czech Republic.

There are ten communities in Bohemia and Moravia in the regional cities of Prague, Plzen, Karlovy Vary, Dêcin, Ústinad Labem, Teplice, Liberec, Brno, Olomouc and Ostrava. There is a kosher kitchens in Prague supervised by the Chief Rabbi and there are plans to open kosher restaurants in Karlovy Vary and Brno.
General inf. from Matana Travel Agency, Maiselova 15, Praha 1. ☎/Fax 232-1049.

BOSKOVICE
Medieval ghetto; 17th c. Synagogue and Jewish cemetery.

BRNO
Syn.: Skorepka 13. Re-development now completed. Com. Centre: Kpt. Jarose 3. Services, Fri. evg. & Sat. morn. ☎ 422-15710. Community President:. ☎ (5) 77-3233.

HOLESOV
The 'Schach' Syn., dating from 1560, now a museum, should be visited. It is

open in the mornings. At other times, the curator will show visitors round, if contacted. The old cemetery is close by.

KARLOVY VARY (KARLSBAD)
Prayer house & Com. Centre, Masaryka 39. Services, Fri. evg. & Sat. morn.

LIBEREC (REICHENBERG)
Prayer house & Comm. Centre, Slavickova 5. ☎ (048) 24 341 or 244-70.

MIKULOV (NIKOLSBURG)
Only one syn., now being restored, remains of the many which flourished here when the town was the spiritual capital of Moravian Jewry and the seat of the Chief Rabbis of Moravia. The cemetery contains the graves of famous rabbis.

OLOMOUC
Prayer house & Com. Centre, Komenskeho 7. ☎ (68) 522-3119.

OSTRAVA
Prayer house & Com. Centre, Ceskobratrska 17. ☎ (69) 611-2389.

PLZEN (PILSEN)
(The Great Synagogue is closed now).
Prayer house & Com. Centre: Smetanovy sady 5. ☎ (019) 72 35749. Services Fri. evg.

PRAGUE
Syns.: Jubilee Syn., Jerusalemskà 7. Services, Fri. evg. & Sat. morn.; Old-New Syn. (Altneuschul), Cervena ul.7 ☎ 231-09-09.
Beth Simcha, Urugayská 7, 2.
Federation of Jewish Coms. in the Czech Republic (Federace zidovskych obc' v CR): 110 01, Maislova 18. Prague 1. Dir. Dr. Tomas Kraus. ☎2481-0130. Fax. 2481-0912. Pres. Jiri Danicek. ☎ 2481-745972. Chief Rabbi: Karol Sidon.
Kosher Restaurant: Shalom, Maislova 18. 11.30 - 8.00 p.m. (Jan-Mar: 12.00-2 p.m. ☎ 2481 0929.
Kosher Shop, Břehová 5, 1. ☎ 232-4729; Osem products are available at KMart at Ovecnytrh.
Jewish Town Hall with Hebrew clock, Maislova 18.
Jewish Museum, Jáchymova 3.
Old Jewish Cemetery, the oldest in Europe, containing the graves of such famous rabbis & scholars as Avigdor Karo (died 1439), Yehuda Löw ben Bezalel (1609), David Gans (1613) & David Oppenheim (1736); High Syn. (the Spanish Syn. is empty, closed now) (exhibition of Jewish synagogue hangings, vestments, and other fine decorated fabrics); Pinkas Syn. (memorial to 77,297 victims of Nazi persecution, under 'renovation' since 1968); Maisl Syn. (silver treasures exhibition); Klaus Syn. (Jewish life and Jewish Holydays); The New Jewish Cemetery, Prague 3-Zizkov, Nad vodovodem 1, contains the grave of Franz Kafka.
Tours organised by Wittmann Tours, Uruguayská 7, 2, Tel/Fax. 251-235 4396293, start at Parizská 28, Prague 1 (in front of Lufthansa office); Heritage Tours, ☎/Fax (422) 4721068.

TEPLICE (TEPLITZ-SCHÖNAU)
Prayer house & Comm. Centre, Lipova 25. ☎ (0417) 265-80.

TEREZIN
There is a new museum in the town Terezin (converted into a ghetto called

Theresienstadt by the Nazis) dedicated to the Jews who were deported from there to Auschwitz death camp. There is also a cemetery in which 11,250 individual and 217 mass graves and the crematorium are placed: 34,000 people died in Terezín.

USTI NAD LABEM (AUSSIG)
Prayer house & Comm. Centre, Moskevska 26. ☎ (047) 520-8082.

DENMARK
There are 8,000 Jews in Denmark today, nearly all of whom live in Copenhagen. A small community of Israelis, Poles and others has been formed in Aarhus.

The Royal Library (Amiliegaden 38, Copenhagen) houses a Jewish collection including the famous 'Bibliotheca Simonseniana' and part of the library of the late Professor Lazarus Goldschmidt. The library has a Jewish Department under the direction of Ulf Haxen. In the Liberty Museum there is a special division devoted to the Resistance Movement, and also a section dealing with 'The Persecution of the Jews.'

General inf. from Danish Tourist Board, 55 Sloane St., SW1X 9SY. ☎ 0171-259 5959. Fax 0171-259 5955.

Travel Guide

A guide to Jewish Denmark, edited by Lisa Goldschmidt Solomon, C.A. Reitzel Ltd.

COPENHAGEN
Synagogues & Religious Organisations
The Chief Rabbi of Denmark is Rabbi Bent Lexner, 9 Oestbaneg., 2100 Ø. ☎ 3526 3540. Fax 3929 2517.

The main syn., with daily and Shabbat services, is at 12 Krystalgade, 1172 K. The Machsike Hadass Syn. at 12 Ole Suhrs Gade, 1354 K, holds regular daily and Shabbat services. ☎ 3315-3117. Rabbi B. Steinhaus, ☎ 3332 5618, & Rabbi M. E. Winkler, ☎ 3313 3933. There is a mikva on the premises. ☎ 3393 7662 or 3332 9443.

From May to Sept., services are held in the syn. at 6 Granvaenget, Hornbaek, N. Seeland.

Representative Organisations
B'nai B'rith. Pres.: Benny Untershlag, Moseagervej 12, 2680 Solrød Strand. ☎ 5614 7203.

Jewish Com. Centre (**Det mosaiske Troessamfund**): Ny Kongensgade 6, 1472 K. ☎ 3312 8868. Fax. 3312-3357. Mikva on premises.

Cultural & Welfare Orgs., etc.
Homes for Elderly People: Raoul Wallenberg Boligerne, Nygårdsvej 14, 2100 Ø
Homes for Aged: Meyers Minde, 12 Krystalgade, 1172 K. ☎ 3312 5523, & N. J. Fraenckels Stiftelse, 93 Skoleholdervej, 2400 NV. ☎ 3834 3168.

Student & Youth Organisations, etc.
B'nei Akiva, 6 Ny Kongensgade, 1472 K.
Hakoah Sports Club. Inq. to Ch.: Alan Melchior, Østerbrogade 21, 2100 Ø. ☎ 3142 3555.
Jewish Youth Club, 6 Ny Kongensgade.

Zionist Organisations
Keren Hayesod. President: Jan Plon, Ny Kongensgade 6, 1472K. ☎ 3393 2466.

Keren Kayemet, Lille Kongensgade 20, 1074 K. ☎ 3391 1991.
WIZO, 6 Ny Kongensgade. ☎ 3393 1965.
Zionist Federation, 6 Ny Kongensgade. ☎ 3393 0093.
Israel Embassy, 4 Lundevangsvej, 2900 Hellerup. ☎ 3962 6288.
Kosher Food: **(K)** Kosher Butcher: Kosher Delikatesse, 87 Lyngbyvej 2100, Ø.
☎ 3118 5777; **(K)** I.A. Samson, Rørholmsgade 3. ☎ 3313-0077. Fax 3314-
8277. **(K)** Mrs Heimann (Bread/cakes). ☎ 3332 9443.

HORNBAEK
Syn. Granavenget 8 (open from Shavuoth to Succoth). ☎ 4220 0731.
Hotel: **(K)** Villa Strand, Kystvej 12. ☎ 4396 9400 and 4220 0088. (Under the
supervision of Rabbi Michael Guttermann.) See advert on p.416.

DOMINICAN REPUBLIC
(Jewish population 400)
SANTO DOMINGO
Syn.: Centro Israelita de la Republica Dominicana, Av. Ciudad de Sarasota 21.
☎ 535-6042.
Israel Embassy, Av. Pedro Henriquez Urena 80, Apartado Postal 1404. ☎(809)
542-1635/1548.
Consejo Dominicano de Mujeres Hebreas. President: M. Lalo, P.O. Box 2189.
Fax. (809) 688-2058.

SOSUA
Felix G. Koch, ☎ (809) 571-2284, welcomes Jewish visitors.

ECUADOR
(Jewish population 1,300)
GUAYAQUIL
Syn. & Com. Centre, cnr. Calle Paradiso & El Bosque. Pres.: Isaac
Pienknaeura, Boyaca 1313, P.O.B. 5976.

QUITO
Com. Centre: Asociación Israelita de Quito, 18 de Septiembre 954, Casilla 17-
03-800. ☎ 502-734. Fax 502-733.
Israel Embassy, Av. Eloy Alfaro 969, Casilla 2463. ☎ 547-322 or 548-431.

EGYPT
There are about 270 Jews in Egypt, 150 in Cairo and 120 in Alexandria.
General inf. from Egyptian State Tourist Office, 170 Piccadilly, W1V 9DD. ☎
0171-493 5282.

ALEXANDRIA
Syn.: Eliahu Hanavi, 69 Nebi Daniel St., Ramla Station. Pres. of Com.:
Clement R. Setton. ☎ 4923974 & 5974438.

CAIRO
Syns.: Shaarei Hashamayim, 17 Adli Pasha St. ☎ 749025. Dir.: (put - for
vacancy); Ben-Ezra, 6 Harett il-Sitt Barbara, Mari Girgés (St. George's), Old
Cairo. ☎ 847695; Meir Enaim, 55 No. 13 Street, Maadi. (This is a small
American-Israeli cong., which holds occasional services.)
Com. Offices: 13 Sebil el-Khazendar St., Midan el-Geish, Abassiya. ☎ 824613
or 824885. Pres.: Emil Rousseau. ☎ 758868. Sec.: ☎ 744850.
Israel Embassy, 6 Ibn Malek St., Gizeh. ☎ 845260, 845205 or 28862.

Israel Government Tourist Office, 6 Ibn Malek St., 4th Floor. ☎ 729734 or 730997.

EL SALVADOR
(Jewish population about 30 families)

SAN SALVADOR
Syn. (Conservative), 23 Blvd. del Hipodromo 626, Colonia San Benito. Fri. evg. services only. Further inf. from Max Starkman. ☎ 237366.
Comunidad Israelita de El Salvador, Aptdo. Postal (06) 182. Pres.: Jean-Claude Kahn, Colonia y Calle Maquilishuat 135. ☎ 981388.
Israel Embassy & Consulate. Colonia Escalon, 85 Av. Norte No. 619. ☎ 238770 or 239221.

ESTONIA
The memorial for Estonian victims of the Holocaust is at Klooga, 35km west of Tallinn. There are Jewish communities in Kohtla-Järve, Narva and Tartu.

TALLIN
Syn.: 9 Magdalena Str., P.O. Box 3576, EE0090. ☎ (372-2) 55-71-54.
Cemetery: Rahumae Str, 5.
Organisation: **Jewish Community of Estonia**, and Jewish Cultural Society, Karu St. 16, P.O. Box 3576, EE0090. Tel/Fax. (372) 2438566. Publishes 'Hashaher' (monthly) in Russian and operates a radio programme on Radio 4 (Thurs 22.15-23.00); Information on vegetarian establishments available.
WIZO, Revekka Blumberg, ☎ (372) 2431817.

ETHIOPIA
The Jews of Ethiopia, who sometimes call themselves Beta Israel, and are known as Falashas, represent one of the oldest Jewish communities in the world. As a result of Operation Moses and extensive emigration to Israel in the past few years and now following a further mass exodus to Israel, the community probably numbers fewer than 1,500, when account is taken of casualties from the famine and the hazards of reaching the refugee camps in the Sudan, estimated at between 3,000 and 4,000. This is about a third of the number in 1981, when the World Ort Union was forced to suspend its aid programme. The Falashas' origin is uncertain, but it is believed that Judaism first reached Ethiopia during the first or second centuries C.E., probably from Egypt, where flourishing Jewish communities existed.

ADDIS ABABA
Com. Centre, P.O. Box 50. ☎ 111725 & 446471.

ASMARA
Syn., Via Hailemariam Mammo 34.

FIJI
Fiji Jewish Association, P.O. Box 882, Suva. President: Cherry Schneider.

FINLAND
The settlement of Jews in Finland dates from about 1850. The original community consisted mostly of Jewish soldiers in the Russian Army in Finland, so-called Cantonists who decided, after 25 years of military service, to settle there with their families. There are about 1,500 Jews in Finland today, about 1,200 of whom live in Helsinki.

General inf. from Finnish Tourist Board, 3rd Flr, 30-35 Pall Mall, SW17 5LP.
☎ 0171-930-5871. Fax. 0171-321-0696.

HELSINKI
Syn. (O) & Com. Centre, school, kindergarten & home for aged, Malminkatu
26. ☎ 6921297 & 6941302. Fax. 6948916. Services, Mon.-Fri., 7.45 a.m..;
Fri. evg., 7.45 p.m. (summer), 5 p.m. (winter); Shabbat & Sun., 9 a.m.
All orgs., including Hazamir Choir, Jewish War Veterans, Keren Kayemet,
Library, Maccabi, WIZO & the Youth Club can be contacted via the above ☎
numbers.
Kosher Deli: **(K)** Malminkatu 24. ☎ 6854584. Open Tues.-Wed., 1 p.m. to 5
p.m.; Thurs., 9 a.m. to 5 p.m.; Fri., 9 a.m. to 2 p.m.
Kosher meals available at the Com. Centre by prior arrangement from: Avi
Hovav, ☎ 6941296 or 877 9627.
Israel Embassy, Vironkatu 5A. ☎ 1356177. Fax. 1356959.

TURKU
Syn.: Brahenkatu 17. The Sec., Mrs. Anneli Zewi, is always pleased to meet
visitors.
Com. Centre, Brahenkatu 17b. ☎ 2312557. Fax. 2334689.

FRANCE
The first Jewish settlers in France arrived with the Greek founders of Marseilles
about 500 B.C.E. After the destruction of the Second Temple, Jewish exiles
established new communities, or reinforced old ones, in the South of France,
where they lived on equal terms with their Gentile neighbours. Rabbis who
become known for their oratory attracted Christians to the synagogues. But
gradually the priesthood inculcated in the masses a hatred of the Jews which,
with the coming of the Crusades, vented itself in pogroms. Yet it was during this
period that French Jewry achieved its noblest spiritual flowering.
Rashi and Rabenu Tam are the best known of hundreds of brilliant medieval
French rabbis and scholars. In 1394 the Jews were banished from the whole of
France, save the small area under the jurisdiction of the Popes of Avignon.
When Alsace-Lorraine became part of France early in the 17th century, the
Jews there were unmolested, and small numbers trickled into the rest of
France. Ten years before the French Revolution, the 500 Jews of Paris built
their first ritual bath. In 1791 the emancipation of French Jewry was the sig-
nal for the ghetto walls to crumble throughout Europe.
During the Second World War, under German occupation, 120,000 Jews were
deported or massacred; but the post-war influx from Central and Eastern
Europe and North Africa has increased the Jewish population to some
700,000.
There are about 380,000 in the Paris area; 85,000 in Marseille; between
30,000 and 35,000 in Lyon; between 25,000 and 30,000 in Nice; between
20,000 and 23,000 in Toulouse; 18,000 in Strasbourg: and about 8,000 each
in Bordeaux and Grenoble.
The Consistoire Central Israélite de France et d'Algérie (17, rue Saint Georges,
75009 Paris) publishes its 'Annuaire', listing all the communal organisations of
France.
General inf. from the French Government Tourist Office, 178 Piccadilly, W1V
0AL. ☎ 0171-499 6911 (recorded message only) or 0171-491 7622 for urgent
messages. Written inquiries dealt with promptly (but £1 in stamps requested
for post & packing for bulky literature).

AGEN (LOT-ET-GARONNE)
Syn. & Com. Centre: 52 rue Montesquieu, 47000. ☎ 5366-24-20.

AIX-EN-PROVENCE (BOUCHES DU RHÔNE)
Syn. & Com. Centre: 3 bis rue de Jérusalem, 13100. ☎ 4226-69-39.
Inf. about kosher butchers from Rabbi H. Harboun.

AIX-LES-BAINS (SAVOIE)
Syn.: Rue Paul Bonna. 73100. ☎ 7935-28-08. Mikva on premises.
Mikva, Pavillon Salvador, rue du Président Roosevelt, 73100. ☎ 7935-38-08.
Rest Home: Maison de Retraite du C.O.J.A.S.O.R., Av. de Berlioz, 73100.
School: Tomer Deborah, Chemin de St. Pol, 73100.
Yeshiva: 25, Montée de la Reine Victoria, Route de Tresserve, 73100. ☎ 7935-03-17.

Kosher Hotel: Auberge de Lebaye, Chemin du Tiraux. ☎ 7934-0417. Fax 7988-4954.
Kosher Meat & Provisions: (K) Berdah, 29 Av. de Tresserve, 73100. ☎ 7961-44-11. (K) Eurocach, Av. d'Italie

AJACCIO
(See under Corsica at end of section on France.)

AMIENS (SOMME)
Syn. & Com. Centre: 38 rue du Port d'Amont, 8000.

ANGERS (MAINE-ET-LOIRE)
Syn.: 12 rue Valdemaine, 49100.

ANNECY (HAUTE-SAVOIE)
Syn. & Com. Centre: 18 rue de Narvik, 74000. ☎ 5045-82-22.

ANNEMASSE (HAUTE SAVOIE)
Kosher Butcher: (K) Yarden, 59 rue de la Libération, 74240 Gaillard. ☎ 5092-64-05.

ANTIBES JUAN-LES-PINS (ALPES-MARITIMES)
Syn.: Villa La Monada. Chemin des Sables, 06600. ☎ 9361-59-34.

Restaurants (Summer only)
(K) Bamboo Grill, 5 rue Alexandre III;
Chez Andre, Chaim's Marchés, 13 Av. Louis Gallet, Juan les Pins. ☎ 9361-4472. Mid-March to Mid-September.
(K) Pizza Beverley, Blvd. Charles Guillaument, which also holds Sephardi services on Shabbat.

Kosher Butchers:
(K) André Sebbah, 28 Av. Maiziers, 06600. ☎ 9334-60-11; (K) Krief, 3 rue Louis-Gallet, 06160. ☎ 9374-73-30.

Kosher Grocery:
Ohayon, 28 Av. Admiral Courbet. ☎ 9367-2508. Fax 9293-0572. (All year).

ARCACHON (GIRONDE)
Syn.: Cours Desbey. Open July & Aug. only.

AVIGNON (VAUCLUSE)
Syn.: 2 Place de Jérusalem, 84000. ☎ 9085-21-24.
Com. Centre: Mikva: 7 rue des Sept-Baisers, 84140 Montfavet. ☎ 9086-30-30.
Kosher Butcher: (K) Chelly, 15 rue Chapeau-Rouge, 84000. ☎ 9082-47-50.

The Conseil Général de Vaucluse, Place Campana, B.P.147, 84008 Avignon (☎ 90.86.43.42) publishes a guide to the Jewish sites of the Vaucluse.

BAR-LE-DUC (MEUSE)
Syn.: 7 Quai Carnot.

BASTIA
(See under Corsica at end of section on France.)

BAYONNE (BASSES-PYRÉNÉES)
Syn. & Com. Centre: 35 rue Maubec, 64100. ☎ 5955-03-95.

BEAUVAIS (OISE)
Syn. & Com. Centre: Rue Jules Isaac, 60000.

BELFORT (TERRITOIRE DE BELFORT)
Syn.: 6 rue de l'As-de-Carreau, 90000. Tel/Fax. (03) 8428-55-41.
Com. Centre: 27 rue Strolz, 90000. ☎ (03) 8428-55-41. Publication 'Notre Communauté' (quart)

BENFELD (BAS-RHIN)
Syn.: 7a rue de la D"me, 67230.
Com. Centre: 6 rue du Grand Rempart, 67230.

BESANÇON (DOUBS)
Syn.: 23c Quai de Strasbourg, 25000.
Com. Centre: 10 rue Grosjean, 25000. ☎ 8180-82-82.
Kosher meat, groceries & frozen food: M. Croppet, 18 rue des Granges. ☎ 8183-35-93. Thurs. only.

BEZIERS (HÉRAULT)
Syn. & Com. Centre: 19 Place Pierre-Sémard, 34500. ☎ 6728-75-98. Operates a kosher food store.

BIARRITZ (BASSES-PYRÉNÉES)
Syn.: rue de Russie (cnr. rue Pellot), 64200. Services, Yom Kippur only.

BISCHHEIM-SCHILTIGHEIM (BAS-RHIN)
Syn. & Com. Centre: 9, Place de la Synagogue, 67800. ☎ 38333-02-87.

BITCHE (MOSELLE)
Syn.: 28 rue de Sarreguemines, 57230. Services, Rosh Hashana & Yom Kippur.

BORDEAUX (GIRONDE)
Syn.: 8 rue du Grand-Rabbin-Joseph-Cohen, 33000. ☎ 5691-79-39.
Com. Centre: 15 Pl. Charles-Gruet, 33000. ☎ 5652-62-69.
Mikva: 213 rue Ste. Catherine, 33000. ☎ 5691-79-39.

Kosher Restaurants:
(K) Mazal Tov, 137 Crs Victor Hugo, 33000. ☎ 56523703.
(K) Sabra, 144, Crs Victor Hugo. ☎ 56928338.

BOULAY (MOSELLE)
Syn.: Rue du Pressoir, 57220. ☎ 8779-28-34.

BOULOGNE-SUR-MER (PAS DE CALAIS)
Syn.: 63 rue Charles Butor.

BOUZONVILLE (MOSELLE)
Syn. & Com. Centre: Rue des Bénédictins, 57320.

BREST (FINISTÈRE)
Syn. & Com. Centre: 40 rue de la République, 29200. Services, Fri., 7.30 p.m.

CAEN (CALVADOS)
Syn. & Com. Centre: 46 Av. de la Libération, 14000. ☎ 3143-60-54.
Kosher Butcher: **(K)** M. Lasry, 26 rue de l'Engannerie, 14000. ☎ 3186-16-25.
Open Thurs.

CAGNES-SUR-MER (ALPES MARITIMES)
Syn.: 5 rue des Capucines, 06800.

CALUIRE ET CUIRE (RHÔNE)
Syn. & Com. Centre: 107 Av. Fleming, 69300. Services. Pres.: J.Wolff. ☎
7823-1237.

CANNES (ALPES-MARITIMES)
Syn.: Habad Lubavitch, 22, Rue Cdt Vidal (Angle Bd. de Lorraine) 06400, ☎
9298-6751; 20 Blvd. d'Alsace, 06400. ☎ 9338-16-54.
Com. Centre: 3 rue de Bône, 06400. ☎ as above.

Restaurant:
(K) Le Tovel, 3 rue Gerard Monod, 06400. ☎ 9339-3625.
Kosher Hotel: **(K) Hotel King David** (60), 16 Blvd. d'Alsace, 06400. ☎ 9399-
16-16. Under the supervision of Rabbi Mordechai Bensoussan, Regional Rabbi
of Nice, Côte d'Azur & Corsica.
Kosher Butchers: **(K)** Marcel Benguigui, 17 rue Maréchal-Joffre, 06400. ☎
9339-57-92; **(K)** J.-Y. Zana, 44 rue Jean-Jaurés, 06400. ☎ 9338-46-59.

CARPENTRAS (VAUCLUSE)
Services are held on festivals in the ancient syn. in the Place de la Mairie,
84200, classed as a national monument. Built in 1367 and rebuilt in 1741, it
is worth a visit. Hours 10-12; 3-5. Inq. to 9063-3997.

CAVAILLON (VAUCLUSE)
The remains of the old syn., built in 1774, are regarded as a French historical
monument. The Musées et Patrimoine de Cavaillon organise tours. Contact 52
Place de Castil-Blaze, 84300. ☎ 9076-0034. Fax 90-71-47-06.

CHALONS-SUR-MARNE (MARNE)
Syn. & Com. Centre: 21 rue Lochet, 51000.

CHALON-SUR-SAONE (SAÔNE-ET-LOIRE)
Syn.: 10 rue Germiny, 71100.

CHAMBÉRY (SAVOIE)
Syn. & Com. Centre: 44 rue St.-Réal. Services, Fri. evg., 7 p.m. and festivals.

CHATEAUROUX (INDRE)
Inq. to Michel Touati, 3 Allée Emile Zola, Montierchaume, 36130 Déols. ☎
5426-05-47.

CLERMONT-FERRAND (PUY DE DÔME)
Syn. & Com. Centre: 6 rue Blatin. ☎ 7393-36-59.
(K) Kosher meat is available at the Com. Centre on alternate Sundays. ☎ 7860-
13-25.

COLMAR (HAUT-RHIN)
Syn.: 3 rue de la Cigogne, 68000. ☎ (03) 8941-38-29. Fax. (03) 8941-1296.
Mikva on premises.

The Chief Rabbi of the Haut-Rhin region is Rabbi Jacky Dreyfus, 1 rue des Jonquilles, 68000. ☎ (03) 8923-13-11.

COMPIÈGNE (OISE)
Syn. & Com. Centre: 4 rue du Dr.-Charles-Nicolle, 60200.

CREIL (OISE)
Syn. & Com. Centre: 1 Place de la Synagogue, 60100. ☎ 4425-16-37. Fax 4425-48-41. M. Rabbin J. Nezri. ☎ 0607-55-9627.

DEAUVILLE
Syn.: 14 rue Castor, 14800. ☎ 3181-2706.

DIEUZE (MOSELLE)
Syn.: Av. Foch, 57260.

DIJON (CÔTE D'OR)
Syn. & Com. Centre: 5 rue de la Synagogue. ☎ 8066-46-47. Mikva. Kosher Butchers: (K) Albert Lévy, 25 rue de la Manutention. ☎ 8030-14-42; (K) Albert Sultan, 4 petite rue Pouffier. ☎ 8073-31-38.

DUNKERQUE (NORD)
Syn. & Com. Centre: 19 rue Jean-Bart, 59140.

ELBEUF (SEINE-MARITIME)
Syn.: 29 rue Grémont, 76500. ☎ 3577-09-11.

EPERNAY (MARNE)
Syn.: 2 rue Placet, 51200. Services, Yom Kippur only. ☎ 2655-24-44.

EPINAL (VOSGES)
Syn.: Rue Charlet, 88000. ☎ 2982-25-23.

ERSTEIN (BAS-RHIN)
Syn.: Rue du Vieux-Marché, 67150. Services, Rosh Hashana & Yom Kippur only.

EVIAN-LES-BAINS (HAUTE-SAVOIE)
Syn.: Adjacent to 1 Av. des Grottes, 74500. ☎ 5075-15-63.

FAULQUEMONT-CREHANGE (MOSELLE)
Syn. & Com. Centre.: Place de l'Hotel de Ville, 57380. Services, festivals & High Holy-days only.

FORBACH (MOSELLE)
Syn. & Com. Centre.: 98 Av. St.-Rémy, 57600. ☎ 8785-25-57.

FRÉJUS (VAR)
Syn.: Villa Ariane, rue du Progrés, Fréjus-Plage, 83600. ☎ 9452-06-87.

GRASSE (ALPES-MARITIMES)
Syn. & Com. Centre: 82 Route de Nice, 06130. ☎ 9336-05-33 after 7 p.m. Services, festivals & High Holy-days only. (Reports on existence of this Centre needed. Ed.)

GRENOBLE (ISÈRE)
Syn. & Com. Centre: 4 rue des Bains, 38000. ☎ 76461514. Rabbinat: 76476372. Rabbi: Dayon Yaakov Levy-Bencheton. Syn & Mikva. 11 rue André-Maginot, 38000. ☎ 7687-02-80. Mikva. ☎ 7687-02-80.

Beit Habad, rue Cazare Carnot. ☎ 7643-3858.
Kosher Butchers: **(K)** C. Cohen, 19 rue Turenne, 38000. ☎ 7646-48-14; **(K)** Sebbag, 6 rue Aubert-Dubayet, 38000. ☎ 7646-40-78.
Kosher Groceries:David France, 75 ave de Vizille. ☎ 7670-4915.
La Rose de Sables, 15 place Gustave Rivet. ☎ 7687-8094.
Aux Délices du Soleil, 49 rue Thiers. ☎ 7646-1960.
Restaurant: Pizzeria Pinocchio, 1 rue des bons Enfants 38000. ☎ 7646-8866.
Radio Kol Hashalom, 4 rue des Bains. ☎ 7687 2122.

GROSBLIEDERSTROFF (MOSELLE)
Syn.: 6 rue des Fermes, 57520.

HAGONDANGE (MOSELLE)
Syn.: Rue Henri-Hoffmann, 57300.

HAGUENAU (BAS-RHIN)
Syn.: 3 rue du Grand-Rabbin-Joseph-Bloch, 67500. ☎ 8873-38-30.
Mikva: 7 rue Neuve. There is an ancient cemetery.
Jewish section at Historical Museum, rue du Maréchal Foch.
Kosher Restaurant: Maison les Cigognes. ☎ 8893-21-58

HYÈRES (VAR)
Syn.: Chemin de la Ritorte, 83400. ☎ 9465-31-97.

INGWILLER (BAS-RHIN)
Syn.: Cours du Château, 67340.

INSMING (MOSELLE)
Syn.: Rue de la Synagogue, 57670.

JUAN-LES-PINS
See Antibes.

LA CIOTAT (BOUCHES DU RHÔNE)
Syn. & Com. Centre: 1 Square de Verdun, 13600. ☎ 4271-92-56. President: Mr C. Michel. Services Friday 7 p.m. (Winter), 7.30 p.m. (Summer). Saturday 9 a.m.

LA ROCHELLE (LOIRE)
Syn. & Com. Centre: For inf. about kosher food, etc., contact Pierre Guedj, 19 rue Bastion d'Evangile, 17000. ☎ 4667-38-91.

LA SEYNE-SUR-MER (VAR)
Syn. & Com. Centre: 5 rue Chevalier-de-la-Barre, 83500. ☎ 9494-40-28.
Kosher Butcher: **(K)** Elie Benhamou, 17 rue Baptistin-Paul, 83500. ☎ 9494-38-60.

LE HAVRE (SEINE-MARITIME)
Syn. & Com. Centre: 38 rue Victor-Hugo, 76600. ☎ 3521-14-59.

LE MANS (SARTHE)
Syn.: 4-6 Blvd. Paixhans, 72000. ☎ 4386-00-96.

LIBOURNE (GIRONDE)
Syn.: 33 rue Lamothe, 33500.

LILLE (NORD)
Syn. & Com. Centre: 5 rue Auguste-Angellier, 59000. ☎ 2030-69-86.
Mikva. ☎ 2085273.

Kosher Grocery: Kosher department at Monoprix, rue du Molinel, carrefour at Shopping Centre Euralille, 59000.

LIMOGES (HAUTE-VIENNE)
Syn. & Com. Centre: 25-27 rue Pierre-Leroux, 87000. ☎ 5577-47-26.
(K) Kosher meat and food products available from the Com. Centre Thurs. afternoon & Sun. morning, as well as by special request.

LIXHEIM (MOSELLE)
Syn.: Rue de la Synagogue, 57110.

LORIENT (MORBIHAN)
Syn.: c/o Mme. Frandji, 18 rue de la Patrie, 56100. Services, festivals & Holydays only.

LUNEVILLE (MEURTHE-ET-MOSELLE)
Syn.: 5 rue Castara, 54300.

LYON (RHÔNE)
Synagogues & Religious Organisations
Regional Chief Rabbi: Rabbi Richard Wertenschlag, 13 Quai Tilsitt, 69002. ☎ 7837 1343.
Consistoire Israélite de Lyon. Same address. ☎ 7837-13-43. Fax 783 82657.
Beth Din, 34 rue d'Armenie, 3e. ☎ 78629763. Fax 78950947.
Consistoire Israélite Sepharade de Lyon, Yaacov Molho Com. Centre, 317 rue Duguesclin, 69007. ☎ 7858-18-74. FAX. 7858 1749.

Synagogues
Ashkenazi, 13 Quai Tilsitt, 69002. ☎ 7837-13-43. This is the city's main syn.
Benarrous, 3-5 rue St.-Jacques, 69003.
Beth David, 202 rue André Philip, 69003. ☎ 6895-28-65.
Chaare Tsedek (N. African), 18 rue St.-Mathieu, 69008. ☎ 7800-72-50.
Jewish Day School, 40 rue Alexandre Boutin, Villeurbanne, 69100. ☎ 7824-38-91.
Lubavitch, 3 passage Cazenove, 69006. ☎ 7889-08-32.
Mizrahi (N. African), 11 rue Ste.-Catherine, 69001. ☎ 7850-87-13.
Neveh Chalom (Sephardi), 317 rue Duguesclin, 69007. ☎ 7858-18-54.
Orah Haim, 17 rue Albert-Thomas, St.-Fons, 69190. ☎ 7251-50-02.
Patah Eliahu, 3 Impasse Professeur-Beauvisage, 69008. ☎ 7800-37-21.
Rav Hida (N. African), La Sauvegarde, La Duchére, 69009. ☎ 7835-14-44.
Synagogue de la Fraternité (Sephardi), 4 rue Malherbe, Villeurbanne, 69100. ☎ 7884-04-32.
Yeshiva Pinto, 20 bis rue des Mûriers, Villeurbanne, 69100. ☎ 7803-89-14.
12 Chemin de la Batterie, Bron, 69500.
48 rue de la Marne, Bron, 69500. ☎ 7826-95-15.
1 rue de Dublin, Rillieux, 69140. ☎ 7888-50-89.
12 Av. Division Leclerc, Vénissieux, 69200. ☎ 7831-69-60.
6 Av. de la Libération, Meyzieu, 69330. ☎ 7804-17-92.
26 rue Chevreul, Villeurbanne, 69100. ☎ 7884-09-55.
7 rue du Docteur Frappaz, Ville-urbanne, 69100. ☎ 7854-12-32.

Mikvaot
Chaare Tsedek. (as above); Jewish Day School (as above); Neveh Chalom (as above); Orah Haim (as above) St.-Fons, 17 rue Albert-Thomas, St. Fons, 69190. ☎ 7867-39-78; Synagogue de la Fraternité (as above); Yeshiva Pinto (as above); Rav Hida (as above); Rillieux (as above).

Representative Organisations
B'nai B'rith, 9 Av. Général Leclerc, 69007.
F.S.J.U., 146 Grande-Rue de la Guillotière, 69007. ☎ 7872-88-23.

Youth Organisations
Betar, 13 Quai Tilsitt 69002. ☎ 78 69 1203.
Bnei Akiva, 317 rue Duguesclin, 69007.
Dror, 18 rue du Bâtiment-d'Argent, 69001. ☎ 7827-35-46.
Eclaireurs et Eclaireuses Israélites de France (Jewish Scouts), c/o Alain
Majerowicz, 13 Quai Tilsitt, 69002. ☎ 7850-29-01.
Lubavitch, 3 Passage Cazenove, 69006.

Zionist Organisations
Jewish Agency, 169 Cours Lafayette, 69006. ☎ 7824-39-02.
WIZO, 18 rue du Bât. d'Argent.

Jewish Media
CIV News, 4 rue Malherbe, Villeurbanne, 69100. ☎ 7884-04-32.
Hachaar, 18 rue St. Mathieu, 69008. ☎ 7800-72-50.
La Voix Sépharade, 317 rue Duguesclin, 69007. ☎ 7858-18-74.
Le Bulletin, 13 Quai Tilsitt, 69002. ☎ 7837-13-43.
Radio Judaïca Lyon (R.J.L.), P.O.B. 7063, 69341. ☎ 7803-99-20. FM 94.5.

Jewish Booksellers
Decitre, Place Bellecour, 69002.
F.N.A.C., rue de la République, 69002.
Levi-Its'hak, 3 Passage Cazenove. ☎ 78931617.
Mazal, 46 rue Jean-Claude-Vivant, Villeurbanne, 69100. ☎ 7852-85-94.
Menorah (Ouaknine), 52 rue Montesquieu, 69007. ☎ 7869-09-35.

Kosher Restaurants
(K) Le Grillon d'Or, 20 rue Terme, 69001. ☎ 7827-33-09.
(K) Jardin d'Eden, 3 Rue Jean Jaurés. ☎ 7233-8565.
(K) Lippmann, 4 rue Tony-Tollet, 69002. ☎ 7842-49-82.
(K) L'Orient Express, 140 rue Dedieu, 69100. ☎ 78.68.99.23.
(K) ORT School, 133 rue Marius Berliet, 69008. ☎ 7874-25-05.
(K) Pizzeria Le Pinnochio, 5 rue Alexandre Boulin, Villeurbanne. ☎ 7868-62-95.
(K) Pizzeria Obadia, 2 rue Jubin Villeurbanne. ☎ 7244-33-62.
Details of kosher bakers, butchers, provision merchants, etc. can be obtained
from the Consistoire Israélite, address & ☎ above.

MÂCON (SAÔNE-ET-LOIRE)
Syn. & Com. Centre: 32 rue des Minimes, 71000.

MARIGNANE (BOUCHES DU RHÔNE)
Syn. & Com. Centre: 9 rue Pilote-Larbonne, 13700.

MARSEILLE (BOUCHES DU RHÔNE)
Synagogues & Religious Organisations
Regional Chief Rabbi: Rabbi Jacques Ouaknin. ☎ 9137-49-64.
Consistoire Israélite de Marseille, 117-119 rue Breteuil, 13006. ☎ 9137-71-84.
Main Synagogue (Sephardi), 117 rue Breteuil, 13006. ☎ 9137-49-64.

Com. Centres: Centre Edmond Fleg, 4 Impasse Dragon,13006. ☎ 9137-42-
01; Centre La Rose, 31 Av. des Olives, 13013. ☎ 9170-05-45; Centre Tif'eret
Israël, 205 Blvd. Sainte Marguerite, 13009.
Mikvaot: Aquarius, 82 Cannebiére. ☎ 9147-40-74; Beth Simha La Rose, 31
Av. des Olives, 13013. ☎ 9170-05-45; Longchamp, 45a rue Consolat, 13001.
☎ 9162-42-61.

Representative Organisation: B'nai B'rith, 41 Cours d'Estienne d'Orves, 13001. ☎ 9133-80-50.

Cultural & Educational Organisations

Assoc. of Cultural & Youth Centres, 67 rue Breteuil, 13006. ☎ 9137-40-57.

Jewish Library, 4 Impasse Dragon, 13006. ☎ 9137-42-01.

Welfare Organisations, Hospitals, etc.

F.S.J.U. (United Jewish Welfare Fund). Representative, H. Zana, 67 rue Breteuil. ☎ 9137-40-57.

C.A.S.I.M. (Marseille Regional Welfare Agency), 61 rue de la Palud, 13006. ☎ 9154-37-36. Dir. H. Zana.

Coopération Féminine. 10, rue St. Jacques, 13006.

Home for Aged, 'Les Oliviers,' 24 Impasse des Joncs. ☎ 9173-04-58.

Student & Youth Organisations

Jeunesse Lubavitch, 73 rue St.-Ferréol, 13006. ☎ 9133-80-96.

Jewish Scouts, 6 Impasse Dragon, 13006. ☎ 9153-54-32.

Maccabi-Sports, 8, rue du Belloi, 13006. ☎ 9181-8103.

Union des Etudiants Juifs de Marseille, 18 Cours Pierre Puget, 13006. ☎ 9133-3762.

Zionist Organisations

A.U.J.F. (United Jewish Appeal), 173 rue Paradis, 13006. ☎ 9137-03-21.

Jewish Agency Immigration Dept., 95 Cours Pierre-Puget, 13006. ☎ 9133-26-26.

WIZO, 2 Blvd. Théodore Thurner, 13006. ☎ 9148-64-26.

Israel Consulate-General, 454 rue Paradis, 13008. ☎ 9177-39-90.

Jewish Media

Radio Juive de Marseille, P.O.B. 243, 13269 Cédex 8. ☎ 9154-12-12. 4, Impasse Dragon, 13006. ☎ 9137-7878.

Bookseller: Librairie Jasyber, 95 rue St. Pierre, 13005. ☎ 9148-17-37.

Kosher Restaurants

(K) Centre Edmund Fleg, 4 Impasse Dragon, 13006. ☎ 9137-42-63.

(K) Eden-Up, 30 rue Tapis-Vert, 13001. ☎ 9191-47-59.

(K) La Crêpe à Musique, 26 rue Sainte, 13001. ☎ 9133-94-46.

(K) Le Dizengoff, 50 Cours Julien, 13006. ☎ 9148-55-45.

(K) Le Liandier restaurant pizzeria, 58 rue Liandier, 13008. ☎ 9178-5839.

(K) Le Lotus de Nissane, 94 Cours Julien, 13006. ☎ 9142-61-60.

(K) Le Sunset Plazza, 24 rue Pavillon, 13001. ☎ 9133-27-77.

(K) ORT, 23 rue des Forges, 13010. ☎ 9179-61-65.

(K) Presto Pizza Cash, Centre Commercial Résidence Bellevue, entrance rue Gaston Berger, 13010. ☎ 9175-19-00.

(K) Snack Chez Alain, 11 rue Glandevés, 13001. ☎ 9189-41-43.

(K) Snack Erets, rue Rouget-de-Lisle, 13001. ☎ 9154-03-70.

(K) Snack Partouche, 5 rue de l'Arc, 13001. ☎ 9133-26-23.

Kosher Butchers

There are 21 kosher butchers licensed by the Chief Rabbinate in various parts of the city, and they display a sign to that effect. Full details from the Consistoire, 117-119 rue Breteuil, 13006. ☎ 9137-71-84.

MELUN (SEINE-ET-MARNE)

Syn. & Com. Centre: Cnr. rues Branly & Michelet, 77000. ☎ (1) 6452-00-05.

MENTON (ALPES-MARITIMES)

Syn. & Com. Centre: Centre Altyner, 106 Cours du Centenaire. ☎ 9335-28-29.

MERLEBACH (MOSELLE)

Syn. & Com. Centre: 19 rue St.-Nicolas, 57800.

METZ (MOSELLE)

Chief Rabbi of Moselle, Rabbi Marc-Raphaël Guedj. ☎ 8775-04-44.
Main Syn.: 39 rue du Rabbin Elie-Bloch, 57000. ☎ 8775-04-44. This street
was renamed from rue de l'Arsenal, in memory of a youth movement rabbi
deported and killed by the Nazis during the Second World War.
Other syns: Adass Yechouroun, 41 rue du Rabbin Elie-Bloch; 2 rue Paul
Michaux; Oratoire Sepharade, 39 rue du Rabbin Elie-Bloch.
Com. Centre: Same address & ☎ as Main Syn.
Mikva: Contact Mme Elalouf. ☎ 8732-3804.

Kosher Restaurant:
(**K**) Galil, 39 rue du Rabbin Elie-Bloch. ☎ 8775-04-44. Open until noon every
weekday.
Kosher sections in supermarkets:
Grotzki, 3 rue du Rabbin Elie-Bloch; Atac, 23 rue de 20e Corps Américain.
(**K**) Butcher: Claude Sebbag, 22 rue Mangin, 57000. Tel 87633350.

MONTAUBAN (TARN-ET-GARONNE)

Syn. & Com. Centre: 14 rue Ste.-Claire, 82000. ☎ 6303-01-37.

MONTBELIARD

Syn.: Rue de la Synagogue, 25200.

MONTPELLIER (HÉRAULT)

Syns.: Ben-Zakai, 7 rue Général-Laffon, 34000. ☎ 6792-92-07; Mazal Tov, 18
rue Ferdinand-Fabre, 34000. ☎ 6779-09-82.
Centre Communautaire et Cultural Juif, 560, blvd. d'Antigone, 3400. ☎ 6715-
0876.
Kosher Butchers: (**K**) Camille Bensoussan, Place Millenaire-Antigone, 34000.
☎ 6766-03-22; Gilbert Bensoussan, 41 rue de Lunaret, 34000. ☎ 6772-67-94.
Cooperative casher, 18 rue Ferdinand Fabre, 3400.

MULHOUSE (HAUT-RHIN)

Syn. & Com. Centre: 2 rue des Rabbins, 68100. ☎ (03) 89662122. Fax (03) 89566349.
Mikva on premises. The old cemetery is also worth a visit - enquire at centre.

Old Age Home Residence, René Hirschler, 111 rue de la République, 68120.
☎ 8950-63-00.

Kosher Butchers:
(**K**) Chez Nessim, Passage des Halles, 68100. ☎ 8966 5565.

NANCY (MEURTHE-ET-MOSELLE)

Syn.: 17 Blvd. Joffre, 54000. ☎ 8332-10-67. Chief Rabbi: Rabbi Edmund
Schwob.
Com. Centre: 19 Blvd. Joffre, 54000. ☎ 8332-10-67.
The Musée Historique Lorrain, 64 Grand' Rue, has an important collection of
sifrei Torah, prayer books & other ritual objects.
Kosher Restaurant: (**K**) Restaurant Universitaire, 19 Blvd. Joffre, 54000. ☎
8332-10-67. Open weekdays until noon.

NANTES (LOIRE-ATLANTIQUE)
Syn. & Com. Centre: 5 Impasse Copernic, 44000. ☎ 4073-48-92. Mikva on premises.

NICE (ALPES-MARITIMES)
The community numbers approx. 30,000

Synagogues & Religious Organisations
Centre Consistorial & Syn.: 22 rue Michelet, 06100. ☎ 9351-89-80. Publishes an annual calendar and guide to Nice and district.
Main Syn.: 7 rue Gustave-Deloye, 06000. ☎ 9392-11-38.
Other Syns. & Com. Centres: 8 rue Marceau, 06000. ☎ 9385 8206; 1 rue Boissy d'Anglas 06000. ☎ 93 80 5896; 9 ave Andre Theuriet. ☎ 9398 47 89.
A.C.I. Aschkenaze, 1 rue Blacas, 06000 ☎ 93623868; Cercle des Etudes Juives, Les Oliviers, 31 Av. Henri Barbasse. ☎ 9351-4363.
Rabbinate: Regional Chief Rabbinate of Nice, Côte d'Azur & Corsica: 1 rue Voltaire 06000. ☎ 0195-82-06.

Mikva: 22 rue Michelet. ☎ 9351-89-80.

General Inf., Tourist Welcome Offices — Pavillon d'Accueil, Av. Thiers, 06000. ☎ 9388-69-63 & 9387-35-44.
Visitors to Nice will appreciate Chagal's Musée Biblique in the town.

Kosher Restaurants
(K) Le cheme Chamayime, 22 rue Rossini. ☎ 9388 4701.
(K) Le Leviathan, 1 ave Georges Clemenceau. ☎ 9387-2264.
(K) Restaurant Mazal, 11 rue Paganini, 06000. ☎ 9387-9350.
(K) Roi David Ten Li Hai, 9 rue Clément-Roassal, 06000. ☎ 9387-65-25. Also take-away.

Groceries etc.
Mickael Supermarket, 37 rue Dabray 06000. ☎ 93 88 81 23; K'gel, 11 rue Fricero, 06000. ☎ 93 86 33 01; Nizzard, 26 rue Pertinax 06000. ☎ 93 62 30 77; Mahédrin, 12 rue Trache 06000. ☎ 93 88 06 96; (K) Super Cash Colbo, 14 rue Michelet, 06100. ☎ 9352-1515.
A list of kosher butchers & bakers can be had from Chief Rabbi Mordehai Bensoussan, ☎ 9385 82 06.

Bookseller: Librairie Tanya, 25 rue Pertinax, 06000. ☎ 9380-21-74.

NÎMES (GARD)
Syn.: 40 rue Roussy, 30000. Mikva on premises. ☎ 6629-51-81.
Com. Centre: 5 rue d'Angoulème, 30000. ☎ 6626-19-51.

OBERNAI (BAS-RHIN)
Syn.: Rue de Sélestat, 67210.

ORLÉANS (LOIRET)
Syn. & Com. Centre: 14 rue Robert-de-Courtenay (to the left of the cathedral), 45000. Kosher meat available every Wed., 4.30 p.m. to 7.30 p.m.
At Pithiviers, near Orléans, there is a monument to the Jewish victims of Nazi persecution.

PARIS
Memorial to the Unknown Jewish Martyr
This stands at the corner of rue Geoffroy l'Asnier and rue Grenier sur l'Eau, Paris 75004, near the Métro Pont-Marie. The memorial, which is open daily, except Saturdays, from 10 a.m. to 12 noon and from 2 to 5 p.m., is one of the

continued from *Paris*

most unusual edifices in Paris. It is divided into two main parts an underground crypt and a four-storey building. The roof of the crypt forms a spacious street-level courtyard, in the middle of which stands a huge bronze cylinder shaped like a crematorium urn. The building contains a library, readingroom and museum devoted to the archives of the Centre de Documentation Juive Contemporaine — which gathers data on Nazi anti-Jewish crimes.

Religious Organisations

The Consistoire Central: Union des Communutés Juives de France, which represents French Jewry in all religious matters, has its headquarters in Paris at 17 rue St. Georges, 75009. ☎ 49 70 8800. Pres.: Jean Kahn. The Chief Rabbi of France, Rabbi Joseph Sitruk, can be contacted at 19 rue St. Georges. Exec. Dir.: Léon Masliah.

In addition, Paris Jewry is represented by the Consistoire de Paris, at 17 rue St. Georges. ☎ 4082-2626. Pres.: Moïse Cohen. Chief Rabbi of Paris: Rabbi David Messos. The Consistoire publishes its supplement to "Information Juive" giving a complete guide to Jewish organisations and institutions in Paris and organisations licensed by the Beth Din.

Communauté Israélite de la Stricte Observance, 10 rue Cadet, 75009. ☎ 4246 3637; Le Conseil Representatif du Judaisme Traditionaliste de France, 23 bis, rue Dufréncy 75016. ☎ 4504 1309; Jeunesse Lubavitch, 8 rue Lamartine 75009 ☎ 4526 8760.

Synagogues

Orthodox

*Belleville, 120 Blvd. de Belleville, 75020. ☎ 4366-66-93.

*Brit Chalom, 18 rue St.-Lazare, 75009. ☎ 4878-45-32.

*Buffault, 28 rue Buffault, 75009. ☎ 4526-80-87.

Chasseloup-Laubat, 14 rue Chasseloup-Laubat, 75015. ☎ 4273-36-29.

*D. I. Abravanel, 84-86 rue de la Roquette, 75011. ☎ 4700-75-95.

Fleischmann, 18 rue des Ecouffes, 75004. ☎ 4887-97-86.

*Fondary, 13 rue Fondary, 75015. ☎ 4059-96-56.

*Julien Lacroix, 75 rue Julien Lacroix, 75020. ☎ 4636-30-10.

*Montmartre, 13 rue Ste.-Isaure, 75018. ☎ 4264-48-34.

Place des Vosges, 14 Place des Vosges, 75004. ☎ 4887-79-45.

*12-14 Cité, Moynet 75012. ☎ 4347-36-78.

*Rue Notre-Dame-de-Nazareth, 15 rue Notre-Dame-de-Nazareth, 75003. ☎ 4278-00-30.

*Rue des Saules, 42 rue des Saules, 75018. ☎ 4606-71-39.

*Rue des Tournelles, 21 bis rue des Tournelles, 75004. ☎ 4274-32-80.

*Rue Vauquelin, 9 rue Vauquelin, 75005. ☎ 4707-21-22.

*Rue Vercingétorix, 223 rue Vercingétorix, 75014. ☎ 4545-03-43.

Rue de la Victoire, 44 rue de la Victoire, 75009. ☎ 4285-71-09.

18 rue Basfroi, 75011. ☎ 4348-82-42.

32 rue Basfroi, 75011. ☎ 4367-89-20.

45 rue de Belleville, 75019.

Beth El, 3 rue Saulnier, 75009. ☎ 4770-09-23.

24 rue Bourg-Tibourg, 75004. ☎ 4307-27-49.

10 rue Cadet, 75009. (Ashkenazi)

Centre Rambam, Synagogue des Originaires du Maroc, 19-21 rue Galvani, 75017. ☎ 4574-51-81.

17 rue de la Cour-des-Noues, 75020. ☎ 4358-14-76.

11-13 rue Curial, 75019.

15 Cour Debille, 75011.

19 rue Domrémy, 75013.

continued from *Paris*

80 rue Doudeauville, 75018.
5 rue Duc, 75018.
9 rue Guy-Patin, 75010.
9 Av. Hoche, 75008.
1 rue Jadin, 75017.
8 rue Lamartine, 75009.
4 rue Martel, 75010.
25 rue Michel-Leconte, 75003.
31 rue de Montevidéo, 75016. (Ashkenazi) ☎ 4504-66-73.
4 rue Pavée, 75004. (Ashkenazi)
13-15 rue des Petites-Ecuries, 75010.
30 Blvd. du Port-Royal, 75005.
Rachi Synagogue, 6 rue Ambroise-Thomas, 75009. (Ashkenazi) ☎ 4824-86-94.
17 rue des Rosiers, 75004.
25 rue des Rosiers, 75004.
4 rue Saulnier, 75009.
70 Av. Secrétan, 75019.
37 Blvd. de Strasbourg, 75010.
51 Blvd. de Strasbourg, 75010.
29 rue de Thionville, 75019.
37 rue des Trois-Bornes, 75011.
61-65 rue Vergniaud, 75013. ☎ 4588-93-84.
6 bis Villa d'Alésia, 75014.
25 Villa d'Alésia, 75014.
Conservative: Adath Shalom. 22bis, rue des Belles Feuilles 75116. ☎ 4553 8409.
Liberal: 24 rue Copernic, 75016. ☎ 4727-25-76.
Syn. & Centre, Mouvement Juif Libéral de France, 11 rue Gaston-de-Caillavet. ☎ 4575-38-09.
*These synagogues are used by the North African community.

Mikvaot
176 rue du Temple, nr. Place de la République, 75003. ☎ 4271-89-28; 6 rue Ambroise Thomas, 75009 (men), ☎ 4824-86-94; 50 rue du Faubourg St.-Martin, 07010. ☎ 4206-43-95; 31 rue Thionville, 75019. ☎ 4245-74-20; 75 rue Julien Lacroix, 75020, ☎ 4636-3920; 10 rue Cadet (men), ☎ 4246-3647; 19-21 rue Gahrani. ☎ 4574-5280; 1, rue des Annelets (men & women), ☎ 4245-5781; 25, rue Riquet (men & women). ☎ 4036-4092; 93, rue des Orteaux (men), ☎ 4024-1060.

Representative Organisations
Anti-Defamation League of B'nai B'rith, 4 bis rue de Lota, 75016. ☎ 4553-03-22.
B'nai B'rith, 38 rue de Clichy, 75009. ☎ 4082-91-11.
Conseil Représentatif des Institutions Juives de France (C.R.I.F.), 19 rue de Téhéran, 75008. ☎ 4561-00-70.
World Jewish Congress, 78 Av. des Champs Elysées, 75008. ☎ 4359-94-63.

Cultural & Educational Organisations
Alliance Israélite Universelle, 45 rue La Bruyère, 75009. ☎ 4280-35-00.
The Alliance is responsible for the maintenance of 124 schools (with 28,000 pupils) in various parts of the Mediterranean.
Alliance Israélite Universelle Library, 45 rue la Bruyére, 75009. (Tues. and Thurs. 1-5 p.m., Wed. 1-7.30 p.m., closed in Aug.). ☎ 4744-75-84.
Association Culturelle des Israélites Nord Africains, 151 Blvd. Magenta, 75010. ☎ 4525-72-76.

continued from *Paris*

Centre de Documentation Juive Contemporaine, 17 rue Geoffroy l'Asnier, 75004. ☎ 4508-06-04. Daily except Sat. and Sun.
Jewish Art Museum, 42 rue des Saules, 75018. (Open Sun., Tues. & Thurs., 3-6 p.m.) (Métro: Lamarck.)
Library of Federation of Jewish Societies of France, 68 rue de la Folie Méricourt, 75011.
Medem Library (Yiddish), 52 rue René Boulanger, 75010.
ORT, 10 Villa d'Eylau, 75016. ☎ 4553-55-16.
Ozar Hatorah, 2 rue Fléchier 75009, ☎ 48-78-77-14 - Recently opened a new network of schools in Paris and throughout France.
Rabbinical Seminary Library, 9 rue Vauquelin, 75005. ☎ 4707-21-22.

Welfare Organisations
American Jewish Joint Distribution Committee (Office for France), 33 rue de Miromesnil, 75008.
C.A.S.I.P. (Paris Jewish Committee for Social Welfare Action), 60 rue Rodier, 75009.
C.O.J.A.S.O.R. (Jewish Committee for Social Welfare Action and Reconstruction), 6 rue Rembrandt, 75008. ☎ 4359-03-63.
F.S.J.U. (Unified Jewish Social Welfare Fund), 19 rue de Téhéran, 75008. ☎ 4563-17-28. Fax. 4563-3462.
O.P.E.J. (Operation for the Protection of Jewish Children), 10 rue Théodore Ribot, 75017. ☎ 4622-00-87 and 00-88.
OSE, 9 Passage de la Boule Blanche, 75012. ☎ 4345-60-07.

Student and Youth Organisations
Centre Edmond Fleg, 8 bis rue de l'Eperon, 75006. Students' clubhouse, (K) restaurant cultural centre, library. ☎ 4633-43-24.
Centre Rachi (Jewish University Students' Centre), 30 Blvd. du Port Royal, 75005. ☎ 4331-98-20.
Eclaireurs Israélites de France (Jewish Scouts), 27 Av. de Ségur, 75007. ☎ 4786-60-33.
Front des Etudiants Juifs (Jewish Students' Front), 59 Blvd. de Strasbourg, 75010. ☎ 4523-14-89.

Jewish Group Holidays:
C.A.E.J., British European Centre for Jewish Youth, 7 rue Marbeuf, 75008. ☎ 4720-81-25, Fax.: 4070-0230; Centres Culturels de Vacances et de Loisirs, 19 rue de Téhéran, 75008. ☎ 4563-49-81 (Dept. of F.S.J.U.), Kosher hotel in the French Alps; A.M.E. Vacances Françaises, 27 Av. de Ségur, 75007. ☎ 4783-63-29.

Jewish Student Hostels:
(K) Foyer-Logement Merkaz Ohr Joseph, 44-48 Quai de la Marne, 75019. (Métro: Ourcq). Male students only. ☎ 4245-83-37. Restaurant on premises. Pension accom. available for students & visitors all year round except Aug.
(K) Jewish Youth Centre & Com. Centre, 19 Blvd. Poissonniére, 75002. ☎ 4233 64-96. Open for lunch at mid-day on the Sabbath, on presentation of pre-paid tickets. These are available at the centre until 1 p.m. on Fri. Centre closed Aug.
Maccabi, 20 rue Nungesser-et-Coli, 75016. ☎ 4605-35-78.
Union des Etudiants Juifs de France (Jewish Students' Union), 47 rue de Chabrol, 75010. ☎ 4523-45-69.

Zionist Organisations
Betar, 59 Blvd. de Strasbourg, 75010. ☎ 4523-14-89.
Bné Akiva, 8 rue Bichat, 75010. ☎ 4240-40-29.

continued from *Paris*

Fédération des Organisations Sionistes de France, 38 rue Turbigo, 75003. ☎ 4274-00-55.

Israël Hatzeira, 47 rue de Chabrol, 75010. ☎ 4770-97-34.

Jewish Agency, 17 rue Fortuny, 75017. ☎ 4766-03-13.

Keren Hayesod & Aide à Israel, 10 rue d'Aumale, 75009. ☎ 4041-91-50

Keren Kayemeth Leisrael, 110 rue de Rivoli, 75001. ☎ 4041-91-50.

Mizrachi-Hapoel Hamizrachi European Office, 4 rue Martel, 75010. ☎ 4521-62-74.

Siona (Sephardi Zionists), 52 rue Richer, 75009. ☎ 4246-04-39.

WIZO, 24 rue du Mont-Thabor, 75001. ☎ 4260-38-19.

Youth Aliyah, 256 rue Marcadet, 75018. ☎ 4229-39-16.

Zionist Movement of France, 38 rue de Turbigo, 75003. ☎ 4272-70-30.

Israel Embassy & Consulate, 3 rue Rabelais, 75008. ☎ 4256-47-47.

Booksellers, etc.

Bibliophane, 26 rue des Rosiers, 75004. ☎ 4887-82-20.

Diasporama, 20 rue des Rosiers, 75004. ☎ 4278-3050. Fax 4274-3876. Judaica Artefacts, music, etc.

Keren Hasefer, 9 rue Vauquelin, 75005 (by correspondence only). Books, records & educational material.

Libermann (Hebraica, Judaica), 12 rue des Hospitaliéres Saint-Gervais, 75004. ☎ 4887-32-20.
Antiquities, Jewish paintings.

Librairie Allouche, 7 rue des Rosiers, 75004.

Librairie Colbo, 3 rue Richer, 75009. ☎ 4770-21-81.

Librairie L. Kra, 6 Pl. d'Estienne d'Orves, 75009. ☎ 4770-41-85.

Librairie du Progrés, 23 rue des Ecouffes, 75004. ☎ 4272-94-44.

Librairie du Temple, 1 rue des Hospitalières St Gervais, 75004. ☎ 4272-3800. Fax 4278-7947.

Service Technique pour l'Education, 19 Blvd. Poissonnière, 75002. ☎ 4508-47-56. Open during Aug. Books and records. Inf. for Jewish tourists.

Jewish Newspapers

Actualité Juive 47 Ave Mathuriu Moreau, 75019. ☎ 4206-03-03. Obtainable from most Jewish shops.

Information Juive, Journal des Communautés, 17 rue St. Georges, 75009. ☎ 4285-71-09.

L'Arche (monthly), 14 rue Georges Berger, 75017. ☎ 4763-70-52.

Tribune Juive (weekly), 29 rue Fbg. Poissonnière 9ᶜ. ☎ 4523-1920. Fax 4523-1304.

Unsere Stime (Yiddish), 20 rue F. Duval, 75004.

Unser Weg (Yiddish), 4 rue Martel, 75010.

Unser Wort (Yiddish), 14 rue du Grand Prieuré, 75011. ☎ 4355-51-99.

Jewish Radio Programme: Radio Communauté Judaïque FM, P.O.B. 124, 75825. ☎ 4763-43-58.

Hotels

(K) Hôtel le Galilée, 8 Ave. de la Soeur Rosalie 75013. ☎ 4354 9387.

(K) Hotel-Restaurant Lebron, 4 rue Lamartine, 75009. ☎ 4878-75-52.

Hotel Concorde St.-Lazare (324), 108 rue St.-Lazare, 75008. ☎ 4294-22-22.

L'Hotel de Mericourt, 50 rue Folie Mericourt, 75011. ☎ 4338-73-63.

Montalembert, 3 rue de Montalembert, 75007. ☎ 4548-68-11 & 4548-61-59.

P.L.M.-Saint Jacques (812), 17 Blvd. St.-Jacques, 75014. (Métro: St.-Jacques). ☎ 4589-89-80.

(K) Kosher kitchen, but catering is for special groups and parties by prior arrangement only at present.

Hotel Touring, 21 rue Buffault 75009. ☎ 4878-0916. Fax. 4878-2774.

continued from *Paris*

Kashrut
For organisations operating under the authority of the Consistoire consult accordingly.

For up-to-date information on provisions and establishments consult Cachère Magazine, 10 rue de Platrières, 75020. ☎ 4040 9808. Fax. 40409522. This is a commercial publication not under any rabbinical authority.

Kosher Restaurants
The **(K)** restaurant at the Jewish Youth Centre & Com. Centre, 19 Blvd. Poissonniére, 75002 (Métro: Bonne Nouvelle), ☎ 4233-64-96, is open from Mon. to Fri. between 12 noon & 2 p.m., and 7 p.m. & 9 p.m. except during Aug., when the centre is closed. Jewish visitors from Britain are especially welcome and are invited to participate in various activities organised at the Centre. Inq. to the manager.
For updated information regarding restaurants, contact ☎ 4285-05-45.
(K) Fri. night & Sat. afternoon meals under the supervision of the Paris Beth Din are available against payment in advance from Beth El Syn., 3 rue Saulnier, 75009. ☎ 4770-09-23.

(K) Adolphe, 14 rue Richer, 75009. ☎ 4770-91-25.
(K) Auberge Ashkefarade, 2 rue Lamartine, 75009. ☎ 4878-42-83.
(K) Aux Iles Philippines, 17 rue Laplace. ☎ 4633-18-59.
(K) Aux Surprises, 40 bis rue du Faubourg-Poissonniére, 75010. ☎ 4770-55-96, 4770-24-19 or 4246-18-02. (Dairy).
(K) Azar & Fils, 6 rue Geoffroy-Marie, 75009. ☎ 4770-08-38.
(K) Berbéche Burger, 47 rue Richer, 75009. ☎ 4770-81-22.
(K) Brasserie de Tunis, 11 rue Geoffroy-Marie, 75009. ☎ 4824-19-03.
(K) Cash Food, 63 Rue de Vinaigriers, 75010. ☎ 4203-95-75.
(K) Centre Comunautaire, 8 Rue de la 8 Mai 1945 94000. ☎ 4377-01-70.
(K) Centre Edmond Fleg, 8 bis rue de l'Eperon, 75006. ☎ 4633-43-31.
(K) Centre Communautaire, 19 Blvd. Poissonniére, 75002. ☎ 4233-64-96.
(K) Centre Rachi, 30 Blvd. du Port Royal, 75005. ☎ 4331-98-20.
(K) Chalom, 10 rue Richer, 75009. ☎ 4246-77-70.
(K) Chez François, 5 rue Ramponeau, 75020. ☎ 4797-87-28.
(K) Chez Gabin, 92 Blvd. de Belleville, 75020. ☎ 4358-78-14.
(K) Chez Harry (Galil), 24 rue Richer, 75009. ☎ 4824-12-50.
(K) Delices de Maroc, 7 rue Montyon, 75009. ☎ 4022-00-17.
(K) Douer Restaurant, 21 rue Bergére, 18 Cité Bergére, 75009. ☎ 4523-53-22.
(K) Eilat's Food, 8 rue Geoffroy-Marie, 75009. ☎ 4246-39-56.
(K) Elygel, 116 Bld. de Belleville, 75020. ☎ 4797-09-73.
(K) Espace Gourmand, 85/89 ave Victor Hugo, Aubervilliers, 93300. ☎ 4834-5422.
(K) Falafel Meny, 39 rue Richer, 75009. ☎ 4246-03-73.
(K) Gagou, 8 rue de la Grange Bateliere, 75009. ☎ 4770-05-02.
(K) Georges de Tunis, 40 rue Richer, 75009. ☎ 4770-43-77.
(K) Habiba, 3 ter rue des Rosiers, 75004. ☎ 4887-39-73.
(K) Hattab Letun, 8 rue du Passage-St.-Martin, 75010. ☎ 4206-42-77.
(K) King Salomon, 46 rue Richer, 75009. ☎ 4246-31-22. (Dairy).
(K) L'Atikva, 3 Cour des Petites Ecouries, 75010. ☎ 4770-67-07.
(K) La Colombe, 46 rue Jules Guesde, Levallois, 92300. ☎ 4270-8035.
(K) La Cave des Amateurs, 48 rue Volta, 75003. ☎ 4277-04-25.
(K) La Grillade, 17 rue Montyon, 75009. ☎ 4824-06-57.
(K) La Halavite, 26 bis rue de l'Ourcq, 75019. ☎ 4034-40-84.
(K) La Parnassa, 53 Bld. Montparnasse, 75006. ☎ 4544-97-47.
(K) La Rose Blanche, 10 bis rue Geoffroy-Marie, 75009. ☎ 4523-37-70.

continued from *Paris*

(K) La Tarteliére, 231 Blvd. Voltaire, 75011. ☎ 4024-14-75. (Dairy).
(K) La Toasterie, 48 rue Richer, 75009. ☎ 4770-55-96, 4770-24-19 or 4246-18-02.
(K) Le Bambou d'Eilat, 2 rue de Nantes, 75019. ☎ 4209-19-14.
(K) Le Chalom, 231 Blvd. Voltaire, 75011. ☎ 4348-29-32.
(K) Le Chandelier, 7 rue Dufresnoy, 75016. ☎ 4504-90-50.
(K) Le Cotel, 5 Bld. Henri Poincarre, 95200. ☎ 3992-42-38. (Dairy).
(K) Le Cristal, 11 rue Montyon, 75009. ☎ 4246-21-65.
(K) Le Gros Ventre, 7-9 rue Montyon, 75009. ☎ 4824-25-34.
(K) Le Laguna, 8 rue d'Estienne d'Orves, 94000. ☎ 4207-10-38. (Dairy).
(K) Le Leviatane, rue St. Blaise, 75020. ☎ 4367-87-09.
(K) Le Milki, 56 rue Richer, 75009. ☎ 4770-24-19. (Dairy).
Le Nouveau Magenta, 73 Blvd. Magenta, 75010. ☎ 4824-70-24.
(K) Le Rolls Pizzeria, 126 Blvd. Voltaire, 75011. ☎ 4086-53-46, 56 Av. de la République, 75011. ☎ 4338-63-18. 27 Bld. de Charonne, 75001. ☎ 4009-71-98. 91 av. Secretan 75019. ☎ 4239-50-41.
(K) Le Shalom, 231 Bld. Volaire, 75001. ☎ 4348-29-32.
(K) Le Takei's, 54 rue Richer, 75009. ☎ 4824-96-05. (Parve).
(K) Le Verre à soi, 9 rue de Cléry, 75002 ☎ 42.36.99.50.
(K) Les Ailes, 34 rue Richer, 75009. ☎ 4770-62-53.
(K) Les Jardins de Nazareth, 44 rue ND de Nazareth, 75003. ☎ 4278-98-22.
(K) Les Relais, 69 Bld. de Belleville, 75020. ☎ 4357-83-91.

continued from *Paris*

(**K**) Les Tables de la Loi, 15 rue St.-Gilles, 75003. ☎ 4804-38-02.
(**K**) Lotus de Nissane, 39 rue Amelot, 75011. ☎ 4355-80-42.
(**K**) Lumiére de Belleville, 102 Blvd. de Belleville, 75020. ☎ 4797-51-83.
(**K**) Maxime Chemama, 16 rue de la Comines, 75003. ☎ 4027-07-07.
(**K**) Mazal Tov, 25 rue des Rosiers, 75004. ☎ 4027-87-40.
(**K**) Mitsou Yan, 18 Faubourg-Montmartre, 75009. ☎ 4523-02-22.
New Beauregard, 18 rue Beauregard, 75002. ☎ 4236-66-30.
(**K**) Nini, 24 rue Saussier-Leroy, 75017. ☎ 4622-28-93.
(**K**) Paparon Follies, 27 rue Richer, 75009. ☎ 4770-81-97.
(**K**) Paris Texas, 101 Av. Jean-Jaurés, 75019. ☎ 4245-48-61.
(**K**) Patrick, 11 rue Montyon, 75009, ☎ 4770-21-20.
(**K**) Resto Flash, 10 rue Lucien Sampaix, 75010. ☎ 4245-03-30.
(**K**) Snack Quick Delight, 24 rue Richer, 75009. ☎ 4523-05-12.
(**K**) Tibi, 128 Blvd. de Clichy, 75018. ☎ 4522-96-99.
(**K**) Yahalom, 24 rue des Rosiers, 75004. ☎ 42.77.12.35.
(**K**) Yris Cash Pates, 10 rue Saulnier, 75009. ☎ 4824-99-64.

Kosher Butchers & Bakers & Patisseries
A list of authorised butchers & bakers and patisseries can be had from the Association Consistoriale Israélite de Paris, 17 rue Saint-Georges, 75009. ☎ 4082-2626.

PARIS SUBURBS
For details of synagogues and facilities in the suburbs of Paris, refer to the synagogue organisations listed on p.270.

PAU (PYRÉNÉES ATLANTIQUES)
Syn. & Com. Centre: 8 rue des Trois-Frères-Bernadac, 64000. ☎ 5962-37-85. Mikva on premises.

PÉRIGUEUX (DORDOGNE)
Syn. & Com. Centre: 13 rue Paul-Louis-Courrier, 24000. ☎ 5353-22-52.

PERPIGNAN (PYRÉNÉES ORIENTALES)
Syn.: 54 rue Arago, 66000.
Kosher butcher:
(**K**) Gilbert Sabbah, 3 rue P.-Rameil, 66000. ☎ 6835-41-23.
There are two monuments of importance in the cemetery of Haut Vernet at Perpignan and in the com. cemetery of Rivesaltes, near the camp from which thousands of Jews were deported to Auschwitz.

PHALSBOURG (MOSELLE)
Syn.: 16 rue Alexandre-Weill, 57370.

POITIERS
Syn. & Com. Centre: 1 rue Guynemer, 86000.

REIMS (MARNE)
Syn. & Com. Centre: 49 rue Clovis, 51100. ☎ 2647-68-47.
There is a war memorial in the Blvd. Général Leclerc with an urn containing ashes from a number of Nazi death camps.

RENNES (ILLE-ET-VILLAINE)
Syn.: 23 rue de la Marbaudais, 35000.

ROANNE (LOIRE)
Syn. & Com. Centre: 9 rue Beaulieu, 42300. ☎ 7771-51-56.

ROUEN (SEINE-MARITIME)
Syn. & Com. Centre: 55 rue des Bons-Enfants, 76100. ☎ 3571-01-44.
The Jewish Youth Club can provide board-residence for student travellers and holiday-makers.

ST. AVOLD (MOSELLE)
Syn.: Pl. du Marché, 57500. ☎ 8791-1616. The American military cemetery here contains the graves of many Jewish soldiers who fell in the Second World War.

ST. DENIS
(See under Réunion at end of section on France.)

ST.-DIE (VOSGES)
Syn.: Rue de l'Evêché, 88100. Services, festivals & Holy-days only.

ST.-ETIENNE (LOIRE)
Syn. & Com. Centre: 34 rue d'Arcole, 42000. ☎ 7733-56-31.

ST.-FONS
Syn. & Religious Assoc. (Association Cultuelle): 17 Av. Albert-Thomas, 69190. ☎ 7867-39-78. Mikva.

ST.-LAURENT DU VAR
Syn. & Com. Centre: Villa 'Le Petit Clos', 35 Av. des Oliviers, 06700.

ST.-LOUIS (HAUT-RHIN)
Syns.: Rue de la Synagogue, 68300; 3 rue de Général Cassagnou, 68300. Com. Centre: 19 rue du Temple, 68300. Kosher products available. ☎ 8970-0048.
The Hegenheim cemetery dates from 1673.

ST.-QUENTIN (AISNE)
Syn. & Com. Centre: 11 ter Blvd. Henri-Martin. ☎ 2308-30-72.

SARREBOURG (MOSELLE)
Syn.: 12 rue du Sauvage.

SARREGUEMINES (MOSELLE)
Syn.: Rue Georges-V, 57200. Mikva on premises. ☎ 8798-81-40.

SAVERNE (BAS-RHIN)
Syn.: Rue du 19 Novembre, 67700.

SEDAN-CHARLEVILLE (ARDENNES)
Syn.: 6 Av. de Verdun, 08200.

SELESTAT (BAS-RHIN)
Syn. & Com. Centre: 4 rue Ste.-Barbe, 67600.

SENS (YONNE)
Syn. & Com. Centre: 14 rue de la Grande-Juiverie, 89100. ☎ 8695-16-65.
The smallest Jewish community in France.

STRASBOURG (BAS-RHIN)
Consistoire Israélite du Bas-Rhin, 23, rue Sellénick, 67000. ☎ (03) 8825-0575. Fax 8825-1275.

Regional Chief Rabbi: Rabbi René Gutman, 5 rue du Général-de-Castelnau, 67000. ☎ (03) 8832-38-97.

Synagogues & Religious Organisations

There are in all more than 15 syns. in Strasbourg; the following are amongst the largest and oldest.

Ashkenazi

Adath Israël, 2 rue St. Pierre-le-Jeune, 67000.
Ets Haïm, 28a rue Kageneck, 67000. Mikva on premises.
Synagogue de la Paix & Com. Centre: 1a rue du Grand-Rabbin-René-Hirschler, 67000. ☎ (03) 8814-4650.

Sephardi

1a rue du Grand-Rabbin-René-Hirschler, 67000.
Mikva: 1a rue du Grand-Rabbin-René-Hirschler, 67000. ☎ (03) 88-14-4668.

Booksellers

Librairie Du Cedrat, 19 rue du Maréchal-Foch, 67000. ☎ (03) 8837960, *and* Librairie Shné-Or, 15 rue de Bitche, 67000. ☎ (03) 8837-32-37
Jewish Newspaper: Echos-Unir (monthly), 1a rue du Grand-Rabbin-René-Hirschler, 67000.

Restaurants

(**K**) Le King, 28 rue Sellénick, 67000. ☎ (03) 8852 1771
(**K**) Le Wilson, 25 Blvd. Wilson, 67000. ☎ (03) 8852-0666.
(**K**) Restaurant Universitaire, 11 rue Sellénick, 67000. ☎ (03) 8825-67-97.

Kosher Food

Meat: (**K**) Buchinger, 63 Faubourg de Pièrre, 67000. ☎ 8832-85-03 & 13 rue Wimpheling, ☎ 8861 0698; (**K**) David, 20 rue Sellénick, 67000. ☎ (03) 8836-75-01.

Groceries:

(**K**) Franc Prix, 31 Faubourg de Saverne, 67000, ☎ (03) 8832-04-40 & 13 rue du Général-Rapp, ☎ (03) 8836-16-51;
(**K**) Yarden, 3 rue Finkmatt. ☎ (03) 8822-49-76, and 13 Blvd. de la Marne. ☎ 8860-1010. Open 9-12.30, 15-19.30pm.

Patisserie:

(**K**) Levy, 4 rue Strauss, Durkheim. ☎ (03) 8835-6821.
(**K**) Meyer, 9 rue de la Nuée-Bleue. ☎ (03) 8832 7379.

Wine

(**K**)Kosher vineyard nearby at Goxwiller, R. Koenig, 35 rue Principale. ☎ 8895-5193.

TARBES (HAUTES-PYRÉNÉES)

Syn. & Com. Centre: Cité Rothschild, 6 rue du Pradeau, 65000.

THIONVILLE (MOSELLE)

Syn. & Com. Centre: 31 Av. Clémenceau, 57100. ☎ 8254-47-89.

TOUL (MERTHE-ET-MOSELLE)

Syn.: Rue de la Halle, 54200.

TOULON (VAR)

Syn. & Com. Centre: Av. Lazare Carnot, 83050. ☎ 9492-61-05. Mikva.
Kosher Butchers:

(K) Abecassis, 8 rue Vincent-Courdouan, 83000. ☎ 9492-39-86.
(K) Fennech, 15 Av. Colbert, 83000. ☎ 9492-70-39.

TOULOUSE (HAUTE-GARONNE)
Regional Chief Rabbi: Rabbi Georges Haik, 17 rue Calvet, 31500. ☎ 6121-5114.
Grand Rabbinet du Toulouse et des Pays de la Garonne, 17, rue Alsace-Lorraine, 31000. ☎ 6121-5114.

Synagogues
Adat Yechouroun (Ashkenazi), 3 rue Jules-Chalande, 31000.
2 rue Palaprat, 31000. ☎ 6162-90-41 (Sephardi).
14 rue du Rempart-St.-Etienne, 31000. ☎ 6121-69-56.
Chaaré Emeth, 35 rue Rembrandt, 31000. ☎ 6140-03-88.
Mikva, 15 rue Francisque Sarcey, 31000. ☎ 6148-8984.
Com. Centre: 14 rue du Rempart-St.-Etienne, 31000. ☎ 6123-36-54.

Kosher Restaurants:
(K) Com. Centre, 14 rue du Rempart-St.-Etienne, 31000. ☎ 6123-36-54.
(Students only); **(K)** Le Kotel, 9 rue Clemence Isaaure. ☎ 61290304.

Kosher Butchers:
(K) Amsellem, 6 rue de la Colombette, 31000. ☎ 6162-97-55; **(K)** Bénichou, 7 rue des Châlets, 31000. ☎ 6163-77-39; **(K)** Cacherout Diffusion, 37 Blvd. Carnot, 31000. ☎ 6123-07-59; **(K)** Carmel, 1 rue Denfert-Rochereau, 31000. ☎ 6162-32-74; **(K)** Ghnassia, 397 Route de St.-Simon, 31000. ☎ 6142-05-81; **(K)** Lasry, 8 rue Matabiau, 31000. ☎ 6162-65-28; Kosher Groceries: **(K)** Novogel, 14, rue E. Guyiaux, 31300. ☎ 61-57-03-19. **(K)** Otguergoust, 21, pl. V. Hugo, 31000. ☎ 61-21-95-36. **(K)** Super Cach, Rondpoint de la Plaine Balma. ☎ 61246675.

TOURS (INDRE-ET-LOIRE)
Syn.: 37 rue Parmentier, 37000. ☎ 4705-56-95.
Com. Centre: 6 rue Chalmel, 37000.

TROYES (CHAMPAGNE-ARDENNES)
Syn. & Com. Centre: 5 rue Brunneval.
Mikva: 1 rue Brunneval, ☎ 2573-34-44.
A memorial statue of Rashi was unveiled at the Troyes cemetery in 1990.

VALENCE (DRÔME)
Syn. & Com. Centre: 1 Place du Colombier, 26000. ☎ 7543-34-43.

VALENCIENNES (NORD)
Syn. & Com. Centre: 36 rue de l'Intendance, 59300. ☎ 2729-11-07.

VENISSIEUX (RHÔNE)
Syn. & Com. Centre: 12 Av. de la Division-Leclerc, 69200. ☎ 7870-69-85.

VERDUN (MEUSE)
Syn.: Impasse des Jacobins, 55100.

VERSAILLES (YVELINES)
Syn.: 10 rue Albert-Joly, 78000. ☎ 39071919. Fax 39509634. Comm. Centre and Mikva.
Butcher: La Versaillaise, 112 rue de la Paroisse, 7800. ☎ 39250066.

VICHY (ALLIER)
Syn.: 2 bis rue du Maréchal Foch, 03200.

VITRY-LE-FRANÇOIS (MARNE)
Syn.: rue du Mouton, 51300. Services Yom Kippur only.

VITTEL (VOSGES)
Syn.: Rue Croix-Pierrot, 88800.

WASSELONNE (HAUT-RHIN)
Syn.: Rue des Bains, 67310.

CORSICA
(Jewish population 150-200)

AJACCIO
There are between 10 and 15 families in the town. Inq. to Jo Michel Reis, La Grande Corniche, Route des Sanguinaires. ☎ 9521-57-52.

BASTIA
This port town has a Jewish population of 25-35 families.
Syn.: 3 rue du Castagno, 20200. Services, Sat. a.m. & festivals.
Com. Pres.: Jacques Ninio, 13 Blvd. Paoli, 20200. ☎ 9531-50-16.

GUADELOUPE
The synagogue, community centre, and restaurant kosher store are located at Bas du Fort in Gosier, a suburb of Point-à-Pitre. ☎ 909908.

MARTINIQUE
FORT-DE-FRANCE
Syn. & Com. Centre: Maison Grambin, Plateau Fofo, Voie 1, 97233. Pres.: André Gabay, 43 Orée du Parc Mongérade, 97200. ☎ 603727.

REUNION
An island département of France in the Indian Ocean, with a Jewish population of about 50, mostly Sephardim. High Holy-day services and communal seder held at Communauté Juive de la Réunion, 8 rue de l'Est, St. Denis, 97400. ☎ (262) 237833. Further inf. from Leon Benamou. ☎ (262) 290545.

(**K**) Hotel Astoria, Paul Djian, 16 rue Juliette Dodu, 97400, St. Denis. ☎ (262) 200-558. Fax (262) 412-630.

TAHITI (FRENCH POLYNESIA)
PAPEETE
A.C.I.S.P.O. (Jewish Religious Assoc.): B.P. rue Morenhout-Pirac, 4821. ☎ 410392. Fax. 420909.

GEORGIA
AKHALTSIKHE
Syn.; 109 Guramishvili St

BATUMI
Syn.: 6 9th March St.

GORI
Syn.: Chelyuskin St.

continued from *Georgia*

KULASHI
Syn.: 170 Stalin St.

ONNI
Syn.: Baazova St.

POTI
Syns.: 23 Ninoshivili,; Tskhakaya St.

SUKHUMI
Syn.: 56 Karl Marx St.

SURAMI
Syn.: Internatsionalnaya St.

TBILISI
Syn.: 45-47 Leselidze St. There is an Ashkenazi syn. near by, at 65 Kozhevenny La. The lane is unmarked, but there is a small drinking fountain on the corner at the entrance to the lane. It is advisable to ask for directions at the Sephardi syn. in Leselidze St.
Organisation: Jews of Georgia Assoc., Tsaritsy Tamari St. 8., 380012. ☎ (883-2) 34-10-57.

TSHKINVALI
Syn.: Isapov St.

TSKHAKAYA
Syn.: Mir St.

VANI
Syn.: 4 Kaikavadze St.

GERMANY
Even the Nazis, with their extermination policy, failed to sever completely Jewish connections with Germany, which go back uninterruptedly to Roman times, although official Jewish communities are of more recent date. In West Berlin, for instance, the community celebrated its 300th anniversary in 1971. Hitler was the latest and most virulent persecutor of German Jewry, but though he came nearest of all to wiping out the country's Jews, he did not succeed in obliterating their incalculable contribution over the centuries to German and world culture, the sciences, the economy and other fields of human endeavour.

When the Nazis gained power in 1933, more than half a million Jews lived in Germany, 160,000 in Berlin. Today there are only some 50,000 registered members of the German community, including some 9,400 in Berlin, 5,300 in Frankfurt & 4,100 in Munich and recent immigrants from Russia.

Buildings, monuments and relics of all kinds abound in Germany today, perpetuating the memory of a great and numerous community reduced to a pale shadow of its former self.

AACHEN
Rep. Organisation: Bundesverband Jüdischer Studenten in Deutschland Oppenhoffallee 50. ☎ (0241) 75998.

ALSENZ
The restored 18th-century syn. in this small village is at Kirchberg 1.

AMBERG
Com. Centre: Salzgasse 5. ☎ (09621) 1-31-40.

ANNWEILER
The oldest cemetery in the Palatinate dating from 16th c. Information: 06235-3333.

ANDERNACH
This Rhine Valley town contains an early 14th-century mikva. Key obtainable from tourist office.

AUGSBURG
Com. Centre: Halderstr. 8. ☎ (0821) 51-79-85. There is a Jewish museum in the restored Liberal syn. See also Ichenhausen below.

BAD KISSINGEN
(K) Eden-Park, Rosenstr. 5-7, D-97688. ☎ 971-7172-00. Fax 971-7172-72.

BAD KREUZNACH
Com. Centre: Gymnasialstr. 11. ☎ (0671) 2-69-91.

BAD NAUHEIM
Syn. (Sabbaths only) & Com. Centre: Karlstr. 34. ☎ (06032) 56-05. M.: Rabbi Wald.
(K) Kosher meals can be obtained at Club Shalom, in the Syn. & Com. Centre bldg., entrance from Friedensstr. Under the supervision of Rabbi Wald. ☎ (06032) 3-11-57;
Kosher Hotel: (K) Accadia, Lindenstr. 15/Frankfurterstr. 22. ☎ (06032) 3-90-68.
Deutscher Koordinierungs Rat der Gesellschaften für Christlich — Jüdische Zusammenarbeit, Otto-Weiß-Str. 2. ☎ (06032) 91-11-0.

BADEN-BADEN
Syn & Community Centre: Werder Str. 2, ☎ 07221-39 1021.

BAMBERG
Com. Centre: Willy-Lessing-Str. 7. ☎ (0951) 2-32-67.

BAYREUTH
Com. Centre: Münzgasse 2. ☎ (0921) 6-54-07.

BERLIN
Synagogues & Religious Organisations
Pestalozzistr. 14 (Liberal), 1000 Berlin 12. ☎ (030) 313-84-11. M.: Rabbi Ernst Stein.
Dernburgstr. 26. 1000 Berlin 19. ☎ (030) 321-20-56.
Fränkelufer 10-12. 1000 Berlin 36. ☎ (030) 614-51-31.
Joachimstaler Str. 13. 1000 Berlin 15. ☎ (030) 880280. Mins.: Rabbi Moshe Dick. ☎ (030) 884-20321, & Rabbi Ernst M. Stein, Joachimstaler Str. 13. ☎ (030) 884-20-321.
Adass Jisroel (est 1869) 40 Tucholsky St., 0-1040 Berlin Mitte. ☎ 281 3135. Fax 281-3122.
Com. Centre: This has been built on the site of a famous syn. destroyed by the Nazis — Fasanenstr. 79-80 (off the Kurfürstendamm). ☎ (030) 88-42-030.
Rykestr. 53, 1055. ☎ 448-52-98.
Neue Synagogue Berlin — Centrum Judaicum, Oranienburger-Str. 28, 1040. ☎ 280-12-50 or 280-12-51. Dir.: Dr. Hermann Simon.

Cemeteries: Heerstr. am Scholzplatz, Berlin-Charlottenburg. ☎ (030) 304-32-34; 2 Wittlicher St, 0-1120, Berlin-Weissensee; Herbert-Baum-Str. 45, 1120 Berlin-Weissensee. ☎ (0372) 365-33-30; Adass Yisroel, Wittlicher Strasse (Falkenberger Chaussee), 1120 Berlin-Weissensee; Schönhauserallee 23, 1058 Berlin-Prenzlauer Berg.

Representative & Student Orgs.
B'nai B'rith Leo Baeck Lodge, Com. Centre, Fasanenstr. 79-80. ☎ (030) 883-53-17; Janusz Korczak Lodge, Passauerstr. 4. ☎ (030) 213-96-26; Raoul Wallenberg Lodge, Kurfürstendamm 48-49. ☎ (030) 881-36-58.
Jüdischer Kulturverein Berlin e. V. Monbijouplatz 4, 10178 Berlin Mitte. ☎ (030) 2826669. Contact: Dr. Irene Runge.
Jüdische Studentenvereinigung in Berlin, Fasanenstr. 79-80, Berlin 12. ☎ (030) 883-17-96.
Makkabi (Jüdischer Turn- und Sportverband), Joachimstaler Str. 13. ☎ (030) 883-17-80. Secretariat: Passauer-Str. 4. ☎ (030) 213-88-89.
Zentralrat der Juden in Deutschland. Berlin Office, Oranienburger Str. 31, 10117. ☎ (030) 282 8714.

Homes, Hospitals, etc.
Homes: Altenheim, Iranische Str. 3, 65. ☎ (030) 492-30-61; Heinrich-Stahl-Wohnheim, Baseler Str. 11, 45. ☎ (030) 833-27-94; Leo-Baeck-Wohnheim, Herbartstr. 26, 19. ☎ (030) 321-20-56; Pflegeheim, Iranische Str. 2, 65. ☎ (030) 492-42-90; Dernburgstr. 36, 19. ☎ (030) 321-20-56.
Hospital: Iranische Str. 2-4, 65. ☎ (030) 492-30-61.

Zionist Organisations
Jewish Agency, Joachimstaler Str. 13. ☎ (030) 881-94-25.
Jewish National Fund, Joachimstaler Str. 13. ☎ (030) 883-43-60.
State of Israel Bonds, Kurfürstendamm 61. ☎ (030) 883-40-91.
United Israel Appeal-Keren Hayesod, Joachimstaler Str. 13, 1000. ☎ (030) 883-52-73.
WIZO, Fäderation Deutschland Joachimsthaler Str. 13, 10719.
Zionist Org. Regional Office, Joachimsthaler Str. 13. ☎ (030) 881-77-97.

Library, Bookshop & Newspapers
Literaturhandlung, Joachimstaler-Str. 13, D-10719. ☎ 030/88 24 250. Fax. 030 88 54 713.
Jewish Library, Oranienburger Str. 28. ☎ 280-12-29.
There is a branch office of the Allgemeine jüdische Wochenzeitung (weekly) at Oranienburger Str. 31, 1040 Berlin (East) 030/238-66-06 & 282 87-42.
The Jüdischer Kulturverein publishes its Jüdische Korrespondenz monthly in German and Russian.

Restaurants, etc.
Cafe Oren, Oranienburger Str. 28, 10117 D. ☎ (030) 282-82-28/2801 201.
(K) Arche Noah Restaurant at Com. Centre, Fasanenstr. 79-80, 12. ☎ (030) 884-20-3/39.
(K) Beth Café, Tucholskystrasse 40, 10117 D. ☎ 281-31-35.
(K) Kolbo, Auguststr. 77/78, 10117 D. ☎ (030) 281-3135.
(K) Schalom Snack Bar, Wielandstr. 43. ☎ (030) 312-11-31.
(K) Kachol Lavan, 4 Passaner Str. ☎ (030) 217 7506 (Supermarket).

BOCHUM
Syn.: Alte Wittener Str. 18, 44 803. Tel (0234) 361563. Fax (0234) 361563. Fax (0234) 360187.

BONN/BAD GODESBERG
Syn. & Com. Centre: Tempelstr. 2-4, cnr. Adenauer Allee, 53113. ☎/Fax(0228) 21-35-60.

Representative Organisation
Zentralrat der Juden in Deutschland (Central Council of Jews in Germany). Secretariat, Rüngsdorfer Str. 6, 53173. ☎ (0228) 35-70-23. Fax. (0228) 36-11-48.

Israel Embassy, Simrockallee 2, 53173. ☎ (0228) 93-46-545.
Jewish Community Fund of N.W. Germany, Rungsdorfer Str. 6, 53173.
Newspaper: Allgemeine jüdische Wochenzeitung (2-weekly), Rüngsdorfer Str. 6, 53173. ☎ (0228) 35-10-21. Fax. (0228) 35-54-69.

BRAUNSCHWEIG
Com. Centre: Steinstr. 4. ☎ (0531) 4-55-36.
The Jewish Museum founded in 1746 was formerly the oldest Jewish museum in the world. It was re-opened in 1987 under the auspices of the Braunschweigisches Landesmuseum at Hinter Aegidien, 3300. ☎ (0531) 484-2602. Hours Tues-Sun: 10-17; Thurs 10-20.00.

BREMEN
Syn. & Com. Centre: Schwachhauser Heerstr. 117. ☎ (0421) 498-51-04. Fax (0421) 498-49-44. M.: Rabbi Dr. B. Z. Barslai. ☎ (421) 440583. Fax (0421) 4986980.

CHEMNITZ
Com. Centre: Stollberger Str. 28. ☎ 3-28-62.

COBLENZ
Com. Centre: Schlachthof Str. 5. ☎ (0261) 4-22-23.

COLOGNE
Syn. & Com. Centre: Roonstr. 50, 50674. ☎ (0221) 9215600. Fax (0221) 9215609. Daily services. There are a youth centre, Jewish museum & library at the same address.
Germania Judaica, Kölner Bibliothek zur Geschichte des Judentums, Josef-Haubrich-Hof 1, 50676, ☎ 0221-232349.
(K) Kosher meals are available at the Com. Centre. ☎/Fax (0221) 240 4440.
Home for Aged, Cologne-Sülz, Berrenratherstr. 480.
Frauenbund, Rovenstr. 50, 50674.
WIZO, Franzstr. 12. ☎ (0221) 40-47-14 & 72-82-84.
Hotel: Leonet (80), Rubensstr. 33. ☎ (0221) 23-60-16.

DARMSTADT
Com. Centre: Wilhelm-Glässing-Str. 26. ☎ (06151) 2 88 97.

DORTMUND
Syn. & Com. Office: Prinz-Friedrich-Karl-Str. 9, 44135. ☎ (0231) 52-84-97. M.: Rabbi Dr. Henry G. Brandt. ☎ (0231) 52-84-96. Fax (0231) 52-13-85.
Landesverband der Jüdischen Kultusgemeinden von Westfalen, Prinz-Friedrich-Karl-Str. 12, 44135. ☎ (0231) 52-84-95. Fax (0231) 58-60-372.

DRESDEN
Syn.: Fiedlerstr. 3. ☎ 69-33-17.
Com. Centre:
Representative Organisation: Landesverband der Jüdischen Gemeinden von

Sachsen, Thüringen, Bautzner Str. 20, 8060 Dresden. ☎ 578691.
A memorial to the six million Jews killed in the Holocaust stands on the site
of the Dresden Synagogue, burnt down by the Nazis in November, 1938.

DUISBURG
Salomon Ludwig Steinheim-Institut für deutsch-jüdische Geschichte (Institute
of German-Jewish History, affiliated to Duisburg University), Geibelstr. 41,
47057. ☎ (203) 37-00-71. Fax (203) 37-33-80. Email: sti@uni-duisberg.de.
www:http://stil.uni.duisberg.de

DÜSSELDORF
Syn. & Com. Office: Zietenstr. 50. ☎ (0211) 461 9120. Fax (0211) 485156.
M. Rabbi Goldberger. ☎ (0211) 46191216.
Representative & Youth Orgs.
B'nai B'rith, Kasernenstr. 23. ☎ (0211) 32-99-11 & 32-48-48.
Landesverband der Jüdischen Gemeinden von Nordrhein, Mauerstr. 41. ☎
(0211) 44-68-09.
Youth & Student Centre, Mauerstr. 41. ☎ (0211) 4691233.
Home for Aged: Nelly Sachs Home for the Aged, Nelly-Sachs-Str. 5. ☎ (0211)
43-42-45.

Zionist Organisations
Jewish National Fund, Kaiserstr. 28. ☎ (0211) 49-40-08.
WIZO, Zietenstr. 50. ☎ (0211) 4417251.
Hotel: Gildors Hotel (under Israeli ownership), Collenbachstr. 51. ☎ (0211)
48-80-05.

EMMENDINGEN/BADENIA
Syn.: Lenzhäusle am Schlossplatz. ☎ (07641) 571989.

ERFURT
Com. Centre: Juri-Gagarin-Ring 16. ☎ 2-49-64.

ESSEN
Com. Centre: Sedanstr. 46. ☎ (0201) 27-34-13.

ESSINGEN
Largest cemetery in the Palatinate, where Anne Frank's ancestors are buried,
16th c. Key at the Mayor's office.

FRANKFURT-AM-MAIN
Synagogues & Religious Organisations
Altkänigstr. 27 (Beth Hamidrash West End). ☎ (069) 72-38-05.
Baumweg 5-7. ☎ (069) 43-93-81 & 49-9-07-58.
Freiherr-vom-Stein-Str. 30 (Westend Syn.). ☎ (069) 72-62-63. This is the city's
main syn.
Röderbergweg 29 (Beth Hamidrash). ☎ (069) 61-59-14/49-04-72.
Com. Centre: Westendstr. 43. ☎ (069) 74-07-21. The com. produces a month-
ly magazine, 'Jüdische Gemeinde-Zeitung Frankfurt'.
The **(K)** com. restaurant, the Sohar, is at the Comm. Centre, entrance in
Savignystr. 66, which see for details. ☎ 75-23-41.
Cemeteries: Eckenheimer Landstr. 238, ☎ (069) 56-18-26; Old Cemetery:
Rat-Beil-Str. ☎ (069) 55-73-59 for appointment; Battonstr. Key obtainable
from Com. Centre.
Mikva: Westend Syn.

Representative Organisations
B'nai B'rith, Liebigstr. 24. ☎ (069) 72-41-37-9.
Landesverband der Jüdischen Gemeinden in Hessen, Hebelstr. 6. ☎ (069) 44-40-49.
Verband jüdischer Akademiker in Deutschland e.V., Im Trierschen Hof 17, ☎ 29 35 17.
Verband Jüdischer Heimatvertriebener und Flüchtlinge in der Bundesrepublik Deutschland, Friedrichstr. 27. ☎ (069) 72-55-30.
Zentralwohlfahrtsstelle der Juden in Deutschland e.V. Hebelstra 6, D 60318. ☎ (069) 944371-0. Fax (069) 49 48 17.

Welfare & Miscellaneous Orgs.
Central Welfare Org. of Jews in Germany. Headquarters: Hebelstr. 6. D-60318. ☎ (069) 244371-0. Fax. (069) 494817.
Homes for Aged: Bornheimer Landwehr 79b. ☎ (069) 43-96-02; Budgestiftung, Wilhelmshäher Str. 279. ☎ (069) 47-87-10.
Jewish Museum, Untermainkai 14-15. ☎ (069) 212-350-00. Sun., Tues. & Thurs., 10 a.m. to 5 p.m.; Wed., 10 a.m. to 8 p.m.; Fri. 10 a.m. to 3 p.m. Closed Mon.
Jewish Restitution Successor Org., Telemannstr, 18. ☎ (069) 714170.
Jüdisches Lehrhaus, c/o R. Karafiat, Lange Str. 28. ☎ (069) 28-85-41.
ORT Germany, Hebelstr. 6. ☎ (069) 44-90-81.

Youth Centre & Students' Association
Savignystr. 66. ☎ (069) 75-13-22. The com. restaurant, the (K) Sohar, ☎ (069) 75-23-41, is open Sun., Tues., Wed. & Thurs. from noon to 3 p.m. & 6 p.m. to 9 p.m., & Fri. from after the evening service until 11 p.m. Closed Mon. It is also closed for the whole of August. Deliveries to hotels may be requested.

Zionist Organisations
Jewish Agency, Hebelstr. 6. ☎ (069) 94-33-340. Fax. 49-0473.
Jewish National Fund. Head Office, Feldbergstr. 5. ☎ (069) 72-05-21.
Makkabi, Westendstr. 43. ☎ (069) 75-19-20.
State of Israel Bonds, Hebelstr. 6. ☎ (069) 49-04-70.
United Israel Appeal-Keren Hayesod. Head Office: Friedrichstr. 27. ☎ (069) 72-90-62.
WIZO, Westendstr. 43. ☎ (069) 75-22-36.
WIZO Aviv, Friedrichstr. 29. ☎ (069) 72-12-01.
Youth Aliyah, Hebelstr. 6. ☎ (069) 4-98-01-51.
Zionist Org. in Germany, Hebelstr. 6. ☎ (069) 4-98-02-51. Fax. 49-0473.
Zionist Youth in Germany, Falkensteiner-Str. 1. ☎ (069) 55-69-63.

Hotels
Hotel Excelsior & Monopol (200), Mannheimer Str. 7-13, 6000, 1. ☎ (069) 25-60-80.
Luxor Hotel, Am Allerheiligentor 2-4. ☎ (069) 29-30-67/69. This hotel, which is under Jewish management, is within walking distance of the Freiherr-vom-Stein-Str. syn.

Kosher Food:
(K) Aviv Butchery & Deli, Hanauer Landstr. 50. ☎ (069) 43-15-39. Kosher bread is obtainable from Donath Werner, Raimundstr. 21. ☎ (069) 52-62-02.

FREIBURG
Com. Centre: Nussmannstr. 14. ☎ (0761) 38-30-96.

FRIEDBERG/HESSEN
The ancient mikva, built in 1260, is at Judengasse 20. The town council has

issued a special explanatory leaflet about it, and it is now scheduled as an historical monument of medieval architecture.

FULDA
Com. Centre; von Schildeckstr. 13. ☎ (0661) 7-02-52. Services first Friday each month, ½ before dusk.
Cemetery: Heidelsteinstr.

FÜRTH
There is a beautifully restored syn. at Julienstr. 2, as well as a historic mikva.
Com. Centre: Blumenstr. 31. ☎ (0911) 77-08-79.

GELSENKIRCHEN
Com. Centre: Von-der-Recke-Str. 9. ☎ (0209) 2-31-43 & 20-66-28.

HAGEN
Com. Centre: Potthofstr. 16. ☎ (02371) 1-32-89.
Hotel: Central, Dahlenkampstr. 2. ☎ (02371) 2-32-58.

HALLE/SAALE
Com. Centre: Grosse Märkerstr. 13. ☎ 2-69-63.

HAMBURG
Syn.: Hohe Weide 34, 20253. ☎ (040) 4409440. Mikva on premises.
Com. Centre: Schäferkampsallee 27, 20357. ☎ (040) 44-09-440. Fax (040) 410 8430. The following organisations are based at the Centre.
B'nai B'rith. Joseph Carlebach Lodge. ☎ (040) 44-09-4448.
Home for Aged: Schäferkampsallee 27, 20357. ☎ (040) 44-09-440.
Union of Jewish Students (JONS): ☎ (040) 44-09-4421.
WIZO, Postfach 202 103, 20214. Kosher food is available upon reservation. ☎ (040) 44-09-4441. Fax (040) 41-08-430.

HANOVER
Syn. & Com. Centre:
Home for Aged: Haeckelstr. 6. ☎ (0511) 81-57-50.
Landesverband der Jüdischen Gemeinden von Niedersachsen, Haeckelstr. 10, 31073. ☎ (0511) 81-27-62.

HEIDELBERG
Com. Centre:
Bundesverband jüdischer Studenten in Deutschland, Landfriedstr. 12, ☎ 18-22-01.
Hochschule für Jüdische Studien (College for Jewish Studies), Friedrichstr. 9. ☎ (06221) 2-25-76. Fax. 167-696. Daily minyan Mon. to Fri. during term-time Apr. 15 to Jul. 15 & Oct. 15 to Feb. 15. (K) Kosher meals available (by arrangement & in advance) Mon.-Fri. at college restaurant, Theaterstr., 100 yds. from college.
Zentralarchiv zur Erforschung der Geschichte der Juden in Deutschland. Dir: Dr. Peter Honigmann, Bienen Str. 5, 69117. ☎ 164-141. Fax. 181-049.

HERFORD
Com. Centre: Keplerweg 11. ☎ (05221) 20-39.

HOF/SAALE
Com. Centre: Am Wiesengrund 20. ☎ (09281) 532-49.

ICHENHAUSEN
Museum of Jewish history in the fine baroque syn. Not far from Ulm.

INGENHEIM
16th century cemetery can be visited; key to be obtained at Klingenerstr. 20.

KAISERSLAUTERN
Com. Centre: Basteigasse 4. ☎ (0631) 6-97-20.

KARLSRUHE
Com. Centre: Knielinger Allee 11. ☎ (0721) 7-20-35.
Oberrat der Israeliten Badens, Knielinger Allee 11. ☎ (0721) 7-20-36.
Landesrabbiner von Baden, Benjamin D. Soussan, c/o Israelitische Gemeinde
Freiburg Nußmannstr. 14. Freiburg. ☎ 0761/392-43

KASSEL
Com. Centre: Bremer Str. 9. ☎ (0561) 1-29-60.

KONSTANZ
Com. Centre: Sigismundstr. 19. ☎ (07531) 2-30-77.

KREFELD
Com. Centre. Wiedstr. 17b. ☎ (02151) 2-06-48.

LANDAU
Prayer room opened in the Frank-Loebsche Haus, Kaufhausgasse 9.

LEIPZIG
Com. Centre: Lährstr. 10. ☎ 29-10-28.

LÜBECK
Syn: Synagogue & Comm. Centre, St. Annen Str. 11, 23552. ☎/Fax (0451)
798-2182. Supervised through the Hamburg community.

MAGDEBURG
Com. Centre: Gräperstr. 1a. ☎ 5-26-65.
Representative Organisations: Landesverband de Jüdischen Gemeinden von
Sachsen-Anhalt, Brandenburg, Mecklenburg-Vorpommern, Gräper Str. 1a
Magdeburg. ☎ 55-2665.

MAINZ
Com. Centre: Forsterstr. 2. ☎ (06131) 61-39-90.
The key to the twelfth-century Jewish cemetery can be obtained at the 'new'
Jewish cemetery, which is at Untere Zahlbacherstr. 11.

MANNHEIM
Com. Centre: F 3-4. ☎ (0621) 15-39-74.

MARBURG/LAHN
Com. Centre: Unterer Eichweg 17. ☎ (06421) 3-28-81.

MINDEN
Com. Centre: Kampstr. 6. ☎ (0571) 2-34-37.

MÖNCHENGLADBACH
Syn. & Com. Centre: Albertusstr. 54, 41363. ☎ (02161) 2-38-79. Fax (02161) 14639.

MÜLHEIM/RUHR-OBERHAUSEN
Com. Centre: Kampstr. 7, Mülheim. ☎ (0208) 3-51-91.

MUNICH
There is a Jewish memorial at the site of the infamous Nazi concentration
camp at Dachau, some 10 miles from Munich. There are trains every half-hour
from Munich main railway station (Hauptbahnhof). From Dachau Station take
the bus going to 'Dachau Ost'.

At the corner of Maxburgstr. and Herzog-Maxstr. is a monument marking the destruction of Munich's synagogues by the Nazis on November 10, 1938. As can be seen from the list below, some have since been rebuilt.

The Israeli sportsmen murdered by Arab terrorists at the 1972 Olympic Games are commemorated by a memorial at Connollystrasse 31.
Syn. Possartstr. 15. Mikva on premises.
Reichenbachstr. 27. Mikva on premises.
Schulstrasse 30. Fri. evenings and Sabbath mornings only.
Schwabing Syn., Georgenstr. 71. Fri. evg. and Sabbath morn. only.
Rabbiner: Itzchak Ehrenberg, Reichenbachstr. 27.

Miscellaneous Organisations
Jüdisches Museum München, Maximilian Str. 36.
B'nai B'rith, Georgenstr. 71. ☎ (089) 2-71-27-74 & 2-71-82-98.
Com. Centre: Reichenbachstr. 27. ☎ (089) 2-01-49-60.
Home for Aged: Kaulbachstr. 65. ☎ (089) 34-75-90.
Makkabi, Hirschgartenallee 14, 80639. ☎ 178-3874.
WIZO, Reichenbachstr. 27. ☎ (089) 2-01-50-91.
Landesverband der Israelitischen Kultusgemeinden in Bayern, Effnerstr. 68. ☎ (089) 98-94-42 & 99-94-43.
Literaturhandlung, Fürstenstr. 17 D-80333 München. ☎ 089/280 01 35 Fax 089/28 16 01.
United Israel Appeal-Keren Hayesod, Reichenbachstr. 27/lll. ☎ (089) 2-01-55-20.
Youth Centre & Union of Jewish Students in Bavaria, Prinzregentenstr. 91. ☎ (089) 47-10-67.
(K) Restaurant run by the com., Reichenbachstr. 27/1. ☎ (089) 2-01-45-65. Hours: 12.00 - 2.30 p.m.; 6.00 p.m. - 9.00 p.m.. Shabbat meals must be ordered by Friday noon. Closed Sunday; August.

MÜNSTER
Com. Centre: Klosterstr. 8-9. ☎ (0251) 4-49-09.

NEUSTADT/RHEINPFALZ
Com. Centre. Ludwigstr. 20. ☎ (06321) 26-52.

NUREMBERG
Com. Centre & Home for Jewish Aged, Johann-Priem-Str. 20. ☎ (0911) 5-62-50.

ODENBACH
There is a historic syn. with baroque paintings in this small village near Bad Kreuznach. Inf. from Bernard Kukatzki, ☎ (06235) 3332; H. Dittrich, ☎ (06753) 2745.

OFFENBACH
Com. Centre: Kaiserstr. 109. ☎ (069) 81-48-74.
David Binzer, Seligenstädter Strasse 153a, ☎ (069) 89-21-98. Fax (069) 898396, will be pleased to meet Jewish visitors.

OSNABRÜCK
Com. Centre: In der Barlage 41, 49078. ☎ (0541) 48420. Fax (0541) 434701.

PADERBORN
Com. Centre: Pipinstr. 32. ☎ (05251) 2-25-96.
Potsdam Com. Centre: Heinrich-Mann- Allee 103, Hans 16, ☎ 87-20-18.

POTSDAM
Comm. Centre: Heinrich-Mann-Allee 103, Haus 16, ☎ 872018.

REGENSBURG
Com. Centre: Am Brixener Hof 2. ☎ (0941) 5-70-93 or 2-18-19.

RÜLZHEIM
The key to the early 19th-century syn. in this village near Karlsruhe is obtainable from the town hall.

SAARBRÜCKEN
Com. Centre: Lortzing Str. 8, 66111. ☎ (0681) 3-51-52.
Synagogengemeinde Saar, Postfach 102838, 66028.
Bundersverband Jüd. Studenten, Kaiserstr. 5, 66111. ☎ 356-800. Fax. 356-840.

SCHWERIN/MECKLENBURG
Com. Centre: Jüdische Gemeinde zu Schwerin, Schlachterstr. 3-5. ☎ (0385) 55-07-345.
Landesverband der Jüdischen Gemeinden in Mecklenburg-Vorpommern, Schlachtermarkt 3-5, 19055.

SPEYER
This town contains the oldest (11th century) mikva in W. Germany, Judenbadgasse. To visit it, obtain the key from the desk at the Hotel Trutzpfuff, in Webergasse, just round the corner, or contact Professor Stein at the Historical Museum. There are some early 19th-century village syns. in the wine-growing region of the Palatinate. For inf., contact B. Kukatzki, ☎ (06235) 3332.

STRAUBING
Com. Centre: Wittelsbacherstr. 2, 94315. ☎ (09421) 13-87.

STUTTGART
Israelitische Religionsgemeinschaft Württembergs: Hospitalstr. 36, D 70174. ☎ (0711) 22-836-0. Fax (0711) 22-836-18. M.: Rabbi Joel Berger.
A H kosher restaurant (closed Mon.) is attached to the Com. Centre.
Rabbiner Konferenz of German Rabbis at same address. ☎ (0711) 22836-20.

SULZBURG
There is a beautifully restored early 19th-century syn. here, some 20 miles from Freiburg. Keys obtainable from Mayor's office.

TRIER
Com. Centre, Kaiserstr. 25. ☎ (0651) 4-05-30 & 3-32-95.

WACHENHEIM
A large 16th c. cemetery. Key available from the Town Hall. First records of registration of Jews in the year 831.

WIESBADEN
Syn.: Friedrichstr. 33. ☎ (06121) 30-18-70 & 30-12-82. Inq. about kosher meals to Communal Offices, Friedrichstr. 33. ☎ (06121) 30-18-70.

WORMS
The original Rashi Synagogue here, built in the eleventh century and the oldest Jewish place of worship in Europe, was destroyed by the Nazis in 1938. After the Second World War it was reconstructed and was reconsecrated in 1961. The bldg. also contains a 12th-century mikva & a Jewish museum. There is also an ancient Jewish cemetery.

WUPPERTAL
Com. Centre: Friedrich-Ebert-Str. 73. ☎ (0202) 30-02-33.

WÜRZBURG
Syn. & Com. Centre: Valentin-Becker-Str. 11, 97072. ☎ (0931) 51190. Fax (0931) 18184.
There is a mikva (for appointment ☎ (0931) 51190) at the same address and the Jewish Dokumentatsionsentrum (Research centre).
Home for Aged, Valentin-Becker-Str. 11.
Kosher meals can be obtained at the Com. Centre, where there are also guest rooms for tourists.
There are old Jewish cemeteries in Würzburg, Heidingsfeld and Höchberg.
Nearby, in Veitshöchheim, the Synagogue and Museum of Jewish Culture has recently been restored at 6 Mühlgasse.

GIBRALTAR

Gibraltar Jewry numbers about 600 families. Sephardi Jews settled there soon after the British occupation in 1704, coming from Italy, North Africa and, later, from England. The Shaar Hashamayim Synagogue was built in the middle of the eighteenth century. Gibraltar Jews are known for their hospitality. The old Jewish cemetery is well worth a visit. It contains the graves of many saintly men, including that of the revered Rev. R. H. M. Benaim.
General inf. from Gibraltar Information Bureau, Arundel Gt. Court, 179 The Strand, WC2R 1EH. ☎ 0171-836 0777. Fax. 0171-240 6612.

Synagogues & Religious Organisations
Abudarham, 20 Parliament Lane. ☎ 78506.
Nefusot Yehuda, 65 Line Wall Rd. ☎ 73037.
Shaar Hashamayim, 19 Engineer Lane. ☎ 78069.
Etz Hayim, Irish Town. ☎ 75955
Chief Rabbi: Rabbi Hassid.
Mikva: 12 Bomb House. Lane. Inf. from Hon. Treas., Mrs. Orovida Hassan, 77 Irish Town. ☎ 77658 (day), 72359 (eves).
Managing Board of Jewish Com. P.O. Box 318. President: Mr. D. Benaim.
Sec.: Mrs. Esther Benady, 10 Bomb House. Lane. ☎ 72606. Fax 40487.
Jewish Social & Cultural Club. Hon. Sec.: S. Attias, 7 Bomb House. Lane. ☎ 72606.
(**K**) Leanse Restaurant. ☎ 41751.
There is a Kosher restaurant in the Jewish Club which opens daily from 10 a.m. to 11 p.m., except Saturdays, but arrangements can be made with this restaurant owner for Shabat meals.
WIZO. Pres.: Mrs. R.Hassan, 2 Victualling Office Lane. ☎ 77417. Hon. Sec.: Mrs S. Cuby 5/3 Jumpers.
Israel Consulate, Marina View, Glacis Rd., P.O. Box 141. Consul: Moses Benaim, 1 Baker's Passage. ☎ 77244.

Recommended Jewish shops:
M. I. Abudarham, 32 Cornwall's Lane (wines & all other kosher products). ☎ 78506; J. Amar 47 Lane Wall Rd., ☎ 73516 (bakery); J. Attias (tailor & outfitter), 6 St George's Lane; Benamor & Co., 133 Main St.; Cohen & Massias Ltd., 52, 142 & 143 Main St., (jewellery & watches); A. Edery (kosher meat, wines & all other products), 26 John Mackintosh Sq.; Annabella's Ladies wear, 10 John Mackintosh Sq.; Garbass Ltd., 82 Irish Town. ☎ 79020 (delicatessen); S. M. Seruya Ltd., 165 Main St.; Teo (men's outfitters), 138 Main St.; Cohen's Camera Centre, 207 Main St.

There are no kosher hotels in Gibraltar, but the White's Hotel and Rock Hotel will provide vegetarian or fish diets.

GREECE

There have been Jewish coms. in Greece since the days of antiquity. Before the Second World War, 76,500 Jews lived in Greece (56,000 in Salonika). Today there are barely 5,000, of whom 2,900 live in Athens, 1,200 in Salonika, 375 in Larissa, 166 in Volos, and the remainder in a number of other towns throughout Greece. General inf. from National Tourist Org. of Greece, 4 Conduit St., W1R 0DJ. ☎ 0171-734 5997-9.

ATHENS

Syn.: Beth Shalom (Sephardi), 5 Odos Melidoni. M.: Rabbi Yaacov Arrar. ☎ 3252-773.
Central Board of the Jewish Coms. of Greece, 2 Sourmeli St. ☎ 8839-951. Fax. 823-4488. Pres.: Nissim Mais.
Jewish Com. of Athens, 8 Odos Melidoni. ☎ 3252-823. Fax. 3220-761.
Jewish Youth Centre, 9 Vissarionis St. & Sina St. ☎ 3637-092. Visiting Jewish young people welcomed.
Jewish Museum, 36 Amalias Av. ☎ 323-1577. Open 9 a.m. to 1 p.m. Sun. to Fri.
B'nai B'rith, 15 Paparigopoulou, ☎ 323-0405.
Israeli Embassy, 1 Marathonodromon, Palaion Psychichon. ☎ 6719-530.
Central Consular Section. ☎ 6719-530.

CHALKIS (HALKIS)

Said to be the oldest Jewish com. in Europe, with an uninterrupted history of more than twenty-two centuries. Jews have lived in Chalkis since 200 B.C.E. Until the last century the com. was called 'Koutsouk Safed' because of its strict religious devotion.
There is a syn. in Kotsou St. which has been rebuilt and renewed many times on its original foundations. Tombstone inscriptions in the cemetery go back more than fifteen centuries.
Community Centre, 46 Kriezotou St., 34100. ☎ 0221-27297. Fax. 0221-76700.
Additional inf. from the Pres. of the com., M. Maissis.
By the main bridge linking Chalkis and the mainland, there is a commemorative bust of Colonel Mordecai Frizis, the first Greek officer to be killed during the Second World War. He was a leading member of the community.

CORFU

There was an ancient syn. and cemetery here on Velissariou St. destroyed by the Nazis. The Pres. of the com. is Raphael Soussis. ☎ 38802.
Moise Soussis, c/o the King Alkinos Hotel, will be pleased to meet Jewish visitors. (☎ 39300).
Community Centre, 5 Riz. Voulefton St., 49100. ☎ 0661-30591. Fax. 0661-31898.

JOANNINA

There is an an ancient syn. here, together with a Com. Centre. 18 Josef Eliyia St, 45221. ☎ 0651-25195. Inf. from the Pres. of the com., Moise Eliassa. ☎ 29429.

LARISSA

Syn. & Com. Centre, 29 Kentavron St. ☎ 226-396. Pres.: Michael Levi.
Jewish Martyrs' Sq. is a memorial to the Jews of the city murdered by the Nazis.

RHODES (DODECANESE ISLANDS)
The syn., built in 1731, is at 1 Simmiou St., in the old Jewish district. Visitors desiring to see round it should contact the caretaker, Lucia Sulan. ☎ 29406. Com. Office: 5 Polydorou St. Pres.: M. Soriano. ☎ 22364.

SALONIKA (THESSALONIKI)
A memorial to the 50,000 Jews who were deported from the city during the Second World War and murdered in the gas chambers of Auschwitz stands in the centre of the cemetery built after the war in the suburb of Stavroupolis. The old cemetery was destroyed in 1943 on the orders of the Nazis.
Syn.: 35, Sigrou, 54630. ☎ 031-524-968.
Yad le Zikaron, 24 Vassileos Irakliou St. M.: Rev. Mois Halegua. Office: 24 Odos Tsimiski, ☎ 275-701.
The Israelite Fraternity House is at the same address. ☎ 221-030. Pres.: Rafael Molho.
The Centre for Historical Studies of Salonika Jews is at 24 Vassileos Irakliou. ☎ 031-223231. Fax. 031-229063.

TRIKKALA
Syn.: Odos Diacou. Pres.: J. Venouziou, Kondili Philippou. ☎ 25834.

VERRIA
Syn. in the ancient Jewish quarter.

VOLOS
Community Centre: 21B Vassani St., 383 33. ☎ 0421-23079.
Inq. to Mr. Raphael Frezis, Com. Pres., 20 Pavlou Mela St. ☎ 25640.
Small Jewish coms. are to be found in Cavala & Carditsa. In Hania, the former capital of the island of Crete, there is an old synagogue in the former Jewish quarter, at 20 Parodos Kondulaki.

GUATEMALA
There are approximately 1,200 Jews in Guatemala.

GUATEMALA CITY
Syns.: Maguen David (Sephardi), 7a Av. 3-80, Zona 2. ☎ (5022) 232-0932; Centro Hebreo (Ashkenazi), 7a Av. 13-51, Zona 9. ☎ (5022) 331-1975.
Zionist Org. of Guatemala, 7a Av. 13-51, Zona 9, P.O.B. 105. ☎ (5022) 363975.
Israel Embassy, 13 Av. 14-07, Zona 10. ☎ (5022) 371305.

HAITI
There are 44 Jews in Haiti, all of them living in Port au Prince, the capital. Religious services are held at the home of the Honorary Consul. Mr. Gilbert Bigio.

HOLLAND
There were some Jews in Holland during the Middle Ages, but Dutch Jewish history effectively began with the settlement of Marranos in Amsterdam at the end of the 16th century. Dutch Jewry was given freedom of worship early in the 17th century and was formally emancipated in 1796. Holland was the first country in the modern world to admit Jews to Parliament (1797).
In 1940 there were approximately 140,000 Jews in the country, but as the result of the Nazi occupation, not more than 30,000 remain, of whom more than half live in the Amsterdam area, where there is much of Jewish interest to be seen.

General inf. from Netherlands Board of Tourism, P.O. Box 523, Buckingham Gate, SW1E 6NT. ☎ 0891-200-277.

For inf. about syns., services & kosher food outside Amsterdam, Rotterdam & The Hague, contact Chief Rabbinate of Holland, ☎ 020-6443868.

AMERSFOORT
Syn.: Drieringensteeg 2. M.: Rabbi J. S. Jacobs. ☎ 033-4726204. Rabbi S. Evers. ☎ 033-720943.

AMSTERDAM/AMSTELVEEN
Synagogues & Religious Organisations
Ashkenazi Chief Rabbinate of Holland. President: M. Just. Sec.: E. M. Maarsen, van der Boechorststr. 26, 1081 BT, P.O.B. 7967, 10008 AD. ☎ 020-6443868.
Ashkenazi Rabbinate of Amsterdam. Rabbis F. Lewis, I. Vorst. Same address & ☎ as above.
Ashkenazi Syns.: Gerard Doustr. 238, Jacob Obrechtplein; Kehilat Jaakow (E. European), Gerrit v. d. Veenstr. 26; Lekstr. 61; van der Boechorststr. 26 (Buitenveldert); Nieuwe Kerkstraat 149 (E. European) (for information ☎ 6766400). Straat van Messina 10, Amsterdam.
Portuguese (Sephardi) Syn. & Com. Centre: Mr. Visserplein 3. ☎ 020-6245351. Texelstr. 82, Amstelveen. ☎ 020-6245351.
Liberal Syn.: Jacob Soetendorpstr. 8. 1079 RM. ☎ 020-6423562. Fax. 020-642-8135. M.: Rabbi David Lilienthal, ☎ 020-6412580; Rabbi M. ten Brink. ☎ 020-6442619.
Mikvaot: Heinzestr. 3. ☎ 020- 6620178 (Ashkenazi); Mr. Visserplein 3. ☎ 020-6245351 (Sephardi).
Ashkenazi Com. Offices, van der Boechorststr. 26. ☎ 020-6460046. Fax. 020-646-4357.
Com. Centre: van der Boechorststr. 26. ☎ 020-6440180.

Representative Organisations
Nederlands Israëlitisch Kerkgenootschap (Organisation of Jewish Communities in the Netherlands), van der Boechorststr. 26, 1081 BT. ☎ 020-6449968. Fax. 020-6442606. Sec-Gen: Dr. J. Sanders. Rabbis M. Just & R. Evers.
Verbond Liberaal Religieuze Joden in Nederland (Fed. of Dutch Liberal Congs.), Jacob Soetendorpstr. 8. ☎ 020-6423562. Chaplaincy: ☎ 070-3167279/070-3166061. Chaplain: ☎ 020-6402546. Rabbi M. ten Brink Carel van Bylandtlaan, 3-5 2596 HP Den Haag.

Cultural Organisations
Anne Frank Foundation, Prinsengracht 263-265. ☎ 020-5567100.
Jad Achat, van de Boechorststr. 26. ☎ 020-6461905.

Welfare Organisations
(K) Beth Shalom Home for Aged, Kastelenstraat 80 (Buitenveldert). ☎ 020-6611516.
(K) CIZ General Hospital, Laan van de Helende Meesters 8, Amstelveen. ☎ 020-5474711.
Joods Maatschapelijk Werk (Jewish Welfare Office), de Lairessestr. 145-147. ☎ 020-6730629.

Student and Youth Organisations
Ijar Student & Youth Org., de Lairessestr. 13. ☎ 020-6768226.
Maccabi. Sec.: Simone Koopman, Koninginneweg 17, Bv 1075 CK. ☎ 6760766.
Sjoeche Youth Society, P.O.B. 71797, 1008 DG. ☎ 020-6446659.

Zionist Organisations
Bnei Akiva, Amstelveenseweg 665. ☎ 020-6463872.
Ichud Haboniem, Landskroon 5. ☎ 644 1406.
Keren Kayemet, van Leyenberghlaan 197, D1082 GG. ☎ 020-646477.
Keren Hayesod Joh. Vermeerstr. 24. ☎ 020-6719123.
Federatie Nederlandse Zionisten (Federation of Dutch Zionists), Joh.
Vermeerstr. 24. ☎ 020-6719126.
Netzer-Kadima, Jacob Soetendorpstr. 8, 1079 RM. ☎ 020-642 3562.
ARZA-Nederland, Jacob Soetendorpstr. 8, 1079 RM. ☎ 020-642 3562.
WIZO, Joh. Siegertstr. 8. ☎ 020-6944269.

Places of Interest
The Portuguese Syn., which has been completely restored, Mr. Visserplein 3,
is open April-Oct: Sun-Fri 10.00-12.30/1.00-4 p.m.; Nov-March: Sun 10.00-
12.00; Mon-Thurs: 10.00-12.30/1.00-4 p.m.; Fri 10.00-12.30/1.00-3 p.m. ☎
624-5351. Fax. 625-4680.

Livraria Montezinos & Ets Haim Library, Mr. Visserplein 3 (open for research
only Mon-Thurs, 9.00-12.30); the Jewish Historical Museum (housed in a
complex of 3 former syns.), Jonas Daniel Meijerplein 2-4. ☎ 020-6269945.
Open daily, 11 a.m.-5 p.m.; the monument in the Meijerplein to the dock
workers of Amsterdam, who went on strike in protest against the Nazi depor-
tation of the Jews; the monument to the Jewish Resistance, Zwanenburgwal
(next to the new Town Hall); the monument in the Weesperstraat to those
who helped the Jews during the Second World War Nazi occupation; the
Hollandse Schouwburg, Plantage, Middenlaan 20, a one-time theatre used as
a collecting point for Jews deported by the Nazis in 1942 and 1943, and converted into an annexe of the Historical Museum; Anne Frank House, the original hiding place of Anne Frank, where she wrote her Diary. Several exhibitions. Prinsengracht 263, near Westermarkt. ☎ 020-5567100. Open weekdays
from 9 a.m.-5 p.m. Suns. & holidays, 10 a.m. – 5p.m.; Bibliotheca
Rosenthaliana (a fine collection of Judaica and Hebraica), in the university
library. Singel 423; the Resistance Museum (housed in the Lekstr. Syn. bldg.),
Lekstr. 61; the Portuguese cemetery, Ouderkerk-on-the-Amstel, 10 miles
south-east of Amsterdam (Manasseh ben Israel is buried here).

The Liberal Synagogue also houses the Judith Druk Library and the Centre for
Jewish Studies.

Booksellers, etc.
Joachimsthal's Boekhandel Europaplein 85, 1078 GZ. ☎ 020-6640017.
Samech Books, Gunterstein 69. ☎ 020-6421424.

Newspaper: Nieuw Israëlietisch Weekblad, Rapenburgerstr. 109. ☎ 020-
6235584.

Hotels
Hotel Arsenal, Frans van Mierisstr. 97. ☎ 020-6792209. Pre-packed kosher
breakfasts available for guests.
Hotel Doria, Damstraat 3. ☎ 020-6388826.
Hotel Golden Tulip, Barbizon Centre, Stadhouderskade 7. ☎ 020-6851351.
(K) Kosher food for groups.
Okura, Ferdinand Bolsstr. 333. ☎ 6787111.

Kosher Meals
(K) Kosher meals are available Mon. to Thurs. from 5.45 p.m. to 7.15 p.m. at
Students' Mensa, Meschibat Nefesh, de Lairessestr. 13 (near Concertgebouw).
☎ 020-6767622. Under supervision of Amsterdam Rabbinate. No accom. is
available. Trams 3, 12, 16; buses 26, 65, 66; (K) Kosher meals available Fri.

night & Shabbat. Kosher meals, sandwiches & lunch boxes delivered to hotels, & Shabbat meals available from Marcus Ritueel. See kosher butchers below.

Kosher Food
(K) Bakeries: Jerusalem Bakery, Scheldestr. 55. ☎ 020-6794764; Theeboom, Bolestein, 45-47. ☎ 020-6427003; Tweede Sweelinckstr. 5. ☎ 020-6627086; Maasstraat 16. ☎ 020-6624827.

Kosher Butchers:
(K) Marcus Ritueel, Ferd. Bolstr. 44. ☎ 020-6719881.
(K) Meyer, Scheldestr. 63. ☎ 020-6640036

Kosher Restaurants:

Carmel, Amstelveensewag 224, 1075XT. ☎ (020) 675-7636; Nieuw Hatikwa (Dairy), Kastelenstraat. 86, 1083. ☎ 020 642 4299. (Apparently open only by special arranagement. Travellers are advised to call in advance.)

(K) Sandwiches, etc.: S. Meyer, Scheldestr. 45, 1078 GG. ☎ 020-6731313; Mouwes Koshere Delicatessen, Kastelenstraat 261, 1082. ☎ 020-6610180.

(K) Mrs. B. Hertzberger, Plantage Westermanlaan 9. ☎ 020-623 4684. 5 minutes from Portuguese Syn. Friday night and Shabbat meals only. Reservation in advance. Also lunchboxes for groups.

(K) Choclatery Bonbon Jeannette, Europaplein 87. ☎ 020-6649638.

ARNHEM

Syn. & Com. Centre: Pastoorstr. 17a. ☎ 026-4425154.

Liberal Cong. Inq. to Dr. H.K.F. Katzenstein, Regentesselaan 18, 7316 AE, Apeldoorn. ☎ 055-5222-332.

Home for Aged: 'Beth Zikna,' Beekstr. 40. ☎ 026-4433788, where arrangements can be made for **(K)** kosher food.

BUSSUM

Syn. & Com. Centre: Kromme Englaan 1a. ☎ 035-691 4882.

DELFT

Hillel House, Beth Studentiem, Jewish students' centre at the Technical University, Koornmarkt 9. ☎ 015-2120300.

(K) Mensa, open Mon-Thurs 18.15 p.m. by previous arrangement.

EINDHOVEN

Syn.: H. Casimirstr. 23. ☎ 040-7511253.

Inq. to Sec. ☎ 040-241 2710.

ENSCHEDE

Syn. & Com. Centre: Prinsestr. 16. ☎ 053-4323479 or 4353336.

Liberal Cong. Inq. to Sec., ☎ 053-4351330. Syn. at Haaksbergen.

GRONINGEN

Syn. & Com. Centre: Folkingestr 60, Postbus 550, 9700AN. ☎ 050-3123151.

HAARLEM

Syn. & Com. Centre: Kenaupark 7. ☎ 023-3326899. ☎ 023-3242051.

HILVERSUM

Syn. & Com. Centre: Laanstr. 30. Inq. to Sec. ☎ 035-6212044.

Inter-Provincial Chief Rabbinate: Laanstraat 30. ☎ 035-6239238. Rabbis J. S. Jacobs, S. Evers, A. L. Heintz.

LEIDEN
Syn. & Com. Centre: Levendaal 16. ☎ 071-5125793.
Jewish Students' Centre, Levendaal 8. ☎ 071-5130382.

MAASTRICHT
Syn. (1840) at Capucijnengang 2.
Nederlands Israelitische Hoofdsynagoge Achter de Comedie 8, 6211 GZ. ☎
43-258125. Fax. 43-218035.

ROTTERDAM
Syn. & Com. Centre: A. B. N. Davidsplein 4. ☎ 010-4669765. Mikva on
premises.
Liberal Syn.: Molenhoek Hillegersberg. Rabbi M. ten Brink. ☎ 020-644-2619.
Inq. to Sec. ☎ 010-4613211.
Kosher Butcher: (**K**) Piket, Walen-burgerweg 97. ☎ 010-4672856 Wed. only.
Kosher groceries available Wed. & Thurs. p.m.

THE HAGUE
Syns.: Syn. & Com. Centre: Corn. Houtmanstr. 11 Bezuidenhout, The Hague.
☎ 070-3473201. Mikva on premises; Beis Jisroël, Doorniksestraat 152, 2587
AZ Scheveningen. ☎ 070-3586363. Min: Dayan P. A. Meijers & Rabbi S.
Katzman. ☎ 070-3473201. Fax. 3479002. Contact: Mrs P. Jacobs. ☎ 3474980
for catering under supervision of the Rabbinate.
Liberal Syn., Prinsessegracht 26, The Hague, M.: Rabbi A. Soetendorp. ☎
070-3656893. Fax. 070-360-3883.
Spinoza House, in Paviljoensgracht, is of special interest, as is the 18th-centu-
ry Portuguese Syn. in the Prinsessegracht, which is now used by the Liberal
cong.
B'nai B'rith Nederland, P.O.B. 96842, 2509 JE. ☎ 070-3247350.
CIDI, Israel Inf. & Documentation Centre, P.O.B. 11646, 2502 AP. ☎ 070-
3646862.
ORT. President: Drs E. L. Berg. ☎ (0318) 610027.
Israel Embassy, Buitenhof 47. ☎ 070-3760500.
(**K**) Jacobs Kosjere Delicatessen, Haverkamp 220. ☎ 070-347-4980. Fax. 383-7909.

TILBURG
Liberal Synagogue Brabant. ☎ 070-365-6893. Inq. ☎ 013-467-5566.

UTRECHT
Syn. & Com. Centre: Springweg 164. M.: Rabbi A. L. Heintz. ☎ 030-
2314742.
Liberal Synagogue. Rabbi S. Herman. ☎ 020-644-2619. Inq. ☎ 030-603-
9343.
Kosher Bakery: (**K**) De Tarwebol, Zadelstr. 19. ☎ 030-2314887.
(**V**) Delicatessen Milk & Honey, Poorstr. 93. ☎ 030-2733114.

ZWOLLE
Syn: Samuel Hirschstr. 8, Postbox 1468, 8001 BL. ☎ 038-211412.

HONDURAS
(Most of the estimated 200 Jews in Honduras are Ashkenazi.)

SAN PEDRO SULA
Com. Sec.: Mauricio Weizenblut. ☎ 530157. Services Fri. & Sat. at syn. &
com. centre.

TEGUCIGALPA

Com. Pres.: Helmut Seidel. ☎ 31-5908. Services usually held in private homes. Israel Embassy & Consulate, Palmira Bldg., 5th Floor. ☎ 32-4232 or 32-5176.

HONG KONG

(Jewish population about 600 families)

The Hong Kong com. dates from about 1857. The syn. was built in 1901. General inf. from Hong Kong Tourist Assoc., 125 Pall Mall, SW1Y 5EA. ☎ 0171-930 4775.

Ohel Leah Syn. and Mikvah, 70 Robinson Rd. ☎ (852) 2589-2615. Fax (852) 2548-4200. M.: Rabbi Shmuel Lopin. Services: Mon & Thu, 7.00 a.m.; Tue, Wed & Fri, 7.15 a.m.; Sat, 9.00 a.m.; Sun & legal holidays, 8.00 a.m.; Friday evening, varies. Serves the mainstream Orthodox community of Hong Kong.

The United Jewish Congregation of Hong Kong (Liberal/Reform). Friday evening services followed by communal Shabbat dinner; periodic Shabbat morning services; holidays. At the Jewish Community Centre. ☎ (852) 2589-2623 or 2735-3037. Fax (852) 2523-3961.

Lubavitch in the Far East (Chabad), 1A Kennedy Heights, Midlevels. Holds regular morning services in the Furama Hotel. Rabbi M. Avtzon. ☎ (852) 2523-9770. Fax (8520 2845-2772.

Shuva Israel Beit Medrash and Community Centre (Orth., Sephardi), 61 Connaught Road Central, 2/F, Fortune House, Central. Rabbi Y. Eliahu. ☎ (852) 2851-7482.

Shuva Israel Synagogue (Orth., Sephardi), 16018 MacDonnel Road, 1-B, Midlevels. Shabbat and holidays. A substantial discount can be arranged at a nearby hotel. Rabbi Y. Eliahu. ☎ (852) 2851-6218. Fax (8520 2851-7482.

Syrian Bet Kenesset, 21 Chatham Rd., 4th Floor, Kowloon. ☎/Fax. 366-6364. M. Rabbi N. Meoded.

Jewish Community Centre, One Robinson Place, 70 Robinson Rd., Mid-Levels, Hong Kong. ☎ (852) 2801-5440. Fax. 2877-0917. Refurbished premises opened in 1995. (K) 2 Kosher Restaurants (under Mashgiach super-vision), Library, Health Club. Temporary membership for travellers.

Israel Consulate-General, Admiralty Centre, Tower II, Room 701, 18 Harcourt Rd. ☎ 2529 6091. Fax. 2865-0220.

Hong Kong Jewish Historical Society. Publishes monographs on subjects of Sino-Judaic interest and maintains an archive. Inf. from Dennis Leventhal. ☎ (852) 2547-2550. Fax (852) 2559-2890.

Jewish Cemetery. Located in Happy Valley. ☎ (852) 2589-2615. Fax (852) 2548-4200.

Jewish Women's Assn. Has 200 members and is affiliated to WIZO and ICJW. Chair: Mrs Rikki Cohen. ☎ (852) 2845-2885. Fax (852)2537-4457. United Israel Appeal. Affiliated to the Keren Hayesod. Info. Mr Sidney Myers. ☎ (852) 2973-0073. Fax (852) 2869-9812.

(K) Shalom Grill Restaurant, 61 Connaught Road, Central 2/f, Fortune House, ☎ 2851-6218. Fax. 2851-7482. Middle Eastern Glatt Kosher cuisine and grocery.

Hotels

Hyatt Regency, 67 Nathan Rd., Kln. ☎ (852) 2311-1234; The Peninsula, Salisbury Rd., TST, Kln. ☎ (852) 2366 6251; The Regent, Salisbury Rd., TST, Kln. ☎ (852) 2721 1211; Sheraton HK, 20 Nathan Rd., Kln. ☎ (852) 2369 1111; Mandarin Oriental, Central, HK. ☎ (852) 2522 0111.

HUNGARY

The Jewish population of Hungary is about 100,000, of whom some 80 % live in the capital, Budapest, and the rest mainly in rural areas. (In 1930 the city had a Jewish population of 230,000 – the second largest in Europe). It is probable that Jews lived in this part of Europe in Roman times. The governing body of Hungarian Jewry is the Central Board of .

The European Council of Jewish Communities has published an extensive directory of communal organisations in Hungary: "Hungarian Jewry in Profile", by David Guttmann, 1994. The National Tourist Board publishes a brochure on Jewish relics in Hungary.

BUDAPEST

Central Board of the Federation of Jewish Communities in Hungary (Magyarországi Zsidb Hitközségek Szövetsége), VII, Sip utca 12. ☎ 342-13-55. Dir.: Gusztav Zoltai. Inf.: Erno Lazarovits. ☎ 322-6478.

The Central Rabbinical Council (Conservative) is at VII, sip utca 12. ☎ 1421-180. Its Pres., Rabbi Dr. Josef Schweitzer, is Chief Rabbi of Hungary and Director of the Rabbinical Seminary.

The Orthodox Central Synagogue is at VII, Kazinczy utca 27. Pres.: Herman Fixler. ☎ 1-324-331.

(K) Kosher milk & cheese are available here three mornings a week.

Heroes Syn., VII Wesselényi u. 5.

The Dohány St. Synagogue, VII, Dohány utca 4-6, was built in 1859, and is the main Conservative synagogue. It is the second largest in the world. In its grounds lie buried the Hungarian Jewish victims of the Nazis. There is also a commemorative plaque to Hanna Senesh, the Jewish girl parachutist who was captured and tortured before being shot by the Nazis. A plaque commemorating Theodor Herzl, the founder of Zionism is in the Jewish Museum.

There are 20 other syns. in the city. Details from the Central Board of Hungarian Jews.

A Gothic syn. dating from the 14th century has been uncovered in Budapest, in Tancsincs Mihaly utca, on the site of the medieval walled town of Budavár, where the Jewish com. lived in the Middle Ages.

Mikva, VII, Kazinczy utca 16.

Jewish Museum (formerly the Herzl House), VII, Dohány utca 2. ☎ 142-8949. Dir.: Robert Turan. Open May to October, 10.00 to 3.00 p.m.

Rabbinical Seminary, Central Archive & Jewish Library, VII, J'zsef körut 27. ☎ 1-342-121. Princ.: Dr. Joseph Schweitzer.

There is a statue of Raoul Wallenberg, the Swedish diplomat in Budapest who saved hundreds of thousands of Hungarian Jews from the Nazis towards the end of the Second World War, at II, Szilagyi Erzsebet Fasor.

The Holocaust Memorial was inaugurated in 1990. It stands at the corner of Rumbach Sebestyén and Wesselényi Streets in the grounds of the former Great Synagogue.
Talmud Torah, VII, Sip utca 12.
Cemeteries: Chevra, X Gránátos u. 12; Farkasréti, XII Erdi u. 9; Kereperi, VIII Solg'tarjani u.; Obudei, III Külsö Bécsi u.369; Rakoskeresztœri u.6.
Jewish Elementary and High School VII Wesseleny U. 44.
Charité Hospital & Nursing Home, XIV, Amerikai ut 53. Superintendent: Dr. András Losonci. ☎ 2-515-518.
Ujpest Home for Aged, IV, Berzeviczy G. utca 8. ☎ 1-293-627.
Fortnightly Newspaper, 'Uj Elet, (New Life)' produced by the Central Board.
Hotel
(K) King's Hotel, Nagydiófa u. 25-27, 1074 ☎/Fax 267-9324.
Kosher Restaurants:
(K) **Hannah**, VII, Dob utca 35. ☎ 1-421-072. Saturday only, and meals need to be ordered in advance.
(K) **Central Kitchen & Food Distribution**, IX, Pava utca 9-11.
There are 12 kosher butchers' shops in Hungary. Inf. from the Central Board.
There is also a (K) kosher bakery at Dob utca 20, and at Kacinczy u. 28. Opening hours and availability are apparently variable.
Koser Bott, Nyar utcal. ☎ 322-9276. Osem products, bread, etc.
Tours of Jewish sites are provided by Chosen Tours. ☎ 185-9499. Fax 166-5165.
Jewish Information Service, Tel/Fax. 166-5165.

SOPRON
Syn.: Jewish Orthodox, Tömolom u.22, H-9400. Head: Mrs Magda Kornfein, Kis János u.3, H-9400. ☎ 3699-313-558.
The Neologue Cemetery dates from the 19th Century. There is a memorial wall dedicated to the 1600 local victims of the holocaust.
Old Synagogue Museum, Új u.22-24, H-9400. ☎ 3699-311-327. Fax 3699-311-347. (A department of the Sopron Museum). Director Dr A. Környei. Medieval Synagogue restored as a museum in 1976. Open daily 9.00 a.m. - 5.00 p.m.
A second medieval Synagogue at Új u.11 which formerly housed the Museum is undergoing restoration and will reopen in 1997.
The ruins of the 1891 synagogue, out of use since 1956 can be seen at Pap-rét, H-9400.

There are also Jewish communities in Debrecen, Györ, Miskolc, Pécs and Szeged, Szombathely and other cities. The beautiful Szeged Syn. has recently been restored.

INDIA
Indian Jewry comprises: (1) The Bene Israel, who form about 92 per cent, with the Bombay region as their main centre; (2) the Jews of Cochin & neighbourhood, on the Malabar Coast; (3) Jews from Iraq, as well as Iran, Bokhara & Afghanistan, who first arrived as a small handful of people some 200 years ago.
There are altogether about 5,500 Jews in India, of whom some 4,350 live in Bombay.
The Bene Israel, according to tradition, arrived in India before the Christian era. The Bene Israel now have more than 20 syns. in India (19 Sephardi and one Liberal). A monument has been erected in the village of Navgaon where they landed.

Jews from Iraq first arrived in about 1796, escaping persecution. They are to be found chiefly in Bombay, Poona and Calcutta. They have two syns. in Bombay, one in Poona, and three in Calcutta. Among the more illustrious of their members were the Sassoon, Ezra and Kadoorie families, who established a large number of mills and other business enterprises.

The Jews of Cochin, on the Malabar Coast, arrived as traders about the first century & have records dating as far back as the eighth century. There are only about 200 Jews in the State of Kerala today, the rest having emigrated to Israel and other countries.

Diplomatic relations have now been established with Israel.

General inf. from Government of India Tourist Office, 7 Cork St., W1X 2AB. ☎ 0171-437 3677-8.

AHMEDABAD
Syn.: Magen Abraham, Bukhara Mohalla, opp. Parsi Agiari.

BOMBAY
Syns.: Beth El Syn., Mirchi Galli, Mahatma Gandhi Rd., Panvel, 410206; Beth El Syn., Rewdanda, Allibag Tehsil, Raigad; Beth Ha-Elohim Syn., Penn; Etz Haeem Prayer Hall, 2nd Lane, Umerkhadi 400009; Gate of Mercy (Shaar Harahamim), 254 Samuel St., Nr Masjid Railway Station, 400003. ☎ 52-20-50. This is the oldest Bene Israel syn. in India, established in 1796 & known as the Samaji Hasaji Syn. or Juni Masjid until 1896 when its name was changed to Shaar Harahamim; Hessed-El Syn., Poynad, Alibag Tehsil; Knesseth Eliahu Syn., Forbes St., Fort, 400001; Kurla Bene Israel Prayer Hall, 275 S.G. Barve Rd. (Pipe Rd.) Kurla, W. Bombay, 400070; Magen Aboth Syn., Alibag; Magen David Syn., opp. Richardson & Cruddas, Byculla, 400008; Magen Hassidim Syn., 8 Mohammed Shahid Marg (formerly Moreland Rd.), Agripada, 400011; Rodef Shalom Syn., Sussex Rd., Byculla, 400027; Shaare Rason Syn., 90 Tantanpura St., 3rd Rd., Don Tad, Israel Mohalla, Khadak, 400009; Shaar Hashamaim Syn., Tembi Naka, opp. Civil Hospital, Thane, 400601; Shahar Hatephilla Syn., Mhasla; Tifereth Israel Syn., 92 K.K. Marg, Jacob Circle, 400011.

The following organisations exist in Bombay: Bene Israel Stree Mandal (Women's Org.). Pres.: Miss Lily Sampson. Sec.: Mrs. Milka Joseph; Bikur Holim, Indu House, Ballard Estate. Sec.: Moses N. J. Sultoon; B'nai B'rith Lodge of India, 2626. Pres.: Basil David. Sec.: Tobias Aaron; Bombay Zionist Assoc. Pres.: E. M. Jacob. ☎ 52-20-50. Sec.: Moses Talegawkar; Central Jewish Board, P.O.B. 539. Pres.: Benjamin Solomon. Hon. Sec.: S. Abraham; Council of Indian Jewry, c/o Jewish Club. Pres.: Professor Nissim Ezekiel. Exec. Ch.: Sec.: Daniel Jacob; Jewish Club, Jeroo Bldg., 137 Mahatma Gandhi Rd. Ch.: Miss S. Kelly. Sec.: E. Mashal. Kosher food available; Jewish Relief Assoc., c/o Feil & Co., Gresham Hse., Sir P. M. Rd. Ch.: Sec. G. Solomon; Jewish Women's League. Pres.: Mrs. M. Sopher. Sec.: Mrs. N. Ezra; ORT India, P.O. Box 16233, 400010. ☎ 862430. Fax 851 1452.

Israel Consulate, 50 Kailash, G. Deshmukh Marg, 26. ☎ 3862793.

Jewish Travel Agent: Tov Tours & Travels (India), 96 Penso Villa, 1st Floor, 400028 (Dadar). ☎ (022) 4450134. Fax (022) 4371700. Tours of Jewish India. Arrangements for the provision of kosher food can be addressed to Pearl Farm, A/1 Ground Floor, Sulabha, Dhobi Alley, Thane 400601, Maharashtra.

CALCUTTA
Syns.: Bethel Syn., 26/1 Pollack St.; Magen David Syn., 109a Peplabi Rash, Bihari Bose Rd. (formerly Canning St.), 1; Neveh Shalome Syn., 9 Jackson Lane, 1.

General inq. to Sec., Jewish Assoc. of Calcutta, 1 & 2 Old Court House Corner. ☎ 22-4861.

COCHIN

Syns.: Chennamangalam, Jew St., Chennamangalam. Built in 1614 & restored in 1916, this syn. has been declared an historical monument by the Govt. of India. A few yards away is a small concrete pillar into which is inset the tombstone of Sara Bat-Israel, dated 5336 (1576); Paradesi, Jew Town, Mattancherry, Cochin 2, the only Cochin syn. still functioning. Built 1568.
Inq. to S. S. Koder, Princess St., Fort, Cochin. ☎ 24288 & 24988.

NEW DELHI

Syn. Judah Hyam Synagogue, 2 Humayun Rd., 110003. ☎ 463-5500. Sec. Ms E. Melekar. Inq. to J. M. Benjamin, Vice-Pres., J.W.A., A/7 Nirman Vihar Patparganj, Delhi 110092. ☎ 2243136.
The Judah Hyam Synagogue Annexe houses a library and centre for Jewish & inter-faith studies.

PUNE

Syns.: Ohel David Syn., Synagogue St., Poona Camp (Cantonment), Pune, 411001; Succath Shelomo Syn., 93 Rasta Peth, Pune 411011. Inq. to Hon. Sec. David Soloman, 247/1 Rasta Peth, Trupti Apt., Pune 411011. Also: Dr. S. B. David, 9 Bund Garden Rd., Pune 411001.

IRAN

There have never been any reliable statistics on the number of Jews living in Iran. Today, there are an estimated 28,000. Most live in Tehran. The Tomb of Daniel is near Ahavaz (Shoush) and that of Mordechai and Esther is venerated at Hamadan.

ISFAHAN

The main syn. is in Shah Abbas St., and there are also some 20 syns. in the old Jewish quarter – called the Mahalleh – near the Friday Mosque.

TEHRAN

The three central syns. are the Haim, in Gavamossaltaneh St., the Iraqi, in Anatole France St., and the Meshedi in Kakh Shomali Av., opposite the Abrishami School.
There are numerous old syns. in what was once the Jewish quarter of Tehran and is still known as the Mahalleh (off Sirus Av.).

IRISH REPUBLIC

A Sephardi community was established in Dublin in the middle of the seventeenth century. In 1918 the office of Chief Rabbi of Eire was established, the first incumbent being Rabbi Isaac Herzog (who became Chief Rabbi of Israel, and died in 1959). Other holders of the office have included Lord Immanuel Jakobovits. The Jewish population is about 1,200, most of whom live in Dublin. General inf. from Irish Tourist Board, 150-151 New Bond St., W1Y 0AQ. ☎ 0171-493 3201.

CORK

In the seventeenth and eighteenth centuries there was a settlement in Cork of Sephardi Jews. Their burial ground has been identified in legal documents – it was a few hundred yards from the present syn. This cong. came into being in the latter part of the nineteenth century, in the days of the exodus from Tsarist Russia. There is a Jewish cemetery in Cork.

Syn.: 10 South Ter. Services: Sabbath morn. 10.30 a.m. and all Holy-days. Pres.: F. Rosehill. ☎ 870413.

DUBLIN
Synagogues & Religious Organisations
Chief Rabbi of Ireland: Rabbi Gavin Broder. Office: Herzog House, 1 Zion Rd., 6. ☎ 492-3751.
Herzog House also houses the JIA and JNF.
Communal M.: Cantor Alwyn Shulman.
Syn.: Dublin Hebrew Congregation, 37 Adelaide Rd. Sec. 661-2408. ☎ 4676-1734.
Terenure Hebrew Cong., Rathfarnham Rd., Terenure 6.
The Jewish Home, 'Denmark Hill', Leinster Rd. West, 6. Admin. ☎ 4976258. Office 4972004. Services are held daily, Fr. evg. at start of Sabbath and Sabbath morn.
Machzikei Hadass, at the rear of 77 Terenure Rd. North, Rathfarnham Rd. Contacts: J. Steinberg. ☎ 4908413; J. Gafason. ☎ 4906130.
Progressive Synagogue, 7 Leicester Av., Rathgar, PO Box 3059, 6. Hon Sec.: Mrs. J. Finkel. ☎ 490-7605. Services are held on Fri. evg. at 8.15 p.m., first Sabbath in the month and Sabbath morn. at 10.30 a.m.
Board of Shechita, 1 Zion Rd., 6. ☎ 492-3751.
Cemeteries: Aughavannagh Rd., ☎ Dolphin's Barn 454-0806. Dolphin's Barn, Dublin, 8. Inq. to caretaker. The old Jewish cemetery at Ballybough (☎ Ballybough: 836-9756), may be visited on application to the caretaker. There is a Progressive cemetery at Woodtown, Co. Dublin.

Cultural & Educational Organisations, Schools, etc.
Com. Centre, 1 Zion Rd., 6. ☎ 492-3751. Fax. 492-4680. Gen. Sec. J. Charry.
Irish Jewish Museum, 3-4 Walworth Rd., 8. Inf. from R. Siev, ☎ 676-0737, S. Siev, ☎ 475-8388. Museum ☎ 453-1797. Curator R. Siev.
Stratford Schools, 1 Zion Rd., 6. ☎ 492-2315.
Talmud Torah, Com. Centre, 1 Zion Rd., 6. ☎ 492-2315.

Welfare Organisations, Homes, etc.
Board of Guardians. Sec.: Mrs. J. Steinberg. ☎ 490-8413.
The Jewish Home, 'Denmark Hill', Leinster Rd. West, 6. ☎ 497-2004.
Student & Youth Organisation:Students' Union: Inf. from Comm. Centre.

Zionist Organisations
J.I.A., J.N.F., Zionist Org. of Ireland, are all at Herzog House, 1 Zion Rd., 6. ☎ 492-2318.

Sport & Miscellaneous Organisations
Edmondstown Golf Club, Edmonstown, Rathfarnham, 14. ☎ 4931082.
Jewish Medical Society. Inf. from Dr. E. Eppel, 202 Kimmage Rd. W., 12. ☎ 490-2427.
Jewish Representative Council of Ireland, 1 Zion Rd., 6. ☎ 492-3751. H. Sec. A. Benson.
Maccabi Assoc., Clubhouse & Sports Ground, Kimmage Rd. West. ☎ 555490.
(K) Kosher meals by arrangement with the Jewish Home.
Booksellers: Barry's Bookshop, Barry Gross, 137 Butterfield Av., Dublin 14. ☎ 493-4211. Fax 493-0899.

Kosher Suppliers
Butchers: (K) Deli Market, 14 Orwell Rd., Rathgar 6. ☎ 490-9911. Fax 490-9917; (K) B. Erlich, 35 Lower Clanbrassil St. ☎ 4542252.
Baker: (K) Bretzel, 1a Lennox St. ☎ 4752724,

ITALY

The Jewish com. of Italy, whose history goes back to very early times, increased considerably at the time of the Dispersion in 70 C.E. During the Middle Ages and the Renaissance there were newcomers from Spain and Germany. Rich syns. as well as rabbinical schools, yeshivot and printing houses were set up and gained wide renown.

A decline of Italian Judaism began during the last century: assimilation, concentration in big towns and emigration reduced many once-flourishing centres. During the first years of fascism Italian Jews did not suffer, but after 1938 – under Nazi pressure – racial laws were introduced and, during the German occupation from 1943 to 1945, nearly 12,000 Jews, especially from Rome, were murdered or banished.

There are 35,000 Jews in Italy today, the most important coms. being in Rome (15,000), Milan (9,500), and Turin (1,285), followed by Florence, Trieste and Venice.

Inf. on Italian Jewry, its monuments and history may be obtained from Unione Comunità Ebraiche Italiane (Union of Italian Jewish Communities), Lungotevere Sanzio 9, Rome. ☎ (06) 580-36-67 & (06) 580-36-70. Fax (06) 5899569. Pres.: Mrs. Tullia Zevi.

General & hotel inf. from Italian State Tourist Office (ENIT), 1 Princes St., W1R 8AY. ☎ 0171-408 1254. Fax. 0171-493 6695.

ANCONA
Syn. & Mikva, Via Astagno. Rabbi.
Com. Offices, Via Fanti 2 bis. ☎ 202638. Pres.: C. Calderoni.

ASTI (TORINO)
Syn., Via Ottolenghi 8.
Museum. V. Ottolenghi 8. ☎ 0141-593281 or 0141-594271.
Cemetery. Via Martiri Israelitici.

BOLOGNA
Syn., Via Mario Finzi. Rabbi M. Saadoun.
Com. Offices, Via Gombruti 9. ☎ 232-066. Com. Pres.: Bianca Finzi.
Kosher Restaurant: (K) Eshel Israel, Via Gombruti 9. ☎ 340-936. Lunch Sun - Fri; Dinner Friday. Closed mid-July and August.

CASALE MONFERRATO
Syn. & Com. Offices, Vicolo Salomone Olper 44. Com Pres.: Dr. Giorgio Ottolenghi. ☎ 0142-71807.
The synagogue, built in 1500 and rebuilt in 1866, also contains a Jewish museum.
Casale-Monferrato is on the Turin-Milan road, and can be reached by turning off it about 13 miles beyond Chivasso.

FERRARA
Syn., Via Mazzini 95. M.: Rabbi Luciano Caro. ☎ 0532-247004. Mikva on premises.
Cemetery, Via delle Vigne 2.
Com. Offices, Via Mazzini 95. Com. Pres.: Celestina Ottolenghi. ☎ 0532-760372.

FLORENCE (FIRENZE)
Syn., Via Luigi Carlo Farini 4. ☎ 245-252. M.: Rabbi Joseph Levi, Via L. C. Farini 2a. ☎ 243164.
Mikva, Via L. C. Farini 4. ☎ 245-252 or 243164.

Com. Offices, Via L. C. Farini 4. ☎ 245-252. Fax 241811. Pres.: Dr Dora Liscia Bemporad.
Jewish Museum, Via L. C. Farini 4. ☎ 2346654. There is a communal religious & artistic souvenir shop on the premises.
B'nai B'rith, Via L. C. Farini 2/a.
Home for Aged, Via Carducci 11/6. ☎ 241-210. Fax 244-044.
Cemeteries: Viale Ludovico Ariosto 14 & Via di Caciolle 13. ☎ 416-723.
Restaurants etc.
(K) Il Cuscussu, Via Farini 2/A. ☎ 241890.
Kosher Butcher, (K) Bruno Falsettini, Mercato Coperto di S. Ambrogio. ☎ 248-0740.
Kosher Poultry, (K) Giovannino, Via Macci 106. ☎ 2480734.

GENOA
Syn., Via Bertora 6. ☎ 8391-513. Fax: 846-1006. Rabbi Giuseppe Momigliano. Pres.: P. dello Strologo. Services every evg. & Shabbat morn. Kosher services available.
Com. Offices, Via Bertora 6, 16122.
Cultural centre, Via I. Frugoni, 15-2. ☎ 541-901.
R. Pacifici School, Via Maragliano 3-4. ☎ 591-402.

GORIZIA (GRADICA)
Syn., Via Ascoli 19. ☎ (3831) 532115.
Cemeteries: Gorizia-Valdirose; (dates back to 1371). Gradisca, Via dei Campi 15. Contact: Associazione Amici di Israele, Via Ascoli 19, 34170. ☎ 0481-532-115. Fax 0481-522-056.

LEGHORN (LIVORNO)
Syn. & Comm. Offices, Piazza Benamozegh 1. ☎ 0586-896290. M.: Rabbi Dr. Isidoro Kahn.
Mikvah: Signora L. Kahn. ☎ 882-584.
Jewish Museum, via Micali 21.
Bnei Akiva, Via Mameli 88.
Com. Pres.: Paola Bedarida Jarach.
Kosher Butcher: (K) Corucci, Banco 25, Mercato Centrale. ☎ 884596.

MANTUA (MANTOVA)
Syn. & Com. Offices, Via G. Govi 11. ☎ 321490. Com. Pres.: F. Norsa.
Cemetery: Via Legnano.

MERANO
Syn. & Com. Offices, Via Schiller 14. ☎ 236-127. Pres.: Federico Steinhaus.
Jewish Museum on the premises.
Cultural Centre "Anne Frank" ☎ 234999. Fax 237520.

MILAN
The Chief Rabbi is Rabbi Dr. Giuseppe Laras. Office: Via Guastalla 19. ☎ 5512-029. Fax. 551-92699.
Synagogues & Religious Organisations
Beth Shelomo, Via Col di Lana 12.
Central Synagogue, Via Guastalla 19. ☎ 5512101. Mikva on premises.
Merkos L'Inyonei Chinuch, Via Carlo Poerio 35, 20129. Pres.: Rabbi G. M. Garelik. ☎ 295-31213.
New Home for Aged, Via Leone XIII 1. ☎ 4982604. Services on Sabbaths and festivals. Mikva on premises.
New Synagogue, Via Eupili 8. Services on Sabbaths and festivals.

Ohel Yacob, Via Benvenuto Cellini 2 (Rabbi G. H. Garelik – Lubavitch). ☎ 545-5076.
Orthodox Sephardi Synagogue, Via Guastalla 19 (Rabbi Y. Haddad).
Persian Synagogues: Angelo Donati Beth Hamidrash, Via Sally Mayer 4-6. Mikva on Premises; Via Montecuccoli 27. ☎ 415-1660; Via Tuberose 14. ☎ 415-1660.

Representative Organisations
B'nai B'rith, Via Eupili 8.
Com. Offices, Sally Mayer, 2. ☎ (02) 483-02-806. Fax (02) 483-04660. Com. Pres.: J.Benatoff.

Welfare Organisations, Homes, etc.
New Home for Aged, Via Leone XIII 1. ☎ 4982604. (Kosher meals by arrangement).
Welfare Committee, Via Guastalla 19. ☎ (02) 551-2029. Fax (02) 55192699.

Zionist Organisations
A.D.E.I.-WIZO, Piazza della Repubblica 6. ☎ (02) 659-8102. Fax (02) 659 7211.
Keren Hayesod, Corso Vercelli 1. ☎ (02) 48021691. Fax (02) 48193376.
Keren Kayemet, Soderini 47. ☎ (02) 418-816.
Zionist Federation of Italy, Via E. de Amicis, 49. ☎ (02) 894-05-692. Fax. (02) 835-7558.

Miscellaneous Organisations
Contemporary Jewish Documentation Centre, Via Eupili 8. ☎ (02) 316-338. Fax (02) 336-02728.
Italian Maccabi Federation, Via Paolo da Cannobio 9. ☎ (02) 877-785. Fax (02) 877-786.

Kosher Restaurants
Giodano Levi, via Cesare da Sesto 7, ☎ (02) 58101011; Moise Malki, via Soncino 3, ☎ (02) 878834; J. Malki, via Montecuccoli 21, ☎ (02) 4159835; "Oriental Market" (Samuele Malki), via Caterina da Forli 58, ☎ (02) 4042977 - 4072788; Eden, viale S. Gimignano 13, ☎ (02) 4122855. Fax (02) 483033517; Eretz, Largo Scalabrini 5, ☎ (02) 4236891; Nuova Residenza per Anziani, via Leone XIII 1, ☎ (02) 4982604; mensa di via cellini 2, ☎ (02) 5455076; pizzeria "Carmel", viale San Gimignano 10, ☎ (02) 416368.

MODENA
Syn. & Com. Offices, Piazza Mazzini 26. ☎ 223-978. Rabbi Dr. R. Lattes.
Kosher Butcher: (**K**) Macelleria Duomo, Mercato Coperto (Covered Market), Stand 25. ☎ 217-269.

NAPLES (NAPOLI)
Syn. & Com. Offices, Via Cappella Vecchia 31. ☎ 764-3480.

OSTIA ANTICA
Here can be found the partially restored excavated remains of a fourth century C.E. synagogue built on the site of another one which stood there 300 years earlier. This is the oldest synagogue site in Europe.
Ostia Antica is about 40 minutes by train from Rome (Termini or Pyramid Stations). To reach the synagogue, cross the footbridge on leaving the station. The entrance to the excavations is straight ahead.

PADUA (PADOVA)
Syn. & Com. Centre, Via S. Martino e Solferino 9. ☎ 875-1106. M.: Mikva. ☎ 871-9501

There are two ancient cemeteries, one near San Leonards and the other in Via Codalunga (near Bastione della Gatta). Isaac Ben Yehuda Abrabanel, Minister of Finance for King Alphonse V of Portugal is buried here.

PARMA
Syn. & Com. Offices, Vicolo Cervi 4.

PERUGIA
Syn., P. della Republica 77 or contact. S. Pacifico. Tel 075-21250.

PISA
Syn. & Com. Offices, Via Palestro 24. ☎ 542-580. Services are held on festivals and Holy-days. During the week the resident beadle will be glad to show visitors round the syn., which is famed for its beauty. It is very near the Teatro Verdi.

RICCIONE
In the summer, (K) kosher food is obtainable at the Vienna Touring Hotel The Hotel Nevada. ☎ 601245 provides vegetarian food and particularly welcomes Jewish guests.

ROME
Synagogues & Religious Organisations
The Chief Rabbi of Rome is Rabbi Dr. E. Toaff, Via Catalana 1.
Lungotevere Cenci (Tempio) 9 (Orthodox Italian service). ☎ 684-0061.
Via Balbo 33 (Orthodox Ashkenazi service).
Via Balbo 33 (Orthodox Italian service). ☎ 475-9881.
Via Catalana (Orthodox Sephardi service). This is in the basement of the main syn. at Lungotevere Cenci (Tempio) 9.
Mikvaot: Lungotevere Cenci (Tempio) 9 and Via Balbo 33.
The Italian Rabbinical Council's headquarters is at Lungotevere Sanzio 9. ☎ 580-3667 & 580-3670.
Beth Din, Lungotevere Cenci (Tempio). ☎ 684-0061.

Representative Organisations
B'nai B'rith, Lungotevere Sanzio 14. ☎ 812-3608 & 812-3655.
Rome Communal Offices: Lungotevere Cenci (Tempio) 9. ☎ 684-0061. Pres.: C. Fano.
Union of Italian Jewish Communities, Lungotevere Sanzio 9. ☎ 580-3667 & 580-3670. Pres.: Mrs. Tullia Zevi.

Cultural & Educational Organisations, Schools, etc.
Davide Almagià Seminary, Lungotevere Sanzio 14. ☎ 580-9196.
Italian Rabbinical College, Lungotevere Sanzio 14. ☎ 580-9196.
Jewish Cultural Centre, Via Arco di Tolomei 1. ☎ 589-7589.
ORT Schools: Via San Francesco di Sales 4-6.

Welfare Organisations, Hospitals, etc.
Hospital & Convalescent Home, Fulda 14. ☎ 6523-2634.
Orphanage, Arco de' Tolomei 1. ☎ 580-0539.
OSE, Viale Trastevere 60. ☎ 581-6486.
Welfare Committee, Viale Trastevere 60. ☎ 580-3657.

Museum, etc.
The Jewish Museum, in the main syn. bldg. at Lungotevere Cenci 9, contains a permanent exhibition covering the 2,000-year history of the Italian Jewish community.
Another link with this long history is the Rome Ghetto almost adjoining. It can be reached by taking buses 44, 56, 60 or 75, near the neighbouring Ponte

Garibaldi. It is a maze of narrow alleys dating from Imperial Roman times, within which, until 1847, all Roman Jews were confined under curfew.
A striking monument has been erected to the memory of 335 Jewish and Christian citizens of Rome who were massacred in 1944 by the Nazis. Named Fosse Ardentine, it lies just outside the Porta San Paolo, a few yards from the main syn.
Jewish Guides: G. Palombo, Via val Maggia 7. ☎ 810-3716 & 993-2074; Ruben E. Popper, 12 Via dei Levii. ☎ (afternoons only) 761-0901.

Zionist Organisations
Bnei Akiva, Com. Centre, Lungotevere Cenci. ☎ 687-5051/2/3.
Hashomer Hatzair, Lungotevere Sanzio 14.
Jewish Agency, Corso Vittorio Emanuele 173. ☎ 654-5290.
Keren Hayesod, Corso Vittorio Emanuele 173. ☎ 656-8564.
Keren Kayemet Leisrael, Via A. Gramsci 42a. ☎ 807-5188.
Israel Embassy, Via Michele Mercati 12. ☎ 322-1541.
Newspaper: 'Shalom', Monthly, Lungotevere Cenci 9. ☎ 687-6816.
Hotels & Restaurants: (K) Da Lisa, Via Foscolo 16-18. ☎ 7049 5456.

Kosher Food
Makolet, Piazza Armellini 6. ☎ 856-862 & 475-5274.
(K) Tavola Calda, via Livorno 10, Piazza Bologna. ☎ (06) 44292025.

Kosher Butchers
(K) Massari, Piazza Bologna 11. ☎ 429-120.
(K) Sion Ben David, Via Filippo Turati 110. ☎ 73-33-58.
(K) Terracina, Via Portico d'Ottavia 1b. ☎ 654-1364.
Bakery: Limentani Settimio, Via Portico d'Ottavia 1.

SENIGALLIA
Syn., Via dei Commercianti.

SIENA
Syn., Vicolo delle Scotte 14. ☎ 284-647. Pres.: Prof. Guiseppe Lattes. The com. has issued a brochure in English, giving the history of the syn., which dates back to medieval times. The Synagogue dates from 1750. Services are held on the Sabbath and High Holy-days. Further inf. from Burroni Bernardi, Via del Porrione. M. Savini, via Salicotta 23. ☎ 283140 (close to the synagogue).
Kosher Butcher: ☎ 281-056.

SPEZIA
Syn., Via 20 Settembre 165.
Talmud Torah, Via 20 Settembre 200. Inq. to Alberto Funaro, Via R. Migliari 32. ☎ 28-504.
Zionist Office: Via 20 Settembre 68.

TRIESTE
Syns., Via Donizetti 2 (Ashkenazi & Sephardi). M.: Rabbi Dr Umberto Piperno. ☎ 631-898.
Com. Offices, Via San Francesco 19. ☎ 371-466.

TURIN (TORINO)
Syn., and Mikvah, P.tta Primo Levi 12, 10125. M.: Rabbi A. Somekh.
Com. Offices, P.tta Primo Levi 12, 10125. ☎ 658-585.
Kosher: Luna, via C.L. Berthollet 23. ☎ (011) 650 2053.
Bookseller: Claudiana, via Principe Tommaso 1, 10125. ☎ (011) 669 2458.

URBINO
Syn., Via Stretta.

VENICE
Synagogues & Religious Organisations
In summer, Sabbath services (Sephardi minhag) are held in the Schola Spagnola, Ghetto Vecchio. In winter all services are held in the Schola Levantina. For details tel: 715-012. There are five syns. (as well as a Jewish museum) in the ghetto.

To reach the ghetto, start out from the railway stn. Facing it and then turning right, go along the Fondamento dei Scalzi, which almost immediately becomes the Lista di Spagna. Continue to the Campo S. Geremia and then, where the street narrows, along the Salizada S. Geremia. You will then come to a bridge. Cross it, and then turn left along the canal for about 75 yards until you see a chemist's shop – Farmacia. Immediately after it you will find the narrow entrance to the ghetto.

To reach the ghetto from the Grand Canal, alight at the San Marcuola landing stage. Walk away from the canal past the church, until you reach the Rio Terra S. Leonardo, a broad shopping thoroughfare. You will then see yellow street signs in Italian and Hebrew directing you to the syns. in the ghetto.

Chief Rabbinate: Ghetto Vecchio 1189. ☎ 715-118. Chief Rabbi: Rav R. Della Rocca.

Mikva: Jewish Rest Home, Ghetto Nuovo 2874. ☎ 715-118.
Com. Offices: Ghetto Nuovo 2899. ☎ 715-012. Pres.: Sandro Romanelli.
Chabad: Ghetto Nuovo, Cannaregio 2915. ☎ 041-716214.
Jewish Library: Ghetto Nuovo, 2899. ☎ 718-833.
Jewish Museum, Schola Tedesca, Ghetto Nuovo, 2902 b. ☎ 715-359.
   Guided visits to the synagogue (in English) start every hour from the Museum. There is also a kosher cafeteria.
Cemeteries: Via Cipro 70 & Riviera San Niccolò 2, Lido, at the corner of Via Cipro. ☎ 5260-142.

(K) Kosher meals and accommodation can occasionally be had in the Jewish Rest Home, Ghetto Nuovo 2874. ☎ 716-002. Very early booking is advised.

(K) Restaurant, books and Judaica available at Beit Chabad, Ghetto Nuovo, Cannaregio 2884. ☎/Fax 041-716214.
Hotels: Buon Pesce, S. Nicolo 50. ☎ 760-533. Open Apr. to Oct.; Danieli. ☎ 26-480; Europa & Regina. ☎ 700-477.

Jewish articles & religious appurtenances are available from Mordehai Fusetti, Ghetto Vecchio 1219. ☎ 714-024 ande from David's, Ghetto Nuovo 2880.

VERCELLI
Syn., Via Foa 70.
Com. Offices, Via Oldoni 20. Pres.: Dario Colombo.

VERONA
Syn., Via Portici 3. M.: Rabbi Dr. C. Piattelli.
Com. Centre, Via Portici 3. ☎ (045) 800-7112. Fax (045) 596627. Email: s.i@intesys.it Pres.: Carlo Rimini.

VIAREGGIO
Com. inq. to Mr. Sananes, via Pacinotti 172/B. ☎ 30777.
Cemetery: Via Marco Polo.

Kosher Meat: Available during the summer from **(K)** Macelleria Corucci, Piazza del Mercato Nuovo. ☎ (0586) 884 596 (Livorno).

SARDINIA

There is no Sardinian Jewish community today, but the island is of more than passing Jewish interest. In 19 C.E. the Emperor Tiberius exiled Jews to Sardinia. There was a synagogue at Cagliari, the island's capital, at least as early as 599, for in that year a convert led a riot against it. Sardinia eventually came under Aragonese rule, and when the edict of expulsion of the Jews from Spain was issued in 1492, the Jews of the island had to leave. Since then there has been no community there.

SICILY

Although there are very few Jews in Sicily today, there is a long and varied history of Jewish settlement on the island stretching back to at least the sixth century C.E. and possibly – according to some scholars – to the first or second centuries.

By the late Middle Ages, the community numbered 40,000. In 1282, Sicily passed under Spanish rule. A century or so later, there was a wave of massacres of Jews, and another in 1474. These culminated in the introduction of the Inquisition in 1479, and the expulsion of the Jews in 1492.

JAMAICA

Jewish settlement in Jamaica, composed in the first instance of fugitives from the Inquisition, goes back to before the period of the British occupation in the mid-seventeenth century. In the eighteenth century there was also a small Ashkenazi influx from England. Jewish disabilities on the island were abolished in 1831.

There were formerly syns. at Port Royal, Spanish Town and Montego Bay. The only one now existing is at Kingston, where the Ashkenazi and Sephardi coms. were combined in 1921. This city contains the majority of the island's 350 Jews.

General inf. from Jamaica Tourist Board, 1-2 Prince Consort Rd., SW7 2BZ. ☎ 0171-224-0505. Fax. 0171-224-0551.

Syn.: Shaare Shalom, Duke & Charles Sts., Kingston (semi-R). Services, Fri. 5.30 p.m. (May to Oct.) & 5 p.m. (Nov. to April). Sabbath 10 a.m; festivals, 9 a.m. all year round. Sec.: Ernest H. de Souza, J.P., 2a King's Dr., Kingston, 6. ☎ 92-77948. Fax 978-6240.

JAPAN

Taking into account businessmen, students, and other professionals with their families in Japan for 3-5 years the Jewish population can easily run to a couple of thousands at any given time. Exact data on permanent residents are not available and there are very few long-time residents who make Japan their permanent domicile. Conservative estimate: about 600 individuals.

General inf. from Japan National Tourist Organisation, 167 Regent St, W1R 7FD. ☎ 0171-734 9638-9.

HIROSHIMA

A Holocaust Education Centre, dedicated to the memory of the child victims of the Holocaust. Dir. Rev. Makoto Otsuka, 866 Nakatsuhara, Miyuki, Fukuyama 720. ☎/Fax. 0849 558001. Open Tues., Wed., Fri. and Sat., 10-30am-4.30pm.

KOBE
There have been Jews in Kobe for more than a century. Today's Jewish population numbers some 15 families.
During the Second World War, Kobe's two synagogues were destroyed. The Ohel Shelomoh Synagogue (Orthodox) and community centre 12/12 Kitano-cho 4-chome, Ikuta-ku (P.O.B. 639). ☎ (078) 221 7236. M3H 3S4. ☎ (416). There is a mikva on the premises. Vice-President: Bruce M. Benson. ☎ (078) 222 3950.

NAGASAKI
There are no Jews living in Nagasaki. The old Jewish cemetery is located at Sakamoto Gaijin Bochi. The site of the first syn. in Japan is Umegasaki Machi.

OKINAWA
While there is no native Jewish com. on Okinawa, there are normally 200-300 Jews serving with the U.S. military on the island. Regular services are conducted by the Jewish chaplain at Camp Smedley D. Butler, and visitors are welcomed.

TOKYO
There are 160 Jewish family members of the Jewish Com. of Japan, Jewish Com. Centre, 8-8 Hiroo, 3-Chome, Shibuya-ku, 150. ☎ 3400-2559 Fax (03) 3400-1827. Pres.: E. Salomon. Beth David Syn. is in the Com. Centre premises. Services held Fri. evg., 6.30 p.m. (7.00 summer); Shabbat morn., 9.30 a.m., and on High Holy-days & festivals. Rabbi James Lebeau. Kosher meals available. Advance notification requested.
Israel Embassy, 3 Niban-cho Chiyodaku. ☎ 3264-0911.

YOKOHAMA
Inf. concerning the Jewish cemetery here may be obtained from the Jewish Community of Japan, in Tokyo.

YOKOSUKA
There is a Jewish chapel at the United States naval base here, and some religious services at the base are open to visitors. Further inf. can be obtained by telephoning (0468) 26-1911, Ext. 6773. Yokosuka is about 1¼ hours' journey south of Tokyo.

KENYA
Jewish settlement in what was British East Africa dates from the beginning of this century. In 1903, when the British Government offered Zionists a territory in Kenya for Jewish settlement, there were already a number of Jews in the capital, Nairobi.

The 'Uganda Plan,' as the offer became known, did not materialise, yet shortly afterwards more Jews settled in the territory. In 1907 the Nairobi Hebrew Congregation was formed, and the foundation-stone for the first synagogue was laid in 1912.

The community was small until 1933, when new immigration started, especially from Central Europe. Today, there are some 500 Jews in the country, including about 400 Israelis. Nearly all live in Nairobi.

NAIROBI
Syn., cnr. University Way & Uhuru Highway. PO Box 40990. ☎ 222770, 219703.

Rosh Kehilla: Vaizman Aharoni. Hon. Sec. Ms A. Zola.
Com. Centre: Vermont Memorial Hall. Open Mon., Tues., Fri., 9.00am-
1.00pm; Wed., 2.30-5.30pm. (Mrs J. Moran). Services Fri. evg. 6.30pm. Sat.
morning 8.00am. All Festivals. Kosher chickens available.

LATVIA

DAUGAVPILS
Syn.: Gogol Str.; Suvorov Str.
Jewish Community, Saules Str., 47. Fax 8 254 24658.

LIEPAJA
Jewish Community, Kungu St. 21. ☎ 25336

REZHITSA
Syn.: Kaleru Str.

RIGA
Syn.: 6/8 Peitavas Str. ☎ 371-2-210827. Fax 371-2-224549.
Organisations:
Jewish Culture Society, Skolas 6, Loek, 226050. ☎ (013-2) 28-95-80. Fax 70
132 289573.
Shamir-M, Dubina Fonds Jewish Community Center, 7 Sporta Str., Riga LV-
1001. ☎ 371-2-334012. Fax 371-2-334382.

LITHUANIA
There are approximately 6,500 Jews in the newly restored Lithuanian
Republic, 4,500 of whom live in Vilnius.

DRUSKININKAI
Jewish Community, 9/15 Sporto Str. ☎ 54-590.

KAUNAS
Syn.: 11 Ozheshkienes Str.
Jewish Community, 26 B Gedimino Str. ☎ 203-717.

KLAIPEDA
Jewish Community, 3 Ziedu Skersqatvis. ☎ 93-758.

PANEVEZYS
Jewish Community, 6/22 Sodu Str., Panevezys 5300. ☎ 68-848.

SHIAULIAI
Jewish Community, 24 Vyshinskio. ☎26-795.

VILNIUS
Main Syn. and matzah bakery: 39 Pylimo Str. ☎ 370-2-612 523.
Zalman Rejzen Foundation Supporting Jewish Culture, Education, and
Science in Lithuania, 4 Pylimo, 1st (British) floor. ☎ 370-2-612 695. P.O. Box
1075, Vilnius 2001.
Jewish Publishing House 'YAD – Yerushalayim de'Lita Publishers', 4 Pylimo,
2nd (Br.) floor, P.O. Box 1075, Vilnius 2001. ☎/fax 370-2-615 758.
WIZO branch in Vilnius, 4 Pylimo, Vilnius 2001. ☎ 611 736.
Jewish Community of Lithuania, 4 Pylimo, Vilnius 2001. Ground floor. ☎
370-2-613 003. Fax 370-2-227-915.
Centre of Yiddish Culture and Musik 'Folkszinger', 4 Pylimo, Vilnius 2001,
2nd floor. ☎ 370-2-227 074 or 412 541.

The Israel Centre of Cultures and Art in Lithuania, 4 Pylimo, Vilnius 2001. 2nd floor. ☎ 370-2-611 736 or 652 139.
Jewish Community of Vilnius, 4 Pylimo, Vilnius 2001. ☎/fax 370-2-632 951.
State Jewish Museum, 4 Pylimo, Vilnius 2001. 1st floor. ☎ 370-2-632 951.

LUXEMBOURG
There are today about 1,000 Jews in Luxembourg, the majority in Luxembourg City.
General inf. from Luxembourg National Tourist & Trade Office, 36-37 Piccadilly, W1V 9PA. ☎ 0171-434 2800. Fax. 0171-734 1205.

ESCH-SUR-ALZETTE
Syn.: 52 rue du Canal. Pres.: Robert Wolf, 19, rue du Nord. Minyan: Friday Evening.

LUXEMBOURG CITY
Syn.: 45 Av. Monterey. ☎ 452914. Fax 250430.
Chief Rabbi emer.: Rabbi Dr. Emmanuel Bulz, 2 rue Marguerite de Brabant. ☎ 442569.
Chief Rabbi: Joseph Sayagh, 34 rue Alphonse Munchen, 2172. ☎ 452366
Cantor: Michel Heymann, 15 Blvd. Grande Duchesse Charlotte. ☎ 452744.
B'nai B'rith: E. Marelli, 39 Ave de la Gare. ☎ 489627.
Jewish Council. Ch.: Guy Aach, 18 rue des Dahlias. ☎ 452458.
WIZO. Mrs. Irmy Mayer, 46 rue du X Septembre. ☎ 452455.
Kosher grocery available at Calon, rue de Reins, 3.

MADEIRA
See under Portugal.

MAJORCA
See under Spain.

MALAWI
LILONGWE
Israel Embassy, P.O. Box 30319. ☎ 731333 & 731789.

MALAYSIA
There are now only three Jewish families in the Malaysian island State of Penang (Pulau Pinang), all resident in the capital of Georgetown. The syn. at 28 Jalan Nagore is closed. There is a cemetery in Jalan Yahudi (Jewish Street).

MALTA
There have been a few Jews in Malta since the Roman period. In the Middle Ages, in addition to the community on Malta itself, there was also one on the nearby island of Gozo, but with the expulsion of the Jews from Sicily in 1492, they both came to an end. From 1492 and thoughout the period of the Knights of St. John (which began in 1530) there were no practising Jews, apart from slaves. A new community originating from North Africa arose at the end of the eighteenth century. There are about 30 Jewish families in Malta today, both Sephardim and Ashkenazim, at present without a Synagogue.
General inf. from Malta National Tourist Office, 36-38 Piccadilly, W1V 0PP. ☎/Fax 0171-734 1880.

Services are held on the first Shabbat of every month and the first days of the main festivals. Sec., Tr. Stanley L. Davis, O.B.E., "Melita", Triq Patri Guze Delia, Balzan BZN 07, Malta. ☎ 445924, will gladly give information on request. Travellers should note that there is no kashrut in Malta.

MEXICO

Marrano Jews went to Mexico with the Spaniards at the beginning of the sixteenth century. Sixty years ago the country had about a thousand Jews, most of them coming from the U.S.A., and others from England and Germany. Today's Jewish population is about 48,000. Those in Mexico City (about 40,000) include Ashkenazim and Sephardim. General inf. from Mexico Ministry of Tourism Office, 7 Cork St., W1X 1PB. ☎ 0171-734 1058-9.

CUERNAVACA
Syn. Madero 404. ☎ 2-05-16 & 2-01-79.

GUADALAJARA
Comunidad Israelita de Guadalajara, Juan Palomar y Arias 651. ☎ (36) 416-463.

MEXICO CITY
The community is increasingly moving out of the city towards the suburbs of Tecamachalco and communal organisation is highly developed.

Synagogues & Religious Organisations
Agudas Achim, Montes de Oca 32, Condesa
Beth Itzhak (O), Eujenio Sue 20, Polence.
Bircas Shumel, Plinio 311, Polanco. ☎ 280-2769.
Cuernavaca, Prolongación Antinea Lote 2, Delicias.
Maguen David (Sephardi), Bernard Shaw 110, Polanco. ☎ 203-9964.
Nidche Israel, Acapulco 70, Condesa. ☎ 211-0575. There is a (K) kosher restaurant on the first floor of the syn. building.
Ramat Shalom, Fuente del Pescador 35, Tecamachalco. ☎ 251-3854.
Sephardi Synagogue, Monterey 359. ☎ 564-11-97 & 564-13-67.
Bet El (C), Horacio 1722, Polanco los Morales. ☎ 281-2592.
Or Damesek, Seneca 343. ☎ 280-6281.
Kolel Aram Zoba, Sofocles 346, Col. Polanco. ☎ 280 2669/4866/8789.
Organizacion T.O.V., Fuente de Concordia 73, Col. Tecamachalco. ☎ 389 8756/66, 2946486. Fax 5899101.
Midrash Latora, Cerrada de Los Morales 8, Col. Polanco. ☎ 280 0875/280 3526.
Shaare Shalom, AV. de Los Bosques 53, Tecamachalco. ☎ 2510973.
Shuba Israel, Edgar Alan Poe 43, Col. Polanco. ☎ 545 8061/280 0136. Mikve for men in premises.
Kolel Maor Abraham, Lafontaine 344, Col. Polanco. ☎ 545 2482.
Bet Midrash Tecamachalco, Fuente de Marcela 23, Col. Tecamachalco. ☎ 251 8454. Mikve for men in premises.
Eliahu Fasja, Fuente de Templanza 13, Col. Tecamachalco. ☎ 294 9388.
Jajam Elfasi (only Shabath services), Fuente Del Pescador 168, Col. Tecamachalco.
Alianza Monte Sinai, Alejandro Dumas 139, Col. Polanco. ☎ 5314932, 5458691.
Monte Sinai, Fuente de Sulpicio, Tecamachalco.
Beth Israel Community Centre (C) – English-speaking – Virreyes 1140, Lomas. ☎ 520-85-15.
Comunidad Monte Sinai, Tennyson 134, Polanco. ☎ 280-9956.
Mikvaot: Banos Campeche 58. ☎ 574-22-04; Platón 413. ☎ 520-9569; Av. de

los Bosques 53, Tecamachalco. ☎ 589-55-30; Bernard Shaw 110, Polanco. ☎ 203-9964.

Representative Organisations

Central Jewish Committee, Cofre de Perote 115, Col. Lomas Barrilaco 11010. Mexico, D.F. ☎ (525) 540-7376, 540 3273. Pres.: Alfredo Achar. International Affairs Director: Susy Norten. ☎ 520-9913. Fax 540-3050.
Tribuna Israelita, Cofre de Perote 115 (as previous). Dr. Dina Siegel. ☎ (525) 520-1044.
B'nai B'rith (same address).
Consejo Mexicano de Mujeres Israelitas, Acapulco 70-60. piso Roma Norte ☎ 211-2733.
Federación Femenina A.C., Luis G. Urbina 58, Polanco Chapultepec. ☎ 280-6874.
Na'amat, Damas Pioneras, A.C., Vicente Suárez 67, Hip'dromo Condesa. ☎ 286-5589

Cultural & Educational Organisations, etc.

Alianza Monte Sinai: Fuente de la Huerta 22, Tecamachelco. ☎ 589-8322.
Colegio Hebreo Maguen David; Antiguo Camino a Tecamachalco no. 370; ☎ 570-0935.
Colegio Hebreo Tarbut, Loma del Parque 116, Vista Hermosa. ☎ 259-4259.
Colegio Israelita, Segundo Retorno del Recuerdo 44, Col.
Vista Hermosa, Cuajimalpa. ☎ 570-3262.
Colegio Monte Sinai, Avenue Parque de Chapultepec 56, Naucalpan de Juarez. ☎ 576-06-21.
Colegio Sefaradi, Progreso 23, Col. Florida Insurgentes. ☎ 524-50-68.
Cultural Centre, Culiacan 71. ☎ 564-52-37.
Federación Mexicana de Estudiantes Universitarios Judíos, Eugenio Sué 353, Polanco. ☎ 280-0780.
Jewish Sports Centre (Centro Deportivo), Blvd. Manuel Arvila Camacho 620, Lomas de Sotelo, D.F. ☎ 557-3000
Nuevo Colegio Israelita, Prolongación Manuel Avila Camacho 30. ☎ 557-5564.
OSE Medical Centre, Mexicali 86, First Floor. ☎ 286-57-52 or 286-52-54.
Yeshiva de México, Anatol France 13. ☎ 520-1219.
Yeshiva Keter Torah; Lago Meru 55. ☎ 531-0973.
Yiddish-Hebrew Teachers' Seminary, Acapulco 70. ☎ 211-09-71.

Zionist Organisations

Bnei Akiva, 191 Av. Amsterdam.
J.N.F. & Zionist Offices, Acapulco 70, Third Floor, Condesa, D.F. ☎ 211-12-22 & 211-27-25.
WIZO Organización Femenina, Monte Blanco 1285, Lomas de Chapultepec. ☎ 540-5861.
Israel Embassy, Sierra Madre 215. ☎ 540-63-40.

Newspapers & Periodicals, etc.

CDI (Spanish weekly), Centro Deportivo, nr. Plaza de Toros of Cuatro Caminos. ☎ 557-30-00.
Di Shtime (Yiddish, weekly). Pedro Moreno 149. ☎ 546-17-20.
Foro de Vida Judia en el Mundo (Spanish monthly), Aviacion Commercial 16, C.P. 15700. ☎ 571-11-14.
Imagen David, Revista, Maguen David; La Fontaine 229. ☎ 203-9964.
Jerusalem de Mexico (Bookshop), Anatore France 359, Local C, Polanco. ☎ 5312269.
Kesher (Spanish monthly), Ap. Postal 41-969, Lomas de Chapultepec. ☎ 203-0517.

La Voz de la Kehila (Spanish monthly), Acapulco 70, Second Floor. ☎ 211-05-01.

Kosher Restaurants
(K) Aladinos; Ingenieros Militares 255; 395-2949.
(K) Centro Social Monte Sinaí, Fuente de la Huerte 22. ☎ 589-8322.
(K) Mac David; Torcuato Tasso 152; 250-8977.
(K) Macabim, 5 de Febrero 36. ☎ 709-1446.
(K) Tauquería Piny, Ejercito Nacional y Emerson; 250-5168.
(K) Sabre Kosher, San Jerónimo 726. ☎ 709-3368.
(K) Shalom, Acapulco 70, First Floor. ☎ (905) 211-19-90. This kosher (dairy only) restaurant is above the Nidche Israel Syn. Under the supervision of Rabbi Abraham I. Bartfeld.
(K) Wendys, Homero & Sofocles, Col. Polanco. ☎ 395-3083.

Kosher Food
Casa Amiga, Horacio 1719, Col. Polanco. ☎ 540-1455.
(K) Super Teca Kosher, Acuezunco 15, San Miguel. ☎ (905) 589-98-23, 98-60 or 32-25.

MONTERREY
Centro Israelita de Monterrey, Canada 207, Nuevo León. ☎ (83) 461-128.

TIJUANA
Syns.: J.C.C Chabad House - Centro Social Israelita de Baja California, Av. 16 Septembre #3000. ☎ 86-26-92 or 86-26-93. Rabbi Mendl Polichenko. Mikva and (K) restaurant on the premises.
Tijuana Hebrew Cong., Amado Nervo 207.

MOLDOVA
CISINAU
Syn.: Yakimovsky per. 8, 277000. ☎ (042-2) 22-12-15.

TELENESHTY
Syn.: 4 28th June St.

TIRASPOL
Details of the Jewish Community from the President: Dr Samuel Vaisman. ☎ 3-36495/ Fax. 3-22208.

MONACO
MONTE CARLO
Syn. & Com. Centre: 15 Av. de la Costa (opp. Balmoral Hotel), MC 98000. ☎ 9330-16-46. Services, Fri. evg. 6.30 p.m., Sat. morn. 8.45 a.m. & 5.30 p.m. M.: Rabbi Isaac Amsellem, 4 Blvd. de Belgique. ☎ 9330-04-76.

MOROCCO
There is a legend that King Solomon sent emissaries to Morocco to raise funds among Israelites living there towards the building of the Temple in Jerusalem, but it is more likely that the first Jewish settlements in Morocco were established by Jewish slaves who accompanied the Phoenicians there in the 3rd century B.C.E. Hebrew grave markers and the ruins of a synagogue have also been found at the Roman colony of Volubilis.

Today's Jewish community is said to have been founded when a hundred Jewish families, fleeing from Roman persecution in Tripolitania during the first century C.E., sought refuge in the High Atlas. Eventually, the neighbour-

ing Berber tribes converted to Judaism, even establishing Jewish kingdoms, it is said. More Jews went to Morocco with the Expulsion from Spain in 1492. At its peak in the 1950s the Moroccan Jewish community numbered some 300,000. Today, it has dwindled through emigration to about 8,000.
General inf. from Moroccan National Tourist Office, 205 Regent St., W1R 7DE. ☎ 0171-437 0073. Fax. 0171-734 8172.

AGADIR
Syn.: Av. Moulay Abdallah, cnr. rue de la Foire. Mikva on premises. ☎ 842 339
Com. Offices, Imm. Arsalane Av. Hassan II. ☎ 840091. Fax 822268. Pres.: Simon Levy, Cite Suisse, Lotissement O.L.M. ☎ 842141.

CASABLANCA
Synagogues & Religious Organisations
There are 25 active syns., of which the principal ones are: Benisty, 13 rue Ferhat Achad; Bennaroche, 24 rue Lusitania; Em Habanim, 14 rue Lusitania; Hazan, rue Roger Farache; Ne'im Zemiroth, 29 rue Jean-Jacques Rousseau; Temple Beth El, 61 rue Jaber ben Hayane.
Mikvaot: 32 rue Officier de Paix Thomas. ☎ 2766-88; 116 rue Galilée; 84 rue des Anglais.
Com. Offices, rue Abbon Abdullah. ☎ 270976 & 2228-61. Fax. 266953.
Council of Moroccan Jewish Communities, same address.

Welfare Organisations
American Joint Distribution Com., 3 rue Rouget de Lisle. ☎ 2747-17 & 2795-63. Fax. 21991.
Jewish Com. Social Service, 1 rue Abbon Abdallah. ☎ 2769-52.
OSE (medical), 203 Blvd. Ziraoui. ☎ 2678-91.
Jewish Home for Aged, rue Verlet Hanus.
Kosher Restaurants:
(K) Bon Délice, 261 Blvd. Ziraoui opp. Lycée Lyautey; (K) La Truffe Blanche, 57 rue Taher Sebti. ☎ 2772-63; (K) Tradition, Centre 2000. ☎ 209310.

EL JADIDA
Com. Offices: P.O. Box 59. Pres.: Simon Bensimon.

ESSAOUIRA (FORMERLY MOGADOR)
Syn.: 2 rue Ziri Ben Atyah. Com. Offices: 29 rue des Syaghines. Pres.: Meyer Cohen.
Meyer Cohen & Simon Look will receive visitors. Inq. to 22 or 29 rue Syaghine. ☎ 22-70.

FEZ
Syns.: Beth El, rue de Beyrouth; Sadoun, ruelle 1, Blvd. Mohammed V.
Talmud Torah: rue Dominique Bouchery. Mikva on premises.
Com. Offices: rue Dominique Bouchery. Kosher Restaurant on the premises.
Mrs. Danielle Mamane, La Boutique, Hotel Palais Jamai, will be pleased to assist Jewish visitors.

KENITRA
Syn.: rue de Lyon. M.: Rabbi Yahia Bennaroche.
Mikva: 58 rue Sallah Eddine.
Com. Offices: 58 rue Sallah Eddine. Pres.: Rabbi Yahia Ben-Harroch.

MARRAKECH
Syns.: Bitton, rue de Touareg; Lazama, rue Talmud Torah; El Fassines; Cadoch and Mikva: Villa Oliviery, Blvd. Zerktouni (Gueliz).

Com. Offices: P.O.Box 515. Pres.: Henri Cadoch, P.O. Box 515. ☎ 44 8754.
Restaurant: Le Viennois, (Hotel Mansour Eddabbi), Ave de France. ☎ (04)
448222. Fax. (04) 448168. Reported to be kosher.

MEKNES
Com. Centre & Syn.: 5 rue de Ghana. ☎ 219-68 or 225-49. Mikva on premises. Mr. Benamram will help tourists if telephoned 24 hours in advance at
either of the above numbers.

OUJDA
Com. Offices: Texaco Maroc, 36 Blvd. Hassan Loukili. Pres.: Henri Amsellem.

RABAT
Syn.: 3 rue Moulay Ismail. Mikva on premises.
Com. Offices: 9 rue Moulay Ismail. ☎ 245-04. Pres.: Albert Derhy.

SAFI
Syns.: Mursiand, rue du R'bat; Beth El, rue du R'bat.
Com. Offices: 1 rue Boussouni. Pres.: J. Cabessa.

TANGIER
Syns.: Shaar Raphael, 27 Blvd. Pasteur. Mikva on premises. ☎ 231-304;
Temple Nahon, rue Moses Nahon.
There are a number of other syns. in the old part of the town in rue des
Synagogues, off rue Siaghines.
Com. Centre, 1 rue de la Liberté. ☎ 316-33 or 210-24. Pres.: Abraham
Azancot.
Nursing Homes: Benchimol, 78 rue Haim Benchimol; Laredo Sabbah, 98 rue
Bourakia.
Hotels: El Minzah (100), 85 rue de la Liberté. ☎ 358-85; La Grande Villa de
France, rue de Belgique; Les Almohades (150), Av. des F.A.R.; Rambrant, Av.
Pasteur. ☎ 378-70/71; Rif, Av. d'Espagne. Mr. A. Serfati will be glad to help
visitors.

TETUAN
Syns.: Benoualid, in the old Mellah; Pintada, in the old Mellah; Yagdil Torah,
adj. Com. Centre.
Com. Offices: 16 rue Moulay Abbas. Pres.: José Bendelac.

MOZAMBIQUE
MAPUTO
Jewish Community of Maputo, c/o Natalie Tenzer-Silva, PO Box 232, Maputo.
☎ (2581) 494413.

UNION OF MYANMAR (BURMA)
(Jewish population about 16)
RANGOON
Syn.: Musmeah Yeshua, 85 26th St. Sec. of Com.: Jack Samuel. ☎ 75062.
Embassy of Israel: 49 Prome Rd. ☎ 22290 or 22291.

NAMIBIA
Some Jewish settlers came to this territory before the First World War, when
it was a German colony. The cemetery at Swakopmund dates from those times.

In 1910 a congregation was established at Keetmanshoop. It had a synagogue and cemetery at one time, but is no longer in existence.
In the 1920s and 1930s there were never more than 100 Jewish families in various centres in Namibia. Today, the figure stands at only 11 families. Efforts are made to arrange services for the High Holy-days.

WINDHOEK
Syn., Corner Tal & Post Sts. P.O.Box 563.
Schools: Jewish Kindergarten; Talmud Torah.
The Sam Cohen Communal Hall is in Louis Botha Av.

NETHERLANDS ANTILLES
ARUBA
There is a syn. in Oranjestad in Adrian Laclé Blvd. ☎ 23272. Services Fri., 8 p.m.

CURAÇAO
Jews first settled on the island in 1651. The Jewish population numbers about 450 today.
Among the items of interest are the famous old sand-floored building of the Mikvé Israel-Emanuel Synagogue in Willemstad and the ancient Jewish cemetery in Blenheim. Both institutions are the oldest of their kind in the Western Hemisphere.
The cong., founded in 1651, is in its fourth building, which dates from 1732. In addition to the syn., the building, at the corner of Columbusstr. & Hanchi di Snoa, also houses a Jewish historical museum.
The Temple Emanuel building (1864) in the Hendrikplein is not in use for worship, but is a tourist attraction. Both buildings are in the centre of Willemstad.
Syns.: United Netherlands Portuguese Cong. 'Mikvé Israel-Emanuel'. (Sephardi, Rec.), P.O. Box 322. ☎ 611067. Fax 611214. M.: Rabbi Y. Feintuch. Pres.: Ronlad Gomes Cassares. ☎ 365121. Sabbath and Holy-day services, Fri. at 6.30 p.m. (second Fri. in month, family service), Sat. at 10 a.m.; Congregation Shaarei Tsedek (O. Ashkenazi) is at Leliweg 1a, P.O.B. 498. ☎ 375738. M. Rabbi R. Poupko. ☎ 369578; Pres.: Isaac Grynsztein. ☎ 368494/617952. ☎ 378505/617333. Services, Fri. at 6.45 p.m., Sat. at 7 a.m.
Community Hebrew School, Gladiolenweg 2. ☎ 375554.
Israel Consulate: Dr. P. Ackerman, Blauwduifweg 5, P.O.B. 3058, Willemstad. ☎ 365088. Fax 370707.
Travel inf. from S. E. L. Maduro & Sons, Inc., Maduro Plaza, Dokweg 19. ☎ 376700. Fax 376131.
There is no kosher restaurant in Curaçao, but kosher food is available at some out-of-town supermarkets.

NEW ZEALAND
There were Jews among the settlers in New Zealand even before the establishment of British sovereignty in 1840. David Nathan founded the Auckland Jewish com., and Abraham Hort the Wellington com. in the early 1840s. The first Mayor of Auckland, under the Municipal Corporations Act, and also the second, were Jews. Among important positions occupied by Jews have been those of Administrator, Prime Minister, and Chief Justice.
New Zealand's Jews number about 5,000. The majority live in Auckland and Wellington provinces.

Immigrants should apply for inf. to the Sec., Auckland Hebrew Cong., P.O.B. 68-224, Auckland, Auckland Jewish Council, P.O.B. 4315, Auckland, or the Jewish Com. Centre, 80 Webb Street, in Wellington, the capital.

AUCKLAND

Auckland Hebrew Cong., 108 Grey's Av., Box 68224. Sec. ☎ 373-2908. Fax. (09) 303-2147, Rabbi: R. Genende.

Progressive Cong. (Temple Shalom), 180 Manukau Rd., Epsom 3. ☎ 524 4139.

Auckland Jewish Council, Auckland Zionist Society, & NZ Zionist Federation, P.O.B. 4315. ☎ 309-9444. Fax. 373-2283. Affiliated orgs.: B'nei Akiva, Friends of the Hebrew University, Habonim, Dror, J.N.F., WIZO, Youth Aliyah.

B'nai B'rith. Lodge Pres.: R. Brami, Chapter Pres.: L. Liebman. ☎ 523-1559.

Chevra Kadisha: Sec.: D. Copeland. ☎ 444-1173.

Syn. Women's Guild. Benita Steingold. ☎ (09) 625-8970.

Council of Jewish Women: Pres.: Mrs. Lesley Eisig, 139c Bassett Rd., Remuera. ☎ 529-1997.

Kadimah College, Box 68224, Newton. ☎ 373 3072.

WIZO: Becky Murray, 6c Rangitoto Tce., Milford. ☎ (09) 410-3698. Sec. Veronica Meltzer. ☎ 575-5506.

Shelleys Catering services provide Kosher meals for all New Zealand Flights, 13 Collingswood St., Freemans Bay. ☎ 360-2989. Fax (09) 623-0073.

CHRISTCHURCH

Syn., 406 Durham St. ☎ 657412. Rev. J. Leverton. ☎ 265543. Pres. S. A. Goldsmith.

Council of Jewish Women. Helene Mautner, 15a Kidson Tce. ☎ 337-0390.

Jewish Council. Regional Chairman: S. A. Goldsmith. ☎ 3588769.

Zionist Soc. Sec.: D. Baruch, 3A Denman St. ☎ 3266458.

DUNEDIN

Syn., Corner George & Dundas Sts.

Council of Jewish Women: Diana Rothstein, 6 Shandon Rd. ☎ 454-5597.

WELLINGTON

Syn., Wellington Jewish Com. Centre, 80 Webb St. Fax. & ☎ 3845-081. Sec. Mrs. E. Gianoutses. The centre contains the Beth El Syn. (Orthodox) of Wellington Hebrew Cong. (M.: Rabbi L. Brown) & the Wellington Jewish Social Club, a Mikva and Kosher Co-op. ☎ 384-3136. Also the Wellington Zionist Society (PO Box 27-156), ☎/Fax 384-4229, and affiliated orgs.: B'nei Akiva, Friends of the Hebrew University, Habonim, Dror, J.N.F., WIZO, Youth Aliyah.

Temple Sinai (Liberal), 147 Ghuznee St., P.O. Box 27-301. ☎ 3850 0720. Fax 385 0572.

Wellington and New Zealand Regional Council, David Zwartz, 54 Central Tce., 5. ☎ 475-7622.

B'nai B'rith. Pres.: Mrs N. Walker. ☎ 476-7625. Fax 384-2401.

Council of Jewish Women. Pres.: Mrs. Shirley Payes, 11 Parnell St., Lower Hutt. ☎ 567-1679. Fax 566-0133. Sec.: Mrs. N. Walker. ☎ 476-7625.

Home for Aged, Rata St., Naenae, Lower Hutt. ☎ 567-8633.

Youth Aliyah & Zionist Soc. of New Zealand. Jewish Com. Centre, Webb St. ☎ 3844-229. Fax. 384-6542.

The monthly 'New Zealand Jewish Chronicle', PO Box 27-211. ☎/Fax 384-4229.

Israel Embassy, DP Tower, 111 The Terrace, PO Box 2171. ☎ 472-2368. Fax 499-0632.

(There is no kosher restaurant in Wellington. Visitors who want kosher meals & kosher food should contact the Jewish Com. Centre Syn., Webb Street. ☎ 384-5081 or 384-3136.)

NORWAY
Norway's Jewish com. is one of Europe's youngest and smallest. Jews first arrived in the country in 1851, but it was not until 1881 that comparatively large-scale Jewish immigration began. The community was founded in 1892. By the beginning of the Second World War, in 1939, there were 1,800 Jews in Norway.
Half of the Norwegian Jewry were killed in Auschwitz, the other half saved by the Norwegian resistance in Sweden. In 1947 the Government invited 500 D.P.s to settle in the country. The Jewish population is now about 1,400, of whom 950 live in Oslo.
General inf. from Norwegian Tourist Board, 5-11 Lower Regent St., SW1Y 4LX. ☎ 0171-839 6255.

OSLO
Syn., & Com. Centre: Bergstien 13-15, 0172. ☎ 2269-6570. M.: Rabbi Michael Melchior, Bergstien 13. ☎ 2269 2612. Pres.: Robert Katz.
There is a Jewish war memorial in Ostre Gravlund Cemetery.
B'nai B'rith. Pres.: M. Levi, Bergstien 13, 0172. ☎ 2228-6217.
Wizo. Marianne Kohn. ☎ 2228-6217.
Help the Jews Home. Mrs Anne Sender, Colletsgt. 43, 0456. ☎ 2269-2370.
Israel Embassy, Drammensveien 82c, 2. ☎ 22447924.
There are no kosher hotels or restaurants in Oslo but there is a (K) kosher food centre at Waldemar Thranesgt. 360171. ☎ 22609166. Open 16-18 Tues.-Thurs., 12-14 Fri. Closed Sat. Under supervision of Rabbi Michael Melchior.
(V) Frishsport Vegeta Vertshus, Munkedamsveien 3B, 0161. ☎ 22834020.

TRONDHEIM
Syn. & Com. Centre, Ark. Christiesgt. 1. Pres.: Julius Paltiel.

PANAMA
(Jewish population 9,000)
The Community has been settled for nearly 150 years.

PANAMA CITY
Inq. to. P.O.Box 6629, 5. Fax (507) 2286796.
Chief Rabbi: Rabbi Sion Levy, Calle 44-40, Bella Vista 85, Apartado 6222, 5. ☎ 2272828.
Syns.: Sociedad Israelita Shevet Ahim (O., Sephardi), Calle 44-27. ☎ 225-5990. Fax 227-1268. Daily services. Mikva on premises; Beneficiencia Israelita Beth El (Ashkenazi), Calle 58E, Urb. Obarrio. ☎ 2233383. Mikva on premises. Koll Sherit Israel (R), Av. Cuba, 354-16. ☎ 225-4100.
Consejo Central Comunitario Hebrew de Panama, Apt. 3309, 4. ☎ (507) 263-8411, Fax: (507) 264-7936
Jewish Centre Centro Cultural Hebreo De Beneficiencía, Calle 50 Final. (K) Restaurant open daily for lunch & supper. Closed Sat. P.O.B 7166, 5. ☎ 226-0455. Fax 226 0869.
Israel Embassy, Edificio Grobman, Calle, Manuel Maria Icaza, 5th Floor. ☎ 264 8257.
Kosher Food & Meat:
(K) **Super Kosher**, Calle San Sebastian, Paitilla. ☎ 236-5254 or 235-5253.
(K) **La Bonbonniere**, Calle Juan XXIII, Paitilla. ☎ 264-5704.

(K) Chocolatier, Calle 53, Urb. Marbella. ☎ 264-4712.
Kosher Restaurants:
(K) Shalom Kosher, Plaza Bal Harbour, Paitilla. ☎ 264-4411.
Kosher Bakery and Dairy Restaurant:
(K) Pita Pan, Plaza Bal Harbour. ☎ 264-2786.
(K) Candies Bazaar, Via Argentina, 155 L-2. ☎ 269-4857.

PARAGUAY
(Jewish population 1,200)
ASUNCION
Syn., General Diaz, 657.
Com. Centre (Consejo Representativo Israelita de Paraguay – Jewish Representative Council of Paraguay), General Diaz 657, P.O.B. 756. ☎ 41744.
Sec.-General: Rolf Kemper.
Israel Embassy, Juan O'Leary y General Diaz, Edificio Lider II-3er. Piso, P.O. Box 1212. ☎ 95097.

PERU
(Jewish population 3,000)
There are about 3,000 Jews in Peru today, nearly all of whom live in Lima, the capital.

IQUITOS
There is a Jewish cemetery in part of the city's burial ground.

LIMA
Synagogues & Religious Organizations
Union Israelita del Peru (O), Jose Quiñones 290, Miraflores 18. ☎ 441-3461. Services are held at the Cento Sharon.
Rabbinate: Av. 2 de Mayo 1815, San Isidro, 27. ☎ 440-0290. Rabbi Yaacov Kraus. ☎ 264-0678.
Centro Social y Cultural Sharon (O), Av. 2 de Mayo 1815, San Isidro, 27. ☎ 440-0290.
Sociedad de Beneficencia Israelita Sefardi (O), Enrique Villar 581, Santa Beatriz, 1. ☎ 471-7230. Rabbi A. Benhamu. ☎ 442-4505.
Asociación Judia de Beneficencia y Culto de 1870 (C), Jose Galvez 282, Miraflores, 18. ☎ 45-1089. Rabbi Guillermo Bronstein. ☎/Fax 445-5148..
Beit Jabad, Salaverry 3095, San Isidro 27. ☎ 264-6060. Rabbi Zalman Blumenfeld. ☎/Fax 442-9441.
The Chief Rabbi of Perú is Rabbi Abraham Benhamu ☎ 42-4505.
Mikvaot: Union Israelita, Ave. Gral. Juan A. Pezet 1472, San Isidro, 27. ☎ 264-2187. Sociedad Israelita Sefardi; Beit Jabad.

Representative Organisations
Asociación Judia del Peru (Representative Body of Peruvian Jewry), Jose Quiñones 290, Miraflores 18. ☎ 441-3461.
Comite de Relaciones Humanas, Av. 2 de Mayo 1815, San Isidro 27. ☎ 440-8291.
Logia B'nai B'rith, Jose Quiñones 290, Miraflores, 18. ☎ 441-3461.
Cultural Organization, Club, etc.:
Asociación Cultural, Deportiva y Social Hebraica (Maccabi), Av. La Molina 318, Ate-Vitarte 3. ☎ 348-0350.

Welfare Organizations, Homes, etc.

Bikur Jolim - Jevra Kadisha, Av. Guardia Civil 175, San Borja, 41. ☎ 475-9005/5430.

Asociacion Filantropica Israelita, Av. Comandante Espinar 150, Miraflores, 18. ☎ 445-4360/4672.

Youth Organization:
Hanoar Hatzioni, c/o Colegia León Pinelo, Maimonides 610, San Isidro, 27. ☎ 445-8291.

Zionist Organizations

Keren Kayemet LeIsrael, Av. 2 de Mayo 1815, San Isidro, 27. ☎ 440-0290.

Naamat - Pioneras, Comandante Jimenez 415, Magadelena del Mar, 17. ☎ 461-7993.

Zionist Federation of Peru, Av. 2 de Mayo 1815, San Isidro, 27. ☎ 40-029

Israel Embassy, Natalio Sanchez 125 6to piso, Santa Beatrice 1. ☎ 433-4431.

Historical Note

Museum of the Inquisition, Junin 548 (in front of the Congress). Dungeon and torture chamber of the headquarters of the Inquisition for all Spanish South America.

Pilatos House, Ancash 390. 17th century private mansion; it is now used by the National Institute of Culture. On the second floor was the synagogue of the Marrano Jews.

Newspapers

J.T.A. - Publicationes Memora S.A., Psje. Malvas 135, Breña, 5. ☎ 424-0534. (Daily).

Shofar, Husares de Junin 163, Jesus Maria, 11. ☎ 24-1412 31-2410. (Monthly).

Hotels: Shabbath observers may wish to stay at the hotels Libertador and Regina, which are a short walk to the Centro Sharon.

Hotel Libertador, Los Eucaliptos 550, San Isidro, 27. ☎ 421-6666. Fax 442-3011.

Hostal Regina, Av. 2 de Mayo 1421, San Isidro, 27. ☎ 441-2541/442-8870. Fax 421-2044.

Kosher Meals

There is no kosher restaurant in Lima. Visitors who want kosher meals should contact Rabbi Yaacov Kraus.

Salon Majestic, Av. Bolivar 965, Pueblo Libre, 21. ☎ 463-0031. Fax 461-8912. Catering for special groups and parties by prior arrangement only, under supervision of Rabbi Abraham Benhamu and Rabbi Yaacov Kraus.

Kosher Food

Minimarket Kasher, Av. Gral. Juan A. Pezet 1472, San Isidro, 27. ☎ 264-2187. Under supervison of Rabbi Yaacov Kraus.

Kosher items available in the supermarket chains Wong and Santa Isabel, and in drugstore Pharmax.

PHILIPPINES REPUBLIC

(Jewish population 225)

MANILA

Syn., & Com. Centre, Jewish Assoc. of the Philippines (Beth Yaacov Syn.), H.V. de la Costa St., cnr. Tordesillas St., Salcedo Village (close to Mandarin

Hotel), Makati, Metro Manila, 1200. ☎ 815-0265 & 815-0263. Fax. 818-9990. Services, Fri., 6.30 p.m.; Sat., 9.30 a.m. Mikva available. Kosher requirements by arrangement.
Embassy of Israel, 23rd floor, Trafalgar Plaza Bldg., HV dela Costa St., Salcedo Village, 1200 Makati City. ☎ (632) 892-5329 to 32, (632) 894-0441/3. Fax (632) 894-1027. Postal address: PO Box 1697, Makati Central Post Office, 1256 Makati City.

POLAND

Jews settled in Poland in the ninth century, coming from Germany, Bohemia and Russia. The first documentary evidence of Polish Jews is dated 1185, and there is also evidence on coins: Jews were in charge of Polish coinage in the twelfth century, and coins bore Hebrew inscriptions.

The Kalisz Statutes of 1264, granted by Duke Boleslaw the Pious, were a charter of Jewish rights. Casimir the Great, the last Polish king of the Piast dynasty (1303-1370), was a protector of the Jews and was, according to legend, married secretly to a Jewess, Esther.

There was persecution under the first Jagiellon kings, and anti-Jewish decrees were issued by the Church in 1420. The granting of rights and privileges (resulting in eras of Jewish freedom and prosperity) alternated in Polish history with the withdrawal of such rights and consequent periods of persecution and, sometimes, expulsion.

Jewish learning flourished from the sixteenth century onwards. Mystic Chasidism, based on the Cabbala, had its wonder-rabbis. Famous Talmudic scholars, codifiers of the ritual, and other eminent men of learning were produced by Polish Jewry.

Of the 3,500,000 Jews in Poland in 1939, about three million were exterminated by Hitler. Many put up a heroic fight, like those of the Warsaw Ghetto in 1943. Fewer than half a million fled to the West and to the Soviet Union. After the Second World War there were several waves of emigration, the last of which was in 1968. Today's ageing Jewish population numbers an estimated 6,000.

Syns. and Social Cultural Societies (TSZK) are known to exist in the following towns: Biala, Bielsko, Bytom, Czestochowa, Dzierzoniów, Gliwice, Katowice, Legnica, Lublin, Milejczyce, Sosnowiec, Swidnica, Szczecin, Tarnów, Tykocin, Walbrzych, Wloclawek, Wroclaw, Zamosc, Zary k/Zag, Zgorzelec.

There are several travel guides to Poland giving directions to Jewish monuments and historical associations in the country. The most thorough in this respect is 'The Rough guide to Poland'.

The Jewish Information and Tourist Bureau has produced several guides including: 'A guide to Jewish Poland' (1993), Lublin (1990), Lodz (1992), Galicia (1993), Bialystok (1992), Cracow (1990) available from the synagogues in the respective towns and in Warsaw, 6 Twarda St., 00950. ☎ (48-22) 200556.

Foreign tourists are advised to address all their queries and requests to the Foreign Tourists' Office, Krakowskie Przedmiescie St., Warsaw 13. ☎ 26-16-68.

BIELSKO-BIALA
Elzbieta Wajs, Ul Mickiewicza 26, 43-300. ☎ 224 38.

BYTOM
(Not available). Ul Smolenia 4, 41902. ☎ 81 3510.

CRACOW
There is a monument in ul. Jerozolimska to the victims of the Nazi death camps. The site of the Auschwitz (Oswiecim) death camp is about 40 miles from Cracow. A Jewish pavilion was inaugurated at the Auschwitz Museum in 1978.

Synagogues
The famous Remuh Synagogue and cemetery, which date from the 15th & 16th centuries, are at ul. Szeroka 40. A number of famous rabbis are buried there. Both the Remuh and the Temple (which dates from 1844) at ul. Miodowa 24 hold services on Sabbaths & Holy-days. There is also a mikva at ul. Miodowa 24. For appointments & inf. ☎ 620-64. The buildings are reported to be currently under reconstruction (late 1996).
The Old Syn. (14th century), ul. Szeroka 2, is one of the oldest syn. buildings in Europe. It has been restored and serves as a Jewish Museum, which is part of Cracow History Museum. The Kuppa Syn. (1595), ul. Miodowa, is now a factory. The Poper Syn. (1620), ul. Szeroka, now serves as a non-Jewish young men's club. The High Syn. (1620), ul. Jozefa, is an architect's home. The Izzaka Syn., ul. Izzak, is an artist's studio.
Cemetery, ul. Miodowa 55. ☎ 545-66.

Religious Org.: Zwiazek Wyznania Mojzeszowego, ul. Skawinska 2. ☎ 66-23-47.
Mr. Jakubowicz, Ul Skawinska 2, 31-006 ☎ 662347.
Secular Org.: Towarzystwo Spoleczno-Kulturalne Zydow (Social and Cultural Assoc. of Jews).
Jewish Club: T. S. K. Z. Krak'w imienia Mordchaja Gebirtiga, ul. Slawkowska 30. ☎ 22-98-41.
Bookshop: Jordan, 2 Szeroka St., Miodowa 41. ☎ 217166.
Ariel Cafe, 17 Szeroka St. ☎ 21-38-70; Restaurant at no. 18.
(**K**) Kazimierz, next door to the Remuh syn. at ul Szeroka 40.
Hadar (Gallery of Modern Jewish Art), 13 Florianska St. ☎ 218-992.

GLIWICE
Mr. Farber. Ul Dolnych Walow 9, 44-100. ☎ 31 47 97.

KATOWICE
Felix Lipman, Ul Mlynska 13, 40-09 8. ☎ 53 7742.

LEGNICA
Mr. Blado, Ul Chojnowska 37, 59-220. ☎ 22730.

LODZ
Jewish Cong., Zachodnia, 78. ☎ 335-156.
Jewish Chd, Sec. Oleg Grinsztajn. ☎ 331-221, 336-825.

LUBLIN
Dr. Weiss. Ul Lubartowska 10, 20-080. ☎ 22353.

RZESZÓW
Two ancient synagogues face each other in ul. Bonicza at the edfe of pl. Ofiara Getta.

SZCZECIN
Ul. Niemcewicza 2, 71-553. ☎ 221674.

TARNÓW
The former Jewish district dating from the 15th Century extends to the east of the town square. There is a functioning synagogue at 1 Goldhammer ul. and a cemetery at ul. Nowodabrowska dating from 1580.

WALBRZYCH
Not available. Ul Moniuszka 13/15. ☎ 25-382.

WARSAW
The Gesia cemetery should be visited. A pilgrimage should also be made to Treblinka, a village situated half-way between Warsaw and Bialystok, about two hours' journey north-east of Warsaw. In 1942-43 it was the site of one of the most infamous extermination camps set up by the Nazis in Europe. About 750,000 Jews, including about 300,000 from the Warsaw Ghetto, perished there. The Ghetto Fighters' Memorial is near Mila Street, in a park bounded by Zamenhof and Anielewicz Streets. At the corner of Mila St. & Dubois is a small monument with an inscription in Polish, Hebrew & Yiddish.
Religious Org.: Zwiazek Religijny Wyznania Mojzeszowego, ul. Krajowej Rady Narodowej 6. ☎ 20-43-24.
Syn. & Vaad Hakehilla, 6 Twarda St., ☎ 204324. Rabbi M. Joskowicz.
Secular Org.: Zarzad Glowny Towarzystwa Spoleczno-Kulturalnego Zydow w Polsce (Main Board of the Cultural & Social Assoc. of Polish Jews), Plac Grzybowski 12. ☎ 200-556.
Society for Polish-Israeli Friendship, ul. Ujazdowskie 47.
The Jewish Historical Institute, 3/5 Tlomackie St., 00-090. ☎ 27-15-30, has a remarkable collection of Judaica. It includes a library of documents on the story of the Warsaw Ghetto and the Ghetto Uprising, and a large collection of manuscripts stolen by the Germans from all over Europe.
Shalom Tours. ☎ 2203037. Fax. 2200559.

(K) Restaurant: **Menora,** Plac Grzybowski, 2. ☎ 203754.
(V) Ekologia Restaurant, Rynek 13, Nowy Miasto.

Cafe Ejlat, ul. Ujazdowskie 47.
Panorama, Al. Witosa 31. ☎ 642-0666.
Salad Bar, ul. Tamka 37. ☎ 635-8463.

WROCKLAW
The Jewish Congregation in Wrocklaw, Ul. Wlodkowica 9, 50072. ☎/Fax 36401. Office hours 9.00 a.m. - 2.00 p.m. Pres.: David Ringel.
Shabbat and Festival services held at 9.30 a.m. in the Comm.Centre. Affiliated organisations include the Union of Jewish Students and Havurah Lelimud Jahadut.
The second largest community in Poland. Restoration of the White Stork Synagogue (1829) at Wlodkowica 9 is in progress. The Old Cemetery (1856) is preserved as part of the city's Historical Museum, Slezna St. 37. ☎ 678236.
The New Cemetery (1900) is being renovated, Lotnicza St., 51. ☎ 36401.

PORTUGAL
Portugal has one of the smallest Jewish communities in Europe (about 700), mostly concentrated in and around Lisbon.
Communal life largely revolves round the Jewish Centre, which, since it was established in 1948 in Lisbon's finest residential quarter, has acted as a strong unifying influence between Sephardim and Ashkenazim. The community maintains a shechita board.
General inf. from Portuguese National Tourist Office, 2nd Flr., 22-25A, Sackville St., W1X 1DE. ☎ 0171-494-1441. Fax. 0171-494-1868.

BELMONTE
Formerly a stronghold of a long standing marrano enclave. There is now an

organised community of some 200 members. Daily services. Jewish Community of Belmonte, Apt. 18, 6250 Belmonte. (Bairo de Santa Maina). ☎/Fax (075) 912465. M.: Rabbi Shlomo Sebag.

FARO
The Jews of the Algarve have recently arranged for the restoration of the cemetery of Faro (1838-1932). It is opposite the Faro Hospital. Details from Ralf Pinto, Rua Infante dom Henrique, 12 30 B, 8500 Portimão. ☎ (82) 416710. Fax. (82) 416515.

LISBON
Main Syn., Rua Alexandre Herculano 59-1250. ☎ 385-06-04. Fax 388-43-04. M.: vacancy. Services on Fri. evg. & Sat. morning.
Avenida Elias Garcia, 110-1°-1050. (Ashkenazi)
Communal Offices, Rua Alexandre Herculano 59-1250. ☎ 385-06-04. Fax 388-43-04.
Jewish Club and Centre, Rua Rosa Araujo 10. ☎ 572041.

Israel Embassy, Rua Antonio Enes 16-4°. ☎ 570251, 570145, 570374 & 570478.

Kosher meals are obtainable if prior notice is given, from **(K)** Mrs. R. Assor, Rua Rodrigo da Fonseca 38.1°D. ☎ 3860396. She can also supply delicatessen. **(K)** kosher meat contact the communal offices.

OPORTO
Syn., Rua Guerra Junqueiro 340.

PONTA DELGADA
Capital of the island of Sao Miguel, in the Azores, a group of Atlantic islands owned by Portugal. Syn., Rua do Brum 16.

TOMAR
The ancient syn. in Rua de Joaquim Jacinto (built 1492-1497) has been reopened as a museum. A Marrano, Luis Vasco, is the custodian and guide. Tomar is north of Lisbon, near Fatima.

MADEIRA
During the war most Gibraltar Jews were evacuated to Madeira, but only a few Jews live there now. There is no organised community.
General information can be obtained from the Portuguese National Tourist Office in London, and in Madeira from Tourismo da Madeira, Av. Arriaga, Funchal.
Vegetarian and fish meals can be had at the Hotel Madeira Palácio (260), P.O. Box 614, ☎ 30001; the Madeira-Sheraton Hotel (292), Largo Antonio Nobre, ☎ 31031; Reid's Hotel and the Savoy Hotel, all in Funchal.

PUERTO RICO
(Jewish population 4,000)

SAN JUAN-SANTURCE
Syns.: Com. Centre-Shaare Zedeck Synagogue (Conservative), 903 Ponce de Leon Av., Santurce, 00907. ☎ 724-4157. M.: Rabbi Alejandro B. Felch. Temple Beth Shalom (Reform), San Jorge Av. & Loiza St., Santurce.
Some major hotels provide kosher style meals in the winter season. Frozen kosher poultry and delicatessen are available at some Pueblo supermarkets.

ROMANIA
There have been Jews in the territory that is now Romania since Roman times. The country's Jewish population today is some 14,000, of whom about 6,500 live in Bucharest. There are 70 functioning synagogues, 4 of them in Bucharest, including two at the two homes for the aged. There are Talmud Torah classes in 24 communities throughout the country.
General inf. from Romanian National Tourist Office, 83A, Marylebone High Street, W1M 3DE.

ARAD
Syns.: Orthodox, 12 Cozia St.; Neologa, 10 Tribunul Dobra St.
Talmud Torah: 10 Tribunul Dobra St.
Com. Office: 10 Tribunul Dobra St. ☎ 281310.
Muzeul Judetean, Piata George Enescu, 1. ☎ 280114.
Home for Aged: 22, 7 Episcopei St.
(K) Restaurant: Ritual, 22, 7 Episcopei St. ☎ 280731.
Hotel Parc, Bd. Dragulina, 25. ☎ 280 820.
Hotel Astoria, Bd. Revolutiei, 79-81. ☎ 281990

BACAU
Syns.: Cerealistilor, 29 Stefan cel Mare St.; Avram A. Rosen Syn., 31 V. Alecsandri St.
Talmud Torah: 11 Alexandru cel Bun St.
Com. Office: 11 Alexandru cel Bun St. ☎ 0341-34-714.
(K) Restaurant: 11 Alexandru cel Bun St.

BORSEC
(K) Transylvania Hotel. Syn. and mikveh on the premises. Contact Interom Tours. ☎ 972-3-9246425. Fax 972-3-5791720.

BOTOSANI
Syns.: Great, 1a Marchian St.; Yiddish, 10 Gh. Dimitrov St.; Mare, 18 Muzicantilor St.
Mikva, 67 7 Aprilie St.
Talmud Torah, 1 Marchian St.
Com. Office, 220 Calea Nationala. ☎ 0315-14-6-59.
(K) Restaurant, 69 7 Aprilie St. ☎ 0315-15-9-17.

BRASOV
Syn.: 27 Poarta Schei St.
Talmud Torah, 27 Poarta Schei St.
Com. Office, 27 Poarta Schei St. ☎ 0681-43-5-32.
(K) Restaurant, 27 Poarta Schei St. ☎ 0681-44440.

BUCHAREST
Chief Rabbi of Romania:- Fed. of Romanian Jewish Coms, Strada Sf. Vineri 9. ☎ 613-2538. Fax 312-0869. Pres.: Dr. N. Cajal. The Fed. publishes a bi-monthly, 'Revista Realitatea Evreiasca' in Romanian, Yiddish, Hebrew & English, with a circulation of 4,500. It is at 24 Popa Rusu St. ☎ 211-80-80.
Jewish Com. of Bucharest, Strada Sf. Vineri 9. ☎ 613-1782.
Principal Synagogues
Choral Temple,Strada Sf. Vineri 9. ☎ 14-72-57. Talmud Torah on premises.
Credinta (Faith), 48 Vasile Toneanu St.
Great Syn. (Sephardi), 9-11 Vasile Adamache St. ☎ 615-08-46.
Ieshua Tova, 9 Nikos Beloiannis St. (near the Lido and Ambassador Hotels). ☎ 659-56-75.
Mikva, 5 Negustori St.

Homes for Aged
Amalia & Chief Rabbi Dr. Moses Rosen Home, 105 Jimbolia St. ☎ 667-3633.
Martin Balus Home, 55 Ripiceni St. ☎ 240-6612.
Both homes have a prayer hall.

Cultural Organisations
Museum of the Jewish Community in Romania, 3 Mamoulari St. ☎ 615-0837.
Open Wed. & Sun., 9.00-13.00.
Romanian Jewish History Research Centre, 12 Juliu Barasch St. ☎ 323-7246.
Jewish State Theatre. ☎ 323-45-30.
Embassy of Israel: 6 Burghelea St. ☎ 613-26-34/5/6.
(K) Restaurant operated by the Jewish com., 18 Popa Soare St. ☎ 322-03-98.

CLUJ NAPOCA
Syns.: Beth Hamidrash Ohel Moshe, 16 David Francisc St.; Sas Hevra, 13 Croitorilor St.; Templul Deportatilor, 21 Horea St.
Mikva, 16 David Francisc St.
Talmud Torah, 16 David Francisc St.
Com. Office, 25 Tipografiei St. ☎ 064-11-667.
(K) Restaurant, 5-7 Paris St. ☎ 064-11-0-26.

CONSTANTA
Syns.: Great Temple, 2 C.A. Rosetti St.; Small, 3 Sarmisagetuza St.
Talmud Torah, 3 Sarmisagetuza St.
Com. Office: 3 Sarmisagetuza St. ☎ 0416-11-5-98.

DOROHOI
Syns.: Great, 4 Piata Unirii St.;
Com. Office, 95 Spiru Haret St. ☎ 0316-11-797.
Home for Aged: 95 Spiru Haret St. ☎ 0316-11-7-97.
(K) Restaurant: 14-18 Dumitru Furtuna St.

GALATI
Syn.: Meseriasilor, 11 Dornei St.
Talmud Torah, 9 Dornei St.
Com. Office: 9 Dornei St. ☎ 0364-13-6-62.
(K) Restaurant, 9 Dornei St. ☎ 0364-13-6-62.

IASI (JASSY)
Syns.: Great, 7 Sinagogilor St.; Schor, 5 Sf. Constantin St.
Mikva, 15 Elena Doamna St.
Talmud Torah, 15 Elena Doamna St.
Com. Office: 15 Elena Doamna St. ☎ 0321-14-4-14.
(K) Restaurant, 15 Elena Doamna St. ☎ 0321-117883.

ORADEA
Syns.: Great, 4 Mihai Viteazu St.; Neolog, 22 Independentei St.; Sas Hevra, 4 Mihai Viteazu St.
Mikva, 5 Mihai Viteazu St.
Talmud Torah, 4 Mihai Viteazu St.
Com. Office: 4 Mihai Viteazu St. ☎ 0591-34-8-43.
(K) Restaurant: 5 Mihai Viteazu St. ☎ 059-31-3-83.

PIATRA NEAMT
Syns.: Leipziger, 12 Meteorului St.; Old Baal Shem Tov, 7 Meteorolui St. (Historical Monument).
Talmud Torah, 7 Petru Rares St.
Com. Office, 7 Petru Rares St. ☎ 0336-23-8-15.

RADAUTI
Syns.: Great, 2, 1 Mai St.; Vijnitzer, 49 Libertatii St.
Com. Office: 11 Aleea Primaverii, Block 14, Apt. 1. ☎ 0304-61-3-33.

SATU MARE
Syn.: Great, 4 Decebal St.
Com. Office: 4 Decebal St. ☎ 0617-43783.

SIGHET
Syn.: Great, 8 Basarabia St.
Talmud Torah, 8 Basarabia St.
Com. Office, 8 Basarabia St. ☎062-511652.
There is a memorial to the Jewish victims of Nazism in Gh. Doja St.

SUCEAVA
Syn.: Gah Chavre, 4 Dimitrie Onciu St.
Talmud Torah, 8 Armeneasca St.
Com. Office, 8 Armeneasca St. ☎ 0302-13-0-84.

TIMISOARA
Syns.: Cetate. 6, Marasesti St.; Fabric, 2 Splaiul Coloniei; Iosefin, 55 Resita St.
Mikva, 55 Resita St.
Talmud Torah, 5 Gh. Lazar St.
Com. Office, 5 Gh. Lazar St. ☎0561-32-8-13.
Home for Aged, 2 Splaiul Coloniei St. ☎ 0561-3-63-48.
(K) Restaurant, 10 Marasesti St. ☎ 0561-36-9-24.

TIRGU MURES
Syn.: 21 Aurel Filimon St.
Talmud Torah, 10 Brailei St. ☎ 065-115001.
Com. Office, 10 Brailei St. ☎ 065-115001.

TUSHNAD
(K) Olt Hotel. Contact Interom Tours. ☎ 972-3-9246425. Fax 972-3-5791720.

VATRA DORNEI
Syns.: Vijnitzer, 14 Luceafarul St.
Com. Office, 54 M Eminescu St. ☎ 0303-71-9-57.

SENEGAL
DAKAR
M. Clement Politis, 13 rue San Diniéry (P.O.B. 449). ☎ 23-27-84 or 23-51-74.
Fax. 23-33-30, will be pleased to receive overseas visitors.

SINGAPORE
The Jewish community of Singapore, numbering about 240, dates from 1840.
The street in which Jewish divine service was first held in a house is now
known as Synagogue Street. The first building to be erected as a synagogue
was Maghain Aboth, opened in 1878. This was rebuilt and enlarged in 1925.
Another synagogue, Chesed-El, was built in 1905. The community is mainly
Sephardi (of Baghdad origin).
The affairs of the community are managed by the annually elected Jewish
Welfare Board, Robinson Rd., P.O. Box 474. Pres.: Mr. Jacob Ballas. Syns.:
Chesed-El, 2 Oxley Rise, S-0923. ☎ 7328832. Services Mon. only; Maghain
Aboth, Waterloo St. ☎ 3360692. Daily & Sabbath services held at Maghain
Aboth Syn.

Talmud Torah: Sir Manasseh Meyer's Hebrew School, 71 Oxley Rise, S-0923. ☎ 7379746.
Israel Embassy, 58 Dalvey Road, Singapore 1025. ☎ 2350966.

SLOVAK REPUBLIC
BRATISLAVA (PRESSBURG)
Syn.: Heydukova 11-13. Services: Mon. Thurs-Sat.
Mikva: Zamocka 13. ☎ 312642. Rabbi Baruch Myers.
(K) Kosher food is obtainable here, also. (Open for lunch only).
Union of Jewish Comm. in Slovakia. Kozia 21/II, 81447. Ch.: Prof. Pavel Traubner. Exec.: Fero Alexander. ☎ 427-312167. Fax 427 311106.
The underground mausoleum contains the graves of 18 famous rabbis, including the Chatham Sepher. The key is available from the Com. Offices.
The Museum of Jewish Culture is on Zidovska Str.
(K) Restaurant Chez David, Zámocká 13, ☎ 316943, 313824. Fax 312-642.

GALANTA
Syn.: Partizanska 907. Daily services are held at the syn. There is also a mikva.

KOSICE (KASCHAU)
Syns.: Puskinova ul. 3; Beth Hamidrash, Zvonarska ul. 5. Rabbi Lazar Kleinman.
Com. Centre: Zvonarska ul. 5, 04001. ☎ 622-1047.
(K) Kosher Restaurant: Zvonarska ul. 5.

PIESTANY
Syn.: Hviezdoslavova 59. Shabbat and festival services.
Old Cemetery: Janosikova ul. 606.

PRESOV
Syn, Community Centre Museum: Sverthova 32. Tel/Fax. 4291-31271.

TRNAVA
Syn.: Kapitulska ul. 7.
Monument to Deportees: in the courtyard of the former syn., at Halenarska ul. 32.

SLOVENIA
Judovska Skupnost Slovenije (Jewish Community of Slovenia), Judovska Obchina Ljubljana (Jewish Community of Ljubljana), P.O. Box 569, 61101 Ljubljana. ☎ 315-884.
The newly independent Republic of Slovenia has a tiny Jewish community of 78 members. There is no synagogue and no kosher restaurant. The nearest synagogue is in Trieste, Italy. Services are also held at the Jewish community office in Zagreb, Croatia. Appointments with Exec. Cttee. members of the Jewish community of Ljubljana by writing only.
The Jewish community of Ljubljana takes care of Jewish cemeteries in Ljubljana, Lendava, Murska Sobota and Rozhna dolina (Nova Gorica). There are monuments to victims of fascism at the Ljubljana and Lendava cemeteries. The Rozhna dolina (Nova Gorica) cemetery is protected as a historic monument. The old synagogue in Maribor, 1429, is currently being renovated by the municipality of Maribor as a historic monument.

SOUTH AFRICA

The Jewish community began as an organised body in Cape Town in 1841, although individual Jews had settled there much earlier. The organisation of religious life varies with the density of the Jewish population (which totals about 100,000). In all, there are about 200 organised communities, most of which have their own synagogues.

The major supermarket chains - Pick and Pay, and Checkers — stock a large range of kosher items.

Kosher meals are available on the following internal aircraft carriers: South African Airways (SAA), Sun Air and Comair. Kosher meals must be booked in advance through your travel agent. It is advisable to confirm both your air-tiket and type of meal 48 hours before departure. When ordering Mehdarin, then a request must be made for a 'special' kosher meal.

General inf. from South African Tourism Board, 5-6 Altgrove, Wimbledon SW19. ☎ 081-944 6646.

CAPE PROVINCE
CAPE TOWN
Synagogues & Religious Organisations
Arthur's Rd., 31 Arthur's Rd., Sea Point. ☎ 434-8680.
Bellville, P.O. Box 41, Bellville, 7535. ☎ 948-3553.
Camps Bay, Chilworth Rd., Camps Bay. ☎ 438-8082.
Cape Town Hebrew Cong., 84 Hatfield St., Gardens. ☎ 45-1405.
Chabad Centre, 6 Holmfirth Rd., Seapoint. ☎ 434-3740.
Claremont, Grove Av., Claremont. ☎ 61-9007.
Constantia, 21 Abbotsford Ave. ☎ 75-2520.
Green and Sea Point Hebrew Cong., Marais Rd., Sea Point. ☎ 439-7543.
Milnerton, 29 Fitzpatrick Rd, Cambridge Estate. ☎ 52-4100.
Muizenberg, Camp Rd., Muizenberg. M.: Rabbi G. Rockman. ☎ 788-7688.
Rondebosch, Stuart Rd., Rondebosch. ☎ 61-3507.
Sephardi Hebrew Cong., 18 Kei Apple Rd., Sea Point. ☎ 439-3127.
Somerset West, Church St., Somerset West. ☎ 024-516316.
Stellenbosch, Van Ryneveld St., Stellenbosch. ☎ 7-1809.
Temple Israel (Reform), Upper Portswood Rd., Green Point. ☎ 434-9721.
Temple Israel (Reform), Salisbury Rd., Wynberg. ☎ 797-3362.
United Orthodox Hebrew Cong., 12 Schoonder St., Gardens, Vredehock. ☎ 45-2239.
Wynberg Hebrew Cong., cnr. Piers & Mortimer Rds., Wynberg. ☎ 797-5029.
Beth Din, 191 Buitenkant St. ☎ 461-6310. Inf. about (**K**) kosher food available from the Beth Din.
Union of Orthodox Syns. of South Africa, Cape Council, 191 Buitenkant St., 8001. ☎ 461-6310. Fax. 461-8320.
Mikva: Arthur's Rd., Sea Point. ☎ 434-3148.

Representative Organisation
S. African Jewish Board of Deputies' Cape Council, 3rd Floor, Leeusig Hse., 4 Leeuwen St. 8001. ☎ 23-2420. Fax. (021) 232-615. Exec. Dir. I. Sacks.

Cultural & Educational Organisations, etc.
Cape Board of Jewish Education, Ground Floor, Leeusig Hse., 4 Leeuwen St. ☎ 23-1825.
Jacob Gitlin Library, Ground Floor, Leeusig Hse., 4 Leeuwen St. ☎ 24-5020.
Jewish Museum, 84 Hatfield St., Gardens. Curator R. Newman; Sec.: Mrs L. Robinson. ☎ 45-1546. Sun. 10 a.m. to 12.30 p.m., Tues. and Thurs. 2 p.m. to 5 p.m., & by appointment. Closed on Jewish and Public holidays.

Miscellaneous Organisations

Cape Jewish Board of Guardians, 4th Floor, Leeusig House, 4 Leewen St. ☎ 23-3783.

Cape Jewish Seniors Org. 3 Bellevue Rd., Sea Point. ☎ 434-9691.

Union of Jewish Women of South Africa (Cape Town Branch), 7 Albany Rd., Sea Point. ☎ 434-9555/6.

Western Province Zionist Council, Leeusig Hse., 4 Leeuwen St. ☎ 24-5020. Fax. 232-615. Also at this address: Betar, Bnei Akiva, Bnoth Zion, Habonim, Israel United Appeal, Jewish National Fund, Maccabi, Magen David Adom, Mizrachi Federation, ORT, Poalei Zion, Revisionist Zionists, S. African Union of Jewish Students, Union of General Zionists, United Zionist Assoc.

Sports & Country Clubs

Glen Country Club, Victoria Rd., Clifton. ☎ 438-1512.

Keurboom Sports Club, Av. de Mist, Rondebosch. ☎ 61-4521.

King David Country Club, Pallotti St., Philippi. ☎ 934-0365.

Delicatessen: (K) Dee's Deli, 359a Main Rd., Sea Point. ☎ 439-1632.

Kosher Restaurant: (K) Belmont Kosher Restaurant, 3 Holmfirth Rd., Sea Point. ☎ 434-0829.

Hotels

(K) Cape Sun, Strand St. ☎ 23-8844.

(K) Belmont Hotel, Aged Home (restaurant for non-residents), Holmfrith Road, Sea Point, 8001. ☎ (021) 439-1155.

Restaurants

Garden of Eden, Glemain, 359a Main Road, Sea Point, 8001. ☎ (021) 439-1632; Dovidil's Pizza, 74 Regent Road, Sea Point, 8001. ☎ (021) 434-1297; Kaplan Student Canteen, University of Cape Town. ☎ (021) 650-3064.

Marrakesh, 315 Main Road, Sea Point, 8001. ☎ (021) 434-0455. Also open for 6 weeks during Dec/Jan in Muizenburg.

Butchery & Bakery

Checkers, Sea Point (Butchery & Bakery). ☎ (021) 439-6159. Fax (021) 439-5630. Also Shoprite, Sea Point.

Claremont Kosher Butcher, Paarden Eiland. ☎ (021) 511-1391. Fax (021) 511-6555.

Pick 'N Pay, Claremont (Butchery). ☎ (021) 683-2900

Pick 'N Pay, Constantia (Butchery). ☎ (021) 794-5690.

Pick 'N Pay, Sea Point (Butchery & Bakery). ☎ (021) 438 2049.

Shoprite, Rondebosch (Bakery). ☎ (021) 689-4563.

EAST LONDON

Syn.: Shar Hashomayim (Orthodox), 56 Park Av., P.O.B. 1043. Inq. to Rabbi Y. Shalpid. ☎ 0431-22071.

Council of Border Jewry, 32 Oxford St., 5200. ☎ (0431) 26151.

KIMBERLEY

Synagogues

Beth Hamedrash, Baronial St. ☎ 5652.

Communal Hall, Voortrekker St.

Griqualand West Hebrew Cong., P.O. Box 68, 8300.

OUDTSHOORN

Syn.: Baron von Rheede St. Communal Hall, P.O.B. 362, 6620. ☎ 2969. There is a Jewish section in the C.P. Nel Museum.

PAARL
Syn.: New Breda St. Communal Hall & Talmud Torah attached. ☎ 24087.

PORT ELIZABETH
Syns.: Port Elizabeth Hebrew Cong. United Syn., Barris Walk, Glendinningvale. ☎ 331332; Summerstrand, Brighton Dr. ☎ 531-651.
Temple Israel (Progressive), Upper Dickens St. ☎ 336642.
Wedgwood Park (Jewish) Country Club. Town office, AA House, Rink St. ☎ 72-1212.
Museum: Raleigh St. Synagogue. ☎ 55-4458.
Eastern Province Council, Rev. Abraham Levy Centre, Barris Walk, Glendinningvale 6001. ☎ (041) 343105.

NATAL
DURBAN
Synagogues, etc.
Great (Orthodox), cnr. Essenwood Rd. & Silverton Rd., P.O.B. 50044, Musgrave Rd., 4062. ☎ 21-5177
Temple David (Progressive), 369 Ridge Rd. ☎ 28-6105.
Com. Centre, Durban Jewish Club, 44 Old Fort Rd., P.O.B. 10797, Marine Parade 4056. ☎ 37-2581.
Council of KwaZulu-Natal Jewry, ☎ 37-2581. Fax. 379-600 & KwaZulu Natal Zionist Council, ☎ 37-1507, both at 44 Old Fort Rd.

Butchery & Bakery
Pick 'N Pay, Musgrave Centre, Berea, 4001. ☎ (031) 21-4208.

ORANGE FREE STATE
BLOEMFONTEIN
O.F.S. & Northern Cape Zionist Council, Com. Centre, 2 Fairview (P.O.B. 564). ☎ (051) 480817. Fax. (051) 480104.
United Hebrew institutions, Com. Centre. ☎ 30-3801.

TRANSVAAL
BENONI
United Hebrew Institutions, 32 Park St. ☎ 845-2850.

BOKSBURG
United Hebrew Institutions, 11 Heidelberg Rd., Parkdene. ☎ 52-6721.

BRAKPAN
United Hebrew Institutions, 664 Voortrekker Rd. ☎ 55-8245.

EDENVALE
Com. Centre, cnr. 3rd St. & 6th Av. ☎ 53-9897.

GERMISTON
United Hebrew Institutions, President St. ☎ 825-2202.

GLEN HAZEL
Beth Harer (Glen Hazel Area Hebrew Congregation, Mikva and Yeshiva College). ☎ 640-5061. Corr. P.O.B. 28836, Sandringham 2131.

JOHANNESBURG
Synagogues & Religious Organisations
Union of Orthodox Syns. of South Africa, Goldberg Centre, 24 Raleigh St.,

Yeoville. ☎ 648-9136. Fax. 648-4014. The Beth Din is at the same address & tel., as is the UOSSA Women's Guilds org.
The Kashrut Dept., issues an annual kosher guide for the whole country.

Orthodox
Adath Jeshurun, P.O.B. 5128. ☎ 648-6300.
Mikva, 41 Hunter St., Yeoville. ☎ 648-6300.
Berea, Tudhope Av. ☎ 642-3825.
Beth Hamedrash Hagadol, Morningside, Sandton. ☎ 883-2747.
Chasidim Cong., Harrow Rd., Yeoville. ☎ 648-7406.
Cyrildene Observatory Hebrew Cong., 32 Aida Av., Cyrildene. ☎ 616-3312.
Emmarentia, 129 Barry Hertzog Av. ☎ 646-6138.
Etz Chayim Cong., 20 Barnato St., Berea. ☎ 642-4548.
Jeppestown Hebrew Cong., P.O.B. 115, Jeppe. ☎ 614-2822.
Kensington Hebrew Cong. ☎ 622-3543.
North-Eastern Hebrew Cong., Orchards. ☎ 640-3101.
Northern Suburbs Hebrew Cong., 5 Kenneth Rd., Bramley. ☎ 786-0437.
Orange Grove Hebrew Cong. 7, 9th St. ☎ 640-3149.
Oxford, 20 North Av., Riviera. ☎ 646-6020.
Parkview-Greenside, Chester Rd. ☎ 788-5036.
Poswohl Shul (National Monument), Mooi St. ☎ 337-6972 (morns. only).
Randburg Hebrew Cong., 94 Blairgowrie Dr., Blairgowrie. ☎ 789-2827.
South-Eastern Hebrew Cong., 198 Prairie St., Rosettenville. ☎ 26-4652.
Sydenham-Highlands North Hebrew Cong., 24 Main Rd., Rouxville. ☎ 640-5021.
Valley-Observatory Hebrew Cong., 11 The Curve, Observatory, P.O.B. 4951. ☎ 648-9900.
Yeoville, Hunter St. & Kenmere Rd. ☎ 648-1210.
Beth Din, Goldberg Centre, 24 Raleigh St., Yeoville. ☎ 648-9136. Fax 648-2325. Dayan: Rabbi M. A. Kurtstag.
Mikva: Goldberg Centre, 24 Raleigh St., Yeoville. ☎ 648-9136.

Progressive
Temple David, Middle Rd., Morningside, Sandton. ☎ 783-7117.
Temple Emanuel, 38 Oxford Rd., Parktown. ☎ 646-6170.
Temple Israel, Cnr. Paul Nel & Claim Sts., Hillbrow. ☎ 484-3003 or 642-1514.
Temple Shalom, 357 Louis Botha Av., Highlands North. ☎ 640-3182.
The Southern African Union for Progressive Judaism, 357 Louis Botha Av., Highlands North. ☎ 640-6614.

Representative Organisations
B'nai Brith Sheffield House, 29 Kruis St. P.O.B. 7065. ☎ 331-6201.
Jewish Ex-Service League. P.O.B. 5254. ☎ 337-6972 (morns. only).
South African Jewish Board of Deputies. P.O.B. 87557, Houghton, 2041. ☎ 486-1434. Fax 646-4940. Publishes 'Guide to Jewish Johannesburg'.
Union of Jewish Women, 1 Oak St., Houghton. ☎ 648-1053.
United Sisterhood. 38 Oxford Rd., Parktown. ☎ 646-2409.

Cultural Organisations
Jewish Library, 4th Floor, Sheffield Hse., Corner Main & Kruis Sts. Mon.-Fri. 9 a.m. to 4 p.m. ☎ 331-0331.

Welfare Organisations
'Arcadia', S.A. Jewish Children's Home, 22 Oxford Rd., Parktown. ☎ 646-6177.
Chabad House, 33 Harley St., Yeoville. ☎ 648-1133.
Jewish Family & Com. Council. ☎ 648-9124.

Witwatersrand Hebrew Benevolent Assoc., 176 Shakespeare Hse. ☎ 838-1283.
Sandringham Gdns. (Home for Aged), George Av., Sandringham. ☎ 640-5187.

Student & Youth Organisations
South African Union of Jewish Students, Students' Union, Witwatersrand
University, 1 Jan Smuts Av., Braamfontein. ☎ 716-3062.
Hillel House, 22 Muller St., Yeoville. ☎ 648-1175.
(K) Restaurant open to public.

Zionist Organisations
South African Zionist Federation, Zionist Centre (and library), 84 De Villiers
St., cnr. Banket St., P.O.B. 18. ☎ 485-1020. Fax. 640-6758. Other Zionist
organisations are also at this address.
South African Zionist Revisionist Org., 100 Plein St., P.O.B. 4474. ☎ 29-3924.

Miscellaneous
Jewish Guild, Rivonia Rd., Morningside. ☎ 783-7109.

Booksellers
Judaica Booksellers, Shop 3, Yeoville Blvd., Kenmere Rd. ☎ 648-7003.
Kollel Bookshop, 22 Muller St., cnr. Grafton Rd., Yeoville. ☎ 648-2707.
L. Rubin, 442 Louis Botha Av., Rouxville. ☎ 640-7615/6.

Media
'Dorem Afrike' (quarterly), 253 Bree St. ☎ 23-3815.
'Tradition', 24 Raleigh St., Yeoville.
'Jewish Affairs' (quarterly magazine of the S.A. Jewish Board of Deputies),
Sheffield Hse., Kruis St.
'The Herald Times', P.O.B. 31015, Braamfontein. ☎ 887-6500.
'Zionist Record', P.O.B. 150.
'The Jewish Sound', Swazi Radio, Atkinson Hse., Eloff St. ☎ 331-0444. Sun.
7 p.m. to 8 p.m. on 1,400 kHz & 49 and 60 metres. Presenter: Rabbi Yossy
Goldman.

Restaurants
(K) Aviv (mehadrin), 444b Louis Botha Avenue, Rouxville, 2192. ☎ 640-4572.
Fax 640-4081.
Courtleigh Hotel, 38 Harrow Rd., Berea. ☎ 648-1140.
(K) Feigel's Kosher Delicattessen, 53 Raleigh St., Yeoville. ☎ 648-3123.
(Closed Shabbat and Yom Tov.)
(K) Hillel House, 22 Muller St., Yeoville. ☎ 648-9601.
(K) Kaufies, 434 Louis Botha Ave., Highlands North. ☎ 640-5065.
(K) King Soloman, Gallaghers Corner, Cnr. Louise Botha St. and 9th St.
Orange Grove. ☎ 728-3000.
(K) Kosher meals can be obtained at the Johannesburg Zionist Assoc.
Luncheon Club. Inq. to Zionist Assoc. ☎ 337-3000, Ext. 214.
(K) King Saul Masada, 45 Raleigh St., Yeoville. ☎ 648-6908.
(K) On the Square, Cradock Ave., Rosebank, 2196. ☎ 880-4153.
MacDavid, Shop No.8, Linsfield Shopping Centre, Club Street, Linksfield,
2198. ☎ 640-4738.
The Pie Works (mehadrin), Shop 35, Greenhill Road, Emmerentia, 2195. ☎
486-1502. Fax 486-0580. Weekdays, 8am to 5pm; close at 4pm on Friday;
Sundays, 8am to 2pm.;Post Office Centre, crn Hopkins & Kenmere Streets,
Yeoville, 2198. ☎ 648-1083. Fax 485-2438. Weekdays and Sundays, 8am to
8pm; close at 4.30pm Fridays; 74 George Avenue, Sandringham, 2192. ☎

485-2447. Weekdays, 8am to 5pm; close at 4pm on Friday; Sundays, 8am to 2pm.

Dairy Restaurants

Cafe Tel Avin (Shula's) (mehadrin), 42 Kenmere St., (Cnr Hunter St.), Yeoville, 2198. ☎ 487-1072/94; 173 Oxford Road, Rosebank, 2196. ☎ 880-6962; 3 Long Avenue (Ctr Summerway St.), Glenhazel, 2192. ☎ 786-5740/1.

Delicatessens and Bakeries

Bolbrand Poultry Shoppe, 74/76 George Ave., Sandringham, 2192. ☎ 640-4080 or 640-4170.

D.H.'s Delicatessen, Shop No. 121, Balfour Park Shopping Centre, Balfour Park, 2090. ☎ 887-8906.

Mama'Les Kitchen, Shop No.38, Morning Glen Shopping Centre (Pick'n Pay), Bowling Ave., Gallo Manor, 2052. ☎ 804-2068.

Feigel's Kosher Delicatessen, Shop No.3, Queen's Place Kingswood Rd., Glenhazel, 2192. ☎ 7887-1364; Bramley Gardens Shopping Centre, Cnr Corlett Drive and 2nd Ave., ☎ 887-9505.

Saveways Spar Supermarket, (Delicatessen, Bakery, Kinneret Butchery (mehadrin)), Fairmount Shopping Centre, cnr Livingston St. and Sandler Ave., Fairmount, 2192. ☎ 640-6592 or 640-3056.

Shirley's Bakery & Deli, 442 Louis Botha Ave., Highlands North, 2192. ☎ 640-4720 or 640-2629.

Toubin's Bakery & deli (Mehadrin & Chalav yisrael), 71 Raleigh St., Yeoville, 2198. ☎ 648-6507.

Yentyl's Deli, 430 Louis Botha St., Highlands North, 2192. ☎ 485-3731.

Butcheries

Pick 'N Pay, Norwood, Gardens Kosher Butchery, Cnr Grant Ave., & 6th St., Norwood, 2192. ☎ 728-6211 (butchery), ☎ 483-3357 (supermarket).

Pick 'N Pay, Gallo Manor, Gardens Kosher Butchery, Braides Ave., Gallo Manor, 2052. ☎ 804-6707.

Checkers, Balfour Park, Rishon Butchery, Balfour Park Shopping Centre, Atholl Road, Balfour Park, 2090. ☎ 885-1930 or 786-9626.

Checkers, Emmerentia, Rishon Butchery, Barry Hertzog Ave., Emmerentia, 2195. ☎ 486-1437 or 646-1525.

Segell's Butchery, 578 Louis Botha Avenue, Gresswold (Savoy), 2090. ☎ 885-2459 or 885-2553.

Maxi Discount Kosher Butcher, 74 George Avenue, Sandringham, 2192. ☎ 6485-1485/6. Fax 485-2991.

Yumpolski's Deli (mehadrin), 5 Durham St., Raedene, 2192. ☎ 485-1045. Fax 485-1082.

N.B. The Capri Hotel and Transvaal Hotel have Kosher facilities (prior arrangement only).

KEMPTON PARK

United Hebrew Institutions, Casuarina St. ☎ 970-1697. (Reported no longer active).

KRUGERSDORP

United Hebrew Institutions, Cilliers St. Monument. ☎ 954-1367.

PRETORIA

Synagogues

Adath Israel, 441 Sibelius St., Lukasrand. ☎ 343-2257.

Pretoria United Hebrew Cong. Great Synagogue, 717 Pretorius St. Arcadia. ☎ 344-3019.
Temple Menorah (Progressive), 315 Bronkhorst St., New Muckleneuk, P.O.B. 1497. ☎ 46-7296.
Sammy Marks Museum. Swartkoppies Hall. ☎ 83-3239.
Info.: Pretoria Council of BOD. ☎ 344-2372. Fax. 344-2059.
Jewish Accommodation for Fellow Aged (JAFFA), 42 Mackie St., Baileys Muckleneuk, 0181. ☎ 346-2006.
Israel Embassy & Consulate-General, 3rd Floor, Dashing Centre, 339 Hilda St., Hatfield. ☎ 421-22227.

Hotel and Restaurant
Jaffa, Old Age Home, 42 Mackie Str., Baileys Muckleneuk, 0181. ☎ 346-2006. Prior booking necessary.

Butchery and Bakery
One Stop Superliner, 217 Bronkhorst Str., Brooklyn, 0181. ☎ 46-3211.

RANDFONTEIN
United Hebrew Institutions, Maugham Rd. ☎ 693-2542.

SPRINGS
United Hebrew Institutions, First Av. ☎ 56-2583.

SOUTH KOREA
There are about 100 families in the Capital, Seoul, including U.S. military personnel and their families.
Religious services are held at the South Post Chapel, building 3702, Yongsan Military Reservation, on Fri. evg. at 7.30 p.m. Further inf. from Jewish Chaplain's office. ☎ 723-9915, Chaplain H. R. White or 793-3728, Fax 796-3805, Larry Rosenberg. Civilians welcome to participate in all Jewish activities, inc. kosher le-Pesach sedarim, meals and services.

SPAIN
There are about 12,000 Jews in Spain: 3,000 in Barcelona, 3,500 in Madrid, 1,500 in Malaga, 1,000 in Marbella, 800 in Ceuta (North Africa), 950 in Melilla (North Africa), and the rest in Alicante, Benidorm, Seville, Valencia and the Balearic and Canary Islands. Newcomers continue to arrive, especially from Morocco and South America. Small communities existed in Seville, Barcelona and Madrid before the Second World War, founded by Sephardim from Morocco, Turkey and Greece, and by Ashkenazim from Eastern and Central Europe.
Today, Spanish Jewry is flourishing, consolidating its communal organisations, and expanding its synagogues and newly created day schools. The various coms. have enjoyed full official recognition as religious associations since June, 1967.
General inf. from Spanish National Tourist Office, 57-58 St. James's St., SW1A 1LD. ☎ 0171-499 0901.

ALICANTE
Communidad Israelita, Apdo. 189, Playa de San Juan 03540. ☎ (96) 515 1572.
Com. Pres.: Elisabet Plom.
Syn.: Da. L. Plon, Avda Santander, 3, Playa de San Juan.

AVILA

The Mosen Rubi Church, cnr. Calle Bracamonte and Calle Lopez Nunez, was originally a syn., built in 1462.

BARCELONA

The ancient community of the city lived in the area of the Calle el Call. The cemetery was in Montjuich (Mountain of the Jews). Most of the tombstones are in the Provincial Archaeological Museum.

Syn.: Calle Porvenir 24. ☎ 200-61-48 & 200-85-13 – the first syn. to be built in Spain since the Inquisition. The building comprises two separate syns., the Sephardi, in the lower part, and the Ashkenazi above it. Services in the Ashkenazi syn. are held only on Rosh Hashana & Yom Kippur, but there is a daily service in the Sephardi syn. The com. headquarters is above the Ashkenazi syn.

M.: Rabbi Salomon Bensabat.

Com. Headquarters & Mikva: Calle de l'Avenir 24. 08071. ☎ 200-61-48 & 200-85-13.

Pres.: Simon Emergui.

Jewish Travel Agency: Viajes Moravia, Consejo de Ciento 380. ☎ 246-03-00.

Vegetarian Restaurant: Calle Canuda 41. Closed during Aug.

BEMBIBRE

The syn. here was converted into a church.

BENIDORM

Enquiries about a newly established synagogue to Tama Cohen. ☎ (96) 522-9360.

BESALU

The Juderia is by the River Fluviá. A mikva was recently discovered there.

BURGOS

The Juderia was in the area of the Calle Fernan Gonzalez.

CACERES

Part of the Juderia still exists. The San Antonio Church on the outskirts of the town is a 13-century former syn.

CEUTA (N. AFRICA)

Inq. to Calle Sargento Coriat 8. Pres.: Menahem Gabizon.

CORDOBA

The ancient syn. (declared a national monument) is at Calle de los Judios 20. Near by, a statue of Maimonides has been erected in the Plazuela de Maimonides. The entrance to the ancient Juderia is near the Almodovar Gate.

EL ESCORIAL

The library of the San Lorenzo Monastery contains a magnificent collection of medieval Hebrew Bibles and illuminated manuscripts. On the walls of the Patio of Kings, in the Palace of Philip II, are sculpted effigies of the six Kings of Judah.

ESTELLA

The Santa Maria de Jus Castillo Church was once a syn.

GIRONA

The Jewish quarter of Girona, known as the Call, is located in the heart of the old town. Its main street exist today, and it is known as Carrer de la Força. The Jewish Quarter of Girona is one of the best-preserved to be found in Europe today.

During the Middle Ages, the Jewish communtiy of Girona achieved considerable importance. It was there that the most important Cabbala school in Western Europe was developed, largely under the guidance of Rabbi Mossé ben Nahman, or Ramban, perhaps its best known representative.
The Bonastruc ça Porta Center houses the Museum of Catalan-Jewish Culture and the Nahmanides Institute for Jewish Studies, on the site where the 15th Century synagogue was located.
In the municipal archives there is an important collection of fragments of Hebrew manuscripts dating from the 13th and 14th Centuries. The Archaeological Museum contains more than 20 medieval gravestones with Hebrew inscriptions, found in the old Jewish cemetery.
Since January 1995, Girona has held the status of Secretary of the Red de Juderías de España, a network of towns and cities within Spain whose common aim is to foster popular knowledge and awareness of Jewish culture in Spain.
Bonastruc ça Porta Center, c/ Sant Llorenç s/n, 17004. ☎/Fax 34-72-216761. Dir.: Assumpció Hosta. Opening Hours: Winter 10.00 a.m. - 6.00 p.m; Summer 10.00 a.m. - 9.00 p.m; Sundays and Holidays 10.00 a.m. - 2.00 p.m.

GRANADA
The Juderia ran from the Corral del Carlon to Torres Bermejas.

HERVAS
This village in the Gredos Mountains, 150 miles west of Madrid, has a well-preserved Juderia, declared a national monument. Its main street has been renamed Calle de la Amistad Judeo Cristiana.

MADRID
The capital's first syn. since the Expulsion of the Jews in 1492 was opened in Dec., 1968, in Calle Balmes 3. The bldg. also houses the Com. Centre, as well as a mikva, library, classrooms, an assembly hall and the offices of the Com. Centre. ☎ 445-9843 & 445-9835. Nearest underground station: Metro Iglesias.
M.: Rabbi Yudah Benasuly Tuati.
Com. Pres.: Maurice Toledano.
Lubavitch Syn.: Chabad Hse., Calle Jordan 9, Apt. 4 Dcha., 28010. ☎ 445-96-29. M.: Rabbi Y. Goldstein.
The com. maintains a Jewish school, Colegio Estrella Toledano, in the suburb of Moraleja.
(K) Kosher meals (apparently for groups only) are available at the Com. Centre at Calle Balmes 3. ☎ 446-7847.
Federación de Comunidades Israelitas d'España, now has its office in Barcelona.
Of special interest to Jewish visitors to Madrid are the following:
Arias-Montano Institute, Calle del Duque de Medinaceli 4 (in front of Palace Hotel & American Express). Library with more than 16,000 volumes about Sephardi history.
Museo Arquelogico (National Archaeological Museum), Calle de Serrano 13. See casts of Hebrew inscriptions from medieval bldgs.
Calle de la Fé (Street of the Faith) facing San Lorenzo Church, is the ancient Jewish quarter.
Israeli Embassy: Velazquez 150, 7th Floor, 28002. ☎ 411-13-57.
Jewish religious articles and Spanish handicrafts are obtainable from Sefarad Handicrafts, Jose Antonio Av. 54. ☎ 548-2577 & 547-6142.

MALAGA
Syn. and Com. Centre: Calle Duquesa de Parcent 8, 3°, 29001. ☎ 221-40-41. Services daily, 8 a.m., Fri. evg. 8.30 p.m., Sat. morn. 9 a.m. M.: Rabbi Joseph Cohen. Pres.: Isaac Benzaquen Pinto.

Mikva: Calle Somera 12, 29001.
Bucher: (**K**) **Carmiceria Kosher**, Calle Somera 14, 29001. ☎ 260-4201.
There is a statue of the 11th-century Hebrew poet, Shlomo Ibn-Gabirol, a
native of Malaga, in the gardens opposite the Roman Theatre which is next to
Alcazaba Castle, in the heart of the city.

MARBELLA
Syn.: Beth El, 21 Calle Jazmines, Urbanizacion El Real, Km. 184, about 2 miles
from the town centre to the east. ☎ 277-40-74, 277-07-57 or 282-49-83.
Services, Fri. evg. 7.00 p.m. (winter), 8.30 p.m. (summer); Shabbat morn. &
all festivals, 10 a.m. Pres.: Leon Amselem. ☎ 277-6334. Mikva on premises.
Com. Centre, Paseo Maritima, "Edificio Marbella 2000".
Community Journal "Focus". P.O.B 145, 29600.
Bakery: La Tahona. ☎ 282-2781.
Kosher poultry, wine: Joelle Kanner. ☎ 277-4074.

MELILLA (N. AFRICA)
Of the 14 syns. in Melilla nine are in the Barrio Poligono. They are open on
festivals and the High Holy-days only. The remaining five, which are open all
year round, are: Yamin Benarroch, Calle Lopez Moreno 8; Isaac Benarroch,
Calle Marina 7; Jacob Almoznino, Calle Luis de Sotomayor 4; Salama, Calle
Alfonso XII 6; Solinquinos, Calle O'Donnell 13.
Inq. to: Calle General Mola 19. Pres.: David Waknin.

MONTBLANC
The Jewish quarter was in the Santa Clara district, where the church was once
a syn.

SANTIAGO DE COMPOSTELA
The cathedral has 24 statues of Biblical prophets framed in the so-called 'Holy
Door'.

SEGOVIA
The Alcazar contains the 16th-century 'Tower of the Jews'.
Calle de la Juderia Vieja and Calle de la Juderia Nueva are the sites of the
medieval Jewish quarters, where the former syn. now houses the Corpus
Christi Convent.

SEVILLE
Syn.: Bustos Tavera, 8, 41003. Services Fri. evg. Pres.: Simon Hassan. ☎ 427-
55-17.
The old syn., now the church of Los Venerables Sacerdotes, is in the Barrio de
Santa Cruz. Seville Cathedral preserves in its treasures two keys to the city
presented to Ferdinand III by the Jews.
The Columbus Archives (Archives of the Indies), 3 Queipo de Llano Av., pre-
serve the account books of Luis de Santangel, financier to King Ferdinand and
Queen Isabella.
Arco & Torreon of the Juderia, in the old Calle de la Juderia, was the gate con-
necting the Alcazar and the Jewish quarter.
There is a Jewish cemetery in part of the city's Christian burial ground in the
Macarena district.

TARAZONA
The Juderia is near the bishop's palace.

TARRAGONA
Tarragona Cathedral, Calle de Escribanias Viejas, has in its cloister a seventh-

century stone inscribed in Latin and Hebrew. Some very old coins are preserved in the Provincial Archaeological Museum. The gate to the medieval Juderia still stands at the entrance to Calle de Talavera.

TOLEDO
Though it now has no established community, Toledo is the historical centre of Spanish Judaism. Well worth a visit are two ancient former syns. One is the El Transito (in Calle de Samuel Levi), founded by Samuel Levi, the treasurer of King Pedro I, in the 14th century. It has been turned by the Spanish Government into a museum of Sephardi culture. The other, now the Church of Santa Maria la Blanca, is the oldest Jewish monument in Toledo, having been built in the 13th century. It stands in a quiet garden in what was once the heart of the Juderia, not far from the edge of the Tagus River. Also of interest is the house of Samuel Levi, in which El Greco, the famous painter, lived. The house is now a museum of his works.

Plaza de la Juderia, half-way between El Transito and Santa Maria la Blanca, was part of the city's two ancient Jewish quarters, where many houses and streets are still much as they were 500 years ago.

TORREMOLINOS
Syn.: Beth Minzi, Calle Skal La Roca 13, (almost opposite the Police Station) a small street at the seaward end of the San Miguel pedestrian precinct. ☎ 383952 (Hon. Sec.). Sephardi/Ashkenazi services held on Sabbath at 9.30 a.m. Friday 6.30 p.m. (winter), 8.30 p.m. (summer)

TORTOSA
The Museum of Santo Domingo Convent preserves the sixth-century gravestone of 'Meliosa, daughter of Judah of blessed memory'.

TUDELA
The remains of the Juderia are near the cathedral. There is a memorial stone to the great Jewish traveller, Benjamin of Tudela.

VALENCIA
Syn.: Calle Asturias 7-4°. Services: Fri. evg. & festivals. Office: Av. Professor Waksman 9. ☎ 33-99-01. Pres.: Samuel Serfaty. ☎ 334.34.16.

VITORIA
The monument on the Campo de Judizmendi commemorates the ancient Jewish cemetery.

ZARAGOZA
This city was once a very important Jewish centre. A mikva has been discovered in the basement of a modern building at 126-132 Calle del Coso.

CANARY ISLANDS
LAS PALMAS DE GRAN CANARIA
Syn.: Calle Leon y Castillo 238, 1st. Fl.
Pres.: Solomon Zrihen, Calle Nestor de la Torre 34. ☎ 24-84-97.

TENERIFE
There are 12 Jewish families in the island capital of Santa Cruz. An official Jewish community was formed in the town in 1972 – Comunidad Israelita de Tenerife. Pres.: Pinhas Abecassis. ☎ 24-72-96 & 24-72-46.

Jacques Benchetrit, Général Mola, 4, Santa Cruz 38006. ☎ 274157 welcomes Jewish visitors.

MAJORCA

Palma Cathedral contains some interesting Jewish relics, including a candelabrum with 365 lights, which was originally in a syn. In the 'Tesoro' room are two unique silver maces over 6 feet long converted from Torah 'rimonim'. The Santa Clara Church stands on the site of another pre-Inquisition syn. The Montezion Church was, in the 14th century, the Great Syn. of this capital. In Calle San Miguel is the Church of San Miguel, which also stands on the site of a former syn. It is not far from the Calle de la Plateria, once a part of the Palma Ghetto.

Majorca's Jewish population today numbers about 300, although fewer than 100 are registered with the com. Founded in 1971, it was the first Jewish com. to be officially recognised since 1435. The Pres. is Boris Ashken. ☎ 28-37-99. The Jewish cemetery is at Santa Eugenia, some 12 miles from Palma. The com. now has a syn., dedicated in June, 1987. It is in Calle Monsenor Palmer, and services are held on Fri. & the High Holy-days. A communal Seder is also held. ☎ 70-02-43.

SRI LANKA

There are only 2 Jewish permanent residents in the country, and no visible transient Jewish population.
Contact Mrs. A. Ranasinghe, 82, Rosmead Place, Colombo 7. ☎ 010-941-695642. Fax. (0094) 698091.

SURINAM

There are about 225 Jews in Surinam.

PARAMARIBO

Syns.: Sedek Ve Shalom, (Sephardi), Herenstr. 20; Neveh Shalom, (Ashkenazi), Keizerstr. 82. Services are held every Shabbat in each synagogue alternately.
Contact Pres: R. Fernandes, Commewijnestraat 21. ☎ 597-400236. Fax 4597-71154.
Mailing address. Jewish Community, P.O.B. 1834, Paramaribo. ☎ 11998.
Mikveh facilities and Kosher bread available.
Sights to see include Joden Savanah (Jewish Savanah) one of the oldest Jewish settlements in the Americas.

SWEDEN

In 1775 the first Jew was granted the right to live in Sweden – Aaron Isaac, of Germany, who founded the Stockholm cong. In 1782 Jews were admitted to Gothenburg and Norrköping, and the com. in Kariskrona was founded not long afterwards. After Sweden's Jews were emancipated in 1870, coms. were founded in Malmö and several other towns. There are some 16,000 Jews in Sweden. About half of them are former victims of the Nazis, and some 2,000 settled in Sweden from Poland after 1968.
General inf. from Swedish National Tourist Office, 73 Welbeck St., W1M 8AN.

BORÅS

Jewish Community of Borås & Synagogue, Varbergsvägen 21, Box 46, 503 05. ☎ (033) 124892. Email: s.rytz@vertextrading.se

GOTHENBURG

Syn.: Storgatan 5 (Orthodox). Östra Larmgatan 12 (C). ☎ (031) 17-72-45.

Jewish Com. Centre and Com. Office: Östra Larmgatan 12, S-41107. ☎ (031) 17-72-45. Fax. (031) 711-93-60.
Kosher Food, Dr. Allardsgata 4. ☎ (031) 82-40-51.
Jewish radio broadcasts, Thurs at 21.00 on 94.4MHz.

HELSINGBORG
Jewish Centre: Springpostgränden 4.

LUND
Syn.: Winstrupsgatan 1. ☎ (046) 14-80-52.
Services on festivals and High Holy-days only.
Com. Centre & Students' Club (Jusil), same address & ☎ as above.
Institute for Jewish Culture, same address & ☎ as above.

MALMÖ
Syn.: Föreningsgatan (cnr. Betaniaplan), Orthodox.
Jewish Com. Centre with old-age home & com. office: Kamrergatan 11. ☎ 11-84-60 & 11-88-60.
Mikva: Kamrergatan 11. ☎ 11-88-60.
Jewish Youth Club, Kamrergatan 11. ☎ 11-84-60.
B'nei Akiva, same address as above.
B'nai B'rith club rooms, Kamrergatan 11.
Wizo, same address as above.
Kosher meat, etc.: Kosher Centre, Carl Herslowsgatan 7. ☎ 23-55-15.

STOCKHOLM
Synagogues
Adas Jeshurun (Orthodox), Riddergatan 5, POB 5053, 102 42. ☎ (08) 611-9161.
Adas Jisroel (Orthodox), St. Paulsgatan 13. ☎ (08) 644-19-95.
Rabbi Moshe Edelmann. ☎ (08) 679-2900.
Great Synagogue (Conservative, organ used), Wahrendorffsgatan 3b. ☎ (08) 679-2900. M.: Rabbi Morton H. Narrowe, Tortstenssonsgatan 4. ☎ (08) 663-95-24. Services Mon., Thur., Fri. evg. & Sat. morn. Open to tourists Mon.-Fri., 10 a.m. & 2 p.m.

Representative Organisations
Com. Centre, Judaica House, Nybrogatan 19, POB 5053, 102 42. ☎ (08) 663-65-66 & (08) 662-66-86. There is a mikva on the premises, as well as a book & gift shop.
Jewish Community of Stockholm, Wahrendorffsgatan 3, POB 7427, 103 91. ☎ (08) 679 2900. Also on premises: library & Raoul Wallenberg Room, named after the Swedish diplomat who saved scores of thousands of Hungarian Jews from the Nazis, was arrested by the Russians in Budapest in 1945 and disappeared.

Cultural Organisations, etc.
Hillel Kindergarten & Day School, Judaica House, Nybrogatan 19. ☎ (08) 662-91-42 (day school), (08) 667-88-94 (kindergarten).
Yiddish Assoc.: Nybrogatan 19. ☎ (08) 663-45-58.
Jewish Museum, Hälsingegatan 2. ☎ (08) 31 01 43.

Student & Youth Organisations
Jewish Students' Club, Judaica House, Nybrogatan 19. ☎ (08) 663-65-66.
Jewish Youth Org., same address.

Zionist Organisations

Bnei Akiva, Judaica House, Nybrogatan 19. ☎ (08) 663-65-75.
Habonim, same address as above. ☎ (08) 663-6566.
Keren Kayemet, same address as above. ☎ (08) 663-6566.
Keren Hayesod, same address as above. ☎ (08) 661 8686.
Maccabi, same address as above. ☎ 6601814.
Magen David Adom. ☎ 6613105.
Solidarity Committee for Israel, same address as above. ☎ (08) 667-0320.
WIZO, same address as above. ☎ (08) 661-39-91.
Zionist Federation of Sweden, same address as above. ☎ (08) 662-60-98.
Israel Embassy, Torstenssonsgatan 4. ☎ (08) 663-04-35.

Travel Agencies

Ritchie Travel, Riddargatan 7A. ☎ (08) 651-2500. Fax. (08) 660-8800;
Sabra Tours, P.O. Box 45119. ☎ (08) 662 6969. Fax 6672444.
Jewish Periodical: Judisk Krönika, P.O.B. 7427, 10391. ☎ (08) 611-8554.
Menorah, P.O. Box 5053, 102 42. ☎ (08) 667 67 70. Fax. (08) 663 76 76.

Kosher Restaurant Food & Supplies

Jewish items are available at the Com. Centre shop: Menorah, Nybrogatan 19, 11439. ☎ (08) 663 6566.
The Judaica House, Nybrogatan 19, offers a meat menu Mon.-Fri. 11.30-1.30pm. Food can also be ordered for takeaways. Information either from Community Centre, ☎ 6636566 or Hillelschool kitchen, ☎ 6623948.
During school term time dairy/vegetarian lunch is available at th School lunch room. Information from Hillelschool kitchen, ☎ 662 3948.
Kosherian, Judaica House, Nybrogatan 19, offers a weekday cold meat buffet as well as burgers, sausages, meat sandwiches and small dishes, ☎ 6636580.
Coffee, cakes and sandwiches (dairy) are available at the Community Centre during opening hours. The Community Centre can also arrange catering for visiting groups.
Kosher Bakery, Nybrogatan 7, has a full range of cakes, bread, sandwiches, salads and diary meals. Restaurant on premises. Takeaway can be arranged, ☎ 6788128.
Kosher Deli, Riddargatan 7, has an extensive range of kosher meats, poultry and delicatessen as well as cheeses, salads and provisions. Meat sandwiches. Takeaways can be arranged, Kosher deli also caters for any funtion and is arranging Shabbat meals for tourists. ☎ 6788127.
All the above premises are under the sueprvision of Rabbi Dr Moshe Edelmann.
SAS, Scandinavian Airlines, serve kosher meals on all flights leaving Swedish airports for abroad, if advance notice of this requirement is given to SAS offices in Sweden or to a Swedish travel agency. Only new crockery and cutlery are used.
There are no kosher restaurants in Stockholm, but (**K**) lunches are under supervision of Rabbi Moshe Edelmann at the Com. Centre during the summer. Dinners can be arranged at the Com. Centre for groups.

UPPSALA

Jewish Students' Club, Dalgatan 15. ☎ (08) 12-54-53.

SWITZERLAND

The Jews were expelled from Switzerland in the 15th century, and it was not until the beginning of the 17th century that they were permitted to settle in

Lengnau and Endingen. Both villages have old syns. In 1856 immigration increased, chiefly from Germany, Alsace, and Eastern Europe. The Jewish population, 3,150 in 1850, is now about 17,600. Zurich, Basle and Geneva have the largest communities. General inf. from Swiss National Tourist Office, Swiss Centre, New Coventry St., W1V 8EE. ☎ 0171-734 1921.

Spectrum Press International, Im Tannegg 1, Friesenbergstrasse, Zurich 8055. ☎ 462 6411/12 publish a quarterly 'Jewish city guide of Switzerland'.

AROSA
Kosher Hotel: **(K)** **Levin's Hotel Metropol.** Open July & Aug., Dec.-Apr. ☎ (081) 31-21-21. Fax 01/291 1919. Mikva on premises and own Kosher bakery.

BADEN
Syn.: Parkstrasse 17. Services on Fri. evg., 18.30 (winter), 19.30 (summer), Sabbath (8.30 a.m.) and all festivals. Pres.: Dr. Josef Bollag, Schartenfelsstr. 47, 5400. ☎ (041) 729-0808 (office), (056) 221-5128 (home). Kosher pre-packed meals available at Schweizerhof, Verenahof and Blume hotels.

BASLE
In 1897 the first Zionist Congress was held in Basle, in the Musiksaal of the Stadt-Casino, in the Steinenberg-Barfusserplatz, and this important event is commemorated by a plaque in German & Hebrew.
Orthodox Synagogues
IBG, Leimenstr. 24, 4003. ☎ (061) 272 9850. Fax (061) 272 7115; Rabbi Dr I.M. Levinger, Leimenstr. 45, 4051. ☎ (061) 272 9170 (office), (061) 271 6024 (private). Fax (061) 272 7151; Mikva, Eulerstr. 10, 4051. ☎ (061) 272 95 48, (061) 301 68 31 (women).
IRG, Ahomstr. 14, 4055. ☎ (061) 301 49 47; Rabbi B.Z. Synders, Rudolfstr. 28, 4045. ☎ (061) 302 1434 (office), (061) 302 53 91 (private). Fax (061) 302 14 37; mikva, Thannerstr. 60, 4054. ☎ (061) 301 22 20. (061) 301 22 18 (women).
Israelitische Gemeinde Basel Com. Centre, Leimenster. 24, 4003. ☎ (061) 272 98 50. Fax (061) 272 7115.
Youth Centre (Miklat), Eullrstr. 12, 4003 ☎ (061) 271 9398. Youth Leader, Jenny Baruch. ☎ (061) 272 2920. Fax (061) 272 7115.
Jewish Museum, Kornhausgasse 8, 4051. ☎ (061) 261 9514. Open; Sun. 10.00am-12.00 noon; Sun., Mon., & Wed., 2.00-5.00pm.
B'nai Brith. Inq. Prof. Dr S. Lauer, Bachlettenstr. 31. ☎ (061) 271 9760.
Old Age Home: La Charmille, Inzlingsrstr. 235, 4125 Riehen. ☎ (061) 641 00 57. Fax (061) 641 0027.
Weekly Newspaper: Jüdische Rundschau Maccabi, Leonhardstr, 37, 4009, ☎ (061) 272 8589.
Hebrew Bookshop & Gifts: Victor Goldschmidt, Mostackerstr. 17, 4051. ☎ (061) 2562 6191. Fax (061) 261 6123.
Union of Jewish Students, Inq. to Michael Bornstein, Hohestr. 238, 4104 Oberwil. ☎ (061) 401 4262.
Restaurant:
(K) Topas, Leimenstr. 24, 4003. ☎ (061) 271 8700. Fax: (061) 271 8701.
Butchers:
(K) Genossenschaftsmetzgerei, Friedrichstr. 26, 4055. ☎ (061) 301 3493. Fax (061) 301 3493. **(K)** H. Hess Metzgerei, Leimenstr. 41, 4051. ☎ (061) 272 8835. Fax (061) 272 2286.

Cemetery: Theodor Herzl Str. 90. ☎ (061) 321 7243. Inq. to IGB office, ☎ (061) 272 9850.

BERNE
Syn. & Com. Centre: Kapellenstr. 2. ☎ (031) 381-49-92. M.: ?
Com. Pres.: R. Heymann, Innerer Giessenweg 23, 3110 Münsingen. ☎ (031) 721-5248.
WIZO: Mrs. Edith Bino. Ahornweg, 50. 3028, Spiegel bei Bern, and Mrs. Brigitte Halpern, Hofmeisterstr. 7. 3006.
Israel Embassy: Alpenstr. 32. 3006. ☎ (031) 351-10-42. Consul Sect.: (031) 352-62-15.

BIEL-BIENNE
Syn., Rüschlistr. 3. Pres.: Klaus Appel, Dufourstr. 68, 2502. ☎ (032) 423670.

BREMGARTEN/AARGAU
Syn.: Luzernstr. 1.
Israelitische Cultusgemeinde, 5620.
Inq. to Com Pres., Werner Meyer-Moses, Ringstr 37, 5620 Bremgarten. ☎ (056) 633-6626.

DAVOS
Syn. and Mikva: Etania Rest Home, Richtstattweg 3, 7270. ☎ (081) 416-54-04. Fax (081) 416 25 92.
(K) Rooms, Kosher meals available. Open all year except Nov. and May.
A range of **(K)** kosher items is available at Konsum Shopping Centre, Davos-Dorf.

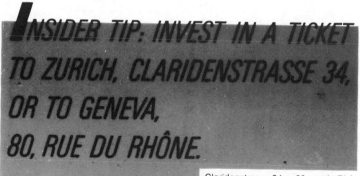

ENDINGEN
Inq. to Com. Pres.: J. Bloch, Buckstr. 2, 5304. ☎ (056) 242 1546, who can also arrange for visits to the old syns. & cemetery.

ENGELBERG
Hotel (K) Marguerite. ☎ (041) 94-25-22. Open Dec.-Apr. & May-Oct. Under supervision of Agudas Achim, Zurich. Mikva on premises.
Kosher items can be obtained at the Rhyner-Fresch and Co-op stores.

FRIBOURG
Syn.: 9 rue Joseph-Piller, 1700. ☎ (037) 322-16-70.
Com. Pres.: Dr. Claude Nordmann, P.O.B. 170, 1701. ☎ (037) 411-29-20.
Société des Dames Israélites. Pres.: Hortense Bollag, 22 Beaumont, 1700. ☎ (037) 424-16-45.
WIZO: Mrs. M. P. Goutenmacher, ch. des Eaux-Vives 21, 1752 Villars-sur-Glâne. ☎ (037) 424 10 37.

GENEVA
Chief Rabbi of Geneva: Rabbi Dr. Alexandre Safran.
Communauté Israélite de Genève, 10 rue St Léger, 1205. ☎ (022) 310-46-86. Fax (022) 3117356. Grand Rabbin of C.I.G.: Marc-Raphael Guedj.
Synagogues
The Geneva Syn. (Ashkenazi), 11 Place de la Synagogue.
Hekhal Haness (Sephardi), 54 Ter route de Malagnou. (on a side alley) ☎ (022) 736-96-32. Mikva on premises.
Liberal (French-speaking), 12 Quai du Seujet. ☎ (022) 732-32-45.
Machsike Hadass (O), 2 Place des Eaux Vives. ☎ (022) 735-2298.
Centre des Jeunes, 24 rue de l'Athénée. ☎ (022) 789-4270.
Representative Organisation:
World Jewish Congress, 1 rue de Varembé, 1211. ☎ (022) 734-13-25. Fax. 733-3985.
Welfare Organisations
American Jewish Joint Distribution Com. Overseas Headquarters, 75 rue de Lyon, 1211. ☎ (022) 344-90-00.
Bnai Brith, 10 rue St. Léger, 1205.
Hias, 75 rue de Lyon, 1203. ☎ (022) 345-9350.
Home for Aged: 'Les Marronniers,' 15 rue Cavour. ☎ (022) 344-87-60.
ORT, 1 rue de Varembé. ☎ (022) 734-14-34.
Ose, rue de Mont Blanc 11, 1201. ☎ (022) 732-3301.
Zionist Organisation
WIZO. Mme. Ruth Rappaport, 14 Chemin Diodati, 1223 Cologny.
Clubs
Jewish students at Centre des Jeunes, 24 rue de l'Athénée. ☎ (022) 789-4270.
Club Maccabi, 54 ter Route de Malagnou. ☎ (022) 736-90-15.

Kosher Bread: Boulangery Pouly, 72 rue des Eaux, Vives. ☎ (022) 736-7078.
Kosher Restaurants:
(K) Le Jardin, 10 rue St Léger. Lunch only. Deliveries to hotels may be requested. ☎ (022) 310-4686. Fax 311-7356.
(K) Kosher meals are available at home for aged (see above), if ordered in advance – for Shabbat, before 9.30 a.m. on Fri.
Kosher Butcher:
(K) Bitton Maghensa, 21 rue Montchoisy. ☎ (022) 736-31-68.

GRINDELWALD
Hotel: (**K**) Wagner-Kahn's Hotel Silberhorn. ☎ (036) 53-28-22. Fax. (036) 53 4822 Mikva on premises. Open mid-December until after Succot.

KREUZLINGEN
Oratory: Hafenstr. 42. Inf. from Louis Hornung, Schulstr 7. ☎ (071) 671-16-30.
WIZO. Inf. from Mme. Erica Marx, Langhaldenstr 6a, 8280. ☎ (071) 688-44-35.

LA CHAUX-DE-FONDS
Syn. & Com. Headquarters: 63 rue du Parc. Spiritual leader: M. Margulies, 27, rue du Parc, 2300. ☎ (039) 231794.
Inq. to Com. Sec.: Laurent Sobel, 50 rue du Chapeau Râblé, 2300. ☎ (039) 261366.

LAUSANNE
Syn.: 1 Av. Juste-Olivier (cnr. Av. J. Olivier/Av. Florimont). ☎ (021) 320-99-11. Mikva: 1 Av. Juste-Olivier (corner Av. J. Olivier/Av. Florimont). ☎ (021) 729-98-20. Rabbi S. Morali, Beau-Séjour 29. ☎ (021) 320-54-94. President: Philippe Joseph. ☎ (021) 729-89-22.
Com. offices: 3, Av. Georgette. ☎ (021) 312-67-33. Com. Center and Restaurant of the Com. Center: 3 Av. Georgette. ☎ (021) 312-67-31. (serves just lunch from 12.00-2.00 p.m.).
Bnai Brith: President: Pierre Ezri. ☎ (021) 617 6454.
WIZO. Inq. to Mrs. M. Guttmann. ☎ (021) 323-56-02 or Mrs. N. Schwed. ☎ (021) 617-90-90.
Union of Jewish Students: Case postale 250, 1009 Pully.
Kosher food available from Kolbo Shalom, 7 Av. Juste-Olivier. ☎ (021) 312-12-65.

LENGNAU
Jewish old people's home headed by Mr Sascha Gelbhaus (Schweizerisches Israelitisches Alters-und Pflegeheim, 5426 Lengnau, ☎ (056) 241 12 (03). Kosher meals available on request. Mr Gelbhaus can also arrange for visits in the old syns. of Lengnau and cemetery. Information concerning the Synagogue of Lengnua is also available from Mr Raymond Benjamin, ☎ (056) 241 2337.

LUCERNE
Syn.: Bruchstr. 51. Rabbi I. Mantel, Berglistr. 22c. ☎/Fax (041) 240-83-05. Pres.: Hugo Benjamin, Bundesplatz 1, 6003. ☎ (041) 210-98-10.
Mikva: Bruchstr. 51. ☎ (041) 320-47-50.
WIZO. Inq. to Maya Bollag, Rütiweidhalde 3, 6033 Buchrain.
There is a Yeshiva at Kriens, near Lucerne (Rosh Yeshiva, Rabbi I. Koppelman). ☎ (041) 320-26-85.
Beth Jacob Seminary, Schlossweg 1. ☎ (041) 310-98-71. Princ.: Rabbi K. Rosen, Bruchstr. 26. ☎ (041) 240-90-39.

Pre-packed kosher meals are available from the restaurant of the Drei Könige Hotel, Bruchstr. 35.
(**K**) Kosher Butcher, Bruchstr. 26. ☎ 240-25-60. Open morns. only.

LUGANO
Syn.: Via Maderno 11, ☎ (091) 23-56-98, has a mikva attached. Mikva appointments: Frau Neuman, ☎ (091) 235309. The minister is Rabbi B. Z. Rabinowitz, 5 Via Marco da Carona. ☎ (091) 23-61-34. The Pres. of the cong. is D. Heller, Via Beltramina 15. ☎ (091) 51-35-31.

WIZO. Inq. to Mme. Fritzi Esther Spitzer, Via Berna 2, 6900. ☎ (091) 23-36-86.
Kosher food obtainable from H. Pollach, via Olgiati 1. ☎ (091) 22 9955.
Kosher Hotel: (**K**) Hotel Dan (34), Via Domenico Fontana 1. Under supervision of Rabbi B. Z. Rabbinowitz. ☎ (091) 54-10-61. Open all year round.

ST. GALLEN
Syn.: Frongartenstr. 18. Rabbi H. Schmelzer, Dierauerstr. 2. ☎ (071) 23-59-23.
Com. Headquarters, Frongartenstr. 16. ☎ (071) 22-71-55. Com. Pres.: Dr. Roland Richter, Merkurstr. 4, 9000. ☎ (071) 22-16-14.

ST. MORITZ
(**K**) Bermann's Hotel Edelweiss, 7500 St. Moritz-Bad. ☎ (081) 833-55-33 or (01) 482-5859. Fax (081) 833-55-73. Kosher Provisions available to visitors. Open July-Aug. & Dec. until after Pesach. Mikva on premises.

SOLOTHURN
Inq. to Robert Dreyfus, Postfach 347, 4502. ☎ (065) 23-23-23.

VEVEY
Syn. & (**K**) Home for Aged: Les Berges du Léman, 3 Blvd. Plumhof. ☎ (021) 923-53-54. Fax (021) 922 5923.
(**K**) Kosher lunch available for tourists; must make reservations and be punctual, 12-12.30 pm, and 6-6.30pm.

WINTERTHUR
Syn.: Rosenstr. 5 (Blaukreuzhaus).
Com. Pres.: Silvain Wyler, Möttelistr. 37, 8400. ☎ (052) 232-81-36 (home).

YVERDON
Com. Pres.: Laurent Ashenden, Chemin du Fontenay 18, 1400 Yverdon-les-Bains. ☎ (022) 364-7323.

ZUG
Restaurant Glashof, Baarerstr. 41, 6301. ☎ 042 221-24-8. Prepared kosher meals are available.

ZURICH
Synagogues & Religious Organisations
Orthodox: Agudas Achim, Erikastr. 8; ☎ (01) 463-57-98. Mikva: ☎ (01) 463-79-25. Bet Chabad, Manessestr. 198. ☎ (01) 201-16-91. Fax. (01) 201-64-33. Rabbi M. Rosenfeld. ☎ (01) 281-14-79; Israelitische Cultusgemeinde, Nüschelerstr 36, (Sec., Lavaterstr. 33, 8002. ☎ (01) 201-16-59); Israelitische Religionsgesellschaft, Freigutstr. 37, 8002. Mikva: ☎ (01) 20121-80 or 201-73-06. (Sec., Manessestr 10. ☎ (01) 241 80 57); Hugo-Mendel-Stiftung, Billeterstr. 10. ☎ (01) 261-19-60; Minyan Sikna, Sallenbachstr. 40. ☎ (01) 462-6123. Fax. (01) 463-10-24.
Minyan Wollishofen, Etzelstr. 6. ☎ (01) 202-45-07 or (01) 482 87 51.
Liberal Cong.: Or Chadasch, Fortunagasse 13, 8001. ☎ (01) 221-11-52.
There is a Jewish prayer room in Terminal B at Zurich airport.

Representative Organisations
B'nai B'rith. Pres.: Dr. Paul Wildman. ☎ (01) 201-16-03.
Federation of Swiss Jewish Communities, Gotthardstr. 65, 8002. ☎ (01) 201-55-83. Fax (01) 202-16-72.
Union of Jewish Students. For inf., contact Lavaterstr. 33, 8002. ☎ (01) 202-66-84.

Welfare Organisation
Swiss Jewish Welfare Fed., Gerechtigkeitsgasse 14, 8002. ☎ (01) 201-58-50.
Fax (01) 202-5877.

Zionist Organisations
Keren Hajessod, ☎ (01) 461 6868. Fax (01) 462-0176.
Keren Kajemet Leisrael, ☎ (01) 211 5885. Fax (01) 211-5049.
Swiss Zionist Fed., (Schweizerischer Zionistenverband), Postfach 676, 8055.
☎ (01) 462-04-07. Fax (01) 462-7775.
WIZO. For inf., ☎ (01) 262-42-43.

Miscellaneous Organisations
Borsalino, Jewish Discothèque & Meeting Place, Tessinerplatz 9, 8002. ☎ (01)
201-18-00.
Maccabi Switzerland. Inq. to Daniel Fischer, Kappelistr. 19. ☎ (01) 281-1880.
Newspaper: 'Israelitisches Wochenblatt' (weekly), Florastr. 14, 8008. ☎ (01)
383-70-94. Fax (01) 383-7800.
Die Judische Zeitung (weekly) Postfach 1012, 8039. ☎ (01) 201-46-17. Fax
(01) 201-4626.
Jewish Bookshops: Victor Goldschmidt, Seestr. 41, 8002. ☎ (01) 202-50-44.
(This is also a gift shop); Morasha, Seestr 11. ☎/Fax (01) 201-1800.
Hotel: **Ascot**, Tessinerplatz 9, 8002. ☎ (01) 201-18-00.

Kosher Restaurants
(K) Schalom Café-Restaurant, Lavaterstr. 33 (near Enge Station). ☎ (01) 201-
14-76.

(K) Restaurant Fein and Schein (dairy), also 'take away fleishig' Schontalstr. 14, 8004. ☎ (01) 241-30-40. Fax (01) 241-2112.

Kosher Food
(K) Metzgerei Adass, Löwenstr. 12. ☎ (01) 211-52-10; Taam-Metzgerei, Aemtlerstr. 8. ☎ (01) 463-90-94.

Kosher Grocer & Provision Merchants:
(K) Aron Herzberg, Zwinglistr. 17. ☎ (01) 242-78-75.
(K) Chaimson, Zentralstr. 10. ☎ (01) 461-2191.
(K) Schleider Kosher Food Supplies, the widest range of food supplies within 100 km, everything under one roof. ☎ (01) 202-44-57.
Kosher food is also available in the grocery dept. of the Jelmoli dept. store in Bahnhofstr., near the main railway station, as well as at Pick & Pay, cnr. Lavaterstr./General Wille-Strasse.

Kosher Bakery:
(K) Ruben Bollag's Kosher Bakery, Waffenplatzstr. 5. ☎ (01) 202-30-45; Brauerstr. 110, cnr. Hohlstr. & Feldstr. ☎ (01) 242-87-00. In addition to chalot, bread, cakes, etc., fresh & tinned kosher food is also available. Under supervision of Rabbi Daniel Levy.
Boxes of **(K)** kosher food can be purchased at Zurich airport by passengers in transit. - unconfirmed, no contract given.

TAIWAN
There are more than 30 families in Taiwan, most of them living in the capital, Taipei.

TAIPEI
Taiwan Jewish Com., Com. Centre: No. 1, Lane 61, Teh Hsing E. Rd, Shihlin, Taipei. Pres.: Don Shapiro. ☎ 886-2-3960159; Fax 886-2-3964022. Sec.: Jacques Bijo. Services are held on most Fri. evg. at 7.30 p.m. Visitors to check in advance. All Holy-days and major festivals are celebrated.
The com. holds brunches & Kabbalat Shabbat dinners several times a month. Only kosher dairy food is served at the Com. Centre. Inq. to: Don Shapiro, as above, or Mrs. F. Chitayat. ☎ 861-6303.
Shabbat & festival services (Orthodox), are held at the Ritz Hotel, 41 Min Chuan E. Rd. ☎ (886-2) 597-1234. Further inf. from Rabbi Dr. E. F. Einhorn. ☎ (886-2) 591-3565
There are no kosher restaurants in Taipei, but Y.Y.'s Steakhouse has a separate kitchen & dining room, where kosher meat meals are served on separate crockery, with separate cutlery. No milk products are available in this section. Chungshan N. Rd., Section 3, cnr. Teh Huei St.

THAILAND
The Jewish community of Thailand numbers about 250. Only a handful are Thai nationals, and they are of European and Asian origin.

BANGKOK
Syns.: Even Chen Syn, (O), Bossotel Inn 55/12-14 Soi Charoenkrung, 42/1 New Road (Silom Road). ☎ 630-6120. Fax. 237-3225. Syn., club and kosher restaurant under supervision of Rabbi Y. Kantor. Daily morn. & evg. minyan. Regular Fri. evg. & Shabbat morn., afternoon & evg. services. Light kosher meal after services, by advance reservation. Further inf.: Rony Avram. ☎ 237-

1697 (office), Motti ben David. ☎ 234-0606 (office), Salim Eubani. ☎ 318-1577 (home).
Beth Elisheva Syn., 121 Soi Sai, Nam Tip 2, (Soi 22) Sukhumvit Rd. ☎ 258-2195. Fax 663-0245.
The Jewish Community of Thailand, Com. Centre, Beth Elisheva Syn. Bldg., address above. ☎ 258-2195. Pres.: Michael Gerson. ☎ 252-7209 252-2809 (h).
(K) Ohr Menachem - Chabad, Kaosarn Rd, 108/1 Ramburthi Rd., Banglampoo. ☎ 282-6388. Daily services, Friday eve. ☎/Fax 282-6388.
Israel Embassy, ☎ 260 4854.

TUNISIA
The Jewish population of Tunisia is approximately 2,000, most of whom live in Tunis. There are also some small communities, mainly in Jerba, Sfax, Sousse and Nabeul.

JERBA
There are Jews in two villages on this small island off the Tunisian coast. There is also a magnificent synagogue, El Ghriba, many hundreds of years old, in the village of Er-Riadh (Hara Sghira). Jewish silversmiths are prominent in Hournt souk on rue Bizerte.

SFAX
Syn.: Azriah, 71 rue Habib Mazoun (near the Town Hall).

TUNIS
Chief Rabbi: Rabbi Haim Madar, 26 rue de Palestine. ☎ 282-406 & 283-540.
Syns.: Grande Synagogue, 43 Av. de la Liberté; Beth Yacob, 3 rue Eve. Nohelle. ☎ 348964.
Com. Offices: 15 rue du Cap Vert. ☎ 282-469 & 287-153.
Lubavitch Yeshiva. Rabbi Nison Pinson, 73 rue de Palestine. ☎ 791-429.
American Joint Distribution Com.: 101 Av. de la Liberté. ☎ 282-835 & 283-208. Local rep.: Gilles Maarek.

TURKEY
After the Expulsion of the Jews from Spain in 1492, at a time when Jews were not tolerated in most of the Christian countries of Western Europe, what was then the Ottoman (Turkish) Empire was their principal land of refuge. In - 1992 they celebrated the 500th anniversary of the establishment of the community. Under the national constitution, their civil rights were reconfirmed. In recent years, many Jews have emigrated to Israel, Western Europe and the United States, and Turkey's Jewish population today numbers about 25,000, of whom 23,000 live in Istanbul.
General inf. from Turkish Tourist Office, 1st Floor, 170-173 Piccadilly, W1V 9DD. ☎ 0171-734 8681-2.

ANKARA
Syn.: Birlik Sokak, Samanpazari. ☎ 311-62-00. This syn. is not easy to find. Off Anafartalar Caddesi in Samanpazari, there is a stairway down at the right of the T. C. Ziraat Bankasi.
The syn. is several buildings along the street on the left, behind a wall. Services every morn. Sabbath morn. services begin at 7 or 7.30 a.m. depending on the time of year.
Israel Legation, Vali Dr. Resit Caddesi, Farabi Sok, No. 43 Cankaya. ☎ 426-49-93.

BURSA

Syn.: Gerush Syn., Kurucesme Caddesi. M.: Rabbi Uriel Arezo. ☎ 368636.
Pres.: Ezra Ventura. ☎ 361584. Services, Fri. evg., Shabbat morn. & festivals.
The syn. is in the old Jewish quarter. There are 180 Jews in the town.

ISTANBUL

Chief Rabbinate: Rabbi David Asseo, Yemenici Sokak, 23, Tünel 80050,
Beyoglu. ☎ 293-8794/95. Fax 244-1980.

Synagogues

Neve Shalom Büyük Hendek Sok, No.61 Galata. ☎ (212) 293 7566 (only
Saturdays).
Beth Israel, Efe Sok, No.4 Şişli. ☎ (212) 240 65 99 (every day).
Askenazi Synagogue, Yüksekkaldinm Sok, No.37 Galata. ☎ (212) 243 6909
(only Saturdays)
Italian Synagogue, Şair Ziya Paşa Yokuşu, No. 29 Galata. ☎ (212) 293 7784
(only Saturdays).
Etz Ahayim Synagogue, Muallim Naci Cad, No.40/1 Ortaköy. ☎ (212) 260 18
96 (every day).
Hemdat Israel Synagogue, Izettin Sok, No.65 Kadiköy. ☎ (216) 336 5293
(every day).
Hesed Leavraam Synagogue, Pancur Sok, No.15 Büyükada. ☎ (216) 382 5788
(June–September including High Holy days).
Caddebostan Synagogue, Taşmektep Sok, Göztepe. ☎ (216) 356 59 22 (every
day).
Com. Centre: Buyuk Hendek, Sokak. No. 61, Galata. ☎ 293-7566. Sec. Gen.
Lina Filiba.
There are also some 10 Jewish institutions in Istanbul, including a hospital,
home for the aged, summer camp for children, a high school, a primary school
& religion classes, as well as 4 Jewish clubs. In addition, there are several old
synagogues in the Balat and Haskoy areas which are worth a visit.
The Chief Rabbinate can supply inf. about a kosher restaurant and kosher
butchers.
Hotel with kosher restaurant: Merit Antique, Ordu Cad. 226, Lalelil. ☎ 513
9300. Fax: 512 6390.
Israel Consulate-General, Elmadag. ☎ 225-1045. Weekly: 'Salom' (Turkish &
Ladino). ☎ 247-3082.

IZMIR

This community, numbering 2,400, is the second largest in Turkey Its institu-
tions include a Jewish School, a hospital and a club.
Syns.: Beth Israel, 265 Mithatpasa St., Karatas, Kanamursil District, nr. the
Asansor (Lift); Shaar Ashamayan, 1390 Sokak 4/2, Alsancak.
Bikur Holim, Esrefpasa Caddesi.
Jewish Com. Council: Azizler Sokak 920/44, Güzelyurt. ☎ 123708.
Kosher Meat: ☎ 148395, Tues. & Thurs., or inquire at syn.

UKRAINE

Pilgrimage to the graves of the Chassidic leaders and their landmarks are now
increasingly underway. Further details of access and contacts in such places as
Ampoli, Berdichev, Hadich, Medzhibuzh, Peremishlani, Pogrebisheh,
Polonnoye, Shepebovka and Uman are required.

BERDICHEV

Syn: 4 Dzherzhinskaya St. ☎ 23938 & 20222. Mikva and kosher kitchen on
premises.

The grave of Levi Isaac ben Meir is in Berdichev. Contact the synagogue for access.

BEREGOVO
Syn.: 17 Sverdlov St.

BERSHAD
Syn.: 25 Narodnaya Str.

CHERNIGOV
Syn.: 34 Kommunisticheskaya Str.

CHERNOVTSY
Syn.: 24 Lukyana Kobylitsa Str. ☎ 54878.

CHMELNITSY
Syn: 58 Komminnestnaya St.

KHARKOV
Syn.: 48 Kryatkovskaya Str.
Orthodox Union Project Reunite, Surnskaya #45. ☎ 408-378. Fax 439-209.

KIEV
Syn.: 29 Shchekovichnaya St. ☎ (044) 4162442/4164430; Reform Cong., 7 Nemanskaya St. ☎ (044) 295-65-39.

KOROSTEN
Syn.: 8 Shchoksa St.

KREMENCHUG
Syn.: 50 Sverdlov Str.

LVIV
Syn: 4 Brativ Mikhnovskykh St., 290018. ☎ 330524. Fax 333-536.
Kosher kitchen available. ☎ 33-35-35.

ODESSA
Syn.: 3 Lesnaya St. There is also a small syn. and matzah bakery at Gazovy La., Moskovskaya St.

SLAVUTA
Syn: Kuzovskaya St. 2. ☎ 25452.
The first edition of the Tanya was printed here by the Shapira family whose tombs are in the cemetery.

ZHITOMIR
Syn.: 59 Lubarskaya Str. ☎ 373468.
Reb Ze'ev Wolf disciple of Dov Baer is buried in the Smolanka cemetery.

URUGUAY
Jewish population about 35,000, mostly living in Montevideo.

MONTEVIDEO
The central body of Uruguayan Jewry is the **Comite Central Israelita**, whose offices are at Rio Negro 1308, Piso 5, Esc. 9. ☎ 916057, 90-6562, 98-2833.
In addition, there are four separate Montevideo Kehillot, each with its own syn.: Comunidad Israelita de Uruguay (Ashkenazi), Canelones 1084, Piso 1. ☎ 92-5750; Comunidad Israelita Hungara, Durazno 972. ☎ 90-8456; Comunidad Israelita Sefaradi, Buenos Aires 234, 21 de Setiembre 3111. ☎ 71-

0179; Nueva Congregacion Israelita (Central European), Wilson F. Aldunete 1168, ☎ 92-6620.
Other syns.: Adat Israel, Democracia 2370; Anshei Jeshurun, Durazno 972; Bet Aharon, Harishona, Inca 2287; Vaad Ha'ir, Canelones 828; Templo Sefaradi de Pocitos L. Franzini 888; Soc. Israelite Adat Yeshurun-Alarcon 1396.
Centro Lubavitch, Av. Brasil 2704. ☎ 79-3444. Dir.: Rabbi Eliezer Shemtov.
ORT: Cuareim 1457. ☎ 92-1505.
Sports Club: Hebraica-Maccabi, Camacua 623. ☎ 96-1246, 96-1249.
Young Zionist Fed., Cipriano Payan 3030.
Zionist Org. of Uruguay, Hector G. Ruiz 1278, Piso 4. ☎ 983482.
Israel Embassy, Bulevar Artigas 1585-89. ☎ 404164, 404165 & 404166.
Jewish Newspaper: 'Semanario Hebreo' (Spanish-language weekly), Soriano 875/201. ☎ 92-5311. Editor J. Jerozolimski, who also directs a daily Yiddish radio programme.
Memorial al Holocausto del Pueblo Judio, at Rambla Wilson, opposite al campo de Golf; Monumento a Golda Meir, Reconquista y Ciudadela; Museo del Holocausto, Canelones 1084, Planta Baja.

Restaurant: **La Vegetariana** (Vegetarian), San Jose 1056 and Avda. Brasil 3086.

VENEZUELA

The Jewish com. of Venezuela now numbers between 20,000 and 23,000, about 90 per cent of whom live in Caracas, the capital, with the rest mainly in the oil centre of Maracaibo. The earliest important Jewish settlement in Venezuela was in the coastal town of Coro, where probably the oldest Jewish cemetery still in use in South America is situated.
While the Coro communtiy was made up of Sephardim from nearby Curaçao, the community in Venezuela today is about equally divided between Sephardim and Ashkenazim.

CARACAS

There are seven syns. in Caracas, three Askhenazi and four Sephardi. The Ashkenazi syns. are:
Great Syn. of Caracas (Gran Rabinato de Caracas). Av. Francisco Javier Ustáriz, San Bernardino. ☎ 51-18-69. Rabbi Tzvi Laufer.
Shomrei Shabbat Assoc. Syn., Av. Anauco, San Bernardino. ☎ 51-71-97. M.: Rabbi Meyer Rosenbaum. Mikva.
Union Israelita de Caracas Syn. & Centre, Av. Marques del Toro, 9 San Bernardino. ☎ 52-8222. M.: Rabbi Pinhas Brener. Mikva on premises. If notified in advance, the Union Israelita office can arrange (**K**) kosher lunches. ☎ 52-6280. There is also a meat snack bar open in the evening. Sabbath observers may wish to stay at the Hotel Avila, which is next door to the synagogue, or the Aventura, which is a short walk away.
The Union building also houses the C.A.I.V., the representative org. of Venezuelan Jewry, WIZO, the Anti-Defamation League and the offices of the newspaper, 'Nuevo Mundo Israelita'.
The Sephardi syns. are:
Shaare Shalom, Av. Bogota, Quinta Julieta, Los Caobos. M.: Rabbi Isaac Sananes.
Bet El, Av. Cajigal, San Bernardino. ☎ 52-20-08.
Keter Tora, Av. Lopez Mendez, San Bernardino.
Tiferet Yisrael, Av. Maripérez, Los Caobos. ☎ 781-19-42. Rabbi I. Cohen. Mikva on premises.
Chabad-Lubavitch Centre, Apartado 5454, 1010A. ☎ 52-38-87.

Yeshiva Guedola de Venezuela, Quinta Lore, Av. Washington, 8, San
Bernardino. ☎ 51-41-67. There is a branch at 12a Avenida, Quinta Mi Reina,
Los Palos Grandes, Altamira, Caracas 1062. ☎ 33 68 86.
B'nai B'rith Centre & Hillel Hse., 9na Transversal entre 7a Av. Avila, Altamira.
☎ 32-65-96.
Kabbalat Shabbat services (Conservative) are held on the first Fri. of every
month at 8.30 p.m. Details of this and other events of interest to Anglo-Jewish
visitors are given in the 'Daily Journal' (in English), which is sold at all major
hotels.
Zionist Fed., Bet-Am Bldg., Ave Washington, San Bernardino. ☎ 51-48-52. All
major Zionist orgs. are housed here.
Bakeries: Le Notre, Avenida Andres Bello, ☎ 782 4448
Pasteleria Kasher, Avenida Los Proceres, ☎ 515086. Take Away: Mini Market,
Avenida Los Caobas, ☎ 7817204.
Israel Embassy & Consulate, Centro Empresarial Miranda, Av. Miranda esq.
Los Ruices, Los Ruices. ☎ 2394110.

Bookshop: Libreria Cultural Maimonides, Av. Altamira, Edif. Carlitos P.B, San
Bernardino. ☎ 519672. Fax 58-2524242.

MARACAIBO
Syn. & Com. Centre: Associaci'n Israelita de Maracaibo, Calle 74 No. 13-26.
☎ 70333.
Jewish School: Colegio Bilu. Address as above.

PORLAMAR
Or Meir Syn. (and Mikva) Margarita Island. Rabbi Y. El-Harrar.

VIRGIN ISLANDS (WEST INDIES)
ST. THOMAS
There have been Jews in the Virgin Islands since the 18th century, and they
played an important part in the life of the islands under Danish rule. The
Virgin Islands have been American territory since 1917. Today the communi-
ty numbers about 450, of whom some 125 families are affiliated to the
Hebrew congregation of St. Thomas.
Inq. to Rabbi Bradd Boxman, St. Thomas Syn., P.O.B. 266, Charlotte Amalie,
V.I., 00804, U.S.A. ☎ 809-774-4312. The syn. was built in 1833.
Information about the Orthodox syn., Khal Hakodesh is available from Herb
Horowitz. ☎ (809) 779-2000. There is a Conservative synagogue on the island
of St. Croix.

YUGOSLAVIA
(The rump of the Federal Republic of Yugoslavia at present comprises only
Serbia and Montenegro. Bosnia Hercegovina, Croatia, Slovenia and
Macedonia are separate republics).
Today the Jews of former Yugoslavia are estimated at no more than 3,500,
organised in 25 coms. In 1941 there were about 82,000, organised in 121
coms.
General inf. from Yugoslav National Tourist Office, 143 Regent St., W1R 8AE.
☎ 071-439 0399.

BELGRADE (BEOGRAD)
The Belgrade com. before the war numbered about 11,000. Today it numbers
about 2,000.
The headquarters of the Fed. of Jewish Coms. in Yugoslavia is in 7 Kralja Petra

St., 71a/lll, 11001. P.O.B. 841. ☎ 624-359 & 621-837. Fax 626-674. Pres.: A. Singer. Sec.: Miroslav Grinvald. Office of the local com. in the same bldg. on the second floor. ☎ 624-289. Pres.: Brane Popovi«c. There is also a Jewish historical museum in 7 Kralja Petra St.,71a/l. ☎ 622-634 It is open daily from 10 a.m. to 12 noon except Mon. The syn. is at Birjuzova St. 19. (Services held on Friday evenings & Jewish holidays) In the Jewish cemetery there are monuments to fallen fighters and martyrs of fascism, and fallen Jewish soldiers in the Serbian army in the 1st World War. In 1990 a new monument to Jews killed in Serbia was erected by the Danube, in the pre-war Jewish quarter Dorcol.

NOVI SAD
Com. Offices, Jevrejska 11. ☎ 613-882. Pres.: Thomir Ungar. Synagogue no longer open, it's reported to be extremely beautiful but is currently being converted to a concert hall! In the Jewish cemetery there is a monument to the Jews who fell in the war and the victims of fascism.

SKOPJE (MACEDONIA)
Since the earthquake disaster of 1963 there have been about 90 Jews in the town. The com. offices are at Borka Talevski St. 24. ☎ 237-543. Pres.: .....

SUBOTICA
Com. offices. Dimitrija Tucovica St 13, ☎ 28-483. Pres.: .....

ZAMBIA
(Jewish population 35)

MIDLANDS
Syn.: Lusaka Hebrew Cong., Chachacha Rd., Lusaka. Ch.: M. C. Galaun, P.O.B. 30020, Lusaka. ☎ 229190. Fax 221428.

ZIMBABWE
(Jewish population approx. 910, of whom 596 live in Harare, 303 in Bulawayo, and about 11 in other centres.) The first cong. was founded in Bulawayo in 1894 & the second in Salisbury (now Harare) a year later.

BULAWAYO
Syn.: Bulawayo Hebrew Cong., Jason Moyo St., P.O.B. 337. ☎ 60829.
Zimbabwe Zionist Organisation, No. 9 Jewish Communal Centre, 44 Jason Moyo St., P.O.B. 1162. ☎ 67383.
Womens Zionist Council, P.O. Box 1162. ☎ 67383.

HARARE
Syns.: Harare Hebrew Cong., Milton Park Jewish Centre, Lezard Av., P.O.B. 342. ☎ 727576 (office); Sephardi Cong., 54 Josiah Chinamano Av., P.O.B. 1051. ☎ 722899 (office); Zimbabwe Jewish Board of Deputies, P.O.B. 342. ☎ 723647.
Central African Zionist Organisation, P.O.B. 1954. ☎ 702506-7
Union of Jewish Women, P.O.B. 2287.

KOSHER FISH AROUND THE WORLD
Courtesy of Kashrut Division, London Beth Din,
and United Synagogue Publications Ltd

UK	France	Holland	Italy	Spain
Anchovy	Anchois	Anchovis	Acciugia	Boqueron
Barbel	Barbue	Barbeel	-	-
Bass	Bar Commun	Baars	Persico, Branzino	Lubina
Bream	Breme	Brasum	-	-
Brill	Barbue	Griet	Rombo, Liscio	-
Brisling	-	-	-	-
Carp	Carpe	Karper	Carpa	-
Coalfish	-	Koolvis	-	-
Cod	Morue, Cabillaud	Kabeljauw	Merluzzo	Bacalao
Dab	Limbaude	Schar	-	-
Dace	-	-	-	-
Flounder	Flet	-	-	-
Grayling	Ombre	Vlagzalm	-	-
Gurnard	Grondin	Poon	Pesce Capone	-
Haddock	Aiglefin	Schelvis	-	-
Hake	Merluche	Kabeljauw	Nasello	Merluza
Halibut	Fletan	Helibot	-	-
Herring	Hareng	Hareng	Aringa	-
John Dory	-	-	-	-
Ling	-	Leng	-	-
Mackerel	Maquereau	Makreel	Sgombro	Caballa
Mullet	Mulet	Baars	-	-
Perch	Perche	Baars	Pesce Persico	-
Pike	Brochet	Snoek	Luccio	-
Pilchard	Pilchard	-	Sardina	Sardina
Plaice	Carrelet, Plie	Schol	-	-
Polack	Lieu Jaune	Pollak	-	-
Roach	Gardon	Blankvoorn	-	-
Saithe	-	-	-	-
Salmon	Saumon	Zalm	Salmone	Salmon
Sardine	Sardine	Sardine	Sardina	Sardina
Shad	Alose	Elft	-	-
Sild	-	-	-	-
Smelt	Eperlan	Spiering	-	-
Snoek	Snoek	Snoek	-	-
Sole	Sole	Tong	Sogliola	Lenguado
Sprat	Sprat	Sprot	Spratto	-
Tench	Tanche	Zeelt	Tinca	-
Trout	Truite	Forel	Trota	Trucha
Tuna	Thon	Tonijin	Tonno	Atun
Whitebait	Blanchaille	-	-	-
Whiting	Merlan	Wijting	Bianchetti	-

Australia

Anchovy
Baramundi
Barracouta
Barracuda
Blue Eye
Blue Grenadier
Bluefin
Bream
Carp
Cod
Coral Perch
Duckfish
Flathead
Flounder
Garfish
Groper
Haddock
Hake
Harpuka
Herring
Jewfish
John Dory
Lemon Sole
Mackerel

Morwong
Mullet
Murray Cod
Murray Perch
Murray Perth Tuna
Northern Blue Fin
Orange Roughy
Perch
Pike
Pilchard
Redfin
Salmon
Sardine
Shad
Sild
Skipjack (Striped)
Snapper
Southern Blue Fin
Tailor
Terakiji
Trevally
Trout
Yellowfin
Yellowtail
Whiting

Hong Kong

Anchovy
Bigeye
Carp
Crevalle
Croaker
Giant Perch
Grey Mullet
Grouper
Japanese Sea Perch
Leopard Coral Trout
Pampano
Pilchard
Red Sea Bream
Round Herring
Sardine
Scad
Whitefish

Japan

Maguro = Tuna

Non-Kosher Fish
(Courtesy of Kashrut Division, London Beth Din)

The following species of fish are non-kosher: abalone (ebi), abbot, allmouth, angelfish, angler, beluga, blonde, catfish, caviar, cockles, conger eel, crabs, dogfish, eelpout, eels, fiddlefish, fishing frog, flake, frog-fish, goosefish, guffer eel, huss, lumpfish, monkfish, mussels, ray, rigg, rock salmon, rockfish, roker, sea devil, sea pout, shellfish, skate, sturgeon, swordfish, thornback ray, turbot.

N.B. Local names for fish vary from region to region and names are repeated for quite different species in different countries.

VEGETARIAN ORGANISATIONS

Extensive information in this section has been compiled with the aid of the Vegetarian Society of the U.K. Ltd., Parkdale, Dunham Rd., Altrincham, Ches. WA14 4QG. ☎ 0161-928 0793, whose Vegetarian Travel Guide, 1991 has been invaluable (edited by Jane Bowler at £4.50 + £1.50 p&p). The Society's magazine gives up to date information on hotels, restaurants etc. More detailed information is available from the Society. (£2 plus £1 p+p). Intending visitors should always inquire first whether accom. is available and not just assume that it is.

There is also a Jewish Vegetarian & Natural Health Society affiliated to the international Vegetarian Union. All inq. to the Sec., International H.Q., Bet Teva, 853-855 Finchley Rd., London NW11 8LX. ☎ 0181-455 0692. ★Dining room open Sun. 12 noon to 3 p.m. & 6 p.m. to 10 p.m., & Mon.-Thurs. 6 p.m. to 10 p.m.

A selection of restaurants, B&B and hotels has been included throughout the U.K. section.

OTHER COUNTRIES

The Vegetarian Travel Guide has an extensive section on facilities for vegetarians overseas and lists vegetarian restaurants in a large number of countries. It recommends "the Vegetarian Passport" compiled by the Dutch Vegetarian Society (De Nederlandse Vegetariesbond, Larensweg 26, 1221 CM Hilversum) as a very comprehensive book which should help you to get by almost anywhere in the world.

The following is a list of national vegetarian societies.

ARGENTINA

Argentinian Vegetarian Society, Sarmiento 1371, Piso No. 705, 1041 Buenos Aires.

AUSTRALIA

The Australian Vegetarian Society, P.O.B. 65, Paddington NSW 2021. ☎ (02) 698-4339.

The Jewish Vegetarian Society, 6/3 Ocean Rd, Bondi, NSW 2062.

AUSTRIA

Österreichische Vegetarier Union, Leechgassen 2, A-8010, Graz.

BELGIUM

Association Internationale des Vegetariens de Langue Française, 25 Avenue Chazal, 1030 Brussels. ☎ 733-6288.

Vegetariersbond van Belgie, Rozenlaan 11, 2232 Schilde. ☎ 03353-6485.

CANADA

Vegetarian Awareness Network (Vegenet). ☎ 800-3288343.

CZECH REPUBLIC

Czech Vegetarian Society, c/o Peter Pribus, Kubelikova 17, Cz 13000 Prague.

DENMARK

Vegetarence Omsorgs and Statteforening, Riskar 14, Smørumndre, 2765 Måløv Smørumneøre.

Dansk Vegetar and Rakostforening, NY Vestergårdsvej 6, 3500 Vaerløse. ☎ 42-48-0267.

FRANCE
Alliance Vegetarienne (ALLVEG), Beauregard, 85240 Saint-Hilaire des Loges.

GERMANY
Vegetarier-Bund Deutschlands, e.V. Blumenstrasse 3, D-30159 Hannover. ☎/Fax 0511-3632050. Email: Vegetarier-Bund@OLN.comlink.apc.org.

INDIA
The Indian Vegetarian Congress, National HQ, 1 Eldams Rd, 600018 Madras. ☎ 450-364.

IRELAND
The Vegetarian Society of Ireland, PO Box 3010, Ballsbridge, Dublin 4. ☎ 01-872 1191.

ISRAEL
Israeli Vegetarian Society, Leventin 2, P.O.B. 2352, 61022 Tel Aviv.

ITALY
Associazione Vegetariana Italiana, Dott Via XXV Aprile 41, 20026 Novate Milanese, Milan.

JAMAICA
Vegetarian Society of Jamaica Ltd, c/o 36 Calypso Crescent, Caribbean Terrace, WI Kingston.

JAPAN
Japanese Vegetarian Union, c/o Japan Medical Centre, 718 Dalsen, 410-21 Nirayama. ☎ 5597-85849.

NEW ZEALAND
New Zealand Vegetarian Society Inc., Box 77-034, Auckland 3.

NORWAY
Norges Vegetariske Landsforbund, Munkedamsveien 3B, 0161 Oslo 1. ☎ 02782-258

PORTUGAL
Associacao Vegetariana Portuguesa, Sede Provisoria, Rua do Salitre 136. Lisbon 1.

SINGAPORE
Food Reform Vegetarian Information Service, Blk 508 West, Coast Drive No. 6-257, 0512 Singapore.

SOUTH AFRICA
Vegetarian Society of South Africa, P.O.B. 23567, Joubert Park, 2044 Johannesburg. ☎ 642-7471.

SPAIN
Federacion Naturista Vegetariana Española, P.O.B. 5326, 08080 Barcelona. ☎ 393-215-6088. http://www.wsite.es/cedel.

SRI LANKA
Sri Lanka Vegetarian Society, 17 Beach Rd, Kotuwegoda, Matara. ☎ 041-3111.

SWEDEN
Svenska Vegetariska Foreningen, Radmansgarten 88, 113 29 Stockholm. ☎ 324929.

SWITZERLAND
Arbeitskreis für Lebenserneuerung, Schwarzenbachweg 16, CH-8049 Zurich. ☎ 01-341-88-47.

THAILAND
Thai Vegetarian Society, Sannak Poo Sawan 270, Soi 65, Petchkasem Rd, Khet, Pasicharoen 10160, Bangkok.

USA
Jewish Vegetarians of North America, c/o 6938 Reliance Rd., Federalsburg, Md. 21632. ☎ (410) 754-5550. Email: imossman@skipjack.bluecrab.org Publishes a quart. newsletter at US$15.

North American Vegetarian Society (NAVS), P.O.B. 72, Dolgeville, N.Y. 13329. ☎ (518) 568-7970.

Vegetarian Awareness Network (Vegenet), P.O.B. 321, Knoxville, TN 37901. ☎ 202-347-8343 and 800-872-8343

HOLIDAY CAMPS

GREAT BRITAIN

Bnei Akiva. Head Office and Email: bnei.akiva@ort.org: 2 Halleswelle Rd., NW11 ODJ. ☎ 0181-209 1319. Leeds Youth Centre: Palestrant Hse., Street Lane Gdns., Street Lane, LS17. ☎ 0532 688290 or 695347. Manchester Youth Centre: 72 Singleton Rd., Salford, M7 OLU. ☎ 061-740 1621. **(K)** Winter & summer camps. Contact the camps organiser, Simon Lawrence for further details.

Camp Aguda, Stamford Hill, N16 5DN. ☎ 0181-800 6688 & 0181-800 0338. **(K)** Camps arranged in two sections for boys: Pirchim (9–15), and Zeirim (15 upwards), in England & on the Continent. Branch office: 35a Northumberland St., Salford, M7, Lancs. **(K)** Ezra Youth Movement, a Alba Gdns., NW11 9NR. ☎ 0181-458 5372. Junior camp, 8-13, in England. Separate intermediate camps for boys & girls, 14-18, in England, Europe & Israel.

Habonim-Dror Camps. 523 Finchley Rd., NW3 7BD. ☎ 0171-435 9033. Fax: 0171-431 4503. Camps for ages 9-22 in Britain, France, Holland & Israel over summer & winter holidays. Year scheme in Israel for post-'A' level students.

Hanoar Hatzioni (Zionist Youth Movement). 31 Tetherdown, Muswell Hill, N10 1ND. ☎ 0181-883 1022. Summer & winter camps. 7-17. European tours 17+ years. Holocaust seminar in Poland 18+ years. Tours/Israel schemes 1 month to 1 year, 15 - 25 years.

Kibbutz Representatives. 1A Accommodation Rd., NW11 8ED. ☎ 0181-458 9235. Fax 0181-455 7930; Email: enquiries@kibbutz.org.uk Kibbutz Ulpan & working programmes all year round. Summer schemes.

Mizrachi-Hapoel Hamizrachi. Gen. Sec.: Simon Kritz. **(K)** Family holiday schemes, tours to Israel, seminars. 2b Golders Green Rd., NW11 8LH. ☎ 0181-455 2243/4.

Union of Jewish Students. B'nai B'rith-Hillel Hse., 1-2 Endsleigh St., WC1H ODS. ☎ 0171-380 0111. Fax 0171-383 0390. Seminars & week-end schools for students. Summer tours to Israel.

ABROAD

CAEJ British European Centre for Jewish Youth, 7 rue Marbeuf, 75008 Paris, France. ☎ 472-08-125. Fax 4070-02-30. For children and students aged 6 to 23, U.S.A, Israel, Canada, UK; Also, kosher hotel in French Alps, under supervision of the Beth Din.

* CCVL Centres Culturels de Vacances et de Loisirs, 19 rue de Téhéran, 75008 Paris, France. ☎ 331-4563 4981. Fax 331-4562 1612. Group holidays for children & teenagers, Feb., Mar., Apr., Jul., Aug. Kosher. Sporting, cultural & Jewish activities. Also for families, Passover & summer.

Merkos L'Inyonei Chinuch: Via Carlo Poerio 35, 20129 - Milan, Italy. Pres.: Rav G. M. Garelik. ☎ 02-225 1213. Hebrew Day School, Yeshiva & High Sch., Kindergarten, Talmud Torah, ☎ 02-5392010; Chabad House Via Fratelli Bronzetti 18. ☎ 02-7010-0080. Lubavitch Youth Org. ☎ 027610531. Summer and winter camps for boys & girls aged 7-13 and summer Yeshiva for boys in Pieve ri Camaiore. ☎ 0584-98-3588 or 027610531. Publications ☎ 02-7010-5168. Chabad House in Venice, (Ghetto). Kosher food available. ☎ 041-716214.

OSE-Italia: **(K)** Viale Trastevere 60, Rome, 00153. ☎ 581-6486. Camps, during July & Aug. at Caletta nr. Leghorn (for children 6-13) and Goria de Veleso, Como (Colonia Enzo Sereni), for children 5-12.

BOOKSELLERS

The booksellers listed below specialise in Jewish books or have extensive Jewish books departments. Many also supply religious requisites.

Greater London

J. Aisenthal, 11 Ashbourne Pde., Finchley Rd., NW11 0AD. ☎/Fax 0181-455 0501.

Blue and White Shop, 6 Beehive La., Gants Hill, Ilford, Essex, IG1 3RD. ☎ 0181-518 1982.

Carmel Gifts, 62 Edgware Way, Edgware, Middx. HA8 8RU ☎ 0181-958 7632. Fax 0181-958 6226.

R. Golub & Co. Ltd., 305 Eastern Av., Gants Hill, Ilford, Essex, IG2 6NT. ☎ 0181-550 6751.

Aubrey Goldstein, 7 Windsor Court, Chase Side, N14 5HT. ☎ 0181-886 4075.

Dillons The Bookstore, 82 Gower St., WC1E 6EG. ☎ 0171-636 1577. Fax 0171 580 7680. Email: enquiries@dillons.co.uk.

Hebrew Book & Gift Centre, 18 Cazenove Rd., N16 6BD. ☎ 0171-254 3963 (day) & 0181-802 4567 (evg.).

B. Hirschler, 62 Portland Av., N16 6EA, & 71 Dunsmure Rd., N16 5PT. ☎ 0181-800 6395. Also maps, ceremonial art, etc.

J. Hochhauser, 61 Lordship Pk., N16 5UP. ☎ 0181-800 8804.

Jerusalem the Golden, 146a Golders Green Rd., NW11 8HE. ☎ 0181-455 4960 or 458 7011. Fax: 0181-203 7808.

Jewish Books & Gifts (Sandra E. Breger), 1 Rosecroft Walk, Pinner, Middx., HA5 1LJ. ☎ 0181-866 6236.

Jewish Memorial Council Bookshop, 25-26 Enford St., W1H 2DD. ☎ 0171-724 7778. Fax 0171-706 1710.

John Trotter Books (Rare and out of print Jewish books, maps and prints), 80 East End Rd., N3 2SY. ☎/Fax 0181-346 7430.

Joseph's Bookstore, 2 Ashbourne Pde., Temple Fortune, NW11 0AD. ☎/Fax 0181-731 7575.

Karnac Books Ltd., 58 Gloucester Rd., SW7 4QY.

Kuperard (London) Ltd., 32-34 Gordon House Rd., NW5 1LP. ☎ 0171-424 0554. Fax 0171-424 0556. (Also distributors and direct mail).

Manor House Bookshop (Jewish books and Judaica), 80 East End Rd., N3 2SY. ☎ 0181-349 9484.

Menorah Book Centre, 16 Russell Parade, Golders Green Rd., NW11 9NN. ☎ 0181-458 8289.

Muswell Hill Bookshop, 72 Fortis Green Rd., N10 3HN. ☎ 0181-444 7588.

George & Vera Nador, 63 Cranbourne Rd., Northwood, Middx., HA6 1JZ. ☎ 01923-821152. Hebraica, Judaica, maps. By appointment only.

M. Rogosnitzky, 20 The Drive, NW11 9SR. ☎ 0181-455 7645 or 4112.

Selfridges Departmental Store, Jewish Section of Book Dept., Oxford St., W1A 1AB. ☎ 0171-629 1234.

S. Simpson, 1a Granville Rd., N. Finchley, N12 0HJ. ☎ 0181-445 6723.

Stamford Hill Stationers, 153 Clapton Common, E5 9AE. ☎ 0181-802 5222. Fax 0181-802 5224.

Swiss Cottage Books, 4 Canfield Gdns., NW6 3BS. ☎ 0171-625 4632.

Torah Treasures, 4 Sentinel Sq., NW4 2EL. ☎ 0181-202 3134. Fax 0181-202 3161.

W. H. Smith, Brent Cross Shopping Centre, NW4. ☎ 0181-202 4226.

Waterstone's Booksellers Ltd., 68 Hampstead High St., NW3 1QP. ☎ 0171 794 1098. Fax 0171-794 7533.

Woburn Bookshop, 10 Woburn Walk, WC1H 0JL. ☎ 0171-388 7278.

Regions

Birmingham
Lubavitch Bookshop, 95 Willows Rd., B12 9QF. ☎ 0121-440 6673. Fax 0121-446 4199.

Gateshead
J. Lehmann (mail order), 20 Cambridge Ter., NE8 1RP. ☎ 0191-490 1692. Fax 0191-477 5431. (retail), 28-30 Grasmere St., NE8 1TS. ☎ 0191-477 3523.

Glasgow
J. & E. Levingstone, 47 & 55 Sinclair Dr., G42 9PT. ☎ 0141-649 2962.

Leicester
Bookshop: Com. Centre, Highfield St., LE2 0NQ. Inq.: J. Markham, 74 Wakerley Rd., LE5 6AQ. ☎ 0116 2737620.

Liverpool
Book & Gift Centre, Jewish Youth & Community Centre, Dunbabin Rd., L15 6XL. ☎ 0151-475-5671. Sun. only, 11 a.m. to 1 p.m.

Manchester & Salford
J. Goldberg, 11 Parkside Av., Salford, M7 0HB. ☎ 0161-740 0732.
Hasefer, 18 Merrybower Rd., Salford, M7 4HE. ☎ 0161-740-3013. Fax 0161-721 4649.
B. Horwitz, (Wholesale & retail Judaica), 20 King Edward Bldgs., Bury Old Rd., MS. ☎ 0161-740 5897.
Jewish Book Centre (Mr Klein), 25 Ashbourne Gr., Salford, M7 4DB. ☎ 0161-792 1253. Fax 0161-773 6502.

Oxford
B. H. Blackwell Ltd., 48-51 Broad St., OXI 3BQ. ☎ 01865 792792, has a Jewish book section.

Southend
Dorothy Young, 21 Colchester Rd., SS2 6HW. ☎ 01702 331218 for appointment.

The Jewish Travel Guide 1998

Advertisement Order Form

Please complete and return this form to us by 1 September 1997.

Please reserve the following advertising space in
The Jewish Travel Guide 1998:

☐ **Full Page** £475 190 x 102mm

☐ **Half Page** £245 93 x 102mm

☐ **Quarter Page** £145 44 x 102mm

A 10% setting charge will be made
Special positions by arrangement
(UK advertisers please note that the above rates are subject to VAT)

☐ **Please insert the attached copy (a 10% setting charge will be made)**

☐ **Copy will be forwarded from our Advertising Agents** *(see below)*

Contact Name: _____

Advertisers Name: _____

Address for invoicing: _____
_____

Tel: _____ Fax: _____

Signed: _____ Title: _____

VAT No: _____

Date: _____

Agency Name (if applicable): _____

Address: _____

Tel: _____ Fax: _____

All advertisements set by the publisher will only be included if they have been signed and approved by the advertiser.

ORDERS TO:
Vallentine Mitchell & Co Ltd
Newbury House, 890-900 Eastern Avenue, Newbury Park, Ilford, Essex IG2 7HH, UK
Tel: 0181-599 8866 Fax: 0181-599 0984 E-Mail: jtg@frankcass.com
VAT Registration No: GB 232 7776 49

Readers are asked kindly to draw attention to any errors or omissions. If errors are discovered, it would be appreciated if you could give up-to-date information, referring to page, place/institution, etc., and return this form to the Editor at the address given below.

With reference to the following entry:

Page:

Country:

Entry should read:

Kindly list on separate sheet if preferred.

Signed: _____   Date: _____

Name (BLOCK CAPITALS) _____

Address: _____

_____

Telephone: _____

Send to: The Editor
　　　　　Jewish Travel Guide
　　　　　Vallentine Mitchell & Co. Ltd.
　　　　　Newbury House, 890–900 Eastern Avenue
　　　　　Newbury Park, Ilford
　　　　　Essex IG2 7HH
　　Fax: 0181 599 0984. E-mail: editors@frankcass.com

Readers are asked kindly to draw attention to any errors or omissions. If errors are discovered, it would be appreciated if you could give up-to-date information, referfing to page, place/institution, etc., and return this form to the Editor at the address given below.

With reference to the following entry:

Page:

Country:

Entry should read:

Kindly list on separate sheet if preferred.

Signed: Date:

Name (BLOCK CAPITALS)

Address:

Telephone:

Send to: The Editor
Jewish Travel Guide
Vallentine Mitchell & Co. Ltd.
Newbury House, 890–900 Eastern Avenue
Newbury Park, Ilford
Essex IG2 7HH
Fax: 0181 599 0984. E-mail: editors@frankcass.com

Readers are asked kindly to draw attention to any errors or omissions. If errors are discovered, it would be appreciated if you could give up-to-date information, referring to page, place/ institution, etc., and return this form to the Editor at the address given below.

With reference to the following entry:

Page:

Country:

Entry should read:

Kindly list on separate sheet if preferred.

Signed: Date:

Name (BLOCK CAPITALS)

Address:

Telephone:

Send to: The Editor
          Jewish Travel Guide
          Vallentine Mitchell & Co. Ltd.
          Newbury House, 890–900 Eastern Avenue
          Newbury Park, Ilford
          Essex IG2 7HH
     Fax: 0181 599 0984. E-mail: editors@frankcass.com

Readers are asked kindly to draw attention to any errors or omissions. If errors are discovered, it would be appreciated if you could give up-to-date information, referfing to page, place/institution, etc., and return this form to the Editor at the address given below.

With reference to the following entry:

Page:

Country:

Entry should read:

Kindly list on separate sheet if preferred.

Signed: Date:

Name (BLOCK CAPITALS)

Address:

Telephone:

Send to: The Editor
    Jewish Travel Guide
    Vallentine Mitchell & Co. Ltd.
    Newbury House, 890–900 Eastern Avenue
    Newbury Park, Ilford
    Essex IG2 7HH
  Fax: 0181 599 0984. E-mail: editors@frankcass.com

Vallentine Mitchell

The Jewish Year Book 1997
Edited by **Stephen W Massil**

'...the Year Book packs a wealth of up-to-date information, statistics, names and addresses. Prominent Jews in government, the professions, academia and the arts are listed in the Who's Who.
Organisations, institutions, libraries and museums appear under their respective interest headings, and among the regional listings. Also noteworthy is the section on Jews throughout the world.'

David Brauner, Jerusalem Post
ISBN 0 85303 326 9   approx 400pp   £24.00/$30.00

The Jewish Year Book 1896
A Centenary Facsimile of the First Jewish Year Book
Preface by **Stephen W Massil**
Historical Introduction by **Anne J Kershen**

Joseph Jacobs' first *Jewish Year Book*, published by Greenburg & Co and Simkin, Marshall & Co was an instant success running to a second impression on publication; it was dubbed *'The Hebrew Whitaker'* by the national press, recognising it as an indispensable guide to the make-up of the Jewish community in the British Isles and the Empire at the time of Queen Victoria's Diamond Jubilee.

'This facsimile edition is a fascinating document and should be on the bookshelf of all those interested in the social, political and religious life of Jews in late-Victorian Britain.'

Cecil Bloom, The Jerusalem Post
ISBN 0 85303 321 8   352pp   cloth £18.50/$25.00
Special Limited Edition Binding
ISBN 0 85303 322 6   £35.00/$49.50

Vallentine Mitchell
UK and overseas orders to: Vallentine Mitchell, Newbury House, 900 Eastern Avenue, London IG2 7HH, England Tel: 0181 599 8866 Fax: 0181 599 0984 E-Mail: sales@frankcass.com
US and North America orders: c/o ISBS, 5804 NE Hassalo Street, Portland, OR 97213-3644, USA Tel: (503) 287-3093, (800) 944 6190 Fax: (503) 280-8832 E-mail: orders@isbs.com

Vallentine Mitchell

Building Jerusalem
Jewish Architecture in Britain
Edited and introduced by Sharman Kadish

The subject of synagogue art and architecture has for too long stood outside the mainstream of architectural history. In the 1990s a series of important conferences in the United States and England has drawn attention th this fact and secured recognition of the Jewish built heritage by the major conservation agencies. Only now is the 'heritage industry' beginning to open up to the reality of a multi-cultural society. In Britain, where Jews have enjoyed 300 years of continuous settlement, the definitive history of Jewish monuments, both sacred and secular, has yet to be written. A comprehensive survey of extant Jewish sites likewise awaits completion. This book aims to fill that gap.

Building Jerusalem is richly illustrated, featuring in particular, original artwork by Beverley-Jane Stewart and photographs by Anthony Harris.

illus 250 pages   90 black & white photographs
ISBN 0 85303 283 1   cloth £45.00/$59.50
ISBN 0 85303 309 9   paper £19.50/$25.00

The Synagogues of London
Paul Lindsay

A fascinating portrait of the capital's diverse Jewish communities through its most important religious buildings. The author describes this rich and varied heritage, often sadly neglected, which is part of the history of London and its architecture. Not only is this abundantly illustrated book a guide to London's synagogues but it also provides an insight into Jewish London today.

144pp illus
ISBN 0 85303 241 6   cloth £27.50/$35.00
ISBN 0 85303 258 0   paper £14.50/$19.50

Vallentine Mitchell
UK and overseas orders to: Vallentine Mitchell, Newbury House, 900 Eastern Avenue, London IG2 7HH, England Tel: 0181 599 8866 Fax: 0181 599 0984 E-Mail: sales@frankcass.com
US and North America orders: c/o ISBS, 5804 NE Hassalo Street, Portland, OR 97213-3644, USA Tel: (503) 287-3093, (800) 944 6190 Fax: (503) 280-8832 E-mail: orders@isbs.com